Time Out

New York

www.timeout.com/newyork

D1386600

Time Out Digital Ltd
4th Floor
125 Shaftesbury Avenue
London WC2H 8AD
United Kingdom
Tel: +44 (0)20 7813 3000
Fax: +44 (0)20 7813 6001
Email: guides@timeout.com
www.timeout.com

Published by Time Out Digital Ltd, a wholly owned subsidiary of
Time Out Group Ltd. Time Out and the Time Out logo are trademarks
of Time Out Group Ltd.

© Time Out Group Ltd 2015
Previous editions 1990, 1992, 1994, 1997, 1998, 1999, 2000, 2001, 2002,
2003, 2004, 2005, 2006, 2007, 2008, 2009, 2011, 2012, 2013, 2014.

10 9 8 7 6 5 4 3 2 1

This edition first published in Great Britain in 2015 by Ebury Publishing.
20 Vauxhall Bridge Road, London SW1V 2SA

Ebury Publishing is part of the Penguin Random House group of companies
whose addresses can be found at global.penguinrandomhouse.com

Distributed in the US and Latin America by Publishers Group West
(1-510-809-3700)

For further distribution details, see www.timeout.com.

ISBN: 978-1-84670-353-9

A CIP catalogue record for this book is available from the British Library.

Printed and bound in China by Leo Paper Products Ltd.

Penguin Random House is committed to a sustainable future for our
business, our readers and our planet. This book is made from Forest
Stewardship Council® certified paper.

MIX
Paper from
responsible sources
FSC® C018179

Contents

136

90

205

370

Time Out New York

Editorial
Editor Lisa Ritchie
Copy Editor Ros Sales
Listings Editor Marcy Franklin
Proofreader Marion Moisy

Editorial Director Sarah Guy
Group Finance Manager Margaret Wright

Design
Senior Designer Kei Ishimaru
Designers Darryl Bell, Christie Webster
Group Commercial Senior Designer Jason Tansley

Picture Desk
Picture Editor Jael Marschner
Deputy Picture Editor Ben Rowe
Picture Researcher Lizzy Owen

Advertising
Managing Director St John Betteridge
Advertising Sales Deborah Maclaren, Helen Debenham at The Media Sales House

Marketing
Senior Publishing Brand Manager Luthfa Begum
Head of Circulation Dan Collins

Production
Production Controller Katie Mulhern-Bhudia

Time Out Group
Founder Tony Elliott
Chief Executive Officer Tim Arthur
Publisher Alex Batho
Managing Director Europe Noel Penzer

Contributors
New York Today Howard Halle. **Diary** Lisa Ritchie and contributors to *Time Out New York* magazine. **Explore** Cristina Alonso, Rheanna O'Neil Bellomo, Howard Halle, Christina Izzo, Marley Lynch, Will Pulos, Lisa Ritchie, Dana Varinsky and contributors to *Time Out New York* magazine. **Children** Alexandra Early. **Film** Joshua Rothkopf. **Gay & Lesbian** Ethan LaCroix. **Nightlife** Adam Feldman, Andrew Frisicano, Christopher Tarantino, Dana Varinsky and contributors to *Time Out New York* magazine. **Performing Arts** Seth Colter Walls, David Cote, Adam Feldman, Gia Kourlas. **Escapes & Excursions** Lisa Ritchie and contributors to *Time Out New York* magazine. **History** Joseph Alexiou, Richard Koss, Kathleen Squires. **Architecture** Eric P Nash. **Hotels** Lisa Ritchie.

Maps JS Graphics Ltd (john@jsgraphics.co.uk)

Cover Photography Jon Arnold/AWL Images Ltd

Back Cover Photography Clockwise from top left: Adrian Gaut; Victoria Lipov/Shutterstock.com; Marco Prati/Shutterstock.com; Songquan Deng/Shutterstock.com; Annie Schlechter.

Photography Pages 2/3 kropic1/Shutterstock.com; 4/5, 28 (right), 136, 288/289, 297, 353 Sean Pavone/Shutterstock.com; 5 (top), 15 (bottom), 44 (bottom), 90, 126, 260 Wendy Connett; 5 (bottom left), 11, 185, 205 alexpro9500/Shutterstock.com; 7, 14 (bottom), 15 (top), 16 (bottom), 17 (bottom), 35, 144, 238/239, 242, 244 littleny/Shutterstock.com; 10 iladm/Shutterstock.com; 10/11 Andrey Bayda/Shutterstock.com; 12 (middle) Adriano Castelli/Shutterstock.com; 12 (bottom) vichie81/Shutterstock.com; 12/13, 166/167 Marco Prati/Shutterstock.com; 13, 55, 348 holbox/Shutterstock.com; 14 (top), 192/193 stockelements/Shutterstock.com; 16 (top), 27, 64, 78, 92, 93, 97, 107, 124, 140, 141, 161, 188, 197 (top), 221 Paul Wagtouicz; 17 (top) Melissa Sinclair; 18/19 Courtesy Related-Oxford; 21 Timothy A. Clary/AFP/Getty Images; 22 Spencer Platt/Getty Images; 24, 56 (bottom), 118, 139, 154 Daniel Krieger Photography; 24/25 (top) duckeesue/Shutterstock.com; 24/25 (bottom) jfk image/Shutterstock.com; 25 Matt Madison-Clark/Below 54; 26 (bottom) mikecphoto/Shutterstock.com; 28 (left), 84, 238 Caroline Voagen Nelson; 29 (bottom), 34 (top), 56 (top), 110, 191, 200, 222, 236, 237, 275 Filip Wolak; 30/31, 34 (bottom) a katz/Shutterstock.com; 33, 36 (bottom), 354/355 lev radin/Shutterstock.com; 37, 301 (top) mandritoiu/Shutterstock.com; 37, 301 (middle) Kevin Yatarola; 38, 328 (bottom) Andrew F. Kazmierski/Shutterstock.com; 39 (top) Alexander Image/Shutterstock.com; 40/41 (top), 88 Benoit Pailley; 40/41 (bottom), 332/333 pisaphotography/Shutterstock.com; 43 Courtesy Opening Ceremony; 45 Oliver Correa; 46/47 Rudy Balasko/Shutterstock.com; 48 Thorsten Nieder/Shutterstock.com; 48/49 Victor Maschek/Shutterstock.com; 50, 57, 394/395 f11photo/Shutterstock.com; 52 Northfoto/Shutterstock.com; 53 (top), 83, 201, 243, 276, 301 (top and bottom), 326 Michael Kirby; 53 (bottom) Rene Pi/Shutterstock.com; 60, 351 Christopher Penler/Shutterstock.com; 63 Ritu Manoj Jethani/Shutterstock.com; 65 Zack Frank/Shutterstock.com; 66 Paul Warchol 66/67 Julien Hautcoeur/Shutterstock.com; 68 Olivier French; 70, 75, 197 (middle and bottom) Jakob N. Layman; 73 Mmuseumm ; 76/77 Ryan DeBerardinis/Shutterstock.com; 80, 164 Jessica Lin; 81 Erika Cross/Shutterstock.com; 84/85 Dean Kaufman; 86 ©Peter Aaron/Esto; 91 (top) Ethan Covey; 91 (bottom) Christa Hamilton Photography; 94 (bottom) Charles Benton; 98 Donny Tsang; 98/99 Getty Images/Hemis.fr; 101 Beyond My Ken/Wikimedia Commons; 104 (top) Noah Kalina; 104 (bottom) Gabriele Stabile; 110/111 Timothy Schenck; 112 lazyllama/Shutterstock.com; 115 Dylan + Jeni; 116 Daniel M. Silva/Shutterstock.com; 117 Bradley Ennis; 120, 121 Cayla Zahoran; 122, 123 Erin Cadigan/Shutterstock.com; 125 (top) Karin Jobst; 125 (bottom left and bottom right) ©Whitney Museum of American Art; 125 (middle) ©Glenn Ligon; 126/127 Barry Winiker/Getty Images; 130 Courtesy Gladstone Gallery, New York and Brussels; 134, 150, 202, 202/203, 246, 253 Leonard Zhukovsky/Shutterstock.com; 134/135, 146/147 Songquan Deng/Shutterstock.com; 138 Igor Khodzinskiy; 145 Ellen Silverman; 146 Igor Sh/Shutterstock.com; 157 Anna Simonak; 158 Dmitro2009/Shutterstock.com; 159 Rob van Esch/Shutterstock.com; 160 Vladimir Korostyshevskiy/Shutterstock.com; 162 Ingfbruno/Wikimedia Commons; 166 Jonathan Bumble; 170 (top) ©AMNH/D. Finnin 170 (bottom) ©AMNH/C. Chesek; 172 ©2012 Francesco Tonelli; 173 (top) Doug Young; 175, 204 Osugi/Shutterstock.com; 176 Tupungato/Shutterstock.com; 178/179, 214, 293, 330 Victoria Lipov/Shutterstock.com; 182, 183 Michael Bodycomb/©The Frick Collection; 186 Cooper Hewitt; 189 ©2015 Estate of Pablo Picasso/Artists Rights Society (ARS), New York/Digital Image ©2004 The Museum of Modern Art; 190 ©Hulya Kolabas for Neue Galerie New York; 192 Tom Stoelker; 194 StefanoT/Shutterstock.com; 198 ©Driely S. 2014 - www.peopleolpado.com; 209 Kristina Williamson; 211 Al Rodriguez Photography; 215 (left) Shannon Taggart; 215 (right) Courtesy of the Morbid Anatomy Museum; 220 BrooklynScribe/Shutterstock.com; 225 Felix Lipov/Shutterstock.com; 226 Gabriela Herman; 226/227 Joel Raskin/Shutterstock.com; 228 Nany New York/Shutterstock.com; 230 Jesse Winter; 233, 270 Liz Clayman; 240 dade72/Shutterstock.com; 246/247 Jannis Tobias Werner/Shutterstock.com; 250/251 Luboslav Tiles/Shutterstock.com; 252, 254 (bottom) CMA; 254 (top) Ken Moore; 255 Nan Palmero/Wikimedia Commons; 257, 286, 324 (top) Ben Rosenzweig; 258 Lee Magill; 261 Everett/REX Shutterstock; 262 Jolie Ruben; 264, 267 Jena Cumbo Photography; 265 Stuart Monk/Shutterstock.com; 268 Magda Biernat; 269 Zenith Richards; 271 Richard Burrowes; 273, 274 David Cova; 278 FashionStock.com/Shutterstock.com; 280 Francine Daveta; 283 JStone/Shutterstock.com; 284 Mindy Tucker; 287 Wendy George; 295, 311 Matthew Murphy; 296 T photography/Shutterstock.com; 298 (top) David Andrako; 298 (bottom), 299 ©2014 Etienne Frossard; 300 Scott Friedlander; 303 Ken Howard; 304 Richard Termine; 307 Courtesy of Harlem Stage; 309 saaton/Shutterstock.com; 310, 312, 315, 316 Joan Marcus; 313 Jacob Cohl; 318 Aislinn Weidele/Ennead Architects; 321 ©Francis Dzikowski/Esto; 322/323 Ivan Cholakov/Shutterstock.com; 324 (bottom) Nancy Kennedy/Shutterstock.com; 325 Allan Bregg/Shutterstock.com; 328 (top) Michael Hynes/Shutterstock.com; 329 Richard Barnes; 331 Nagel Photography/Shutterstock.com; 334/335 Apic/Getty Images; 336 Jean Leon Gerome Ferris/Wikimedia Commons; 338 (top) Alex Florez courtesy the Office of Council Member Daniel Dromm; 338 (bottom) Wikimedia Commons; 341 ©Everett Collection Historical/Alamy; 346/347 Pete Spiro/Shutterstock.com; 357 Douglas Lyle Thompson; 360, 361 (bottom) Stephen Smith; 361 (top left and top right) Annie Schlechter; 373 Matthew Williams

The following images were supplied by the featured establishments: 5 (bottom right), 26 (top), 29 (top), 39 (bottom), 44 (top), 59, 89, 94 (top), 95, 96, 109, 133, 142, 165, 174, 178, 215, 223, 231, 234, 259, 263, 277, 327, 356, 359, 362, 365, 366, 369, 370

About the Guide

GETTING AROUND

Each sightseeing chapter contains a street map or maps of the area marked with the locations of sights and museums (❶), restaurants (❶), cafés and bars (❶) and shops (❶). There are also street maps of New York, along with subway maps, at the back of the book, plus an overview map of the city on pages 8 and 9. In addition, there is a detachable fold-out street map inside the back cover.

THE ESSENTIALS

For practical information, including visas, disabled access, emergency numbers, lost property, websites and local transport, see the Essential Information section. It begins on page 354.

THE LISTINGS

Addresses, phone numbers, websites, transport information, hours and prices are all included in our listings, as are selected other facilities. All were checked and correct at press time. However, business owners can alter their arrangements at any time, and fluctuating economic conditions can cause prices to change rapidly.

The very best venues in the city, the must-sees and must-dos in every category, have been marked with a red star (★). In the sightseeing chapters, we've also marked venues with free admission with a FREE symbol.

PHONE NUMBERS

New York has a number of area codes. Manhattan uses 212 and 646, while Brooklyn, Queens, the Bronx and Staten Island are served by 718 and 347. Even if you're dialling from within the area you're calling, you'll need to use the area code, always preceded by 1.

From outside the US, dial your country's international access code (00 from the UK) or a plus symbol, followed by the number as listed in the guide; here, the initial '1' serves as the US country code. So, to reach the Metropolitan Museum of Art, dial +1-212 535 7710. For more on phones, see p383.

FEEDBACK

We welcome feedback on this guide, both on the venues we've included and on any other locations that you'd like to see featured in future editions. Please email us at guides@timeout.com.

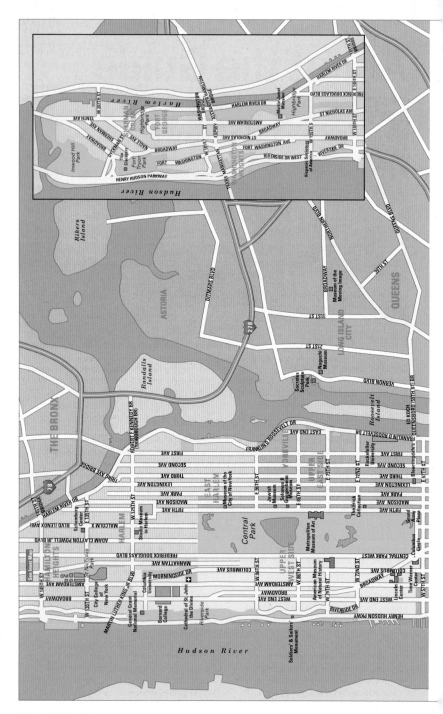

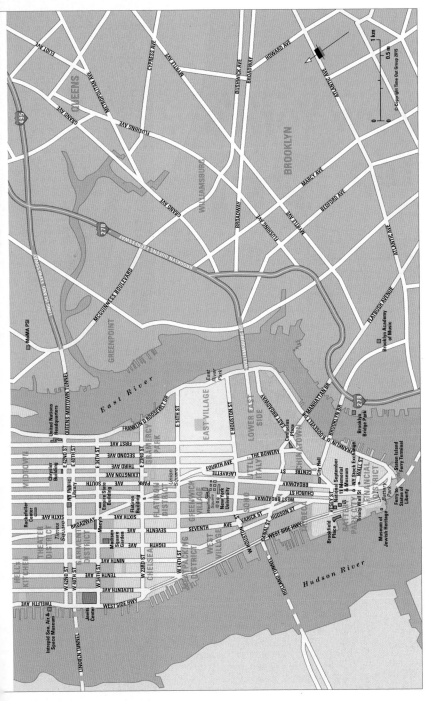

QUEENS

ELIOT AVE

METROPOLITAN AVE

GRAND AVE

495

CYPRESS AVE

MYRTLE AVE

HOWARD AVE

BUSHWICK AVE

BROADWAY

ATLANTIC AVE

1 km

0.5 m

© Copyright Time Out Group 2015

FLUSHING AVE

GRAND AVE

WILLIAMSBURG

BROADWAY

MARCY AVE

BROOKLYN

MYRTLE AVE

BEDFORD AVE

ATLANTIC AVE

278

BROOKLYN-QUEENS EXPRESSWAY

FLUSHING AVE

FLATBUSH AVENUE

MoMA PS1

McGUINNESS BOULEVARD

GREENPOINT

Brooklyn Academy
of Music

WILLIAMSBURG BR

East River

East
River
Park

MANHATTAN BR

BROOKLYN BR

270

Brooklyn
Bridge Park

United Nations
Headquarters

QUEENS-MIDTOWN TUNNEL

FRANKLIN D. ROOSEVELT DR

E 14TH ST

EAST VILLAGE

E HOUSTON ST

LOWER EAST
SIDE

EAST BROADWAY

CHINATOWN

Confucius
Plaza

Staten Island
Ferry Terminal

Chrysler
Building

E 42ND ST

E 40TH ST

E 34TH ST

FIRST AVE

SECOND AVE

THIRD AVE

GRAMERCY
PARK

E 23RD ST

LEXINGTON AVE

FOURTH AVE

THE BOWERY

LAFAYETTE

LITTLE ITALY

CENTRE ST

City Hall

National September
11 Memorial

NY Stock Exchange

WALL ST

FINANCIAL
DISTRICT

MIDTOWN

NY Public
Library

Empire State
Building

SOUTH

AVE

FLATIRON
DISTRICT

Flatiron
Building

Union
Square

NOHO

New York
University

Washington
Square

GREENWICH
VILLAGE

SOHO

BROADWAY

WEST BROADWAY

CHURCH ST

VESEY ST

Trinity
Church

Brookfield
Place

Museum of
Jewish Heritage

BATTERY
PARK CITY

Battery
Park

Statue of
Liberty

Rockefeller
Center

Times
Square

THEATER
DISTRICT

BROADWAY

SIXTH AVE

Macy's

Madison
Square
Garden

SEVENTH

AVE

VARICK ST

HUDSON ST

W HOUSTON ST

WEST
VILLAGE

CANAL ST

WEST SIDE HWY

HELL'S
KITCHEN

W 42ND ST

W 40TH ST

GARMENT
DISTRICT

NINTH AVE

EIGHTH

AVE

W 34TH ST

W 23RD ST

MEATPACKING
DISTRICT

CHELSEA

TENTH AVE

ELEVENTH AVE

TWELFTH AVE

WEST SIDE HWY

LINCOLN TUNNEL

HOLLAND TUNNEL

Hudson River

Intrepid Sea, Air &
Space Museum

Javits
Center

Time Out New York **9**

New York's
Top **20**

*City essentials, from
iconic skyscrapers to
massive sandwiches.*

1 Empire State Building
(page 157)

King Kong recognised the Empire
State's skyscraper supremacy when he
commandeered the iconic tower. It may
no longer be the city's tallest building,
but it has more than 80 years of movie
cameos over 1 World Trade Center. Brave
the crowds to escape the urban jungle
and get a pigeon's-eye panorama of
the metropolis and beyond.

2 Statue of Liberty
(page 55)

Symbolic and surreal (a monumental statue-cum-lighthouse?), Lady Liberty was a beacon to millions of immigrants who subsequently shaped the city, and America. Impressive viewed from land, up close she is an immense marvel. A climb to the crown affords an exhilarating view of New York Harbor and the chance to see the literal nuts and bolts of Frédéric Auguste Bartholdi's creation.

3 Metropolitan Museum of Art (page 185)

Not only does this massive institution – comprising 17 curatorial collections and more than two million objects – preserve such treasures as an Egyptian temple from c15 BC, but it is also in a state of constant self-improvement. The American Wing, the European Paintings Galleries and the Costume Institute have all received impressive revamps, and in spring 2016 the museum opens Met Breuer, showcasing contemporary art and performances in the old Whitney space. Since the suggested admission now grants you entry to the Cloisters, the Met's uptown medieval outpost, in the same week, the sum doesn't seem quite so steep.

4 Museum of Modern Art
(page 157)

You could spend a day getting lost in the permanent collection, which showcases some of the best-known works by Picasso, Van Gogh and other modern masters. But equally essential are the museum's other elements, including an attached cinema that combines arthouse fare and more accessible offerings, a sculpture garden with works by Rodin and Moore, and fine-dining destination the Modern.

5 Solomon R Guggenheim Museum (page 188)

When it was completed in 1959, Frank Lloyd Wright's curved concrete edifice ruffled a few art-world feathers, including those of Willem de Kooning and Robert Motherwell, who complained their art was not best appreciated from the museum's ramps. Today, the iconic spiral – Wright's only building in Manhattan – is considered as much a work of art as are the paintings it houses (which include masterpieces by Picasso, Chagall and Kandinsky).

6 Central Park
(page 175)

Urban visionaries Frederick Law Olmsted and Calvert Vaux sought a harmonious balance of scenic elements: pastoral (the open lawn of the Sheep Meadow), formal (the linear, tree-lined Mall) and picturesque (the densely wooded paths of the Ramble). Today, the 843-acre plot draws millions of visitors to

bridge in the world. Stride along its wide wood-planked promenade from lower Manhattan and discover the pleasure of arriving at a completely different and very pleasant destination (Dumbo) on foot – with an expansive vista of New York Harbor, the Statue of Liberty and downtown's skyscrapers along the way.

8 National September 11 Memorial & Museum
(page 60)

It was a decade in the making, but New York finally got a suitably awe-inspiring memorial of the terrible event that shook the city to its core. It's impossible not to feel moved as you gaze at the monumental waterfalls cascading down the sides of the vast chasms where the Twin Towers once stood. Above you, the soaring 1 World Trade Center serves as a reminder that this town never stays down for long. Below ground, in the fallen towers' foundations, the 9/11 Memorial Museum brings home the immense scale and far-reaching repercussions of the tragedy.

its skyscraper-bordered vistas in all seasons: sunbathers and picnickers in summer, ice-skaters in winter, and bird-watchers in spring and autumn. It's also an idyllic venue for beloved cultural events like Shakespeare in the Park and the New York Philharmonic's annual open-air performances.

7 Brooklyn Bridge
(page 205)

No mere river crossing, this span is an elegant reminder of New York's history of architectural innovation. When it opened in 1883, the Brooklyn Bridge was the longest suspension

9 Times Square
(page 151)

Larger than life, brash, lurid and utterly hypnotic. For more than a century, the Crossroads of the World has provided an eye-popping arena for news, entertainment and advertising. Even the most jaded New Yorkers have to admit that the ever-shifting illuminated tableau is dazzling viewed from the top of the red steps behind TKTS – and you can pick up some cheap theatre tickets while you're there. The crowds in today's family-friendly Times Square can be infuriating (about 300,000 people pass through daily), but new pedestrian plazas and granite seating have improved the experience.

(10)

10 Soho shopping

(page 70)

Yes, the former artists' enclave has become an outdoor shopping mall. But have you ever seen one so exquisite? Avoid the Saturday crowds and wander amid the pristine warehouses hung with fire escapes like so much costume jewellery, popping in and out of the ground-level retail ranging from cult designer boutiques (Alexander Wang, Rachel Comey) to luxury labels (Prada, Chanel) and

(11)

cheaper chains (Madewell, Topshop). There are even outposts of Barneys and Bloomingdale's, and plenty of good brunch choices – we recommend Jack's Wife Freda (see p70) – in the area.

11 Lincoln Center

(page 396)

The largest campus of its kind in the world, this Upper West Side institution is home to a staggering array of theatre, music, dance and film. Construction began in 1959 with the help of John D Rockefeller III, largely in an effort to provide new stomping grounds for the Metropolitan Opera, the New York Philharmonic and the Juilliard School. Today the complex encompasses 30 venues and 11 world-class resident organisations that mount thousands of events each year. After a campus-wide renovation, it's looking better than ever. Standing in Josie Robertson Plaza at twilight, with the fountain spouting white-lit jets of water and the lobby of the Met glowing golden behind it, is one of Manhattan's more transporting experiences.

The pathway takes you above the city while keeping you rooted in urban life – where else can you walk through a field of wildflowers or sprawl on a lush lawn as taxis zoom along the street beneath you? Keep an eye out for iconic sights (from the Statue of Liberty to the Empire State Building) and intriguing art installations. And it now has one of the city's most important art hubs, the Whitney Museum of American Art, at its foot.

13 Katz's Delicatessen
(page 85)

New York may be known for its delis, but these kosher canteens are a dying breed, and some celebrated pastrami purveyors don't live up to their overstuffed reputations. Plastered with shots of famous noshers, Katz's delivers on more than 125 years of history. Hand-carved and bookended with rye bread, the tender smoked meat is piled high and served with just a slick of mustard.

14 Washington Square Park (page 112)

The beatniks, folkies and hippies who flocked to this park are still there, though sporting slightly different facial hair from their predecessors. During warmer months, the park is one of the city's best people-watching spots, as musicians and street artists perform in the shadow of the Stanford White-designed Washington Arch. The park is still fresh from a controversial, multimillion-dollar renovation, which spruced it up with more benches, lawns and flower beds.

12 The High Line (page 123)

There's something uniquely New York about this eyrie. Built on an abandoned railway track, the space is ingenious in its use of reclaimed industrial detritus, a necessity in footage-starved Manhattan.

15 Chelsea gallery district
(page 128)

We're not suggesting you skip the essential museums on our list, but in west Chelsea's contemporary-art mecca you can often catch museum-calibre shows without spending a dime. The former industrial buildings have been converted into more than 200 galleries, from sleek blue-chip salons to densely packed warrens of smaller art spaces.

16 Brooklyn Flea
(page 35)

New Yorkers aren't content with merely shopping at the weekend, they want a complete cultural experience that involves local artisans, people-watching and cult eats. Since its debut more than a half-dozen years ago, the Flea has elevated the vintage-and-craft market concept, spawning several offshoots as well as imitators. The food-only spin-off Smorgasburg – a glutton's paradise packed with up to 100 vendors – gives you the opportunity to taste your way across the city in one convenient spot.

17 Panorama of the City of New York
(page 237)

Located on the grounds of two World's Fairs, the Queens Museum holds one of Gotham's most intriguing curiosities: The Panorama of the City of New York, a 9,335-square-foot scale model of the five boroughs, created for the 1964 exposition and featuring Lilliputian models of landmarks. And following the museum's recent renovation and expansion, the Little Apple debuted a new mini skyscraper – a replica of 1 World Trade Center.

18 Roberta's (page 220)

Chef Carlo Mirarchi and two partners took locavore aspirations to a new stratosphere with this ramshackle Brooklyn pizzeria. A DIY ethos pervades the spot, with plates incorporating pickings from the backyard garden and a food-centric radio station. But the menu evokes a focused simplicity, even as it evolved to encompass locally cured meats, thoughtful salads and handmade pastas. Playing the dual role of hipster clubhouse and required stop for visiting food-world dignitaries like Alice Waters, the joint transformed Bushwick from desolate outer-borough 'hood into a legit dining destination. The team has since opened sleek on-site tasting-menu restaurant Blanca, which baits well-heeled gastronauts to a fringe locale for exceptional fare.

19 Radio City Music Hall
(page 289)

New York City is full of legendary performance venues, but few match Radio City Music Hall in terms of sheer elegance. Designed by Donald Deskey, the art deco interior features opulent chandeliers, while the stage and proscenium are meant to resemble a setting sun. Although it's probably best known as the home of the Rockettes, a plethora of noteworthy performers have graced its boards, including Leonard Cohen, Tony Bennett and Lady Gaga.

20 Williamsburg clubbing
(page 217)

With its largely low-rise architecture (for now, before the condos take over), Williamsburg feels like a small town with an unusually high concentration of bars and gig spots. Hop from laid-back spaces showcasing local talent to megaclubs like Output (see p275) and Verboten (see p277).

New York Today

In Gotham, money still talks.

TEXT: HOWARD HALLE

When Democrat Bill de Blasio was elected as New York's mayor in 2013, it was widely expected that he'd move City Hall away from catering to Wall Street bankers, real estate developers and other species of the mega-rich – players whose interests had come to dominate the economic and political life of the city over the previous decades. He'd run on a promise to end the NYPD's controversial stop-and-frisk policy, which overwhelmingly impacted men of colour by subjecting them to arbitrary police searches. He also vowed to create more affordable housing in an effort to staunch the exodus of middle- and working-class New Yorkers. Given that De Blasio had garnered 73 per cent of the vote, it seemed like a good bet that he could transform New York. But nearly two years into his first term, the most remarkable thing about New York is how little it seems to have changed from the city led by former mayor Michael Bloomberg, a Republican who once opined that New York needed more billionaires like himself to create jobs and pump money into the economy.

From the start, De Blasio departed from his image as an unalloyed liberal, most conspicuously by appointing William Bratton as police commissioner. Bratton had occupied the post under the law-and-order administration of Mayor Rudy Giuliani. He was a proponent of the 'broken windows' theory, which postulated that decreasing major crime started with stopping petty offences – like those of the myriad 'squeegee men', who'd shake down drivers by washing their windshields without permission before demanding money. This sense of a city out of control provided the rationale for stop-and-frisks meant to uncover drugs and firearms.

Still, Bratton has curtailed the practice, despite warnings that ending it would unleash a wave of mayhem. In fact, crime has only continued to decline, making New York one of the safest cities in the world. Even so, New York's citizens of colour disproportionately attract the attention of law enforcement. The NYPD apparently hasn't got the message that New York is no longer the lawless frontier town that necessitated an ends-justify-the-means approach to public order.

NYPD BLUES
All of which was crystallised by an incident that unleashed a political furore and led to a showdown between police and the mayor – the death of a man named Eric Garner at the hands of cops in Staten Island. Thanks to a bystander's video that went viral, New Yorkers saw Garner, an African-American, as he was swarmed by officers, put in a chokehold and wrestled to the ground. He could be heard repeatedly saying that he couldn't breathe. He fell unconscious, but neither the police nor arriving emergency medical technicians performed CPR. Garner later died at the hospital. His crime: allegedly selling 'loosies', or loose cigarettes, a practice common in poorer neighbourhoods. Although chokeholds were against department guidelines, Daniel Pantaleo, the patrolman responsible for applying it, wasn't indicted by a grand jury, even though the medical examiner had ruled Garner's death a homicide.

Scores of protests ensued, including a mass 'die-in' in Grand Central Terminal. De Blasio, whose wife is African-American, expressed sympathy for the demonstrators, going so far as to say that he'd told his own

son to be careful around the police. This sparked outrage from the NYPD's union representatives, most notably the voluble Patrick Lynch, head of the Patrolmen's Benevolent Association, who accused the mayor of calling the police racist. Things came to an ugly head when a deranged African-American man from Baltimore shot two patrolmen (one Hispanic, the other Chinese) as they sat in their squad car – ostensibly to avenge Garner. Lynch railed that De Blasio had the blood of the two officers on his hands, and when the mayor attended their funerals, dozens of police turned their backs on him. For several weeks, cops in certain precincts operated a slowdown on summons for misdemeanours, before the commissioner stepped in and ordered them back to doing their jobs. Eventually, tensions between the NYPD and the mayor subsided, though distrust for De Blasio continues to simmer among the NYPD's rank-and-file.

'Despite the city's rent stabilisation ordinance, the average cost of an apartment rose 75 per cent between 2000 and 2012 while wages only increased by 31 per cent.'

THE RENT IS TOO DAMN HIGH
Public safety has, of course, had a symbiotic relationship with New York's rising tide of gentrification over the past 30 years, and the concomitant increase in rents over the same period. Despite the city's rent stabilisation ordinance, the average cost of an apartment rose 75 per cent between 2000 and 2012 while wages only increased by 31 per cent. In an effort to reverse the trend, De Blasio has proposed building 80,000 new low-cost homes, and retaining 120,000 more. Critics contend that these figures aren't nearly

'Die-in' at Grand Central Terminal

enough to solve the problem, and that the mayor's decision to rely on private sector developers to create units (through a programme of subsidies, tax breaks and incentives such as permitting larger buildings than zoning allows) compromises the plan from the start. Also, they ask, what assurance is there that affordable rents wouldn't eventually be raised to market rates (currently a median of $3,000 a month)?

The upward pressure on rents overall has been driven by skyrocketing prices at the top of the food chain. Buildings that were once landmarks of New York's commercial skyline are now being turned into high-rise residences, with the priciest units commanding formerly inconceivable prices. One such project, the conversion of the iconic Woolworth Building, is asking for $125 million for its prime penthouse space. Another changeover will combine three floors of midtown's famed Chippendale building – once the headquarters of AT&T and the Sony corporation – into a 30,000-square-foot unit with a price tag of $150 million. Most buyers for such castles in the sky are wealthy foreigners – from the Middle East, Russia and elsewhere – looking to shelter their money from economic and political upheavals back home. Prestige is another motivation: the

buyer of the largest unit in the glossy new One57 tower on 57th Street (who paid, it's estimated, a relatively reasonable sum of $90 million) said he bought the place because it was the Mona Lisa of New York City apartments. Perhaps, but only for the time being.

The most prominent symbol of this excess is 432 Park Avenue, designed by international starchitect Rafael Viñoly. The slender, boxy tower rises to a height equal to that of 1 World Trade Center, minus the latter's spire. Its construction costs rivalled those of the entire real estate in an average, mid-size American city. And while it can be seen from all five boroughs, 432 Park Avenue will soon be eclipsed by other luxury towers in terms of height.

GREEN FOR GREEN

All of this money has radically transformed nearly every pocket of the city over the past decade – in some cases for the good. This is especially true of public parks and cultural institutions. The High Line, for instance, has been completed, running its full length from the Meatpacking District to its northern terminus at West 34th Street and Eleventh Avenue. Next door, the sprawling Hudson Yards is well under way with the completion

Mayor Bill de Blasio and family. *See p20.*

of its first tower, 10 Hudson Yards, along with an adjacent retail podium, in 2015. However, while work on the 7 subway line extension into the area has been completed, its official opening has been delayed several times. The Culture Shed, a spectacular, retractable performing arts and exhibition centre that will be sited behind 10 Hudson Yards, recently named its artistic director, Alex Poots. Meanwhile, at the southern – Gansevoort Street – end of the High Line, the Whitney Museum of American Art opened its new industrial-chic, Renzo Piano-designed home. Its former Madison Avenue digs are being taken over for eight years by the Metropolitan Museum of Art, which also recently received an upgrade to its Fifth Avenue Plaza courtesy of billionaire patron of the arts David Koch.

In fact, private donors are being increasingly tapped for projects that were once the domain of the state and City Hall. One such case is Hudson River Park, a narrow recreational strip that runs uptown from Battery Park City in the Financial District. Plans for its continued development have stalled over recent years, but billionaire media mogul Barry Diller and his spouse,

the legendary fashion maven Diane von Furstenberg, have stepped in to pay for Pier 55 near Chelsea, a brand new riverside park within the Hudson River Park area. The project boasts an elevated, sci-fi design, in which a series of plant-shaped concrete pilings projecting into the river will support a bowl-like, undulating green space.

Brooklyn Bridge Park is continuing to expand with a three-and-a-half-acre site at Main Street in Dumbo. Not far from Jane's Carousel, it will include a nautically themed playground. But here again, private enterprise plays a huge part: part of the deal for the park's funding involves high-end construction, including a nine-storey 'eco-luxe' hotel called the Pierhouse. Nearby residents have attempted to get a stop-work order on the project because it had exceeded its planned height, blocking views of the East River, but the Pierhouse has proceeded apace.

Besides the aforementioned Hudson Yards, New York's other mega-developments are slowly but surely coming to fruition, despite delays and cost overruns. The most important is the World Trade Center (*see p57*), whose progress has seemed agonisingly slow since the 9/11 attacks. It's finally seen the completion of its most controversial element, the Santiago Calatrava-designed transport hub, which has cost $4 billion dollars, twice the original budget; its futuristic exo-skeleton structure has led people to compare it to a Stegosaurus. Unbelievably, given his reputation for burning money, Calatrava has been awarded the design for rebuilding nearby St Nicholas Greek Orthodox Church, also destroyed on 9/11. Costing around $38 million, his plan looks like an extraterrestrial version of the Hagia Sofia in Istanbul. World Trade 3, designed by Richard Rogers, has restarted after being stuck at seven storeys for several years. It's slated to open in 2018. Still missing in action are World Trade Center 2, designed by Lord Norman Foster, and a proposed performing arts centre that was originally going to be the work of Frank Gehry; he's since been taken off the project.

It's a truism in New York construction that the absence of lawsuits doesn't guarantee progress. Exhibit A is Brooklyn's once hotly contested Atlantic Yards, which has rebranded itself Pacific Park in hopes of a fresh start. In its dozen-year history, the project has only produced one visible accomplishment: the Barclays Center Arena, which opened in 2012. Since then, momentum on a series of residential towers using modular construction instead of conventional on-site construction has been hampered by design flaws.

EXIT FROM BROOKLYN?

Speaking of the Borough of Kings, no other part of New York City has undergone as much of an image makeover over the past quarter-century, going from a place to escape from to the world capital of cool. This transformation was entirely due to the arrival of the creative classes – artists and writers – expelled from Manhattan by rising rents. As usual in the gentrification process, developers have been in hot pursuit. High-rises are springing up all over downtown Brooklyn (now known as DoBro), each one challenged by the next for the title of tallest building in Brooklyn. The Fulton Mall, once a funky shopping street of sneaker and cell-phone emporia patronised mainly by African-Americans, is being reshaped by an influx of high-end shops culminating in City Point, a massive mixed-use complex that will stretch from Flatbush

to DeKalb Avenues. Court and Smith Streets, the main retail arteries of Cobble Hill and Boerum Hill, have seen mom-and-pop stores pushed out by such luxe purveyors as Barneys New York and Rag and Bone. The surrounding neighbourhoods, once largely Italian-American, have been settled increasingly by financial-industry types and even in some cases, celebrities. Famed British author Martin Amis is now a Cobble Hill resident. In an interview he once said that he was drawn to Brooklyn because of its 'prelapsarian' qualities.

That view may no longer be shared by the people who set the table for Brooklyn's renaissance, and are being pushed further south into Borough Park and as far East as Ridgewood, Queens. All of which raises the question: can the borough still claim its cool rep?

The answer for the moment appears to be yes and no. Bushwick continues to boast a lively gallery scene, for instance. Gowanus has pockets of hipster activity such as music venues and bars – though even here, an enormous Whole Foods supermarket opened in 2013. But it's become abundantly clear that the increasing costs of living in Brooklyn have made it untenable for those who pioneered it to remain. Recently, Galapagos, a long-established performance arts centre in Dumbo, pulled up stakes and left New York altogether – for Detroit! It's settled into a 40,000-square-foot home that would have been unaffordable in New York for anyone but a multi-billionaire.

Money, the old saying goes, changes everything, and that has been startlingly clear in New York for a long time. The city is safer and cleaner that ever before, and now hosts ever more extraordinary attractions for visitors. Attempts have begun to steer the city away from its dependence on finance towards a tech economy (Cornel University's extension on Roosevelt Island; a proposed technology park in Red Hook) but as the example of San Francisco shows, Silicon Valley-type industry will only add to the problem of wealth throttling cultural vitality where it starts: among those who have nothing, risking everything for their art. It's ironic that in a city where crime was once out of control, money now seems to be, presenting a challenge for any mayor, regardless of how progressive they aim to be.

Itineraries

Make the most of every New York minute with our three-day tour of the metropolis.

9AM

NOON

1PM

Day 1

9AM A disused freight-train track reborn as a public park-cum-promenade, the High Line (p123) has existed in its current incarnation for little more than half a decade, but it is already one of the most popular spots for both visitors and locals. Before you embark on your journey, boost your calorie intake with a made-to-order pastry from the new Dominique Ansel Kitchen (p118) in the West Village.

10AM Walk north along leafy West 4th Street with its picturesque townhouses, then take a left at Jane Street and continue north into the Meatpacking District. Here, upscale shops include cool designer boutique Owen (p124) and antique jewellers Doyle & Doyle (p124). But if you'd rather peruse paintings and sculptures than fashionable goods, spend a couple of hours in the new Whitney Museum of American Art (p125), which sits at the southernmost

7PM

Clockwise from far left: **Dominique Ansel Kitchen**; **High Line**; **54 Below** (see p26); **Empire Diner**.

entrance to the High Line, at Gansevoort and Washington Streets. If you don't want to make a commitment, you can check out the free lobby gallery without buying a ticket.

NOON As you stroll north on the High Line, keep an eye out for several interesting features. Commanding an expansive river view, the 'sun deck' between 14th and 15th Streets has wooden deck chairs that can be rolled along the original tracks, plus a water feature for cooling your feet. Just past 15th Street, the High Line cuts through the loading dock of the former Nabisco factory. This conglomeration of 18 structures, built between the 1890s and the 1930s, now houses Chelsea Market (p128). Alight here if you want to shop in the ground-floor food arcade for artisanal

bread, wine, baked goods and freshly made ice-cream, among other treats. From around late April until late October, however, food vendors set up on the High Line itself, and you can stop for a tipple at seasonal open-air vino spot Terroir.

The elevated walkway provides a great vantage point for viewing the surrounding architecture; you will see not only iconic structures like the Statue of Liberty and the Empire State Building, but also newer buildings such as Frank Gehry's 2007 headquarters for Barry Diller's InterActiveCorp (555 W 18th Street, at West Side Highway), which comprises tilting glass volumes that resemble a fully rigged tall ship.

1PM Stop for lunch at the iconic Empire Diner (p131) at 22nd Street. Now helmed by celebrity chef Amanda Freitag, it offers fresh seasonal spins on classic eats. Fortified, you're ready for some cultural sustenance. In the 1980s, many of New York's galleries left Soho for what was then an industrial wasteland on the western edge of Chelsea.

Today, blue-chip spaces and numerous less exalted ones attract swarms of art aficionados to the area between Tenth and Eleventh Avenues from 19th to 29th Streets (see p130 for our picks). If you want to pick up a souvenir, stop by arty bookshop Printed Matter (p132) or constantly changing concept store Story (p132).

4PM Your art tour isn't over when you resume your High Line perambulation (there are stairs at 23rd and 26th Streets). The park has a dedicated curator of temporary site-specific installations, so keep an eye out for temporary works along its length. The final section of the High Line skirts the under-construction mixed-use complex Hudson Yards, which over the next few years will be populated with retailers including a Neiman Marcus department store. You'll come to the end of the line at 34th Street and Eleventh Avenue.

5PM From here, you can walk or take a taxi to Hell's Kitchen. At Gotham West Market (p153), a contemporary take on a food court, you can choose from several cult eateries including Tokyo transplant Ivan Ramen. Otherwise, Ninth Avenue in the 40s and 50s is packed with inexpensive restaurants serving just about any ethnic cuisine you can think of.

7PM After dinner, the bright lights of Broadway (and Off Broadway), a few blocks away, beckon. Score cut-price Broadway tickets at TKTS (p309), or see high-level cabaret at 54 Below (p294), in the bowels of legendary nightspot Studio 54.

9AM

Day 2

9AM A short break in the Big Apple involves some tough choices: the Upper East Side's Museum Mile alone is lined with half a dozen world-class institutions. Fortify yourself with sumptuous pastries and exquisite coffee at Café Sabarsky (p188) as you mull over your itinerary. The newly expanded Cooper Hewitt, Smithsonian Design Museum (p186) is a must for design aficionados. If you opt for the Metropolitan Museum of Art (p185), you can either take a brisk two-hour essentials tour or forget the rest of the itinerary entirely – the vast museum is home to more than two million objects. Don't miss the recently rehung European Paintings Galleries, the Temple of Dendur and the Costume Institute among the many highlights. The Iris & B Gerald Cantor Roof Garden offers a view over Central Park, as well as a new installation each year, in the warmer months. Afterwards, even if you decide you can't manage another Museum Mile institution, walk a few blocks north to the Guggenheim (p188) to admire the curvaceous lines of its Frank Lloyd Wright-designed

1PM

exterior. Now it's time to ease your art-saturated brain with a stroll in the park. Enter at 79th or 76th Street and walk south to admire the picturesque Conservatory Water, or cross East Drive and try to snag a table at the outdoor bar at the Loeb Boathouse to gaze at the somewhat incongruous sight of gondolas on the lake over drinks.

1PM Grab a taxi on Fifth Avenue (or walk through the park) to the Museum of Modern Art (p157). If you happen to be in town on a Friday, it's worth noting it

Clockwise from top left: **Cooper Hewitt, Smithsonian Design Museum**; **Betony**; **MoMA**.

8PM

stays open until 8pm. Before you take in the superb collection of art and design, lunch at the more affordable bar of MoMA's destination restaurant, the Modern.

5PM Once you've had your fill of modern masterpieces, it's time to get high. Rockefeller Center's Top of the Rock (p158) is a less-mobbed alternative to the Empire State Building – and affords a good view of the latter iconic structure.

8PM Evening brings more dilemmas. Should you head back uptown for a global contemporary twist on soul food and live music at Red Rooster in Harlem (p198)? Or maybe it would be better to stick to midtown for a slap-up meal at Betony (p160), followed by a Broadway or Off-Broadway show. It's simply a matter of taste.

No sleep till Brooklyn

It's hard to imagine that in the early years of this millennium, visitors who ventured into Brooklyn tended to be diehard urban explorers or staying with friends. These days, if you're in town for any period longer than a weekend, an excursion to the second borough is essential. Newcomers are discovering it's not as far from Manhattan as they thought – one of the nicest ways to get there is on foot. This full-day itinerary links two historic, culture-rich and fashionable neighbourhoods – with some exhilarating views in the middle.

New York's character has been shaped by successive waves of immigrants, from the Dutch settlers who invaded the domain of the Lenape Indians in the 16th century to more recent Asian and Latino arrivals. But in the early 20th century, the Lower East Side was home to the world's largest Jewish community, most of them from Eastern Europe. Some of the businesses started by those enterprising arrivals are still going strong, including Yonah Schimmel Knish Bakery (p92) – named after the rabbi who originally sold the namesake nosh from a pushcart – and smoked-fish specialists Russ & Daughters, which has been run by the same family since 1914. In its centenary year, the original Russ's great-grandchildren opened a café (p92) in the

Russ & Daughters Café.

Lower East Side Tenement Museum.

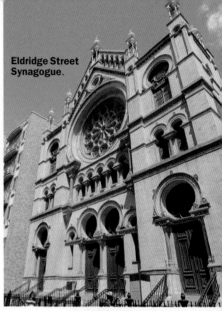

Eldridge Street Synagogue.

same spirit as the throwback shop around the corner. In homage to the old country, start your day with the Shtetl sandwich: smoked sable and goat's milk cream cheese on a bialy.

On Orchard Street, you can pick out a few old-school survivors among the stylish new boutiques and galleries, including Orchard Corset (no.157, between Rivington & Stanton Streets, 1-212 674 0786, www.orchard corset.com; closed Sat), which was opened by corset-factory pattern cutter Isaiah Bernstein in the 1960s.

For a window into how locals lived – and worked – in the 19th and early 20th centuries, the Lower East Side Tenement Museum (p87) conducts tours of apartments once occupied by documented residents, some of whom operated businesses on the site. If you'd rather contemplate the provenance of impeccably selected vintage wares, head to Edith Machinist (p95) and David Owens Vintage (p95). Combining retail past and present, seasonal fixture Hester Street Fair (p35), on the site of a former pushcart market at Hester and Essex Streets, sells a mix of vintage, crafts and artisanal food.

Four blocks west and one block south, on the edge of Chinatown, admire the Eldridge Street Synagogue (p88), which has an impressive façade combining Moorish, Romanesque and Gothic details and an opulent interior. A stained-glass window, added in 2010, was designed by prominent New York artist Kiki Smith.

Second only to Chelsea, today's Lower East Side is a major contemporary art hub, home to some of the city's most cutting-edge galleries, along with the New Museum of Contemporary

Art (p88). After popping into a few (consult our gallery-hopping guide on p94), pick up a one-of-a-kind souvenir at Objectify 139 (p95), where artist-made, NYC-themed items trump foam Statue of Liberty crowns and I Love NY T-shirts.

Before you trek to Brooklyn, you'll want to stop for lunch. With a wealth of restaurants crammed into these streets, it's tough to choose, but since every trip to NYC must include at least one classic deli, we recommend a corned beef sandwich at cavernous no-frills canteen Katz's Delicatessen (p90).

When the Williamsburg Bridge was completed in 1903, it was the longest suspension bridge in the world. Soon after, it became known as the 'Jews' Highway' because it provided an exodus for Lower East Side residents into Brooklyn; Williamsburg retains a Hasidic community among its diverse demographic. The bridge's chief engineer was Leffert Lefferts Buck. In 1898, he also built an ill-fated 'honeymoon' bridge at Niagara Falls, which collapsed into the falls when a run of ice came down from Lake Erie. But don't let that scare you – hoof it uphill on the two-way bike- and footpath straight up the centre, and you'll get an expansive skyline vista.

When you arrive in Brooklyn, take a left on to Havemeyer Street and you'll reach the City Reliquary (p217) at Metropolitan Avenue. This small, volunteer-run museum preserves all kinds of urban artefacts and Gotham relics and hosts temporary shows spotlighting such quirky local collections as historic pizza boxes amassed by Scott Weiner of Scott's Pizza Tours (www.scottspizzatours.com). Mirroring the Lower East Side's evolution, Williamsburg became colonised by artists, musicians and other nonconformists before luxury apartments started taking root. Like its counterpart across the East River, it has a mix of indie boutiques, vintage shops and glossier businesses. But the neighbourhood is probably best known for its indie-rock and club scene. Head north then back towards the river on North 9th Street to browse vinyl and maybe catch a free show at NYC's outpost of London music emporium Rough Trade (p224). There's no shortage of dinner options in the area – you might choose a dozen oysters and absinthe at Nola-inspired Maison Premiere (p222), or perhaps dinner and a movie – simultaneously – at Nitehawk Cinema (p260). But for a truly unique dining experience, secure a table at Semilla (p220) – the 'vegetable forward' tasting menu may not be cheap, but it's a great deal compared with others of this calibre. If you can still move after this bi-borough odyssey, end the night at one of New York's best clubs, Verboten (p277), or catch a gig at one of many music venues in this rockin' part of town.

Rough Trade.

Semilla.

NEW YORK FOR FREE
Some of the best things in the city are literally priceless.

SUMMER SAVINGS
When the temperature soars, the populace heads outside for superb events, from the star-studded plays of Shakespeare in the Park to big-name concerts in venues throughout the city at SummerStage and the River to River Festival. Outdoor film series bring big screens to several parks.

CASHLESS CULTURE
Time it right and you can visit many top institutions at no charge. On Friday nights, the Museum of Modern Art stays open late and admission – including films – is waived, while on the first Saturday of most months the Brooklyn Museum lays on live performances in addition to evening admission. New York also has many fine museums that are always free, including the National Museum of the American Indian, the Museum at FIT and the American Folk Art Museum.

CHEAPSKATES' CRUISE
It's no secret that the Staten Island Ferry provides thrilling panoramas of New York Harbor and the Statue of Liberty during its brief crossing. You can also cruise to Red Hook, Brooklyn on New York Water Taxi's IKEA Express Shuttle (p375), which is free on weekends and has an outdoor deck to take in the skyline en route.

GARDEN VARIETY
Offering more than mere greenery, New York's parks are filled with diversions, from the art-studded High Line to Brooklyn Bridge Park's vintage carousel.

GET IN ON THE ACT
Free entertainment isn't only on the streets. At some of the Upright Citizens Brigade Theater's long-running comedy shows, the laughs are on them, and you can catch gratis concerts at Lincoln Center's David Rubenstein Atrium – they're usually held on Thursday nights.

Diary

*Our year-round
guide to the city's best
festivals and events.*

New Yorkers hardly struggle to find something to celebrate. The venerable citywide traditions are well known, but there are also numerous offbeat shindigs brimming with character. Soak up the local vibe at quirky annual events such as Brooklyn's Mermaid Parade or the Jazz Age Lawn Party on Governors Island, and take advantage of free summer concerts and outdoor films in the city's green spaces, such as Bryant, Central and Madison Square Parks. For more festivals and events, check out the other chapters in the Arts & Entertainment section. Before you set out or plan a trip around an event, it's wise to call or check online first as dates, times and locations are subject to change. For the latest listings, consult *Time Out New York* magazine or www.timeout.com/newyork.

New Year's Eve in Times Square.
See p39.

Spring

Armory Show
*Piers 92 & 94, Twelfth Avenue, at 55th Street,
Hell's Kitchen (1-212 645 6440, www.thearmory
show.com). Subway C, E to 50th Street.* **Date**
early Mar.
Although its name pays homage to the 1913 show
that introduced avant-garde European art to an
American audience, this contemporary interna-
tional art mart debuted in 1999. It's now held on the
Hudson River.

St Patrick's Day Parade
*Fifth Avenue, from 44th to 79th Streets, Midtown
to Upper East Side (www.nycstpatricksparade.org).*
Date 17 Mar.
This massive march is even older than the United
States – it was started by a group of homesick Irish
conscripts from the British army in 1762. If you feel
like braving huge crowds and potentially nasty
weather, you'll see thousands of green-clad merry-
makers strutting to the sounds of pipe bands.

PUBLIC HOLIDAYS

Memorial Day
30 May 2016, 29 May 2017

Independence Day
4 July

Labor Day
7 Sept 2015, 5 Sept 2016

Columbus Day
12 Oct 2015, 10 Oct 2016

Veterans Day
11 Nov

Thanksgiving Day
26 Nov 2015, 24 Nov 2016,

Christmas Day
25 Dec

New Year's Day
1 Jan

Martin Luther King, Jr Day
18 Jan 2016, 16 Jan 2017

Presidents Day
15 Feb 2016, 20 Feb 2017

THE BEST OF BROADWAY

FINAL BROADWAY PERFORMANCE

SEPTEMBER 5, 2015

♿ **BROADHURST THEATRE**
MammaMiaNorthAmerica.com

"**EXACTLY WHAT YOU WISHED FOR!**"
NBC-TV

Disney *Aladdin*

BROADWAY'S NEW MUSICAL COMEDY

New Amsterdam Theatre, Broadway & 42nd Street • 866-870-2717
AladdinTheMusical.com ✦ 🐦 📷

© Disney

"THERE IS SIMPLY
NOTHING ELSE LIKE IT."
THE NEW YORK TIMES

Disney PRESENTS
THE LION KING

THE AWARD-WINNING BEST MUSICAL

Ⓝ Minskoff Theatre, B'way & 45th St.
866-870-2717 | lionking.com ✦ 🐦 📷

©Disney

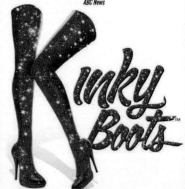

"*Cyndi Lauper delivers the best Broadway score in years!*"
ABC News

Kinky Boots™

**BROADWAY'S HUGE-HEARTED,
TONY-WINNING BEST MUSICAL!**

KINKYBOOTSTHEMUSICAL.COM
TELECHARGE.COM or +1-212-239-6200 • ♿ AL HIRSCHFELD THEATRE, 302 W. 45ᵀᴴ ST.

Easter Parade

Fifth Avenue, from 49th to 57th Streets, Midtown.
Subway E, M to Fifth Avenue-53rd Street. **Date** late
Mar/early Apr.

From 10am on Easter Sunday, participants gather to
show off elaborately constructed hats – we're talking noggin-toppers shaped like the NYC skyline or
the Coney Island Cyclone. Fifth Avenue becomes a
car-free promenade of gussied-up crowds milling
around and showing off their extravagant bonnets.

Tribeca Film Festival

Date Apr.
See p263.

Sakura Matsuri (Cherry Blossom Festival)

For listings, *see p214* **Brooklyn Botanic Garden**.
Date late Apr.

The climax to the cherry blossom season, when
more than 200 trees are in flower, the annual Sakura
Matsuri celebrates both the blooms and Japanese culture with concerts, traditional dance, cosplay fashion
shows, manga exhibitions and tea ceremonies.

TD Five Boro Bike Tour

Lower Manhattan to Staten Island (1-212 870 2080,
www.bikenewyork.org). **Date** early May.

Thousands of cyclists take over the city for a
40-mile, car-free Tour de New York. Advance
registration is required if you want to take part.
The route begins near Battery Park, moves up
through Manhattan and makes a circuit of the
boroughs before winding up at Staten Island's Fort
Wadsworth for a festival.

Frieze Art Fair New York

Randalls Island Park (www.friezenewyork.com).
Date early/mid May.

The New York edition of the tent-tastic London art
fair first arrived on Randalls Island in 2011. A global
array of around 190 galleries sets up shop under a
temporary structure overlooking the East River, and
several contemporary artists are commissioned to
create site-specific works.

Washington Square Outdoor Art Exhibit

Various streets surrounding Washington Square
Park, from University Place, at 13th Street, to
Schwartz Plaza, at 3rd Street, Greenwich Village
(1-212 982 6255, www.wsoae.org). Subway A, B, C,
D, E, F, M to W 4th Street; N, R to 8th Street-NYU.
Date late May/early June & early/mid Sept.

In 1931, Jackson Pollock and Willem de Kooning
propped up a few of their paintings on the pavement
near Washington Square Park and called it a show. A
lot has changed since then: now, more than 125 artists and artisans exhibit here. If you miss it in May
and June, you'll have another chance to browse in late
summer/early autumn.

Frieze Art Fair New York.

Summer

SummerStage

Rumsey Playfield, Central Park, entrance on Fifth
Avenue, at 72nd Street, Upper East Side (1-212 360
2777, www.summerstage.org). Subway 6 to 68th
Street-Hunter College. **Date** late May-early Oct.

Rockers, world music stars, orchestras and performers in various disciplines take over the main stage in
Central Park – and green spaces across the five boroughs – for this very popular and mostly free annual
series, which marked its 30th season in 2015. Show
up early or listen from outside the enclosure gates.

Shakespeare in the Park

Date June-Aug.
See p319.

Celebrate Brooklyn!

Prospect Park Bandshell, Prospect Park West, at 9th
Street, Park Slope, Brooklyn (1-718 855 7882, www.
bricartsmedia.org). Subway F to Seventh Avenue.
Date June-Aug.

Community arts organisation BRIC launched
this series of outdoor performances to revitalise
Prospect Park, and now the festival is Brooklyn's
premier summer fête. It includes music, dance, film
and spoken word acts. A $3 donation is requested
and there's an admission charge for some shows.

Jazz Age Lawn Party

Governors Island, see p55 (www.jazzagelawnparty.
com). **Date** mid June & mid Aug.

Young hepcats in period garb gather on the green
pastures of Colonels Row to drink cocktails and look

clockwise
from left:
**Jazz Age
Lawn Party**
(see p33);
**Brooklyn
Flea**;
**Mermaid
Parade**.

fantastic. Held twice during the summer, the weekend event includes Charleston contests, old-timey swimsuit competitions, vintage portraits and a DJ spinning 78rpm records, among other activities.

National Puerto Rican Day Parade

Fifth Avenue, from 44th to 79th Streets,
Midtown to Upper East Side (www.nprdpinc.org).
Date early/mid June.
A whopping 80,000 Nuyoricans take part in the march, including *vejigantes* (carnival dancers), colourful floats and live salsa and reggaetón bands at this celebration of the city's largest Hispanic community and its culture.

Egg Rolls & Egg Creams Festival

Museum at Eldridge Street. For listings, see p88.
Date early June.
This block party organised by the Museum at Eldridge Street celebrates the convergence of Jewish and Chinese traditions on the Lower East Side, with klezmer music, acrobats, Chinese opera, tea ceremonies and, of course, plenty of the titular treats.

Governors Ball Music Festival

Randalls Island Park (www.governorsball
musicfestival.com). **Date** early June.
NYC still can't boast a summer music fest as iconic as Coachella or Bonnaroo, but with every year, Gov Ball inches closer to that status. The eclectic slate of crowd-pleasers has recently included Drake, the Black Keys, Deadmau5, Lana Del Rey, Florence and the Machine, My Morning Jacket and Björk. There are plenty of cool names further down the bill too.

Big Apple Barbecue Block Party

Madison Square Park, Flatiron District
(www.bigapplebbq.org). Subway N, R, 6 to 23rd
Street; 6 to 28th Street. **Date** early/mid June.
Get your fill of the best 'cue around as the country's top pit masters band together for this two-day outdoor carnivore's paradise. Live music, chefs' demos and tips are also on the menu.

Museum Mile Festival

Fifth Avenue, from 82nd to 105th Streets,
Upper East Side (1-212 606 2296, www.
museummilefestival.org). **Date** early June.
Nine of the city's most prestigious art institutions – including the Guggenheim, the Met and the Museum of the City of New York – open their doors to the public free of charge. Music, dance and children's activities turn this into a 23-block-long celebration, but you'll have to arrive early to stand a chance of getting into the museums themselves.

New York Philharmonic Concerts in the Parks

Date mid/late June.
See p301 **Everything Under the Sun.**

★ River to River Festival

Various venues along the West Side & southern
waterfronts of Manhattan (1-212 219 9401,
www.rivertorivernyc.com). **Date** mid-late June.
Lower Manhattan organisations present dozens of free events – from visual arts to all sorts of

FLEA SEASON
Spring brings cool markets across the city.

BROOKLYN FLEA
Launched in 2008 by Jonathan Butler, founder of real-estate blog Brownstoner.com, and Eric Demby, former PR man for the Brooklyn borough president, the Brooklyn Flea was the first of a new breed of bazaar in NYC, offering high-quality crafts, locally designed fashion and gourmet snacks alongside vintage wares and bric-a-brac. The original location, which has around 150 vendors, operates in a Fort Greene schoolyard from April through November. Several spin-offs include the nosh-only Smorgasburg, and in winter the market moves to an indoor space.
176 Lafayette Avenue, between Clermont & Vanderbilt Avenues, Fort Greene (www.brooklynflea.com; see website for other locations).

BROOKLYN NIGHT BAZAAR
On Friday and Saturday nights all year round, Brooklyn Night Bazaar features a locally focused line-up of art, crafts and food in a 24,000-square-foot warehouse. A beer garden and music add to the mix – four to five bands play each night.
165 Banker Street, at Norman Avenue, Greenpoint (www.bkbazaar.com).

HESTER STREET FAIR
You can sample everything from Brooklyn-made popsicles to lobster rolls as you browse vintage fashion, hand-crafted jewellery, ceramics and more from 60-plus vendors. Located on the site of a former pushcart market, Hester Street Fair is open Saturdays from late April to the end of October.
Hester Street, at Essex Street, Lower East Side (www.hesterstreetfair.com).

LIC FLEA & FOOD
The brainchild of local publisher Josh Schneps, Long Island City's market is strong on vintage wares, but you'll also find vendors of everything from locally made jewellery to international food. The on-site beer garden serves suds from all six of the borough's breweries. The open-air bazaar runs from mid April to the end of October, then moves indoors during November and December.
5-25 46th Avenue, between Vernon Boulevard and 5th Street, Long Island City, Queens (www.licflea.com).

performances – at various venues. Past participants have included Patti Smith, Laurie Anderson and Angélique Kidjo.

★ Mermaid Parade
Coney Island, Brooklyn (1-718 372 5159, www.coneyisland.com). Subway D, F, N, Q to Coney Island-Stillwell Avenue. **Date** 3rd Sat in June.
Glitter-covered semi-nude revellers, aquatically adorned floats and classic cruisers fill Surf Avenue for this annual art parade.

★ Midsummer Night Swing
Damrosch Park at Lincoln Center Plaza, W 62nd Street, between Columbus & Amsterdam Avenues, Upper West Side (1-212 721 6500, www.midsummer nightswing.org). Subway 1 to 66th Street-Lincoln Center. **Date** late June-mid July.
Lincoln Center's Damrosch Park is turned into a giant dancefloor as bands play salsa, Cajun, swing and other music. For three weeks (Tue-Sat), each night's party is devoted to a different dance style, and is preceded by lessons. Beginners are welcome, of course.

★ NYC LGBT Pride March
From Fifth Avenue, at 36th Street, to Christopher Street, Midtown to West Village (1-212 807 7433, www.nycpride.org). **Date** late June.

clockwise
from right:
**Macy's
Fourth of
July
Fireworks;
Lincoln
Center Out
of Doors;
US Open**.

Downtown Manhattan becomes a sea of rainbow flags as lesbian, gay, bisexual and transgendered people from the city and beyond parade down Fifth Avenue in commemoration of the 1969 Stonewall Riots. After the march, there's a massive street fair and a dance on the West Side piers.

Warm Up
Date late June-early Sept.
See p280.

Howl! Festival
Various East Village locations (1-212 466 6666, www.howlfestival.com). **Date** July.
A reading of Allen Ginsberg's seminal poem kicks off this three-day arts fest – a grab bag of art events, film screenings, poetry readings, performance art and much more.

Macy's Fourth of July Fireworks
Various East River locations (www.macys.com/fireworks). **Date** 4 July.
After a few years on the Hudson, NYC's main Independence Day attraction moved back to the East River, where fireworks are launched from barges and the Brooklyn Bridge. The pyrotechnics start at around 9pm, but you'll need to scope out your vantage point much earlier. Spectators are packed like sardines at prime spots.

Harlem Week
Various Harlem locations (1-877 427 5364, www. harlemweek.com). Subway B, C, 2, 3 to 135th Street. **Date** late July-late Aug.
Get into the groove at this massive culture fest, which began in 1974 as a one-day event. Harlem Day is still the centrepiece, but 'Harlem Week' is now a misnomer; besides the street fair serving up music, art and food along 135th Street, a wealth of

concerts, films, dance performances, fashion and sports events are on tap for around a month.

Summer Restaurant Week
www.nycgo.com/restaurantweek. **Date** late July/early Aug.
Twice a year, for two weeks or more at a stretch, some of the city's finest restaurants dish out three-course prix-fixe lunches for $25; some also offer dinner for $38. For the full list of participating restaurants, visit the website. Make reservations well in advance.

Lincoln Center Out of Doors
For listings, *see p296* **Lincoln Center**.
Date late July-early Aug.
Free dance, music, theatre, opera and more make up the programme over the course of three weeks at this ambitious and family-friendly festival.

New York International Fringe Festival
Various venues (1-212 279 4488, www.fringenyc. org). **Date** mid-late Aug.

Wacky and sometimes wonderful, downtown's Fringe Festival – inspired by the Edinburgh original – shoehorns hundreds of arts performances into 16 theatre-crammed days.
▶ *See p321 for more information on Off-Off Broadway shows.*

US Open
USTA Billie Jean King National Tennis Center, Flushing Meadows Corona Park, Queens (1-718 760 6200, www.usopen.org). Subway 7 to Mets-Willets Point. **Date** late Aug-mid Sept.
For two weeks every summer, Flushing, Queens, becomes the centre of the tennis universe when it hosts the final Grand Slam event of the year.

Autumn

West Indian-American Day Carnival Parade
Eastern Parkway, from Schenectady Avenue to Flatbush Avenue, Crown Heights, Brooklyn (1-718 467 1797, www.wiadcacarnival.org). Subway 2, 3 to Grand Army Plaza; 3, 4 to Crown Heights-Utica Avenue. **Date** early Sept.
This annual Caribbean celebration is never short on costumed stilt dancers, floats blaring soca and calypso music, and plenty of flags from Caribbean countries like Trinidad & Tobago, Jamaica and elsewhere. Look out for vendors stationed along Eastern Parkway selling island eats such as jerk chicken, curry goat and oxtail.

Electric Zoo
Randall's Island (www.electriczoofestival.com). **Date** early Sept.
Don your Day-Glo shades and head for this three-day outdoor EDM rager. The line-up is heavy on superstar DJs such as Armin Van Buuren, David Guetta and Dimitri Vegas & Like Mike.

Feast of San Gennaro
Mulberry Street, between Canal & Houston Streets; Grand Street, between Baxter & Mott Streets; Hester Street, between Baxter & Mott Streets, Little Italy (1-212 768 9320, www.sangennaro.org). Subway B, D, F, M to Broadway-Lafayette Street; J, N, Q, R, Z, 6 to Canal Street. **Date** mid-late Sept.
Celebrate the martyred third-century bishop and patron saint of Naples at this 11-day festival that fills the streets of Little Italy every year. Come after dark, when sparkling lights arch over Mulberry Street and the smells of frying *zeppole* (custard- or jam-filled fritters) and sausages hang in the sultry air. On the offical feast day, a statue of San Gennaro is carried in a Grand Procession outside the Most Precious Blood Church.

Brooklyn Book Festival
Brooklyn Borough Hall & Plaza, 209 Joralemon Street, at Court Street, Downtown Brooklyn (www.brooklynbookfestival.org). Subway 2, 3, 4, 5 to Borough Hall. **Date** mid-late Sept.
The city's largest (and free) literary fest takes over Brooklyn Borough Hall and Plaza every autumn for a full day of panels and readings, bibliophile swag and inordinate book buying.

Next Wave Festival
For listings, *see p295* **Brooklyn Academy of Music**. **Date** Sept-Dec.
The festival is among the most highly anticipated of the city's autumn culture offerings, as it showcases only the very best in avant-garde music, dance, theatre and opera. Legends like John Cale, Meredith Monk and Steve Reich are among the many luminaries the festival has hosted.

Atlantic Antic
Atlantic Avenue, from Fourth Avenue to Hicks Street, Brooklyn (1-718 875 8993, www.atlanticave.org). Subway B, Q, 2, 3, 4, 5 to Atlantic Avenue; D, N, R to Pacific Street. **Date** late Sept.
More than 500 food and craft vendors and a dozen stages close down a busy Brooklyn artery for the annual Atlantic Antic. Spanning ten blocks and cutting through four neighbourhoods, it's billed as NYC's largest street fair, and features local bands and cult Brooklyn food and drink.

★ New York Film Festival
Date late Sept-mid Oct.
See p263.

★ Open House New York Weekend
1-212 991 6470, www.ohny.org. **Date** mid Oct.
Around 200 of the city's coolest and most exclusive architectural sites, private homes and landmarks open their doors during a weekend of urban exploration. Behind-the-scenes tours and educational programmes are also on offer.

CMJ Music Marathon

Various venues (1-212 235 7027, www.cmj.com).
Date mid Oct.
The annual *College Music Journal* schmooze-fest draws fans and music-industry types to one of the best showcases for new rock, indie, hip hop and electronica acts.

New York City Wine & Food Festival

Various locations (www.nycwff.org). Date mid Oct.
The Food Network's epicurean fête offers four belt-busting days of tasting events and celebrity-chef demos.

Tompkins Square Park Halloween Dog Parade

Tompkins Square Park, East Village (www.tompkinssquaredogrun.com). Subway L to First Avenue; 6 to Astor Place. **Date** late Oct.
To see a plethora of puppies in adorable outfits, head to this canine costume parade, which has been an East Village institution for more than two decades. The get-ups are remarkably elaborate and conceptual and have included Evita, ET and one of the sandworms from *Beetlejuice*. Enterprising owners win prizes if their dog is selected Best in Show.

★ Village Halloween Parade

Sixth Avenue, from Spring to 16th Streets, Greenwich Village (www.halloween-nyc.com).
Date 31 Oct.
The sidewalks at this iconic Village shindig are always packed beyond belief. For the best vantage point, don a costume and watch from inside the parade (the line-up starts at 6.30pm on Sixth Avenue, at Spring Street; the parade kicks off at 7pm).

Winter

New York Comedy Festival

Various venues (www.nycomedyfestival.com).
Date early-mid Nov.
This five-day laugh fest features both big names (Jerry Seinfeld, Larry David, Bill Cosby and Amy Schumer in recent years) and up-and-comers.

New York City Marathon

Staten Island side of the Verrazano-Narrows Bridge to Tavern on the Green in Central Park (1-212 423 2249, www.tcsnycmarathon.org). **Date** early Nov.
Around 50,000 runners hotfoot it through all five boroughs over a 26.2-mile course. For a good view, we recommend staking out a spot on First Avenue between 60th and 96th Streets, Central Park South, or Fourth Avenue in Park Slope, Brooklyn.

Macy's Thanksgiving Day Parade & Balloon Inflation

Central Park West, at 77th Street, to Macy's, Broadway, at 34th Street, Upper West Side

to Midtown (1-212 494 4495, www.macys.com/parade). **Date** late Nov.
At 9am on Thanksgiving Day, the stars of this nationally televised parade are the gigantic balloons, the elaborate floats and good ol' Santa Claus. The evening before, New Yorkers brave the cold night air to watch the rubbery colossi take shape at the inflation area around the Museum of Natural History (beginning at 79th Street & Columbus Avenue).

Rockefeller Center Tree-Lighting Ceremony

Rockefeller Center, Fifth Avenue, between 49th & 50th Streets, Midtown (1-212 332 6868, www.rockefellercenter.com). Subway B, D, F, M to 47th-50th Streets-Rockefeller Center. **Date** early Dec.
Proceedings start at 7pm, but this festive celebration is always mobbed, so get there early. Most of the two-hour event is devoted to celebrity performances, then the 30,000 LEDs covering the massive ever-green are switched on.

Unsilent Night

Washington Square Arch, Fifth Avenue, at Waverly Place, to Tompkins Square Park, Greenwich Village to East Village (www.unsilentnight.com). Subway A, B, C, D, E, F, M to W 4th Street. **Date** mid Dec.
This trippy musical performance piece, dreamed up by composer Phil Kline, is downtown's arty, secular

clockwise
from far left:
**Rockfeller
Center Tree-
Lighting
Ceremony;
Chinese
New Year;
Unsilent
Night.**

New Year's Day Marathon Reading

Poetry Project at St Mark's Church, 131 E 10th Street, at Second Avenue (1-212 674 0910, www.poetryproject.org). Subway L to Third Avenue; 6 to Astor Place. **Date** 1 Jan.

Around 140 of the city's best poets, artists and performers gather at St Mark's Church in-the-Bowery and, one after another, recite their work to a hall full of listeners. Big-name bohemians such as Anne Waldman and Patti Smith have stepped up to the mic during this spoken-word spectacle, organised by the Poetry Project.

No Pants Subway Ride

www.improveverywhere.com. **Date** early Jan.

Improv Everywhere's annual barefaced, bare-legged mission began in January 2002 with a handful of operatives in one car on the downtown 6 train, but it's grown into a well-publicised mass event. Admittedly, it's not the mildly subversive, playful prank it was – it's now a chance for New Yorkers to perform a cheeky feat while supported by thousands of fellow residents. For unsuspecting visitors, it's a surreal spectacle.

Winter Restaurant Week

For listings, *see p36* **Summer Restaurant Week**. **Date** late Jan/early Feb.

The Winter Restaurant Week provides yet another opportunity to sample delicious gourmet food at highly palatable prices.

Chinese New Year

Around Mott Street, Chinatown (www.better chinatown.com). Subway J, N, Q, R, Z, 6 to Canal Street. **Date** early Feb.

Gung hay fat choy!, the greeting goes. Chinatown bustles with colour and is charged with energy during the two weeks of the Lunar New Year. The firecracker ceremony – which includes lion dances and food and craft vendors as well as the pyrotechnics – and parade are key events.

answer to Christmas carolling. Boom-box-toting participants gather under the Washington Square Arch, where they are given a cassette or CD of one of four different atmospheric tracks; you can also download the Unsilent Night app and sync up via smartphone. Everyone then presses play at the same time and marches through the streets of New York, blending their music and filling the air with a beautiful, echoing 45-minute piece.

New Year's Eve in Times Square

Times Square, Theater District (1-212 768 1560, www.timessquarenyc.org). Subway N, Q, R, S, 1, 2, 3, 7 to 42nd Street-Times Square. **Date** 31 Dec.

Get together with a million others and watch the giant illuminated Waterford Crystal ball descend amid a blizzard of confetti and cheering. Arrive by 3pm at the latest to stake out a spot in the Broadway-Seventh Avenue bowtie and be prepared to stay put. There are no public restrooms or food vendors, and leaving means giving up your spot. Your endurance will be rewarded with celebrity performances held across two stages, beginning at 6pm. Forget toasting the new year with champagne, though: public drinking is illegal in NYC. *Photo p31.*

New York's Best

Check off the essentials with our list of hand-picked highlights.

New Museum of Contemporary Art.

Sightseeing

VIEWS

One World Observatory p59
Whizz up the western hemisphere's tallest tower.

Empire State Building p157
No longer the highest viewpoint, but still the top.

Brooklyn Heights Promenade p204
Postcard-worthy views from this riverside strip.

Brooklyn Bridge p205
The city's most scenic pedestrian crossing.

Times Square p151
Climb the TKTS steps for a 360-degree light show.

Rockefeller Center p158
Great views from the 70th-floor Top of the Rock observation deck.

ART

Metropolitan Museum of Art p185
A mammoth era- and globespanning collection.

Museum of Modern Art p157
Modern masterpieces and much more.

Solomon R Guggenheim Museum p188
Frank Lloyd Wright's building is the real treasure.

Whitney Museum of American Art p123
A major art hub beside the High Line.

The Cloisters p200
A magical melange of medieval buildings set in a riverside park.

New Museum of Contemporary Art p88
Ground-breaking art in a striking structure.

National September 11 Memorial & Museum.

Noguchi Museum p232
A serene sanctuary for
sculpture in Queens.

HISTORY
**Lower East Side Tenement
Museum** p87
See how immigrants lived in
this erstwhile slum.
New-York Historical Society
p171
A revamp shook the dust from
this impressive collection.
**Museum of the City of New
York** p187
Engaging city-centric
exhibitions.
**American Museum of Natural
History** p170
The famous dioramas have
been restored.

OUTDOORS
Central Park p175
Manhattan's back yard.
Governors Island p53
An island retreat just minutes
from lower Manhattan.
Brooklyn Bridge Park p205
Lush lawns, knockout views
and NYC's coolest carousel.
The High Line p123
All aboard the elevated
park-cum-walkway.

RELIGIOUS BUILDINGS
St Patrick's Cathedral p159
A white marble confection
with a Tiffany altar.
**Cathedral Church of St John
the Divine** p177
Unfinished but awe-inspiring.
St Paul's Chapel p56
One of the finest Georgian
buildings in America.
Eldridge Street Synagogue
p88
A major restoration included a
Kiki Smith-designed window.

ICONS
Statue of Liberty p55
This American icon is truly
a marvel.

**National September 11
Memorial & Museum** p60
A monumental tribute as
dramatic as it is moving.
Chrysler Building p161
A dazzling art deco homage
to the automobile.
Flatiron Building p136
This early skyscraper still
impresses.
Yankee Stadium p241
The new limestone arena is
a worthy successor to the
'House that Ruth Built'.
Coney Island Cyclone p225
Take a teeth-rattling ride on
this classic roller coaster.

CURIOSITIES
Mmuseumm p73
A bizarre collection displayed
in a disused elevator shaft.
City Reliquary p218
All manner of Gotham
ephemera and memorabilia.
Morbid Anatomy Museum
p214
Displays that illuminate the
dark side.

CHILDREN
**Children's Museum of
Manhattan** p253
Educational and entertaining
exhibits for each age group.
Sony Wonder Technology Lab
p254
Virtual fun for little techies.
New Victory Theater p255
Exciting international youth-
targeted productions.

Eating &
drinking

INSTITUTIONS
Barney Greengrass p171
Massive egg and fish platters
and delightfully gruff staff.
Katz's Delicatessen p90
Film-set looks and celebrated
pastrami sandwiches.

RADIO CITY
═ STAGE DOOR ═
TOUR™

MEET A ROCKETTE!

GO BEHIND THE SCENES OF THE SHOWPLACE OF THE NATION!

TOURS RUN DAILY FROM 10:00AM TO 5:00PM

1260 AVENUE OF THE AMERICAS AT 50TH STREET

── PURCHASE TICKETS TODAY! ──

INFO	VISIT	GROUPS
212-247-4777	StageDoorTour.com	212-465-6080

Peter Luger p220
Steakhouses come and go, but Luger is the original.
Grand Central Oyster Bar & Restaurant p163
The classic spot for bivalves and cocktails.
McSorley's Old Ale House p106
Houdini was just one of the regulars at this historic pub.

BLOWOUTS
Carbone p114
The food is as satisfying as the retro setting at this reimagined mob supper club.
Narcissa p105
Sublime cuisine outshines an unremarkable dining room.
The NoMad p141
Elegant dining in plush, Paris-inspired surroundings.
Semilla p220
Destination-worthy vegetable dishes.

AMERICAN
The Dutch p68
A raucous restaurant and oyster bar from hot chef Andrew Carmellini.
Shake Shack p173
Danny Meyer's burger stand is now a chain, but still delivers prime patties.
Empire Diner p131
A chrome NYC icon with a celeb chef in the kitchen.

MODERN MELTING POT
Cosme p139
Mexican goes modern.
Ivan Ramen p89
A culture-crossing bowl.
Momofuku Ssäm Bar p105
Contemporary Korean from David Chang.
Pok Pok NY p210
A renowned Portland chef brings his personal touch to Thai cuisine.
RedFarm p120
Imaginative riffs on dim sum.

Opening Ceremony.

Red Rooster Harlem p198
Soul food from a Swedish-raised, Ethiopian toque.
Roberta's p220
Imaginative, seasonal spins on pizza and more.

BRUNCH
Allswell p218
Reliable diner-style dishes in Williamsburg.
Benoit p159
The all-you-can-eat dessert bar is a sweet-tooth's delight.
Jack's Wife Freda p70
Creative riffs on late-morning grub at great prices.
Cookshop p129
Seasonal variations on classics like French toast.
Lafayette p104
A lively spot for top-notch pastries and egg dishes.

BARS
Raine's Law Room p142
Exquisite cocktails are mixed in the 'kitchen' of this bar-less speakeasy.
PDT p106
The phonebooth entry is fun, but the drinks are serious.

Sunny's Bar p212
A time-warp waterside tavern.
Bohemian Hall & Beer Garden p234
A remnant of Queens quaffing history.

Shopping
CONCEPT
Dover Street Market p165
Rei Kawakubo's arty Comme mega-boutique.
Fivestory p184
Chic clothing and homewares in a townhouse setting.
Opening Ceremony p72
Gold-standard avant-garde looks, books and music.
Story p132
The ever-changing concept means it never gets old.
Modern Anthology p209
Everything that a fashionable male needs.

FOOD & DRINK
Eataly p143
An entire country's worth of flavours under one roof.

clockwise from top left: **Objectify 139**; **Verboten**; **Mantiques Modern**.

Bond Street Chocolate p107
Decadent sweets for grown-up tastes
Dominique Ansel Bakery p71
Home of the cult Cronut.
Russ & Daughters p96
Superb smoked fish and other delicacies at this 100-year-old purveyor.

GIFTS & SOUVENIRS
Magpie p174
Eco-friendly handmade goods.
Bowne & Co Stationers p63
Hand-printed cards and stationery in a wonderfully old-fashioned store.
Objectify 139 p95
Unique, artist-made NYC-themed wares.
Aedes de Venustas p122
A boudoir-style stash of hard-to-find scents.
By Brooklyn p212
Gifts from bags to edibles, all made in the borough.

BOOKS & MUSIC
Other Music p108
Genre-crossing indie fare.
Strand Book Store p109
A browser's paradise on several floors.
Housing Works Bookstore Café p71
A great literary hangout that's all in a good cause.

Rough Trade p224
Vinyl lives at this UK import, which also hosts gigs.

LOCAL DESIGNERS
Erica Weiner p83
Unusual, affordable baubles.
Rachel Comey p72
The indie favourite recently debuted her Soho flagship.
(3x1) p70
Made-in-New York denim.
In God We Trust p71
Well-priced gear for guys and gals.

ANTIQUES & VINTAGE
Brooklyn Flea p35
A mix of bric-a-brac, locally designed wares and artisanal food.
Grand Street Bakery p224
A trove of denim and other American classics.
Mantiques Modern p132
A mad mix of bizarre and beautiful items.
What Goes Around Comes Around p72
The fashion insiders' choice for era-spanning clothing.

CHILDREN
Books of Wonder p143
An indie bookstore just
for young readers.
Egg p209
Classic kids' clothing with
contemporary flair.
FAO Schwarz p160
The ultimate New York City
toy box.

DEPARTMENT STORES
Barneys New York p183
A contemporary twist on
the department store.
Bergdorf Goodman p160
The ultimate Upper East
Side designer institution.
Century 21 p61
Bargains galore at this
rummagers' paradise.

Nightlife

CLUBS
Verboten p277
The roving party finally put
down roots in Brooklyn.
Comedy Cellar p280
Your best chance to have
a laugh with local greats.

Slipper Room p279
The city's burlesque bastion
is better than ever.

MUSIC
Bowery Ballroom p285
Prime venue for indie bands.
Rockwood Music Hall p289
Sample a smorgasbord of
upand coming acts.
Radio City Music Hall
p289
The glitzy setting turns a
concert into an event.
Small's p293
The authentic hole-in-the-wall
Village jazz joint you've been
looking for.
54 Below p294
Broadway names belt out
show tunes at this cabaret
supper club.

GENRE-CROSSING VENUES
Le Poisson Rouge p289
A varied programme in a
historic Village space.
Joe's Pub p286
Performers of all genres:
alt-cabaret, comedy, rock
and more.

Arts

FESTIVALS
River to River p34
Partake of free culture at
dozens of downtown events.
Shakespeare in the Park
p319
It's worth queuing for hours
(take a picnic!) for these
gratis al fresco shows.
Next Wave Festival p37
Adventurous theatre, dance
and music at BAM.
Mermaid Parade p35
Exotic sea creatures parade
around Coney Island in this
flamboyant fête.

THEATRE
Public Theater p318
The East Village landmark
stages ambitious works.
Brooklyn Academy of Music
p295
Big stars are often on the bill
of BAM's reworked classics.
Sleep No More p315
An immersive, eerie riff
on Macbeth.
Soho Rep p319
Diverse offerings are to be
found at this innovative Off
Broadway stage.

FILM
Film Forum p260
A well-loved non-profit cinema
with exciting programming.
**Film Society of Lincoln
Center** p262
Host of the prestigious
New York Film Festival.
Nitehawk Cinema p260
Get dinner and a movie.

CLASSICAL & DANCE
Lincoln Center p296
Home of the Metropolitan
Opera, New York Phil and
New York City Ballet.
Carnegie Hall p296
A grand setting for luminaries
and emerging stars alike.

Explore

The Financial District

Commerce has been the backbone of New York's prosperity since its earliest days as a Dutch colony. The southern tip of Manhattan quickly evolved into the Financial District because, in the days before telecommunications, banks put their headquarters near the port. The oldest part of the city, lower Manhattan is the city's financial, legal and political powerhouse, but as the arrival point for the 19th-century influx of immigrants, it played another vital role in the city's evolution.

This part of town is still in flux, as more than a decade of construction moves towards completion. At the new World Trade Center, you can now ascend to One World Observatory, the city's highest vantage point. And the South Street Seaport is gradually being transformed from a touristy eyesore into a waterfront destination with bars, shops and areas for outdoor lounging that are also a hit with locals.

EXPLORE

Statue of Liberty.

Don't Miss

1 **Governors Island** A tranquil retreat minutes from Manhattan (p55).

2 **Statue of Liberty** Ascend to the crown for a breathtaking vista (p55).

3 **Dead Rabbit Grocery & Grog** A lesson in booze history (p57).

4 **National September 11 Memorial & Museum** A suitably monumental tribute (p60).

5 **Century 21** Paradise for bargain lovers (p61).

Bowling Green

BATTERY PARK TO WALL STREET

Subway J, Z to Broad Street; R to Whitehall Street-South Ferry; 1 to South Ferry; R, 1 to Rector Street; 2, 3, 4, 5 to Wall Street; 4, 5 to Bowling Green.

It's easy to forget that Manhattan is an island – what with all those gargantuan skyscrapers obscuring your view of the water. Until, that is, you reach the southern point, where salty ocean breezes are reminders of the millions of immigrants who travelled on steamers in search of prosperity, liberty and a new home. This is where they landed, after passing through Ellis Island's immigration and quarantine centres.

On the edge of Battery Park, **Castle Clinton** was one of several forts built to defend New York Harbor against attacks by the British in the War of 1812 (others included Castle Williams on Governors Island, Fort Gibson on Ellis Island and Fort Wood, now the base of the Statue of Liberty). After serving as an aquarium, immigration centre and opera house, the sandstone fort is now a visitors' centre and ticket booth for **Statue of Liberty** and **Ellis Island** tours, as well as an intimate, open-air setting for concerts.

Joining the throngs making their way to Lady Liberty, you'll head south-east along the shore, where several ferry terminals jut into the harbour. Among them is the **Whitehall Ferry Terminal**, the boarding place for the famous **Staten Island Ferry**. Constructed in 1907, the terminal was severely damaged by fire in 1991, but was completely rebuilt in 2005. More than 75,000 passengers take the free, 25-minute journey to Staten Island each day; most are commuters but many are tourists, taking advantage of the views of the Manhattan skyline and the Statue of Liberty. Before the Brooklyn Bridge was completed in 1883, the **Battery Maritime Building** (10 South Street, between

Broad & Whitehall Streets) served as a terminal for the ferry services between Manhattan and Brooklyn. Now, it's the launch point for a ferry to tranquil **Governors Island** (*see p53* **Island Getaway**). On the park's northern waterfront, the 1886 **Pier A Harbor House**, once the HQ for the harbour police, has been reinvented as a massive dining and drinking destination.

Just north of Battery Park you'll find the triangular **Bowling Green**, the city's oldest park and a popular lunchtime spot for Financial District workers; it's also the front lawn of the **Alexander Hamilton US Custom House**, now home to the **National Museum of the American Indian**.

Dwarfed by the surrounding architecture, the **Stone Street Historic District** is a small pocket of restored 1830s buildings on the eponymous winding cobblestoned lane, also encompassing South William and Pearl Streets and Coenties Alley. Office workers and tourists frequent its restaurants and bars, including the boisterous **Ulysses' Folk House** (95 Pearl Street, between Broad Street & Hanover Square, 1-212 482 0400, www.ulyssesnyc.com) and **Stone Street Tavern** (52 Stone Street, between Broad Street & Hanover Square, 1-212 785 5658, www.stonestreettavernnyc.com).

IN THE KNOW THE BULL'S BALLS

On Bowling Green's northern side stands a three-and-a-half-ton bronze sculpture of a bull (symbolising the bull, or rising, share market). The statue was deposited without permission outside the Stock Exchange by guerrilla artist Arturo di Modica in 1989 and has since been moved by the city to its current location. The bull's enormous balls are often rubbed for good luck by tourists (and perhaps the occasional broker).

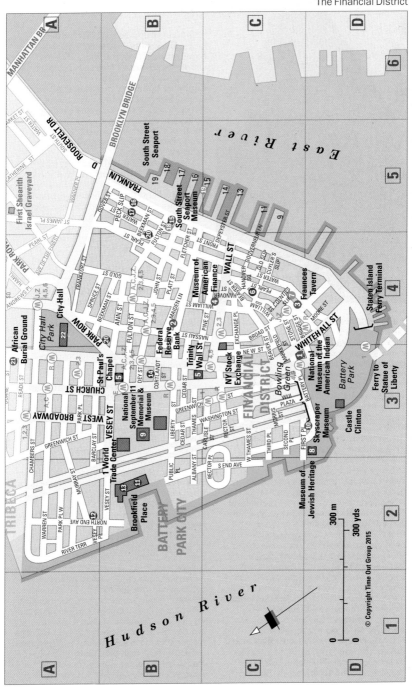

EXPLORE

Manhattan Br

Brooklyn Bridge

D Roosevelt Dr

Franklin

South Street Seaport

East River

South Street Seaport Museum

Wall St

Museum of American Finance

Fraunces Tavern

Staten Island Ferry Terminal

Federal Reserve Bank

Trinity Wall St

NY Stock Exchange

Financial District

National Museum of the American Indian

Whitehall St

Battery Park

Ferry to Statue of Liberty

First Shearith Israel Graveyard

Park Row

City Hall Park

African Burial Ground

St Paul's Chapel

Church St

Broadway

West St

Vesey St

National September 11 Memorial & Museum

1 World Trade Center

Brookfield Place

Tribeca

Battery Park City

Bowling Green

Skyscraper Museum

Castle Clinton

Museum of Jewish Heritage

Hudson River

300 m
300 yds

© Copyright Time Out Group 2015

Federal Reserve Bank. *See p55.*

State trounced them both in 1931); and the former **Merchants' Exchange** at 55 Wall Street (between Hanover & William Streets), with its stacked rows of Ionic and Corinthian columns. Back around the corner is the **Equitable Building** (120 Broadway, between Cedar & Pine Streets), whose greedy use of vertical space helped to instigate the zoning laws that now govern skyscrapers; stand across the street from the building to get the best view. Nearby is the **Federal Reserve Bank**, with its huge gold vault.

The nerve centre of the US economy is the **New York Stock Exchange** (11 Wall Street, between Broad & New Streets, www.nyse.nyx. com). For security reasons, the Exchange is no longer open to the public, but the street outside offers an endless pageant of brokers, traders and their minions. For a lesson on Wall Street's influence over the years, visit the **Museum of American Finance**.

Sights & Museums

Although the neighbourhood is bisected vertically by the ever-bustling Broadway, it's the east–west **Wall Street** (or 'the Street' in trader lingo) that's synonymous with the world's greatest den of capitalism. The name derives from a defensive wooden wall built in 1653 to mark the northern limit of New Amsterdam, and despite its huge significance, the thoroughfare is less than a mile long. At its western intersection with Broadway, you'll find the Gothic Revival spire of **Trinity Wall Street**. The original church burned down in 1776, and a second was demolished in 1839; the current version became the island's tallest structure when it was completed in 1846. **St Paul's Chapel**, the church's older satellite, is one of the finest Georgian structures in the US.

A block to the east of Trinity is the **Federal Hall National Memorial** (26 Wall Street, at Nassau Street, 1-212 825 6990, www.nps.gov/feha, closed Sat, Sun), an august Greek Revival building and – in a previous incarnation – the site of George Washington's first inauguration. It was along this stretch that corporate America made its first audacious architectural statements; a walk eastwards offers much evidence of what money can buy. Structures include the **Bankers Trust Building** at 14 Wall Street (at Broad Street), completed in 1912 and crowned by a seven-storey pyramid modelled on the Mausoleum of Halicarnassus; **40 Wall Street** (between Nassau & William Streets), which battled the Chrysler Building in 1929 for the title of world's tallest building (the Empire

FREE Alexander Hamilton US Custom House/National Museum of the American Indian

1 Bowling Green, between State & Whitehall Streets (1-212 514 3700, www.nmai.si.edu). Subway R to Whitehall Street-South Ferry; 1 to South Ferry; 4, 5 to Bowling Green. **Open** 10am-5pm Mon-Wed, Fri-Sun; 10am-8pm Thur. **Admission** free. **Map** p51 C3 ❶

Cass Gilbert's magnificent Beaux Arts Custom House, completed in 1907, housed the Customs Service until 1973, when the federal government moved it to the newly built World Trade Center complex. Four monumental figures by Lincoln Memorial sculptor Daniel Chester French – representing America, Asia, Europe and Africa – flank the impressive entrance. The panels surrounding the elliptical rotunda dome were designed to feature murals, but the plan wasn't realised until the 1930s, when local artist Reginald Marsh was commissioned to decorate them under the New Deal's Works Progress Administration; the paintings depict a ship entering New York Harbor.

In 1994, the National Museum of the American Indian's George Gustav Heye Center, a branch of the Smithsonian, moved into the first two floors of the building. On the second level, the life and culture of Native Americans are illuminated in three galleries radiating out from the rotunda. In addition to a roster of changing shows, the permanent exhibition, 'Infinity of Nations', displays 700 of the museum's wide-ranging collection of Native American art and objects, from decorated baskets to elaborate ceremonial headdresses, organised by geographical region. On the ground floor, the Diker Pavilion for Native Arts & Culture is the city's only dedicated showcase for Native American performing arts.

ISLAND GETAWAY

The former military HQ is now an arty seasonal sanctuary.

A 172-acre chunk of prime waterside real estate that can never be developed into luxury condos, **Governors Island** (see p55) is a secluded anomaly a scant 800 yards from lower Manhattan. The verdant commons and stately red-brick buildings evoke an Ivy League campus by way of a colonial New England village – oddly emptied of its inhabitants.

The peaceful backwater has had a tumultuous history. Initially a seasonal fishing and gathering ground for the Lenape Indians, it had plentiful nut trees, earning it the name 'Noten Eylant' when the Dutch arrived in the 1620s. In 1674, the British secured it for 'the benefit and accommodation of His Majesty's Governors'. Perhaps the most colourful of these was Edward Hyde, Viscount Cornbury, Governor of New York and New Jersey from 1702 to 1708. A cousin of Queen Anne, he was alleged to be a cross-dresser (a portrait, said to be of Lord Cornbury in drag, is in the collection of the New-York Historical Society, see p171).

The island's strategic position cemented its future as a military outpost (by the late 19th century it was the army's headquarters

for the entire eastern US), and it still retains a significant chunk of its military-era construction, including Fort Jay, started in 1776, and Castle Williams, completed in 1812. When the army began to outgrow the space, excavated soil from the Lexington Avenue subway line was used to enlarge the island by 103 acres.

The modest patch has been the backdrop for some huge events. In 1909, it launched the first overwater flight, when Wilbur Wright circled the Statue of Liberty before flying back. Such legendary figures as Generals Ulysses S Grant and Douglas MacArthur had stints on the island. Today, as well as providing a peaceful setting for cycling (bring a bike, or rent one on arrival), the island hosts a programme of events, including the popular Jazz Age Lawn party (see p34). There are even plans for a day spa. In 2012, construction began on a new park, and 30 acres of green space have since opened to the public, including lawns, two ball fields and the Hammock Grove for shady reclining. By 2016, new hills constructed from the debris of demolished buildings will provide even more spectacular viewpoints for harbour panoramas.

EXPLORE

GET AN ALL ACCESS LOOK AT THE WORLD'S MOST FAMOUS ARENA®!

Explore exclusive VIP areas in the state-of-the-art arena and commemorate over 130 years of legendary Garden history. Visit the spectacular Chase Bridges, explore the Knicks and Rangers locker rooms^, and experience the iconic Arena bowl, where some of the world's greatest concerts have taken place.

TOURS RUN DAILY STARTING AT 10:30AM

4 PENNSYLVANIA PLAZA (32nd St. & 7th Ave.)

PURCHASE TICKETS TODAY!

INFO: 212-465-6741   **VISIT:** MSGAllAccessTour.com   **GROUPS:** 212-465-6080

Ellis Island National Museum of Immigration.

FREE Federal Reserve Bank

Visitors' entrance: 44 Maiden Lane, between Nassau & William Streets (www.ny.frb.org/ aboutthefed/visiting.html). Subway 2, 3, 4, 5 to Wall Street. **Tours** *vary (reservations required).* **Map** p51 B4 ❷

It's no surprise that tours of this important financial institution must be booked in advance on the website (up to a month ahead) and a photo ID presented before admission. Descend 80ft below street level and you'll find the world's largest known supply of monetary gold (more than 530,000 bars, worth more than $300 billion), stored in a gigantic vault that rests on the solid bedrock of Manhattan Island. Visitors learn about the New York Fed's safeguarding of the precious metal, and the responsibilities and actions of the Federal Reserve. *Photo p52.*

Fraunces Tavern Museum

2nd & 3rd Floors, 54 Pearl Street, at Broad Street (1-212 425 1778, www.frauncestavernmuseum. org). Subway J, Z to Broad Street; 4, 5 to Bowling Green. **Open** *noon-5pm daily.* **Admission** $7; $4 reductions; free under-6s & active military.* **Map** p51 C4 ❸

True, George Washington slept here, but there's little left of the original 18th-century tavern he favoured during the Revolution. Fire-damaged and rebuilt in the 19th century, it was reconstructed in its current Colonial Revival style in 1907. Step into a period perfect recreation of the Long Room, where Washington took tearful farewell of his troops after the British had been defeated and vowed to retire from public life. (Luckily, he had a change of heart six years later and became the country's first president.) The museum also contains a collection of 5,000 Revolutionary

War objects, including muskets, prints and such Washington relics as a lock of his hair. And you can still raise a pint in the bar and restaurant, which is run by Dublin's Porterhouse Brewing Company.

★ FREE Governors Island

1-212 440 2202, www.govisland.com. Subway R to Whitehall Street-South Ferry; 1 to South Ferry; 4, 5 to Bowling Green. Then take ferry from Battery Maritime Building at Slip no.7. **Open** *Late May-late Sept 10am-6pm Mon-Fri; 10am-7pm Sat, Sun (see website for hours and ferry schedule). Closed late Sept-late May.* **Admission** *Ferry $2 round trip; free under-12s; free 10am-noon Sat, Sun. See p53* **Island Getaway***.

Museum of American Finance

48 Wall Street, at William Street (1-212 908 4110, www.moaf.org). Subway R, 1 to Rector Street; 2, 3, 4, 5 to Wall Street. **Open** *10am-4pm Tue-Sat.* **Admission** *$8; $5 reductions; free under-7s.* **Map** p51 C4 ❹

Situated in the stately former headquarters of the Bank of New York, the museum brings the world of money to life with a lively schedule of exhibitions. Tracing the history of Wall Street and America's financial markets, the permanent collection includes a bearer bond made out to President George Washington and ticker tape from the morning of the stock market crash of 1929.

★ Statue of Liberty & Ellis Island National Museum of Immigration

Liberty Island (1-212 363 3200, www.nps.gov/stli). Subway R to Whitehall Street-South Ferry; 1 to South Ferry; 4, 5 to Bowling Green; then take

EXPLORE

Statue of Liberty ferry (1-201 604 2800, 1-877 523 9849, www.statuecruises.com), departing roughly every 30mins from gangway 4 or 5 in southernmost Battery Park. **Open** ferry runs 9.30am-3.30pm daily (extended hrs in summer; see website). Purchase tickets online, by phone or at Castle Clinton in Battery Park. **Admission** $18; $9-$14 reductions; free under 4s.

The sole occupant of Liberty Island, Liberty Enlightening the World stands 305ft tall from the bottom of her base to the tip of her gold-leaf torch. Intended as a gift from France on America's 100th birthday, the statue was designed by Frédéric Auguste Bartholdi (1834-1904). Construction began in Paris in 1874, her skeletal iron framework crafted by Gustave Eiffel (the man behind the Tower), but only the arm with the torch was finished in time for the centennial in 1876. In 1884, the statue was finally completed – only to be taken apart to be shipped to New York, where it was unveiled in 1886. It served as a lighthouse until 1902, and as a welcoming beacon for millions of immigrants. These 'tired…poor…huddled masses' were evoked in Emma Lazarus's poem 'The New Colossus', written in 1883 to raise funds for the pedestal and engraved inside the statue in 1903.

With a free Monument Pass, available only with ferry tickets reserved in advance, you can enter the pedestal and view the interior through a glass ceiling. Access to the crown costs an extra $3 and must be reserved in advance.

A half-mile across the harbour from Liberty Island is the 32-acre Ellis Island, gateway for over 12 million people who entered the country between 1892 and 1954. In the National Museum of Immigration (a former check-in depot), three floors of photos, interactive displays and exhibits pay tribute to the hopeful souls who made the voyage. Tickets can be purchased online, by phone or at Castle Clinton in Battery Park.

FREE Trinity Wall Street & St Paul's Chapel

Trinity Wall Street *75 Broadway, at Wall Street (1-212 602 0800, www.trinitywallstreet.org). Subway R, 1 to Rector Street; 2, 3, 4, 5 to Wall Street.* **Open** 7am-6pm Mon-Fri; 10am-4pm Sat; 7am-4pm Sun. See website for cemetery hours. **Admission** free. **Map** p51 E33.
St Paul's Chapel *209 Broadway, between Fulton & Vesey Streets (1-212 602 0800, www.trinitywallstreet.org). Subway A, C, J, Z, 2, 3, 4, 5 to Fulton Street.* **Open** 10am-6pm Mon-Sat; 7am-6pm Sun. **Admission** free. **Map** p51 B3 ⑤

Trinity Church was the island's tallest structure when it was completed in 1846 (the original burned down in 1776; a second was demolished in 1839). A set of gates north of the church on Broadway allows access to the adjacent cemetery, where cracked and faded tombstones mark the final resting places of dozens of past city dwellers, including such notable New Yorkers as founding father Alexander Hamilton, business tycoon John Jacob Astor and steamboat inventor

Dead Rabbit Grocery & Grog.

Robert Fulton. The church museum displays historic diaries, photographs, sermons and burial records.

Six blocks to the north, Trinity's satellite, St Paul's Chapel, is more important architecturally. The oldest building in New York still in continuous use (it dates from 1766), it is one of the nation's most valued Georgian structures.

► *For Trinity's free concert series, see p302.*

Restaurants & Cafés

Adrienne's Pizzabar

54 Stone Street, between Coenties Alley & Mill Street (1-212 248 3838). Subway R to Whitehall Street-South Ferry; 2, 3 to Wall Street. **Open** 11am-midnight Mon-Sat; 11am-10pm Sun. **Pizzas** $15-$24. **Map** p51 C4 ⑨ **Pizza**

Good, non-chain eateries are scarce in the Financial District, but this bright, modern pizzeria on quaint Stone Street provides a pleasant break from the crowded thoroughfares – there are outside tables from April through November. The kitchen prepares nicely charred pies with delectable toppings such as the rich *quattro formaggi*. If you're in a hurry, you can eat at the 12-seat bar, or opt for the sleek, wood-accented dining room to savour small plates and main courses such as potato gnocchi and ravioli *al formaggio*.

Bars

★ Dead Rabbit Grocery & Grog
*30 Water Street, at Broad Street (1-646 422 7906,
www.deadrabbitnyc.com). Subway R to Whitehall
Street-South Ferry.* **Open** 11am-4am daily. **Map**
p51 C4 ❼
At this time-capsule nook, you can drink like a boss
– Boss Tweed, that is. Belfast bar vets Sean Muldoon
and Jack McGarry have conjured up a rough-and-
tumble 19th-century tavern in a red-brick landmark.
Resurrecting long-forgotten quaffs is nothing new
in NYC, but the Dead Rabbit's sheer breadth of mid
19th-century libations eclipses the competition,
spanning 60-odd bishops, fixes, nogs and smashes.
Cocktails make good use of seasonal produce and
esoteric ingredients, such as the summertime Little
White Rabbit (gin, cream sherry, orange sherbet,
tarragon and fresh parsnip juice).

WORLD TRADE CENTER & BATTERY PARK CITY

*Subway A, C, 1, 2, 3 to Chambers Street; A, C,
J, Z, 2, 3, 4, 5 to Fulton Street; E to World Trade
Center; R to Cortlandt Street; R, 1 to Rector
Street; 2, 3 to Park Place; 4, 5 to Bowling Green.*

On a date now etched into our collective memory,
the worst attack on US soil took nearly 3,000 lives
and left a gaping hole where the Twin Towers
had once helped to define the New York skyline.
Today, walking through the World Trade Center's
tree-shaded memorial plaza, with its monumental
waterfalls, it's hard to believe that this area was a
gaping hole, then a fenced-off construction site,
for most of the previous decade. Spring 2014 saw

the opening of the long-anticipated **National
September 11 Museum**, which serves a
threefold function as memorial tribute, historical
record and mind-boggling evocation of the
immense scale of the disaster. In addition to
memorialising the tragedy, the rebuilt World
Trade Center has more impressive visitor
attractions than its previous incarnation. As this
guide went to press, **One World Observatory**
(*see p59* **Going Up!**) was due to open on floors
100 to 102 of the 1,776-foot-high 1 World Trade
Center, which counts media giant Condé Nast
among its tenants. Also on the horizon is a multi-
level shopping and dining complex – larger than
six football fields – operated by shopping-mall
giant Westfield and spread across the WTC's
towers and starchitect Santiago Calatrava's bird-
like transit hub; its attractions will include a
branch of Italian-food mecca **Eataly** (*see p143*).

A 600-foot-long, marble-clad pedestrian
corridor links the PATH station and **Brookfield
Place**. The granite-and-glass corporate/retail/
dining complex abuts **Battery Park City**, a
92-acre planned community devised in the 1950s
to replace decaying shipping piers with new
apartments, green spaces and schools. It's a man-
made addition to the island, built on soil and rocks
excavated from the original World Trade Center
construction site and sediment dredged from New
York Harbor. Visitors can enjoy its esplanade, a
favoured route for bikers, skaters and joggers,
and a string of parks that runs north along the
Hudson River from Battery Park.

Providing expansive views of the Statue of
Liberty and Ellis Island at its southernmost
reaches, the stretch is dotted with monuments
and sculptures. Close by the marina is the 1997

EXPLORE

Battery Park.

Police Memorial (Liberty Street, at South End Avenue), a granite pool and fountain that symbolically trace the lifespan of a police officer through the use of moving water, with names of the fallen etched into the wall. The **Irish Hunger Memorial** (Vesey Street, at North End Avenue) is here too, paying tribute to those who suffered during the famine from 1845 to 1852. Designed by artist Brian Tolle and landscape architect Gail Wittwer-Laird, the quarter-acre memorial incorporates vegetation, soil and stones from Ireland's 32 counties, and a reproduction of a 19th-century Irish cottage.

To the north, **Nelson A Rockefeller Park** (north end of Battery Park City, west of River Terrace) attracts sun worshippers, kite flyers and soccer players in the warm-weather months. Look out for Tom Otterness's whimsical sculpture installation, *The Real World*. Just east is **Teardrop Park** (between Warren & Murray Streets, east of River Terrace), a two-acre space designed to evoke the bucolic Hudson River Valley, and to the south are the inventively designed **South Cove** (on the Esplanade, between First & Third Place), with its quays and island, and **Robert F Wagner Jr Park** (north of Historic Battery Park, off Battery Place), where an observation deck offers fabulous views of both the harbour and the Verrazano-Narrows Bridge; below it, Louise Bourgeois's *Eyes* gaze over the Hudson from the lawn. The **Museum of Jewish Heritage**, Gotham's memorial to the

GOING UP!

Look out, Empire State – there's a new observation deck in town.

Since the 9/11 Memorial debuted in 2011, featuring man-made waterfalls that drop to 30 feet below street level, visiting the World Trade Center site has been mainly about what lies beneath. The 9/11 Memorial Museum reinforced the below-ground focus when it opened in the foundations of the fallen Twin Towers. By the time you read this, however, you'll be able to gain a far more elevated perspective – from a height of more than 1,250 feet to be precise. Due to open as this guide went to press, **One World Observatory** – perched on floors 100 to 102 of the tallest skyscraper in the western hemisphere – gives the Empire State Building some serious competition. In fact, it's now the highest observation deck in the city.

Getting up there is an experience in itself – Sky Pod elevators, featuring a lightning-fast floor-to-ceiling simulation of New York City's development, whisk visitors to the top of the building in a mere minute. When you arrive on the 102nd floor, a high-tech two-minute video presentation whets your appetite for the main attraction before screens rise to reveal the panoramic view. Two levels down, those not prone to vertigo can step on to the Sky Portal, a 14ft-wide circular disc displaying an HD real-time image of the street below. On the middle level, a restaurant, casual café and bar let you relax and take in the incredible vistas over a snack, cocktails or a full meal.

1 World Trade Center, 285 Fulton Street (1-844 696 1776, www.oneworldobservatory.com). **Admission** $32; $26-$30 reductions; free under-6s, 9/11 family members and 9/11 rescue and recovery workers.

EXPLORE

Holocaust, is on the edge of the green. Across the street at the **Skyscraper Museum**, you can learn about the buildings that have created the city's iconic skyline.

Sights & Museums

Museum of Jewish Heritage: A Living Memorial to the Holocaust

Edmond J Safra Plaza, 36 Battery Place, at First Place (1-646 437 4202, www.mjhnyc.org). Subway 4, 5 to Bowling Green. **Open** 10am-5.45pm Mon, Tue, Thur, Sun; 10am-8pm Wed; 10am-5pm Fri (until 3pm Nov-mid Mar); 10am-3pm eve of Jewish hols. **Admission** $12; $7-$10 reductions; free under-13s; free 4-8pm Wed. **Map** p51 D3 ❽

This museum explores Jewish life before, during and after the Nazi genocide. The permanent collection includes nearly 25,000 photographs, documents, films and artefacts – many of them donated by Holocaust survivors and their families – which are displayed on rotation. The Keeping History Center brings the collection to life with interactive displays, including 'Voices of Liberty', a soundscape of émigrés' and refugees' reactions to arrival in the United States – made all the more poignant juxtaposed with the museum's panoramic views of Ellis Island and the Statue of Liberty. Special exhibitions tackle historical events or themes. The Memorial Garden features English artist Andy Goldsworthy's *Garden of Stones*, 18 fire-hollowed boulders embedded with dwarf oak saplings.

★ National September 11 Memorial & Museum

Various entry points on Greenwich, Liberty & West Streets (1-212 312 8800, www.911memorial.org). Subway A, C, 1, 2, 3 to Chambers Street; A, C, J, Z, 2, 3, 4, 5 to Fulton Street; E to World Trade Center; R to Cortlandt Street; 1 to Rector Street; 2, 3 to Park Place. **Open** *Memorial plaza* 7.30am-9pm daily. *Museum* 9am-8pm Mon-Thur, Sun; 9am-9pm Fri, Sat (hours vary seasonally; see website for updates). **Admission** *Memorial plaza* free. *Museum* $24; $12-$18 reductions; free under-6s, 9/11 family members, rescue workers and US military. Free 5-8pm Tue. **Map** p51 B3 ❾

In a city known for its sky-high aspirations, Ground Zero was a potent symbol of grief, and for most of the decade following 9/11, it felt as if the gaping wound in lower Manhattan would never be healed. A decade later, however, the National September 11 Memorial opened on the tenth anniversary of the attacks and in spring 2014, the long-awaited museum opened to the public.

Surrounded by a tree-shaded plaza, the memorial itself, Reflecting Absence, created by architects Michael Arad and Peter Walker, comprises two one-acre 'footprints' of the destroyed towers, with 30ft man-made waterfalls cascading down their sides. Bronze parapets around the edges are inscribed with

National September 11 Memorial & Museum.

the names of the 2,983 victims of the 2001 attacks at the World Trade Center, the Pentagon and the passengers of United Flight 93, as well as those who lost their lives in the bombing on 26 February 1993.

The museum pavilion, designed by Oslo-based firm Snøhetta, rises between the pools. Its web-like glass atrium houses two steel trident-shaped columns salvaged from the base of the Twin Towers. Visitors descend to the vast spaces of the WTC's original foundations alongside a remnant of the Vesey Street staircase known as the Survivors' Stairs, which was used by hundreds of people escaping the carnage. Massive pieces of twisted metal and a fallen segment of the North Tower's radio/TV antenna bring home the enormous scale of the disaster.

Around 1,000 artefacts, plus images, documents and oral histories chronicle events leading up to the attacks, commemorate the victims and document how the world changed after 9/11. Items vividly evoke individual stories, from private voicemails

EXPLORE

left by people in the towers to the East Village's Ladder Company 3 fire truck, dispatched with 11 firefighters who died during the rescue effort. The In Memoriam exhibition pays tribute to each victim with a portrait, bio and audio remembrances.

Skyscraper Museum

39 Battery Place, between Little West Street & 1st Place (1-212 968 1961, www.skyscraper.org). Subway 4, 5 to Bowling Green. **Open** noon-6pm Wed-Sun. **Admission** $5; $2.50 reductions. **Map** p51 D3 ⑩

The only institution of its kind in the world, this modest space explores high-rise buildings as objects of design, products of technology, real-estate investments and places of work and residence. A large part of the single gallery (a mirrored ceiling gives the illusion of height) is devoted to temporary exhibitions. A substantial chunk of the permanent collection relates to the Word Trade Center, including original models of the Twin Towers and the new 1 World Trade Center. Other highlights of the display are large-scale photographs of lower Manhattan's skyscrapers from 1956, 1976 and 2004, and a 1931 silent film documenting the Empire State Building's construction.

▶ For more, see p351 **Race to the Top**.

Restaurants & Cafés

Hudson Eats

Brookfield Place, 230 Vesey Street, between West Street & the Hudson River (1-212 417 2445, www. brookfieldplaceny.com). Subway A, C, 1, 2, 3 to Chambers Street; A, C, J, Z, 2, 3, 4, 5 to Fulton Street; E to World Trade Center; R to Cortlandt Street; R, 1 to Rector Street; 2, 3 to Park Place. **Open** 7am-9pm Mon-Fri; 10am-9pm Sat; 11am-7pm Sun. **Main courses** varies. **Map** p51 B2 ⑪ **Eclectic**

Carved out from the second floor of a monster retail complex, the glossy, 600-seat dining terrace upgrades food-court schlock with white-marble counters, 17ft-high windows offering gobsmacking waterfront views and 14 chef-driven kiosks, including branches of Mighty Quinn's (*see p104*) for Texas-meets-Carolina 'cue, Dos Toros (*see p103*) for tacos and burritos, Num Pang (*see p114*) for Cambodian sandwiches and lox-and-schmear outfit Black Seed (*see p82*).

IN THE KNOW
THE GHOST SUBWAY STATION

If you take the 6 train to its last downtown stop, Brooklyn Bridge-City Hall, ignore the recorded entreaty to get off. Stay aboard while the train makes its U-turn loop before heading uptown and you'll get a glimpse of the original 1904 City Hall Station (out of use since 1945) and its brass chandeliers, vaulted ceilings, tile mosaics and skylights.

North End Grill

104 North End Avenue, at Murray Street (1-646 747 1600, www.northendgrillnyc.com). Subway A, C to Chambers Street; E to World Trade Center; 2, 3 to Park Place. **Open** 11.30am-10pm Mon-Thur; 11.30am-10.30pm Fri; 11am-10.30pm Sat; 11am-9pm Sun. **Main courses** $27-$54. **Map** p51 A2 ⑫ **American**

This instant classic has all the hallmarks of a Danny Meyer joint: effortless, affable service; a warm, buzzy space; and cooking that's easy and accessible. Eric Korsh has replaced Floyd Cardoz in the kitchen, putting a French-accented spin on the seasonal menu (which incorporates produce from the eaterie's rooftop farm). The chef has introduced charcuterie and a raw bar dispensing lavish shellfish platters and a weeknight $1 oyster happy hour. Wood-fired grills and mesquite charcoal ovens impart a smoky finish to dishes like Berkshire tomahawk pork chop with pickled chillies and the whole free-range chicken for two.

Shops & Services

Brookfield Place

230 Vesey Street, between West Street & the Hudson River (1-212 417 2445, www. brookfieldplaceny.com). Subway A, C, 1, 2, 3 to Chambers Street; A, C, J, Z, 2, 3, 4, 5 to Fulton Street; E to World Trade Center; R to Cortlandt Street; R, 1 to Rector Street; 2, 3 to Park Place. **Open** 10am-9pm Mon-Sat; 11am-7pm Sun (restaurant hours vary). **Map** p51 B2 ⑬ **Mall**

Directly across West Street from the World Trade Center, this sprawling office, retail and dining complex has the distinction of being the only mall with a view of the Statue of Liberty. The first of several new upscale shopping centres to hit the city, it caters to the WTC's stylish new tenants (the likes of Condé Nast) with a mix of luxe designer names like Hermès, Bottega Veneta and Burberry, contemporary fashion brands including DVF, Bonobos and Vince, plus Saks Fifth Avenue (opening early 2016), family-owned Posnan Books, cool Tribeca-born kids' shop Babesta and a 30,000sq ft French-food market, Le District. Multiple refuelling options range from chic food court Hudson Eats (*see left*) to haute-cuisine destination L'Atelier de Joël Robuchon. Brookfield Place also hosts numerous free arts events in its Winter Garden atrium and waterfront plaza (see website calendar), which overlooks a marina.

Century 21

22 Cortlandt Street, between Broadway & Church Street (1-212 227 9092, www.c21stores.com). Subway A, C, J, Z, 2, 3, 4, 5 to Fulton Street; E to World Trade Center; R to Cortlandt Street. **Open** 7.45am-9pm Mon-Wed; 7.45am-9.30pm Thur, Fri; 10am-9pm Sat; 11am-8pm Sun. **Map** p51 B3 ⑭ **Fashion**

EXPLORE

A Marc Jacobs cashmere sweater for less than $200? Stella McCartney sunglasses for a mere $40? No, you're not dreaming – you're shopping at Century 21. You may have to rummage to unearth a treasure, but with savings of up to 65% off regular prices, it's worth it. In our experience, the smaller, more upscale, less chaotic Upper West Side location doesn't yield as many steals as the original.
Other locations 1972 Broadway, between 66th & 67th Streets, Upper West Side (1-212 518 2121); 472 86th Street, between Fourth & Fifth Avenues, Bay Ridge, Brooklyn (1-718 748 3266).

SOUTH STREET SEAPORT

Subway A, C, J, Z, 2, 3, 4, 5 to Fulton Street.

New York's fortunes originally rolled in on the swells that crashed into its harbour. The city was perfectly situated for trade with Europe and, after 1825, goods from the Western Territories arrived via the Erie Canal and the Hudson River. By 1892, New York was also the point of entry for millions of immigrants. The **South Street Seaport** is the best place to appreciate this port heritage.

If you enter the Seaport area from Water Street, the first thing you're likely to spot is the whitewashed **Titanic Memorial Lighthouse**. It was originally erected on top of the Seaman's Church Institute (Coenties Slip & South Street) in 1913, the year after the great ship sank, but was moved to its current location at the intersection of Pearl and Fulton Streets in 1976. Check out the magnificent views of the Brooklyn Bridge from this bit of the district.

When New York's role as a vital shipping hub diminished during the 20th century, the South Street Seaport area fell into disuse, but a massive redevelopment project in the mid 1980s saw old buildings converted into restaurants, bars, chain stores and the **South Street Seaport Museum. Pier 17** once supported the famous Fulton Fish Market, a bustling, early-morning trading centre dating back to the mid 1800s. However, in 2006 the market relocated to a larger facility in the Hunts Point area of the Bronx. Pier 17 was redeveloped into a mall in the 1980s, which is now shuttered. A plan by SHoP Architects to replace it with a mixed-use complex has been stalled due to local opposition to a 42-storey tower, which preservationists feel would destroy the character of the historic area. The city's East River Esplanade and Piers Project has landscaped the stretch of waterfront between the Battery Maritime Building and Fulton Street and will continue up to the Lower East Side's Pier 35. **Pier 15** has been transformed into a bi-level lounging space, comprising a lawned viewing deck above a maritime education centre and the **Watermark**, a stylish glass-enclosed bar.

Sights & Museums

South Street Seaport Museum
12 Fulton Street, between South & Water Streets (1-212 748 8600, www.southstreetseaport museum.org). Subway A, C, J, Z, 2, 3, 4, 5 to Fulton Street. **Open & Admission** Call or see website for information. **Map** p51 B5 ⓯
Founded in 1967, the South Street Seaport Museum celebrates the maritime history of New York City's 19th-century waterfront. However, at time of writing it was still closed due to damage from 2012's Hurricane Sandy and a reopening date had yet to be determined. The museum shop, comprising Bowne Printers and Bowne & Co Stationers (*see p63*), has remained open. The institution also has a fleet of historic vessels on Pier 16, including the 1607 lightship *Ambrose* and the 1885 schooner *Pioneer*, which offers excursions along the East River from May through October.

Restaurants & Cafés

Barbalu
225-227 Front Street, between Beekman Street & Peck Slip (1-646 918 6565, www.barbalu.com). Subway A, C, J, Z, 2, 3, 4, 5 to Fulton Street. **Open** 10am-10pm daily. **Main courses** $14-$24. **Map** p51 B5 ⓰ Italian
After their restaurant, Barbarini, was destroyed by Hurricane Sandy, owners Stefano Barbagallo and Adriana Luque opened this 120-seat Italian eaterie at the same location. The husband-and-wife team expanded the bar area, where you can order charcuterie and cheese plates to accompany the Italian wine. Slide into a brown banquette in the skylighted dining room for classics like mozzarella-and-eggplant *caponatina*, fettuccine with shrimp and tomatoes, and *torta di pinoli* (pine-nut cake).

Jack's Stir Brew Coffee
222 Front Street, between Beekman Street & Peck Slip (1-212 227 7631, www.jacksstirbrew.com). Subway A, C, J, Z, 2, 3, 4, 5 to Fulton Street. **Open** 7am-6pm Mon-Fri; 8am-6pm Sat, Sun. **Coffee** $2.50-$5.50. **Map** p51 B5 ⓱ Café
Java fiends convene at this award-winning caffeine spot that offers organic, shade-grown beans and a homey vibe. Coffee is served by espresso artisans with a knack for oddball concoctions, such as the super-silky Mountie latte, infused with maple syrup.
Other locations 138 W 10th Street, between Greenwich Avenue & Waverly Place, West Village (1-212 929 0821); 10 Downing Street, between Bedford Street & Sixth Avenue, West Village (1-212 929 6011).

Bars

Ambrose Hall
18 Fulton Street, between Front & South Streets (1-212 785 0018, www.ambrosehall.theluregroup.com).

Subway A, C, J, Z, 2, 3, 4, 5 to Fulton Street; 2, 3 to Wall Street. **Open** noon-10pm Mon-Wed, Sun; noon-1am Thur-Sat. **Map** p51 B5 ⑱
Named after the South Street Seaport Museum's lightship *Ambrose*, which is docked nearby, the space at Ambrose Hall is split into three locales: a nautical-ish hall inside the historic Schermerhorn Row building, a revved-up surf club atop shipping containers and an easygoing outdoor beer garden. In the no-fuss mess hall, coastal lunch fare such as lobster rolls is served on paper plates. Though the twinkly lights and sea-kissed air are intoxicating at night, it's best to avoid happy hour, when the bustling beach house can feel more cramped than cool. The splashy raised cabana deck – kitted out with kitschy surfboards and a driftwood bar – is prime for soaking up rays and people-watching from above.

Watermark
Pier 15, between Fletcher Street & Maiden Lane (1-646 742 8200, www.watermarkny.com). Subway A, C, J, Z, 2, 3, 4, 5 to Fulton Street; 2, 3 to Wall Street. **Open** *Apr-Oct* noon-11pm daily. *Nov-Mar* noon-7pm daily. **Map** p51 C5 ⑲
Sip beer by the bucket or cocktails accompanied by casual bites like lobster rolls and burgers at this contemporary waterfront bar – the skyline views through the floor-to-ceiling windows are spectacular. Although the bar is generally open year-round, it's a good idea to call or check the website if you plan to visit during winter.
▶ *For more waterside options, see p64* **NY Sea***.*

Shops & Services

★ Bowne Printers and Bowne & Co Stationers
209-211 Water Street, between Fulton & Beekman Streets (1-646 628 2707). Subway A, C, J, Z, 2, 3, 4, 5 to Fulton Street. **Open** 11am-7pm daily. **Map** p51 B5 **Gifts & stationery** ⑳
The South Street Seaport Museum shop comprises Bowne Printers and Bowne & Co Stationers. The re-creation of a 19th-century print shop doesn't just look the part: the platen presses – hand-set using antique letterpress and type from the museum's collection – also turn out stationery and cards. Next door, Bowne & Co Stationers, founded in 1775, sells hand-printed cards, prints, journals and other gifts.

CIVIC CENTER & CITY HALL PARK
Subway J, Z to Chambers Street; R to City Hall; 2, 3 to Park Place; 4, 5, 6 to Brooklyn Bridge-City Hall.

The business of running New York takes place in the grand buildings in and around **City Hall Park**, an area that formed the budding city's northern boundary in the 1700s. The park itself was renovated just before the millennium.
At the park's southern end, a granite 'time wheel' tracks its history. At the northern end of the park, **City Hall** houses the mayor's office and the chambers of the City Council. When City Hall was completed in 1812, its architects were so

EXPLORE

South Street Seaport.

NY SEA

Waterside watering holes play up Manhattan's nautical side.

Grand Banks.

Given the fact that lower Manhattan is surrounded by water, there are surprisingly few options for tasteful harbourside eating and drinking. But a new wave of nautical-inspired establishments has dropped anchor along the shore. The ongoing redevelopment of the esplanade and piers on the East Side brought the **Watermark** (see p63) to South Street Seaport's Pier 15, while across the island, the *Sherman Zwicker* sailed into the Hudson River in summer 2014, blowing trashy party-boat clichés about plastic chairs and beer-swilling masses out of the water. The 1940s schooner is home to seasonal oyster bar **Grand Banks** (May-Oct, 1-212 960 3390, www.grandbanks.org), co-captained by Mark Firth, one of the founders of popular Williamsburg eaterie Marlow & Sons. Docked just above Battery Park City at Tribeca's Pier 25, the elegant vessel has an out-to-sea feel, but with the glittering World Trade Center and spotlighted Statue of Liberty still in sight. Two brass-tapped bars flank the ship's bow and mizzen-mast, offering prime seating even without reservations, while the yellow-and-white-striped awning and business-casual crowd hint at the Hamptons. The waitstaff, like a well-groomed crew outfitted in navy striped shirts, deliver the likes of baked oysters in shallot marmalade, bacon-

flecked fluke crudo, seasonal salads and daily cocktail specials such as a white-wine Sherman's Cup with fresh berries.

To the south, the commanding 1886 **Pier A Harbor House** (22 Battery Place, at Pier A, 1-212 785 0153, www.piera.com), juts out into the harbour alongside Battery Park, anchored by its distinctive clocktower. The former harbour police HQ had been vacant since the early 1990s and left to deteriorate. But in winter 2014, it was reinvented as a three-level drinking and dining destination by a team including restaurateur Peter Poulakakos, who was also behind the Dead Rabbit (see p57). Decked out with nautical relics like pipes from steamship engine rooms, the ground level includes a long beer hall pouring old-world European suds and a raw bar shucking oysters and clams. While the refit feels a bit too slick to convey an authentic sense of history, the cavernous interior and expansive deck – with Lady Liberty views – can accommodate huge crowds without feeling cramped. We have higher hopes for the upper level, due to open as this guide went to press, which includes two smaller bars and an upscale restaurant spotlighting Hudson Valley-sourced produce.

Pier A Harbor House.

EXPLORE

confident that the city would grow no further north that they didn't bother to put any marble on its northern side. Nevertheless, the building is a beautiful blend of Federalist form and French Renaissance detail. Overlooking the park from the west is Cass Gilbert's famous **Woolworth Building** (233 Broadway, between Barclay Street & Park Place), the tallest building in the world when it opened in 1913. The neo-Gothic skyscraper's grand spires, gargoyles, vaulted ceilings and church-like interior earned it the moniker 'the Cathedral of Commerce'.

Behind City Hall, on Chambers Street, is the 1872 Old New York County Courthouse; it's popularly known as the **Tweed Courthouse**, after William 'Boss' Tweed (*see p340*), leader of the political machine Tammany Hall, who pocketed some $10 million of the building's $14 million construction budget. What he didn't steal bought a beautiful edifice, with exquisite Italianate detailing. These days, it houses the city's Department of Education and a New York City public school, but it's also open for tours by reservation (1-212 788 2656, www.nyc.gov/designcommission). To the east, other civic offices and services occupy the one million square feet of office space in the 1914 **Manhattan Municipal Building** at 1 Centre Street. This landmark limestone structure, built by McKim, Mead & White, also houses New York City's official gift shop (www.nyc.gov/citystore, closed Sat, Sun).

The houses of crime and punishment are located in the **Civic Center**, near Foley Square, once the site of the city's most notorious 19th-century slum, Five Points. These days, you'll find the State Supreme Court in the **New York County Courthouse** (60 Centre Street, at Pearl Street), a hexagonal Roman Revival building; the rotunda is decorated with a mural called *Law Through the Ages*. The **Thurgood Marshall United States Courthouse** (40 Centre Street, between Duane & Pearl Streets) is a Corinthian temple crowned with a golden pyramid.

The **Criminal Courts Building & Manhattan Detention Complex** (100 Centre Street, between Leonard & White Streets) is still known as 'the Tombs', a nod to the original 1838 Egyptian Revival building – or, depending on who you ask, its current grimness. There's no denying that the hall's great granite slabs and looming towers are downright lugubrious. Nearby, the **African Burial Ground** was officially designated a National Monument in 2006.

Sights & Museums

African Burial Ground National Monument

Visitor centre: 290 Broadway, between Duane & Reade Streets (1-212 637 2019, www.nps.gov/afbg).

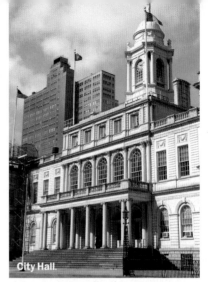

City Hall.

Subway J, Z to Chambers Street; R to City Hall; 4, 5, 6 to Brooklyn Bridge-City Hall. **Open** *Apr-Oct* 9am-5pm Mon-Sat. Closed Nov-Mar. *Visitor centre year-round* 10am-4pm Tue-Sat. **Admission** free. **Map** p51 A3 ㉑

The African Burial Ground is a small remnant of a 6.6-acre unmarked gravesite where between 10,000 and 20,000 enslaved Africans were buried. The burial ground, which closed in 1794, was unearthed during the construction of a federal office building in 1991 and later designated a National Monument. In 2007, a stone memorial, designed by architect Rodney Leon, was erected; the tall, curved structure draws heavily on African architecture and contains a spiral path leading to an ancestral chamber.

City Hall

City Hall Park, from Vesey to Chambers Streets, between Broadway & Park Row (1-212 788 2656, www.nyc.gov/designcommission). Subway J, Z to Chambers Street; R to City Hall; 2, 3 to Park Place; 4, 5, 6 to Brooklyn Bridge-City Hall. **Open** *Tours* (individuals) noon Wed, 10am Thur; (groups) 10.30am Mon, Tue. Reservations required.
Admission free. **Map** p51 A4 ㉒

Designed by French émigré Joseph François Mangin and John McComb Jr, the fine, Federal-style City Hall was completed in 1812. Tours take in the rotunda, with its splendid coffered dome, the City Council Chamber and the Governor's Room, with its collection of American 19th-century political portraits and historic furnishings (including George Washington's desk). The Thursday morning tour must be booked in advance; alternatively, sign up for the first come, first-served Wednesday noon tour between 10am and 11.30am at the NYC tourism kiosk at the southern end of City Hall Park on the east side of Broadway, at Barclay Street.

Soho & Tribeca

I n the 1960s and '70s, artists colonised what had become a post-industrial wasteland south of Houston Street, squatting in abandoned warehouses. Eventually, they worked with the city to rezone and restore them. Others followed suit in the Triangle Below Canal, which was once the site of the city's main produce market. Today, many of the old factory buildings in Soho and Tribeca are occupied by designer stores and high-end restaurants, and those once-spartan loft spaces are among the most desirable real estate in the city. But you can still find pockets of experimental culture in this consumer paradise, in the form of scattered art galleries and Off and Off-Off Broadway theatres. Even if you're not shopping or dining, take a walk in the area to admire a well-preserved architectural legacy with a uniquely New York character.

Drawing Center.

Don't Miss

1 **Drawing Center** A bastion of culture in shop-saturated Soho (p68).

2 **Dominique Ansel Bakery** Exquisite, boundary-pushing pastries (p71).

3 **Opening Ceremony** A diverse mix of designers go for gold (p72).

4 **Mmuseumm** Mini masterpiece (p74).

5 **Brushstroke** This East-West collaboration serves a truly memorable feast (p74).

EXPLORE

SOHO

*Subway A, C, E, 1 to Canal Street; C, E, 6
to Spring Street; N, R to Prince Street; 1 to
Houston Street.*

Now a retail mecca, Soho was once a hardscrabble
manufacturing zone with the derisive nickname
Hell's Hundred Acres. In the 1960s, it was
earmarked for destruction by over-zealous
urban planner Robert Moses, but its signature
cast-iron warehouses were saved by the artists
who inhabited them as cheap live-work spaces.
The **King & Queen of Greene Street**
(respectively, 72-76 Greene Street, between
Broome & Spring Streets, and 28-30 Greene
Street, between Canal & Grand Streets) are
both fine examples of the area's beloved
architectural landmarks. The most celebrated
of Soho's cast-iron edifices, however, is the five-
storey **Haughwout Building**, at 488-492
Broadway, at Broome Street. Designed in 1857,
it featured the world's first hydraulic lift (still
in working condition).

After landlords sniffed the potential for profits
in converting old loft buildings, Soho morphed
into a playground for the young, beautiful and
rich. It can still be a pleasure to stroll around the
cobblestoned side streets, and there are some
standout shops in the area, but the large chain
stores and sidewalk-encroaching street vendors
along Broadway create a shopping-mall-at-
Christmas crush on weekends. Although many
of the galleries that made Soho an art capital in
the 1970s and '80s decamped to Chelsea and, more
recently, the Lower East Side, a few excellent art
spaces remain, including the recently expanded
Drawing Center.

Sights & Museums

★ Drawing Center

*35 Wooster Street, between Broome & Grand Streets
(1-212 219 2166, www.drawingcenter.org). Subway
A, C, E, 1 to Canal Street.* **Open** noon-6pm Wed, Fri-
Sun; noon-8pm Thur. **Admission** $5; $3 reductions;
free under-12s. Free 6-8pm Thur. **Map** p69 C2 ❶
Established in 1977, the Drawing Center showcases
the broadly defined art form in its three galleries.
The non-profit standout assembles shows of
museum-calibre legends such as Philip Guston,
James Ensor and Willem de Kooning, but also
'Selections' surveys of newcomers. Art stars such as
Kara Walker and Chris Ofili received some of their
earliest NYC exposure here.

New York City Fire Museum

*278 Spring Street, between Hudson & Varick
Streets (1-212 691 1303, www.nycfiremuseum.
org). Subway C, E to Spring Street; 1 to Houston
Street.* **Open** 10am-5pm daily. **Admission** $8; $5
reductions. **Map** p69 B1 ❷

Soho Cigar Bar.

An active firehouse from 1905 to 1959, this museum
is filled with all manner of life-saving gadgetry,
from late 18th-century hand-pumped fire engines to
present-day equipment.

Restaurants & Cafés

Balthazar

*80 Spring Street, between Broadway & Crosby
Street (1-212 965 1414, www.balthazarny.com).
Subway N, R to Prince Street; 6 to Spring Street.*
Open 7.30-11.30am, noon-midnight Mon-Thur;
7.30-11.30am, noon-1am Fri; 8am-4pm, 6pm-1am
Sat; 8am-4pm, 5.30pm-midnight Sun. **Main
courses** $20-$45. **Map** p69 D1 ❸ **French**
At dinner, this iconic eaterie is perennially packed
with rail-thin lookers dressed to the nines. But it's
more than simply fashionable – the kitchen rarely
makes a false move and the service is surprisingly
friendly. The $170 three-tiered seafood platter
casts an impressive shadow, and the roast chicken
with garlic mashed potatoes for two is *délicieux*.

★ The Dutch

*131 Sullivan Street, at Prince Street (1-212 677
6200, www.thedutchnyc.com). Subway C, E to
Spring Street.* **Open** 11.30am-3pm, 5.30-11pm

Mon-Wed; 11.30am-3pm, 5.30pm-midnight Thur, Fri; 10am-3pm, 5.30pm-midnight Sat; 10am-3pm, 5.30pm-11pm Sun. **Main courses** $26-$49. **Map** p69 C1 ❹ American

From the moment it opened, Andrew Carmellini's rollicking Soho eaterie seemed destined to join the ranks of neighbourhood classics. The virtuoso chef offers diners an exuberant gastro-tour of the American melting pot, including mini fried-oyster sandwiches on house-made buns and superb dry-aged steaks. That everything tastes good and somehow works well together explains why reservations are hard to come by. Wait for your table in the airy oak bar (with adjacent oyster room) with one of the extensive selection of American whiskeys.

Ed's Lobster Bar

222 Lafayette Street, between Kenmare & Spring Streets (1-212 343 3236, www.lobster barnyc.com). Subway 6 to Spring Street. **Open** noon-3pm, 5-11pm Mon-Thur; noon-3pm, 5pm-midnight Fri; noon-midnight Sat; noon-9pm Sun. **Main courses** $18-$36. **Map** p69 D1 ❺ Seafood

If you secure a place at the 25-seat marble seafood bar or one of the few tables in the narrow, whitewashed space, expect superlative raw-bar

eats, delicately fried clams and lobster served every which way: steamed, grilled, broiled, stuffed into a pie and – the crowd favourite – the lobster roll. Here, it's a buttered bun stuffed with premium chunks of meat and a light coating of mayo. Note that the place serves lobster rolls only at the bar on weekday afternoons (3-5pm).

$ La Esquina

114 Kenmare Street, between Cleveland Place & Lafayette Street (1-646 613 7100, www. esquinanyc.com). Subway 6 to Spring Street. **Open** *Taqueria* 11am-2am daily. *Café* noon-midnight Mon-Thur; noon-1am Fri; 11am-1am Sat; 11am-midnight Sun. *Restaurant* 6pm-2am daily. **Tacos** $3.25-$4. **Main courses** *Café* $10-$24. *Restaurant* $18-$32. **Map** p69 D1 ❻ Mexican

La Esquina comprises three dining and drinking areas: first, a street-level *taqueria*, serving a short-order menu of tacos and Mexican *tortas*. Around the corner is a 30-seat café, its shelves stocked with books and old vinyl. Lastly, there's a dungeonesque restaurant and lounge accessible through a back door of the *taqueria* (to enter, you have to confirm that you have a reservation). It's worth the hassle: a world of Mexican murals, fine tequilas, chicken *mole* and crab *tostadas* awaits.

EXPLORE

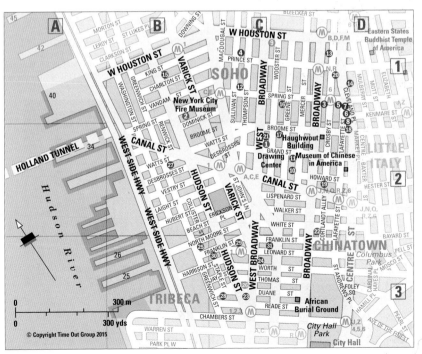

EXPLORE

Jack's Wife Freda

*224 Lafayette Street, between Kenmare & Spring
Streets (1-212 510 8550, www.jackswifefreda.com).
Subway 6 to Spring Street.* **Open** 9am-midnight
Mon-Sat; 9am-10pm Sun. **Main courses** $18-$25.
Map p69 D1 ❼ Café
Keith McNally protégé Dean Jankelowitz
(Balthazar, Schiller's Liquor Bar) is behind this
charming café. Decked out with dark-green leather
banquettes, brass railings and marble counters,
the classic yet cosy spot serves homey fare like
Jankelowitz's grandmother's matzo ball soup made
with duck fat or skirt steak sandwich with hand-
cut fries. In a prime shopping area, between Soho
and Nolita, it's also a great brunch spot.
Other location 50 Carmine Street, between
Bedford & Bleecker Streets, West Village
(1-646 669 9888)

★ Osteria Morini

*218 Lafayette Street, between Broome & Spring
Streets (1-212 965 8777, www.osteriamorini.com).
Subway 6 to Spring Street.* **Open** 11.30am-11pm
Mon-Thur; 11.30am-midnight Fri, Sat; 11.30am-
10pm Sun. **Main courses** $28-$38. **Map** p69 D2 ❽
Italian
Michael White is one of New York's most prolific
and successful Italian-American chefs, and this
terrific downtown homage to a classic Bolognese
tavern is his most accessible restaurant. White
spent seven years cooking in Italy's Emilia-
Romagna region, and his connection to the
area surfaces in the restaurant's rustic food.
Handmade pastas are fantastic across the board,
while superb meat dishes might include porchetta
with crisp, crackling skin and potatoes bathed in
pan drippings.

Bars

★ Pegu Club

*2nd Floor, 77 W Houston Street, at West Broadway
(1-212 473 7348, www.peguclub.com). Subway B,
D, F, M to Broadway-Lafayette Street; N, R to Prince
Street.* **Open** 5pm-2am Mon-Wed, Sun; 5pm-4am
Thur-Sat. **Map** p69 C1 ❾
It's easy to miss the discreet entrance of this bar,
which was inspired by a British officers' club
in Burma. Once you've found it, you'll be glad
you persevered. The sophisticated second-floor
destination, helmed by cocktail maven Audrey
Saunders, focuses on classics culled from decades-
old booze bibles. Gin is the key ingredient – these are
serious drinks for grown-up tastes.

Shops & Services

Soho's converted warehouses are packed with just
about every major fashion brand you can think of,
from budget and mid-priced international chains
like H&M, COS and Topshop to contemporary
stars **Alexander Wang** and **Rachel Comey**
and A-list designer labels like Balenciaga, Chanel
and Prada, plus stores selling home goods,
cosmetics, food and more. Listed below is a
selection of our favourite independent shops.

(3x1)

*15 Mercer Street, between Howard & Grand Streets
(1-212 391 6969, www.3x1.us). Subway A, C, E, J,
N, Q, R, Z, 1, 6 to Canal Street.* **Open** 11am-7pm
Mon-Sat; noon-6pm Sun. **Map** p69 C2 ❿ **Fashion**
Denim obsessives who are always looking for the
next It jeans have another place to splurge: (3x1)
creates entirely limited-edition styles sewn in the

Jack's Wife Freda.

store. Designer Scott Morrison, who previously launched Paper Denim & Cloth and Earnest Sewn, fills the large, gallery-like space with a variety of jeans (prices start at $195 for women, $245 for men) and other denim pieces such as shorts and miniskirts. Watch the construction process take place in a glass-walled design studio in the middle of the boutique.

Alexander Wang

103 Grand Street, between Greene & Mercer Streets (1-212 977 9683, www.alexanderwang.com). Subway J, N, Q, R, Z, 6 to Canal Street. **Open** 11am-7pm Mon-Sat; noon-6pm Sun. **Map** p69 C2 ⓫ Fashion

Anna Wintour-approved designer Alexander Wang has amassed a cultlike following of vogueish downtown types. He launched his eponymous line in 2007, and was propelled to fashion royalty in 2008 after scoring a Council of Fashion Designers of America award. With chalky-white marble display pedestals and overstuffed leather couches, his luxurious and spacious flagship boutique offers the wunderkind's chic-but-casual men's and women's clothing, handbags and showstopping shoes, plus the lower-priced T by Alexander Wang line.

★ Dominique Ansel Bakery

189 Spring Street, between Sullivan & Thompson Streets (1-212 219 2773, www.dominiqueansel. com). Subway C, E to Spring Street. **Open** 8am-7pm Mon-Sat; 9am-7pm Sun. **Map** p69 C1 ⓬ Food & drink

Dominique Ansel honed his skills as executive pastry chef at Daniel for six years before opening this innovative patisserie. In 2013, his croissant-doughnut hybrid, the Cronut, created a frenzy in foodie circles and put his ingenious creations into the spotlight. If you can't get your hands on a Cronut, try the DKA – a caramelised, flaky take on the croissant-like Breton speciality *kouign amann*. And his cotton-soft mini cheesecake, an ethereally light gâteau with a brûléed top, leaves the dense old New York classic sputtering in its dust.

▶ *For the dessert wizard's latest venture, see p118* **Short-Order and Sweet**.

Housing Works Bookstore Café

126 Crosby Street, between Houston & Prince Streets (1-212 334 3324, www.housingworks bookstore.org). Subway B, D, F, M to Broadway-Lafayette Street; N, R to Prince Street; 6 to Bleecker Street. **Open** 9am-9pm Mon-Fri; 10am-5pm Sat, Sun. **Map** p69 D1 ⓭ **Books & music**

This popular two-level store – which stocks literary fiction, non-fiction, rare books and collectibles – is also a peaceful spot for a coffee (or wine) break. All proceeds go to providing support services for people living with HIV/AIDS. Emerging writers and the literati take the mic at the regular readings.

IN THE KNOW
SOHO'S ITALIAN LEGACY

Just west of West Broadway, tenement- and townhouse-lined streets contain remnants of the Italian community that once dominated the area, such as **St Anthony of Padua** Roman Catholic Church (154 Sullivan Street, at Houston Street), dedicated in 1888. You'll still find old-school neighbourhood flavour at **Pino's Prime Meat Market** (149 Sullivan Street, 1-212 475 8134, closed Sun).The iconic Vesuvio Bakery is now occupied by **Birdbath Neighborhood Green Bakery** (160 Prince Street, between Thompson Street & West Broadway, 1-646 556 7720, www.thecity bakery.com), which has kept the old-fashioned façade intact.

In God We Trust

265 Lafayette Street, between Prince & Spring Streets (1-212 966 9010, www.ingodwetrust nyc.com). Subway N, R to Prince Street; 6 to Spring Street. **Open** noon-8pm Mon-Sat; noon-7pm Sun. **Map** p69 D1 ⓮ **Fashion/Accessories**

Designer Shana Tabor's cosy antique-furnished stores cater to that appealing vintage-intellectual aesthetic, offering locally crafted collections for men and women. The store's line of well-priced, cheeky accessories is a highlight – for example, gold heart-shaped pendants engraved with blunt sayings like 'Boring' or 'Blah Blah Blah', rifle-shaped tie bars, and a wide selection of retro sunglasses for only $20 a pair.

Other locations 129 Bedford Avenue, between North 9th & 10th Streets, Williamsburg, Brooklyn (1-718 384 0700); 70 Greenpoint Avenue, between Milton & Franklin Streets, Greenpoint, Brooklyn (1-718 389 3545).

Jacques Torres Chocolate

350 Hudson Street, between Charlton & King Streets, entrance on King Street (1-212 414 2462, www.mrchocolate.com). Subway 1 to Houston Street. **Open** 8.30am-7pm Mon-Fri; 9am-7pm Sat; 10.30am-6.30pm Sun. **Map** p69 B1 ⓯ Food & drink

Walk into Jacques Torres's glass-walled shop and café, and you'll be surrounded by a Willy Wonka-esque factory that turns raw cocoa beans into luscious chocolate goodies before your eyes. As well as selling the usual assortments, truffles and bars (plus more unusual delicacies such as chocolate-covered cornflakes and Cheerios), the shop serves deliciously rich hot chocolate, steamed to order.

Other locations throughout the city.

EXPLORE

EXPLORE

Kiki de Montparnasse

79 Greene Street, between Broome & Spring
Streets (1-212 965 8150, www.kikidm.com).
Subway N, R to Prince Street; 6 to Spring Street.
Open 11am-7pm Mon, Sun; 11am-8pm Tue-Sat.
Map p69 C1 ⑯ **Lingerie**
This impeccably tasteful erotic boutique channels
the spirit of its namesake, a 1920s sexual icon and
Man Ray muse, with an array of subtly provocative
contemporary lingerie in silk and French lace. Look
out for novelties such as fine cotton tank tops with
built-in garters and exquisitely crafted corsets, crops,
ticklers and other bedroom accoutrements. Prices
reflect the high quality and luxurious materials.

Kirna Zabête

477 Broome Street, between Greene & Wooster
Streets (1-212 941 9656, www.kirnazabete.com).
Subway N, R to Prince Street; 6 to Spring Street.
Open 11am-7pm Mon-Sat; noon-6pm Sun.
Map p69 C2 ⑰ **Fashion**
Former fashion editor Beth Buccini and designer-
wholesale vet Sarah Easley showcase more than
100 labels in this 10,000sq ft boutique. Although the
stock leans towards pricey designer wares – Euro
heavyweights such as Alaïa, Saint Laurent and
Valentino, new American classics including Proenza
Schouler and Altuzarra, plus newer names like Wes
Gordon and Baja East – this is no hushed fashion
temple. The playful, colourful interior is decorated
with six-foot wooden 'chandeliers', black-and-white
striped hardwood floors and neon signs displaying
quirky mantras including 'Life is short, buy the
shoes'. Unusual jewellery and accessories, plus
coffee-table books, stationery and novelties provide
plenty of scope for style-minded gifts.

Odin

199 Lafayette Street, between Broome & Kenmare
Streets (1-212 966 0026, www.odinnewyork.com).
Subway 6 to Spring Street. **Open** 11am-8pm Mon-
Sat; noon-7pm Sun. **Map** p69 D2 ⑱ **Fashion**
The Norse god Odin is often portrayed sporting an eye
patch and shabby robes. That may have been stylish
in medieval Scandinavia, but to make it in NYC,
he'd have to pick up some Engineered Garments,
Rag & Bone or Band of Outsiders gear from this
upscale men's boutique. Also look out for White
Mountaineering, a Japanese brand that combines
high-function fabrics with a fashionable aesthetic.
Other locations 328 E 11th Street, between First
& Second Avenues, East Village (1-212 475 0666);
106 Greenwich Avenue, between Jane & W 13th
Streets, West Village (1-212 243 4724).

★ Opening Ceremony

33-35 Howard Street, between Broadway &
Lafayette Street (1-212 219 2688, www.opening
ceremony.us). Subway J, N, Q, R, Z, 6 to Canal
Street. **Open** 11am-8pm Mon-Sat; noon-7pm
Sun. **Map** p69 D2 ⑲ **Fashion**

The Olympics-referencing name reflects Opening
Ceremony's multinational approach to fashion. The
mega-concept store sprawls over two storefronts
and four floors, each with a noticeably different
atmosphere, eye-catching installations and eclectic
stock. The constantly rotating mix of labels veers
from experimental to refined, and under-the-
radar to iconic. You'll find the popular Opening
Ceremony collection and big names like Kenzo and
Loewe, but also some you might not recognise – for
example, Adam Selman, who created sensational
outfits for Rihanna before launching his own line;
Shane Oliver's cult androgynous streetwear, Hood
By Air (HBA); and vintage-looking Korean label
Fleamadonna. Shoes, accessories and OC-approved
periodicals and music bump up the browse factor.
▶ *There's an additional OC outpost at the Ace*
Hotel, see p363.

Rachel Comey

95 Crosby Street, between Prince & Spring
Streets (1-212 334 0455, www.rachelcomey.com).
Subway N, R to Prince Street; 6 to Spring Street.
Open 11am-7.30pm Mon-Sat; noon-6pm Sun.
Map p69 D1 ⑳ **Fashion**
A certain arty, indie sensibility in this NYC design-
er's output can be traced to her fine-arts background
and a stint creating stage gear for downtown bands.
Comey has amassed a devoted following and, since
summer 2014, fans can flock to this Soho flagship.
In addition to the complete collection of vintage-
inspired women's clothing and the hugely popular
footwear, the store is reintroducing the men's line.

What Goes Around Comes Around

351 West Broadway, between Broome & Grand
Streets (1-212 343 1225, www.whatgoesaround
nyc.com). Subway A, C, E, 1 to Canal Street. **Open**
11am-8pm Mon-Sat; noon-7pm Sun. **Map** p69 C2 ㉑
Fashion
A favourite among the city's fashion cognoscenti,
this downtown vintage destination sells highly
curated stock alongside its own retro label. Style
mavens particularly recommend it for 1960s, '70s
and '80s rock T-shirts, pristine Alaïa clothing and
vintage fur coats.

TRIBECA

Subway A, C, E, 1 to Canal Street; 1 to Franklin
Street; 1, 2, 3 to Chambers Street.

In just two decades, the Triangle Below Canal
Street morphed from an isolated, run-down
corner to a wealthy enclave with a family- and
celebrity-heavy demographic. Robert De Niro
has been a key figure in the area's transformation,
founding the **Tribeca Film Center** (375
Greenwich Street, at Franklin Street) with
partner Jane Rosenthal in 1988, which contains
industry magnet **Tribeca Grill** (1-212 941 3900).

SMALL WONDER

NYC's tiniest museum occupies a Tribeca elevator shaft.

Institutions like the Metropolitan Museum of Art are home to thousands of treasures. At the other end of the spectrum, there's **Mmuseumm** (*see p74*), a 60-square-foot repository in an abandoned Tribeca freight elevator. The walk-in-closet-size space, founded by indie filmmakers Alex Kalman, Josh Safdie and Benny Safdie, showcases a mishmash of found objects and artefacts donated by hobbyists. Although Mmuseumm is only open at weekends, viewers can also get a peek at the space when it's closed – look for the small peepholes in a metal door on the narrow throughway between Franklin and White Streets.

Mmuseumm was a logical extension of the filmmaking process, explains Alex Kalman. 'We've made a lot of work that is very much rooted in exploring the humanity of the world around us, so in a way we've been collecting moments by capturing them on video. Then at a certain point we started collecting actual objects – objects that we would consider proof of things, or that blew our minds – so we started amassing them over a couple of years. Then we said, let's open an institution for this language.'

Holdings include an index card detailing a pot dealer's pricing scale, and – allegedly – the shoe that was thrown at President George W Bush in Iraq in 2008. The exhibits for each season, lasting roughly six months, are acquired in various ways, including via a submissions email address, and have included such varied ephemera as a selection of *Screw* magazine founder Al Goldstein's transcribed personal Dictaphone notes, memorabilia from one of Saddam Hussein's palaces, fake vomit from around the world, and part of a collection charting the evolution of the coffee-cup lid, amassed by two architects. In spring 2015, the minuscule museum was preparing to open a new 'wing' in an even smaller adjacent space. The inaugural show is a recreation of the pristine closet of Sara Berman (artist Maira Kalman's mother and Alex's grandmother), who always wore white.

Although Kalman acknowledges the humour inherent in many of Mmuseumm's displays, he stresses it's not merely an esoteric joke. 'We know that it's small, but it's basically saying, these are not the things we're creating in society because we think they're important or valuable, these are the things we're creating because they are the things we want and need, and that tells us a lot about our psychology and who we are. It's trying to paint a very big portrait of humanity through the collection of our smallest things.'

EXPLORE

A few blocks away, De Niro's **Tribeca Cinemas** (54 Varick Street, at Laight Street, 1-212 941 2001, www.tribecacinemas.com) hosts premières and glitzy parties, when it isn't serving as a venue for the **Tribeca Film Festival** (*see p263*). In 2008, the actor opened the **Greenwich Hotel** (*see p357*).

The preponderance of large, hulking former industrial buildings gives Tribeca an imposing profile, but fine small-scale cast-iron architecture still stands along White Street and the parallel thoroughfares. Upscale eateries and, increasingly, shops cater to the well-heeled locals.

Sights & Museums

★ FREE Mmuseumm
Cortlandt Alley, between Franklin & White Streets (no phone, www.mmuseumm.com). Subway J, N, Q, R, Z, 6 to Canal Street. **Open** noon-6pm Sat, Sun. Admission free. **Map** p69 D2 ☻
See p73 **Small Wonder**.

Restaurants & Cafés

★ Brushstroke
30 Hudson Street, at Duane Street (1-212 791 3771, www.davidbouley.com). Subway 1, 2, 3 to Chambers Street. **Open** 5.30-10.30pm Mon; 11.30am-2.45pm, 5.30-10.30pm Tue-Thur; 11.30am-2.45pm, 5.30-11pm Fri, Sat. **Tasting menus** $90-$250. **Map** p69 C3 ☻ **Japanese**
Prominent local chef David Bouley's name may be behind this venture, but he's not in the kitchen, having handed the reins over to talented import Isao Yamada, who turns out some of the most accomplished Japanese food in the city. The ever-changing seasonal menu is best experienced as an intricate multicourse feast inspired by the Japanese *kaiseki*. A meal might start with crab *chawanmushi* (egg custard) with Oregon black truffles, before building slowly towards a subtle climax. In keeping with the basic tenets of this culinary art form, the savoury procession concludes with a rice dish – top-notch *chirashi* or seafood and rice cooked in a clay casserole – and delicate sweets such as creamy soy-milk panna cotta. The sushi bar is run by Tokyo-trained chef Eiji Ichimura, who serves a traditional Edomae-style *omakase*.

Landmarc Tribeca
179 West Broadway, between Leonard & Worth Streets (1-212 343 3883, www.landmarc-restaurant.com). Subway 1 to Franklin Street. **Open** 11am-11pm daily. **Main courses** $27-$38. **Map** p69 C3 ☻ **Eclectic**
This downtown dining destination distinguished itself among its Tribeca competitors with heady bistro dishes (bone marrow, crispy sweetbreads) and a wine list stocked with reasonably priced half bottles. Chef-owner Marc Murphy focuses on

the tried and trusted: *frisée aux lardons*, braised lamb shank and several types of mussels. Metal beams and exposed brick add an unfinished edge to the elegant bi-level space. Those who have little restraint when it comes to sweets will appreciate the dessert menu: miniature portions cost just $4 a pop and a tasting of six goes for $20.
Other location 3rd Floor, Time Warner Center, 10 Columbus Circle, at Broadway, Upper West Side (1-212 823 6123).

Locanda Verde
377 Greenwich Street, at North Moore Street (1-212 925 3797, www.locandaverdenyc.com). Subway 1 to Franklin Street. **Open** 7-11am, 11.30am-3pm, 5.30-11pm Mon-Thur; 7am-3pm, 5.30-11.30pm Fri; 8am-3pm, 5.30-11.30pm Sat; 8am-3pm, 5.30-11pm Sun. **Main courses** $22-$37. **Map** p69 B3 ☻ **Italian**
This buzzy eaterie in Robert De Niro's Greenwich Hotel features bold family-style fare that's best enjoyed as a bacchanalian banquet. Waygu beef *tartara* piedmontese with hazelnuts and truffles won't last long in the middle of the table. Nor will the 'grandmother's' ravioli, stuffed with veal, pork and beef. This is one of those rare Italian restaurants with desserts worth saving room for, including decadent confections for two.

Bars

Weather Up Tribeca
159 Duane Street, between Hudson Street & West Broadway (1-212 766 3202, www.weatherupnyc.com). Subway 1, 2, 3 to Chambers Street. **Open** 5pm-midnight Mon-Wed; 5pm-2am Thur-Sat. **Map** p69 C3 ☻
At Kathryn Weatherup's tony Manhattan drinkery, a spin-off of her popular Prospect Heights bar, the well-balanced cocktail list features a regularly rotating mix of classics and original quaffs. Pair the booze with smart snacks such as grilled cheese sandwiches and steak tartare.
Other location 589 Vanderbilt Avenue, between Bergen & Dean Streets, Prospect Heights, Brooklyn (no phone).

Shops & Services

La Garçonne

465 Greenwich Street, at Watts Street (1-646 553 3303, www.lagarconne.com). Subway 1 to Canal Street. **Open** 11am-7pm Mon-Sat; noon-6pm Sun. **Map** p69 B2 ❷ **Fashion**

After nine years as an online boutique, La Garçonne opened this chic brick-and-mortar version. The minimal, refined aesthetic is reflected in both the space and the stock, which includes such labels as Comme des Garçons, Proenza Schouler, Marni, Jil Sander, and the in-house collection, La Garçonne Moderne, alongside newer names. While catering mainly to women, there is a smaller selection of menswear.

Nili Lotan

188 Duane Street, between Greenwich & Hudson Streets (1-212 219 8794, www.nililotan.com). Subway 1, 2, 3 to Chambers Street. **Open** noon-7pm Mon-Sat; noon-6pm Sun. **Map** p69 C3 ❷ **Fashion**

The sparsely hung women's garments in Israeli designer Nili Lotan's airy, all-white store and studio look like art pieces on display in a gallery. Perfectly cut, largely monochrome wardrobe staples such as silk camisoles and dresses, oversized cashmere sweaters and crisply tailored menswear-inspired shirts appeal to minimalists with a penchant for luxury.

Patron of the New

151 Franklin Street, between Hudson & Varick Streets (1-212 966 7144, www.patronofthenew.us). Subway A, C, E to Canal Street; 1 to Franklin Street. **Open** noon-8pm Mon-Sat; noon-6pm Sun. **Map** p69 C3 ❷ **Fashion**

This avant-garde fashion emporium showcases a collection of unique guys' and gals' clothing, beauty products, accessories and housewares from both illustrious and under-the-radar designers, including Balmain, Nicolas Andreas Taralis and Denis Colomb. Goods are pricey, but there are some affordable accessories, jewellery and gifts like soaps and candles.

Shinola

177 Franklin Street, between Greenwich & Hudson Streets (1-917 728 3000, www.shinola.com). Subway A, C, E to Canal Street; 1 to Franklin Street. **Open** 11am-7pm Mon-Sat; noon-6pm Sun. **Map** p69 C3 ❸ **Fashion**

Detroit-based brand Shinola is a Motor City success story. Peruse the range of American-manufactured watches, bicycles, leather goods and other items, all with a sturdy, midcentury aesthetic, in the industrial-edged NYC flagship. But that's not all: you can also admire a 1930s bronze map that used to hang in Rockefeller Center and stop for coffee at the in-store outpost of cult East Village café the Smile.

Steven Alan

103 Franklin Street, between West Broadway & Church Street (1-212 343 0692, www.stevenalan. com). Subway 1 to Franklin Street. **Open** 11.30am-7pm Mon-Wed, Fri, Sat; 11.30am-8pm Thur; noon-6pm Sun. **Map** p69 C3 ❸ **Fashion**

Known for well-crafted cotton shirts in an array of stripes, checks and solid colours, Steven Alan also assembles cultish boutique brands for men and women in its flagship store. In addition to the house label, browse clothing by Acne, Band of Outsiders and Engineered Garments, and handbags and shoes.

Brushstroke.

EXPLORE

Chinatown, Little Italy & Nolita

Take a walk in the area south of Broome Street and east of Broadway, and you'll feel as though you've entered a different continent. The streets of Manhattan's Chinatown are packed with exotic-produce stands, herb emporiums, cheap jewellers, snack vendors and, of course, restaurants. As New York City's largest Asian community continues to grow, it merges with neighbouring Little Italy. Squeezed between Chinatown's sprawl and the multiplying boutiques and hotspots of Nolita (North of Little Italy), the historically Italian district has long been shrinking, but you can still get a taste of the old neighbourhood in its classic cafés and red-sauce eateries.

Estela.

Don't Miss

1 Museum of Chinese in America The Chinese-American story, stylishly told (p78).

2 Nom Wah Tea Parlor Superior dim sum in a vintage setting (p80).

3 Xi'an Famous Foods Celeb chef-approved cheap eats (p81).

4 Estela Imaginative Med-influenced fare (p82).

5 Erica Weiner Unique (and affordable) local trinkets (p83).

EXPLORE

CHINATOWN

Subway F to East Broadway; J, N, Q, R, Z, 6 to Canal Street.

A steady flow of new arrivals keeps this neighbourhood – one of the largest Chinese communities outside Asia – full to bursting, with thousands of residents packed into the area surrounding the eastern stretch of Canal Street. Some eventually decamp to one of NYC's three other Chinatowns, in Sunset Park, Brooklyn, and Flushing and Elmhurst in Queens.

Mott and Grand Streets are lined with fish-, fruit- and vegetable-stocked stands selling some of the best and most affordable seafood and produce in the city – you'll see buckets of live eels and crabs, square watermelons and piles of hairy rambutans. Street vendors sell satisfying snacks such as pork buns and sweet egg pancakes by the bagful. Canal Street glitters with cheap jewellery and gift shops, but beware furtive vendors of (undoubtedly fake) designer goods. Between Kenmare and Worth Streets, Mott Street is lined

with restaurants representing the cuisine of virtually every province of mainland China and Hong Kong; the Bowery, East Broadway and Division Street are just as diverse. Adding to the mix are myriad Indonesian, Malaysian, Thai and Vietnamese eateries and shops.

At the engaging **Museum of Chinese in America**, you can learn about the Chinese experience on these shores. The **Eastern States Buddhist Temple of America** (64 Mott Street, between Bayard & Canal Streets, 1-212 966 6229), founded in 1962, is one of the country's oldest Chinese Buddhist temples.

Sights & Museums

Museum of Chinese in America
215 Centre Street, between Grand & Howard Streets (1-212 619 4785, www.mocanyc.org). Subway J, N, Q, R, Z, 6 to Canal Street. **Open** 11am-6pm Tue, Wed, Fri-Sun; 11am-9pm Thur. **Admission** $10; $5 reductions; free under-12s. Free 1st Thur of mth. **Map** p79 A3 ❶

Designed by prominent Chinese-American architect Maya Lin, MoCA reopened in an airy former machine shop in 2009. Its interior is loosely inspired by a traditional Chinese house, with rooms radiating off a central courtyard and areas defined by screens. The core exhibition traces the development of Chinese communities in the US from the 1850s to the present through objects, images and video. Innovative displays (drawers open to reveal artwork and documents, portraits are presented in a ceiling mobile) cover the development of industries such as laundries and restaurants in New York, Chinese stereotypes in pop culture, and the suspicion and humiliation Chinese-Americans endured during World War II and the McCarthy era. A mocked-up Chinese

Nom Wah Tea Parlor. *See p80.*

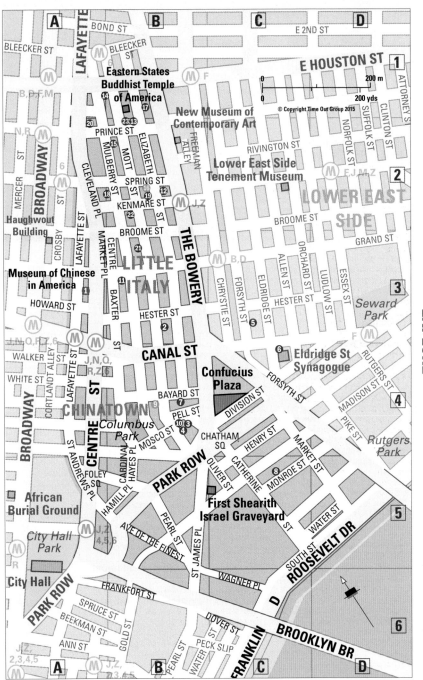

EXPLORE

Big Wing Wong.

general store evokes the feel of these multi-purpose spaces, which served as vital community lifelines for men severed from their families under the 1882 Exclusion Act that restricted immigration. There's also a gallery for special exhibitions.

Restaurants & Cafés

$ Big Wing Wong

102 Mott Street, between Canal & Hester Streets (1-212 274 0696). Subway J, N, Q, R, Z, 6 to Canal Street. **Open** 9am-10.30pm daily. **Main courses** $5-$20. **No credit cards. Map** p79 B3 ❷ **Chinese**
You'll be confused when you show up at this old-school Cantonese joint – the outside inexplicably says 102 Noodles Town. But the real speciality is clear when you taste a slice of the roasted duck, with its fatty, succulent meat and crackly, burnished mahogany skin. You can get the bird over rice or congee, but purists stick to a mere drizzle of hoisin.

★ $ Nom Wah Tea Parlor

13 Doyers Street, between Bowery & Pell Street (1-212 962 6047, www.nomwah.com). Subway J, N, Q, R, Z, 6 to Canal Street; J, Z to Chambers Street. **Open** 10.30am-9pm Mon-Thur, Sun; 10.30am-10pm Fri, Sat. **Main courses** $3.50-$12. **Map** p79 B4 ❸ **Chinese**
New York's first dim sum house, Nom Wah opened in 1920 and was owned by the same family for more than three decades. The current owner, Wilson Tang, has revamped it in a vintage style true to the restaurant's archival photographs. The most important tweaks, though, were behind the scenes: Tang updated the kitchen and did away with the procedure of cooking dim sum en masse. Now, each plate (ultra-fluffy oversized roasted-pork buns, flaky fried crêpe egg rolls) is cooked to order. *Photo p78.*

Ping's

22 Mott Street, between Mosco & Pell Streets (1-212 602 9988). Subway J, N, Q, R, Z, 6 to Canal Street. **Open** 10.30am-11pm Mon-Fri; 9am-11pm Sat, Sun. **Main courses** $9-$29. **Map** p79 B4 ❹ **Chinese**
The bank of fish tanks near the entrance suggests the speciality. Bite-sized pieces of boneless smelt are deep-fried to a golden yellow and served with a mix of Szechuan peppercorns and salt. Big steamed oysters benefit from a splash of Ping's celebrated house-made XO sauce – a spicy condiment made of dried shrimp, scallops and garlic. The sliced sautéed conch is set off by snappy snow peas and a tangy fermented shrimp sauce. Those exotic flavours, plus refinements like tablecloths, justify prices that are a notch above the Chinatown norm.

$ Prosperity Dumpling

46 Eldridge Street, between Canal & Hester Streets (1-212 343 0683). Subway J, N, Q, R, Z, 6 to Canal Street. **Open** 7.30am-10pm daily. **Dumplings** $1-$2/4. **No credit cards. Map** p79 C3 ❺ **Chinese**
This pint-size dumpling den serves one of the best budget meals in Chinatown: four pan-fried pot stickers for a buck or two. A plump, handmade wrapper – chewy with crisp, griddle-pressed edges – is folded around a juicy pork-and-chive filling, its rich flavour at odds with the cheap price.

$ Super Taste Restaurant

26 Eldridge Street, at Canal Street (1-646 283 0999). Subway F to East Broadway. **Open** 10am-11pm daily. **Main courses** $4-$6. **No credit cards. Map** p79 C4 ❻ **Chinese**
In a sea of cheap Chinatown noodle bars, Super Taste stands out. Watch the cook hand pull your Lanzhou-style *la mian*, the Chinese relative of Japanese ramen, which is served in a soup with toppings that vary from beef tendon to eel – for little more than $5.

$ Xi'an Famous Foods

67 Bayard Street, between Elizabeth & Mott Streets (no phone, www.xianfoods.com). Subway J, N, Q, R, Z, 6 to Canal Street. **Open** 11.30am-9pm Mon-Thur, Sun; 11.30am-9.30pm Fri, Sat. **Main courses** $3-$10. **No credit cards. Map** p79 B4 ❼ **Chinese**
This cheap Chinese chainlet, which got the seal of approval from celebrity chef Anthony Bourdain, highlights the mouth-tingling cuisine of Xi'an, an ancient capital along China's Silk Road. Claim one of the 35 stools and nosh on spicy noodles or a cumin-spiced burger for less than ten bucks.
Other locations throughout the city.

Shops & Services

Downtown Music Gallery

13 Monroe Street, between Catherine & Market Streets (1-212 473 0043, www.downtownmusic gallery.com). Subway J, Z to Chambers Street; 4, 5, 6 to Brooklyn Bridge-City Hall. **Open** noon-6pm daily. **Map** p79 C5 ❾ **Books & music**
Many landmarks of the so-called downtown music scene have shuttered, but as long as DMG persists, the community will have a sturdy anchor. The shop stocks the city's finest selection of avant-garde jazz, contemporary classical, progressive rock and related styles.

★ Sun's Organic Garden

79 Bayard Street, between Mott & Mulberry Streets (1-212 566 3260). Subway J, N, Q, R, Z,

Little Italy.

6 to Canal Street. **Open** 10am-7.30pm daily. **Map** p79 B4 ❾ **Food & drink**
Owner Lorna Lai knows tea the way a sommelier knows terroir. Curious sippers peruse the well-stocked shelves of the Hong Kong native's nook, which boasts more than a thousand jarred loose-leaf varieties from around the world, available by the ounce. Lai's house-made herbal blends are stand-outs, in exotic flavours like holy basil and bilberry.

Uniqulee

36 Mott Street, at Pell Street (1-212 323 2870). Subway J, N, Q, R, Z, 6 to Canal Street. **Open** noon-9pm Mon-Sat; noon-8pm Sun. **Map** p79 B4 ❿
Lee Chan's Chinatown design store is the antithesis of the neighbourhood's stock-in-trade cheap gift emporiums. As the name asserts, Uniqulee focuses on one-of-a-kind finds. Look for locally designed dish towels, Selenite candle holders, cast-iron piggy banks, hand-crafted banana fibre bowls and more.

LITTLE ITALY & NOLITA

Subway B, D, F, M to Broadway-Lafayette Street; J, N, Q, R, Z, 6 to Canal Street; J, Z to Bowery; N, R to Prince Street; 6 to Spring Street.

Abandoning the dismal tenements of the Five Points district (in what is now the Civic Center and part of Chinatown), immigrants from Naples and Sicily began moving to **Little Italy** in the 1880s. The area once stretched from Canal Street to Houston Street, between Lafayette Street and the Bowery, but as families prospered in the 1950s, they moved to the outer boroughs and suburbs. These days a strong Italian presence can only be observed on the blocks immediately surrounding Mulberry Street. Yet ethnic pride remains: Italian-Americans flood in from across the city during the 11-day **Feast of San Gennaro** (*see p37*).

Completed in 1809 and restored after a fire in 1868, **St Patrick's Old Cathedral** (260-264 Mulberry Street, between Houston & Prince Streets) was the city's premier Catholic church until it was demoted upon consecration of the Fifth Avenue cathedral of the same name. Touristy cafés and restaurants line Mulberry Street between Broome and Canal Streets, but pockets of the past linger nearby. Long-time residents still buy fresh mozzarella from **DiPalo's Fine Foods** (200 Grand Street, at Mott Street, 1-212 226 1033). Legend has it that the first pizzeria in New York was opened by Gennaro Lombardi on Spring Street in 1905. **Lombardi's** moved down the block in 1994 (32 Spring Street, at Mott Street, 1-212 941 7994), but still serves its signature clam pies. Today the area's restaurants are largely undistinguished grills and pasta houses, but two reliable choices are **Il Cortile** (125 Mulberry Street, between Canal & Hester Streets, 1-212 226 6060, www.ilcortile.com) and **La Mela** (167 Mulberry Street, between

EXPLORE

Broome & Grand Streets, 1-212 431 9493, www. lamelarestaurant.com). Drop in for dessert at **Caffè Roma** (385 Broome Street, at Mulberry Street, 1-212 226 8413), which opened in 1891.

Nolita became a magnet for independent boutiques and trendy eateries in the 1990s. Elizabeth, Mott and Mulberry Streets, between Houston and Spring Streets, in particular, are home to hip shops.

Restaurants & Cafés

Baz Bagel & Restaurant
181 Grand Street, between Baxter & Mulberry Streets (1-212 335 0609, www.bazbagel.com). Subway J, N, Q, R, Z, 6 to Canal Street. **Open** 7am-4pm Mon-Fri; 8am-6pm Sat, Sun. **Bagels** $1.25-$26. **Map** p79 B3 ⓫ **Café**
See p97 **Bagel Boom.**

Black Seed
170 Elizabeth Street, between Kenmare & Spring Streets (1-212 730 1950, www.blackseedbagels. com). Subway J, Z to Bowery. **Open** 7am-4pm daily. **Bagels** $1.50-$15. **Map** p79 B2 ⓬ **Café**
See p97 **Bagel Boom.**

$ Café Habana
17 Prince Street, at Elizabeth Street (1-212 625 2001, www.cafehabana.com). Subway N, R to Prince Street; 6 to Spring Street. **Open** 9am-midnight daily. **Main courses** $10-$19. **Map** p79 B2 ⓭ **Cuban**
Since 1998, this converted corner diner has been drawing crowds for its addictive corn, doused in fresh mayo, chargrilled, and generously sprinkled with chilli powder and grated cotija cheese. Other staples include a Cuban sandwich of roasted pork, ham, melted swiss and sliced pickles, and crisp beer-battered catfish with spicy mayo.

Estela
47 E Houston Street, between Mott & Mulberry Streets (1-212 219 7693, www.estelanyc.com). Subway B, D, F, M to Broadway-Lafayette Street; 6 to Bleecker Street. **Open** 5.30pm-midnight Mon-Thur; 5.30pm-1am Fri; 11am-2.30pm, 5.30pm-1am Sat; 11am-2.30pm, 5.30pm-midnight Sun. **Main courses** $16-$34. **Map** p79 A1 ⓮ **American creative**
The fashionable cookie-cutter decor – exposed brick, globe lights, hulking marble bar – may suggest you've stumbled into yet another bustling rustic restaurant-cum-bar that's not worth the wait. But there is more to this Mediterranean-tinged spot than meets the eye: primarily, the talent of imaginative Uruguayan-born chef Ignacio Mattos. An ever-changing, mostly small-plates menu pivots from avant-garde towards intimate. Highlights might include beef tartare with tart pickled elderberries, a musty baseline note from fish sauce and crunchy sunchoke (Jerusalem artichoke) chips; egg with gigante beans and cured tuna; and a creamy panna cotta with honey.

Parm
248 Mulberry Street, between Prince & Spring Streets (1-212 993 7189, www.parmnyc.com). Subway N, R to Prince Street; 6 to Spring Street. **Open** 11am-11pm Mon-Thur, Sun; 11am-midnight Fri-Sat. **Sandwiches** $9-$19. **Map** p79 B2 ⓯ **Italian**
Mario Carbone and Rich Torrisi, two young fine-dining chefs, brought a cool-kid sheen to red-sauce plates in 2010, when they debuted Torrisi Italian Specialties, a deli by day and haute eaterie by night. People lined up for their buzzworthy sandwiches (outstanding herb-rubbed roast turkey, classic cold cuts or chicken parmesan), packing the joint until it outgrew the space. Although the original is no more, the superlative sandwiches are still served in these fetching diner digs, plus a new location on the Upper West Side. Together with partner Jeff Zalaznick, the duo now has several restaurants around town, including the excellent Carbone (*see p114*) and Santina (*see p123*).
Other location 235 Columbus Avenue, between 70th & 71st Streets, Upper West Side (1-212 776 4921).

Bars

Mother's Ruin
18 Spring Street, between Elizabeth & Mott Streets (no phone, www.mothersruinnyc.com). Subway J, Z to Bowery; 6 to Spring Street. **Open** 11am-4am daily. **Map** p79 B2 ⓰
At this airy Nolita drinkery, co-owners Timothy Lynch and Richard Knapp bring in a rotating cast of star bartenders to sling classic and contemporary drinks. The laid-back space – done up with a cream tin ceiling, exposed brick and weathered-wood bar – also offers a full menu of globally inflected bites.

Shops & Services

Christian Siriano
252 Elizabeth Street, between E Houston & Prince Streets (1-212 775 8494, www.christiansiriano. com). Subway B, D, F, M to Broadway-Lafayette Street. **Open** 11.30am-7pm Mon-Sat; noon-6pm Sun. **Map** p79 B1 ⓱ **Fashion**
This 1,000sq ft flagship boutique was personally designed by the hotshot *Project Runway* winner. You'll find the glam evening wear that propelled Siriano to success, such as beaded gowns and cocktail dresses, on display. But if you don't have a red-carpet event on your calendar, there are plenty of reasonably priced separates and accessories to paw through, along with his Payless footwear collection (starting at just $30).

Creatures of Comfort
205 Mulberry Street, between Kenmare & Spring Streets (1-212 925 1005, www.creatures ofcomfort.us). Subway 6 to Spring Street; N, R to Prince Street. **Open** 11am-7pm Mon-Sat; noon-6pm Sun. **Map** p79 B2 ⓲ **Fashion**

Café Habana.

Jade Lai opened Creatures of Comfort in Los Angeles in 2005 and brought her cool-girl aesthetic east five years later. In the former home of the 12th police precinct, the New York store offers a similar collection of pricey, wearably nonconformist fashion for both genders. Rubbing shoulders on the racks with the eponymous house label are pieces by Christophe Lemaire, Acne, Dana Lee and Isabel Marant Etoile, among others. Shoes and accessories – from Robert Clergerie, Common Projects, Piece A Conviction and more – also reflect the boutique's effortless left-of-mainstream style.

★ Erica Weiner
173 Elizabeth Street, between Kenmare & Spring Streets (1-212 334 6383, www.ericaweiner.com). Subway C, E to Spring Street. **Open** *noon-8pm daily* **Map** p79 B2 ⑲ **Accessories**
Erica Weiner sells her own bronze, brass, silver and gold creations – many under $100 – alongside vintage and reworked baubles. Old wooden cabinets and stacked crates showcase rings and charm-laden necklaces, the latter dangling the likes of tiny pretzels and vintage NYC subway tokens (a quaint anachronism since the introduction of the MetroCard). Other favourites include brass ginkgo-leaf earrings, and moveable-type-letter necklaces – the perfect gift for your favourite wordsmith.

McNally Jackson
52 Prince Street, between Lafayette & Mulberry Streets (1-212 274 1160, www.mcnallyjackson. com). Subway N, R to Prince Street; 6 to Spring Street. **Open** *10am-10pm Mon-Sat; 10am-9pm Sun.* **Map** p79 A2 ⑳ **Books & music**
An appealing indie bookstore, with one of the city's most thoughtfully curated selections of nonfiction, novels, hard-to-find magazines, children's books and, most notably, poetry, plus a café. Readings and events – which have included such literary luminaries as Hari Kunzru, Martin Amis and Siri Hustvedt – take place in its comfortable downstairs space.

New & Almost New
171 Mott Street, between Broome & Grand Streets (1-212 226 6677, www.newandalmostnew.com). Subway B, D to Grand Street; J, Z to Bowery; 6 to Spring Street. **Open** *noon-6.30pm Tue-Sat; 1-5pm Sun.* **Map** p79 B3 ㉑ **Fashion**
Germophobe bargain-hunters will be delighted to find that much of the merchandise on sale at this resale shop is actually brand new. Owner Maggie Chan hand-selects every piece, ensuring its quality and authenticity, and stock frequently includes lofty labels such as Prada, Chanel and Hermès. Prices range from as low as $15 up to around $600.

Warm
181 Mott Street, between Broome & Kenmare Streets (1-212 925 1200, www.warmny.com). Subway J, Z to Bowery; 6 to Spring Street. **Open** *noon-7pm Mon-Sat; noon-6pm Sun.* **Map** p79 B2 ㉒ **Fashion/accessories**
The husband-and-wife owners of this appealing boutique, Rob Magnotta and Winnie Beattie, bring together an eclectic selection of women's, men's and kids' threads, accessories and home items, all informed by their globe-trotting surfer lifestyle. The laid-back looks include urban boho-chic clothing from the likes of Vanessa Bruno, Giada Forte, the Elder Statesman and former childrenswear designer Ryan Roche.

Will Leather Goods
29 Prince Street, at Mott Street (1-212 925 2824, www.willleathergoods.com). Subway 6 to Spring Street. **Open** *11am-8pm daily.* **Map** p79 B2 ㉓
Accessories
Will Adler's eponymous line was previously sold only at high-end retailers such as Barneys New York and Saks Fifth Avenue. Now the globally influenced designer has a spacious NYC flagship to display the brand's full collection of rustic leather accessories for men and women. Wares include wallets, belts and bags, such as canvas-and-leather totes and duffles crafted from vintage Mexican wool and leather.

EXPLORE

Lower East Side

Once better known for bagels and bargains, the Lower East Side is now brimming with vintage and indie-designer boutiques, fashionable bars and contemporary art galleries. In fact, the former slum has been so radically altered by the forces of gentrification that in 2008 it was placed on the National Trust for Historic Preservation's annual list of the 11 most endangered historic places. But new development hasn't yet destroyed the character of the erstwhile centre of immigrant life. You can still explore remnants of the old Jewish neighbourhood that the Marx Brothers and George Gershwin called home, including 100-year-old food purveyors, a magnificently restored synagogue and recreated tenement apartments.

Lower East Side Tenement Museum.

Don't Miss

1 Lower East Side Tenement Museum See how the other half really lived (p87).

2 Museum at Eldridge Street This restored synagogue is an inspirational sight (p88).

3 New Museum of Contemporary Art Cutting-edge exhibitions in a cool building (p88).

4 Katz's Delicatessen Your chance to have what she had (p90).

5 Russ & Daughters Get a new-school bagel at this old-school shop (p96).

Museum at Eldridge Street. See p88.

LOWER EAST SIDE

Subway B, D to Grand Street; F to East Broadway; F to Delancey Street or Lower East Side-Second Avenue; J, Z to Bowery; J, M, Z to Delancey-Essex Streets.

In the 19th century, tenement buildings were constructed on the Lower East Side, a roughly defined area south of Houston Street and west of the East River, to house the growing number of German, Irish, Jewish and Italian immigrants – by 1900 it was the most populous neighbourhood in the US. The appalling conditions of these overcrowded, unsanitary slums were captured by photographer and writer Jacob Riis in *How the Other Half Lives* in 1890; its publication spurred activists and prompted the introduction of more humane building codes. The dwellings have since been converted or demolished, but you can see how newcomers once lived by visiting

IN THE KNOW GRAVE SECRETS

Although the gate is usually locked, catch a glimpse of the **First Shearith Israel Graveyard** (55-57 St James Place, between James & Oliver Streets), the final resting place for members of the country's first Jewish community; some gravestones date from 1683, including those of Spanish and Portuguese Jews who fled the Inquisition.

the recreated apartments of the **Lower East Side Tenement Museum**.

The neighbourhood was also the focal point of Jewish culture in New York. Between 1870 and 1920, hundreds of synagogues and religious schools thrived alongside Yiddish newspapers, social-reform societies and kosher bakeries. Vaudeville and classic Yiddish theatre also prospered here. Today, most of these places are long gone, but vestiges of Jewish life can be found amid the Chinese businesses spilling over from sprawling Chinatown and the area's ever-multiplying boutiques, restaurants and bars. The magnificent **Eldridge Street Synagogue**, now a museum open to the public, still has a small but vital congregation. On the corner of Orchard and Canal Streets, the 1912 premises of the **Sender Jarmulowsky Bank**, which catered to Jewish immigrants until its collapse in 1914, is being restored as a luxury hotel. The **Forward Building** (175 E Broadway, at Canal Street) was once the headquarters of the *Jewish Daily Forward*, a Yiddish-language paper that had a peak circulation of 275,000 in the 1920s; it's now home to multimillion-dollar condominiums. You can still get a taste of the old neighbourhood at local institutions **Katz's Delicatessen**, **Russ & Daughters** and **Yonah Schimmel Knish Bakery**.

By the 1980s, when young artists and musicians began moving into the area, the Lower East Side was a patchwork of Asian, Latino and Jewish enclaves. Hipster bars and music venues sprang up on and around Ludlow Street, creating an annex to the East Village. That scene still survives, at spots like the **Mercury Lounge**, but rents have risen dramatically and some stalwarts have closed.

These days, visual art is the Lower East Side's main cultural draw. Dozens of storefront galleries have opened in the vicinity over the past decade (for our picks, *see p94* **Gallery-Hopping Guide**). In 2007, the **New Museum of Contemporary Art** decamped here from Chelsea, opening a $50-million building on the Bowery, and the **International Center of Photography Museum** (www.icp.org) is relocating nearby, at 250 Bowery, in autumn 2015.

A proliferation of indie boutiques hasn't yet pushed out the **Orchard Street** bargain district – a row of shops selling utilitarian goods such as socks, sportswear and luggage, beloved of hagglers. But more mainstream commercial gloss is on the rise, including a mega-development, Essex Crossing, which over the next decade will bring apartments, a movie theatre, an outpost of Pittsburgh's Andy Warhol Museum, and a new location for **Essex Street Market** (www.essexstreetmarket.com) to a series of vacant lots. The current indoor market, at Essex and Delancey Streets, opened in 1940 as part of La Guardia's plan to get pushcarts off the streets, and houses high-quality vendors of cheese, produce, fish, meat and sweets.

Sights & Museums

★ Lower East Side Tenement Museum

Visitors' centre, 103 Orchard Street, at Delancey Street (1-212 982 8420, www.tenement.org). Subway F to Delancey Street; J, M, Z to Delancey-Essex Streets. **Open** *Museum shop & ticketing* 10am-6.30pm Mon-Wed, Fri-Sun; 10am-8.30pm Thur. **Tours** 10.30am-5pm Mon-Wed, Fri-Sun; 10am-8pm Thur (see website for schedule). **Admission** $25; $20 reductions. **Map** p87 B2 ❶

This fascinating museum – actually a series of restored tenement apartments at 97 Orchard Street – is accessible only by guided tour. These start at the visitors' centre at 103 Orchard Street, and often sell out, so it's wise to book ahead. 'Hard Times' visits the homes of an Italian and a German-Jewish clan; 'Sweatshop Workers' explores the apartments of two Eastern European Jewish families as well as a garment shop where many of the locals would have found employment; and 'Irish Outsiders' unfurls the life of the Moore family, who are coping with the loss of their child. 'Shop Life' explores the diverse retailers that occupied the building's storefronts, including a 19th-century German saloon. 'Live at the Tenement' lets you interact with actors channelling the original occupants (on select dates; see website). From mid March to December, the museum also

EXPLORE

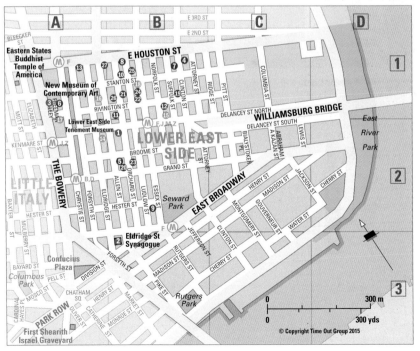

conducts themed daily walking tours of the Lower East Side ($25-$45; $20-$40 reductions).

★ Museum at Eldridge Street (Eldridge Street Synagogue)

12 Eldridge Street, between Canal & Division Streets (1-212 219 0302, www.eldridgestreet.org). Subway F to East Broadway. **Open** 10am-5pm Mon-Thur, Sun; 10am-3pm Fri. **Admission** $12; $8-$10 reductions; free under-5s. Free Mon. **Map** p87 B3 ❷

With an impressive façade that combines Moorish, Gothic and Romanesque elements, this opulent house of worship is now surrounded by dumpling shops and Chinese herb stores, but rewind about a century and you would have found delicatessens and *mikvot* (ritual bathhouses). For its first 50 years, the 1887 synagogue had a congregation of thousands and doubled as a mutual-aid society for new arrivals in need of financial assistance, healthcare and employment. But as Jews left the area and the congregation dwindled, the building fell into disrepair. A 20-year, $20-million facelift has restored its splendour; the soaring main sanctuary, designed by high-society interior decorators the Herter Brothers, features hand-stencilled walls and a resplendent stained-glass rose window with Star of David motifs. The renovations were completed in autumn 2010, with the installation of a second stained-glass window designed by artist Kiki Smith and architect Deborah Gans. The admission price includes a guided tour (see website for schedule). Downstairs, an orientation centre helps to illuminate the Jewish faith and local history through historic documents, artefacts and interactive displays. *Photo p86.*

★ New Museum of Contemporary Art

235 Bowery, between Prince & Stanton Streets (1-212 219 1222, www.newmuseum.org). Subway N, R to Prince Street; 6 to Spring Street.

New Museum of Contemporary Art.

Open 11am-6pm Wed, Fri-Sun; 11am-9pm Thur.
Admission $16; $10-$14 reductions; free under-
19s. Pay what you wish 7-9pm Thur. **Map** p87 A1 **❸**
Having occupied various sites for 30 years, New
York City's only contemporary art museum got its
own purpose-built space in late 2007. Dedicated
to emerging media and under-recognised artists,
the New Mu also hosts a triennial for young talent.
The seven-floor building is worth a look for the
architecture alone – it's a striking, off-centre stack
of aluminium-mesh-clad boxes designed by the
cutting-edge Tokyo architectural firm Sejima
+ Nishizawa/SANAA. Two ongoing exterior
installations by Chris Burden add to the drama:
the artist's 36ft-high *Twin Quasi Legal Skyscrapers*
(2013) perch on the roof and his 30ft-long *Ghost Ship*
(2005) hangs on the façade. The museum's café is run
by the folks behind the area's popular Hester Street
Market, offering artisanal eats by a selection of local
vendors. At weekends, don't miss the fabulous views
from the minimalist seventh-floor Sky Room.

Restaurants & Cafés

Clinton Street Baking Company & Restaurant
*4 Clinton Street, between E Houston & Stanton
Streets (1-646 602 6263, www.dintonstreetbaking.
com). Subway F to Lower East Side-Second
Avenue or Delancey Street; J, M, Z to Delancey-
Essex Streets.* **Open** 8am-4pm, 6-11pm Mon-
Fri; 9am-4pm, 6-11pm Sat; 9am-6pm Sun. **Main
courses** $13-$23. **No credit cards** before 6pm.
Map p87 B1 **❹ Café**
The warm buttermilk biscuits and fluffy plate-size
pancakes at this pioneering little eaterie are reason
enough to face the brunch-time crowds. If you want
to avoid the onslaught, the homey place is just as
reliable for both lunch and dinner; drop in for the $15
beer and burger special (6-8pm Mon-Thur).

Dirt Candy
*86 Allen Street, between Broome & Grand
Streets (1-212 228 7732, www.dirtcandynyc.com).
Subway F to Delancey Street; J, M, Z to Delancey-
Essex Streets.* **Open** 5.30-11pm Tue-Sat. **Main
courses** $21-$30. **Map** p87 B2 **❺ Vegetarian**
Fuelled by the ambition to make people crave vegetables, Amanda Cohen has revived her beloved
East Village eaterie on the Lower East Side with a
ramped-up menu and a space three times the size
of the 18-seat original. Emblazoned with a mural
of greenery by graffiti artist Noah McDonough,
the sprawling dining room is focused on the open
kitchen at its heart, complete with a chef's counter.
Each dish is anchored by one vegetable, but the
chef's retooled offerings layer multiple ingredients.
The portobello-mushroom mousse starter, for example, rejigs a dish from the initial menu, breaking
down the ginger-cherry compôte into individual
parts: ginger cream, cherry purée and dehydrated

Freemans.

pears. Shareable plates, including brussels-sprout
tacos folded into lettuce wraps, are fresh to Cohen's
lineup. Brunch is in the works, so call or check the
website for updates.

Freemans
*2 Freeman Alley, off Rivington Street, between
Bowery & Chrystie Street (1-212 420 0012,
www.freemansrestaurant.com). Subway F to
Lower East Side-Second Avenue; J, Z to Bowery.*
Open 11am-4pm, 6-11.30pm Mon-Fri; 10am-4pm,
6-11.30pm Sat, Sun. **Main courses** $16-$32.
Map p87 A1 **❻ American creative**
Located at the end of a graffiti-marked alley,
Freemans, with its colonial tavern meets hunting
lodge style, is an enduring hit with retro-loving New
Yorkers. Garage-sale oil paintings and moose antlers
serve as backdrops to a curved zinc bar, while the
menu recalls a simpler time – devils on horseback
(prunes stuffed with stilton cheese and wrapped in
bacon), four different types of house-made sausages,
and stiff cocktails that'll get you good and sauced.

★ Ivan Ramen
*25 Clinton Street, between E Houston & Stanton
Streets (1-646 678 3859, www.ivanramen.com).
Subway F to Lower East Side-Second Avenue or
Delancey Street; J, M, Z to Delancey-Essex Streets.*
Open noon-3.30pm, 5.30pm-midnight daily. **Main
courses** $15-$16. **Map** p87 B1 **❼ Japanese**
Ivan Orkin has never been one to play by the rule-
book – the brash Long Islander first built his food-
world fame 6,000 miles away in Tokyo, where he

Katz's Delicatessen

stirred up Japan's devout ramen congregation with his light, silky slurp bowls in 2007. Seven years later, he opened this narrow slip of a *ramen-ya* on the Lower East Side. The vibrant 60-seat parlour tangles together the noodle virtuoso's all-American roots and Japanophile leanings – a massive, papier-mâché mural in front features a kaleidoscope of Dolly Parton, John Wayne, waving lucky cats and Technicolor geishas. The menu follows culture-crossing suit: along with his seminal rye-flour noodles (in both *shio* and *shoyu* varieties), there's four-cheese *mazemen*, like ramen gone Kraft, and fried chicken hearts – double-dipped à la KFC – with ponzu honey mustard.

★ Katz's Delicatessen

205 E Houston Street, at Ludlow Street (1-212 254 2246, www.katzsdelicatessen.com). Subway F to Lower East Side-Second Avenue. **Open** 8am-10.45pm Mon-Wed; 8am-2.45am Thur; 24 hrs Fri-Sun (8am Fri-10.45pm Sun). **Sandwiches** $12-$22. **Map** p87 B1 ❽ American

A visit to Gotham isn't complete without a stop at a quintessential New York deli, and this Lower East Side survivor, which opened in 1888, is the real deal. You might get a kick out of the famous faces (from Bill Clinton to Ben Stiller) plastered to the panelled walls, or the spot where Meg Ryan faked it in *When Harry Met Sally...*, but the real stars of this cavernous cafeteria are the thick-cut pastrami sandwiches and crisp-skinned all-beef hot dogs – the latter a mere $3.75.

Meow Parlour

Cat club *46 Hester Street, between Essex & Ludlow Streets.* **Open** noon-8pm Mon, Tue, Thur; noon-10pm Fri-Sun. **Admission** $4/30mins.
Pâtisserie *34 Ludlow Street, between Grand & Hester Streets.* **Open** 10am-8pm Mon, Tue, Thur; 10am-10pm Fri-Sun. **Macarons** $2.50.
Both *No phone, www.meowparlour.com. Subway F to East Broadway or Delancey Street; J, M, Z to Delancey-Essex Streets.* **Map** p87 B2 ❾ Bakery/café
See p91 **Pussies Galore**.

Mission Cantina

172 Orchard Street, at Stanton Street (1-212 254 2233, www.missioncantinany.com). Subway F to Lower East Side-Second Avenue. **Open** 9am-11.30pm, noon-4pm, 5pm-midnight daily. **Tacos** $5-$6. **Shared plates** $35. **Map** p87 B1 ❿ Mexican

Danny Bowien, the chef behind San Francisco import Mission Chinese Food, changed the tune for his second act, turning from Szechuan eats to South of the Border fare. At this 40-seat hangout, he puts his own spin on Mexican dishes, such as crisp chicken wings dry-rubbed with *mole* spices, and riffs on the famed Mission District burrito with fillings like gamey lamb or pulled pork trotter.

EXPLORE

PUSSIES GALORE

The city's first feline café is the cat's whiskers.

The antics of Grumpy Cat, Maru, Lil Bub and numerous breakout YouTube stars are fuelling a worldwide cat craze. Tokyo's popular *neko* cafés have inspired similar establishments in Amsterdam, London and now NYC. Co-founded by Christina Ha, owner of nouveau pâtisserie Macaron Parlour (www.macaronparlour.com), who has four cats and a certificate in animal care and handling, **Meow Parlour** (*see p90*) allows the cat-obsessed to commune with around a dozen felines for anything from 30 minutes to five hours. Since entry is limited to 15 people at a time to maintain a calm atmosphere, slots are booked in advance on the website, and the current wait is around two months. Visitors must read the rules (no flash photos, no tail pulling) and sign a waiver before admittance.

Due to NYC Department of Health regulations, which prohibit animals on the premises of a facility where food is prepared, the actual café is around the corner, but you can have cute cat-shaped cookies, kitty-face macarons and even, sometimes,

limited-edition dark-chocolate brownie 'poops' delivered to the 'cat club', along with cult Blue Bottle coffee and tea.

With high tables for enjoying the treats out of reach of curious paws, the 800-square-foot space – larger than many NYC apartments – was designed with cats in mind. Enclosed beds with glass tops let you observe napping moggies and reach into a side opening to stroke them. There are plenty of dangling toys on hand, an exercise wheel and a wall of shelving, which residents enjoy scaling. Decorated with cat-themed items such as locally designed pillows by Meowingtons (www.meowingtons.com), the unit also has secret passageways behind it where cats can retreat from attention. Framed profiles detail their likes (for example, jingle bells, head massages) and dislikes (bubble wrap) for your purr-usal before making overtures. Good news for those who make a connection – the café is in partnership with rescue group KittyKind, which means that all the inhabitants are available for adoption.

EXPLORE

Other location Mission Chinese Food, 171 East Broadway, between Jefferson & Rutgers Streets, (1-212 432 0300).

Russ & Daughters Café

127 Orchard Street, between Delancey & Rivington Streets (1-212 475 4881, www.russanddaughters cafe.com). Subway F to Delancey Street; J, M, Z to Delancey-Essex Streets. **Open** 10am-10pm Mon-Fri; 8am-10pm Sat, Sun. **Main courses** $16-$22. **Shared Platters** $70-$90. **Map** p87 B1 ⓫ Café. *See p97* Bagel Boom.

Schiller's Liquor Bar

131 Rivington Street, at Norfolk Street (1-212 260 4555, www.schillersny.com). Subway F to Delancey Street; J, M, Z to Delancey-Essex Streets. **Open** 11am-1am Mon-Thur; 11am-3am Fri; 10am-3am Sat; 10am-midnight Sun. **Main courses** $13-$26. **Map** p87 B1 ⓬ Eclectic

At this artfully reconstructed faux-vintage hangout, the menu is a mix of French bistro (steak frites), British pub (fish and chips) and good ol' American (cheeseburger), while the wine menu famously hawks a down-to-earth hierarchy: Good, Decent, Cheap. As at Keith McNally's other establishments, folks pack in for the scene, triple-parking at the curved central bar for elaborate cocktails and star sightings.

$ Yonah Schimmel Knish Bakery

137 E Houston Street, between Eldridge & Forsyth Streets (1-212 477 2858, www.knishery.com). Subway F to Lower East Side-Second Avenue. **Open** 9am-7pm Mon-Thur, Sun; 9am-9pm Fri,

Sat (extended hours in summer). **Knishes** $3.50-$5. **Map** p87 A1 ⓭ Bakery/café

Born from the namesake rabbi's pushcart, this neighbourhood stalwart has been doling out its carb-laden goodies since 1910. More than a dozen rotating varieties are available, including blueberry, chocolate-cheese and 'pizza', but traditional potato, kasha and spinach knishes are the most popular.

Bars

Attaboy

134 Eldridge Street, between Broome & Delancey Streets (no phone). Subway F to Delancey Street; J, M, Z to Delancey-Essex Streets. **Open** 6pm-3.30am daily. **Map** p87 A2 ⓮

Occupying the original location of Milk and Honey (www.mlkhny.com) and run by alums Sam Ross and Michael McIlroy, Attaboy has a livelier, lighter air than Sasha Petraske's big-league cocktail den. The tucked-away haunt has kept the same bespoke protocol as its forebear: at the brushed-steel bar, drinks slingers stir off-the-cuff riffs to suit each customer's preference. Nostalgic boozers can seek solace in Petraske-era standard-bearers, like Ross's signature Penicillin, a still-inspiring blend of Laphroaig ten-year, honey-ginger syrup and lemon.

Backroom Bar

102 Norfolk Street, between Delancey & Rivington Streets (1-212 228 5098, www.backroomnyc.com). Subway F to Delancey Street; J, M, Z to Delancey-Essex Streets. **Open** 7.30pm-2am Mon, Sun; 7.30pm-3am Tue-Thur; 7.30am-4am Fri, Sat. **Map** p87 B1 ⓯

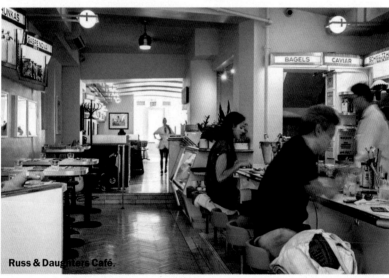

Russ & Daughters Café.

Copper & Oak

Unlike NYC's other ersatz speakeasies, this place has roots in the Prohibition era, when it was the illicit booze-dispensing back room of (now defunct) Ratner's deli. For access, look for a sign that reads 'The Lower East Side Toy Company'. Pass through the gate, down an alleyway and up a metal staircase, and open an unmarked door to find a replica of a 1920s watering hole. Cocktails are poured into teacups, and bottled beer is brown-bagged before being served. Patrons must be 25 or older on Fridays and Saturdays. The dress code is casual, but in a departure from the Jazz Age sensibility, real fur is banned in the bar.

Copper & Oak
157 Allen Street, between Rivington & Stanton Streets (1-212 460 5546). Subway F to Lower East Side-Second Avenue; J, Z to Bowery. **Open** *5pm-1am Wed-Sat.* **Map** *p87 A1* 16
With walls made from deconstructed bourbon barrels and lined with backlit shelves, Copper & Oak could pass for a small library – but instead of books this whisky den is crammed with 600 bottles of dark-hued elixirs. Dive deep into the collection of hard-to-find Japanese whiskies including Suntory's Yamazaki Puncheon, fragrant with vanilla and citrus, or the 12-year-old blended Hibiki, partly matured in plum wine barrels to give it notes of oak and fruit.

Loreley
7 Rivington Street, between Bowery & Chrystie Street (1-212 253 7077, www.loreleynyc.com). Subway J, Z to Bowery. **Open** *noon-1am Mon, Tue, Sun; noon-2am Wed; noon-3am Thur; noon-4am Fri, Sat.* **Map** *p87 A1* 17

Perhaps bar owner Michael Momm, aka DJ Foosh, wanted a place where he could spin to his heart's content. Maybe he missed the *biergartens* of his youth in Cologne. Whatever. Just rejoice that he opened Loreley. Twelve draughts and eight bottled varieties of Germany's finest brews are available, along with wines from the country's Loreley region and a full roster of spirits. Or try one of the speciality cocktails, such as the Zimtschnitte, with Captain Morgan, Cointreau, cinnamon and fresh orange. *Photo p95.*

Two-Bit's Retro Arcade
153 Essex Street, between Rivington & Stanton Streets (1-212 477 8161, www.twobitsretroarcade. com). Subway F to Lower East Side-Second Avenue or Delancey Street; J, M, Z to Delancey-Essex Streets. **Open** *5pm-2am Mon-Thur; 5pm-4am Fri; 1pm-4am Sat; 1pm-2am Sun.* **Map** *p87 B1* 18
Joystick addicts, take note: this gamer haven offers titles dating back to the 1980s (Pac-Man, Popeye, Final Fight, Donkey Kong), as well as pinball (Fun House, Twilight Zone). After you've grabbed a beer, pause for a moment to admire the video-game-character illustrations inlaid in the bar. One tip: try to make it here by early evening, before the queues to play become three dudes deep.

Shops & Services

★ Alife Rivington Club
158 Rivington Street, between Clinton & Suffolk Streets (1-212 432 7200, www.alifenewyork.com). Subway F to Delancey Street; J, M, Z to

EXPLORE

GALLERY-HOPPING GUIDE

Plan a culture crawl of this hot art 'hood with our curated list.

Over the past ten years, the Lower East Side has seen a steady incoming migration of young dealers, aided by the relocation of the New Museum of Contemporary Art to the Bowery. These are a few of our favourites.

Canada *333 Broome Street, between Bowery & Chrystie Street (1-212 925 4631, www.canadanewyork.com).* **Open** 11am-6pm Wed-Sun.
One of the first of the Lower East Side galleries, Canada continues to keep it real with a programme that reflects a funky DIY aesthetic.

Eleven Rivington *11 Rivington Street, between Bowery & Chrystie Street (1-212 982 1930, www.elevenrivington.com).* **Open** noon-6pm Wed-Sun.
The offshoot of the Van Doren Waxter Gallery offers an impeccable uptown vibe in small-storefront form.

Lisa Cooley *107 Norfolk Street, between Delancey & Rivington Streets (1-212 680 0564, www.lisa-cooley.com).* **Open** 10am-6pm Wed-Sun (call for summer hrs).
Lisa Cooley's roster of artists seems to share a penchant for Conceptualist sleight of hand, mixed with unexpected materials.

Miguel Abreu Gallery *36 Orchard Street, between Canal & Hester Streets (1-212 995 1774, www.miguelabreugallery.com).* **Open** 10.30am-6.30pm Wed-Sun.
A filmmaker as well as founding member of the legendary Threadwaxing alternative space in Soho (now closed), Miguel Abreu

Rachel Uffner Gallery.

represents conceptually inspired artists. He also has a second gallery at 88 Eldridge Street, between Hester & Grand Streets.

Rachel Uffner Gallery *70 Suffolk Street, between E Houston & Stanton Streets (1-212 274 0064, www.racheluffnergallery.com).* **Open** 10am-6pm Wed-Sun.
Uffner, who cut her teeth at Christies, showcases a small but eclectic stable.

Sperone Westwater *257 Bowery, between E Houston & Stanton Streets (1-212 999 7337, www.speronewestwater.com).* **Open** 10am-6pm Tue-Sat.
Started in 1975, this gallery now occupies a purpose-built showcase designed by starchitect Norman Foster. The high-profile stable includes Bruce Nauman, Susan Rothenberg and William Wegman.

Eleven Rivington.

EXPLORE

Loreley. See p93.

Delancey-Essex Streets. **Open** noon-7pm Mon-Sat; noon-6pm Sun. **Map** p87 B1 ⑲ **Accessories**
Whether you're looking for simple white trainers or a trendy graphic style, you'll want to gain entry to this 'club', which stocks a wide range of major brands such as Adidas, Puma Asics and Nike (including sought-after re-issues like Air Jordan). You'll also find lesser-known names including the shop's own label.

The Cast
71 Orchard Street, between Broome & Grand Streets (1-212 228 2020, www.thecast.com). Subway B, D to Grand Street; F to Delancey Street; J, M, Z to Delancey-Essex Streets. **Open** 11.30am-7.30pm Mon-Sat; noon-6pm Sun. **Map** p87 B2 ⑳ **Fashion**
At the core of Chuck Guarino and Elisa Maldonado's rock 'n' roll-inspired collection is the trinity of well-cut denim, superior leather jackets based on classic motorcycle styles, and the artful T-shirts that launched the label in 2004. The couple caters to a range of budgets – the off-the-peg Cast Off line of jackets for men and women starts at $650, but you'll pay at least $1,500 for a bespoke leather made in NYC. Supple skirts, trousers and a range of accessories are also available.

David Owens Vintage
154 Orchard Street, between Rivington & Stanton Streets (1-212 677 3301). Subway F to Lower East Side-Second Avenue. **Open** noon-8pm Mon-Sat; 11am-7pm Sun. **Map** p87 B1 ㉑ **Fashion**
Unlike many vintage stores that traffic in 1980s and '90s garb, David Owens's eponymous boutique carries items exclusively from the '40s to the '70s. The small space is stuffed to the gills with rare and unique pieces, such as a '30s printed dress with the original store tags attached and a '60s clutch made to look like a rolled-up *Harper's Bazaar* magazine. Men will find just as many interesting items, including pin-up girl ties and leather motorcycle jackets.

Edith Machinist
104 Rivington Street, between Essex & Ludlow Streets (1-212 979 9992, www.edithmachinist. com). Subway F to Delancey Street; J, M, Z to Delancey-Essex Streets. **Open** noon-6pm Mon, Fri, Sun; noon-7pm Tue-Thur, Sat. **Map** p87 B1 ㉒ **Fashion/accessories**
An impeccable, eclectic assemblage of leather bags, shoes and boots is the main draw of this vintage trove, but you'll also find a whittled-down collection of clothes, including a small men's section.

Moo Shoes
78 Orchard Street, between Broome & Grand Streets (1-212 254 6512, www.mooshoes.com). Subway F to Delancey Street; J, M, Z to Delancey-Essex Streets. **Open** 11.30am-7.30pm Mon-Sat; noon-6pm Sun. **Map** p87 B2 ㉓ **Accessories**
Cruelty-free footwear is far more fashionable than it used to be. Moo stocks a variety of brands for men and women, such as Vegetarian Shoes and Novacas, plus styles from independent designers such as Elizabeth Olsen, whose arty OlsenHaus line of high heels and handbags is anything but hippyish.

Objectify 139
139 Essex Street, between Rivington & Stanton Streets (1-646 370 6993, www.objectify139.com). Subway F to Delancey Street. **Open** noon-8pm daily. **Map** p87 B1 ㉔ **Gifts & souvenirs**

EXPLORE

Objectify 139. *See p95.*

At her badass boutique, artist Maria Candanoza sells some of the city's coolest collectible books, prints and baubles, all at affordable prices. Pick up unique art and kitchy gifts that you won't find anywhere else, such as Statue of Liberty candles, Sparkle Diva mink coozies and Leonardo DiCaprio tees. And you can meet the artists during in-store meet-ups scheduled each month.

Obsessive Compulsive Cosmetics
174 Ludlow Street, between E Houston & Stanton Streets (1-212 675 2404, www.occmakeup.com). Subway F to Lower East Side-Second Avenue. **Open** 11am-7pm Mon-Sat; noon-6pm Sun. **Map** p87 B1 ㉕ **Health & beauty**
Creator David Klasfeld founded OCC in the kitchen of his Lower East Side apartment in 2004. The make-up artist has since expanded his 100% vegan and cruelty-free cosmetics line from just two shades of lip balm to an extensive assortment of bang-for-your-buck beauty products. In the downtown flagship, you can browse more than 40 shades of nail polish and nearly 40 loose eye-shadow powders, among other products, but we especially like the Lip Tars, which glide on like a gloss but have the matte finish and saturated pigmentation of a lipstick.

Reed Space
151 Orchard Street, between Rivington & Stanton Streets (1-212 253 0588, www.thereedspace.com). Subway F to Delancey Street; J, M, Z to Delancey-Essex Streets. **Open** 1-7pm Mon-Fri; noon-7pm Sat, Sun. **Map** p87 B1 ㉖ **Fashion/accessories**
Reed Space is the brainchild of Jeff Ng (AKA Jeff Staple), who has worked on product design and branding with the likes of Nike and Timberland. The store stocks local and international urban clothing brands – such as 10.Deep and Stussy – and footwear, including exclusive Staple collaborations. Art books and culture mags are shelved on an eye-popping installation of four stacked rows of white chairs fixed to one wall.

★ Russ & Daughters
179 E Houston Street, between Allen & Orchard Streets (1-212 475 4880, www.russanddaughters. com). Subway F to Lower East Side-Second Avenue. **Open** 8am-8pm Mon-Fri; 9am-7pm Sat; 8am-5.30pm Sun. **Map** p87 A1 ㉗ **Food & drink**
The daughters in the name have given way to great-grandchildren, but this Lower East Side institution (est 1914) is still run by the same family. Specialising in smoked and cured fish and caviar, it sells about a dozen varieties of smoked salmon, eight types of herring (pickled, salt-cured, smoked and so on) and many other Jewish-inflected Eastern European delectables. Filled bagels like the amazing Super Heebster (baked salmon, whitefish salad, horseradish cream cheese and wasabi flying-fish roe) are available to take away, but a new café (*see p92*) offers a more extensive menu and table service.

BAGEL BOOM

Neo nosh spots bring the NYC staple back into the spotlight.

Don't call it a comeback – bagels, introduced by late 19th-century Polish Jewish immigrants, have long been a quintessential NYC food. Yet their handcrafted heyday ended in the 1960s with the advent of automated bagel-making machines. That spawned five decades of far too many steam-baked, dough-conditioned pucks, puffier than an ageing screen star's face and stripped of taste and tradition. Now the New York bagel is returning to form, with a fresh batch of downtown shops giving the icon its due.

At newfangled Nolita bagelry **Black Seed** (*see p82*), from Mile End's Noah Bernamoff and the Smile impresario Matt Kliegman, the hand-rolled rounds merge two disciplines: they're honey-enhanced à la Bernamoff's native Montreal, but with an eggless, touch-of-salt bite to satisfy lifelong Gothamite Kliegman. Kettle-boiled and wood-fired, the small but mighty bagels are crowned with house-made toppings both classic (scallion cream cheese, silky cold-smoked salmon) and fanciful (salty tobiko caviar, crisp watermelon radishes).

Bari Musacchio – longtime general manager at Italian restaurant Rubirosa – is also tackling the old-fashioned boil-and-bake technique at nearby diner upgrade **Baz Bagel & Restaurant** (*see p82*). Partnering with Barney Greengrass vet David Heffernan,

Musacchio's operation is, as in the old days, small-batch and labour-intensive: slow-rising dough rings are set on burlap-covered boards and given a spin in a rotating tray oven, resulting in springy-yet-crusty vehicles for the house nova (cold-smoked salmon) and chive spread.

Lower East Side institution **Russ & Daughters** (*see p97*) debuted a café (*see p92*) in its centennial year, where open-faced sandwich boards let you sample some of the store's famous fish: melt-in-your-mouth sable meets decadent goat's-milk cream cheese on a bagel or bialy in the Shtetl; or go classic with silky, saline nova, piled high with tomatoes, capers and onions.

Meanwhile, bread savant Melissa Weller, the Per Se and Roberta's vet behind Smorgasburg's acclaimed East River Bagels, is collaborating with heavy hitters Rich Torrisi, Mario Carbone and Jeff Zalaznick (Carbone, Parm, Santina) to open **Sadelle's** in Soho (463 West Broadway, between Prince & W Houston Streets) by publication of this guide. Named after Zalaznick's great-grandmother and inspired by Jewish 'appetising stores' – traditionally purveyors of fish and dairy products for eating with bagels – the full-service restaurant will serve such delicacies as blintzes, smoked fish and tangy, sourdough-based versions of those ubiquitous discs.

EXPLORE

Above: **Black Seed**.
Below: **Baz Bagel & Restaurant**.

East Village

Originally part of the Lower East Side, the East Village developed its distinct identity as a countercultural hotbed in the 1960s. By the dawning of the Age of Aquarius, rock clubs thrived on almost every corner. But in the '70s, the neighbourhood took a dive as drugs and crime prevailed – although that didn't stop the influx of artists and punk rockers. In the early '80s, East Village galleries were among the first to display the work of groundbreaking artists like Jean-Michel Basquiat and Keith Haring.

The blocks east of Broadway between Houston and 14th Streets may have lost some of their edge, and the former tenements are increasingly occupied by young professionals and trust-fund kids, but humanity in all its guises converges in the parks, bargain restaurants, indie record stores and grungy watering holes on First and Second Avenues and St Marks Place. Chic shops and eateries have taken up residence on Bond and Great Jones Streets in the enclave also known as Noho.

EXPLORE

Big Gay Ice Cream Shop.

Don't Miss

1 Merchant's House Museum Visit the past via this time capsule (p101).

2 Big Gay Ice Cream Shop It's out, it's proud and it's delicious (p102).

3 Narcissa Turn a blind eye to the bland setting – the food is sublime (p105).

4 McSorley's Old Ale House The only spirits are the spooky kind (p106).

5 Strand Book Store The well-stacked indie is an NYC institution (p109).

EAST VILLAGE

Subway B, D, F, M to Broadway-Lafayette Street; F to Lower East Side-Second Avenue; N, R to 8th Street-NYU; L to First Avenue or Third Avenue; 6 to Astor Place or Bleecker Street.

From the 1950s to the '70s, **St Marks Place** (E 8th Street, between Lafayette Street & Avenue A) was a hotbed of artists, writers, radicals and musicians, including WH Auden, Abbie Hoffman, Lenny Bruce, Joni Mitchell and GG Allin. The grungy strip still fizzes with energy well into the wee hours, but these days, it's packed with cheap eateries, tattoo parlours and shops selling T-shirts, tourist junk and pot paraphernalia.

A short walk north brings you to **St Mark's Church in-the-Bowery** (131 E 10th Street, at Second Avenue, 1-212 674 6377, www.stmarks bowery.org). Built in 1799, the Federal-style church sits on the site of Peter Stuyvesant's farm; the old guy himself, one of New York's first governors, is buried in the adjacent cemetery. Regular services are still held, and the church is home to several cultural organisations, including the Poetry Project and Danspace Project.

Cutting between Broadway and Fourth Avenue south of East 8th Street, **Astor Place** is the site of the **Cooper Union**. Comprising schools of art, architecture and engineering, it was the only free private college in the United States until 2014, when the institution started charging partial tuition fees. It was here, in February 1860, that Abraham Lincoln gave his celebrated Cooper Union Address, which argued for the regulation (though not abolition) of slavery and helped to propel him into the White House.

During the 19th century, Astor Place marked the boundary between the slums to the east and some of the city's most fashionable homes. **Colonnade Row** (428-434 Lafayette Street, between Astor Place & E 4th Street) faces the distinguished Astor Public Library building, which theatre legend Joseph Papp rescued from demolition in the 1960s. Today, the old library houses the **Public Theater** (*see p318*), a platform for first-run American plays, and cabaret venue **Joe's Pub** (*see p286*). Nearby, the **Merchant's House Museum** is a perfectly preserved specimen of upper-class domestic life in the 1800s.

Below Astor Place, Third Avenue (one block east of Lafayette Street) becomes the **Bowery**. For decades, the street languished as a seedy strip and the home of missionary organisations catering to the down and out. Although the sharp-eyed can find traces of the old flophouses and the more obvious Gothic Revival headquarters of **Bowery Mission** at no.227 (between Rivington & Stanton Streets), the thoroughfare has been cleaned up and repopulated with high-rise condo buildings, restaurants, nightspots and hotels.

Elsewhere in the neighbourhood, East 7th Street is a stronghold of New York's Ukrainian community, of which the focal point is the Eastern Catholic **St George's Ukrainian Catholic Church** at no.30. The **Ukrainian Museum** (222 E 6th Street, between Second & Third Avenues, 1-212 228 0110, www. ukrainianmuseum.org, closed Mon, Tue) houses folk and fine art and archival materials from that country. One block over, there's often a long line of loud fraternity types waiting at weekends to enter **McSorley's Old Ale House**. Festooned with aged photos, yellowed newspaper articles and dusty memorabilia, the 1854 Irish tavern is purportedly the oldest continually operating pub in New York and the spot where Lincoln repaired after giving his Cooper Union Address. Representing a different corner of the globe, **Curry Row** (East 6th Street, between First & Second Avenues) is lined with Indian restaurants that are popular with budget-minded diners.

Alphabet City (which gets its name from its key avenues: A, B, C and D) stretches towards the East River. It was once an edgy Puerto Rican neighbourhood with links to the drugs trade, but its demographic has dramatically shifted over the past 20 years. Avenue C is also known as Loisaida Avenue, a rough approximation of 'Lower East Side' when pronounced with a Hispanic accent. The **Nuyorican Poets Café** (236 E 3rd Street, between Avenues B & C, 1-212 505 8183, www. nuyorican.org), a clubhouse for espresso-drinking wordsmiths since 1974, is known for its Friday-night poetry slams, in which performers wage lyric battles before a score-keeping audience.

Dating from 1834, **Tompkins Square Park** (from 7th to 10th Streets, between Avenues A & B), honours Daniel D Tompkins, governor of New York from 1807 to 1817, and vice-president during the Monroe administration. Over the

IN THE KNOW ROCK RELICS

Pay your respects to the neighbourhood's late, legendary music venues, including the Dom (23 St Marks Place, between Second & Third Avenues), where the Velvet Underground headlined – the building is now a condo. CBGB, once the unofficial home of US punk, which fostered the Ramones, Talking Heads and Patti Smith, is now occupied by swanky menswear shop John Varvatos (315 Bowery, at Bleecker Street, 1-212 358 0315, www.johnvarvatos.com). The store has preserved a section of the club's flyer-plastered wall behind glass.

years, this 10.5-acre park has been a site for demonstrations and rioting. The last major uprising occurred in 1991, when the city evicted squatters from the park and renovated it to suit the influx of affluent residents. Along with dozens of 150-year-old elm trees (some of the oldest in the city), the landscaped green space has basketball courts, playgrounds and dog runs, and remains a place where bongo beaters, guitarists, multi-pierced teenagers, hipsters, local families and vagrants mingle.

North of Tompkins Square are remnants of earlier communities: discount fabric dealers; Italian cheese shops; Polish butchers, and a great Italian coffee and cannoli house, **Veniero's Pasticceria & Caffè** (342 E 11th Street, between First & Second Avenues, 1-212 674 7070, www.venierospastry.com).

Sights & Museums

Merchant's House Museum

29 E 4th Street, between Lafayette Street & Bowery (1-212 777 1089, www.merchantshouse. org). Subway B, D, F, M to Broadway-Lafayette Street; 6 to Bleecker Street. **Open** noon-5pm Mon, Thur-Sun. *Guided tour* 2pm. **Admission** $10; $5 reductions; free under-12s. **Map** p101 A2 ❶

Merchant's House Museum

EXPLORE

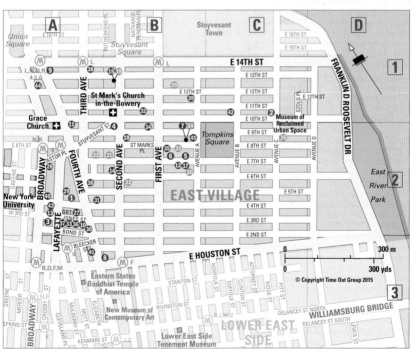

Merchant's House Museum, the city's only fully preserved 19th-century family home, is an elegant, late Federal-Greek Revival property kitted out with the same furnishings and decorations it contained when it was inhabited from 1835 by hardware tycoon Seabury Tredwell and his family. Three years after Tredwell's eighth daughter died in 1933, it opened as a museum. Gertrude Tredwell is said to haunt her home of 93 years (check the website for details of the candlelight ghost tours, held one evening of most months). During regular hours, you can peruse the house at your own pace, following along with the museum's printed guide, or opt for the 2pm guided tour. Be sure to ascend to the servants' quarters on the fourth floor, and note the original bell that summoned the four Irish maids at the top of the stairs.

Museum of Reclaimed Urban Space

155 Avenue C, between 9th & 10th Streets (1-646 833 7764, www.morusnyc.org). Subway L to First Avenue. **Open** 11am-7pm Tue, Thur-Sun. **Admission** *Suggested donation* $5. **Map** p101 C1 ❷
Co-founded by Bill Di Paola, director of advocacy group Time's Up!, this monument to local activism is housed in C-Squat, a five-floor walk-up that has sheltered activists, down-on-their-luck artists and members of several punk bands (including Leftover Crack, Old Skull and Nausea) from the 1970s to the present. Artefacts from Occupy Wall Street (including an energy bike that helped to power Zuccotti Park during its occupation in 2011) and earlier causes show how city residents, both past and present, created, protected and took back community spaces.

Restaurants & Cafés

Acme

9 Great Jones Street, between Broadway & Lafayette Street (1-212 203 2121, www.acmenyc.com). Subway B, D, F, M to Broadway-Lafayette Street; 6 to Bleecker Street. **Open** 6-11pm Mon-Wed; 6pm-midnight Thur, Fri; 11am-3pm, 6pm-midnight Sat; 11am-3pm, 6-11pm Sun. **Main courses** $12-$38. **Map** p101 A2 ❸ Scandinavian
Danish chef Mads Refslund, who co-founded Copenhagen's Noma with superstar René Redzepi, is behind this chic bistro. The menu delivers an easy introduction to the avant-garde cuisine of northern Europe, unpretentious and moderately priced. Even the most oddball combinations work. The chef's spin on steak tartare marries hand-cut raw bison with delicious sweet shrimp – an elemental surf-and-turf spooned like retro canapés into bitter endive and radicchio leaves. The big family-style portions of meat, fish and fowl that round out the collection of shareable plates are even more down-to-earth.

Alder

157 Second Avenue, between 9th & 10th Streets (1-212 539 1900, www.aldernyc.com). Subway L to Third Avenue; 6 to Astor Place. **Open** 6-11pm

Mon-Sat; noon-4pm, 5-9pm Sun. **Main courses** $11-$20. **Map** p101 B2 ❹ Gastropub
James Beard Award-winning chef Wylie Dufresne cultivated his modernist, tongue-in-cheek approach at wd~50 (now closed), creating curiosities such as deep-fried mayonnaise and scrambled-egg ravioli. At his gastropub, Dufresne is still challenging the orthodoxy of serious cooking, presenting familiar flavours in new frameworks: the wrappers in a pigs-in-blankets riff are Pepperidge Farm hot-dog buns, flattened in a pasta machine and fried into crisp jackets as gratifying as any puff pastry. But you can also eat quite simply here if you want to, with a pub cheese platter or 'French Onion Soup' onion rings. Intriguing tapped cocktails like the Dr Dave's 'Scrip Pad, made with rye, amaro, smoked maple and yuzu, are sold in full-size or short portions, so you can taste your way through the lot.

★ Big Gay Ice Cream Shop

125 E 7th Street, between First Avenue & Avenue A (1-212 533 9333, www.biggayicecream.com). Subway L to First Avenue. **Open** 1-10pm Mon-Thur, Sun; 1-11pm Fri, Sat. **Ice-cream** $4-$8. **Map** p101 B2 ❺ Ice-cream
Ice-cream truckers Doug Quint and Bryan Petroff now have two bricks-and-mortar shops in NYC dispensing their quirky soft-serve creations. Toppings run the gamut from cayenne pepper to bourbon-butterscotch sauce, or opt for one of the signature combos like the Salty Pimp (vanilla ice-cream, dulce de leche, sea salt and chocolate dip) or the Bea Arthur (vanilla ice-cream, dulce de leche and crushed Nilla wafers).
Other location 61 Grove Street, at Seventh Avenue South, West Village (1-212 533 9333).

$ Caracas Arepa Bar

93½ E 7th Street, between First Avenue & Avenue A (1-212 228 5062, www.caracasarepabar.com). Subway F to Lower East Side-Second Avenue; 6 to Astor Place. **Open** noon-11pm daily. **Arepas** $7.25-$8.50. **Map** p101 B2 ❻ Venezuelan
This endearing spot, with bare-brick walls and tables covered with flower-patterned vinyl, zaps you straight to Caracas. Each *arepa* is made from scratch daily; the pita-like pockets are stuffed with a choice of a dozen fillings, such as the classic beef with black beans, cheese and plantain, or chicken with chorizo and avocado. Top off your snack with a *cocada*, a thick and creamy coconut milkshake made with freshly grated cinnamon.

Other location 291 Grand Street, between Havemeyer & Roebling Streets, Williamsburg, Brooklyn (1-718 218 6050).

$ Crif Dogs

113 St Marks Place, between First Avenue & Avenue A (1-212 614 2728, www.crifdogs.com). Subway L to First Avenue; 6 to Astor Place. **Open** noon-2am Mon-Thur, Sun; noon-4am Fri, Sat. **Hot dogs** $2.50-$5. **Map** p101 B2 **❼ American**

You'll recognise this place by the giant hot dog outside, bearing the come-on 'Eat me'. Crif offers the best New Jersey-style dogs this side of the Hudson: handmade smoked-pork tube-steaks that are deep-fried until they're bursting out of their skins. While they're served in various guises, among them the Spicy Redneck (wrapped in bacon and covered in chilli, coleslaw and jalapeños), we're partial to the classic with mustard and kraut. If you're wondering why there are so many people hanging around near the public phone booth at night, it's because there's a trendy cocktail bar, PDT (*see p106*), concealed behind it.

Other location 555 Driggs Avenue, at North 7th Street, Williamsburg, Brooklyn (1-718 302 3200).

DBGB Kitchen & Bar

299 Bowery, at E Houston Street (1-212 933 5300, www.dbgb.com/nyc). Subway B, D, F, M to Broadway-Lafayette Street; 6 to Bleecker Street. **Open** 5-11pm Mon; 5pm-midnight Tue-Thur; noon-3pm, 5pm-1am Fri; 11am-3pm, 5pm-1am Sat; 11am-3pm, 5-11pm Sun. **Main courses** $16-$48. **Map** p101 B3 **❾ French**

This big, buzzy brasserie – chef Daniel Boulud's most populist venture – stands out for its kitchen-sink scope. Around ten kinds of sausage, from Thai-accented to Tunisienne, are served alongside burgers, offal and haute bistro fare. The best way to get your head around the schizophrenic enterprise is to bring a large group and try to sample as much of the range as possible, including ice-cream sundaes or sumptuous cakes for dessert.

▶ *For more of Daniel Boulud's output, see p171 and p182.*

Dos Toros

137 Fourth Avenue, between 13th & 14th Streets (1-212 677 7300, www.dostoros.com). Subway L to Third Avenue; L, N, Q, R, 4, 5, 6 to 14th Street-Union Square. **Open** 11.30am-10.30pm Mon; 11.30am-11pm Tue-Fri; noon-11pm Sat; noon-10.30pm Sun. **Burritos** $7-$9. **Map** p101 A1 **❾ Mexican**

This bright little Cal-Mex taqueria has expanded into a mini chain, but still serves bangin' burritos. The fillings – juicy flap steak, moist grilled chicken, smooth guacamole – are among the best in town. **Other locations** throughout the city.

Il Buco Alimentari & Vineria

53 Great Jones Street, between Bowery & Lafayette Streets (1-212 837 2622, www.ilbucovineria.com). Subway B, D, F, M to Broadway-Lafayette Street; 6 to Bleecker Street. **Open** 7am-11pm Mon-Thur; 7am-midnight Fri; 9am-midnight Sat; 9am-11pm Sun. **Main courses** $19-$59. **Map** p101 A2 **❿ Italian**

Il Buco has been a mainstay of the downtown dining scene since the 1990s and a pioneer in the sort of rustic Italian food now ubiquitous in the city. Owner Donna Lennard took her sweet time (18 years, to be exact) to unveil her first offshoot, Il Buco Alimentari & Vineria. It was worth the wait: the hybrid bakery, food shop, café and trattoria is as confident as its

Mighty Quinn's. See p104.

decades-old sibling, with sure-footed service, the familial bustle of a neighbourhood pillar, and heady aromas of wood-fired short ribs and salt-crusted fish drifting from an open kitchen.
Other location Il Buco, 47 Bond Street, between Bowery & Lafayette Street, East Village (1-212 533 1932).

Ippudo NY

65 Fourth Avenue, between 9th & 10th Streets (1-212 388 0088, www.ippudony.com). Subway 6 to Astor Place. **Open** 11am-3.30pm, 5-11.30pm Mon-Thur; 11am-3.30pm, 5pm-12.30am Fri, Sat; 11am-10.30pm Sun. **Ramen** $15-$17. **Map** p101 A2 ⓲ **Japanese**
This sleek outpost of a Japanese ramen chain is packed mostly with Nippon natives who queue up for a taste of 'Ramen King' Shigemi Kawahara's *tonkotsu* – a pork-based broth. About half a dozen varieties include the Akamaru Modern, a smooth, buttery soup topped with scallions, cabbage, a slice of roasted pork and pleasantly elastic noodles. Avoid non-soup dishes such as the oily fried-chicken wings. Long live the Ramen King – just don't ask him to move beyond his speciality.
Other location 321 W 51st Street, between Eighth & Ninth Avenues, Midtown West (1-212 974 2500).

★ Kyo Ya

94 E 7th Street, between First Avenue & Avenue A (1-212 982 4140). Subway 6 to Astor Place. **Open** 5.30-11.30pm Tue-Sat. **Main courses** $28-$42. **Map** p101 B2 ⓴ **Japanese**
The city's most ambitious Japanese speakeasy is marked only by an 'Open' sign, but in-the-know diners still find their way inside. The food, presented on beautiful handmade plates, is gorgeous: maitake mushrooms are fried in the lightest tempura batter and delivered on a polished stone bed. Sushi is pressed with a hot iron on to sticky vinegar rice. The few desserts are just as ethereal as the savoury food.

Lafayette

380 Lafayette Street, at Great Jones Street (1-212 533 3000, www.lafayetteny.com). Subway B, D, F, M to Broadway-Lafayette Street; 6 to Bleecker Street. **Open** 7.30-11.30am, noon-11pm Mon-Fri; 8am-11pm Sat; 8am-10.30pm Sun. **Main courses** $28-$38. **Map** p101 A2 ⓳ **French**
Ace culinary crew Andrew Carmellini, Josh Pickard and Luke Ostrom – the winning team behind blockbusters Locanda Verde and the Dutch – followed up with this souped-up, all-day French bistro, which marks Carmellini's return to his Francophilic roots (exemplified by runs at Café Boulud and Lespinasse). The changing menu focuses on the country's rustic south. In the spacious, mahogany-floored eaterie, a zinc-hooded rotisserie twirls roast chicken *pour deux*, while an in-house bakery churns out Provençal staples like *pain de campagne* and pretty people gab

Momofuku Ssäm Bar.

over their niçoise salads. While some dishes fail to excite, it's a solid choice for brunch.

Mighty Quinn's

103 Second Avenue, at E 6th Street (1-212 677 3733, www.mightyquinnsbbq.com). Subway 6 to Astor Place. **Open** 11.30am-11pm Mon-Thur, Sun; 11.30am-midnight Fri, Sat. **Main courses** $7.50-$9.25/single serving; $12.50-$23/lb. **Map** p101 B2 ⓴ **American**
Drummer-turned-chef Hugh Mangum first hawked his Texalina (Texas spice meets Carolina vinegar) specialities at his immensely popular stand at Smorgasburg (*see p35*). When the operation went bricks-and-mortar, the hungry throngs followed. Lines of customers snake through the steel-tinged joint, watching as black-gloved carvers give glistening meat porn a dash of Maldon salt before slinging it down the assembly line. Dry-rubbed brisket is slow-smoked for 22 hours, and the Jurassic-sized beef rib is so impossibly tender that one bite will quiet the pickiest barbecue connoisseur. *Photo p103.*

EXPLORE

Other locations 75 Greenwich Avenue, at Seventh Avenue (1-646 524 7889); Hudson Eats, Brookfield Place (*see p61*).

★ Momofuku Ssäm Bar
207 Second Avenue, at 13th Street (1-212 254 3500, www.momofuku.com). Subway L to First or Third Avenue; L, N, Q, R, 4, 5, 6 to 14th Street-Union Square. **Open** 11.30am-3.30pm, 5pm-midnight Mon-Thur, Sun; 11.30am-3.30pm, 5pm-1am Fri, Sat. **Main courses** $19-$36. **Map** p101 B1 ⑮ **Korean**
At chef David Chang's second modern Korean restaurant, waiters hustle to noisy rock music in the 50-seat space, which feels expansive compared with the crowded counter dining of its nearby predecessor, Momofuku Noodle Bar. Try the wonderfully fatty pork-belly steamed bun with hoisin sauce and cucumbers, or one of the ham platters. But you'll need to come with a crowd to sample the house speciality, *bo ssäm* (a slow-roasted pork shoulder that is consumed wrapped in lettuce leaves, with a dozen oysters and other accompaniments); it serves eight people and must be ordered in advance. David Chang has further expanded his E Vill empire with a bar, Booker and Dax (*see right*) at this location, and a sweet annexe, Milk Bar (one of several in the city), across the street. **Other locations** Má Pêche, 15 West 56th Street, between Fifth & Sixth Avenues, Midtown West (1-212 757 5878); Momofuku Ko, 8 Extra Place, between Bowery & Second Avenue, East Village (1-212 500 0831); Momofuku Noodle Bar, 171 First Avenue, between 10th & 11th Streets, East Village (1-212 777 7773).

★ Narcissa
Standard East Village, 25 Cooper Square, between 5th & 6th Streets(1-212 228 3344, www.narcissa restaurant.com). Subway 6 to Astor Place. **Open** 11.30am-3pm, 5.30-11pm Mon-Thur; 11.30am-3pm, 5.30pm-midnight Fri; 10.30am-4pm, 5.30pm-midnight Sat; 10.30am-4pm, 5.30-11pm Sun. **Main courses** $24-$58. **Map** p101 A2 ⑯ **American**
Chef John Fraser, who also owns Michelin-starred Dovetail on the Upper West Side, is the latest adopter of the vegetable high altar. At Narcissa, dishes such as carrots Wellington – sweet, brined carrots tinged hauntingly bitter by a coffee-cocoa rub and encased in buttery puff pastry – are fittingly sublime. The restaurant space is less than transcendent, however, with a carpeted main dining area that would look like a Marriott breakfast buffet were it not filled with black-clad art directors and Coen brothers lookalikes. But a card-carrying locavore chef couldn't ask for a better home than the Standard East Village hotel, whose proprietor André Balazs owns an upstate farm that funnels produce directly to the kitchen. Fraser also works wonders with meat. Charred rotisserie rib eye tastes so rich, you'd think the cow had been taking daily marrow supplements.

★ $ Porchetta
110 E 7th Street, between First Avenue & Avenue A (1-212 777 2151, www.porchettanyc.com). Subway F to Lower East Side-Second Avenue; L to First Avenue; 6 to Astor Place. **Open** 11.30am-10pm Mon-Thur, Sun; 11.30am-11pm Fri, Sat. **Sandwiches** $7-$15. **Map** p101 B2 ⑰ **Café**
This small, subway-tiled space has a narrow focus: central Italy's boneless roasted pork. The meat, available as a sandwich or a platter, is amazingly moist and tender, having been slowly roasted with rendered pork fat, seasoned with fennel pollen, herbs and spices and flecked with brittle shards of skin. Pair it with sides like crispy potatoes, and kale and broccoli rabe topped with roasted garlic.

Veselka
144 Second Avenue, at 9th Street (1-212 228 9682, www.veselka.com). Subway L to Third Avenue; 6 to Astor Place. **Open** 24hrs daily. **Main courses** $14-$18. **Map** p101 B2 ⑱ **Eastern European**
When you need food to soak up the mess of drinks you've consumed in the East Village in the early hours, it's worth remembering Veselka: a relatively inexpensive Eastern European restaurant with plenty of seats, which is open 24 hours a day. Hearty appetites can get a platter of classic Ukrainian grub: *pierogies*, goulash, *kielbasa*, beef stroganoff or *bigos* stew. For dessert, try the *kutya* (traditional Ukrainian pudding made with berries, walnuts, poppy seeds and honey).

Bars

Booker and Dax
207 Second Avenue, at 13th Street (entrance on 13th Street) (1-212 254 3500, www.momofuku. com). Subway L to Third Avenue; L, N, Q, R, 4, 5, 6 to 14th Street-Union Square. **Open** 5pm-1am Mon-Thur, Sun; 5pm-2am Fri, Sat. **Map** p101 B1 ⑲
This tech-forward cocktail joint, housed next to Momofuku Ssäm Bar (*see left*), showcases the boozy tinkerings of wizardly Dave Arnold, the International Culinary Center director of culinary technology. Glasses are chilled with a pour of liquid nitrogen, and winter warmers, like the Friend of the Devil (Campari, sweet vermouth, rye, Pernod, bitters, absinthe), are scorched with a Red Hot Poker, a rod with a built-in 1,500-degree heater created by Arnold. He also showcases new techniques for creating fizzy drinks, like the Gin and Juice, made with Tanqueray gin and grapefruit juice that is clarified in a centrifuge, then carbonated in a CO^2-pressurised cocktail shaker.

Death & Company
433 E 6th Street, between First Avenue & Avenue A (1-212 388 0882, www.deathandcompany.com). Subway F to Lower East Side-Second Avenue; 6 to Astor Place. **Open** 6pm-1am Mon-Thur, Sun; 6pm-2am Fri, Sat. **Map** p101 B2 ⑳

EXPLORE

EXPLORE

IN THE KNOW SPIN THE ALAMO

Astor Place is marked by a steel cube that has sat on a traffic island by the entrance to the 6 train since 1968. With a little elbow grease, the cube, whose proper title is *Alamo*, will spin on its axis.

The nattily attired mixologists are deadly serious about drinks at this pseudo speakeasy with gothic flair (don't be intimidated by the imposing wooden door). Black walls and cushy booths combine with chandeliers to set a luxuriously sombre mood. The inventive cocktails, including some neat twists on the classics, are matched by a changing selection of top-notch bar bites, such as Welsh rarebit and spicy fried cornichons.

Jimmy's No.43

43 E 7th Street, between Second & Third Avenues (1-212 982 3006, www.jimmysno43.com). Subway F to Lower East Side-Second Avenue; 6 to Astor Place. **Open** 4pm-1.30am Mon; 4pm-2.30am Tue-Thur; 4pm-4am Fri, Sat; 3pm-12.30am Sun. **Map** p101 B2 ㉔

You could easily miss this worthy subterranean spot if it weren't for the sign painted on a doorway over an inconspicuous set of stairs. Descend them and you'll encounter mismatched wood tables, burnt-yellow walls displaying taxidermy and medieval-style arched passageways that lead to different rooms. Beer is a big attraction here, with about a dozen quality selections on tap (and more in the bottle), many of which also make it into the slow-food dishes filled with organic ingredients.

Mayahuel

304 E 6th Street, between First & Second Avenues (1-212 253 5888, www.mayahuelny.com). Subway F to Lower East Side-Second Avenue; 6 to Astor Place. **Open** 6pm-2am daily. **Map** p101 B2 ㉒

Tequila and its cousin, mezcal, are the focus at this haute cantina. The inventive cocktail menu features Green Gloves, a spicy mix of jalapeño-infused tequila blanco, green chartreuse, celery and lime; and the smoky but sweet Ron's Dodge Charger, made with chile de árbol-infused mescal, pineapple, agave nectar and smoked salt. The craftsmanship in the drinks is equalled in the bar menu, which features juicy pork belly with papaya and mango salsa.

★ McSorley's Old Ale House

15 E 7th Street, between Second & Third Avenues (1-212 473 9148). Subway F to Lower East Side-Second Avenue. **Open** 11am-1am Mon-Sat; 1pm-1am Sun. **No credit cards**. **Map** p101 A2 ㉓

Ladies should probably leave the Blahniks at home. In traditional Irish-pub fashion, McSorley's floor has been thoroughly scattered with sawdust to take care of the spills and other messes that often accompany the consumption of large quantities of cheap beer. Established in 1854, McSorley's became an institution by remaining steadfastly authentic and providing only two choices: McSorley's Dark Ale and McSorley's Light Ale. A fascinating cast of characters has raised a glass here, from Tammany Hall politicians to purported regular Harry Houdini (look for his handcuffs above the bar).

★ PDT

113 St Marks Place, between First Avenue & Avenue A (1-212 614 0386, www.pdtnyc.com). Subway L to First Avenue; 6 to Astor Place. **Open** 6pm-2am Mon-Thur, Sun; 6pm-4am Fri, Sat. **Map** p101 B2 ㉓

The word is out about 'Please Don't Tell', the faux speakeasy inside gourmet hot dog joint Crif Dogs (*see p103*), so it's a good idea to reserve a booth in advance. Once you arrive, you'll notice people lingering outside an old wooden phonebooth near the front. Slip inside, pick up the receiver and the host opens a secret panel to the dark, narrow space. The serious cocktails surpass the gimmicky entry: try the house old-fashioned, made with bacon-infused bourbon, which leaves a smoky aftertaste.

Proletariat

102 St Marks Place, between First Avenue & Avenue A (1-212 777 6707, www.proletariatny.com). Subway 6 to Astor Place. **Open** 5pm-2am Mon-Thur; 2pm-2am Fri-Sun. **Map** p101 B2 ㉕

Proletariat is a much-deserved look into no-holds-barred beer geekdom, blissfully free of TVs and generic pub grub. With just 12 stools and a space so tight that menus have been replaced with a QR code (scan it with your smartphone), brewhounds get the type of intimacy usually reserved for the cocktail and wine crowds. The expert servers have a story for every keg they tap, from the newest local brews to obscure New Zealand ales and deep cuts from the Belgian canon.

Wayland

700 E 9th Street, at Avenue C (1-212 777 7022, www.thewaylandnyc.com). Subway L to First Avenue. **Open** 5pm-4am daily. **Map** p101 C2 ㉖

East Village bar crawlers have been stumbling further down the alphabet for years now, but it's taken Avenue C time to develop the critical mass necessary to attract a late-night buzz. At this fun-loving bar, solicitous staff, a young crowd and the likelihood of a spontaneous sing-along around the piano all contribute to a convivial vibe that makes you want to call for another round. An old-fashioned riff called I Hear Banjos (apple pie moonshine, rye whiskey and apple-spice bitters) comes with a ceremonious puff of applewood smoke, captured in an overturned glass that's placed over the drink.

Shops & Services

3.1 Phillip Lim
48 Great Jones Street, between Bowery & Lafayette Street (1-212 334 1160, www.31philliplim.com). Subway B, D, F, M to Broadway-Lafayette; 6 to Bleecker Street. **Open** 11am-7pm Mon-Sat; noon-6pm Sun. **Map** p101 A2 ❷ **Fashion**
The New York-based designer has amassed a devoted international following for his simple yet strong silhouettes and beautifully constructed tailoring with a twist. His spacious, all-white flagship showcases his collections for men and women, alongside accessories including his highly sought-after handbags.

Astor Place Hairstylists
2 Astor Place, at Broadway (1-212 475 9854, www.astorplacehairnyc.com). Subway N, R to 8th Street-NYU; 6 to Astor Place. **Open** 8am-8pm Mon, Sat; 8am-9pm Tue-Fri; 9am-6pm Sun. **No credit cards. Map** p101 A2 ❷ **Health & beauty**
The army of barbers at Astor Place does everything from neat trims to more complicated and creative shaved designs. There are no reservations; just take a number and wait outside with the crowd. Sunday mornings are usually quieter. Cuts start at $17.

Astor Wines & Spirits
399 Lafayette Street, at 4th Street (1-212 674 7500, www.astorwines.com). Subway N, R to 8th Street-NYU; 6 to Astor Place. **Open** 9am-9pm Mon-Sat; noon-6pm Sun. **Map** p101 A2 ❷ **Food & drink**
High-ceilinged, wide-aisled Astor Wines is a terrific place to browse for wines of every price, vineyard and year. Sakés and spirits are also well represented.

Bond No.9
9 Bond Street, between Broadway & Lafayette Street (1-212 228 1732, www.bondno9.com). Subway B, D, F, M to Broadway-Lafayette Street; 6 to Bleecker Street. **Open** 11am-8pm Mon-Fri; noon-7pm Sat; noon-6pm Sun. **Map** p101 A2 ❸ **Health & beauty**
The Bond No.9 fragrance collection pays olfactory homage to New York City. Choose from more than 60 'neighbourhoods' and 'sensibilities', including Wall Street, Park Avenue, Eau de Noho, High Line, Brooklyn – even Chinatown (but don't worry, it smells of peach blossoms, gardenia and patchouli, not fish stands). The arty bottles and neat, colourful packaging are particularly gift-friendly.
Other locations throughout the city.

★ Bond Street Chocolate
63 E 4th Street, between Bowery & Second Avenue (1-212 677 5103, www.bondstchocolate.com). Subway 6 to Bleecker Street. **Open** noon-8pm Tue-Sat; 1-5pm Sun. **Map** p101 A2 ❸ **Food & drink**
Former pastry chef Lynda Stern's East Village spot is a grown-up's candy store, with quirky chocolate confections in shapes ranging from gilded Buddhas (and other religious figures) to skulls, and flavours from elderflower to bourbon and absinthe.

Buffalo Exchange
332 E 11th Street, between First & Second Avenues (1-212 260 9340, www.buffaloexchange.com). Subway L to First Avenue. **Open** 11am-8pm Mon-Sat; noon-7pm Sun. **Map** p101 B1 ❷ **Fashion**
This popular buy-sell-trade clothing shop spans all sartorial tastes, from Forever 21 to Marc Jacobs. You could score a pair of cult jeans for $25, current-season Manolo Blahniks for $250 or a Burberry men's wool coat for $135.
Other locations throughout the city.

★ Dear: Rivington
37 Great Jones Street, between Bowery & Lafayette Street (1-212 673 3494, www.dearrivington.com). Subway B, D, F, M to Broadway-Lafayette; 6 to Bleecker Street. **Open** 11am-7pm Mon-Sat; noon-6pm Sun. **Map** p101 A2 ❸ **Fashion**
A utilitarian white space provides a stage for Moon Rhee and Hey Ja Do's installation-like displays, incorporating industrial furniture, manufacturing

relics and other curios. Hanging on an assortment of period rolling racks, the duo's own line of one-of-a-kind garments is interspersed with select pieces by the likes of Comme des Garçons and Yohji Yamamoto; the Dear label combines a Japanese minimalist aesthetic with Victorian and 1950s influences, often incorporating salvaged trimmings like beaded collars and lace. A large collection of pristine vintage handbags is scattered around the store – hung like art objects on one wall, arranged in an antique display case with other accessories, and even dangling from a weathered iron bedstead.

★ Fabulous Fanny's

335 E 9th Street, between First & Second Avenues (1-212 533 0637, www.fabulousfannys.com). Subway L to First Avenue; 6 to Astor Place. **Open** noon-8pm daily. **Map** p101 B2 ㉞ **Accessories**
Formerly a Chelsea flea market booth, this two-room shop is the city's best source of period glasses, stocking more than 30,000 pairs of spectacles, from Jules Verne-esque wire rims to 1970s rhinestone-encrusted Versace shades.

Fun City Tattoo

94 St Marks Place, between First Avenue & Avenue A (1-212 353 8282, www.funcitytattoo. com). Subway N, R to 8th Street-NYU; 6 to Astor Place. **Open** noon-10pm daily. **No credit cards. Map** p101 B2 ㉟ **Tattoo parlour**
Jonathan Shaw started inking locals from his apartment in the mid-1970s (when tattooing was illegal) before opening this store in the 1990s. The legendary figure has retired to South America, but his New York City institution – which has served the likes of Johnny Depp, Jim Jarmusch, Dee Dee Ramone and Sepultura's Max Cavalera – continues its operations in the East Village. Fun City's six current artists – 'Big' Steve Pedone, Mina Aoki, Claire Vuillemot, Benjamin Haft, Amanda Wachob, and Andrew Mann – can do most anything, from lettering and Japanese to American traditional.

Future Perfect

55 Great Jones Street, between Bowery & Lafayette Street (1-212 473 2500, www.thefutureperfect. com). Subway 6 to Bleecker Street. **Open** 10am-7pm Mon-Fri; noon-7pm Sat. **Map** p101 A2 ㊱ **Homewares**
Championing avant-garde interior design, this innovative store specialises in artist-made, limited-edition and one-of-a-kind pieces. The Future Perfect is the exclusive US stockist of Dutch designer Piet Hein Eek's elegant woodwork and pottery, but it also showcases local talent. Check out beautifully simple hand-thrown and -glazed bowls by Jason Miller, spare gold jewellery and branching metal light fixtures by Lindsey Adelman, and extraordinary dripped-concrete vases made in Brooklyn by Chen Chen and Kai Williams.

★ Great Jones Spa

29 Great Jones Street, at Lafayette Street (1-212 505 3185, www.greatjonesspa.com). Subway 6 to Astor Place. **Open** 9am-10pm daily. **Map** p101 A2 ㊲ **Health & beauty**
Harnessing the wellbeing-boosting properties of water, Great Jones is outfitted with a popular wet lounge complete with subterranean pools, saunas, steam rooms and a three-and-a-half-storey waterfall. Access to the 15,000sq ft paradise is complimentary with spa services over $100 – treat yourself to a divinely scented body scrub, a massage or one of the many indulgent packages. Alternatively, a three-hour pass costs $55.

Kiehl's

109 Third Avenue, between 13th & 14th Streets (1-212 677 3171, www.kiehls.com). Subway L to Third Avenue; N, Q, R, 4, 5, 6 to 14th Street-Union Square. **Open** 10am-8pm Mon-Sat; 11am-6pm Sun. **Map** p101 A1 ㊳ **Health & beauty**
The apothecary founded on this site in 1851 has morphed into a major skincare brand, but the products, in their minimal packaging, are still good value and effective. Lip balms and the thick-as-custard Creme de Corps have become cult classics. **Other locations** throughout the city.

★ Obscura Antiques & Oddities

207 Avenue A, between 12th & 13th Streets (1-212 505 9251, www.obscuraantiques.com). Subway L to First Avenue. **Open** noon-8pm Mon-Sat; noon-7pm Sun. **Map** p101 B1 ㊴ **Gifts & souvenirs/ homewares**
Housed inside a former funeral home, this eccentric shop, immortalised in a Science Channel reality TV series, specialises in bizarre items like medical and scientific antiques, human skulls and taxidermied animals dating from the 19th century. Owners Evan Michelson and Mike Zohn scour flea markets, auctions and even museums for rare artefacts like jarred piranhas, 1920s decorative 'boudoir dolls' and a mummified cat.

★ Other Music

15 E 4th Street, between Broadway & Lafayette Street (1-212 477 8150, www.othermusic.com). Subway B, D, F, M to Broadway-Lafayette Street; 6 to Bleecker Street. **Open** 11am-9pm Mon-Fri; noon-8pm Sat; noon-7pm Sun. **Map** p101 A2 ㊵ **Books & music**
Other Music opened in the shadow of Tower Records in the mid 1990s, a pocket of resistance to chain-store tedium. All these years later, the Goliath across the street is gone, but tiny Other Music carries on. Whereas the shop's mishmash of indie rock, experimental music and stray slabs of rock's past once seemed adventurous, the curatorial foundation has proved prescient, amid the emergence of mixed-genre venues in the city.

Patricia Field
*306 Bowery, between Bleecker & E Houston Streets
(1-212 966 4066, www.patriciafield.com). Subway
6 to Bleecker Street.* **Open** 11am-8pm Mon-Thur,
Sun; 11am-9pm Fri, Sat. **Map** p101 A3 ⚐ **Fashion/
Health & beauty**
The iconic redheaded designer and stylist moved her
boutique two doors down from the original, into a
space that's nearly double the size, combining Field's
former apartment with a vacated store behind it –
her old bedroom is now a full-service hair salon. In
addition to funky, flamboyant threads for men and
women, stock up on whimsical accessories such as
polka-dot heart-shaped shades and beaded yellow
taxi cab-shaped handbags.

Rue St Denis
*170 Avenue B, between 10th & 11th Streets
(1-212 260 3388, www.ruestdenis.com). Subway
L to First Avenue.* **Open** noon-8pm Mon-Fri;
noon-7.30pm Sat, Sun. **Map** p101 C1 ⚐ **Fashion**
Jean-Paul Buthier searches the US and Europe for
unworn dead-stock garb, from long-closed factories
and stores. Film, TV and Broadway costume departments frequently source pieces here. Menswear is
the speciality – the back room is filled with pristine
suits from the 1940s to the '90s, organised by era –
but ladies will also find plenty to ogle.

Screaming Mimi's
*382 Lafayette Street, at 4th Street (1-212 677
6464, www.screamingmimis.com). Subway B, D,
F, M to Broadway-Lafayette Street; N, R to Prince
Street; 6 to Bleecker Street.* **Open** noon-8pm
Mon-Sat; 1-7pm Sun. **Map** p101 A2 ⚐ **Fashion**
This vintage mecca has been peddling men's and
women's clothing and accessories since 1978. Owner
Laura Wills travels the world, scouting eclectic

finds that span the 1920s to the '90s, and organises
clothing racks by decade. Do you need sunglasses
from the 1970s? How about a Duran Duran T-shirt
from the '80s? Head upstairs to check out higher-end
garments by designers such as Moschino, Jean Paul
Gaultier and Vivienne Westwood.

★ Strand Book Store
*828 Broadway, at 12th Street (1-212 473 1452,
www.strandbooks.com). Subway L, N, Q, R, 4,
5, 6 to 14th Street-Union Square.* **Open** 9.30am-
10.30pm Mon-Sat; 11am-10.30pm Sun. **Map** p101
A1 ⚐ **Books & music**
Established in 1927, the Strand has a mammoth
collection of more than two million discount
volumes (both new and used), and the store is made
all the more daunting by its chaotic, towering
shelves and sometimes crotchety staff. You can
find just about anything here, from that out-of-
print Victorian book on manners to the kitschiest
of sci-fi pulp. Note that the rare book room upstairs
closes at 6.15pm.
► *There's a seasonal Strand kiosk on the edge
of Central Park at Fifth Avenue and 60th Street
(Apr-Dec 10am-dusk, weather permitting).*

Sustainable NYC
*139 Avenue A, between 9th Street & St Marks
Place (1-212 254 5400, www.sustainable-nyc.
com). Subway L to First Avenue; 6 to Astor Place.*
Open 8am-10pm Mon-Fri; 9am-10pm Sat, Sun.
Map p101 B2 ⚐ **Gifts & souvenirs**
This gift-friendly shop houses a wealth of eco-
minded goods within its green walls: organic beauty
products, soy candles and locally made soaps,
frames, jewellery, clutch bags and other gifts made
from recycled materials. The on-site café serves Fair
Trade coffee, sandwiches and vegan treats.

EXPLORE

Strand Book Store.

Greenwich Village & West Village

EXPLORE

Anchored by New York University, Greenwich Village, along with its western adjunct the West Village, is one of the most picturesque parts of the city. The stomping ground of the Beat Generation is no longer a cheap-rent bohemian paradise, but it's still a pleasant place for idle wandering, dining in excellent restaurants and hopping between bars and cabaret venues. The Meatpacking District, which over the past two decades has evolved from gritty industrial zone to gay cruising spot to hedonistic consumer playground, has a flashier feel. But the 2015 opening of the Whitney Museum is bringing culture to the neighbourhood.

Carbone.

Don't Miss

1 **Washington Square Park** The heart of Village life (p112).

2 **Caffe Reggio** Forgo artisanal beans to soak up a vintage vibe (p114).

3 **Carbone** A cinematic replica of an old-school red-sauce joint (p114).

4 **High Line** The elevated park is insanely popular (p123).

5 **Whitney Musem of American Art** The city's newest art temple (p123).

Washington Square Park.

EXPLORE

GREENWICH VILLAGE

Subway A, B, C, D, E, F, M to W 4th Street; L, N, Q, R, 4, 5, 6 to 14th Street-Union Square; N, R to 8th Street-NYU; 1 to Christopher Street-Sheridan Square.

Stretching from Houston Street to 14th Street, between Broadway and Sixth Avenue, **Greenwich Village** has been inspiring bohemians for more than a century. Now that it has become one of the most expensive neighbourhoods in the city, you need a lot more than a struggling artist's or writer's income to inhabit its leafy streets.

Great for people-watching, **Washington Square Park** attracts a disparate cast of characters that takes in hippies, students and street musicians. Skateboarders clatter near the base of the Washington Arch, a modestly sized replica of Paris's Arc de Triomphe, built in 1895 to honour George Washington. The 9.75-acre green space recently received a $16-million redesign.

In the 1830s, the wealthy began building handsome townhouses around the square. A few of those properties are still privately owned and occupied, but many others have become part of the ever-expanding NYU campus. The university also owns the Washington Mews, a row of charming 19th-century former stables that line a tiny cobblestoned alley just to the north of the park between Fifth Avenue and University Place. Several famed literary figures, including Henry James (author of the celebrated novel that took its title from the square), Herman Melville, Edith Wharton, Edgar Allan Poe and Eugene O'Neill, lived on or near the square. In 1871, the local creative community founded the **Salmagundi**

Club (47 Fifth Avenue, between 11th & 12th Streets, 1-212 255 7740, www.salmagundi.org), America's oldest artists' club. Now situated north of Washington Square on Fifth Avenue, it has galleries that are open to the public.

Greenwich Village continues to change with the times, for the better and for the worse. In the 1960s, **8th Street** was the closest New York got to San Francisco's hippie magnet, Haight Street; Jimi Hendrix's **Electric Lady Studios** is still at 52 West 8th Street, between Fifth & Sixth Avenues. For years, the run-down strip has been a procession of piercing parlours, smoke shops and shoe stores, but it's been smartened up with the arrival of popular purveyors like **Stumptown Coffee Roasters** and a boutique hotel, the **Marlton** (*see p361*).

Once the dingy but colourful domain of Beat poets and folk and jazz musicians, the well-trafficked section of **Bleecker Street** between La Guardia Place and Sixth Avenue is now an overcrowded stretch of poster shops, cheap restaurants and music venues for the college crowd. Renowned hangouts such as Le Figaro Café (184 Bleecker Street, at MacDougal Street), Kerouac's favourite, are no more, but a worthy alternative is **Caffe Reggio**, the oldest coffeehouse in the village. Although 1960s hotspot **Cafe Wha?** (115 MacDougal Street, between Bleecker & W 3rd Streets, 1-212 254 3706, www.cafewha.com) is now running on the fumes of its illustrious past, it has a decent house band. Nearby, the **Bitter End** (147 Bleecker Street, between La Guardia Place & Thompson Street, 1-212 673 7030, www.bitterend.com) has proudly championed the singer-songwriter – including a young Bob Dylan – since 1961.

The famed Village Gate jazz club at the corner of Bleecker and Thompson Streets – which staged performances by Miles Davis, Nina Simone and John Cage – closed in 1993. However, in 2008, **Le Poisson Rouge** (*see p289*) opened on the site with a similar mission to present diverse genres under one roof.

Not far from here, in the triangle formed by Sixth Avenue, Greenwich Avenue and 10th Street, you'll see the Gothic-style **Jefferson Market Library** (a branch of the New York Public Library). The lovely flower-filled garden facing Greenwich Avenue was once the site of the Women's House of Detention, which was torn down in 1974. Mae West did a little time there in 1926, on obscenity charges stemming from her Broadway show *Sex*.

Just behind the library, off 10th Street, lies **Patchin Place**, which was home to some of the leading luminaries of New York's literary pantheon. This cul-de-sac lined with brick houses built during the mid 19th century is off limits to the public, but through the gate you can make out no.4, where the poet and staunch foe of capitalisation ee cummings resided from 1923 to 1962; and no.5, where Djuna Barnes, author of *Nightwood*, lived from 1940 to 1982.

Sights & Museums

FREE AIA Center for Architecture
536 La Guardia Place, between Bleecker & W 3rd Streets (1-212 683 0023, http://cfa.aiany.org). Subway A, B, C, D, E, F, M to W 4th Street. **Open** 9am-8pm Mon-Fri; 11am-5pm Sat. **Admission** free. **Map** p113 D2 ❶
Redesigned by architect Andrew Berman in 2003, the Center is home to the New York chapter of the American Institute of Architects. Berman cut away large slabs of flooring at the street and basement levels, converting underground spaces into bright, museum-quality galleries; exhibitions here focus on both local and international themes.

Restaurants & Cafés

★ Blue Hill
75 Washington Place, between Washington Square West & Sixth Avenue (1-212 539 1776, www.bluehillfarm.com). Subway A, B, C, D, E, F, M to W 4th Street. **Open** 5-11pm daily. **Set meals** $85-$98. **Map** p113 C2 ❷ **American**
More than a mere crusader for sustainability, Dan Barber is also one of the most talented cooks in town, building his menu around whatever's at its peak on the family farm in Great Barrington, Massachusetts,

EXPLORE

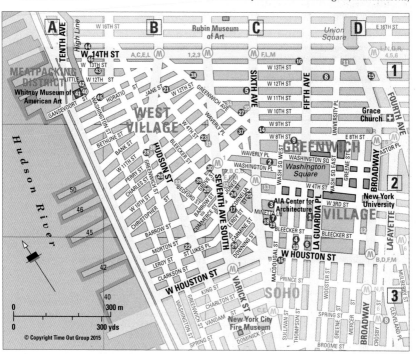

and the not-for-profit Stone Barns Center for Food and Agriculture in Westchester, New York (home to a sibling restaurant), among other suppliers. The evening may begin with a sophisticated seasonal spin on a pig's-liver terrine and move on to a sweet slow-roasted parsnip 'steak' with creamed spinach and beet ketchup, or grass-fed lamb.

Caffe Reggio

119 MacDougal Street, at W 3rd Street (1-212 475 9557, www.caffereggio.com). Subway A, B, C, D, E, F, M to W 4th Street. **Open** 8am-3am Mon-Thur; 8am-4am Fri, Sat; 9am-3am Sun. **Main courses** $10-$11. **No credit cards. Map** p113 C2 ❸ Café
Legend has it that the original owner of this classic café introduced Americans to the cappuccino in 1927 and, apart from its acquired patina, we bet the interior hasn't changed much since then. Although it's traded in the coal-fuelled espresso machine for a sleeker Caffe Sacco model, you can still admire the old custom chrome-and-bronze contraption on the bar. Sip espresso and tuck into a house-made tiramisu under the Italian Renaissance-style paintings.

★ Carbone

181 Thompson Street, between Bleecker & Houston Streets (1-212 254 3000, www.carbonenewyork. com). Subway C, E to Spring Street. **Open** noon-2pm, 5.30pm-midnight Mon-Fri; 5.30pm-midnight Sat, Sun. **Main courses** $21-$57. **Map** p113 C3 ❹ Italian
Red sauce revivalists Rich Torrisi and Mario Carbone honour Gotham's legendary Italian joints (Rao's, Bamonte's) with their high-profile revamp of historic Rocco's Ristorante. Suave, tuxedo-clad waiters – Bronx accents intact, but their burgundy threads designed by Zac Posen – tote an avalanche of complimentary extras: chunks of chianti-infused parmesan, olive-oil-soaked 'Grandma Bread' and slivers of smoky prosciutto. Follow updated renditions of classic pasta, such as a spicy, über-rich rigatoni vodka, with mains like sticky cherry-pepper ribs and lavish takes on tiramisu for dessert.

Kin Shop

469 Sixth Avenue, between 11th & 12th Streets (1-212 675 4295, www.kinshopnyc.com). Subway F, M to 14th Street; L to Sixth Avenue. **Open** 11.30am-3pm, 5.30-10pm Mon-Wed; 11.30am-3pm, 5.30-11pm Thur-Sat; 11.30am-3pm, 5-10pm Sun. **Main courses** $20-$29. **Map** p113 C1 ❺ Thai
Top Chef champ Harold Dieterle channels his Southeast Asian travels into the menu at this eatery, which serves classic Thai street food alongside more upmarket Thai-inspired dishes. The traditional fare seems extraneous, but Dieterle's creations are often inspired. A salad of crispy oysters, slivered celery and fried pork belly is bright and refreshing, while a chefly riff on massaman curry features long-braised goat with a silky sauce infused with toasted coconut, fried shallots and purple yams.

Lupa

170 Thompson Street, between Bleecker & W Houston Streets (1-212 982 5089, www.lupa restaurant.com). Subway A, B, C, D, E, F, M to W 4th Street. **Open** 11.30am-11pm Mon-Thur, Sun; 11.30am-midnight Fri, Sat. **Main courses** $21-$34. **Map** p113 C3 ❻ Italian
No mere 'poor man's Babbo' (Mario Batali's other, pricier restaurant around the corner), this convivial trattoria offers communal dining, reasonably priced wines and hit-the-spot comfort food. Come for classic Roman fare such as *pollo alla diavola* ('the devil's chicken', seasoned with black and crushed red pepper), or gumdrop-shaped ricotta gnocchi.
▶ *For Mario Batali's sprawling Italian food emporium Eataly, see p143; for Casa Mono, the celeb chef's take on a tapas bar, see p145.*

Minetta Tavern

113 MacDougal Street, between Bleecker & W 3rd Streets (1-212 475 3850, www.minetta tavernny.com). Subway A, B, C, D, E, F, M to W 4th Street. **Open** 5.30pm-1am Mon, Tue; noon-3pm, 5.30pm-1am Wed-Fri; 11am-3pm, 5.30pm-1am Sat, Sun. **Main courses** $20-$35. **Map** p113 C2 ❼ Eclectic
Restaurateur Keith McNally brought the buzz back to this erstwhile literati hangout once frequented by Hemingway and Fitzgerald. In line with the spot-on restoration of its vintage interior, the big-flavoured bistro fare includes classics such as roasted bone marrow, trout meunière topped with crabmeat, and the airy Grand Marnier soufflé. But the most illustrious thing on the menu is the Black Label burger. You might find the $28 price tag a little hard to swallow, but the superbly tender sandwich – essentially chopped steak in a bun smothered in caramelised onions – is worth every penny.
▶ *For less expensive but equally acclaimed burgers, see Corner Bistro (p119) and Shake Shack (p173).*

$ Num Pang Sandwich Shop

28 E 12th Street, between Fifth Avenue & University Place (1-646 791 0439, www.num pangnyc.com). Subway L, N, Q, R, 4, 5, 6 to 14th Street-Union Square. **Open** 11am-10pm Mon-Sat; noon-9pm Sun. **Sandwiches** $7.50-$12. **No credit cards. Map** p113 D1 ❽ Cambodian
At this small shop, the rotating varieties of *num pang* (Cambodia's answer to the Vietnamese *banh*

EXPLORE

mi) include pulled *duroc* pork with spiced honey, peppercorn catfish, or hoisin veal meatballs, each stuffed into crusty baguettes. There's limited seating, so if you can't find a space at the counter, get it to go and eat in Union or Washington Square Park. **Other locations** throughout the city.

Stumptown Coffee Roasters
30 W 8th Street, at MacDougal Street (1-347 414 7802, www.stumptowncoffee.com). Subway A, B, C, D, E, F, M to W 4th Street. **Open** 7am-8pm daily. **Coffee** $2.50-$6. **Map** p113 C2 **❾** Café
The lauded Portland, Oregon, outfit expanded its New York holdings – which include a branch inside the Ace Hotel (*see p363*) – with this standalone café. The wood-panelled counter and old-fashioned cabinetry nod to classic coffee houses, but purists can savour single-origin espresso from a La Marzocco GS3 machine and slow brews prepared via java-geek speciality drips like Chemex pourovers, ceramic filter-cone Bee House drippers or a siphon vacuum brewer. The low-key hangout offers the chain's full line of more than 20 seasonal coffees, plus pastries from Momofuku Milk Bar and Ovenly.

ZZ's Clam Bar
169 Thompson Street, between Bleecker & W Houston Streets (1-212 254 3000, www.zzs dambar.com). Subway B, D, F, M to Broadway-Lafayette Street; 6 to Bleecker Street. **Open** 6pm-1am Tue-Sat. **Main courses** $18-$105. **Map** p113 C3 **❿** Seafood
This 12-seat spot from powerhouse trio Rich Torrisi, Mario Carbone and Jeff 'ZZ' Zalaznick highlights first-rate cocktails and *crudo*. At the marble bar, acclaimed barman Thomas Waugh concocts the likes of rum, house-made coconut cream, acacia

honey and lime juice served in a frozen coconut. Bar-friendly small plates explore raw fish in all forms, from East Coast oysters on the half-shell to *shimaaji* (striped horse mackerel) tartare topped with whipped ricotta and Petrossian caviar.

Bars

Corkbuzz Wine Studio
13 E 13th Street, between Fifth Avenue & University Place (1-646 873 6071, www.cork buzz.com). Subway L, N, Q, R, 4, 5, 6 to 14th Street-Union Square. **Open** 4.30pm-midnight Mon-Wed; 4.30pm-1am Thur, Fri; 2pm-1am Sat; noon-3pm, 4.30pm-midnight Sun (hrs vary seasonally). **Map** p113 D1 **⓫**
This intriguing and elegant hybrid, owned by one of the world's youngest female master sommeliers, Laura Maniec, comprises a restaurant, wine bar and educational centre. Staff preach the Maniec gospel to patrons as they navigate more than 50 by-the-glass options and around 250 bottles.
Other location Chelsea Market, 75 9th Avenue, between 15th & 16th Streets, Chelsea (1-646 237 4847).

Sweetwater Social
643 Broadway, at Bleecker Street (1-212 253 0477, www.sweetwatersocial-hub.com). Subway B, D, F, M to Broadway-Lafayette Street; 6 to Bleecker Street. **Open** 5pm-2am Mon-Sat; noon-2am Sun. **Map** p113 D2 **⓬**
Channelling a 1980s basement rec room, cocktail-world vets Tim Cooper and Justin Noel concoct a lively playground of game-hall amusements and well-executed quaffs at this throwback bar. The witty drinks menu is laid out on a New York

EXPLORE

ZZ's Clam Bar.

subway map, with each cocktail reminiscent of a particular stop: the Ivan Drago, for example, a nod to Russian-heavy Brighton Beach and the Soviet opponent in Rocky IV, updates a classic Moscow mule with aromatic cardamom, clove and cinnamon. Leather-jacketed gents huddle over foosball tables – unearthed from Cooper's own childhood basement – while off-duty suits loosen their ties during high-octane Galaga game play.

Vol de Nuit Bar (aka Belgian Beer Lounge)

148 W 4th Street, between Sixth Avenue & MacDougal Street (1-212 982 3388, www.volde nuitbar.com). Subway A, B, C, D, E, F, M to W 4th Street. **Open** 4pm-midnight Mon-Wed, Sun; 4pm-1am Thur; 4pm-2am Fri, Sat. **Map** p113 C2 ⑱
Duck through an unmarked doorway and find yourself in a red-walled Belgian bar that serves brews exclusively from the motherland. Clusters of European grad students knock back glasses of Corsendork and Lindeman's Framboise – just two of 13 beers on tap and nearly 30 by the bottle. Moules and frites – served with one of a dozen sauces – are available most nights.

Shops & Services

CO Bigelow Chemists

414 Sixth Avenue, between 8th & 9th Streets (1-212 533 2700, www.bigelowchemists.com). Subway A, B, C, D, F, M to W 4th Street; 1 to Christopher Street. **Open** 7.30am-9pm Mon-Fri; 8.30am-7pm Sat; 8.30am-5pm Sun. **Map** p113 C2 ⑭
Health & beauty
Established in 1838, Bigelow is the oldest apothecary in America. Its appealingly old-school line of toiletries includes such tried-and-trusted favourites as Mentha Lip Shine, Barber Cologne Elixirs and Lemon Body Cream. The spacious, chandelier-lit store is packed with natural and homeopathic remedies, organic skincare products and drugstore essentials – and the place still fills prescriptions.

Forbidden Planet

832 Broadway, between 12th & 13th Streets (1-212 473 1576, www.fpnyc.com). Subway L, N, Q, R, 4, 5, 6 to 14th Street-Union Square. **Open** 9am-10pm Mon, Tue, Sun; 8am-midnight Wed; 9am-midnight Thur-Sat. **Map** p113 D1 ⑮
Books & music
Embracing pop culture and the cult underground, Forbidden Planet takes comics very seriously. You'll also find graphic novels, manga, action figures, DVDs and more.

Harry's Corner Shop

64 MacDougal Street, at Houston Street (1-646 964 5193, www.harrys.com/cornershop). Subway 1 to Houston Street. **Open** 11am-8pm Mon-Fri; 10am-6pm Sat-Sun. **Map** p113 C3 ⑯ **Barber**

CO Bigelow Chemists.

Warby Parker co-founder Jeff Raider and business partner Andy Katz-Mayfield launched grooming brand Harry's in 2013 and opened the e-commerce platform's first 1920s-esque barbershop. Aside from affordable cuts ($40) and shaves ($35), the shop offers clients a completely individualised appointment: barbers use iPads to snap headshots and update digital profiles of each customer. The merchandise stocked on ash-wood shelves includes Harry's razors and shave cream, plus gents' essentials like Hanes white cotton tees, Sleepy Jones boxer shorts, and Makr small leather goods.

Murray's Cheese

254 Bleecker Street, between Sixth & Seventh Avenues (1-212 243 3289, www.murrayscheese. com). Subway A, B, C, D, E, F, M to W 4th Street. **Open** 8am-9pm Mon-Sat; 9am-7pm Sun. **Map** p113 C2 ⑰ **Food & drink**
For the last word in curd, New Yorkers have been flocking to Murray's since 1940 to sniff out the best international and domestic cheeses. The helpful staff will guide you through hundreds of stinky, runny, washed-rind and aged comestibles.
▶ *Murray's also has an outpost in Grand Central Terminal, plus a Cheese Bar at 264 Bleecker Street.*

Porto Rico Importing Co

201 Bleecker Street, between Sixth Avenue & MacDougal Street (1-212 477 5421, www. portorico.com). Subway A, B, C, D, E, F, M to W 4th Street. **Open** 8am-9pm Mon-Fri; 9am-9pm Sat; noon-7pm Sun. **Map** p113 C2 ⑱
Food & drink
This small, family-run store, established in 1907, has earned a large following for its terrific range of coffee beans, including its own prepared blends. Prices are reasonable, and the selection of teas also warrants exploration.
Other locations 40 ½ St Marks Place, between First & Second Avenues, East Village (1-212 533 1982); Essex Market, 120 Essex Street, between Delancey & Rivington Streets, Lower East Side (1-212 677 1210); 636 Grand Street, between Manhattan Avenue & Leonard Street, Williamsburg, Brooklyn (1-718 782 1200).

Stieber's Sweet Shoppe

195 Bleecker Street, between MacDougal Street & Sixth Avenue (1-646 439 7903, http://stiebers. com). Subway A, B, C, D, E, F, M to W 4th Street. **Open** noon-9pm Mon-Sat; noon-8pm Sun.
Map p113 C2 ⑲ **Food & drink**
Inhale the intoxicating aromas of freshly baked fudge while you agonise over the huge selection of old-fashioned candies at this well-stocked sweet spot. Around 250 types of gummies include such unexpected flavours as red-hot chilli pepper. Die-hard cocoa fans will no doubt gravitate towards the display case containing chocolate-dipped Oreos and pretzels encrusted with M&M's.

WEST VILLAGE

Subway A, C, E, 1, 2, 3 to 14th Street; L to Eighth Avenue; 1 to Christopher Street-Sheridan Square.

In the early 20th century, the **West Village** was largely a working-class Italian neighbourhood. These days, the highly desirable enclave is home to numerous celebrities (including Claire Danes and Hugh Jackman), but a low-key, everyone-knows-everyone feel remains. One of the oldest parts of the Village, the area west of Sixth Avenue to the Hudson River, from 14th Street to Houston Street, retains a street layout based on the original settlers' horse paths. Only here could West 10th Street cross West 4th Street, and Waverly Place cross… Waverly Place.

Locals and visitors crowd bistros along Seventh Avenue and Hudson Street, and patronise the high-rent boutiques on this stretch of Bleecker Street, including no fewer than four Marc Jacobs shops. Venture on to the side streets for interesting discoveries, such as sumptuous perfume parlour **Aedes de Venustas** on Christopher Street. The area's bohemian population may have dwindled years ago, but a few old landmarks remain. Solemnly raise a glass in the **White Horse Tavern**, a favourite of such literary luminaries as Ezra Pound, James Baldwin, Norman Mailer and Dylan Thomas, who included it on his last drinking binge before his death in 1953. On and just off Seventh Avenue South are jazz and cabaret clubs, including the **Village Vanguard** (*see p294*).

EXPLORE

Stieber's Sweet Shoppe.

SHORT-ORDER AND SWEET

Dominique Ansel's pastry kitchen gives new meaning to 'freshly baked'.

Dominique Ansel is a dough-wielding wizard. After the madcap pastry chef dreamed up the highly sought after croissant-doughnut hybrid, the Cronut, at his Soho bakery (*see p71*), he developed the chocolate-chip cookie milk shot, skewered frozen iterations of campfire classic s'mores, and even hawked house-made canned sundaes from an ice-cream truck in the Hamptons. At his new venture, Dominique Ansel Kitchen, poised to open in the West Village at the time of writing, the concept is less experimental and sans Cronut – but injected with a bit of booze.

The 20-seat bakery-bar focuses on made-to-order desserts and pastries, such as millefeuille, flaky croissants and the warm, four-minute madeleine cookies he doles out at the Soho shop. His inspiration? Time spent behind the burners. 'I've worked in the kitchen for over 20 years and I've found little details are lost when something sits – like the texture and the flavour of chocolate mousse,' he says. 'I want to change that. Making it to order intensifies the chocolate and you can taste the difference because time is a main ingredient.'

That difference is evident in his fresh, hot-out-of-the-oven chocolate croissant: after getting dolloped with orange-blossom butter, the pastry arrives sprinkled with sea salt and topped with shards of chocolate that begin to melt across its flaky top. Ansel's made-to-order lemon tart is served immediately rather than getting chilled, so its emulsified custard filling is creamy and smooth instead of firm and bouncy. Ice-cream gets a makeover as well, showered with fresh Tahitian vanilla bean shavings. 'It's all about freshness, just like coffee,' Ansel says. 'People want a cup made to order, not a pot that's sitting around.'

Taking the place of a traditional kitchen, a series of service stations dole out different desserts. Order at the counter, then take a seat at one of the stainless-steel tables in the white-subway-tiled café space to watch the chefs at work. Savoury options include a breakfast sandwich that layers black squid ink brioche with poached egg, garlic mashed potato, mushroom béchamel sauce and shaved parmesan, but the spotlight remains on sweets. Dessert diehards can take part in six- to eight-course nighttime tastings ($65) at an intimate, ten-seat communal table upstairs called Unlimited Possibilities. Boozy bakeries may not be new – predecessors include fellow Villager Sweet Revenge (*see p120*) and spiked Brooklyn pie spot Butter & Scotch (818 Franklin Avenue, between Eastern Parkway & Union Street, Crown Heights, 1-347 350 8899, www.butterandscotch.com) – but Ansel's after-dark affair pairs cocktails with exclusive confections unavailable in the shop below. *137 Seventh Avenue South, between 10th & Charles Streets (1-212 219 5111, www.dominiqueanselkitchen.com).*

Dominique Ansel's lemon tart.

EXPLORE

The West Village is also a historic gay neighbourhood, although the current scene has mostly migrated north to Hell's Kitchen. The **Stonewall Inn** (*see p270*), on Christopher Street, was the site of the 1969 riots that marked the birth of the modern gay-rights movement. The street's pivotal role is commemorated in **Christopher Park**, which faces the bar, by George Segal's *Gay Liberation*, a piece comprising plaster sculptures of two same-sex couples.

Restaurants & Cafés

Buvette

42 Grove Street, between Bedford & Bleecker Streets (1-212 255 3590, www.ilovebuvette.com). Subway 1 to Christopher Street-Sheridan Square. **Open** 8am-2am Mon-Fri; 9am-2am Sat, Sun. **Main courses** $8-$16. **Map** p113 C2 ② **French**

Chef Jody Williams has filled every nook of tiny, Gallic-themed Buvette with old picnic baskets, teapots and silver trays, among other vintage ephemera. The food is just as thoughtfully curated – Williams's immaculate renditions of coq au vin, duck rillettes or intense, lacquered wedges of tarte tatin arrive on tiny plates, in petite jars or in miniature casseroles.

$ Corner Bistro

331 W 4th Street, at Jane Street (1-212 242 9502). Subway A, C, E to 14th Street; L to Eighth Avenue. **Open** 11.30am-4am Mon-Sat; noon-4am Sun. **Burgers** $8-$10. **No credit cards. Map** p113 B1 ② **American**

There's one compelling reason to come to this legendary pub: it serves what some New Yorkers say are the city's best burgers – plus the beer is just $3 for a mug of McSorley's. The patties are no-frills and served on a flimsy paper plate. To get one, you may have to queue for a good hour, especially on weekend nights; if the wait is too long for a table, try to slip into a space at the bar.

Other location 47-18 Vernon Boulevard, at 47th Road, Long Island City, Queens (1-718 606 6500).

▶ *For other top-ranking burgers, see Minetta Tavern (see p114) and Shake Shack (p173).*

EN Japanese Brasserie

435 Hudson Street, at Leroy Street (1-212 647 9196, www.enjb.com). Subway 1 to Houston Street. **Open** noon-2.30pm, 5.30-10.30pm Mon-Thur; noon-2.30pm, 5.30-11.30pm Fri; 11am-2.30pm, 5.30-11.30pm Sat; 11am-2.30pm, 5.30-10.30pm Sun. **Main courses** $18-$34. **Map** p113 B3 ② **Japanese**

The owners of this popular spot aim to evoke a sense of Japanese living in the multi-level space. On the ground floor are tatami-style rooms; on the mezzanine are recreations of a living room, dining room and library of a Japanese home from the Meiji era. But the spacious main dining room is where the action is. Highlights of chef Abe Hiroki's menu

include freshly made scooped tofu served with *wari-joyu* sauce (a mix of soy sauce and *dashi*, a fish broth); miso-marinated, broiled Alaskan black cod; and Berkshire pork belly braised in sansho miso. Try the Japanese whisky, saké and shochu flights.

Fedora

239 W 4th Street, between Charles & W 10th Streets (1-646 449 9336, www.fedoranyc.com). Subway A, B, C, D, E, F, M to W 4th Street; 1 to Christopher Street-Sheridan Square. **Open** 5.30pm-2am Mon, Thur-Sat; 5.30pm-midnight Tue, Wed. **Main courses** $24-$30. **Map** p113 B2 ② **Eclectic**

This French-Canadian knockout is part of restaurateur Gabriel Stulman's West Village mini-empire (his other eateries in the 'hood are Joseph Leonard, Jeffrey's Grocery, Italian spot Perla and Bar Sardine; *see p121*). Chef Mehdi Brunet-Benkritly produces some of the most exciting toe-to-tongue cooking in town, plying epicurean hipsters with Quebecois party food that's eccentric, excessive and fun – crisp pig's head with flageolet beans and ranch dressing, for example, or maple-smoked salmon with almonds and curry cream.

★ Kesté Pizza & Vino

271 Bleecker Street, between Cornelia & Jones Streets (1-212 243 1500, www.kestepizzeria.com). Subway 1 to Christopher Street-Sheridan Square. **Open** noon-3.30pm, 5-11pm Mon-Thur; noon-11.30pm Fri, Sat; noon-10.30pm Sun. **Pizzas** $13-$26. **Map** p113 C2 ② **Pizza**

If anyone can claim to be an expert on Neapolitan pizza, it's Kesté's Roberto Caporuscio: as president of the US branch of the Associazione Pizzaiuoli Napoletani, he's the top dog for the training and certification of *pizzaioli*. At his intimate, 46-seat space, it's all about the crust – blistered, salty and elastic, it could easily be eaten plain. Add ace toppings such as sweet-tart San Marzano tomato sauce, milky mozzarella and fresh basil, and you have one of New York's finest pies.

▶ *Roberto Caporuscio also had a hand in superior Theater District pizza place, Don Antonio by Starita (see p153).*

Pearl Oyster Bar

18 Cornelia Street, between Bleecker & W 4th Streets (1-212 691 8211, www.pearloysterbar. com). Subway A, B, C, D, E, F, M to W 4th Street. **Open** noon-2.30pm, 6-11pm Mon-Fri; 6-11pm Sat. **Main courses** $23-$36. **Map** p113 C2 ② **Seafood**

There's a good reason this convivial, no-reservations, New England-style fish joint always has a queue – the food is outstanding. Signature dishes include the lobster roll (sweet, lemon-scented meat laced with mayonnaise on a butter-enriched bun) and a contemporary take on bouillabaisse: a briny lobster broth packed with mussels, cod, scallops and clams, topped with an aïoli-smothered croûton.

EXPLORE

Happiest Hour. See p122.

★ RedFarm

529 Hudson Street, between Charles & W 10th Streets (1-212 792 9700, www.redfarmnyc.com). Subway 1 to Christopher Street-Sheridan Square. **Open** 5-11.45pm Mon-Fri; 11am-2.30pm, 5-11.45pm Sat; 11am-2.30pm, 5-11pm Sun. **Main courses** $17-$32. **Map** p113 B2 ㉖ **Chinese**

The high-end ingredients and whimsical plating at Ed Schoenfeld's interpretive Chinese restaurant have helped to pack the dining room since opening night. Chef Joe Ng is known for his dim sum artistry, including Katz's pastrami-stuffed egg rolls and shrimp dumplings decorated with 'eyes' and pursued on the plate by a sweet-potato Pac-Man. **Other location** 2170 Broadway, between 76th & 77th Streets, Upper West Side (1-212 724 9700).

Rosemary's

18 Greenwich Avenue, at 10th Street (1-212 647 1818, www.rosemarysnyc.com). Subway A, B, C, D, E, F, M to W 4th Street. **Open** 8am-4.30pm, 5pm-midnight Mon-Fri; 10am-4pm, 5pm-midnight Sat, Sun. **Main courses** $18-$32. **Map** p113 C1 ㉗ **Italian**

While gastronomy isn't the primary focus in most of the pheromone factories clustered near this stretch of Seventh Avenue, this rustic, farmhouse-vibe celebrity magnet is an exception. Chef Wade Moises, who worked for Mario Batali at Babbo and Lupa, turns out superb pasta and showstopping platters for two that in fact serve three or four. The menu changes seasonally, but house-made *cavatelli* or *orchiette* with broccoli rabe act as a mellow foil for the

chef's *secondi* course, which may include a porcini-rubbed strip steak or smoked lamb.

Spotted Pig

314 W 11th Street, at Greenwich Street (1-212 620 0393, www.thespottedpig.com). Subway A, C, E to 14th Street; L to Eighth Avenue. **Open** noon-5pm, 5.30pm-2am Mon-Fri; 11am-5pm, 5.30pm-2am Sat, Sun. **Main courses** $21-$38. **Map** p113 B2 ㉘ **Eclectic**

With a creaky interior that recalls an ancient pub, this Anglo-Italian hybrid from Ken Friedman and James Beard Award-winning chef April Bloomfield is still hopping more than a decade after opening. The gastropub doesn't take reservations and a wait can always be expected. The burger is a must-order: a secret blend of ground beef grilled rare covered with gobs of pungent roquefort and accompanied by a tower of shoestring fries tossed with rosemary. Bloomfield's predilection for offcuts, in dishes like the crispy pig's ear salad, helped usher in the city's pork-and-offal era.

$ Sweet Revenge

62 Carmine Street, between Bedford Street & Seventh Avenue (1-212 242 2240, www.sweet revengenyc.com). Subway A, B, C, D, E, F, M to W 4th Street; 1 to Christopher Street-Sheridan Square. **Open** 7am-11pm Mon-Thur; 7am-12.30am Fri; 10.30am-12.30am Sat; 10.30am-10pm Sun. **Cupcakes** $4-$5. **Map** p113 C3 ㉙ **Café**

Baker Marlo Scott steamrollered over the cupcake's innocent charms: at her café/bar, she pairs her

confections with wine or beer; where there were pastel swirls of frosting, there are now anarchic spikes of peanut butter, cream cheese and milk-chocolate icing. In the process, she saved the ubiquitous treat from becoming a cloying cliché. Gourmet sandwiches and other plates cater to non-sweet-tooths.

★ Via Carota
51 Grove Street, between Bleecker Street & Seventh Avenue South (no phone, www.viacarota.com). Subway 1 to Christopher St-Sheridan Square. **Open** 8am-midnight Mon-Wed; 8am-1am Thur, Fri; 9am-1am Sat; 9am-midnight Sun. **Main courses** $17-$25. **Map** p113 C2 ③⓪ **Italian**

The soulful Italian plates served at this glass-fronted *gastroteca*, the first joint effort from chef power couple Jody Williams and Rita Sodi, prove that simple food can be anything but basic. Pastas are satisfying but safe – what really stands out is the *verdure*. Fuss-free provincial stunners include *barbabietola*, a toss of tender beets and pickled apples flecked with fragrant thyme and tangy pebbles of goat's-milk feta. You can make an excellent meal here on vegetable dishes alone, but then you'd miss out on the house *svizzerina*, a bunless, hand-chopped round of New York strip steak that arrives flash-seared and nearly naked, save a few husk-on garlic cloves and a salty, rosemary-licked pool of fat. The chefs operate with an unflappable disregard for 'cool' that nearly borders on subversive – the knickknacky room is garnished with more bowls of fruit than a Nancy Meyers movie kitchen.

Bars

Bar Sardine
183 W 10th Street, at W 4th Street (1-646 360 3705, www.barsardinenyc.com). Subway A, B, C, D, E, F, M to W 4th Street; 1 to Christopher Street-Sheridan Square. **Open** noon-midnight Mon-Wed, Sun; noon-2am Thur-Sat. **Map** p113 C2 ③①

After shuttering for two weeks in summer 2014, Chez Sardine traded in its Asian influences for a more playful snack menu and a heavier concentration on cocktails. Chef Mehdi Brunet-Benkritly (of Fedora; *see p119*) remains in the kitchen to dispatch elevated bar bites like black-garlic devilled eggs, herbed french fries with maple-mustard aioli and cod fritters with lemon mayo, but the mid-20th-century space now has a larger bar, where you can order such creative tipples as a Black Pepper Grasshopper made with mint soft-serve ice-cream, cocoa and cream liqueurs.

Blind Tiger Ale House
281 Bleecker Street, at Jones Street (1-212 462 4682, www.blindtigeralehouse.com). Subway A, B, C, D, E, F, M to W 4th Street; 1 to Christopher Street-Sheridan Square. **Open** 11.30am-4am daily. **Map** p113 C2 ③②

Brew geeks descend on this hops heaven for boutique ales and more than two dozen daily rotating, hard-to-find drafts (like Southern Tier Krampus and Singlecut Half-Stack). The clubby room features windows that open on to the street. Late afternoons and early evenings are ideal for serious sippers enjoying plates of charcuterie and cheese, while the after-dark set veers dangerously close to Phi Kappa territory.

Employees Only
510 Hudson Street, between Christopher & W 10th Streets (1-212 242 3021, www.employeesonlynyc.com). Subway 1 to Christopher Street-Sheridan Square. **Open** 6pm-4am daily. **Map** p113 B2 ③③

This Prohibition-themed bar cultivates an exclusive vibe, but there's no cover and no hassle at the door. Pass by the palm reader in the window (it's a front) and you'll find an amber-lit art deco interior where formality continues to flourish: servers wear custom-designed frocks and bartenders are in waitstaff whites. But the real stunners are cocktails such as the West Side, a lethal mix of lemon vodka, lemon juice, fresh mint and club soda.

Gottino
52 Greenwich Avenue, between Charles & Perry Streets (1-212 633 2590, www.gottinony.com). Subway 1 to Christopher Street-Sheridan Square. **Open** 8am-2am Mon-Fri; 10am-2am Sat, Sun. **Map** p113 C1 ③④

Jockey for a seat at this narrow enoteca – there are just five tables, plus a long marble bar. It's worth the crush. The all-Italian wine list is complemented by a menu of choice nibbles, divided into salumi and cheese on one side, and delectable prepared bites on the other.

EXPLORE

Happiest Hour

121 W 10th Street, at Greenwich Avenue (1-212 243 2827, www.thehappiesthournyc. com). Subway 1 to Christopher Street-Sheridan Square. **Open** 5pm-4am daily. **Map** p113 C1 ㉟
A 1960s pop soundtrack sets the mood at this retro-kitted tiki lounge crammed with midcentury curios. Renowned barman Jim Kearns (Pegu Club, the NoMad) mans the horseshoe-shaped bar, offering a clever list of cocktails that can be customised with a choice of spirits. The breezy vibe attracts an eclectic young crowd: off-hours suits sipping scotch on the rocks, bubbly girl groups clinking wine glasses, polo-clad bros glugging Miller High Life and couples getting cosy in the half-moon booths. *Photo p120.*

White Horse Tavern

567 Hudson Street, at 11th Street (1-212 989 3956). Subway 1 to Christopher Street-Sheridan Square. **Open** 11am-2am Mon-Thur, Sun; 11am-4am Fri, Sat. **No credit cards. Map** p113 B2 ㊱
Popular lore tells us that in 1953, Dylan Thomas knocked back 18 straight whiskeys here before expiring in his Chelsea Hotel residence – a portrait of him now hangs in the middle room, above his favourite table in the corner. Now the old-school bar and its adjacent outdoor patio play host to a yuppie crowd and clutches of tourists, drawn by the outdoor seating, a fine selection of beers – and the legend.

Shops & Services

Aedes de Venustas

9 Christopher Street, between Greenwich Avenue & Waverly Place (1-212 206 8674, www.aedes. com). Subway A, B, C, D, F, M to W 4th Street; 1 to Christopher Street-Sheridan Square. **Open** noon-8pm Mon-Sat; 1-7pm Sun. **Map** p113 C2 ㊲
Health & beauty
Decked out like a 19th-century boudoir, this perfume collector's palace devotes itself to ultra-sophisticated fragrances and high-end skincare lines, such as Diptyque, Santa Maria Novella and its own glamorously packaged range of fragrances, candles and room sprays. Hard-to-find scents, such as Serge Lutens perfumes, line the walls.

Flight 001

96 Greenwich Avenue, between Jane & W 12th Streets (1-212 989 0001, www.flight001.com). Subway A, C, E to 14th Street; L to Eighth Avenue. **Open** 11am-8pm Mon-Sat; noon-6pm Sun. **Map** p113 B1 ㊳ **Travel**
As well as a tasteful selection of luggage by the likes of Lipault, Rimowa and Hideo, this one-stop shop carries everything for the chic jet-setter. The range of fun and functional travel products includes novelty patterned eye masks, emergency totes that squash down to tennis ball size, expanding hand-towel tablets and battery backups for your gadgets.

Other location 132 Smith Street, between Bergen & Dean Streets, Boerum Hill, Brooklyn (1-718 243 0001).

Whittemore House

45 Grove Street, at Bleecker Street (1-212 242 8880, www.whittemorehousesalon.com). Subway 1 to Christopher Street-Sheridan Square. **Open** 10am-8pm Tue; noon-8pm Wed-Thur; 10am-9pm Fri; 10am-6pm Sat. **Map** p113 B2 ㊴
Health & beauty
Victoria Hunter and Larry Raspanti, who each spent more than 15 years at Bumble & Bumble, opened their own hair salon in an 1830s mansion. The decor features faux-decayed stencilled walls and boudoir chairs. Cuts (from $110) and natural-looking colour come courtesy of some of New York's best stylists.

MEATPACKING DISTRICT

Subway A, C, E to 14th Street; L to Eighth Avenue.

The north-west corner of the West Village has been known as the **Meatpacking District** since the area was dominated by the wholesale meat industry in the early 20th century. As business waned, gay fetish clubs took root in derelict buildings and, until the 1990s, the area was a haunt for transsexual prostitutes. In more recent years, however, hip eateries and designer boutiques have moved in. Frequent mentions on *Sex and the City*, along with the arrival of

High Line.

EXPLORE

swanky hotel **Gansevoort Meatpacking NYC** (*see p362*) in the noughties, cemented the area's reputation as a mainstream consumer playground. Nightclubs, including **Cielo** (*see p274*) and **Le Bain** (*see p273*), continue to draw after-dark pleasure seekers.

The 2009 opening of freight-track-turned-park the **High Line** has brought even bigger crowds to the area and, as of spring 2015, the attractions have been boosted by the new **Whitney Museum of American Art**. Slick style hotel the **Standard** (*see p362*) straddles the elevated park at West 13th Street, and its Biergarten, nestled beneath it, is a great spot for a pint.

Sights & Museums

★ High Line
1-212 500 6035, www.thehighline.org. **Open** usually 7am-10pm daily (hours vary seasonally; see website for updates). **Map** p113 A1 ⓭
Running from Gansevoort Street in the Meatpacking District through Chelsea's gallery district to 34th Street, this slender, sinuous green strip – formerly an elevated freight train track – has been designed by landscape architects James Corner Field Operations and architects Diller Scofidio + Renfro. *See also p256 and p352.*

★ Whitney Museum of American Art
99 Gansevoort Street, between Washington & West Streets (1-212 570 3600, www.whitney.org). Subway A, C, E to 14th St; L to Eighth Avenue.

Open Call or see website. **Admission** $22; $18 reductions; free under-10s. Pay what you wish 7-10pm Fri. **Map** p113 A1 ⓭
See p125 **An Art Hub on the Hudson.**

Restaurants & Cafés

Santina
820 Washington Street, between Gansevoort & Little West 12th Streets (1-212 254 3000, www.santinanyc.com). Subway A, C, E to 14th Street; L to Eighth Avenue. **Open** 11.30am-2.30pm, 5.30pm-midnight Mon-Fri; 5.30pm-midnight Sat, Sun. **Main courses** $23-$28. **Map** p113 A1 ⓭ **Italian**
For their latest, and largest, eatery so far, Mario Carbone, Rich Torrisi and Jeff Zalaznick (Carbone, ZZ's Clam Bar) bring the flavours of the Italian coast to this Hudson-hugging locale. Named after Carbone's Sicilian grandmother, Santina sits under the High Line next to the Whitney Museum. The Renzo Piano-designed glass cube is decked out with with Murano-glass chandeliers and seascape paintings crafted from ceramic plates. Fish and vegetables feature prominently on the menu, and while it's refreshing to see the team lighten up, we expect more heft. The house speciality, the surf-and-turf Chitarra Santina, boasts lovely egg-yolk strands tangled around plump mussels and merguez sausage, but the spare tossing of olive oil and garlic is so minimal, it barely registers. At the time of writing, the new restaurant was planning to open for breakfast and weekend brunch; call or see website for hours. *Photo p124.*

EXPLORE

Santina. *See p123.*

Shops & Services

★ Doyle & Doyle
412 W 13th Street, between Ninth Avenue & Washington Street (1-212 677 9991, www. doyledoyle.com). Subway A, C, E to 14th Street; L to Eighth Avenue. **Open** noon-7pm Mon-Wed, Fri-Sun; noon-8pm Thur. **Map** p113 A1 ㊽
Accessories
Whether your taste is art deco or nouveau, Victorian or Edwardian, Elizabeth and Pamela Doyle are bound to have that one-of-a-kind piece you're looking for, including engagement and eternity rings. The gemologist sisters, who specialise in vintage and antique jewellery, have also launched their own collection of new heirlooms.

Jeffrey New York
449 W 14th Street, between Ninth & Tenth Avenues (1-212 206 1272, www.jeffreynewyork.com). Subway A, C, E to 14th Street; L to Eighth Avenue. **Open** 10am-8pm Mon-Wed, Fri; 10am-9pm Thur; 10am-7pm Sat; 12.30-6pm Sun. **Map** p113 A1 ㊹ **Fashion**
Jeffrey Kalinsky, a former Barneys shoe buyer, was a Meatpacking District pioneer when he opened his namesake store in 1999. Designer clothing abounds here – by Saint Laurent, Givenchy and Christopher Kane, among others. The centrepiece is the shoe salon, which features the work of Manolo Blahnik, Christian Louboutin and Gianvito Rossi, as well as newer names.

Owen
809 Washington Street, between Gansevoort & Horatio Streets (1-212 524 9770, www.owennyc. com). Subway A, C, E to 14th Street; L to Eighth Avenue. **Open** 11am-7pm Mon-Sat; noon-6pm Sun. **Map** p113 B1 ㊺ **Fashion**
FIT grad Phillip Salem assembles a well-honed selection of emerging and established brands at his upscale boutique. Contemporary threads for both genders are displayed atop quartz slab tables and hung on blackened steel bars. Womenswear includes sophisticated pieces from NYC labels Cushnie et Ochs, Jonathan Simkhai, SUNO and Tanya Taylor, and cool, urban menswear comes courtesy of 3.1 Phillip Lim, Tim Coppens and Acne.

★ Rag & Bone General Store
425 W 13th Street, at Washington Street (1-212 249 3331, www.rag-bone.com). Subway A, C, E to 14th Street. **Open** 11am-8pm Mon-Sat; noon-7pm Sun. **Map** p113 A1 ㊻ **Fashion**
The downtown outpost of this enduringly hip brand, which began as a denim line in 2002, was once a meat factory, and it retains much of that industrial vibe with unfinished concrete floors, brick walls and an original Dave's Quality Veal sign. Sip a latte from the in-store Jack's Stir Brew Coffee before or after browsing the impeccably cut jeans, classic T-shirts, luxurious knitwear and well-tailored jackets for both sexes. **Other locations** throughout the city.

AN ART HUB ON THE HUDSON

The Whitney Museum moves into new downtown digs.

Once the gritty domain of wholesale butchers and gay nightspots with evocative names such as the Mineshaft and the Ramrod, the Meatpacking District became a fashionable hub in the 1990s and early noughties before giving way to more mainstream popularity. What the neighbourhood has lacked, however, is culture – though since 2009, the High Line has provided a direct pedestrian link to Chelsea's galleries (and plenty of temporary public art installations along its length). But, as of spring 2015, it has an illustrious institution: the **Whitney Museum of American Art** (see p123), in its striking new digs at the southern foot of the park.

Founded by sculptor and art patron Gertrude Vanderbilt Whitney in 1931, the museum holds more than 20,000 pieces by around 3,000 artists, including Willem de Kooning, Edward Hopper, Jasper Johns, Georgia O'Keeffe and Claes Oldenburg. Yet, until now, its reputation has rested primarily on its temporary shows – particularly the prestigious and controversial Whitney Biennial, held in even-numbered years.

The nine-storey, steel-and-glass building, designed by Renzo Piano, is roughly three times the size of the old Upper East Side premises. For the first time, there will be space for a comprehensive display of the collection, including such iconic works as Alexander Calder's *Circus* and Jasper Johns's *Three Flags*.

The dramatic, asymmetrical structure features a series of outdoor terraces that rise like steps above the High Line. The art isn't restricted to the museum's interior. On the fifth, sixth and seventh floors you can take in

alfresco sculptures and installations while admiring views of the Hudson River and city landmarks including the Empire State Building and 1 World Trade Center. An 8,500-square-foot public plaza beneath the High Line leads to the cantilevered glass entrance. Inside, you'll find a ground-floor restaurant helmed by dining guru Danny Meyer, a gift shop and a free-admission lobby gallery. Four elevators, commissioned from Richard Artschwager before his death in 2013, have a dual function as passenger lifts and an art installation, entitled *Six in Four*. Using six themes that have featured in the artist's work since the 1970s – door, window, table, basket, mirror and rug – they transport visitors not only to the upper floors, but also to an alternative reality.

EXPLORE

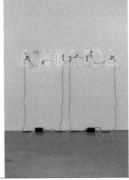

Chelsea

Formerly a working-class Irish and Hispanic neighbourhood, the corridor between 14th and 29th Streets west of Sixth Avenue emerged as the nexus of New York's queer life in the 1990s. Due to rising housing costs and the protean nature of the city's cultural landscape, it's since been eclipsed by Hell's Kitchen to the north (just as Chelsea overtook the West Village), but you'll still find bars, restaurants and shops catering to the once-ubiquitous 'Chelsea boys'. The cityscape shifts from leafy side streets lined with pristine 19th-century brownstones to an array of striking industrial and contemporary architecture on the far west side. In recent years, the local buzz has shifted to the previously neglected Hudson-hugging strip that has evolved into the city's main gallery district. But it's the transformation of a disused elevated freight train track snaking through the area into one of the city's most popular parks that's really drawing crowds to this patch.

Mantiques Modern.

Don't Miss

1 Chelsea gallery district Around 200 art spaces in just ten blocks (p128).

2 Museum at FIT A must for fashion-conscious folk – and it's free (p128).

3 Empire Diner A reinvigorated Chelsea classic (p131).

4 Story The concept store, reinvented (p132).

5 Mantiques Modern An atmospheric trove of unique objects (p132).

CHELSEA

Subway A, C, E, 1, 2, 3 to 14th Street;
C, E, 1 to 23rd Street; L to Eighth Avenue;
1 to 18th Street or 28th Street.

In the 1990s, many of New York's contemporary galleries left Soho for the once-desolate western edge of Chelsea (*see p130* **Gallery-Hopping Guide**). Today, internationally recognised spaces such as **Mary Boone Gallery**, **Gagosian Gallery** and **Gladstone Gallery**, as well as numerous less exalted names, attract swarms of art aficionados. The High Line has brought even more gallery-goers to the area as it provides a verdant pathway from the boutique- and restaurant-rich Meatpacking District to the art enclave. Traversing the elevated promenade, you'll pass through the old loading dock of the former Nabisco factory, where the first Oreo cookie was made in 1912. This conglomeration of 18 structures, built between the 1890s and the 1930s, now houses **Chelsea Market** (75 Ninth Avenue, between 15th & 16th Streets, www.chelseamarket.com). The ground-floor food arcade offers artisanal bread, wine, baked goods and freshly made ice-cream, among other treats. The complex houses bars, restaurants and the **Artists & Fleas** designer/vintage/craft market.

Also among the area's notable industrial architecture is the **Starrett-Lehigh Building** (601 W 26th Street, at Eleventh Avenue). The stunning 1929 structure was left in disrepair until the dot-com boom of the late 1990s, when media companies, photographers and designers snatched up its loft-like spaces.

While some of the Hudson River piers, which were once terminals for the world's grand ocean liners, remain in a state of ruin, the four that lie between 17th and 23rd Streets have been transformed into mega sports centre **Chelsea Piers**.

To get a glimpse of how Chelsea looked back when it was first developed in the 1880s, stroll along **Cushman Row** (406-418 W 20th Street,

between Ninth & Tenth Avenues) in the Chelsea Historic District. Just to the north is the block-long **General Theological Seminary of the Episcopal Church** (440 W 21st Street, between Ninth & Tenth Avenues). The seminary's land was part of the estate known as Chelsea, owned by poet Clement Clarke Moore, author of *A Visit from St Nicholas* (more commonly known as *'Twas the Night Before Christmas*), and the guest wing has been converted into the **High Line Hotel** (*see p363*).

A hostelry with a more notorious history is nearby. The **Chelsea Hotel** on West 23rd Street has been a magnet for creative types since it first opened in 1884; Mark Twain was an early guest. The list of those who have stayed here reads like an international *Who's Who* of the artistic elite: Sarah Bernhardt (who slept in a coffin), William Burroughs (who wrote *Naked Lunch* here), Dylan Thomas, Janis Joplin and Jimi Hendrix, to name a few. In the 1960s, it was the stomping ground of Andy Warhol's coterie of superstars, and the location of his 1966 film *The Chelsea Girls*. In the midst of a makeover by a boutique-hotel developer, the Chelsea (www.chelseahotels.com) is expected to reopen in 2016.

The weekend **flea markets** in the area have shrunk in recent years (casualties of development), but you'll still find one on West 25th Street, between Sixth Avenue and Broadway (www.annexmarkets.com). Not far from here, the Fashion Institute of Technology, on 27th Street, between Seventh and Eighth Avenues, counts Calvin Klein, Nanette Lepore and Michael Kors among its alumni. The school's **Museum at FIT** mounts free exhibitions.

Sights & Museums

FREE Museum at FIT

Building E, Seventh Avenue, at 27th Street
(1-212 217 4558, www.fitnyc.edu/museum).
Subway 1 to 28th Street. **Open** noon-8pm
Tue-Fri; 10am-5pm Sat. **Admission** free.
Map p129 D1 ❶

The Fashion Institute of Technology owns one of the largest and most impressive clothing collections in the world, with some 50,000 garments and accessories dating from the 18th century to the present. Under the directorship of fashion historian Dr Valerie Steele, the museum showcases a rotating selection from the permanent collection, as well as a programme of temporary exhibitions focusing on individual designers or spotlighting fashion from cultural angles.

Rubin Museum of Art

150 W 17th Street, at Seventh Avenue (1-212
620 5000, www.rmanyc.org). Subway A, C,
E to 14th Street; L to Eighth Avenue; 1 to 18th
Street. **Open** 11am-5pm Mon, Thur; 11am-9pm
Wed; 11am-10pm Fri; 11am-6pm Sat, Sun.

IN THE KNOW STREET ART

While in Chelsea's gallery district, don't overlook the outdoor art installation *7000 Oaks* by German artist Joseph Beuys: 18 pairings of basalt stones and trees on W 22nd Street, between Tenth and Eleventh Avenues. Maintained by Dia Art Foundation (www.diaart.org), the piece is a spin-off of a five-year international effort, begun in 1982 at Germany's Documenta 7 exhibition, to enact social and environmental change by planting 7,000 trees.

Admission $15; $10 reductions; free under-13s.
Free 6-10pm Fri. **Map** p129 D3 ❷
Dedicated to the art of the Himalayan region, the
Rubin is a very stylish museum – a fact that falls
into place when you learn that the six-storey space
was once occupied by fashion store Barneys. The
ground-floor Indian- and Tibetan-inflected café used
to be the accessories department, and retail lives on
in the colourful gift shop. In the galleries, rich-toned
walls are classy foils for the serene statuary and
intricate, multicoloured textiles. Annually rotating
selections from the permanent collection of more
than 2,500 pieces from the second century to the
present day are highlighted in 'Gateway to Himalayan
Art'. A recreation of a Tibetan Buddhist shrine
room lets visitors see sculptures, paintings, textiles,
furnishings and ritual objects in context. The Rubin's
temporary shows often extend beyond the museum's
primary focus to contemporary art and photography.

Restaurants & Cafés

Co
*230 Ninth Avenue, at 24th Street (1-212 243 1105,
www.co-pane.com). Subway C, E to 23rd Street.*
Open 5-11pm Mon; 11.30am-11pm Tue-Fri;
11am-11pm Sat; 11am-10pm Sun. **Pizzas** $9-$20.
Map p129 C2 ❸ **Pizza**

This unassuming pizzeria was the restaurant
debut of Jim Lahey, whose Sullivan Street Bakery
supplies bread to many top restaurants. Lahey's
crust is so good, in fact, it doesn't need any toppings
(try the Pizza Bianca, sprinkled with sea salt and
olive oil). The most compelling individual-sized
pies come from non-traditional sources, such as
the ham and cheese, essentially a croque-monsieur
in pizza form.

★ Cookshop
*156 Tenth Avenue, at 20th Street (1-212 924
4440, www.cookshopny.com). Subway C, E to
23rd Street.* **Open** 8-11am, 11.30am-4pm, 5.30-
11.30pm Mon-Fri; 10.30am-4pm, 5.30-11.30pm
Sat, Sun. **Main courses** $18-$38. **Map** p129 B2 ❹
American creative

Chef Marc Meyer and his wife Vicki Freeman want
their restaurant to be a platform for sustainable
ingredients from independent farmers. True to
this mission, the ingredients are consistently top-
notch, and the menu changes daily. While organic
ingredients alone don't guarantee a great meal,
Meyer knows how to let the flavours speak for
themselves, and Cookshop scores points for getting
the house-made ice-cream to taste as good as Ben &
Jerry's. The buzzing art world favourite is always
packed for its excellent weekend brunch.

EXPLORE

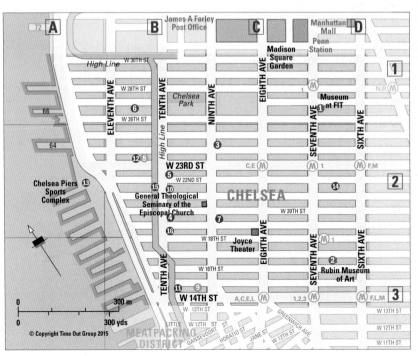

GALLERY-HOPPING GUIDE

Hit these essential stops in the city's premier contemporary art hub.

From West 19th Street to West 29th Street, between Tenth and Eleventh Avenues, converted industrial spaces are crammed with around 200 art spaces. Here, you'll find group shows by up-and-comers, blockbuster exhibitions from big names and a slew of provocative work. Note that galleries are generally closed or operate on an appointment-only basis on Mondays, and are open 10am-6pm Tuesday to Saturday. In summer, however, many keep different hours and close at weekends. Some may shut up shop for two weeks or a month at a stretch in July or August, so call before visiting. Below are our highlights.

Cheim & Read *547 W 25th Street, between Tenth & Eleventh Avenues (1-212 242 7727, www.cheimread.com).*
The international artists here include such superstars as Diane Arbus and Jenny Holzer.

David Zwirner *519, 525 & 533 W 19th Street, between Tenth & Eleventh Avenues (1-212 727 2070, www.davidzwirner.com).*
Zwirner mixes museum-quality shows of historical figures with a head-turning array of contemporary artists.

Gagosian Gallery *555 W 24th Street, between Tenth & Eleventh Avenues (1-212 741 1111, www.gagosian.com).*
Larry Gagosian's mammoth (20,000sq ft) contribution to 24th Street's galleries opened in 1999.

Gladstone Gallery *515 W 24th Street, between Tenth & Eleventh Avenues (1-212 206 9300, www.gladstonegallery.com).*
Gladstone is strictly blue-chip, with an emphasis on daring conceptual art.

Luhring Augustine *531 W 24th Street, between Tenth & Eleventh Avenues (1-212 206 9100, www.luhringaugustine.com).*
An impressive index of artists includes Rachel Whiteread, Christopher Wool and Pipilotti Rist.

Mary Boone Gallery *541 W 24th Street, between Tenth & Eleventh Avenues (1-212 752 2929, www.maryboonegallery.com).*
Boone made her name in the 1980s, representing Julian Schnabel and Jean-Michel Basquiat, among others, and continues to produce hit shows featuring young artists.

Matthew Marks Gallery *523 W 24th Street, between Tenth & Eleventh Avenues (1-212 243 0200, www.matthewmarks.com).*
Opened in 1991, the Matthew Marks gallery was a driving force behind Chelsea's transformation into an art destination. There's a second location at 522 W 22nd Street.

Tanya Bonakdar Gallery *521 W 21st Street, between Tenth & Eleventh Avenues (1-212 414 4144, www.tanyabonakdargallery.com).*
This elegant space reps such powerhouse names as *New York City Waterfalls* maestro Olafur Eliasson.

Yossi Milo *245 Tenth Avenue, between West 24th & West 25th Streets (1-212 414 0370, www.yossimilo.com).*
Yossi Milo's impressive roster of camera talent encompasses emerging artists as well as more established photographers.

Gladstone Gallery.

EXPLORE

Empire Diner

210 Tenth Avenue, at 22nd Street (1-212 596 7523, www.empire-diner.com). Subway C, E to 23rd Street. **Open** 7.30am-4.30pm, 5-11pm Mon-Wed; 7.30am-4.30pm, 5pm-midnight Thur, Fri; 11am-4pm, 5pm-midnight Sat; 11am-4pm, 5-10pm Sun. **Main courses** $17-$26. **Map** p129 B2 **❺**
American

Despite attaining celebrity-chef status through appearances on *Chopped* and *Iron Chef*, Amanda Freitag (formerly of the Harrison) had one space left to fill on her résumé – running her own restaurant. In 2013, the Chelsea resident took over this shuttered local fixture. Freitag preserved the classic looks of the 1940s Fodero dining car – immortalised by Woody Allen in the 1979 movie *Manhattan* – but gave the menu a contemporary, locavore revamp. The seasonally changing fare includes the likes of smoked whitefish and radish crêpes and Greek salad studded with charred octopus, and the ice-cream for the banana splits is churned in house.

Heath

McKittrick Hotel, 530 W 27th Street, between Tenth & Eleventh Avenues (1-212 564 1662, www.theheathnyc.com). Subway 1 to 28th Street. **Open** 6-11pm Wed-Sat; 11.30am-3.30pm Sun. **Main courses** $23-$38. **Map** p129 B1 **❻**
American/British

Punchdrunk – the London troupe behind the hit *Macbeth*-inspired production *Sleep No More* (*see p315*) – opened this 150-seat restaurant underneath its seasonal rooftop bar, Gallow Green. Chef RL King crafts a menu of modern American and British fare, such as beef and ale pie and roast chicken with gruyère grits. Cocktails like the gin-based King's Cross and the Aberdonian Sour (Scotch, orgeat syrup, red wine float) nod to the company's UK roots.

Tipsy Parson

156 Ninth Avenue, between 19th & 20th Streets (1-212 620 4545, www.tipsyparson.com). Subway C, E to 23rd Street. **Open** 11.30am-11pm Mon-Thur; 11.30am-midnight Fri; 10am-3.30pm, 5.30pm-midnight Sat; 10am-3.30pm, 5.30-10pm Sun. **Main courses** $24-$40. **Map** p129 C2 **❼**
American regional

Julie Wallach's restaurant channels the experience of dining at home – if your home happens to be a charming country cottage, that is. The nostalgic

---

N THE KNOW VINO AL FRESCO

From around late April until late October, food vendors set up on the High Line, and you can stop for a tipple at seasonal open-air café, the Porch, at 15th Street, which serves local wine and beer from cult vino spot Terroir (www.wineisterroir.com).

Empire Diner.

food is grounded firmly in the Deep South. A tasty down-home twist on a burger comes topped with a potato bun (pimento cheese and/or bacon optional). Macaroni and cheese features a complex medley of cheddar, gruyère and grana padano, with crumbled corn bread and fresh *cavatelli*. For dessert, try the namesake Tipsy Parson – a boozy trifle.

Bars

Half King

505 W 23rd Street, between Tenth & Eleventh Avenues (1-212 462 4300, www.thehalfking.com). Subway C, E to 23rd Street. **Open** 11am-4am Mon-Fri; 9am-4am Sat, Sun. **Map** p129 B2 **❽**

Don't let their blasé appearance fool you – the creative types gathered at the Half King's yellow pine bar are probably as excited as you are to catch a glimpse of the part-owner, author Sebastian Junger. While you're waiting, order one of the 15 draught beers – including several local brews – or a seasonal cocktail.

Tippler

Chelsea Market, 425 W 15th Street, between Ninth & Tenth Avenues (1-212 206 0000, www.thetippler. com). Subway A, C, E to 14th Street; L to Eighth Avenue. **Open** 4pm-2am Mon-Thur, Sun; 4pm-4am Fri, Sat. **Map** p129 B3 ⑨

Even at its most packed, there's still a fair amount of room to manoeuvre in this expansive lounge, so you won't have too much trouble accessing the long marble bar. The menu includes draft and bottled beers, plus wines from around the world, but it would be remiss not to try at least one of the speciality cocktails, such as the Booty Collins (vodka, green tea, passionfruit, lemon juice and cayenne pepper).

Shops & Services

192 Books

192 Tenth Avenue, between 21st & 22nd Streets (1-212 255 4022, www.192books.com). Subway C, E to 23rd Street. **Open** 11am-7pm daily. **Map** p129 B2 ⑩ **Books & music**

In an era when many an indie bookshop has closed, 192, open since 2003, is proving that quirky boutique booksellers can make it after all. Owned by art dealer Paula Cooper and her husband, editor Jack Macrae, the store offers a strong selection of art books and literature, as well as tomes on history, current affairs, music, science and nature. The phenomenal reading series brings in top authors of the calibre of Anne Rice, Mark Strand and Colm Tóibín.

Artists & Fleas

88 Tenth Avenue, at 15th Street (1-917 488 0044, www.artistsandfleas.com). Subway A, C, E to 14th Street; L to Eighth Avenue. **Open** 10am-9pm Mon-Sat; 10am-8pm Sun. **Map** p129 B3 ⑪ **Accessories/ gifts & souvenirs**

New Yorkers love Artists & Fleas (it's one of the most searched-for stores on *Time Out New York*'s website) – and it's easy to see why: every weekend, a rotating selection of around 100 vendors, including local craftspeople, designers and artists, sets up shop in a Williamsburg warehouse. The Chelsea Market outpost is smaller, but it's oh so convenient and open seven days a week. The browsable mix includes everything from original T-shirts and handmade jewellery to home-decor items and vinyl. **Other location** 70 North 7th Street, between Kent & Wythe Avenues, Williamsburg, Brooklyn (1-917 488 4203).

Chamber

515 W 23rd Street, between Tenth & Eleventh Avenues (1-212 206 0236, www.chambernyc.com). Subway C, E to 23rd St. **Open** 10am-6pm Tue-Sat. **Map** p129 B2 ⑫ **Gifts & souvenirs/homewares** *See p133* **The Art of Shopping**.

Chelsea Piers

Piers 59-62, W 18th to 23rd Streets, at Twelfth Avenue (1-212 336 6666, www.chelseapiers.com). Subway C, E to 23rd Street. **Open** varies; call or check website for details. **Map** p129 A2 ⑬ **Sport**

Chelsea Piers is the most impressive all-in-one athletic facility in New York. Between the ice rink (Pier 61, 1-212 336 6100), the bowling alley (between Pier 60, 1-212 835 2695), the driving range (Pier 59, 1-212 336 6400) and scads of other choices, there's an activity for everyone. The Field House (between Piers 61 & 62, 1-212 336 6500) has a climbing wall, a gymnastics centre, batting cages and basketball courts. At the Sports Center Health Club (Pier 60, 1-212 336 6000), you'll find classes covering everything from boxing to triathlon training in the pool, as well as a gym with comprehensive weight deck and cardiovascular machines.

★ Mantiques Modern

146 W 22nd Street, between Sixth & Seventh Avenues (1-212 206 1494, www.mantiques modern.com). Subway 1 to 23rd Street. **Open** 10.30am-6.30pm Mon-Fri; 11am-7pm Sat, Sun. **Map** p129 D2 ⑭ **Homewares**

Walking into this two-level shop is like stumbling on the private collection of a mad professor. Specialising in industrial and modernist art, objects, furnishings and accessories from the 1880s to the 1980s, it's a fantastic repository of beautiful and bizarre items, from kinetic sculptures and early 20th-century wooden artists' mannequins to a Soviet World War II telescope. Pieces by famous designers like Hermès sit side by side with natural curiosities. Skulls (in metal or Lucite), crabs, animal horns and robots are recurring themes.

★ Printed Matter

195 Tenth Avenue, between 21st & 22nd Streets (1-212 925 0325, www.printedmatter.org). Subway C, E to 23rd Street. **Open** 11am-7pm Mon-Wed, Sat; 11am-8pm Thur, Fri. **Map** p129 B2 ⑮ **Books & music**

This non-profit organisation is devoted to artists' books – from David Shrigley's deceptively naïve illustrations to provocative photographic self-portraits by Matthias Herrmann. Works by little-known talents share shelf space with those by veterans such as Yoko Ono and Edward Ruscha.

★ Story

144 Tenth Avenue, at 19th Street (1-212 242 4853, www.thisisstory.com). Subway A, C, E to 14th Street; L to Eighth Avenue. **Open** 11am-7pm Mon-Wed, Fri-Sun; 11am-8pm Thur. **Map** p129 B2 ⑯ **Accessories/fashion/homewares** *See p133* **The Art of Shopping**.

THE ART OF SHOPPING
Innovative concept stores give new meaning to 'curated' stock.

Story.

EXPLORE

The western fringe of Chelsea has been a gallery hub since the 1990s, but recently shops have been moving in. In addition to arty bookstores **Printed Matter** (*see 132*) and **192 Books** (*see p132*) and a smattering of boutiques, a couple of retail concepts playing on the idea of curation have taken root on Tenth Avenue. Every four to six weeks, **Story** (*see p132*) shuts down and reopens with a totally new theme. Combining the editorial style of a magazine with splashy installations, the store collaborates with a different partner for each cycle, changing not only the products but the entire interior. Motifs have included 'Love Story', featuring chocolates and other tokens of affection, and 'Cool Story' spotlighting a new air-conditioner from Quirky, beach bags and other hot-weather gear. 'Your Story' focused on cult NYC brands and products favoured by YouTube personalities, from Vintage Twin reworked flannel shirts to sweets from Dylan's Candy Bar and BaubleBar jewellery. But whatever the theme, you're bound to find an appealing mix of goods, engaging displays and NYC-specific merch.

In contrast, **Chamber** (*see p132*), tucked under the High Line in Neil Denari's space-agey steel-and-glass HL23 building, feels more like a contemporary art gallery. Each year, a collection is compiled by a creative individual or company – Dutch design duo Studio Job for the first iteration, for example – and a rotating selection of objects is displayed during the run. Founder Juan Garcia Mosqueda was inspired by the idea of a 'cabinet of curiosities', so you might see vintage or found items alongside pricey, limited-edition art and design pieces by the likes of Tord Boontje, Tom Dixon and Stefan Sagmeister. But like Story's founder Rachel Shechtman, Mosqueda is interested in the narratives behind these objects, which make them so desirable to collectors. The details are all documented in a hardcover tome, available for purchase in the space.

Chamber.

Gramercy & Flatiron

Lying east of Chelsea, the Gramercy and Flatiron neighbourhoods contain some of the city's most distinctive architecture – including the famous wedge-shaped building that gave the Flatiron District its name – and several inviting green spaces. Unfortunately, you'll probably only get tantalising over-the-gate glimpses of pretty Gramercy Park, which remains the exclusive preserve of residents of the surrounding buildings. But in recent years, the attractions for visitors have multiplied in this part of town, with the arrival of new museums and shops, including the country's first Museum of Mathematics and Italian-food mecca Eataly. Some of the city's best new eateries, from contemporary taverns to decadent fine-dining rooms, have taken root here, cementing the area's reputation as a gastronomic hotspot.

EXPLORE

Madison Square Park

Don't Miss

1 Flatiron Building The lovely structure that gave the nabe its name (p136).

2 Madison Square Park A picturesque patch with an adventurous public-art programme (p136).

3 Cosme Market-fresh, modern Mexican small plates (p139).

4 Dear Irving Time-travelling tipples (p145).

5 ABC Carpet & Home You'll find far more than furnishings here (p142).

Union Square.

FLATIRON DISTRICT & UNION SQUARE

Subway F, M to 14th Street; L, N, Q, R, 4, 5, 6 to 14th Street-Union Square; L to Sixth Avenue; N, R, 6 to 23rd Street or 28th Street.

EXPLORE

Taking its name from the distinctive wedge-shaped **Flatiron Building**, this district extends from 14th to 29th Streets, between Sixth and Lexington Avenues. (However, as with many NYC neighbourhoods, the borders are disputed and evolving – NoMad is slowly catching on as the new name for the blocks north of Madison Square Park.) The area was once predominantly commercial, home to numerous toy manufacturers and photography studios – it's still not uncommon to see models and actors strolling to and from their shoots. However, in the 1980s, the neighbourhood became more residential,

IN THE KNOW
MYSTERIES OF THE METRONOME

It's not uncommon to see passers-by perplexed by the Metronome, a massive sculptural installation attached to 1 Union Square South that bellows steam and generates a barrage of numbers on a digital read-out. Although they appear strange, they're not random numbers – the 15-digit display is actually a clock indicating the time relative to midnight. There's a detailed explanation at the website of Kristin Jones and Andrew Ginzel, the artists responsible; see www.jonesginzel.com.

as buyers were drawn to its 19th-century brownstones and early 20th-century industrial architecture. Clusters of restaurants and shops soon followed. By the turn of the millennium, many internet start-ups had moved to the area, earning it the nickname 'Silicon Alley'.

There are two major public spaces in the locale: Madison Square Park and Union Square. Opened in 1847, **Madison Square Park** (from 23rd to 26th Streets, between Fifth & Madison Avenues) is the more stately of the two. In the 19th century, the square was a highly desirable address. Winston Churchill's grandfather resided in a magnificent but since-demolished mansion at Madison Avenue and 26th Street; Edith Wharton also made her home in the neighbourhood and set many of her high-society novels here. By the 1990s, the park had become a decaying no-go zone given over to drug dealers and the homeless, but it got a much-needed makeover in 2001 thanks to the efforts of the Madison Square Park Conservancy (www.madisonsquarepark.org), which has created a programme of cultural events, including Mad Sq Art, a year-round 'gallery without walls', featuring sculptural, video and installation exhibitions from big-name artists. A further lure is the original **Shake Shack**, the burger stand that spawned the popular chain (for a review of the large Upper West Side location, *see p173*). It still attracts a perpetual queue.

The square is surrounded by illustrious buildings. Completed in 1909, the **Metropolitan Life Tower** (1 Madison Avenue, at 24th Street) was modelled on the Campanile in Venice's Piazza San Marco (an allusion as commercial as it was architectural, for Met Life Insurance wanted to remind people that it had raised funds for the

Campanile after its fall two years earlier). The **Appellate Division Courthouse** (35 E 25th Street, at Madison Avenue) features one of the most beautiful pediments in the city, while Cass Gilbert's **New York Life Insurance Company Building** (51 Madison Avenue, at 26th Street) is capped by a golden pyramid that's one of the skyline's jewels.

The most famous of all Madison Square's edifices, however, lies at the southern end. The **Flatiron Building** (175 Fifth Avenue, between 22nd & 23rd Streets) was the world's first steel-frame skyscraper, a 22-storey Beaux Arts edifice clad conspicuously in white limestone and glazed terracotta. But it's the unique triangular shape that has drawn sightseers since it opened in 1902. Legend has it that a popular 1920s catchphrase originated at this corner of 23rd Street – police would give the '23 skidoo' to ne'er-do-wells trying to peek at ladies' petticoats as the unique wind currents that swirled around the building blew their dresses upward. Speaking of rampant libidos: the nearby **Museum of Sex** houses an impressive collection of salacious ephemera.

In the 19th century, the neighbourhood went by the moniker of Ladies' Mile, thanks to the ritzy department stores that lined Broadway and Sixth Avenue. These retail palaces attracted the 'carriage trade', wealthy women who bought the latest imported fashions and household goods. By 1914, most of the department stores had moved north, leaving their proud cast-iron buildings behind. Today, the area is peppered with chain clothing stores, bookshops and tasteful home-furnishing shops such as **ABC Carpet & Home**.

The Flatiron District's other major public space, **Union Square** (from 14th to 17th Streets, between Union Square East & Union Square West) is named after neither the Union of the Civil War nor the labour rallies that once took place here, but simply for the union of Broadway and Bowery Lane (now Fourth Avenue). Even so, it does have its radical roots: from the 1920s until the early '60s, it was a favourite spot for tub-thumping political oratory. Following 9/11, the park was home to candlelit vigils and became a focal point for the city's grief. Formerly grungy, the park is fresh from a rolling renovation project started in the 1980s and is the home of the **Union Square Greenmarket**. The square is flanked by a variety of large businesses, including a **Barnes & Noble** bookstore (www.barnesandnoble.com) that hosts an excellent programme of author events.

EXPLORE

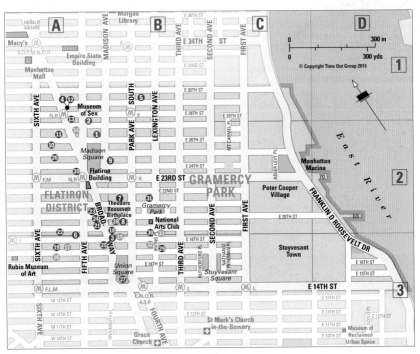

Sights & Museums

Museum of Mathematics (MoMath)

11 E 26th Street, between Fifth & Madison Avenues (1-212 542 0566, www.momath.org). Subway N, R, 6 to 23rd Street. **Open** 10am-5pm daily (10am-2.30pm 1st Wed of each mth). **Admission** $16; $10 reductions. **Map** p137 A2 ❶

Designed for visitors of all ages, the country's first Museum of Mathematics replaces lectures and textbooks with more than 30 eclectic, interactive exhibits covering such topics as algebra and geometry. Think a ride on a square-wheeled trike could never be smooth? Find out just how bump-free it can be when you take said tricycle over a sunflower-shaped track, where the petals create strategically placed catenaries – curves used in geometry and physics – that make a level ride possible. Elsewhere, you can pass 3-D objects (or even your own body) through the laser-light 'Wall of Fire', and the lasers will display the objects as two-dimensional cross-sections (a cone becomes a triangle and circle, for instance). Or collaborate with a pair of fellow visitors to pan, zoom and rotate your own video cameras to create a single composite image, which can be manipulated into a bevy of interesting 'Feedback Fractals' (or fragmented shapes).

Museum of Sex

233 Fifth Avenue, at 27th Street (1-212 689 6337, www.museumofsex.com). Subway N, R, 6 to 28th Street. **Open** 10am-8pm Mon-Thur, Sun; 10am-9pm Fri, Sat. **Admission** $17.50; $15.25 reductions. Under-18s not admitted. **Map** p137 A1 ❷

Situated in the former Tenderloin district, which was bumping and grinding with dance halls and brothels in the 1800s, MoSex explores its subject within a cultural context. Rotating highlights of the permanent collection of more than 15,000 objects range from the tastefully erotic to the outlandish: an 1890s anti-onanism device looks as uncomfortable as the BDSM gear donated by a local dominatrix, and a pair of male and female RealDolls are disturbingly lifelike. You may see naughty French postcards or kinky art courtesy of Picasso and Keith Haring. Special exhibitions in the three-level space include the likes of 'The Sex Lives of Animals'. The gift shop stocks books and arty sex toys, while Play, the museum's bar-café combo, serves aphrodisiac cocktails, coffee, sweets and light bites.

Restaurants & Cafés

★ ABC Kitchen

35 E 18th Street, between Broadway & Park Avenue South (1-212 475 5829, www.abckitchennyc.com). Subway L, N, Q, R, 4, 5, 6 to 14th Street-Union Square. **Open** noon-3pm, 5.30-10.30pm Mon-Wed; noon-3pm, 5.30-11pm Thur; noon-3pm, 5.30-10pm Fri; 11am-3pm, 5.30-11.30pm Sat; 11am-3pm, 5.30-10pm Sun. **Main courses** $15-$35. **Map** p137 B2 ❸ **Eclectic**

The haute green cooking at Jean-Georges Vongerichten's artfully decorated restaurant is based on the most gorgeous ingredients from up and down the East Coast. The local, seasonal bounty finds its way into dishes like a mushroom pizza, topped with parmesan, oregano and a farm egg, or roasted black sea bass infused with chillies and herbs. A signature sundae of salted caramel ice-cream, candied peanuts and popcorn with chocolate sauce reworks the kids' classic to thrill a grown-up

Museum of Sex.

palate. ABC delivers one message overall: food that's good for the planet needn't be any less flavourful or stunning to look at. The team's Latin-accented ABC Cocina is around the corner at 38 E 19th Street, and a vegetarian spinoff is in the works.

Breslin Bar & Dining Room
Ace Hotel New York, 16 W 29th Street, at Broadway (1-212 679 1939, www.thebreslin.com). Subway N, R to 28th Street. **Open** *7am-4pm, 5.30pm-midnight daily.* **Main courses** *$21-$48.* **Map** p137 A1 ❹
Eclectic
The third project from restaurant savant Ken Friedman and Anglo chef April Bloomfield, the Breslin broke gluttonous new ground. Start as you mean to continue by accompanying your pre-dinner drinks with an order of scrumpets (fried strips of lamb belly). The overall ethos might well be described as late-period Henry VIII: groaning boards of house-made terrines feature thick slices of guinea hen, rabbit and pork. The menu changes frequently, but you'll always find hearty staples, such as the popular lamb burger, or the pig's foot for two – half a leg, really, which could feed the full Tudor court. Desserts include amped-up childhood treats like ice-cream and cookies.

$ Cannibal
113 E 29th Street, between Park & Lexington Avenues (1-212 686 5480, www.cannibalnyc.com). Subway 6 to 28th Street. **Open** *11am-11.30pm daily.* **Small plates** *$11-$18.* **Map** p137 B1 ❺
American creative
Run by restaurateur Christian Pappanicholas and connected to his Belgian-American eatery, Resto, the Cannibal is an unusual retail-restaurant hybrid – a beer store and a butcher but also a laid-back place to eat and drink. The meat counter supplies whole beasts for Resto's large-format feasts, but the carnivore's paradise is otherwise autonomous, with its own chef, Francis Derby (formerly of Wylie Dufresne's wd~50), and beer master, Julian Kurland. The food is best ordered in rounds, pairing beer and bites – wispy shavings of Kentucky ham, pâtés, sausages and tartares – as you sample some of the 450 selections on the drinks list.
Other location Gotham West Market, 600 Eleventh Avenue, between 44th & 45th Streets, Hell's Kitchen (1-212 582 7947).

$ City Bakery
3 W 18th Street, between Fifth & Sixth Avenues (1-212 366 1414, www.thecitybakery.com). Subway L, N, Q, R, 4, 5, 6 to 14th Street-Union Square. **Open** *7.30am-7pm Mon-Fri; 8am-7pm Sat; 9am-6pm Sun.* **Salad bar** *$14/lb.* **Map** p137 A3 ❻ Café
Pastry genius Maury Rubin's loft-size City Bakery is jammed with shoppers loading up on creative baked goods such as maple bacon biscuits and unusual salad bar choices (grilled pineapple with ancho chilli, or beansprouts with smoked tofu, for example).

Cannibal.

There's also a small selection of soups, pizzas and hot dishes. But never mind all that: the thick, incredibly rich hot chocolate with fat house-made marshmallows is justly famed, and the moist 'melted' chocolate-chip cookies are divinely decadent.

★ Cosme
35 E 21st Street, between Broadway & Park Avenue South (1-212 913 9659, www.cosmenyc.com). Subway 6 to 23rd Street. **Open** *5.30-11pm daily.* **Main courses** *$15-$35.* **Map** p137 A2 ❼ Mexican
Enrique Olvera is the megawatt Mexico City talent behind Pujol, regularly ranked one of the 20 best restaurants in the world. His stateside debut – a bare-concrete dining room – is the Mexican restaurant New York has been missing. Olvera's elegant, high-gear small plates are pristine, pricey and as market-fresh as anything coming out of Thomas Keller's kitchen. Tacos make a solitary appearance on the menu, in a generous portion of duck carnitas, cooked to the sinful midpoint of unctuous fat and seared flesh. Single-corn tortillas pop up frequently, from a complimentary starter of crackly blue-corn tortillas with chilli-kicked pumpkin-seed butter to dense, crispy tostadas dabbed with bone-marrow salsa and creamy tongues of sea urchin. But it's

EXPLORE

Cosme. See p139.

the face-melting, savoury-sweet, Instagrammed-to-death husk meringue, with its fine hull giving way to a velvety, supercharged corn mousse, that cements Olvera's status as a premier haute-Mex ambassador.

élan

43 East 20th Street, between Broadway & Park Avenue South (1-646 682 7105, www.elannyc. com). Subway N, R, 6 to 23rd Street. **Open** 11.30-3pm, 5.30-10.30pm Mon-Wed; 11.30-3pm 5.30-11pm Thur, Fri; 11am-3pm, 5.30-11pm Sat; 11am-3pm, 5.30-10pm Sun. **Main courses** $27-$38. **Map** p137 A2 ❽ **American creative**
David Waltuck has never been one to shirk decadence – at his late, great Chanterelle, a 30-year-old Tribeca trailblazer that deftly married fine-dining finesse with mom-and-pop familiarity until it shuttered in 2009, zucchini blossoms came gorged with black truffles, and sausages famously burst with lobster beneath their casings. This follow-up is just as unabashedly awash in duck fat but heaps more playful: guacamole swirled with ocean-brine uni; potato pot stickers – hitting the sweet spot between pan-fried crisp and dumpling chew – stuffed with delicate summer truffles; and tender General Tso's-style sweetbreads, boosted from the takeout container with a ginger-carrot mirepoix and a pep of fresh chillies.

Eleven Madison Park

11 Madison Avenue, at E 24th Street (1-212 889 0905, www.elevenmadisonpark.com). Subway N, R, 6 to 23rd Street. **Open** 5.30-10pm Mon-Wed, Sun; noon-1pm, 5.30-10pm Thur-Sat. **Tasting menu** $225. **Map** p137 B2 ❾ **American creative**
Chef Daniel Humm and impresario Will Guidara – who bought Eleven Madison Park from their old boss, restaurateur Danny Meyer – are masters of reinvention. And once again, they've hit on a winning formula, this time for a 16-course Gotham-themed meal – marked by stagecraft and tricks

– that departs from the city's upper echelons of Old World-dominated fine dining. During a recent meal, a glass cloche rose over a puff of smoke, unveiling smoked sturgeon above smouldering embers. Rib eye, aged an astonishing 140 days, was served with a side of oxtail jam with melted foie gras and whipped potato icing that's as rich as it sounds, and a waiter performed a card trick with a chocolate pay off – a nod to the city's old street-corner shysters.

Hanjan

36 W 26th Street, between Broadway & Sixth Avenue (1-212 206 7226, www.hanjan26.com). Subway N, R to 28th Street. **Open** noon-2.30pm, 5pm-midnight Mon-Fri; 5pm-1am Sat. **Main courses** $16-$38. **Map** p137 A2 ❿ **Korean**
Hanjan is a shining example of a *joomak*, the Korean equivalent of the English gastropub. Expect a barrage of deeply satisfying dishes: glutinous rice cakes licked with spicy pork fat; crispy spring onion pancakes studded with local squid; and skewers of fresh chicken thighs that you can swab with *ssamjang*. Each plate packs its own surprises, but the whole feast is tied together by a soulful bass note melding sweetness, spice and just the right amount of fishy funk.

Hill Country

30 W 26th Street, between Broadway & Sixth Avenue (1-212 255 4544, www.hillcountryny.com). Subway N, R to 28th Street. **Open** noon-10pm Mon-Wed, Sun; noon-11pm Thur-Sat. **Main courses** $8-$29. **Map** p137 A2 ⓫ **American barbecue**
The guys behind Hill Country are about as Texan as Donald Trump in a stetson, but the cooking is an authentic, world-class take on the restaurant's namesake region. Dishes feature sausages imported from barbecue stalwart Kreuz Market of Lockhart, Texas, and two options for brisket: go for the 'moist' (read: fatty) version for full flavour. Beef shoulder emerges from the smoker in 20lb slabs, and tips-on

pork ribs are hefty, with just enough fat to imbue them with proper flavour. Desserts, such as jelly-filled cupcakes with peanut butter frosting, live out some kind of *Leave It to Beaver* fantasy, though June Cleaver wouldn't approve of the two dozen tequilas and bourbons on offer.

Other location 345 Adams Street, between Willoughby Street & Tech Plaza, Downtown Brooklyn (1-718 885 4608).

John Dory Oyster Bar

Ace Hotel New York, 1196 Broadway, at 29th Street (1-212 792 9000, www.thejohndory.com). Subway N, R to 28th Street. **Open** noon-midnight daily. **Small plates** $11-$29. **Map** p137 A1 ⑫ **Seafood**
April Bloomfield and Ken Friedman's original John Dory in the Meatpacking District was an ambitious, pricey endeavour, but its reincarnation in the Ace Hotel is an understated success. Tall stools face a raw bar stocked with a rotating mix of East and West Coast oysters, all expertly handled and impeccably sourced. True to form, the rest of Bloomfield's tapas-style seafood dishes are intensely flavoured – cold poached lobster with tomalley vinaigrette, for example, or chorizo-stuffed squid with smoked tomato.

★ NoMad

1170 Broadway, at 28th Street (1-212 796 1500, www.thenomadhotel.com). Subway N, R to 28th Street. **Open** 7-10am, noon-2pm, 5.30-10.30 Mon-Thur; 7-10am, noon-2pm, 5.30-11pm Fri; 7-10am, 11am-2.30pm, 5.30-11pm Sat; 7-10am,

11am-2.30pm, 5.30-10pm Sun. **Main courses** $22-$37. **Map** p137 A1 ⑬ **American**
Another restaurant from Daniel Humm and Will Guidara, the duo behind Eleven Madison Park *(see p140)*, the NoMad features plush armchairs around well-spaced tables and a stylish return to three-course dining. The food, like the space, exudes unbuttoned decadence: a slow-cooked egg stars in one over-the-top starter, with mushrooms, black garlic and kale for crunch. And while there are plenty of rich-man roast chickens for two in New York, the amber-hued bird here – with a foie gras, brioche and black truffle stuffing under the skin – is surely the new gold standard, well worth its $82 price tag. For the leaner of wallet, the elegant NoMad Bar serves lofty pub grub and smart cocktails.

Bars

230 Fifth

230 Fifth Avenue, at 27th Street (1-212 725 4300, www.230-fifth.com). Subway N, R to 28th Street. **Open** 4pm-4am Mon-Fri; 10am-4am Sat, Sun. **Map** p137 A2 ⑭
Perched atop an anonymous office building, the 14,000sq ft roof garden dazzles with spectacular views, including a close-up of the Empire State Building. While the sprawling outdoor space gets mobbed on sultry nights, it's less crowded during the cooler months when heaters, fleece robes and hot ciders make it a winter hotspot. For those who prefer to drink indoors, there's a glitzy lounge below, with wraparound sofas and floor-to-ceiling windows.

EXPLORE

élan.

EXPLORE

Old Town Bar & Grill

45 E 18th Street, between Broadway & Park Avenue South (1-212 529 6732, www.oldtownbar.com). Subway L, N, Q, R, W, 4, 5, 6 to 14th Street-Union Square. **Open** 11.30am-1am Mon-Fri; noon-2am Sat; 1pm-midnight Sun. **Map** p137 B3 ⓯

Amid the swank food and drink sanctums sprouting around Park Avenue South, this classic tavern remains a shrine to unchanging values. Grab a sweet wooden booth or belly up to the long bar and drain a few pints alongside the regulars who gather on stools 'south of the pumps' (their lingo for taps). If you work up an appetite, skip the much-praised burger in favour of the chilli dog: a grilled and scored all-beef Sabrett with spicy house-made beef-and-red-kidney-bean chilli.

★ Raines Law Room

48 W 17th Street, between Fifth & Sixth Avenues (no phone, www.raineslawroom.com). Subway F, M to 14th Street; L to Sixth Avenue. **Open** 5pm-2am Mon-Thur; 5pm-3am Fri, Sat; 7pm-1am Sun. **Map** p137 A3 ⓰

There's no bar at this louche lounge. In deference to its name (which refers to an 1896 law that was designed to curb liquor consumption), drinks are prepared in a half-hidden back room known as 'the kitchen', surrounded by gleaming examples of every tool and gizmo a barkeep could wish for. From this gorgeous tableau comes an austere cocktail list. Kick back in the plush, upholstered space to sip classics, and variations thereof.

Other location The William, 24 E 39th Street, between Madison & Park Avenues (1-646 922 8600, www.thewilliamnyc.com).

Rye House

11 W 17th Street, between Fifth & Sixth Avenues (1-212 255 7260, www.ryehousenyc.com). Subway F, M to 14th Street; L to Sixth Avenue. **Open** noon-2am Mon-Fri; 11am-2am Sat; 11am-midnight Sun. **Map** p137 A3 ⓱

As the name suggests, American spirits are the emphasis at this dark, sultry bar. As well as bourbons and ryes, there are gins, vodkas and rums, most distilled in the States. Check out the jalapeño-infused Wake-up Call, one of the venue's most popular bourbon cocktails. While the focus is clearly on drinking, there's excellent upscale pub grub, such as truffle grilled cheese or potato pierogi.

Shops & Services

★ ABC Carpet & Home

888 Broadway, at 19th Street (1-212 473 3000, www.abchome.com). Subway L, N, Q, R, 4, 5, 6 to 14th Street-Union Square. **Open** 10am-7pm Mon-Wed, Fri, Sat; 10am-8pm Thur; 11am-6.30pm Sun. **Map** p137 B2 ⓳ **Homewares**

Most of ABC's 35,000-strong carpet range is housed in the store across the street at no.881 – except the rarest rugs, which reside on the sixth floor of the main store. Browse everything from organic soap to hand-beaded lampshades on the bazaar-style ground floor. On the upper floors, furniture spans every style, from slick European minimalism to antique oriental and mid-century modern. The Bronx warehouse outlet has discounted furnishings, but prices are still steep.

Other location ABC Carpet & Home Outlet, 1055 Bronx River Avenue, between Bruckner Boulevard & Westchester Avenue, Bronx (1-718 842 8772).

Lulu Shop.

Books of Wonder

18 W 18th Street, between Fifth & Sixth Avenues,
(1-212 989 3270, www.booksofwonder.com).
Subway F, M to 14th Street; L to Sixth Avenue;
1 to 18th Street. **Open** *10am-7pm Mon-Sat;*
11am-6pm Sun. **Map** p137 A3 ⑲ **Books & music**
This large independent children's bookstore sells
rare and out-of-print editions as well as new titles,
plus a special collection of Oz books. The store
also always has a good stock of signed books and
children's book art.

Eataly

200 Fifth Avenue, between 23rd & 24th Streets
(1-212 229 2560, www.eataly.com). Subway F,
M, N, R to 23rd Street. **Open** *10am-11pm daily.*
Map p137 A2 ⑳ **Food & drink**
A spin-off of an operation by the same name just
outside of Turin, this massive foodie destination
from Mario Batali and Joe and Lidia Bastianich
sprawls across 50,000sq ft. The Italian gastro-com-
plex encompasses six sit-down restaurants and a
rooftop beer garden. Adjacent retail areas offer gourmet provisions, including artisanal breads baked
on the premises, fresh mozzarella, salumi and a vast
array of olive oils.

Fishs Eddy

889 Broadway, at 19th Street (1-212 420
9020, www.fishseddy.com). Subway N, R to
23rd Street. **Open** *9am-9pm Mon-Thur; 9am-*
10pm Fri, Sat; 10am-8pm Sun. **Map** p137 A2 ㉑
Homewares
Penny-pinchers frequent this barn-like space
for sturdy dishware and glasses – surplus stock
or recycled from restaurants, ocean liners and
hotels (plain white side plates start at a mere $1.99
here). But there are plenty of affordable, freshly
minted goods too. Add spice to mealtime with
glasses adorned with male or female pole-dancers;
dinnerware and mugs printed with the Manhattan
or Brooklyn skyline; and studio floor plan side
plates – at just $10, NYC real estate has never been
so cheap.

Idlewild Books

12 W 19th Street, between Fifth & Sixth Avenues
(1-212 414 8888, www.idlewildbooks.com).
Subway F, M to 14th Street; L to Sixth Avenue.
Open *noon-7.30pm Mon-Thur; noon-6pm Fri-*
Sun. **Map** p137 A2 ㉒ **Books & music**
Opened by a former United Nations press officer,
Idlewild stocks travel guides to more than 100
countries and all 50 states, which are grouped with
related works of fiction and non-fiction. It also has
a large selection of works in French, Spanish and
Italian. Fun fact: Idlewild was the original name for
JFK Airport.
Other location 249 Warren Street, between
Court & Smith Streets, Cobble Hill, Brooklyn
(1-718 403 9600).

LA Burdick

5 E 20th Street, between Fifth Avenue & Broadway
(1-212 796 0143, www.burdickchocolate.com).
Subway N, R to 23rd Street. **Open** *9am-7pm*
Mon-Wed; 9am-8pm Thur-Sat; 10am-7pm Sun.
Map p137 A2 ㉓ **Food & drink**
Best known for its petite ganache-filled chocolate
penguins and mice, the family-owned, New
Hampshire-based chocolatier also has a shop and
café in NYC. Display cases showcase a tempting
array of marzipan, dipped caramels and truffles.
Ponder the choices over a cup of dark, white or milk
hot chocolate, or plump for dealer's choice with one
of the classy gift boxes or baskets.

Lulu Shop

12 E 20th Street, between Fifth Avenue &
Broadway (1-212 965 0075, www.lulufrost.com).
Subway N, R to 23rd Street. **Open** *11am-6pm*
Mon-Fri. **Map** p137 A2 ㉔ **Accessories**
Lisa Salzer launched her jewellery line in 2004,
fashioning baubles with a dazzling combination of
vintage and modern elements. Peruse the label's first
boutique for deco-inspired tassel necklaces, oxidised
silver drop earrings and a range of unisex pieces,
like hand-wrapped embroidered bracelets made
from horse hair and leather. For customised jewels,
browse the make-your-own jewellery station, where
you can embellish 18-carat gold earrings with your
pick of fine gemstones.

Paragon Sporting Goods

867 Broadway, at 18th Street (1-212 255 8889,
www.paragonsports.com). Subway L, N, Q, R, 4,
5, 6 to 14th Street-Union Square. **Open**
10am-8.30pm Mon-Fri; 10am-8pm Sat; 11am-7pm
Sun. **Map** p137 A3 ㉕ **Sports equipment**
Established in 1908, Paragon Sporting Goods offers
three floors of equipment and clothing for almost
every activity, from the everyday (workout-wear and
trainers) to the more niche (badminton sets, kayaking accessories).

Showplace Antique & Design Center

40 W 25th Street, between Fifth & Sixth Avenues
(1-212 633 6063, www.nyshowplace.com). Subway
F, M to 23rd Street. **Open** *10am-6pm Mon-Fri;*
8.30am-5.30pm Sat, Sun. **Map** p137 A2 ㉖
Fashion/homewares
Set over four expansive floors, this indoor market
houses more than 200 high-quality dealers selling
everything from Greek and Roman antiquities to
vintage furniture. Among the highlights are Joe
Sundlie's spot-on-trend designer vintage pieces
(Chanel, Oscar de la Renta, Jean Paul Gaultier), and
Mood Indigo – arguably the best source in the city
for collectable bar accessories and dinnerware. The
array of Bakelite jewellery and table accessories,
Fiestaware and novelty cocktail glasses is dazzling,
and it's a wonderful repository of art deco cigarette
cases, lighters and New York memorabilia.

EXPLORE

Union Square Greenmarket.

Union Square Greenmarket
From 16th to 17th Streets, between Union Square East & Union Square West (1-212 788 7476, www. grownyc.org/greenmarket). Subway L, N, Q, R, 4, 5, 6 to 14th Street-Union Square. **Open** *8am-6pm Mon, Wed, Fri, Sat.* **Map** p137 B3 ② **Market**
Shop elbow-to-elbow with top chefs for locally grown produce, handmade breads and baked goods, preserves and cheeses at the city's flagship farmers' market on the periphery of Union Square Park. Between Thanksgiving and Christmas, a holiday market sets up shop here too.

GRAMERCY PARK

Subway L to Third Avenue; L, N, Q, R, 4, 5, 6 to 14th Street-Union Square; N, R, 6 to 23rd Street.

A key to **Gramercy Park**, the tranquil, gated square at the bottom of Lexington Avenue, between 20th and 21st Streets, is one of the most sought-after treasures in all the five boroughs. For the most part, only residents of the beautiful surrounding townhouses and apartment buildings have access to the park, which was developed in the 1830s to resemble a London square. The park is flanked by two private clubs. The **Players Club** (16 Gramercy Park South, between Park Avenue South & Irving Place, 1-212 475 6116, www.the playersnyc.org) was inspired by London's Garrick Club. It's housed in an 1847 brownstone formerly owned by Edwin Booth, the celebrated 19th-century actor and brother of John Wilkes Booth, Abraham Lincoln's assassin. Next door at no.15 is the Victorian Gothic Revival Samuel J Tilden House, which houses the **National Arts Club** (1-212 475 3424, www.nationalartsclub.org, closed Sat, Sun & July, Aug). The busts of literary greats (Shakespeare, Dante) along the façade were chosen to reflect Tilden's library, which, along with his

fortune, helped to create the New York Public Library. The NAC's galleries are open to non-members, but call before visiting as they may close for private events or between shows.

Leading south from the park to 14th Street, Irving Place is named after author Washington Irving (although he never actually lived here). Near the corner of 15th Street sits **Irving Plaza** (*see p286*), a music venue. At the corner of Park Avenue South and 17th Street is the final base of the once-omnipotent Tammany Hall political machine. Built in 1929, it now houses the New York Film Academy. A few blocks away from here is the **Theodore Roosevelt Birthplace**, a national historic site.

The largely residential area bordered by 23rd and 30th Streets, Park Avenue and the East River is known as **Kips Bay** after Jacobus Kip, whose farm covered the area in the 17th century. Third Avenue is the district's main thoroughfare, and a locus of restaurants representing a variety of eastern cuisines, including Afghan, Tibetan and Turkish.

Sights & Museums

FREE Theodore Roosevelt Birthplace National Historic Site
28 E 20th Street, between Broadway & Park Avenue South (1-212 260 1616, www.nps.gov/ thrb). Subway 6 to 23rd Street. **Open** *Closed until 2016 (call or see website for updates).* **Admission** *free.* **Map** p137 B2 ㉓
The brownstone where the 26th President of the United States was born and raised until the age of 14 was demolished in 1916. But it was recreated after his death in 1919, complete with authentic period furniture (some from the original residence). The house can only be explored by guided tour. However, as of May 2015, the site is closed for at least a year while it undergoes renovation.

Restaurants & Cafés

Casa Mono
52 Irving Place, at 17th Street (1-212 253 2773, www.casamononyc.com). Subway L to Third Avenue; N, Q, R, 4, 5, 6 to 14th Street-Union Square. **Open** noon-midnight daily. **Small plates** $5-$30. **Map** p137 B3 ㉙ **Spanish**
In 2003 offal-loving chef-partners Mario Batali and Andy Nusser broke new ground in NYC with their adventurous Spanish fare – dishes include mussels with chorizo and cava, fried sweetbreads with fennel, foie gras with *cinco cebollas* (five types of onion), and fried duck egg with black truffles. For a slightly cheaper option, the attached Bar Jamón (125 E 17th Street; open 5pm-2am Mon-Fri; noon-2am Sat, Sun) offers tapas, Ibérico hams and Spanish cheeses.

$ Irving Farm Coffee Roasters
71 Irving Place, between 18th & 19th Streets (1-212 995 5252, www.irvingfarm.com). Subway L, N, Q, R, 4, 5, 6 to 14th Street-Union Square. **Open** 7am-10pm Mon-Fri; 8am-10pm Sat-Sun. **Sandwiches** $9-$12. **Map** p137 B2 ㉚ **Café**
Irving Farm's beans are roasted in a 100-year-old carriage house in the Hudson Valley. The rural connection is reflected in the rustic feel of this café, set within a stately brownstone. Breakfast, baked goods, sandwiches and salads accompany the excellent java. **Other locations** 88 Orchard Street, at Broome Street, Lower East Side (1-212 228 8880); 89 E 42nd Street, Grand Central Terminal, Midtown (1-212 983 4242); 224 W 79th Street, between Amsterdam Avenue & Broadway, Upper West Side (1-212 874 7979).

Maialino
Gramercy Park Hotel, 2 Lexington Avenue, between E 21st & E 22nd Streets (1-212 777 2410, www. maialinonyc.com). Subway 6 to 23rd Street. **Open** 7.30-10am, noon-2pm, 5.30-10.30pm Mon-Thur; 7.30-10am, noon-2pm, 5.30-11pm Fri; 10am-2.30pm, 5.30-11pm Sat; 10am-2.30pm, 5.30-10.30pm Sun. **Main courses** $17-$72. **Map** p137 B2 ㉛ **Italian**
Danny Meyer's first full-fledged foray into Italian cuisine is a dedicated homage to the neighbourhood trattorias that kept him well fed as a 20-year-old tour guide in Rome. Salumi and bakery stations between the front bar and the wood-beamed dining room – hog jowls and sausages dangling near shelves stacked with crusty loaves of bread – mimic a market off the Appian Way. Executive chef Nick Anderer's menu has exceptional facsimiles of dishes specific to Rome, such as carbonara, braised tripe and suckling pig.

Bars

Dear Irving
55 Irving Place, between 17th &18th Streets (no phone, www.dearirving.com). Subway L, N, Q, R, 4, 5, 6 to 14th Street-Union Square. **Open** 5pm-2am Mon-Thur; 5pm-3am Fri, Sat; 5pm-1am Sun. **Map** p137 B3 ㉜
All golden-age yearning and space-time shuffling, this dapper Gramercy lounge is the work of Raines Law Room operators Alberto Benenati and Yves Jadot. The railroad space is divided into period-piece quarters, including a tufted Victorian parlour and an ashtray-dotted hooch den worthy of Don Draper. Spend an hour at this luxe oasis sipping tried-and-true classics (Gibson, Paloma) and house creations, and you'll completely lose track of time.

Pete's Tavern
129 E 18th Street, at Irving Place (1-212 473 7676, www.petestavern.com). Subway L, N, Q, R, W, 4, 5, 6 to 14th Street-Union Square. **Open** 11am-2.30am daily. **Map** p137 B3 ㉝
According to history buffs, in 1904, O Henry wrote his sentimental short story 'The Gift of the Magi' in what was then a quiet Gramercy pub. Today it's three deep at the bar, and O Henry would have a hard time parking it anywhere. Although Pete's – a Civil War-era survivor – draws its share of tourists, you'll also rub shoulders with neighbourhood types who slide into the wooden booths to snack on affordable Italian eats with standard suds (16 beers on tap include a hoppy house ale) bubbling in frosty mugs.

EXPLORE

Maialino.

Midtown

Soaring office towers, crowded pavements and taxi-choked streets – that's the image most people have of the busy midsection of Manhattan. This part of town draws visitors to some of the city's best-known landmarks, including iconic skyscrapers like the Empire State Building and the Chrysler Building, the dazzling electronic spectacle that is Times Square, and Rockefeller Center, with its picturesque seasonal ice-skating rink. Fifth Avenue, the dividing line between Midtown West and Midtown East, is continuously clogged with shoppers from all over the world. But there's more to midtown than iconic architecture and commerce. On the far west side, the northern extension of the High Line is attracting galleries and shops, and rapidly gentrifying Hell's Kitchen has emerged as the city's hottest gaybourhood. The character of this area will continue to evolve with the construction of Hudson Yards – the largest development in the city since Rockefeller Center.

Times Square.

Don't Miss

1 Times Square The bright lights still razzle-dazzle (p151).

2 Empire State Building The world's most iconic skyscraper (p157).

3 Museum of Modern Art (MoMA) Art primer from the 19th century to the present (p157).

4 Don Antonio by Starita Pedigree pizza a block from Broadway (p153).

5 Dover Street Market The classy, kooky Comme concept store is an essential browse (p165).

EXPLORE

EXPLORE

HERALD SQUARE & THE GARMENT DISTRICT

Subway A, C, E, 1, 2, 3 to 34th Street-Penn Station; B, D, F, M, N, Q, R to 34th Street-Herald Square.

Seventh Avenue, aka Fashion Avenue, is the main drag of the **Garment District** (roughly from 34th to 40th Streets, between Broadway & Eighth Avenue). Although manufacturing in the area has decreased, it's still where designers – and their seamstresses, fitters and assistants – feed America's multi-billion-dollar clothing industry. Delivery trucks and workers pushing racks of clothes clog streets lined with wholesale trimming, button and fabric shops. Many showrooms hold sample sales (*see p163* **In the Know**).

Taking up an entire city block, from 34th Street to 35th Street, between Broadway and Seventh Avenue, is the legendary **Macy's**. With one million square feet of selling space spread across nine floors, it's the biggest and busiest department store in the world. Facing Macy's, at the intersection of Broadway, 34th Street and Sixth Avenue, is **Herald Square**, named after a long-gone newspaper, the *New York Herald*. The lower section is known as **Greeley Square** after editor and reformer Horace Greeley, owner of the *Herald*'s rival, the *New York Tribune* (the two papers merged in 1924). Once seedy, the square now offers bistro chairs and tables that get crowded with shoppers and office lunchers in the warmer months. To the east, the many spas, restaurants and karaoke bars of small enclave **Koreatown** line 32nd Street, between Broadway and Fifth Avenue.

Located not in Madison Square but on Seventh Avenue, between 31st and 33rd Streets, **Madison Square Garden** (*see p282*) is home for the Knicks and Rangers, and has welcomed rock icons from Elvis to Lady Gaga, as well as the Barnum & Bailey Circus and other big events. The massive arena is actually the fourth building to bear that name (the first two were appropriately located in the square after which they were named) and opened in 1968, replacing the grand old Pennsylvania Station razed four years earlier. This brutal act of architectural vandalism spurred the creation of the city's Landmarks Preservation Commission, which has saved many other edifices from a similar fate.

Beneath Madison Square Garden stands **Penn Station**, a claustrophobic catacomb serving 600,000 Amtrak, Long Island Rail Road and New Jersey Transit passengers daily and the busiest train station in America. A proposal to relocate the station across the street to the stately **James A Farley Post Office** (421 Eighth Avenue, between 31st & 33rd Streets) was championed by the late Senator Patrick Moynihan in the early 1990s. The project, which has stalled over the years, finally got the necessary funding and government approval, and Moynihan Station is expected to be completed in 2016.

Restaurants & Cafés

Keens Steakhouse

72 W 36th Street, at Sixth Avenue (1-212 947 3636, www.keens.com). Subway B, D, F, M, N, Q, R to 34th Street-Herald Square. **Open** 11.45am-10.30pm Mon-Fri; 5-10.30pm Sat; 5-9.30pm Sun. **Main courses** $33-$58. **Map** p149 D4 **❶** Steakhouse

The ceiling and walls are hung with pipes, some from such long-ago Keens regulars as Babe Ruth, JP Morgan and Teddy Roosevelt. Even in these non-smoking days, you can catch a whiff of the restaurant's 130 years of history. Bevelled-glass doors, two working fireplaces and a forest's worth of dark wood suggest a time when 'Diamond Jim' Brady piled his table with bushels of oysters, slabs of seared beef and troughs of ale. The menu still lists a three-inch-thick mutton chop, and the porterhouse (for two or three) holds its own against any steak in the city.

$ Mandoo Bar

2 W 32nd Street, between Fifth Avenue & Broadway (1-212 279 3075, www.mandoobarnyc.com). Subway B, D, F, M, N, Q, R to 34th Street-Herald Square. **Open** 11.30am-10pm Mon; 11.30am-3am Tue-Thur; 11.30am-4am Fri, Sat; 11.30am-midnight Sun. **Main courses** $12-$20. **Map** p149 D4 **❷** Korean

If the staff members filling and crimping dough squares in the front window don't give it away, we will – this wood-wrapped industrial-style spot elevates *mandoo* (Korean dumplings) above mere appetiser status. Six varieties of the tasty morsels are filled with such delights as subtly piquant kimchi, juicy pork, succulent shrimp and vegetables. Try them miniaturised, as in the Baby Mandoo, swimming in a soothing beef broth or atop soupy ramen noodles.

Shops & Services

B&H

420 Ninth Avenue, at 34th Street (1-212 444 6615, www.bhphotovideo.com). Subway A, C, E to 34th Street-Penn Station. **Open** 9am-7pm Mon-Thur; 9am-1pm Fri; 10am-6pm Sun. **Map** p149 D2 **❸** Electronics & photography

This huge store is the ultimate one-stop shop for all your photographic, video and audio needs. Adding to the character of the place, goods are transported from the stock room via an overhead conveyor belt. Note that due to the largely Hasidic Jewish staff, it's closed on Saturdays and Jewish holidays.

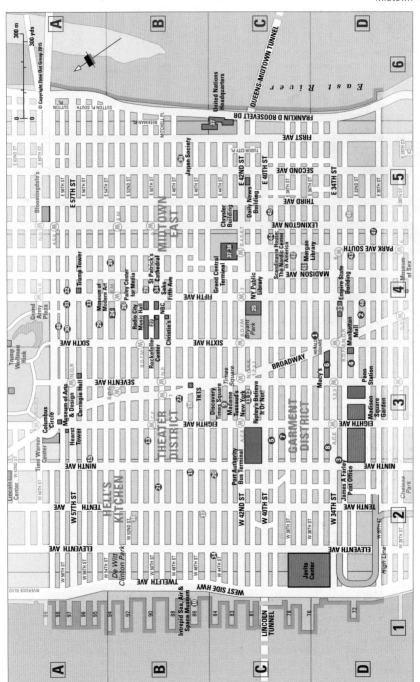

EXPLORE

Macy's

Juvenex
5th Floor, 25 W 32nd Street, between Fifth Avenue & Broadway (1-646 733 1330, www.juvenexspa. com). Subway B, D, F, M, N, Q, R to 34th Street-Herald Square. **Open** 24hrs daily. **Map** p149 D3 ❹
Health & beauty
This bustling Koreatown relaxation hub may be slightly rough around the edges (frayed towels, dingy sandals), but we embrace it for its bathhouse-meets-Epcot feel (igloo saunas, tiled 'soaking ponds' and a slatted bridge), and 24-hour availability (it's women only between 7am and 5pm). A basic Purification Program – including soak and sauna, face, body and hair cleansing and a salt scrub – is great value at $115.

Kee's Chocolates
315 W 39th Street between Eighth & Ninth Avenues (1-212 967 8088, www.keeschocolates.com). Subway A, C, E to 42nd Street-Port Authority. **Open** 9am-6.30pm Mon-Fri; 10am-5pm Sat. **Map** p149 C3 ❺
Food & drink
Every piece of Kee Ling Tong's exquisite confectionery is tempered and dipped by hand to create a thick, smooth shell that encloses either silky cream filling, fluffy mousse or rich ganache. The 48 bonbon flavours rotate daily, and crème brûlée, passionfruit and Thai chilli are among the most popular. But all of them, including green tea, key lime, blood orange and black sesame, are worth investigating.
Other locations 80 Thompson Street, between Broome & Spring Streets, Soho (1-212 334 3284); HSBC, 452 Fifth Avenue, between 39th & 40th Streets, Murray Hill (1-212 525 6099).

Macy's
151 W 34th Street, between Broadway & Seventh Avenue (1-212 695 4400, www.macys.com). Subway B, D, F, M, N, Q, R to 34th Street-Herald Square; 1, 2, 3 to 34th Street-Penn Station. **Open** 9am-9.30pm Mon-Fri; 10am-9.30pm Sat; 11am-8.30pm Sun. **Map** p149 D3 ❻
Department store
It may not be as glamorous as New York's other famous stores but for sheer breadth of stock, the 34th Street behemoth is hard to beat. Mid-price fashion for all ages, big beauty names and housewares have traditionally been the store's bread and butter, but a $400 million redesign, wrapping up in late 2015, has introduced new luxury boutiques including Gucci and Burberry. The cosmetics department has been luxed-up with high-end brands such as Jo Malone London and Laura Mercier.
▶ *If you need tourist guidance, stop by the store's Official NYC Information Center.*

Nepenthes New York
307 W 38th Street, between Eighth & Ninth Avenues (1-212 643 9540, www.nepenthesny.com). Subway A, C, E, 1, 2, 3 to 34th Street-Penn Station. **Open** noon-7pm Mon-Sat; noon-5pm Sun. **Map** p149 C3 ❼ **Fashion**
Well-dressed dudes with an eye on the Japanese style scene will already be familiar with this Tokyo fashion retailer. The narrow Garment District shop – its first US location – showcases expertly crafted urban-rustic menswear from house label Engineered Garments, such as plaid flannel shirts and workwear-inspired jackets. There is also a small selection of women's clothing.

Sam Ash Music
333 W 34th Street, between Eighth & Ninth Avenues (1-212 719 2299, www.samashmusic. com). Subway A, C, E to 34th Street-Penn Station. **Open** 10am-8pm Mon-Sat; 11am-7pm Sun. **Map** p149 D3 ❽ **Books & music**

EXPLORE

Established in Brooklyn in 1924, this musical instrument emporium moved from Times Square's now-silent 'music row' in 2013. The 30,000sq ft store offers new, vintage and custom guitars of all varieties, along with amps, DJ equipment, drums, keyboards, recording equipment, turntables and an array of sheet music. **Other location** 113-25 Queens Boulevard, at 76th Road, Forest Hills, Queens (1-718 793 7983).

THE THEATER DISTRICT & HELL'S KITCHEN

Subway A, C, E to 42nd Street-Port Authority; C, E to 5th Street; N, Q, R to 49th Street; N, Q, R, S, 1, 2, 3, 7 to 42nd Street-Times Square.

Times Square's evolution from a traffic-choked fleshpot to a tourist-friendly theme park has accelerated in the past few years. Not only has 'the Crossroads of the World' gained an elevated viewing platform atop the TKTS discount booth, from which visitors can admire the surrounding light show (*see p154* **Times Square Survival Guide**), but also stretches of Broadway, from 47th to 42nd Streets and from 35th to 33rd Streets, have been designated pedestrian zones, complete with seating, in an effort to streamline midtown traffic and create a more pleasant environment. Permanent plazas, designed by National September 11 Museum architects Snøhetta, are being developed in the 'Bowtie' from 42nd to 47th Streets, featuring continuous paved areas and granite benches. Much of the work has been completed, and the project will wrap up in 2016.

Originally Longacre Square, the junction of Broadway and Seventh Avenue, stretching from 42nd to 47th Streets, was renamed after the *New York Times* moved here in the early 1900s. The first electrified billboard graced the district in 1904, on the side of a bank at 46th and Broadway. The same year, the inaugural New Year's Eve party in Times Square doubled as the *Times*'s housewarming party in its new HQ. Today, about a million people gather here to watch an illuminated Waterford Crystal ball descend every 31 December.

The paper left the building only a decade after it had arrived (it now occupies an $84-million tower on Eighth Avenue, between 40th and 41st Streets). However, it retained ownership of its old headquarters until the 1960s, and erected the world's first scrolling electric news 'zipper' in 1928. The readout, now sponsored by Dow Jones, still trumpets the latest breaking stories.

Times Square is also the gateway to the **Theater District**, the zone between 41st Street and 53rd Street, from Sixth Avenue to Ninth Avenue, where extravagant shows are put on six days a week (Monday is the traditional night off). While numerous venues stage first-rate productions in the area, only 39 are officially Broadway theatres. The distinction is based on size rather than location or quality – Broadway theatres must have more than 500 seats.

The Theater District's transformation from the cradle of New York's sex industry began in 1984, when the city condemned properties along 42nd Street ('Forty Deuce', or 'the Deuce' for short), between Seventh and Eighth Avenues. A change in zoning laws meant adult-oriented venues must now subsist on X-rated videos rather than live 'dance' shows; the square's sex trade is now relegated to short stretches of Seventh and Eighth Avenues, just north and south of 42nd Street.

The streets to the west of Eighth Avenue are filled with eateries catering to theatregoers, especially the predominantly tourist-oriented, pricey places along **Restaurant Row** (46th Street, between Eighth and Ninth Avenues). Locals tend to walk west to Ninth Avenue – in the 40s and 50s, the Hell's Kitchen strip is tightly packed with inexpensive restaurants serving a variety of ethnic cuisines.

Recording studios, record labels, theatrical agencies and other entertainment and media companies reside in the area's office buildings. The **Brill Building** (1619 Broadway, at 49th Street) was once a hive of music publishers and producers; such luminaries as Jerry Lieber, Mike Stoller and Carole King wrote and auditioned their hits here.

Flashy attractions and huge retail stores strive to outdo one another in hopes of snaring the tourist throngs. The vast **Toys 'R' Us** (1514 Broadway, at 44th Street, 1-646 366 8800) boasts a 60-foot indoor Ferris wheel and a two-floor Barbie emporium.

West of the Theater District lies **Hell's Kitchen**. The precise origins of the name are unclear, but are no doubt connected to its emergence as an Irish-mob-dominated neighbourhood in the 19th-century. In the 1950s, clashes between Irish and recently arrived Puerto Rican factions were dramatised in the musical *West Side Story*. It was a particularly violent incident in 1959, in which two teenagers died, that led to an attempt by local businesses to erase the stigma associated with the area by renaming it Clinton (taken from a park named after one-time

EXPLORE

IN THE KNOW LOFTY RETREAT

If you need respite from the traffic in Midtown East, slip into **Tudor City** *(see p161)*, which perches on a hill between First and Second Avenues. The peaceful residential enclave features a charming park where you can rest your feet. Head for the development's east-facing terrace for an impressive view of the United Nations complex.

Antique Chic.

10%
Off
Special
*

mayor DeWitt Clinton). The new name never really took, and gang culture survived until the 1980s.

Today, the area has emerged as New York's hottest queer neighbourhood, with numerous bars and the city's first gay-oriented luxury hotel, the **Out NYC** (*see p266*). As gentrification takes hold, new apartment blocks are also springing up in the former wasteland near the Hudson River. This area is dominated by the massive, black-glass **Jacob K Javits Convention Center** (Eleventh Avenue, between 34th & 39th Streets). A couple of major draws are also here: the **Circle Line Terminal** (*see p376*), at Pier 83, the departure point for the cruise company's three-hour circumnavigation of Manhattan Island, and the **Intrepid Sea, Air & Space Museum**, a retired aircraft carrier-cum-naval museum.

Sights & Museums

Discovery Times Square
226 W 44th Street, between Seventh & Eighth Avenues (1-866 987 9692, www.discoverytsx.com). Subway A, C, E to 42nd Street-Port Authority; N, Q, R, S, 1, 2, 3, 7 to 42nd Street-Times Square. **Open** 10am-7pm Mon, Tue, Sun; 10am-8pm Wed, Thur; 10am-9pm Fri, Sat. **Admission** $27; $19.50-$23.50 reductions; free under-4s. **Map** p149 C3 **9**
This Discovery Channel-sponsored exhibition centre stages big shows on such crowd-pleasing subjects as King Tut, Pompeii, the *Titanic* and the *Hunger Games* franchise.

Intrepid Sea, Air & Space Museum
USS Intrepid, Pier 86, Twelfth Avenue & 46th Street (1-212 245 0072, www.intrepidmuseum. org). Subway A, C, E to 42nd Street-Port Authority, then M42 bus to Twelfth Avenue or 15min walk. **Open** Apr-Oct 10am-5pm Mon-Fri; 10am-6pm Sat, Sun. Nov-Mar 10am-5pm daily. **Admission** $24; $12-$20 reductions; free under-3s, active & retired US military. **Map** p149 B1 **10**
Commissioned in 1943, this 27,000-ton, 898ft aircraft carrier survived torpedoes and kamikaze attacks in World War II, served during the Vietnam War and the Cuban Missile Crisis, and recovered two space capsules for NASA. It was decommissioned in 1974, then resurrected as an educational institution. On its flight deck and portside aircraft elevator are top-notch examples of American military might, including the US Navy F-14 Tomcat (as featured in *Top Gun*), an A-12 Blackbird spy plane and a fully restored Army AH-1G Cobra gunship helicopter. In 2011, the museum became home to the Enterprise (OV-101), the retired prototype NASA Orbiter (entry to the Space Shuttle Pavilion costs extra).

Madame Tussauds New York
234 W 42nd Street, between Seventh & Eighth Avenues (1-866 841 3505, www.madametussauds. com/newyork). Subway A, C, E to 42nd Street-Port
Authority; N, Q, R, S, 1, 2, 3, 7 to 42nd Street-Times Square. **Open** 10am-8pm Mon-Thur, Sun; 10am-10pm Fri, Sat. **Admission** $36; $29 reductions; free under-4s. **Map** p149 C3 **11**
With roots in 18th-century Paris and founded in London in 1802, the world's most famous wax museum now draws celebrity-hungry crowds to more than a dozen locations worldwide. At the New York outpost, you can get a stalker's-eye view of paraffin doppelgangers of an array of political, sports, film and pop stars, from Barack Obama and Carmelo Anthony to Leonardo DiCaprio and Lady Gaga. A new crop of freshly waxed victims debuts every few months.

Ripley's Believe It or Not!
234 W 42nd Street, between Seventh & Eighth Avenues (1-212 398 3133, www.ripleysnewyork. com). Subway A, C, E to 42nd Street-Port Authority; N, Q, R, S, 1, 2, 3, 7 to 42nd Street-Times Square. **Open** 9am-1am daily (last entry midnight). **Admission** $33; $25 reductions; free under-4s. **Map** p149 C3 **12**
Times Square might be a little whitewashed these days, but you can get a feel for the old freak show at this repository of the eerie and uncanny. Marvel at such bizarre artefacts as a six-legged cow, the world's largest collection of shrunken heads and a cache of weird art that includes a portrait of President Obama composed of 12,600 gumballs.

Restaurants & Cafés

★ Don Antonio by Starita
309 W 50th Street, between Eighth & Ninth Avenues (1-646 719 1043, www.donantonio pizza.com). Subway C, E to 50th Street. **Open** 11.30am-11pm Mon-Thur; 11.30am-3.30pm, 4.30pm-midnight Fri; 11.30am-midnight Sat; 11.30am-10.30pm Sun. **Pizzas** $9-$25. **Map** p149 B3 **13** Italian/pizza
It may not be trendy, but pizza aficionados flock to this pedigreed eaterie, a collaboration between Kesté's (*see p119*) talented Roberto Caporuscio and his decorated Naples mentor, Antonio Starita. Start with tasty bites like the *fritattine* (a deep-fried spaghetti cake oozing *prosciutto cotto* and mozzarella sauce). The main event should be the habit-forming Montanara Starita, which gets a quick dip in the deep fryer before hitting the oven to develop its puffy, golden crust. Topped with tomato sauce, basil and intensely smoky buffalo mozzarella, it's a worthy addition to the pantheon of classic New York pies.

★ Gotham West Market
600 Eleventh Avenue, between 44th & 45th Streets (1-212 582 7940, www.gothamwestmarket.com). A, C, E to 42nd Street-Port Authority. **Open** 7am-11pm Mon-Thur; 7am-midnight Fri; 8am-midnight Sat; 8am-11pm Sun. **Map** p149 C2 **14** Eclectic

EXPLORE

TIMES SQUARE SURVIVAL GUIDE

Avoid Crossroads of the World rage with these tips.

RISE ABOVE IT ALL

After you've queued to score cheap theatre tickets at the TKTS in Duffy Square (Broadway, at 47th Street; *see p309*), ascend the ticket booth's red glass structural steps for an eye-popping panorama of the Great White Way. The glowing staircase, which debuted in 2008, was the brainchild of Australians John Choi and Tai Ropiha, who won a globe-spanning competition for a new design.

STOP AND LISTEN

Steal a moment of relative quiet amid the clamour of this bustling intersection and experience sound in the name of art. Rising from a metal subway grate on Broadway, between 45th and 46th Streets, a 1977 sound installation by Max Neuhaus titled *Times Square* often competes with – but also depends upon – its environment. The surrounding architecture and a series of underground spaces amplify the piece, which evokes ringing church bells.

RETREAT TO A DIVE BAR

The trad interior of 1950s survivor **Smith's Bar** (701 Eighth Avenue, at 44th Street, 1-212 247 2161) has been smartened up, but the vintage neon sign still glows and the standard pub grub (burgers, nachos) are mostly under $15. For an even more authentic dive-bar experience (but no food), stop by slender boxing shrine **Jimmy's Corner** (140 W 44th Street, between Broadway & Sixth Avenue, 1-212 221 9510), where the walls are plastered with photos of right-hook big shots and the customers are, well, plastered.

FILL UP AT A NEO-FOOD COURT

For an inexpensive pre- or post-theatre bite, head to **Gotham West Market** (*see p153*) – the hip Hell's Kitchen food court recently extended its hours and debuted a late-night menu from Ivan Ramen, the Cannibal and others. If you don't want to walk that far, **City Kitchen**, at behemoth hotel Row NYC (700 8th Avenue, at 44th Street, http://citykitchen.rownyc.com), contains nine popular NYC purveyors including Luke's Lobster, Whitman's burgers and Dough doughnuts in sleek, subway-tiled stations.

ENJOY THE VIEW WITH A BREW

The surprisingly unhyped **R Lounge** in the Renaissance Hotel (714 Seventh Avenue, at 48th Street, 1-212 261 5200, www.rlounge timessquare.com) provides a ringside view of the bright lights and snacks by the Bromberg brothers, the team behind the popular Blue Ribbon eateries. In warm weather, slip up to the sprawling **St Cloud** rooftop bar at the new Knickerbocker Hotel (6 Times Square, 1-212 204 4980, www.theknickerbocker.com), which offers a menu of small plates designed by Aureole toque Charlie Palmer and close-ups of the world's most famous crystal ball.

Gotham West Market.

In 2013, Hell's Kitchen welcomed this hip take on a food court, perfect for lunch or a quick pre-theatre bite. The 15,000sq ft retail-dining mecca is divided into eight culinary stalls as well as a full-service NYC Velo bike shop. Dine-in or take-out options include Ivan Ramen Slurp Shop, where Tokyo noodle guru Ivan Orkin offers his famed *shio*, shoyu and chilli-sesame varieties; El Colmado tapas bar from Seamus Mullen of Tertulia; Blue Bottle Coffee; and a cocktail-and-charcuterie outpost of the Cannibal (*see p139*). Seating is at chefs' counters or communal tables.

Kashkaval Garden

852 Ninth Avenue, between 55th & 56th Streets (1-212 245 1758, www.kashkavalgarden.com). Subway C, E to 50th Street. **Open** 11am-2am Mon-Thur; 11am-3am Fri, Sat; 11am-1am Sun. **Main courses** $12-$21. **Map** p149 A2 ⑮
Mediterranean
This charming tapas and wine bar evokes fondue's peasant origins, with deep cast-iron pots and generous baskets of crusty bread. Steer clear of the bland and rubbery kashkaval (a Balkan sheep's-milk cheese) and order the gooey gruyère and truffle. Or choose from the selection of tangy Mediterranean spreads – roasted artichoke dip with breadcrumbs or beet houmous – and the impressive roster of skewers.

Bars

For gay bars in Hell's Kitchen, *see pp271-272*.

★ Ardesia

510 W 52nd Street, between Tenth & Eleventh Avenues (1-212 247 9191, www.ardesia-ny.com). Subway C, E to 50th Street. **Open** 4pm-midnight Mon-Wed; 4pm-2am Thur, Fri; 2pm-2am Sat; 2-11pm Sun. **Map** p149 B2 ⑯
Le Bernardin vet Mandy Oser's iron-and-marble gem offers superior wines in a relaxed setting. The 85-strong collection of international bottles is a smart balance of Old and New World options that pair beautifully with the artisanal cheeses, charcuterie, salads and a constantly changing choice of small plates, such as the daily selection of croquettes and house-made NYC-style pretzels. One for the serious oenophile.

Pony Bar

637 Tenth Avenue, at 45th Street (1-212 586 2707, www.theponybar.com). Subway C, E to 50th Street. **Open** 3pm-4am Mon-Fri; noon-4am Sat, Sun. **Map** p149 B2 ⑰
The Theater District isn't known for civilised, non-chain bars, so walk a couple of blocks west to this convivial paean to American microbrews. Choose from a constantly changing selection of two cask ales and 20 beers on tap; daily selections are artfully listed on signboards according to provenance and potency. Despite the expert curation, the prices are kept low (all beers cost $7, or $5 during happy hour).

Other location 1444 First Avenue, at 75th Street, Upper East Side (1-212 288 0090).

Rum House

228 W 47th Street, between Seventh & Eighth Avenues (1-646 490 6924, www.edisonrumhouse.com). Subway N, Q, R to 49th Street. **Open** noon-4am daily. **Map** p149 B3 ⑱
In 2011, this rakish, 1970s-vintage piano bar in the Edison Hotel seemed destined to go the way of the Times Square peep show. But the team behind Tribeca mixology den Ward III ushered in a second act, introducing key upgrades (including serious cocktails) while maintaining the charmingly offbeat vibe. Sip dark, spirit-heavy tipples, such as a funky old-fashioned riff that showcases a sultry aged rum, while listening to live music most nights of the week.

Shops & Services

Amy's Bread

672 Ninth Avenue, between 46th & 47th Streets (1-212 977 2670, www.amysbread.com). Subway C, E to 50th Street; N, Q, R to 49th Street. **Open** 7.30am-10pm Mon, Tue; 7.30am-11pm Wed-Fri; 8am-11pm Sat; 8am-10pm Sun. **Map** p149 B2 ⑲
Food & drink
Whether sweet (double-chocolate pecan Chubbie cookies) or savoury (black olive bread twists), Amy's never disappoints. Breakfast and snacks such as grilled cheese sandwiches (made with New York State cheddar and spicy chipotle-pepper purée) are served. **Other locations** Chelsea Market, 75 Ninth Avenue, between 15th & 16th Streets, Chelsea (1-212 462 4338); 250 Bleecker Street, at Leroy Street, West Village (1-212 675 7802).

EXPLORE

★ Domus

413 W 44th Street, at Ninth Avenue (1-212 581 8099, www.domusnewyork.com). Subway A, C, E to 42nd Street-Port Authority. **Open** noon-8pm Tue-Sat; noon-6pm Sun. **Map** p149 C2 ➋⓪ **Homewares**
Scouring the globe for unusual design products is nothing new, but owners Luisa Cerutti and Nicki Lindheimer take the concept a step further; each year they visit a far-flung part of the world to forge links with and support co-operatives and individual craftspeople. The beautiful results, such as vivid baskets made from telephone wire by South African Zulu tribespeople, carved soapstone boxes from Vietnam or handwoven Tunisian bath towels, reflect a fine attention to detail and a sense of place. It's a great place to pick up reasonably priced gifts.

Fine and Dandy

445 W 49th Street, between Ninth & Tenth Avenues (1-212 247 4847, www.fineanddandyshop.com). Subway C, E to 50th Street. **Open** noon-8pm Mon-Sat; 1-8pm Sun. **Map** p149 B2 ➋➒ **Accessories**
Following several pop-ups around the city, owner Matt Fox opened his first permanent location in Hell's Kitchen. The accessories-only shop – decked out with collegiate trophies and ironing boards repurposed as tables – is a prime location for the modern gent to score of-the-moment retro accoutrements like bow ties, suspenders (braces) and spats. House-label printed ties are hung in propped-open vintage trunks; patterned socks are displayed in old briefcases.

Skagen

1585 Broadway, between 47th & 48th Streets (1-845 384 1221, www.skagen.com). Subway N, Q, R to 49th Street; N, Q, R, S, 1, 2, 3, 7 to 42nd Street-Times Square. **Open** 9am-midnight Mon-Thur, Sun; 9am-1am Fri, Sat. **Map** p149 B3 ➋➋ **Accessories**

Yes, this accessories store is in the heart of Times Square, but the interior, which channels the seaside village on the coast of Denmark, is a pocket of calm amid the chaos. The space pays homage to the famous Skagen beaches in the form of modernised pebble-shaped tables and natural wood surfaces. Digital displays detail the stories behind items in the shop, which include watches and jewellery as well as a collection of leather bags that range from backpacks to satchels for men and women.

FIFTH AVENUE & AROUND

Subway B, D, F, M, N, Q, R to 34th Street-Herald Square; Subway B, D, F, M to 42nd Street-Bryant Park; B, D, F, M to 47-50th Streets-Rockefeller Center; E, M to Fifth Avenue-53rd Street; 7 to Fifth Avenue.

The city's central thoroughfare is the main route for public processions, such as the **St Patrick's Day Parade** (*see p31*), the **LGBT Pride March** (*see p36*) and many others. But even without floats or marching bands, the sidewalks are generally teeming with shoppers and tourists. The most famous skyscraper in the world also has its entrance on Fifth Avenue: the **Empire State Building**, located smack-bang in the centre of midtown.

A pair of impassive stone lions, which were dubbed Patience and Fortitude by Mayor Fiorello La Guardia during the Great Depression, guard the steps of the beautiful Beaux Arts humanities and social sciences branch of the **New York Public Library** at 42nd Street, now officially named the Stephen A Schwarzman Building. Just behind the library is **Bryant Park**, a manicured lawn that hosts a popular outdoor film series in summer and an ice-skating rink in winter.

The luxury **Bryant Park Hotel** (*see p367*) occupies the former American Radiator Building on 40th Street. Designed by architect Raymond Hood in the mid 1920s, the structure is faced with near-black brick and trimmed in gold leaf. Alexander Woollcott, Dorothy Parker and her 'vicious circle' held court and traded barbs at the nearby **Algonquin** (59 W 44th Street, between Fifth & Sixth Avenues, 1-212 840 6800, www.algonquinhotel.com)); the lobby is still a great place to meet for a drink.

Step off Fifth Avenue into **Rockefeller Center** and you'll find yourself in a 'city within a city', an interlacing complex of 19 buildings housing corporate offices, retail space and Rockefeller Plaza. After plans for an expansion of the Metropolitan Opera on the site fell through in 1929, John D Rockefeller Jr set about creating the complex to house radio and television corporations. Designed by Raymond Hood and many other prominent architects, Rock Center grew over the decades, with each new building conforming to the original master plan and art

IN THE KNOW PUBLIC ART

While you're walking around midtown, keep an eye out for famous pieces of public art such as Robert Indiana's 12-foot-high, red-and-blue *LOVE* (Sixth Avenue at 55th Street) and Alexander Calder's red, mobile-like yet static *Saurien* (Madison Avenue at 57th Street). Next to Grand Central Terminal, the Grand Hyatt (109 E 42nd Street, 1-212 883 1234, www.grandhyattnewyork.com) has two ethereal marble heads by Barcelona-based artist Jaume Plensa. Other intriguing works, hidden within office buildings, need to be sleuthed out, such as the life-size nude sculpture between the revolving doors of 747 Third Avenue (between 46th & 47th Streets) – you get a surreal double-take glimpse as you pass through.

Fine and Dandy.

deco design. On weekday mornings, a crowd gathers at the NBC network's glass-walled, ground-level studio (where the *Today* show is shot), at the south-west corner of Rockefeller Plaza and 49th Street. The complex is also home to art auction house **Christie's** (20 Rockefeller Plaza, 49th Street, between Fifth & Sixth Avenues, 1-212 636 2000, www.christies.com; closed Sat, Sun); pop into the lobby to admire a mural by conceptualist Sol LeWitt.

When it opened on Sixth Avenue (at 50th Street) in 1932, **Radio City Music Hall** (*see p289*) was designed as a showcase for high-end variety acts, but the death of vaudeville led to a quick transition into what was then the world's largest movie house. Today, the art deco jewel hosts concerts and a traditional Christmas Spectacular featuring renowned precision dance troupe the Rockettes. Visitors can get a peek backstage, and meet one of the high-kicking dancers, on the Stage Door tour (every 30mins, 11am-3pm daily; $20, $15 reductions; see www.radiocity.com/tours.html for details).

Facing Rockefeller Center is the beautiful **St Patrick's Cathedral**. Famous couples from F Scott and Zelda Fitzgerald to Liza Minnelli and

David Gest have tied the knot here; funeral services for such notables as Andy Warhol and baseball legend Joe DiMaggio were held in its confines. A few blocks north is the **Museum of Modern Art** (MoMA) and the **Paley Center for Media**.

The stretch of Fifth Avenue between Rockefeller Center and Central Park South (59th Street) showcases retail palaces bearing names that were famous long before the concept of branding was developed. Along with Madison Avenue uptown, this is the centre of high-end shopping in New York, and the window displays – particularly during the frenetic Christmas shopping season – are worth a look even if you're not buying. A block from the park, Grand Army Plaza is presided over by a gilded statue of General William Tecumseh Sherman. To the west stands the **Plaza** (*see p367*), the famous hotel that was home to fictional moppet Eloise. Stretching north is **Central Park** (*see pp175-176*).

Sights & Museums

★ Empire State Building

350 Fifth Avenue, between 33rd & 34th Streets (1-212 736 3100, www.esbnyc.com). Subway B, D, F, M, N, Q, R to 34th Street-Herald Square. **Open** 8am-2am daily (last elevator 1.15am). **Admission** *86th floor* $32; $26-$29 reductions; free under-6s. *102nd floor* $20 extra. **Map** p149 D4 ㉓

Financed by General Motors executive John J Raskob at the height of New York's skyscraper race, the Empire State sprang up in a mere 14 months, weeks ahead of schedule and $5 million under budget. Since its opening in 1931, it's been immortalised in countless photos and films, from the original *King Kong* to *Sleepless in Seattle*. Following the destruction of the World Trade Center in 2001, the 1,250ft tower resumed its title as New York's tallest building but has since been overtaken by the new 1 World Trade Center. The nocturnal colour scheme of the tower lights – upgraded to flashy LEDs – often honours holidays, charities or special events.

The enclosed observatory on the 102nd floor is the city's highest lookout point, but the panoramic deck on the 86th floor, 1,050ft above the street, is roomier. From here, you can enjoy views of all five boroughs and five neighbouring states too (when the skies are clear). For tips on how to beat the queues, *see p158* **In the Know**.

★ Museum of Modern Art

11 W 53rd Street, between Fifth & Sixth Avenues (1-212 708 9400, www.moma.org). Subway E, M to Fifth Avenue-53rd Street. **Open** Sept-June 10.30am-5.30pm Mon-Thur, Sat, Sun; 10.30am-8pm Fri. *July, Aug* 10.30am-5.30pm Mon-Wed, Sat, Sun; 10.30am-8.30pm Thur; 10.30am-8pm Fri. **Admission** (incl admission to film programmes) $25; $14-$18 reductions; free under-17s; free 4-8pm Fri. **Map** p149 B4 ㉔

EXPLORE

Museum of Modern Art. See p257.

After a two-year renovation based on a design by Japanese architect Yoshio Taniguchi, MoMA reopened in 2004 with almost double the space to display some of the most impressive artworks from the 19th, 20th and 21st centuries. On the horizon is another expansion project, which will extend the museum into adjoining sites, but the time frame hadn't been determined at time of writing. MoMA's permanent collection encompasses seven curatorial departments: Architecture and Design, Drawings, Film, Media, Painting and Sculpture, Photography, and Prints and Illustrated Books. Highlights include Picasso's *Les Demoiselles d'Avignon*, Van Gogh's *The Starry Night* and Dali's *The Persistence of Memory*, as well as masterpieces by Giacometti, Hopper, Matisse, Monet, O'Keeffe, Pollock, Rothko, Warhol and many others. Outside, the Philip Johnson-designed Abby Aldrich Rockefeller Sculpture Garden contains works by Calder, Rodin and Moore. The destination museum also contains a destination restaurant, the Modern, which overlooks the garden. If you find the prices too steep, dine in the bar, which shares the kitchen.

▶ *For MoMA PS1 in Queens, see p228.*

★ FREE New York Public Library

Fifth Avenue, at 42nd Street (1-917 275 6975, www.nypl.org). Subway B, D, F, M to 42nd Street-Bryant Park; 7 to Fifth Avenue. **Open** *Sept-June* 10am-6pm Mon, Thur-Sat; 10am-8pm Tue, Wed; 1-5pm Sun. *July, Aug* 10am-6pm Mon, Thur-Sat; 10am-8pm Tue, Wed (see website for gallery hours). **Admission** free. **Map** p149 C4 ㉕

Guarded by the marble lions Patience and Fortitude, this austere Beaux Arts edifice, designed by Carrère

and Hastings, was completed in 1911. The building was renamed in honour of philanthropist Stephen A Schwarzman in 2008, but Gothamites still know it as the New York Public Library (although the citywide library system consists of 92 locations). Free hour-long tours (11am, 2pm Mon-Sat; 2pm Sun, except July & Aug) take in the Rose Main Reading Room on the third floor, which at 297ft long and 78ft wide is almost the size of a football field. Specialist departments include the Map Division, containing some 431,000 maps and 16,000 atlases, and the Rare Books Division boasting Walt Whitman's personal copies of the first (1855) and third (1860) editions of *Leaves of Grass*. The library also stages major exhibitions and events, including the excellent 'Live from the NYPL' series of talks and lectures from big-name authors and thinkers (see the website for the schedule).

Paley Center for Media

25 W 52nd Street, between Fifth & Sixth Avenues (1-212 621 6800, www.paleycenter.org). Subway B, D, F, M to 47-50th Streets-Rockefeller Center; E, M to Fifth Avenue-53rd Street. **Open** noon-6pm Wed, Fri-Sun; noon-8pm Thur. **Admission** $10; $5-$8 reductions. **No credit cards. Map** p149 B4 ㉖

Nirvana for telly addicts and pop-culture junkies, the Paley Center houses an immense archive of more than 160,000 radio, TV and online shows and commercials. Head to the fourth-floor library to search the system for your favourite episode of *Seinfeld*, *Mad Men*, or rarer fare, and watch or listen to it on your assigned console. A theatre on the concourse level is the site of frequent screenings, premières and high-profile panel discussions.

★ Rockefeller Center

From 48th to 51st Streets, between Fifth & Sixth Avenues (tours & Top of the Rock 1-212 698 2000, www.rockefellercenter.com). Subway B, D, F, M to 47-50th Streets-Rockefeller Center. **Open** *Tours* vary. *Observation deck* 8am-midnight daily (last elevator 11pm). **Admission** *Rockefeller Center tours* $17 (under-6s not admitted). *Observation deck* $29; $18-$27 reductions; free under-6s. **Map** p149 B4 ㉗

IN THE KNOW
EMPIRE STATE EXPRESS

If you're visiting the **Empire State Building** (see p157), allow at least two hours for queueing and viewing. To save time, bypass one of three lines by buying tickets online (but not the others, for security and entry), and visit late at night. Alternatively, springing for an express pass ($55, or $75 for both the 86th and 102nd floors) allows you to cut to the front.

Constructed under the aegis of industrialist John D Rockefeller in the 1930s, this art deco city-within-a-city is inhabited by NBC, Simon & Schuster, McGraw-Hill and other media giants, as well as Radio City Music Hall, Christie's auction house, and an underground shopping arcade. Guided tours of the entire complex are available daily, and there's a separate NBC Studio tour, which was closed for a revamp at time of writing but due to reopen at some point in 2015 (call 1-212 664 3700 or check www. nbcstudiotour.com) for updates.

The buildings and grounds are embellished with works by several well-known artists; look out for Isamu Noguchi's stainless-steel relief, *News*, above the entrance to 50 Rockefeller Plaza, and José Maria Sert's mural *American Progress* in the lobby of 30 Rockefeller Plaza (also known as the GE Building). But the most breathtaking sights are those seen from the 70th-floor Top of the Rock observation deck (combined tour/observation deck tickets are available). From around mid October to April, the Plaza's sunken courtyard – eternally guarded by Paul Manship's bronze statue of Prometheus – becomes a picturesque, if crowded, ice-skating rink. *Photo p160.*

FREE St Patrick's Cathedral
Fifth Avenue, between 50th & 51st Streets (1-212 753 2261, www.saintpatrickscathedral. org). Subway B, D, F, M to 47-50th Streets-Rockefeller Center; E, M to Fifth Avenue-53rd Street. **Open** 6.30am-8.45pm daily. **Admission** free. **Map** p149 B4 ㉓

The largest Catholic church in America, St Patrick's counts presidents, business leaders and movie stars among its past and present parishioners. The newly cleaned Gothic-style façade features intricate white-marble spires, but equally impressive is the interior, including the Louis Tiffany-designed altar, solid bronze baldachin, and the rose window by stained-glass master Charles Connick.

▶ *Further uptown is another awe-inspiring house of worship, the Cathedral Church of St John the Divine; see p177.*

Restaurants & Cafés

Benoit
60 W 55th Street, between Fifth & Sixth Avenues (1-646 943 7373, www.benoitny.com). Subway E, M to Fifth Avenue-53rd Street; F to 57th Street. **Open** 11.45am-3pm, 5.30-11pm Mon-Sat; 11.30am-3.30pm, 5.30-11pm Sun. **Main courses** $26-$48. **Map** p149 A4 ㉙ **French**
Alain Ducasse's classic brasserie attempts to reclaim 55th Street's former Francophile row. Come for successful, seasonality-snubbing classics like a cassoulet packed with pork loin, garlic sausage and duck confit under a canopy of white beans. At the Sunday brunch, the dessert bar ($5 per item, $16 all-you-can-eat) offers a dozen seasonal pastries and tarts.

New York Public Library.

★ Betony

41 W 57th Street, between Fifth & Sixth Avenues (1-212 465 2400, www.betony-nyc.com). Subway F, N, Q, R to 57th Street. **Open** *noon-2pm, 5.30-10pm Mon-Thur; noon-2pm, 5.30-10.30pm Fri; 5.30-10.30pm Sat.* **Main courses** *$28-$37.* **Map** p149 A4 ㉚ **American creative**

Eleven Madison Park alums Bryce Shuman and Eamon Rockey have created a rare treat: a serious New American restaurant that doesn't take itself too seriously. In the glam dining room, with its ornately carved wood walls, hyper-professional service is softened with a heaping dose of humanity, and the fun-loving, changing à la carte menu may include stellar riffs on salad with green goddess dressing and toasty tuna melts. Dishes such as seared foie gras plugged with smoked ham hock and draped with crisp, vinegar-twanged kale combine upmarket cachet with down-home comforts.

Shops & Services

Bracketed by **Saks Fifth Avenue** and **Bergdorf Goodman**, the prime shopping stretch of Fifth Avenue is chock-a-block with luxury designer flagships (Gucci, Prada, Tiffany & Co, Valentino) and mall-level brands (Gap, Forever 21, Uniqlo), not to mention a 24-hour, subterranean Apple Store (www.apple.com), entered via a 32-foot glass cube. The parade of big names continues east along 57th Street.

Rockefeller Center. *See p158.*

★ Bergdorf Goodman

754 Fifth Avenue, between 57th & 58th Streets (1-212 753 7300, www.bergdorfgoodman.com). Subway E, M to Fifth Avenue-53rd Street; N, Q, R to Fifth Avenue-59th Street. **Open** *10am-8pm Mon-Fri; 10am-7pm Sat; 11am-6pm Sun.* **Map** p149 A4 ㉛ **Department store**

Synonymous with understated luxury, Bergdorf's is known for designer clothes (the fifth floor is dedicated to younger, trend-driven labels) and accessories. For something more unusual, seek out Kentshire's wonderful cache of vintage jewellery on the seventh floor. Descend to the basement for the wide-ranging beauty department. The men's store is across the street at 745 Fifth Avenue. *Photo p162.*

★ FAO Schwarz

767 Fifth Avenue, at 58th Street (1-212 644 9400, www.fao.com). Subway N, Q, R to Lexington Avenue-59th Street; 4, 5, 6 to 59th Street. **Open** *10am-7pm Mon-Thur, Sun; 10am-8pm Fri, Sat.* **Map** p149 A4 ㉜ **Children**

Although it's now owned by the ubiquitous Toys 'R' Us, this three-storey emporium is still the ultimate NYC toy box. Most people head straight to the 22ft-long floor piano that Tom Hanks famously tinkled in the film *Big*. Kids will marvel at the giant stuffed animals, and the detailed and imaginative Lego figures.

Henri Bendel

712 Fifth Avenue, at 56th Street (1-212 247 1100, www.henribendel.com). Subway E, M to Fifth Avenue-53rd Street; N, Q, R to Fifth Avenue-59th Street. **Open** *10am-8pm Mon-Sat; noon-7pm Sun.* **Map** p149 A4 ㉝ **Department store**

While Bendel's merchandise (a mix of jewellery, fashion accessories, cosmetics and fragrances) is comparable to that of other upscale stores, it somehow seems more desirable when viewed in its opulent premises, a conglomeration of three 19th-century townhouses – and those darling brown-and-white striped shopping bags don't hurt, either. Bendel's is also the home of celebrity hairdresser Frédéric Fekkai's flagship salon.

Saks Fifth Avenue

611 Fifth Avenue, between 49th & 50th Streets, (1-212 753 4000, www.saksfifthavenue.com). Subway E, M to Fifth Avenue-53rd Street. **Open** *10am-8.30pm Mon-Sat; 11am-7pm Sun.* **Map** p149 B4 ㉞ **Department store**

Although Saks has 39 locations nationwide, the Fifth Avenue flagship is the original, established in 1924 by New York retailers Horace Saks and Bernard Gimbel. The store features all the big names in fashion, from Armani to Zac Posen, including an expansive luxury shoe salon on the eighth floor. The opulent beauty hall is fun to peruse, and customer service is excellent, though some people might find it too aggressive.

EXPLORE

Betony.

MIDTOWN EAST

Subway E, M to Lexington Avenue-53rd Street; S, 4, 5, 6, 7 to 42nd Street-Grand Central; 6 to 51st Street.

Shopping, dining and entertainment options wane east of Fifth Avenue in the 40s and 50s. However, the area has some striking architecture, including several iconic landmarks. The 1913 **Grand Central Terminal** is the city's most spectacular point of arrival, although these days it welcomes only commuter trains from Connecticut and upstate New York. Looming behind the terminal, the **MetLife Building** (formerly the Pan Am Building) was the world's largest office tower when it opened in the 1960s. Other must-see buildings in the vicinity include **Lever House** (390 Park Avenue, between 53rd & 54th Streets), the **Seagram Building** (375 Park Avenue, between 52nd & 53rd Streets), the slanted-roofed **Citigroup Center** (from 53rd Street to 54th Street, between Lexington & Third Avenues) and the stunning art deco skyscraper that anchors the corner of Lexington Avenue and 51st Street, formerly the **General Electric Building** (and before that, the RCA Victor Building). A Chippendale crown tops the **Sony Building** (550 Madison Avenue, between 55th & 56th Streets), Philip Johnson's postmodern icon.

East 42nd Street has a wealth of architectural distinction, including the Romanesque Revival hall of the former **Bowery Savings Bank** (no.110) and the art deco details of the **Chanin Building** (no.122). Completed in 1930 by architect William Van Alen, the gleaming **Chrysler Building** (at Lexington Avenue) is a pinnacle of the art deco style, paying homage to the automobile with vast radiator-cap eagles in lieu of traditional gargoyles and a brickwork relief sculpture of racing cars complete with chrome hubcaps. The **Daily News Building** (no.220), another art deco gem designed by Raymond Hood, was immortalised in the *Superman* films. Although the namesake tabloid no longer has its offices here, the lobby still houses its giant globe and weather instruments.

To the east lies the literally elevated **Tudor City** (between First & Second Avenues, from E 41st to E 43rd Streets), a pioneering 1925 residential development that resembles high-rise versions of England's Hampton Court Palace.

Bergdorf Goodman. See p160.

At the end of 43rd Street is a terrace overlooking, and stairs leading down to, the **United Nations Headquarters**. Not far from here is the **Japan Society**, designated an official landmark in 2011.

Sights & Museums

FREE Grand Central Terminal

From 42nd to 44th Streets, between Vanderbilt & Lexington Avenues (audio tours 1-917 566 0008, www.grandcentralterminal.com). Subway S, 4, 5, 6, 7 to 42nd Street-Grand Central. **Map** p149 C4 ⑯

Each day, the world's largest rail terminal sees more than 750,000 people shuffle through its Beaux Arts threshold – many of them sightseers. Designed by Warren & Wetmore and Reed & Stern, the gorgeous transport hub opened in 1913 with lashings of Botticino marble and staircases modelled after those of the Paris opera house. After midcentury decline, the terminal underwent extensive restoration and is now a destination in itself, with shopping and dining options, including the Campbell Apartment (1-212 953 0409), the Grand Central Oyster Bar & Restaurant (*see p163*), and a sprawling Apple Store (1-212 284 1800) on the East Balcony. Visit the website for information about self-guided audio tours ($9; $7 reductions), or download the $5 smartphone app.

▶ *For trains from Grand Central, see p374.*

Japan Society

333 E 47th Street, between First & Second Avenues (1-212 832 1155, www.japansociety.org). Subway E, M to Lexington Avenue-53rd Street; 6 to 51st Street. **Open** hrs vary. Gallery 11am-6pm Tue-Thur; 11am-9pm Fri; 11am-5pm Sat, Sun. **Admission** $12; $10 reductions; free under-16s; free 6-9pm Fri. **Map** p149 B5 ㊱

Founded in 1907, the Japan Society moved into its current home in 1971. Designed by Junzo Yoshimura, it was the first contemporary Japanese building in New York, complete with a waterfall and bamboo garden. The gallery mounts temporary exhibitions on such diverse subjects as depictions of cats in *Ukiyo-e* woodblock prints, textile design and works by prominent contemporary artists.

United Nations Headquarters

Visitors' entrance: First Avenue, between 45th & 46th Streets (tours 1-212 963 8687, http://visit. un.org). Subway S, 4, 5, 6, 7 to 42nd Street-Grand Central. **Open** Visitor centre 9am-4.30pm Mon-Fri; 10am-4.30pm Sat, Sun. Tours 9.30am-4.45pm Mon-Fri. **Admission** $18; $9-$11 reductions (under-5s not admitted). **Map** p149 C5 ㊲

The UN has wrapped up extensive renovations to its complex and Le Corbusier's Secretariat building is gleaming. The iconic skyscraper is off-limits to the public, however, so you can only admire the exterior. Hour-long tours discuss the history and role of the UN, and visit the Security Council Chamber and the General Assembly Hall (when they're not in session). Artworks are back on view for the first time in years, including Norman Rockwell's mosaic *The Golden Rule*, and José Vela Zanetti's epic, 64ft-long 1953 mural *Mankind's Struggle for a Lasting Peace*. Note that while tickets may be available on site (cash only), it's advisable to book online. The UN is closed for two weeks in September for the General Debate.

EXPLORE

Restaurants & Cafés

Grand Central Oyster Bar & Restaurant

Grand Central Terminal, Lower Level, 42nd Street, at Park Avenue (1-212 490 6650, www.oyster barny.com). Subway S, 4, 5, 6, 7 to 42nd Street-Grand Central. **Open** 11.30am-9.30pm Mon-Sat. **Main courses** $18-$32. **Map** p149 C4 ❸ **Seafood**

The legendary Grand Central Oyster Bar has been a fixture since 1913. The surly countermen at the mile-long bar (the best seats in the house) are part of the charm. Avoid the more complicated fish concoctions and play it safe with a reliably awe-inspiring platter of iced, just-shucked oysters (there can be a whopping 30 varieties to choose from, including many from nearby Long Island).

▶ *For more on the iconic transport hub, see p162.*

Monkey Bar

Hotel Elysée, 60 E 54th Street, between Madison & Park Avenues (1-212 288 1010, www.monkeybar newyork.com). Subway E, M to Lexington Avenue-53rd Street; 6 to 51st Street. **Open** 11.30am-10pm Mon-Fri; 5.30-10pm Sat. **Main courses** $22-$46. **Map** p149 B4 ❸ **American**

After the repeal of Prohibition in 1933, this one-time piano bar in the swank Hotel Elysée (*see p368*) became a boozy clubhouse for the glitzy artistic figures of the age, among them Tallulah Bankhead, Dorothy Parker and Tennessee Williams. The Monkey Bar is now owned by publishing titan Graydon Carter, who brought new buzz to the historic space. Perched at the bar with a pitch-perfect glass of Gonet-Medeville champagne or ensconced in a red leather booth with a plate of fettuccine carbonara with bacon lardons, you'll find yourself seduced by that rare alchemy of old New York luxury and new-school flair.

IN THE KNOW SAMPLE SALES

Home to numerous designer studios and showrooms, New York's **Garment District** (*see p148*) hosts a weekly spate of sample sales. The best are listed in the Shopping & Style section of *Time Out New York* magazine and www.timeout.com/new york. Other good resources are **Racked** (www.ny.racked.com), **Top Button** (www.topbutton.com) and **Clothing Line** (1-212 947 8748, www.clothingline.com), which holds sales for a variety of labels – from J Crew and Milly to Helmut Lang and Rag & Bone, at its showroom (Second Floor, 261 W 36th Street, between Seventh & Eighth Avenues). Another prime sample-sale spot is further east, in the Flatiron District at **260 Fifth Avenue** (1-212 725 5400, www.260samplesale.com).

Quality Meats

57 W 58th Street, between Fifth & Sixth Avenues (1-212 371 7777, www.qualitymeatsnyc.com). Subway F, N, Q, R to 57th Street; N, Q, R to Fifth Avenue-59th Street. **Open** 11.30am-3pm, 5-10.30pm Mon-Wed; 11.30am-3pm, 5-11.30pm Thur, Fri; 5-11.30pm Sat; 5-10pm Sun. **Main courses** $21-$47. **Map** p149 A4 ❹ **Steakhouse**

Michael Stillman – son of the founder of landmark steakhouse Smith & Wollensky – is behind this highly stylised industrial theme park complete with meat-hook light fixtures, wooden butcher blocks, white tiles and exposed brick. Lespinasse-trained chef Craig Koketsu nails the steaks (including a $110 double-rib steak) and breathes new life into traditional side dishes like airy 'gnocchi & cheese', a clever take on mac and cheese. The list of unusual ice-cream flavours includes the outstanding coffee-and-doughnuts, crammed with chunks of the treat.

Shops & Services

For our pick of the department stores on Fifth Avenue, *see p160*.

MURRAY HILL

Murray Hill spans 30th to 40th Streets, between Third and Fifth Avenues. Townhouses of the rich and powerful were once clustered around Madison and Park Avenues, including the home of Pierpont Morgan; his private library is now the **Morgan Library & Museum**, which houses some 500,000 rare books, prints, manuscripts and objects. These days, the neighbourhood is populated mostly by upwardly mobiles fresh out of university, and only a few streets retain their former elegance. One is **Sniffen Court** (150-158 E 36th Street, between Lexington & Third Avenues), an unspoiled row of 1864 carriage houses located within earshot of the Queens Midtown Tunnel's ceaseless traffic.

Sights & Museums

★ Morgan Library & Museum

225 Madison Avenue, at 36th Street (1-212 685 0008, www.themorgan.org). Subway 6 to 33rd Street. **Open** 10.30am-5pm Tue-Thur; 10.30am-9pm Fri; 10am-6pm Sat; 11am-6pm Sun. **Admission** $18; $12 reductions; free under-13s; free 7-9pm Fri. **Map** p149 C4 ❹

This Madison Avenue institution began as the private library of financier Pierpont Morgan, and is his cultural gift to the city. Building on the collection Morgan amassed in his lifetime, the museum houses first-rate works on paper, including drawings by Michelangelo, Rembrandt and Picasso; three Gutenberg Bibles; a copy of *Frankenstein* annotated by Mary Shelley; manuscripts by Dickens, Poe, Twain, Steinbeck and Wilde; sheet music

EXPLORE

handwritten by Beethoven and Mozart; and an original edition of Dickens's *A Christmas Carol* that's displayed every Yuletide. A massive renovation and expansion orchestrated by Renzo Piano brought more natural light into the building and doubled the available exhibition space. The final phase restored the original 1906 building, designed by McKim, Mead & White. Visitors can now see Morgan's spectacular library (the East Room), with its 30ft-high book-lined walls and murals designed by Henry Siddons Mowbray (who also painted the ceiling of the restored Rotunda).

Scandinavia House – The Nordic Center in America

58 Park Avenue, at 38th Street (1-212 779 3587, www.scandinaviahouse.org). Subway S, 4, 5, 6, 7 to 42nd Street-Grand Central. **Open** varies. *Gallery* noon-6pm Tue, Thur-Sat; noon-7pm Wed. **Admission** varies. **Map** p149 C4 ❷
One of the city's top cultural centres, Scandinavia House serves as a link between the US and the Scandinavian nations, and offers a full schedule of film screenings, lectures and book talks, concerts and art exhibitions. An outpost of Smörgås Chef (open 11am-10pm Mon-Sat, 11am-5pm Sun), serves tasty Swedish meatballs, and the shop is a showcase for chic Scandinavian design.

EXPLORE

Restaurants & Cafés

Artisanal

2 Park Avenue, at 32nd Street (1-212 725 8585, www.artisanalbistro.com). Subway 6 to 33rd Street. **Open** 11.45am-2.45pm,5-9.45pm Mon-Wed; 11.45am-2.45pm, 5-10.45pm Thur, Fri; 11am-3.45pm, 5-10.45pm Sat; 10.30am-3.45pm, 5-8.45pm Sun. **Main courses** $21-$75. **Map** p149 D4 ❸ **French**
While many NYC bistros veer towards uniformity, Terrance Brennan's high-ceilinged deco gem makes its mark with an all-out homage to fromage. Skip the appetisers and open with fondue, which comes in three varieties. Familiar bistro fare awaits, with such dishes as steak frites, mussels, and chicken baked 'under a brick', but the curd gets the last word with the cheese and wine pairings. These themed selections (for example, 'sinful' or 'feisty') of three combinations make a sumptuous and intriguing finale. You can also consult the in-house fromager to create your a personalised combo.

★ Kajitsu

125 E 39th Street, between Park & Lexington Avenues (1-212 228 4873, www.kajitsunyc.com). Subway S, 4, 5, 6, 7 to 42nd Street-Grand Central. **Open** 11.45am-1.45pm, 5.30-10pm Tue-Sat; 5.30-10pm Sun (closed 1st day of each month). **Tasting menus** $55-$95. **Map** p149 C4 ❷
Japanese/vegetarian
There's no shortage of cheap ramen joints in postgrad mecca Murray Hill, but house-made soba crowned

Salvation Taco.

with shaved black truffles? That's only at Kajitsu. The minimalist, Michelin-starred den displays a devotion to produce, influenced by the monk-approved *shojin-ryori* (vegetarian) tradition. The sublime fare has made it a cult favourite among top-notch toques like Momofuku's David Chang. In the small, bare dining room or at the eight-seat chef's counter, choose from two ever-changing menus – four or eight courses – each paired with sake if you like.

Salvation Taco

145 E 39th Street, between Lexington & Third Avenues (1-212 865 5800, www.salvationtaco. com). Subway S, 4, 5, 6, 7 to 42nd Street-Grand Central. **Open** 7am-5pm, 5.30pm-midnight daily. **Main courses** $12-$42. **Map** p149 C5 ❹ **Mexican**
The decor – coloured Christmas lights, fake fruit – may evoke that Cancun vacation, but the fiesta fare doled out at this Murray Hill cantina off the lobby of the Pod 39 hotel (*see p368*) has an upscale bent, thanks to April Bloomfield and Ken Friedman (of the Spotted Pig and the Ace Hotel's Breslin). Exotic fillings include Moroccan-spiced lamb and Korean-barbecue-style beef. Even a margarita gets a chefly update with a zippy guajillo chili salt rim.

Bars

Middle Branch

154 E 33rd Street, between Lexington & Third Avenues (1-212 213 1350). Subway 6 to 33rd Street. **Open** 5pm-2am daily. **Map** p149 D5 ❹

In 2000, visionary barman Sasha Petraske paved the way for the modern cocktail bar with members-only Milk & Honey; since then, he and his acolytes have spread the liquid gospel with a rapidly expanding web of standout watering holes. Middle Branch plants a flag for artisanal cocktails in post-frat epicentre Murray Hill. Unlike Petraske's Little Branch, this is no sly speakeasy, hidden from the masses with a windowless façade and an unmarked ingress: the bi-level drinkery, sporting French doors that offer a glimpse inside, practically beckons passersby to come in. But it has the same focus of the mixology master's other highfalutin' joints: classic cocktails and riffs, built with hand-cut ice and superior spirits.

Other location Little Branch, 20 Seventh Avenue South, at Leroy Street, West Village (1-212 929 4360).

Shops & Services

★ Dover Street Market New York

160 Lexington Avenue, at 30th Street (1-646 837 7750, http://newyork.doverstreetmarket.com). Subway 6 to 28th or 33rd Street. **Open** 11am-7pm Mon-Sat; noon-6pm Sun. **Map** p149 D5 **47** **Fashion/accessories**

In December 2013, Comme des Garçons designer Rei Kawakubo brought her quirky, upscale interpretation of a London fashion market to the former New York School of Applied Design, complete with an outpost of the cult Paris eaterie, Rose Bakery. One of three offspring of the original location on Mayfair's

Dover Street (the others are in Tokyo and Beijing), DSMNY is a multilevel store that blurs the line between art and commerce. A transparent elevator whisks shoppers through the seven-floor consumer playground. Three pillars running through six of the levels have been transformed into art installations: a stripey patchwork knitted sheath by Magda Sayeg, London Fieldworks' wooden metropolis, and 3D collages by 'junk sculptor' Leo Sewell. All of the Comme lines are here, alongside mini boutiques for luxury labels like Prada and Azzedine Alaïa, newer names such as Simone Rocha and Greg Lauren, streetwear brands including Nike and Supreme, an entire floor spotlighting emerging talent, and a raft of cool names and exclusive items.

★ JJ Hat Center

310 Fifth Avenue, between 31st & 32nd Streets (1-212 239 4368, www.jjhatcenter.com). Subway B, D, F, M, N, Q, R to 34th Street-Herald Square. **Open** 9am-6pm Mon-Fri; 9.30am-5.30pm Sat. **Map** p149 D4 **48** **Accessories**

Traditional hats may currently be back in fashion, but this venerable shop, in business since 1911, is oblivious to passing trends. Dapper gents sporting the shop's wares will help you choose from more than 4,000 fedoras, pork pies, caps and other styles on display in the splendid, chandelier-illuminated, wood-panelled showroom. Prices start at around $45 for a wool-blend cap.

Other location Pork Pie Hatters, 440 East 9th Street, between 1st Avenue & Avenue A, East Village (1-212 260 0408).

EXPLORE

Dover Street Market.

Upper West Side & Central Park

In the late 19th century, lavish apartment buildings sprang up alongside newly completed Central Park, luring well-heeled New Yorkers north. And in the decades that followed, immigrants brought diverse shops and eateries to the neighbourhood's avenues. While a few character-filled institutions survive, the arrival of new real estate and chain stores has had a homogenising effect. But the four-mile-long stretch between the park and the Hudson River is still culturally rich and cosmopolitan. The area is home to the American Museum of Natural History, the New-York Historical Society and venerated performing-arts complex Lincoln Center.

EXPLORE

Barney Greengrass.

Don't Miss

1 American Museum of Natural History Nature comes to life at this revitalised classic (p170).

2 Museum of Arts & Design Curators get creative with inventive themed shows (p171).

3 Barney Greengrass The 'Sturgeon King' has reigned since 1908 (p171).

4 Central Park From formal gardens and follies to rustic woodland (p171).

5 Cathedral Church of St John the Divine Prepare to be awed (p177).

UPPER WEST SIDE

Subway A, B, C, D, 1 to 59th Street-Columbus Circle; B, C to 72nd Street, 81st Street-Museum of Natural History, 86th Street, 96th Street or 103rd Street; 1, 2, 3 to 72nd Street or 96th Street; 1 to 66th Street-Lincoln Center, 79th Street, 86th Street or 103rd Street.

The gateway to the Upper West Side is **Columbus Circle**, where Broadway meets 59th Street, Eighth Avenue, Central Park South and Central Park West – a rare roundabout in a city of right angles. The architecture around it could make anyone's head spin. At the entrance to Central Park, a 700-ton statue of Christopher Columbus is dwarfed by the **Time Warner Center** across the street, which houses offices, apartments, a luxury hotel and Jazz at Lincoln Center's stunning **Frederick P Rose Hall** (*see p292*). The first seven levels of the enormous glass complex are filled with high-end retailers and gourmet restaurants, such as **Per Se**. In 2008, the **Museum of Arts & Design** opened in a landmark building on the south side of the circle, itself the subject of a controversial redesign.

A few blocks north, **Lincoln Center** (*see p296*), a complex of concert halls and auditoriums built in the early 1960s, is the home of the New York Philharmonic, the New York City Ballet, the Metropolitan Opera and a host of other notable arts organisations. The big circular fountain in the central plaza is a popular gathering spot and should be even more so when a planned alfresco champagne bar opens by the time this guide is published.

The centre has completed a major overhaul that included a redesign of public spaces, refurbishment of the various halls and a new visitor centre, the **David Rubenstein Atrium** (Broadway, between W 62nd & W 63rd Streets). Conceived as a contemporary interior garden with lush planted walls, the Atrium stages free genre-spanning concerts and events, and sells discounted tickets to performances at Lincoln Center, plus other Manhattan venues (see www. lincolncenter.org for details). It's also the starting point for guided tours of the complex (1-212 875 5350, $18, $15 reductions), which, in addition to the hallowed concert halls, contains several notable artworks, including Henry Moore's *Reclining Figure* in the plaza near Lincoln Center Theater, and two massive music-themed paintings by Marc Chagall in the lobby of the Metropolitan Opera House. Nearby is the **New York Public Library for the Performing Arts** (40 Lincoln Center Plaza, at 65th Street, 1-212 870 1630, www.nypl.org, closed Sun); alongside its extraordinary collection of films, letters, manuscripts, videos and sound recordings, it stages concerts and lectures.

Around Sherman and Verdi Squares (from 70th to 73rd Streets, where Broadway and Amsterdam Avenue intersect), classic early 20th-century buildings stand cheek-by-jowl with newer high-rises. The jewel is the 1904 **Ansonia Hotel** (2109 Broadway, between 73rd & 74th Streets). Over the years, Enrico Caruso, Babe Ruth and Igor Stravinsky have lived in this Beaux Arts masterpiece; it was also the site of the Continental Baths, the gay bathhouse and cabaret where Bette Midler got her start, and Plato's Retreat, a swinging 1970s sex club.

After Central Park was completed, magnificently tall residential buildings rose up along **Central Park West** to take advantage of the views. The first of these great apartment blocks was the **Dakota** (at 72nd Street), so named because its location was considered remote when it was built in 1884. The fortress-like building is known as the setting for *Rosemary's Baby* and the site of John Lennon's murder in 1980 (Yoko Ono still lives there); other residents have included Judy Garland, Rudolf Nureyev, Lauren Bacall and Boris Karloff – but not Billy Joel, who was turned away by the co-op board when he tried to buy an apartment. You might recognise **55 Central Park West** (at 66th Street) from the movie *Ghostbusters*. Built in 1930, it was the first art deco building on the block. Heading north on Central Park West, you'll spy the massive twin-towered **San Remo Apartments** (at 74th Street), which also date from 1930. Rita Hayworth, Steven Spielberg, Tiger Woods and U2's Bono have been among the building's many celebrity residents.

A few blocks to the north, the **New-York Historical Society** is the city's oldest museum, founded in 1804. Across the street, at the glorious **American Museum of Natural History**, dinosaur skeletons, a planetarium and an IMAX theatre lure visitors of all ages.

To see West Siders in their natural habitat, queue at the perpetually jammed gourmet market **Zabar's**. The legendary (if scruffy) restaurant and delicatessen **Barney Greengrass**, the self-styled 'Sturgeon King', has specialised in smoked fish, knishes and what may be the city's best chopped liver since 1908.

IN THE KNOW BOATS & BEER

From late March through October (weather permitting), you can take in the view of the **79th Street Boat Basin** (*see p170*) with a beer and a burger at the no-reservations **Boat Basin Café** (www.boatbasincafe.com). The patio of this extremely popular spot overlooks the marina, but there's also an adjacent covered rotunda.

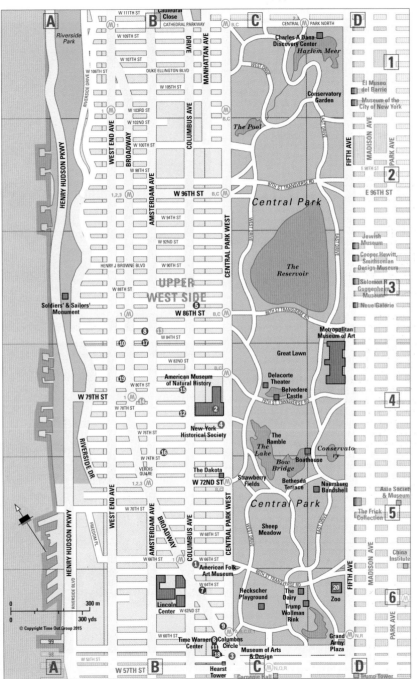

EXPLORE

Riverside Park, a sinuous stretch of riverbank along the Hudson from 59th Street to 155th Street, was originally designed by Central Park's Frederick Law Olmsted, and subsequently extended. You'll probably see yachts, along with several houseboats, berthed at the **79th Street Boat Basin**. Several sites provide havens for quiet reflection. The **Soldiers' & Sailors' Monument** (89th Street, at Riverside Drive), built in 1902 by French sculptor Paul EM Duboy, honours Union soldiers who died in the Civil War; and a 1913 memorial (100th Street, at Riverside Drive) pays tribute to fallen firemen.

Sights & Museums

FREE American Folk Art Museum
2 Lincoln Square, Columbus Avenue, at 66th Street (1-212 595 9533, www.folkartmuseum.org). Subway 1 to 66th Street-Lincoln Center. **Open** noon-7.30pm Tue-Sat; noon-6pm Sun. **Admission** free. **Map** p169 B5 ❶
The small space is misleading – the American Folk Art Museum's unparalleled holdings of folk art include more than 5,000 works dating from the late 18th century to the present. Changing exhibitions explore the work of self-taught and outsider artists, as well as showing traditional folk art such as quilts and needlework, and other decorative objects. You can purchase original handmade pieces in the large gift shop, and the museum regularly hosts free musical performances and other events.

★ American Museum of Natural History/ Rose Center for Earth & Space
Central Park West, at 79th Street (1-212 769 5100, www.amnh.org). Subway B, C to 81st Street-Museum of Natural History. **Open** 10am-5.45pm daily. **Admission** *Suggested donation* $22; $12.50-$17 reductions. **Map** p169 C4 ❷
The American Museum of Natural History's fourth-floor dino halls are home to the largest and arguably most fabulous collection of dinosaur fossils in the world. Nearly 85% of the bones on display are original, but during the museum's mid 1990s renovation, several specimens were remodelled to incorporate more recent discoveries. The Tyrannosaurus rex, for instance, was once believed to have walked upright, Godzilla-style; it now stalks prey with its head lowered and tail raised parallel to the ground.

The Hall of North American Mammals reopened in autumn 2012 after extensive restoration of its formerly faded 1940s dioramas. A life-size model of a blue whale hangs from the cavernous ceiling of the Hall of Ocean Life, while in the Hall of Meteorites, the focal point is Ahnighito, the largest iron meteor on display in the world, weighing in at 34 tons. Other halls explore human origins, world ecosystems and environmental preservation.

The spectacular Rose Center for Earth & Space offers insight into recent cosmic discoveries via

American Museum of Natural History.

EXPLORE

shows in the Hayden Planetarium and a simulation of the origins of the Universe in the Big Bang Theater. The museum also screens digital nature films in 3D, and the roster of temporary exhibitions is thought-provoking for all ages.

★ Museum of Arts & Design

2 Columbus Circle, at Broadway (1-212 299 7777, www.madmuseum.org). Subway A, B, C, D, 1 to 59th Street-Columbus Circle. **Open** 10am-6pm Tue, Wed, Sat, Sun; 10am-9pm Thur, Fri. **Admission** $16; $12-$14 reductions; free under-19s; pay what you wish 6-9pm Thur, Fri. **Map** p169 C6 ❸

This institution celebrates creative practice with a permanent collection of art, craft and design items dating from 1950 to the present. MAD brings together contemporary objects created in a wide range of media – including clay, glass, wood, metal and cloth – with a strong focus on materials and process. In 2008, after an extensive redesign of Edward Durell Stone's 1964 windowless monolith at 2 Columbus Circle, including a new façade, the museum moved to the site. The ten-storey building now has four floors of exhibition galleries, including the Tiffany & Co Foundation Jewelry Gallery. Curators are able to display more of the 3,000-piece permanent collection, which includes porcelain ware by Cindy Sherman, stained glass by Judith Schaechter and ceramics by James Turrell. In addition to checking out temporary shows, you can watch resident artists create works in studios on the sixth floor, while the ninth-floor bistro has views over the park.

★ New-York Historical Society

170 Central Park West, between 76th & 77th Streets (1-212 873 3400, www.nyhistory.org). Subway B, C to 81st Street-Museum of Natural History. **Open** 10am-6pm Tue-Thur, Sat; 10am-8pm Fri; 11am-5pm Sun. **Admission** $19; $6-$15 reductions; free under-4s. Pay what you wish 6-8pm Fri. **Map** p169 C4 ❹

Founded in 1804 by a group of prominent New Yorkers that included Mayor DeWitt Clinton, the New-York Historical Society is the city's oldest museum, originally based at City Hall. In autumn 2011, the society's 1904 building reopened after a three-year, $70-million renovation that opened up the interior spaces to make the collection more accessible to a 21st-century audience. The Robert H and Clarice Smith New York Gallery of American History provides an overview of the collection and a broad sweep of New York's place in American history – Revolutionary-era maps are juxtaposed with a piece of the ceiling mural from Keith Haring's Pop Shop (the artist's Soho store, which closed after his death in 1990). Touch-screen monitors offer insight into artwork and documents, and large HD screens display a continuous slide show of highlights of the museum's holdings, such as original watercolours from Audubon's *Birds of America* and some of its 132 Tiffany lamps. The auditorium screens an 18-minute film tracing the city's development, while downstairs, the DiMenna Children's History Museum engages the next generation. The upper floors house changing exhibitions.

Restaurants & Cafés

★ Barney Greengrass

541 Amsterdam Avenue, between 86th & 87th Streets (1-212 724 4707, www.barneygreengrass. com). Subway B, C, 1 to 86th Street. **Open** 8am-6pm Tue-Sun. **Sandwiches** $9-$21. **No credit cards. Map** p169 B3 ❺ American

Despite decor that Jewish mothers might call 'schmutzy', this legendary deli is a madhouse at breakfast and brunch. Enormous egg platters come with the usual choice of smoked fish (such as sturgeon or Nova Scotia salmon). Prices are on the high side, but portions are large, and that goes for the sandwiches too. Soup – matzo-ball or cold pink borscht – is a less costly option.

$ Bouchon Bakery

3rd Floor, Time Warner Center, 10 Columbus Circle, at Broadway (1-212 823 9366, www. bouchonbakery.com). Subway A, B, C, D, 1 to 59th Street-Columbus Circle. **Open** 8am-9pm Mon-Sat; 8am-7pm Sun. **Pastries** $1-$7. **Map** p169 C6 ❻ Café

Chef Thomas Keller's café, in the same mall as his lauded fine-dining room Per Se (*see p173*), lacks ambience, and the menu (soups, tartines, salads, sandwiches) is basic. But prices are much more palatable – a dry-cured ham and emmenthal baguette is around a tenner. Baked goods, including Keller's takes on American classics like Oreo cookies, are the highlights.

Other locations 1 Rockefeller Plaza, at 49th Street, Midtown (1-212 782 3890).

Boulud Sud

20 W 64th Street, between Broadway & Central Park West (1-212 595 1313, www.bouludsud.com). Subway 1 to 66th Street-Lincoln Center. **Open**

IN THE KNOW
NEW-YORK, NEW-YORK

The name of the **New-York Historical Society** (*see p171*) is itself a historical preservation – placing a hyphen between 'New' and 'York' was common in the early 19th century. In fact, according to the Society, *The New York Times*, the paper of record, maintained the convention until 1896.

EXPLORE

Jean-Georges

11.30am-2.30pm, 5-11pm Mon-Wed; 11.30am-2.30pm, 5-11.30pm Thur, Fri; 11am-3pm, 5-11.30pm Sat; 11am-3pm, 5-10pm Sun. **Main courses** $21-$39. **Map** p169 B6 **❼ Mediterranean**
At his most international restaurant yet, superchef Daniel Boulud highlights the new French cuisine of melting-pot cities like Marseille and Nice. With his executive chef, Travis Swikard, he casts a wide net – looking to Egypt, Turkey and Greece. Diners can build a full tapas meal from shareable snacks like octopus *à la plancha*, with marcona almonds and arugula. Heartier dishes combine Gallic finesse with polyglot flavours: sweet-spicy chicken tagine with harira soup borrows from Morocco. Desserts – such as grapefruit *givré* stuffed with sorbet, sesame mousse and rose-scented nuggets of Turkish delight – take the exotic mix to even loftier heights.

Celeste
502 Amsterdam Avenue, between 84th & 85th Streets (1-212 874 4559, www.celestenewyork. com). Subway 1 to 86th Street. **Open** 5-11pm Mon-Thur; 5-11.30pm Fri; noon-3pm, 5-11.30pm Sat; noon-3pm, 5-10.30pm Sun. **No credit cards. Map** p169 B3 **❽ Italian**
This popular spot, offering authentic fare in a rustic setting, doesn't take reservations so a wait is to be expected. Once you're in, start with *carciofi fritti*: fried artichokes that are so light, they're evanescent. Three house-made pastas are prepared daily – the tagliatelle with shrimp, cabbage and pecorino stands out. Those who can manage a few more bites are advised to try the *pastiera*, a grain-and-ricotta cake flavoured with candied fruit and orange-blossom water.

Jean-Georges
Trump International Hotel & Tower, 1 Central Park West, at Columbus Circle (1-212 299 3900, www. jean-georgesrestaurant.com). Subway A, B, C, D, 1 to 59th Street-Columbus Circle. **Open** 11.45am-2.30pm, 5.30-11pm Mon-Thur; 11.45am-2.30pm,

5-11pm Fri-Sun. **Three-course prix fixe** $128. **Seven-course prix fixe** $208. **Map** p169 C6 **❾ French**
Unlike many of its vaunted peers, the flagship of celebrated chef Jean-Georges Vongerichten has not become a shadow of itself: the top-rated food is still breathtaking. Velvety foie gras terrine is coated in a thin brûlée shell; other signature dishes include ginger-marinated yellowfin tuna ribbons with avocado and spicy radish. Pastry chef Joseph Murphy's inventive seasonal quartets, comprising four mini desserts, are always a delight. The more casual on-site Nougatine café is less expensive, but still provides a taste of its big brother.

Ouest
2315 Broadway, between 83rd & 84th Streets (1-212 580 8700, www.ouestny.com). Subway 1 to 86th Street. **Open** 5.30-9.30pm Mon-Wed; 5.30-10pm Thur, Fri; 5-11pm Sat; 11am-2pm, 5-9pm Sun. **Main courses** $27-$36. **Map** p169 B4 **❿ American creative**
A prototypical local clientele calls chef-owner Tom Valenti's uptown stalwart – one of the neighbourhood's most celebrated restaurants – its local canteen. And why not? The friendly servers ferry pitch-perfect cocktails and rich, Italian-inflected cuisine from the open kitchen to immensely comfortable round red booths. Valenti adds some

---

IN THE KNOW PARK AND REFUEL

Near the Sheep Meadow, mid-park at 69th Street, you'll find an outpost of popular café **Le Pain Quotidien** in the former mineral springs (which once served health-giving water to park-goers). Indoor and outdoor seating is available for coffee, pastries, salads or the chain's signature tartines.

EXPLORE

unexpected flourishes to the soothing formula: salmon gravadlax is served with a chickpea pancake topped with caviar and potent mustard oil, while the house-smoked sturgeon presides over frisée, lardons and a poached egg.

★ Per Se

4th Floor, Time Warner Center, 10 Columbus Circle, at Broadway (1-212 823 9335, www. perseny.com). Subway A, B, C, D, 1 to 59th Street-Columbus Circle. **Open** 5.30-10pm Mon-Thur; 11.30am-1.30pm, 5.30-10pm Fri-Sun. **Main courses** (in lounge) $30-$125. **Set lunch** $205 (5 courses, Fri-Sun only), **Tasting menu** $310 (9 courses). **Map** 169 C6 ⓰ **French**

Expectations are high at Per Se – and that goes both ways. You're expected to wear the right clothes (jackets are required for men), pay a non-negotiable service charge, and pretend you aren't eating in a shopping mall. The restaurant, in turn, is expected to deliver one hell of a tasting menu for $310. And it does. Dish after dish is flawless, beginning with Thomas Keller's signature Oysters and Pearls (a sabayon of pearl tapioca with oysters and caviar); an all-vegetable version is also available.

★ $ Shake Shack

366 Columbus Avenue, at 77th Street (1-646 747 8770, www.shakeshack.com). Subway B, C to 81st Street-Museum of Natural History; 1 to 79th Street. **Open** 10.45am-11pm daily. **Burgers** $5-$9. **Map** p169 B4 ⓬ **American**

The spacious offspring of Danny Meyer's wildly popular Madison Square Park concession stand is now one of several locations across the city (and beyond). Shake Shack still gets several local critics' votes for New York's best burger. Patties are made from fresh-ground, all-natural Angus beef, and the franks are served Chicago-style on potato buns and topped with Rick's Picks Shack relish. Frozen-custard shakes hit the spot, and there's beer and wine if you want something stronger.
Other locations throughout the city.

Bars

Jacob's Pickles

509 Amsterdam Avenue, between 84th and 85th Streets (212 470 5566, www.jacobspickles.com). Subway 1 to 86th Street. **Open** 10am-2am Mon-Thur; 10am-4am Fri; 9am-4am Sat; 9am-2am Sun. **Map** p169 B3 ⓭

This craft-beer-and-biscuit-slinging gastropub shoehorns a grab bag of tippling memes – Dixieland grub, house-made bitters, local wines on tap – into one rustic barroom. But while it may be trying a little too hard, there's plenty for brew geeks to get excited about, with more than two dozen taps offering an all-domestic lineup. The list is broken down by state, with a stable of Empire State breweries (Barrier, Radiant Pig, Single-Cut) complemented by

a constantly rotating roster of cross-country favourites. If you're feeling peckish, go for the namesake pickles or the biscuits in sausage gravy.

Manhattan Cricket Club

226 W 79th Street, between Amsterdam Avenue & Broadway (1-646 823 9252, www.mccnewyork. com). Subway 1 to 79th Street. **Open** 6pm-2am daily. **Map** p169 B4 ⓮

Upstairs from Australian bistro Burke & Wills, this gold-brocaded, cricket-inspired cocktail parlour is a polished upgrade from the shrimp-on-the-barbie kitsch that often plagues Aussie efforts. Summit Bar founder Greg Seider offers pricey but potent quaffs inspired by cricket hubs like India and South Africa. The I'll Have Another jolts a dark-and-stormy base of sweet rum and shaved ginger with the spice-heavy bite of garam masala-infused agave, while the kafir lime's sweetness tempers a smoky spritz of campfire essence in the vodka-based Bonfire of the Calamities.

Jacob's Pickles.

EXPLORE

Shops & Services

Alexis Bittar

*410 Columbus Avenue, at 80th Street (1-646 590
4142, www.alexisbittar.com). Subway B, C to
81st Street-Museum of Natural History.* **Open**
11am-7pm Mon-Sat; noon-6pm Sun. **Map** p169 B4
⓯ **Accessories**

Alexis Bittar started out selling his jewellery from
a humble Soho street stall, but now the designer
has four shops in which to show off his flamboyant pieces, such as sculptural Lucite cuffs and
oversized crystal-encrusted earrings. This uptown
boutique is twice the size of the West Village,
Upper East Side and Soho locations, and is meant to
resemble a 1940s powder room, with silk wallpaper
and art deco-style lights.
Other locations 465 Broome Street, between
Greene & Mercer Streets, Soho (1-212 625 8340);
353 Bleecker Street, between Charles & 10th
Streets, West Village (1-212 727 1093); 1100
Madison Avenue, between 82nd & 83rd Streets,
Upper East Side (1-212 249 3649).

Levain Bakery

*167 W 74th Street, between Columbus
& Amsterdam Avenues (1-212 874 6080,
www.levainbakery.com). Subway 1 to 79th
Street.* **Open** 8am-7pm Mon-Sat; 9am-7pm
Sun. **Map** p169 B4 ⓰ **Food & drink**

Levain sells breads, muffins, brioche and other
delectable baked goods, but we're crazy about the
cookies. A full 6oz each, the massive mounds stay
gooey in the middle. The lush, brownie-like double-
chocolate variety, made with extra-dark French
cocoa and semi-sweet chocolate chips, is a truly
decadent treat.
Other locations 2167 Frederick Douglass
Boulevard (Eighth Avenue), between 116th & 117th
Streets, Harlem (1-646 455 0952).

Magpie

*488 Amsterdam Avenue, between 83rd & 84th
Streets (1-646 998 3002, www.magpienewyork.
com). Subway 1 to 86th Street.* **Open** 11am-7pm
Tue-Sat; 11am-6pm Sun. **Map** p169 B3 ⓱
Homewares

Sylvia Parker worked as a buyer at the American
Folk Art Museum gift shop before opening this
eco-friendly boutique. The slender space, which is
decorated with bamboo shelving and Hudson River
driftwood, is packed with locally made, handcrafted,
sustainable and fair-trade items. Finds include hand-
embellished cushions and ceramics, recycled-resin
jewellery, attractively packaged soaps and candles.

Shops at Columbus Circle

*Time Warner Center, 10 Columbus Circle, at
59th Street (1-212 823 6300, www.theshops
atcolumbuscircle.com). Subway A, B, C, D,
1 to 59th Street-Columbus Circle.* **Open**

Magpie.

10am-9pm Mon-Sat; 11am-7pm Sun (hours
vary for some shops, bars and restaurants).
Map p169 C6 ⓲ **Mall**
The classy retail contingent of the 2.8 million-sq-ft
Time Warner Center features upscale stores alongside shopping centre staples. Notable tenants include
Coach, Cole Haan and LK Bennett for accessories
and shoes, London shirtmaker Thomas Pink, Bose
home entertainment, cult candle maker Diptyque,
French confectioner La Maison du Chocolat, fancy
kitchenware purveyor Williams-Sonoma and
organic grocer Whole Foods. Some of the city's top
restaurants (including Thomas Keller's gourmet
destination Per Se, *p173*, and his café Bouchon
Bakery, *p171*) have made it a dining destination that
transcends the stigma of eating at the mall.
▶ *The Museum of Arts & Design next door has a
gift shop selling handcrafted jewellery and design
items; see p171.*

Zabar's

*2245 Broadway, at 80th Street (1-212 787 2000,
www.zabars.com). Subway 1 to 79th Street.* **Open**
8am-7.30pm Mon-Fri; 8am-8pm Sat; 9am-6pm Sun.
Map p169 B4 ⓳ **Food & drink**
Zabar's is more than a shop – it's a New York City
landmark. It began life in 1934 as a tiny storefront
specialising in Jewish 'appetising' delicacies, and
has gradually expanded to take over half a block
of prime Upper West Side real estate. What never
cease to surprise, however, are the reasonable
prices – even for high-end foods. Besides the famous
smoked fish and rafts of delicacies, Zabar's has
fabulous bread, cheese, olives and coffee, and an
entire floor dedicated to gadgets and homewares.

CENTRAL PARK

Numerous subway stations on multiple lines.

In 1858, the newly formed Central Park Commission chose landscape designer Frederick Law Olmsted and architect Calvert Vaux to turn a vast tract of rocky swampland into a rambling oasis of lush greenery. Inspired by the great parks of London and Paris, the Commission imagined a place that would provide city dwellers with respite from the crowded streets. It was a noble thought, but one that required the eviction of 1,600 mostly poor or immigrant inhabitants, including residents of Seneca Village, the city's oldest African-American settlement. Still, clear the area they did: when it was completed in 1873, it became the first man-made public park in the US.

Although it suffered from neglect at various points in the 20th century (most recently in the 1970s and '80s, when it gained a reputation as a dangerous spot), the park has now been returned to its green glory thanks largely to the Central Park Conservancy. Since this not-for-profit civic group was formed in 1980, it has been instrumental in the park's restoration and maintenance.

The 1870 Victorian Gothic **Dairy** (midpark at 65th Street, 1-212 794 6564, www.centralpark nyc.org, open 10am-5pm daily) houses one of Central Park Conservancy's five visitor centres and a gift shop; there are additional staffed information booths dotted around the park.

The southern section abounds with family-friendly diversions, including the **Central Park Zoo** (between 63rd & 66th Streets); the **Carousel** (midpark, at 64th Street); and the **Trump Wollman Rink** (between 62nd & 63rd Streets), which doubles as a small children's amusement park in the warmer months. For all, *see p257* **Central Park Seven**. Come summer, kites, Frisbees and soccer balls seem to fly every which way across **Sheep Meadow**, the designated quiet zone that begins at 66th Street. Sheep did indeed graze here until 1934, but they've since been replaced by sunbathers improving their tans and scoping out the throngs. **Tavern on the Green** (Central Park West, at 67th Street, www.tavernon thegreen.com), the landmark restaurant housed in the former shepherd's residence, closed in 2009, and a new incarnation was panned by critics before former Chez Panisse chef Jeremiah Tower was hired to reinvent the menus. East of Sheep Meadow, between 66th and 72nd Streets, is the **Mall**, an elm-lined promenade that attracts street performers and in-line skaters. And just east of the Mall's Naumburg Bandshell is **Rumsey Playfield** – the main venue of the annual **SummerStage** series (*see p33*), an eclectic roster of free and benefit concerts in the city's parks.

One of the park's most popular meeting places (and loveliest spots) is north of here, overlooking

Bethesda Fountain & Terrace.

the lake: the grand **Bethesda Fountain & Terrace**, near the midpoint of the 72nd Street Transverse Road. *Angel of the Waters*, the sculpture in the centre of the fountain, was created by Emma Stebbins, the first woman to be granted a major public art commission in New York City. Be sure to admire the Minton-tiled ceiling of the ornate passageway that connects the plaza around the fountain to the Mall – after years of neglect in storage, the tiles, designed by Jacob Wrey Mould, were restored and reinstated in 2007. Mould also designed the intricate carved ornamentation of the stairways leading down to the fountain.

To the west of the fountain, near the West 72nd Street entrance, sits **Strawberry Fields**, which memorialises John Lennon, who lived in, and was shot in front of, the nearby Dakota Building (*see p168*). It features a mosaic of the word 'imagine' that was donated by the city of Naples. More than 160 species of flowers and plants from all over the world flourish here, strawberries among them. Just north of the fountain is the **Loeb Boathouse** (midpark, between 74th & 75th Streets, 1-212 517 2233, www.thecentralparkboathouse.com). From here, you can take a rowing boat or a gondola out on the lake, which is crossed by the elegant Bow Bridge. The Loeb houses a restaurant and bar (closed dinner Nov-Mar), and lake views make it a lovely place for brunch or drinks.

Further north, the popular **Belvedere Castle** (*see p257*), a restored Victorian folly, sits atop the park's second-highest peak. Besides offering excellent views and a terrific setting for a picnic, it also houses the Henry Luce Nature Observatory. The nearby Delacorte Theater

EXPLORE

hosts **Shakespeare in the Park** (*see p33*), a summer run of free open-air performances of plays by the Bard and others. Further north still sits the **Great Lawn** (midpark, between 79th & 85th Streets), a sprawling stretch of grass that doubles as a rallying point for political protests and a concert spot for just about any act that can attract six-figure audiences. At other times, it's put to use by seriously competitive soccer, baseball and softball teams. East of the Great Lawn, behind the **Metropolitan Museum of Art** (*see p185*), is the **Obelisk**, a 69-foot hieroglyphics-covered granite monument dating from around 1500 BC, which was given to the US by the Khedive of Egypt in 1881.

In the mid 1990s, the **Reservoir** (midpark, between 85th & 96th Streets) was renamed in honour of the late Jacqueline Kennedy Onassis, who used to jog around it. A turn here gives great views of the skyscrapers rising above the park; in spring, the cherry trees that ring the reservoir path and the bridle path below it make it particularly beautiful.

In the northern section, the exquisite **Conservatory Garden** (entrance on Fifth Avenue, at 105th Street) comprises formal gardens inspired by English, French and Italian styles. At the top of the park, next to the Harlem Meer, the **Charles A Dana Discovery Center** (entrance at Malcolm X Boulevard/Lenox Avenue, at 110th Street, 1-212 860 1374, www.centralparknyc.org, open 10am-5pm daily) operates a roster of activities, events and exhibitions. It also lends out fishing rods and bait (for 'catch and release' fishing, Apr-Oct); prospective fishermen need to take photo ID.

Sights & Museums

Central Park Zoo

830 Fifth Avenue, between 63rd & 66th Streets (1-212 439 6500, www.centralparkzoo.org). Subway N, Q, R to Fifth Avenue-59th Street.

Open *April-Nov* 10am-5pm Mon-Fri; 10am-5.30pm Sat, Sun. *Nov-Apr* 10am-4.30 daily. **Admission** (under-16s must be accompanied by an adult) $12; $7-$9 reductions; free under-3s. **Map** p169 D6 ⑳
A collection of animals has been kept in Central Park since the 1860s. But in its current form, Central Park Zoo dates only from 1988; it was renovated when operation of the zoo was assumed by the Wildlife Conservation Society. More than 180 species inhabit its 6.5-acre corner of the park, snow leopards and penguins among them. The Tisch Children's Zoo (*see p257*) is home to kid-friendly species, and the roving characters on the George Delacorte Musical Clock – perched atop a brick arcade between both zoos – delight little ones every half-hour.

MORNINGSIDE HEIGHTS

Subway B, C, 1 to 110th Street-Cathedral Parkway; 1 to 116th Street.

Morningside Heights runs from 110th Street (also known west of Central Park as Cathedral Parkway) to 125th Street, between Morningside Park and the Hudson River. The campus of **Columbia University** exerts a considerable influence over the surrounding neighbourhood, while the Cathedral Church of St John the Divine draws visitors from all over the city.

One of the oldest universities in the US, Columbia was initially chartered in 1754 as King's College (the name changed after the Revolutionary War). It moved to its present location in 1897. If you wander into Columbia's campus entrance at 116th Street, you won't fail to miss the impressive **Low Memorial Building**, modelled on Rome's Pantheon. The former library, completed in 1897, is now an administrative building. The list of illustrious graduates includes Alexander Hamilton, Allen Ginsberg and Barack Obama.

Thanks to the large student population of Columbia and its sister school, Barnard College, the area has an academic feel, with bookshops, inexpensive restaurants and coffeehouses lining Broadway between 110th and 116th Streets. The façade of **Tom's Restaurant** (2880 Broadway, at 112th Street, 1-212 864 6137) will be familiar to *Seinfeld* aficionados, but the interior doesn't resemble Monk's Café, which was created on a studio set for the long-running sitcom.

The **Cathedral Church of St John the Divine** is the seat of the Episcopal Diocese of New York. Subject to a series of construction delays and misfortunes, the enormous cathedral (larger than Paris's Notre Dame) is on a medieval schedule for completion: work is set to continue for a couple more centuries, although it has wrapped up for the time being. Just behind is the green expanse of **Morningside Park** (from 110th to 123rd Streets, between Morningside Avenue & Morningside Drive).

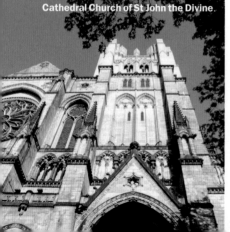

Cathedral Church of St John the Divine.

North of Columbia, **General Grant National Memorial** (aka Grant's Tomb), the mausoleum of former president Ulysses S Grant, is located in Riverside Park. Across the street stands the towering Gothic-style **Riverside Church** (490 Riverside Drive, at 120th Street, 1-212 870 6700, www.the riversidechurchny.org), built in 1930. The tower contains the world's largest carillon: 74 bronze bells, played every Sunday at 10.30am, 12.30pm and 3pm.

Sights & Museums

★ Cathedral Church of St John the Divine

1047 Amsterdam Avenue, at 112th Street (1-212 316 7540, www.stjohndivine.org). Subway B, C, 1 to 110th Street-Cathedral Parkway. **Open** 7.30am-6pm daily. **Admission** *Suggested donation* $10. *Tours* $8-$17; $7-$15 reductions. **Map** p177 B2 ⓴

Construction of this massive house of worship, affectionately nicknamed St John the Unfinished, began in 1892 following a Romanesque-Byzantine design by George Heins and Christopher Grant LaFarge. In 1911, Ralph Adams Cram took over with a Gothic Revival redesign. Work came to a halt in 1941, when the US entered World War II. It resumed in earnest in 1979, but a fire in 2001 that destroyed the church's gift shop and damaged two 17th-century Italian tapestries further delayed completion. It's still missing a tower and a north transept, among other things, but the nave has been restored and the entire interior reopened and rededicated. No further work is planned... for now. In addition to Sunday services, the cathedral hosts concerts and tours (the Vertical Tour, which takes you the top of the building, is a revelation). It bills itself as a place for all people – and it certainly means it. Annual events include both winter and summer solstice celebrations, the Blessing of the Animals during the Feast of St Francis, which draws pets and their people from all over the city, and even a Blessing of the Bicycles every spring.

FREE General Grant National Memorial

Riverside Drive, at 122nd Street (1-212 666 1640, www.nps.gov/gegr). Subway 1 to 125th Street. **Open** *Visitor centre* 9am-5pm Wed-Sun. **Admission** free. **Map** p177 A1 ㉒

Although he was born in Ohio, Civil War hero and 18th president Ulysses S Grant lived in New York for the last five years of his life. More commonly referred to as Grant's Tomb, the neoclassical granite and marble mausoleum was completed in 1897; his wife, Julia, is also laid to rest here. The tomb is open for self-guided tours between 10am to 5pm, except for an hour between 1pm and 2pm. The visitor centre offers exhibits and free talks by National Park Service rangers at 11.15am, 1.15pm and 3.15pm.

Restaurants & Cafés

Community Food & Juice

2893 Broadway, between 112th & 113th Streets (1-212 665 2800, www.communityrestaurant.com). Subway 1 to 110th Street-Cathedral Parkway. **Open** 8am-3.30pm, 5-9.30pm Mon-Thur; 8am-3.30pm, 5-10pm Fri; 9am-3.30pm, 5-10pm Sat; 9am-3.30pm, 5-9.30pm Sun. **Main courses** $14-$30. **Map** p177 A2 ㉓ **American**

Clinton Street Baking Company's UWS sibling is a neighbourhood brunch destination, but there's more to eating here than eggs and pancakes. Chef-co-owner Neil Kleinberg's dinner menu of global comfort food includes a formidable matzo-ball soup and a top-notch grass-fed burger with caramelised onions and Vermont cheddar. Vegetarians will be pleased by a range of creative dishes.

Hungarian Pastry Shop

1030 Amsterdam Avenue, between 110th & 111th Streets (1-212 866 4230). Subway 1 to 110th Street-Cathedral Parkway. **Open** 8am-11.30pm Mon-Fri; 8.30am-11.30pm Sat; 8.30am-10.30pm Sun. **Pastries** $1-$4. **Map** p177 B2 ㉔ **Café**

A Columbia University neighbourhood institution. The java is strong enough to make up for the erratic array of pastries, and the Euro feel is enhanced by the view of the cathedral from outdoor tables.

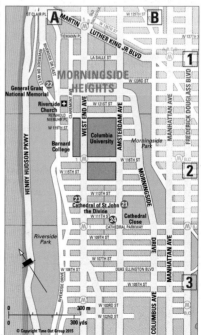

EXPLORE

Upper East Side

Luxurious pre-war apartments owned by blue-blooded socialites, soigné restaurants filled with Botoxed ladies-who-lunch, exclusive designer boutiques… this is the clichéd image of the Upper East Side, and you'll see a lot of supporting evidence on Fifth, Madison and Park Avenues. Although Manhattan's super-rich now live all over town, the air of old money is most palpable in the area east of Central Park. Drawn to the freshly landscaped green space in the late 19th century, the city's more affluent residents began building mansions and townhouses along Fifth Avenue. Many of these buildings now house foreign consulates and some of the world-class institutions that draw hordes of visitors and New Yorkers to Museum Mile.

EXPLORE

Lexington Candy Shop.

Don't Miss

1 Metropolitan Museum of Art The globe- and era-spanning behemoth (p185).

2 Solomon R Guggenheim Museum A stunning Frank Lloyd Wright building (p188).

3 Lexington Candy Shop A portal to classic NYC (p182).

4 Bar Pleiades Sophisticated sipping (p183).

5 Barneys New York The city's most fashionable department store (see p183).

SOLOMON R GUGGENHEIM M

LENOX HILL

Subway F to Lexington Avenue-63rd Street; 6 to 68th Street-Hunter College or 77th Street.

The swathe between Fifth and Lexington Avenues in the 60s and 70s, Lenox Hill encapsulates the classic Upper East Side. Along Fifth, Madison and Park, stately mansions and townhouses rub shoulders with deluxe apartment buildings guarded by uniformed doormen. The 1916 limestone structure at 820 Fifth Avenue (at 63rd Street) was one of the earliest luxury apartment buildings on the avenue, and still has just one residence per floor. And further north, Stanford White designed 998 Fifth Avenue (at 81st Street) in the image of an Italian Renaissance palazzo. The neighbourhood's gilded past is also reflected in the impressive 1881 **Park Avenue Armory**.

If you head east on 59th Street, you'll eventually reach the **Ed Koch Queensboro Bridge**, which was renamed in 2011 to honour the former mayor, and links to Queens. Nearby, admire the handsome stone façade of the **Mount Vernon Hotel Museum & Garden** (421 E 61st Street, between First & York Avenues, 1-212 838 6878, www.mvhm. org; closed Mon). The 1799 carriage house, which operated as a bucolic retreat in the early 19th century, is open for guided tours of eight period rooms. At Second Avenue you can catch the overhead tram to **Roosevelt Island**. The two-mile-long isle between Manhattan and Queens is largely residential. However, from 1686 to 1921, it went by the name of Blackwell's Island, during which time it was the site of an insane asylum, a smallpox hospital and a prison – notable inmates included Mae West, who served eight days here after being moved from the Women's House of Detention in the Village, and Emma Goldman, the anarchist, feminist and political agitator. In autumn 2012, **Franklin D Roosevelt Four Freedoms Park** (www.fdrfourfreedomspark. org) finally opened on the island's southern tip, 40 years after Mayor John Lindsay and Governor Nelson A Rockefeller announced the memorial. The plans languished until 2005, when an exhibition at Cooper Union revived interest in the project. Commemorating the 32nd President's famous 'four freedoms' speech, the park offers postcard-worthy skyline views.

IN THE KNOW
ROOSEVELT ISLAND TRAM

Suspended on a cable, the tram to Roosevelt Island reaches a height of 250 feet on its brief journey. The fare is the same as a subway ride – MetroCards are accepted – and the views are spectacular.

Sights & Museums

Asia Society & Museum

725 Park Avenue, at 70th Street (1-212 288 6400, www.asiasociety.org). Subway 6 to 68th Street-Hunter College. **Open** *July, Aug* 11am-6pm Tue-Sun. *Sept-June* 11am-6pm Tue-Thur, Sat, Sun; 11am-9pm Fri. **Admission** $12; $7-$10 reductions; free under-16s (must be accompanied by an adult). Free 6-9pm Fri. **Map** p181 B5 ❶

The Asia Society sponsors study missions and conferences while promoting public programmes in the US and abroad. The headquarters' striking galleries host exhibitions of art from dozens of countries and time periods (from ancient India and medieval Persia to contemporary Japan); some are assembled from public and private collections, including the permanent Mr and Mrs John D Rockefeller III collection of Asian art. Break for sushi or dim sum at the atrium-like pan-Asian café.

China Institute

125 E 65th Street, between Park & Lexington Avenues (1-212 744 8181, www.chinainstitute. org). Subway F to Lexington Avenue-63rd Street; 6 to 68th Street-Hunter College. **Open** *Galleries* 10am-5pm Mon, Wed, Fri-Sun; 10am-8pm Tue, Thur. **Admission** $7; $4 reductions; free under-12s. Free 6-8pm Tue, Thur. **Map** p181 B5 ❷

With two small galleries, the China Institute is somewhat overshadowed by the nearby Asia Society, but the organisation mounts two substantial exhibitions a year, which include high-profile collections on loan from Chinese institutions. The institute also offers courses and arts events such as concerts and films.

★ Frick Collection

1 E 70th Street, at Fifth Avenue (1-212 288 0700, www.frick.org). Subway 6 to 68th Street-Hunter College. **Open** 10am-6pm Tue-Sat; 11am-5pm Sun. **Admission** (under-10s not admitted) $20; $10-$15 reductions. Pay what you wish 11am-1pm Sun. **Map** p181 B5 ❸

Industrialist, robber baron and collector Henry Clay Frick commissioned this opulent mansion with a view to leaving his legacy to the public. Designed by Thomas Hastings of Carrère & Hastings (the firm behind the New York Public Library) and built in 1914, the building was inspired by 18th-century British and French architecture.

In an effort to preserve the feel of a private residence, labelling is minimal, but you can opt for a free audio guide, download the app or pay $2 for a booklet. Works spanning the 14th to the 19th centuries include masterpieces by Rembrandt, Vermeer, Whistler, Gainsborough, Holbein and Titian, and exquisite period furniture, porcelain and other decorative objects. Aficionados of 18th-century French art will find two rooms especially enchanting: the panels of the Boucher Room (1750-52) depict

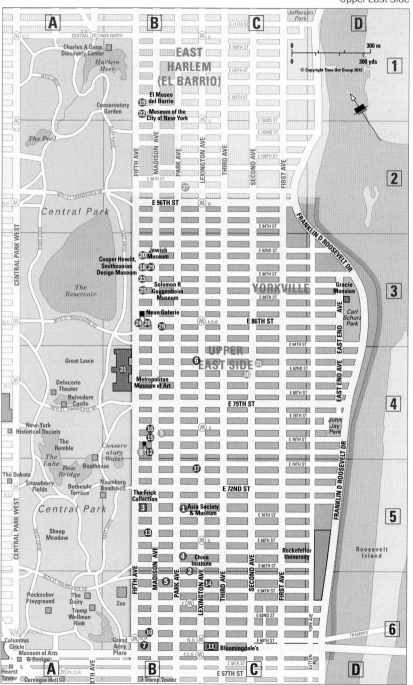

EXPLORE

Frick Collection. *See p180.*

children engaged in adult occupations; the Fragonard Room contains the artist's series *Progress of Love* – four of the paintings were commissioned (and rejected) by Louis XV's mistress Madame du Barry. A gallery in the enclosed garden portico is devoted to decorative arts and sculpture.

▶ *For the Frick's excellent concert series, see p299.*

Park Avenue Armory

643 Park Avenue, between 66th & 67th Streets (1-212 616 3930, www.armoryonpark.org). Subway 6 to 68th Street-Hunter College. **Open** during events; see website for details. *Tours* $10; free-$5 reductions. **Map** p181 B5 ❹

Once home to the Seventh Regiment of the National Guard, this impressive 1881 structure contains a series of period rooms dating from the late 19th century, designed by such luminaries as Louis Comfort Tiffany and the Herter Brothers. The vast Wade Thompson Drill Hall has become one of the city's premier alternative spaces for art, concerts and theatre.

Restaurants & Cafés

Daniel

60 E 65th Street, between Madison & Park Avenues (1-212 288 0033, www.danielnyc.com). Subway F to Lexington Avenue-63rd Street; 6 to 68th Street-Hunter College. **Open** 5.30-10.30pm Mon-Sat. **Set dinner** $135. **Map** p181 B6 ❺

French

The cuisine at Daniel Boulud's elegant fine-dining flagship, designed by Adam Tihany, is rooted in French technique with contemporary flourishes like fusion elements and an emphasis on local produce. Although the menu changes seasonally, it always includes a few signature dishes, such as the chef's

oven-baked black sea bass with Syrah sauce, or the duo of beef – a sumptuous pairing of Black Angus short ribs and seared Wagyu tenderloin.

Other locations Café Boulud, 20 E 76th Street, between Fifth & Madison Avenues, Upper East Side (1-212 772 2600); Bar Boulud, 1900 Broadway, at 64th Street, Upper West Side (1-212 595 0303); DB Bistro Moderne, 55 West 44th Street, between Fifth & Sixth Avenues, Midtown West (1-212 391 2400).

▶ *For Boulud's Bowery brasserie DBGB, see p103; for Boulud Sud, see p171.*

★ Lexington Candy Shop

1226 Lexington Avenue, at 83rd Street (1-212 288 0057, www.lexingtoncandyshop.net). Subway 4, 5, 6 to 86th Street. **Open** 7am-7pm Mon-Sat; 8am-6pm Sun. **Main courses** $6-$15. **Map** p181 B4 ❻

American

You won't find much candy for sale at this well-preserved retro lunchroom, which opened in 1925. But in addition to the usual diner fare (burgers, egg creams), the extensive menu lists such old-fashioned items as Lime Rickeys and liverwurst sandwiches. If you come for breakfast, order the doorstop slabs of french toast.

Rôtisserie Georgette

14 E 60th Street, between Fifth & Madison Avenues (1-212 390 8060, www.rotisserieg.com). Subway N, Q, R to Fifth Avenue-59th Street. **Open** noon-2.30pm, 5.45-10pm Mon; noon-2.30pm, 5.45-11pm Tue-Fri; noon-3pm, 5.45-11pm Sat; 5.45-10pm Sun. **Main courses** $24-$49. **Map** p181 B6 ❼ **French/American**

Georgette Farkas, who was Daniel Boulud's publicist for nearly two decades, opened this 90-seat rotisserie, furnished with caramel-coloured

banquettes and showcasing spit-fired roasts. Former Daniel sous chef Chad Brauze heads the kitchen, turning out organic Zimmerman Farm chicken and rib-eye steak with béarnaise sauce. Seasonal sides include pancetta-studded brussels sprouts and three takes on potatoes (traditional roasted, twice-baked with parmesan mashed potatoes, or baked with apples and tarragon). The vino list showcases lesser-known French producers.

Bars

★ Bar Pleiades
The Surrey, 20 E 76th Street, between Fifth & Madison Avenues (1-212 772 2600, www. barpleiades.com). Subway 6 to 77th Street. **Open** noon-midnight daily. **Map** p181 B4 ❸
Designed as a nod to Coco Chanel, Daniel Boulud's bar is framed in black lacquered panels that recall an elegant make-up compact. The luxe setting and moneyed crowd might seem a little stiff, but the seasonally rotating cocktails are so exquisitely executed you probably won't mind. Light eats are provided by Café Boulud next door.

Bemelmans Bar
The Carlyle, 35 E 76th Street, at Madison Avenue (1-212 744 1600, www.thecarlyle.com). Subway 6 to 77th Street. **Open** noon-1am Mon-Thur, Sun; noon-1.30am Fri, Sat. **Map** p181 B4 ❾
The Plaza may have Eloise, but the Carlyle has its own children's book connection – the wonderful 1947 murals of Central Park by *Madeline* creator Ludwig Bemelmans in this, the quintessential classy New York bar. A pianist adds to the atmosphere in the early evening and a jazz trio takes up residence later (9pm Mon, Sun; 9.30pm Tue-Sat), when a $15-$35 cover charge kicks in.

Shops & Services

Madison Avenue, between 57th and 86th Streets, is packed with international designer names: Alexander McQueen, Chloé, Derek Lam, Gucci, Fendi, Helmut Lang, Prada, Lanvin, Ralph Lauren, Valentino and many more.

★ Barneys New York
660 Madison Avenue, at 61st Street, Upper East Side (1-212 826 8900, www.barneys.com). Subway N, Q, R to Fifth Avenue-59th Street; 4, 5, 6 to 59th Street. **Open** 10am-8pm Mon-Fri; 10am-7pm Sat; 11am-7pm Sun. **Map** p181 B6 ❿ **Department store**
Barneys has a reputation for spotlighting more independent designer labels than other upmarket department stores, and also has its own trend-driven collection. The ground floor showcases luxe accessories, and cult beauty brands are in the basement. Head to the seventh and eighth floors for contemporary designer and denim lines.
Other locations 2151 Broadway, at 76th Street, Upper West Side (1-646 335 0978); 194 Atlantic Avenue, at Court Street, Cobble Hill, Brooklyn (1-718 637 2234).

Bloomingdale's
1000 Third Avenue, at 59th Street (1-212 705 2000, www.bloomingdales.com). Subway N, Q, R to Lexington Avenue-59th Street; 4, 5, 6 to 59th Street. **Open** 10am-8.30pm Mon-Sat; 11am-7pm Sun. **Map** p181 C6 ⓫ **Department store**
Ranking among the city's top tourist attractions, Bloomie's is a gigantic, glitzy department store stocked with everything from handbags to home furnishings. The glam beauty section includes an outpost of globe-spanning apothecary Space NK, and you can get a mid-shopping sugar fix at the on-site Magnolia Bakery. The hipper, compact Soho outpost concentrates on contemporary fashion and accessories, denim and cosmetics.
Other location 504 Broadway, between Broome & Spring Streets, Soho (1-212 729 5900).

Cornelia Spa at the Surrey
2nd Floor, 20 E 76th Street, between Fifth & Madison Avenues (1-646 358 3600, www. corneliaspaatthesurrey.com). Subway 6 to 77th Street. **Open** 10am-8pm Mon-Fri; 9am-7pm Sat, Sun. **Map** p181 B4 ⓬ **Health & beauty**
Husband and wife Rick Aidekman and Ellen Sackoff reopened their popular boutique spa, which closed in 2009, in a smaller space in upscale hotel the Surrey. The intimate yet luxurious oasis is designed to make you feel as if you're lounging in your own living space, complete with savoury and sweet post-treatment bites. Splurge on the Reparative Caviar and Oxygen Quench facial ($325), or a signature massage ($175 for an hour), which combines deep-tissue, Swedish and shiatsu techniques.

EXPLORE

Fivestory

*18 E 69th Street, between Fifth & Madison Avenues
(1-212 288 1338, www.fivestoryny.com). Subway 6
to 68th Street-Hunter College.* **Open** 10am-6pm
Mon-Wed, Fri; 10am-7pm Thur; noon-6pm Sat.
Map p181 B5 ⓭ **Fashion**
At just 26 (with a little help from her fashion-
industry insider dad), Claire Distenfeld opened
this glamorous, grown-up boutique, which
sprawls over two and a half floors of – yes – a
five-storey townhouse. The hand-selected stock
spans American and European fashion, shoes and
accessories for men, women and children, plus select
home items. You might find clothing by Alexander
Wang, Jason Wu, Giambattista Valli and Narciso
Rodriguez, jewellery by Aurélie Bidermann and
Delfina Delettrez and footwear by Gianvito Rossi
and Laurence Dacade.

Fix Beauty Bar

*2nd Floor, 847 Lexington Avenue between 64th &
65th Streets (1-212 744 0800, www.fixbeautybar.
com). Subway F to Lexington Avenue-63rd Street.*
Open 9am-7pm Mon, Tue; 9am-8pm Wed, Thur;
9am-9pm Fri, Sat; 9am-6pm Sun. **Map** p181 C6 ⓮
Health & beauty
This multitasking beauty spot takes the blow-
dry bar phenomenon a step further, offering
manicures ($15) and pedicures ($35) to accompany
the flat-rate blow-dries ($40) that take place in the
chic lavender-and-grey surroundings. Hairstyles
are named after celebrities with instantly
recognisable tresses, such as the Jen (sleek and
pin-straight), the Taylor (soft, styled curls) and the
Kim (full, dramatic waves).

Gagosian Shop

*976 Madison Avenue, between 76th & 77th Streets
(1-212 796 1224, www.gagosian.com). Subway 6 to
77th Street.* **Open** 10am-7pm Mon-Sat. **Map** p181
B4 ⓯ **Gifts & souvenirs**
The art gallery giant recently opened a 600sq ft
gift shop, designed by Selldorf Architects, on
the ground floor of its Upper East Side location.
Posters, prints and publications are the main focus,
but artist-designed home decor and objects pepper
the offerings.

Lisa Perry

*988 Madison Avenue, at 77th Street (1-212 431
7467, www.lisaperrystyle.com). Subway 6 to 77th
Street.* **Open** 10am-6pm Mon-Sat; noon-5pm Sun.
Map p181 B4 ⓰ **Fashion**
Upon graduation from FIT in 1981, designer Lisa
Perry launched her line of retro women's threads
inspired by her massive personal collection of
1960s and '70s fashion. Ultrabright pieces, such
as her signature colour-blocked minidresses, pop
against the stark white walls of her Madison Avenue
flagship. You'll also find the designer's cheerful
accessories and mod home collection.

Paul Molé Barber Shop

*1034 Lexington Avenue, at 74th Street (1-212 535
8461). Subway 6 to 77th Street.* **Open** 7.30am-8pm
Mon-Fri; 8am-5.30pm Sat, Sun (hrs vary). **No
credit cards. Map** p181 B5 ⓱ **Health & beauty**
Best known for its precise shaves, this nostalgic barber
has been grooming men since 1913 (John Steinbeck
used to come here). As well as its signature Deluxe
Open Razor Shave ($40), you can get a haircut (from
$39) and other services such as a scalp massage ($10).

MUSEUM MILE & CARNEGIE HILL

*Subway 4, 5, 6 to 86th Street; 6 to 96th Street
or 103rd Street.*

Philanthropic gestures made by the moneyed
classes over the past 130-odd years have helped
to create an impressive cluster of art collections,
museums and cultural institutions on the Upper
East Side. Indeed, Fifth Avenue from 82nd to
105th Streets is known as **Museum Mile**, and
for good reason: it's lined with more than half
a dozen celebrated institutions. **El Museo del
Barrio** used to define the Mile's northern border,
but the strip is lengthening: the future home of
the **New Africa Center** (www.theafricacenter.
org), which will contain exhibition galleries, is
at the corner of 110th Street, though the opening
has been delayed by lack of funding.

    Carnegie Hill, the northern blocks of the
Upper East Side between Fifth and Lexington
Avenues, takes its name from early resident Andrew
Carnegie. The Scottish philanthropist bought a
large chunk of then-rural land in 1898 to build a
64-room mansion, which is now home to the **Cooper
Hewitt, Smithsonian Design Museum**.

Sights & Museums

Cooper Hewitt, Smithsonian Design Museum

*2 E 91st Street, at Fifth Avenue (1-212 849 8400,
www.cooperhewitt.org). Subway 4, 5, 6 to 86th
Street.* **Open** 10am-6pm Mon-Fri, Sun; 10am-9pm
Sat. **Admission** $18; $9-$12 reductions; free under-
18s. Pay what you wish 6-9pm Sat. **Map** p181 B3 ⓭
The museum began as a collection created for
students of the Cooper Union for the Advancement
of Science and Art by the Hewitt sisters – grand-
daughters of the institution's founder, Peter
Cooper – and opened to the public in 1897. Part of
the Smithsonian since the 1960s, the Cooper Hewitt
is the only museum in the US solely dedicated
to historic and contemporary design. In 1976,
it took up residence in the former home of steel
magnate Andrew Carnegie. Following a three-year
renovation, which has increased the exhibition
space by 60%, the museum reopened in December
2014. *See also p186* **Grand Designs**.

EXPLORE

IN THE KNOW
NIGHT AT THE MUSEUM

Most of the city's major museums are free or pay what you wish one evening (usually Thursday or Friday) or afternoon of the week. Some enhance the experience with musical and other performances.

El Museo del Barrio

1230 Fifth Avenue, at 104th Street (1-212 831 7272, www.elmuseo.org). Subway 6 to 103rd Street. **Open** *11am-6pm Tue-Sat.* **Admission** *Suggested donation $9; $5 reductions; free under-12s; free over-65s Wed. Free 3rd Sat each mth.* **Map** p181 B1 ⓳

Founded in 1969 by the artist and former MoMA curator Rafael Montañez Ortiz, El Museo del Barrio takes its name from its East Harlem locale (though this stretch of Fifth Avenue is an extension of the Upper East Side's Museum Mile). Dedicated to the art and culture of Puerto Ricans and Latin Americans all over the US, El Museo reopened in autumn 2009 following a $35-million renovation. The redesigned spaces within the museum's 1921 Beaux Arts building provide a polished, contemporary showcase for the diversity and vibrancy of Hispanic art. The new galleries allow more space for rotating exhibitions from the museum's 6,500-piece holdings – from pre-Columbian artefacts to contemporary installations – as well as temporary shows.

Jewish Museum

1109 Fifth Avenue, at 92nd Street (1-212 423 3200, www.thejewishmuseum.org). Subway 4, 5, 6 to 86th Street; 6 to 96th Street. **Open** *11am-5.45pm Mon, Tue, Sat, Sun; 11am-8pm Thur; 11am-5.45pm Fri (11am-4pm Nov-Mar). Closed Jewish holidays.* **Admission** *$15; $7.50-$12 reductions; free under-19s. Free Sat. Pay what you wish 5-8pm Thur.* **Map** p181 B3 ⓴

The Jewish Museum is housed in a magnificent 1908 French Gothic-style mansion – the former home of the financier, collector and Jewish leader Felix Warburg. Inside, 'Culture and Continuity: the Jewish Journey' traces the evolution of Judaism from antiquity to the present day. The two-floor permanent exhibition comprises thematic displays of 800 of the museum's cache of more than 30,000 works of art, artefacts and media installations. The excellent temporary shows, which spotlight Jewish artists or related themes, appeal to a broad audience. By publication of this guide, you should be able to nosh on bagels and knishes at a new outpost of famed Lower East Side purveyor, Russ & Daughters (*see p96*).

▶ *The Museum of Jewish Heritage: A Living Memorial to the Holocaust (see p60) and the Museum at Eldridge Street (see p88), both Downtown, further explore Jewish culture.*

★ Metropolitan Museum of Art

1000 Fifth Avenue, at 82nd Street (1-212 535 7710, www.metmuseum.org). Subway 4, 5, 6 to 86th Street. **Open** *10am-5.30pm Mon-Thur, Sun; 10am-9pm Fri, Sat.* **Admission** *Suggested*

EXPLORE

Metropolitan Museum of Art.

GRAND DESIGNS

NYC's premier design institution debuts a dramatic restoration.

Home to 217,000 objects, the **Cooper Hewitt, Smithsonian Design Museum** (*see p184*) occupies the Carnegie mansion – itself an example of ground-breaking design. The 64-room Georgian-style pile was among the first private homes to have a lift, central heating and even a precursor of air-conditioning. Historic spaces such as the Teak Room, with its intricately carved wall panelling and cabinets, have been painstakingly restored, and the addition of a 6,000-square-foot gallery on the third floor – formerly occupied by the National Design Library, now housed in an adjacent building – provides more room for rotating exhibitions. The reopening also sees the continuation of the excellent Selects series, in which a prominent artist, designer, architect or other tastemaker curates their favourite items from the collection.

Architects Diller Scofidio + Renfro have created contemporary, interactive displays that respect the period surroundings. Each visitor receives a high-tech pen, allowing them to 'collect' objects, explore them and even create their own designs on high-definition screens on tables. The entire second floor now showcases objects from the permanent collection, with wall coverings, textiles, product design, decorative arts, drawings, prints and graphic design, organised by theme. Items from different eras and geographical areas are attractively grouped together, creating interesting juxtapositions and revealing links – the mesh-like quality of a 2007 stainless-steel bowl designed by the

Brazilian Campana brothers echoes the surface of a turn-of-the-20th-century porcelain fruit basket from Northern Ireland, for example. The varied holdings include oil sketches by Hudson River School painter Frederic Church (1826-1900), which reflect the museum's origins as a 'visual library' for Cooper Union students that included preparatory drawings as well as completed works. 'The real strength of our collection is 19th century,' says curatorial director Cara McCarty, 'although in recent years we've been making a concerted effort to add to the contemporary collection.'

You'll also see a 1996 concept design for the Air Jordan XIII sneaker, by the shoe's original designer, Tinker Hatfield – emphasising the Cooper Hewitt's commitment to collecting drawings and prototypes that illuminate the design process. The reimagined museum includes a Models & Prototypes Gallery, a hands-on Process Lab and a digital Immersion Room that lets you fully experience the institution's impressive collection of wallcoverings – the largest in the US.

EXPLORE

donation (incl same-week admission to the Cloisters) $25; $12-$17 reductions; free under-12s. **Map** p181 B4 ㉑
Now occupying 13 acres of Central Park, the Met opened in 1880. The original Gothic Revival building was designed by Calvert Vaux and Jacob Wrey Mould, but is now almost hidden by subsequent additions. The museum's four-block-long plaza has recently been spruced up with new fountains and tree-shaded seating. The first floor's north wing contains the collection of ancient Egyptian art and the glass-walled atrium housing the Temple of Dendur, moved en masse from its original Nile-side setting and now overlooking a reflective pool. In the northwest corner is the American Wing, which underwent a multi-phase renovation that culminated in 2012 with the reopening of its Galleries for Paintings, Sculpture and Decorative Arts; the centrepiece is Emanuel Gottlieb Leutze's iconic 1851 painting *Washington Crossing the Delaware*. The wing's grand Engelhard Court is flanked by the salvaged façade of Wall Street's Branch Bank of the United States and a stunning loggia designed by Louis Comfort Tiffany for his Long Island estate.

In the southern wing are the halls housing Greek and Roman art. Turning west brings you to the Arts of Africa, Oceania and the Americas collection; it was donated by Nelson Rockefeller as a memorial to his son Michael, who disappeared while visiting New Guinea in 1961. A wider-ranging bequest, the two-storey Robert Lehman Wing, is at the western end of the floor. This eclectic collection is housed in a recreation of the Lehman family townhouse and features works by Botticelli, Bellini, Ingres and Rembrandt, among others. At ground level, the renovated and rechristened Anna Wintour Costume Center is the site of the Met's blockbuster fashion exhibitions.

Upstairs, the central western section is dominated by the recently expanded and rehung European Paintings galleries, which hold an amazing reserve of old masters – the museum's five Vermeers are now shown together for the first time. To the south, the 19th-century European galleries contain some of the Met's most popular works – in particular the two-room Monet holdings and a colony of Van Goghs that includes his oft-reproduced *Irises*.

Walk eastward and you'll reach the galleries of the Art of the Arab Lands, Turkey, Iran, Central Asia and Later South Asia. In the north-east wing of the floor, you'll find the sprawling collection of Asian art; be sure to check out the ceiling of the Jain Meeting Hall in the South-east Asian gallery. Rest your feet in the Astor Court, a tranquil recreation of a Ming Dynasty garden, or head up to the Iris & B Gerald Cantor Roof Garden (usually open May-Oct).

In March 2016, the Met Breuer opens in the old Whitney building (945 Madison Avenue, at 75th Street), spotlighting modern and contemporary art and performances for the next eight years.
▶ *For the Cloisters, which houses the Met's medieval art collection, see p200.*

Museum of the City of New York
1220 Fifth Avenue, between 103rd & 104th Streets (1-212 534 1672, www.mcny.org). Subway 6 to 103rd Street. **Open** 10am-6pm daily. **Admission** *Suggested donation* $14; $10 reductions; free under-20s. **Map** p181 B1 ㉒
A great introduction to Gotham, this institution contains a wealth of city history. *Timescapes*, a 22-minute multimedia presentation that illuminates the growth of NYC, is shown free with admission every half hour. The museum's holdings include prints, drawings and photos, decorative arts and furnishings, and a large collection of toys. The undoubted jewel is the amazing Stettheimer Dollhouse: it was created in the 1920s by Carrie Stettheimer, whose artist friends reinterpreted their masterpieces in miniature to hang on the walls. Look closely and you'll even spy a tiny version of Marcel Duchamp's famous *Nude Descending a Staircase*. Temporary shows, on such varied subjects as graffiti and the gilded age, spotlight the metropolis from different angles. The culmination of a rolling $95 million renovation in autumn 2016 will bring a permanent core exhibition about New York.

National Academy Museum
1083 Fifth Avenue, at 89th Street (1-212 369 4880, www.nationalacademy.org). Subway 4, 5, 6 to 86th Street. **Open** 11am-6pm Wed-Sun. **Admission** Pay what you wish; free under-12s. **Map** p181 B3 ㉓
Founded in 1825, the National Academy combines an art school, a museum and a professional association – academicians include Bill Viola, Chuck Close, Cindy Sherman and Frank Gehry, to name but a few. Housed in an elegant Fifth Avenue townhouse, the museum holds more than 7,000 works of American art, from the 19th century to the present, including paintings, sculptures, engravings and architectural drawings by the likes of Louise Bourgeois, Jasper Johns, Robert Rauschenberg and John Singer Sargent, and regularly hosts temporary shows.

Neue Galerie
1048 Fifth Avenue, at 86th Street (1-212 628 6200, www.neuegalerie.org). Subway 4, 5, 6 to 86th Street. **Open** 11am-6pm Mon, Thur-Sun; 11am-8pm 1st Fri of the mth. **Admission** (under-12s not admitted) $20; $10 reductions. Free 6-8pm 1st Fri of the mth. **Map** p181 B3 ㉔

EXPLORE

IN THE KNOW POP ARTIST'S PAD

A sedate Upper East Side address might seem at odds with Andy Warhol's avant-garde image, but the artist lived at 57 East 66th Street from 1974 to 1987.

Set within a refined 1914 mansion designed by New York Public Library architects Carrère & Hastings, the elegant Neue Galerie showcases early-20th-century German and Austrian fine art, objects and furnishings in several exquisitely restored rooms. The creation of the late art dealer Serge Sabarsky and cosmetics mogul Ronald S Lauder, it has the largest concentration of works by Gustav Klimt and Egon Schiele outside of Vienna, including Klimt's gorgeous *The Woman in Gold* – the portrait of Adele Bloch-Bauer that was returned to the subject's family (and subsequently purchased by the Neue Galerie) after being stolen by the Nazis in World War II. Factor in a stop at the chic Café Sabarsky (*see right*) for coffee and ravishing Viennese pastries, or something more substantial. *Photo p190.*

★ Solomon R Guggenheim Museum

1071 Fifth Avenue, between 88th & 89th Streets (1-212 423 3500, www.guggenheim.org). Subway 4, 5, 6 to 86th Street. **Open** 10am-5.45pm Mon-Wed, Fri, Sun; 10am-7.45pm Sat. **Admission** $25; $18 reductions; free under-12s. Pay what you wish 5.45-7.45pm Sat. **Map** p181 B3 ㉕

The Guggenheim is as famous for its landmark building as it is for its impressive collection and daring temporary shows. Frank Lloyd Wright's dramatic structure, with its winding, cantilevered curves, caused quite a stir when it debuted in 1959. In 1992, the addition of a ten-storey tower

provided space for a sculpture terrace, a café and an auditorium; the museum also has a more upscale restaurant. Solomon R Guggenheim's original founding collection, amassed in the 1930s, includes 150 works by Kandinsky, in addition to pieces by Chagall, Picasso, Franz Marc and others; the Solomon R Guggenheim Foundation's holdings have since been enriched by subsequent bequests, including the Thannhauser Collection – which includes paintings by Impressionist and post-Impressionist masters such as Manet, Cézanne and Gaugin – and the Panza di Biumo Collection of American minimalist and conceptual art from the 1960s and '70s.

Restaurants & Cafés

★ Café Sabarsky

Neue Galerie, 1048 Fifth Avenue, at 86th Street (1-212 288 0665, www.neuegalerie.org/cafes/sabarsky). Subway 4, 5, 6 to 86th Street. **Open** 9am-6pm Mon, Wed; 9am-9pm Thur-Sun. **Main courses** $16-$30. **Map** p181 B3 ㉖ Austrian/café

Purveyor of indulgent pastries and whipped cream-topped *einspänner* coffee for Neue Galerie patrons by day, this sophisticated, high-ceilinged restaurant, inspired by a classic Viennese *kaffeehaus*, is helmed by chef Kurt Gutenbrunner of modern Austrian restaurant Wallsé. Appetisers are most adventurous – the creaminess of the spätzle is a perfect base for sweetcorn, tarragon and wild mushrooms – while main course specials, such as wiener schnitzel tartly garnished with lingonberries, are capable yet ultimately feel like the calm before the *Sturm und Drang* of dessert. Try the *klimttorte*, which masterfully alternates layers of hazelnut cake with chocolate. Note: the eaterie is closed on Tuesdays.

Bars

Earl's Beer & Cheese

1259 Park Avenue, between 97th & 98th Street (1-212 289 1581, www.earlsny.com). Subway 6 to 96th Street. **Open** 4pm-midnight Mon, Tue; 11am-midnight Wed, Thur, Sun; 11am-2am Fri, Sat. **Map** p181 B2 ㉗

Tucked into the no-man's land between the Upper East Side and Spanish Harlem, this craft-beer cubby hole has the sort of community-hub vibe that makes you want to settle in. The well-priced, rotating selection of American craft brews and slapdash set-up appeal to a neighbourhood crowd, but the madcap bar menu makes it destination-worthy. Try the NY State Cheddar – a grilled cheese sandwich with braised pork belly, fried egg and house-made kimchi. (Be advised that the kitchen closes at 11pm.) The crew has since opened a cocktail bar, the Guthrie Inn, next door (at the same address, 1-212 423 9900).

Earl's Beer & Cheese.

BRUSH WITH GREATNESS

The five paintings you must see in NYC.

With eight institutions on Museum Mile alone, and many more scattered throughout the city, it can be tough to narrow down which museums, let alone which masterpieces, to seek out on a short visit. We're here to help. In spring 2015, *Time Out New York* magazine surveyed a distinguished group of 34 artists, critics, journalists, curators and gallery dealers – among them photographer David LaChapelle, MoMA painting and sculpture curator Laura Hoptman, Brooklyn Museum director Arnold Lehman and *Time Out New York* art editor Howard Halle – to come up with the top 100 paintings in NYC. We've whittled the list down to five; for the full countdown, go to www.timeout.com/newyork/100bestpaintings.

1 Les Demoiselles d'Avignon (1907), Pablo Picasso

This masterpiece (*pictured*) ushered in the modern era by decisively splitting with the representational tradition of Western painting. The women of the title are actually prostitutes in a brothel. Originally the work was also going to feature the figure of a man – a medical student, apparently – making his selection for the night. Picasso decided to omit him from the final composition, leaving only Avignon in the title as a clue to his subjects – it's the name of a street in the artist's native Barcelona, famous for its brothels.
See it at the Museum of Modern Art (p157).

2 St Francis in the Desert (1475–78), Giovanni Bellini

One of the most treasured Renaissance paintings in the US. The subject, an animal-friendly friar, is shown in the wilderness, bearing the stigmata. The landscape is filled with Franciscan symbolism and a supernatural light.
See it at the Frick Collection (p180).

3 Comtesse d'Haussonville (1845), Jean-Auguste-Dominique Ingres

The granddaughter of French intellectual Madame de Staël, the Comtesse was a woman (and a writer) with a deep sense of her own sensuality. Leaning suggestively in a corner of her boudoir, she appears almost surprised that the artist has burst into her chambers. In reality, Ingres spent

more than three years capturing the intriguing expression.
See it at the Frick Collection (p180).

4 The Duchess of Alba (1797), Francisco Goya

Recognised as a great beauty in her day, and also as one of the richest women in Spain, the duchess was a fixation for the artist. Want proof? Check out the sand at her feet. It reads 'solo goya'. And if you look closely at the Duchess's rings, they read 'alba' and 'goya', sparking rumours about romantic ties.
See it at the Hispanic Society of America (see p200).

5 A Storm in the Rocky Mountains (1866), Albert Bierstadt

Manifest Destiny is both an integral part of American identity and also a source of everlasting national shame. This sense is captured perfectly in this work, which the artist completed three years after travelling through and sketching the eponymous terrain. Although Bierstadt took some licence with the landscape, he captures the grandeur that must have struck Western migrants dumb as they pushed aside the Native Americans on their way to the Pacific.
See it at the Brooklyn Museum (p214).

EXPLORE

Neue Galerie. *See p187.*

EXPLORE

Shops & Services

Chuckies New York

1169 Madison Avenue, between 85th & 86th Streets (1-212 249 2254, www.chuckiesnewyork. com). Subway 4, 5, 6 to 86th Street. **Open** 10am-7pm Mon-Sat; noon-6pm Sun. **Map** p181 B3 ㉘ **Accessories**

Only the most exquisite women's footwear gains shelf space in this compact, bi-level shoebox. The finely tuned international stock spans cool contemporary labels like Alexander Wang, Isabel Marant and Jérôme Dreyfuss, and coveted designer lines including Lanvin, Balenciaga and Valentino. **Other locations** 1052 Lexington Avenue, between 74th & 75th Streets (1-212 861 1415).

Malin + Goetz

1270 Madison Avenue, between 90th & 91st Streets (1-212 328 9347, www.malinandgoetz. com). Subway 4, 5, 6 to 86th Street. **Open** 11am-7pm Mon-Fri; noon-7pm Sat; noon-6pm Sun. **Map** p181 B3 ㉙ **Health & beauty**

The third Manhattan location of Matthew Malin and Andrew Goetz's modern apothecary showcases their natural, locally manufactured line of unisex

skin and hair products. Aluminium towers hold the full collection, including glycolic-acid peel pads, aluminium-free eucalyptus deodorant and sage styling cream. An alcove in the back wall displays candles and fragrances in unusual scents.

YORKVILLE

The atmosphere becomes noticeably less rarefied as you walk east from Central Park, with grand edifices giving way to bland modern apartment blocks and walk-up tenements. Not much remains of the old German and Hungarian immigrant communities that once filled **Yorkville**, the neighbourhood above 79th Street between Third Avenue and the East River, with delicatessens, beer halls and restaurants. However, one such flashback, open since 1936, is **Heidelberg** (1648 Second Avenue, between 85th & 86th Streets, 1-212 628 2332, www.heidelberg-nyc.com), where dirndl-wearing waitresses serve up steins of Spaten and platters of sausages from the wurst-meisters at butcher shop **Schaller & Weber** a few doors up (1654 Second Avenue, 1-212 879 3047, closed Sun). Second Avenue in the 70s and 80s throbs with rowdy pick-up bars frequented by preppy, twentysomething crowds. But new craft-beer and cocktail bars are bringing an indie-cool downtown vibe to the area.

The only Federal-style mansion in Manhattan, **Gracie Mansion** stands at the eastern end of 88th Street. The stately pile has served as New York's official mayoral residence since 1942 – except during billionaire Michael Bloomberg's time in office. Following Bill de Blasio's election in 2013, it is once again occupied. The mansion is fenced off, but much of the exterior can be seen from surrounding **Carl Schurz Park**.

One block from Gracie Mansion, the **Henderson Place Historic District** (at East End Avenue, between 86th & 87th Streets) contains 24 handsome Queen Anne row houses – commissioned by furrier and noted real-estate developer John C Henderson as servants' quarters – with their original turrets, double stoops and slate roofs.

Bars

Gilroy
1561 Second Avenue, at 81st Street (1-212 734 8800, www.thegilroynyc.com). Subway 4, 5, 6 to 86th Street; 6 to 77th Street. **Open** 5pm-4am daily. **Map** p181 C4 ❸⓪
Decorated with art deco chandeliers and red brocade wallpaper, this dimly lit drinkery brings high-wire cocktail culture to the Upper East Side with seven variations on the negroni, a piña colada-margarita hybrid with a coconutty cloud of tech-geek 'salt air' and chocolate-banana juleps vacuum-sealed into individual packets, among other creations. Cocktails aren't

the whole story, though. Behind the copper-topped bar lies the custom Hoppinator, the latest in a growing line of NYC draft-line gadgetry. Hooked up to the taps, the suds system can adjust a beer's hops to amp up its flavour and intensity.

Penrose
1590 Second Avenue, between 82nd & 83rd Streets (1-212 203 2751, www.penrosebar.com). Subway 4, 5, 6 to 86th Street. **Open** 3pm-4am Mon-Thur; noon-4am Fri; 10.30am-4am Sat, Sun. **Map** p181 C4 ❸①
Named for a neighbourhood in Cork, Ireland, where two of the owners grew up, the Penrose stands apart from the Upper East Side's sports bars and fancier joints – its exposed-brick walls, retro decorative touches and curved wooden bar are casually sophisticated. The changing craft-brew list includes the malty NewBurgh Brown Ale from upstate New York; there's also Murphy's Stout and an extensive whiskey selection (Irish, American and Scotch). The comfort-food-heavy menu includes a thick, juicy Pat LaFrieda blend house burger.

EXPLORE

Gilroy.

Harlem & Upper Manhattan

Harlem is the cultural capital of black America – a legacy of the Harlem Renaissance, the cultural movement that spanned the 1920s. During the Jazz Age, white New Yorkers accepted Ellington's famous invitation to 'Take the A Train' uptown to the neighbourhood's celebrated nightclubs, but in the 1960s and '70s, crime and urban decay kept non-residents away. Today, Harlem is seeing a second renaissance. The area isn't packed with sights, but it's worth visiting for its eclectic architecture, theatrical street life, historic churches with exuberant gospel choirs and rejuvenated restaurant and bar scene.

Morris-Jumel Mansion.

Welcome to the World Fam...
APOLLO THEAT...

Don't Miss

1 **Studio Museum in Harlem** Work by prominent and emerging black artists (p196).

2 **Red Rooster Harlem** Savour gourmet soul food at this cross-cultural canteen (p198).

3 **Harlem Haberdashery** If it's good enough for Jay Z… (p199).

4 **Morris-Jumel Mansion** George Washington slept here (p201).

5 **The Cloisters** A fairytale castle houses the Met's medieval collection (p200).

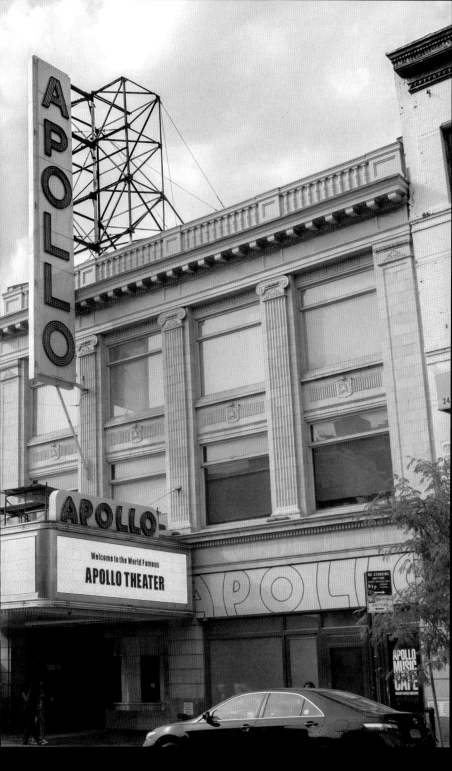

Harlem.

Harlem

WEST & CENTRAL HARLEM

Subway A, B, C, D to 125th Street; B, C to 116th Street or 135th Street; 1, 2, 3 to 125th Street.

The village of Harlem, named by Dutch colonists after their native Haarlem, was annexed by the City of New York in 1873. The extension of the elevated subway two decades later brought eager developers who overbuilt in the suddenly accessible suburb. The consequent housing glut led to cheap rents, and Jewish, Italian and Irish immigrants escaping the tenements of the Lower East Side snapped them up.

Around the turn of the 20th century, black Americans joined the procession into Harlem, their ranks swelled by the Great Migration from the Deep South. By 1914, the black population of Harlem had risen well above 50,000; by the 1920s, Harlem was predominately black and the country's most populous African-American community. This prominence soon attracted some of black America's greatest artists: writers such as Langston Hughes and Zora Neale Hurston and musicians including Duke Ellington, Louis Armstrong and Cab Calloway. The unprecedented cultural gathering was known as the Harlem Renaissance. White New York took notice, venturing uptown – where the enforcement of Prohibition was lax – to enjoy the Cotton Club, Connie's Inn, Smalls Paradise and the Savoy Ballroom, which supplied the beat for the city that never sleeps.

The Depression killed the Harlem Renaissance, and deeply wounded Harlem. By the 1960s, the community had been ravaged by middle-class flight and municipal neglect. Businesses closed, racial tensions ran high, and the looting during the 1977 blackout was among the worst the city had seen. However, as New York's economic standing improved in the mid '90s, investment began slowly spilling into the area, spawning new businesses and the phalanxes of renovated brownstones that beckon the middle class (white and black). This moneyed influx's coexistence with Harlem's long-standing residents can be tense, but it is seldom volatile.

On 125th Street, Harlem's main artery, street preachers and mix-tape hawkers vie for the attentions of the human parade and the celebrated **Apollo Theater** (*see p283*) hosts concerts, a syndicated TV show and the classic Amateur Night every Wednesday – James Brown, Ella Fitzgerald, Michael Jackson and Lauryn Hill are among its starry alumni. A block east is the highly regarded **Studio Museum in Harlem**.

Although new apartment buildings, boutiques, restaurants and cafés are scattered throughout the neighbourhood, Harlem has retained many of the buildings that went up around the turn of the century because redevelopers shunned it for so long. Of particular interest, the **Mount Morris**

IN THE KNOW HALLELUJAH!

In the 1930s, the **Abyssinian Baptist Church** (132 Odell Clark Place/W 138th Street, between Malcolm X Boulevard/ Lenox Avenue & Adam Clayton Powell Jr Boulevard/Seventh Avenue, 1-212 862 7474, www.abyssinian.org) was under the leadership of legendary civil rights crusader Adam Clayton Powell Jr. From the staid gingerbread Gothic exterior, you'd never suspect the energy that charges the church when the gospel choir gets into swing. Visitors are welcome to attend most 11am Sunday services, but get there early, and don't wear shorts or flip-flops.

EXPLORE

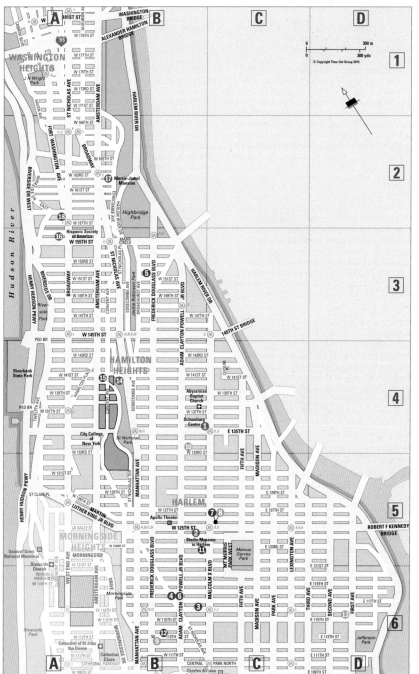

EXPLORE

EXPLORE

Historic District (from 119th to 124th Streets, between Malcolm X Boulevard/Lenox Avenue & Mount Morris Park West) contains charming brownstones and a collection of religious buildings in a variety of architectural styles.

The section of W 116th Street between St Nicholas Avenue and Morningside Park is known as **Little Senegal**, a strip of West African shops and restaurants. Continue east along 116th Street, past the domed **Masjid Malcolm Shabazz** (no.102), the mosque of Malcolm X's ministry, to the **Malcolm Shabazz Harlem Market** (no.52, 1-212 987 8131), an outdoor bazaar that buzzes with vendors, most from West Africa, selling clothes, jewellery and other goods from covered stalls. While most of the storied jazz clubs have closed, **Showman's Bar** (375 W 125th Street, between St Nicholas & Morningside Avenues, 1-212 864 8941, www.showmansjazzclub.com, closed Sun) is a neighbourhood old-timer.

Further north is **Strivers' Row**, also known as the St Nicholas Historic District. On 138th and 139th Streets, between Adam Clayton Powell Jr Boulevard (Seventh Avenue) and Frederick Douglass Boulevard (Eighth Avenue), these harmonious blocks of brick townhouses were developed in 1891 by David H King Jr and designed by three different architects, one of whom was Stanford White. The enclave is so well preserved that the alleyway sign advising you to 'walk your horses' is still visible.

Harlem's rich history is stored in the archives of the nearby **Schomburg Center for Research in Black Culture**. This branch of the New York Public Library contains more than five million documents, artefacts, films and prints relating to the cultures of peoples of African descent, with a strong emphasis on the African-American experience.

Sights & Museums

FREE Schomburg Center for Research in Black Culture

515 Malcolm X Boulevard (Lenox Avenue), between 135th & 136th Streets (1-917 275 6975, www.nypl. org/locations/schomburg). Subway 2, 3 to 135th Street. **Open** *General & gallery* 10am-6pm Mon, Fri, Sat; 10am-8pm Tue-Thur. *Other departments* times vary. **Admission** free. **Map** p195 C4 ❶

Part of the New York Public Library, this institution holds an extraordinary trove of vintage literature and historical memorabilia relating to black culture and the African diaspora, much of which was amassed by notable bibliophile Arturo Alfonso Schomburg, who was curator from 1932 until his death in 1938. (It was posthumously renamed in his honour.) Note that parts of the collection can only be viewed on certain days by appointment; call or refer to the website. The centre also hosts regular exhibitions, concerts, films, lectures and other events.

Studio Museum in Harlem

144 W 125th Street, between Adam Clayton Powell Jr Boulevard (Seventh Avenue) & Malcolm X Boulevard (Lenox Avenue) (1-212 864 4500, www.studiomuseum.org). Subway 2, 3 to 125th Street. **Open** noon-9pm Thur, Fri; 10am-6pm Sat; noon-6pm Sun. **Admission** *Suggested donation* $7; $3 reductions; free under-12s. Free Sun. **Map** p195 B5 ❷

The first black fine arts museum in the United States when it opened in 1968, the Studio Museum is an important player in the art scene of the African diaspora. Under the leadership of director and chief curator Thelma Golden (formerly of the Whitney), this vibrant institution, housed in a stripped-down, three-level space, presents shows in a variety of media by black artists from around the world. The museum supports emerging visual artists of African descent through its coveted artist-in-residence programme.

Restaurants & Cafés

Amy Ruth's

113 W 116th Street, between Malcolm X Boulevard (Lenox Avenue) & Adam Clayton Powell Jr Boulevard (Seventh Avenue) (1-212 280 8779, www.amyruthsharlem.com). Subway 2, 3 to 116th Street. **Open** 11.30am-11pm Mon; 8.30am-11pm Tue-Thur; 8.30am-5.30am Fri; 7.30am-5.30am Sat; 7.30am-11pm Sun. **Main courses** $13-$24. **Map** p195 B6 ❸ **American regional**

This popular no-reservations spot is the place for soul food. Delicately fried okra is delivered without a hint of slime, and the mac and cheese is gooey inside and crunchy-brown on top. Dishes take their names from notable African-Americans – vote for the President Barack Obama (fried, smothered, baked or barbecued chicken) or celebrate hip hop's NYC roots over the Afrika Bambaataa (fried whiting).

Cecil

210 W 118th Street, between Adam Clayton Powell Jr Boulevard (Seventh Avenue) & St Nicholas Avenue (1-212 866 1262, www.thececilharlem. com). Subway B, C to 116th Street. **Open** 5pm-midnight Mon-Thur; 5pm-1am Fri; 11am-1am Sat; 11am-11pm Sun. **Main courses** $19-$36. **Map** p195 B6 ❹ **Eclectic**

See p197 **Harlem Gets Its Groove Back**.

$ Charles' Country Panfried Chicken

2839 Frederick Douglass Boulevard (Eighth Avenue), between 151st & 152nd Streets (1-212 281 1800). Subway B, D to 155th Street. **Open** 11am-1am Mon-Sat; 11am-8pm Sun. **Main courses** $10.50-11.50. **Map** p195 B3 ❺ **American regional**

Fried chicken guru Charles Gabriel's no-frills eaterie is far from any tourist attractions, but devotees rave about his speciality's moist flesh and crackly skin. In

HARLEM GETS ITS GROOVE BACK

The neighbourhood is hopping again, with lively eateries and nightspots.

Red Rooster Harlem.

Nearly a century after its famed cultural surge, Harlem is experiencing another renaissance, this time of the culinary variety. Buzzy eateries are popping up throughout the area, especially on Frederick Douglass and Malcolm X Boulevards. Marcus Samuelsson helped to pioneer the movement in 2011 when he opened his comfort-food sensation, **Red Rooster Harlem** (*see p198*), named after a legendary Harlem speakeasy once located at 138th Street and Seventh Avenue. The Ethiopian-born, Swedish-raised chef – himself a Harlem resident – created a destination as cool as any downtown spot, but with a distinctly uptown vibe, raking in critical acclaim for his refined soul food that honours both the nabe's history, with classics like fried chicken and waffles, and its multicultural residents with eclectic influences. A year later, Samuelsson expanded his Harlem holdings with **Ginny's Supper Club** (*see p198*), a jazzy ode to the swinging speakeasies and live-music lounges of the 1920s. At press time, he opened **Streetbird Rotisserie** (2149 Frederick Douglass Boulevard, between 115th & 116th Streets, 1-212 206 2557, www.streetbirdnyc.com), featuring the titular chicken in globe-spanning dishes. The restaurant is decked out with hip hop paraphernalia and historic Harlem elements, including a floor-to-ceiling installation of boom-box stereos and a vintage marquee sign recovered from the iconic M&G Diner that reads 'old fashion' but good'.

In autumn 2013, Richard Parsons and Alexander Smalls paid tribute to Harlem cuisine and music with two notable openings. Inside the historic Cecil Hotel space, the twosome revived Minton's Playhouse, the

1930s jazz lounge where Thelonious Monk served as house pianist and Dizzy Gillespie invented bebop. Their supper club, **Minton's** (*see p198*), tips a hat to this musical past – a 1948 mural of Hot Lips Page anchors the stage where jazz bands play most nights. Next door, the **Cecil** (*see p196*) braids together the far-reaching flavours of the African diaspora (citrus jerk bass, roasted poussin yassa) in a polished, gold-accented dining room. In 2014, the owners of Brooklyn stalwart **Madiba** (*see p217*) brought their successful combination of South African grub and live music uptown to multi-purpose events/studio complex **My Image Studios** (46 W 116th Street, between Fifth Avenue & Malcolm X Boulevard/Lenox Avenue, 1-646 738 3043, www.madibaharlem.com). Performers at the upbeat eaterie have included such luminaries as Lauryn Hill.

Ginny's Supper Club.

EXPLORE

EXPLORE

addition to the poultry, you can feast on barbecued ribs, mac and cheese, collard greens, yams and other Southern favourites.

Minton's

206 W 118th Street, between Adam Clayton Powell Jr Boulevard (Seventh Avenue) & St Nicholas Avenue (1-212 243 2222, www.mintonsharlem.com). Subway B, C to 116th Street. **Open** 6-11pm Tue-Thur; 6pm-1am Fri, Sat; noon-3.30pm, 5-10pm Sun. **Main courses** $22-$36. **Map** p195 B6 **❻** American
See p197 **Harlem Gets Its Groove Back.**

★ Red Rooster Harlem

310 Malcolm X Boulevard (Lenox Avenue), between 125th & 126th Streets (1-212 792 9001, www.red roosterharlem.com). Subway 2, 3 to 125th Street. **Open** 11.30am-10.30pm Mon-Thur; 11.30am-11.30pm Fri; 10am-11.30pm Sat; 10am-10pm Sun. **Main courses** $18-$37. **Map** p195 C5 **❼** American
With its hobnobbing bar scrum, potent cocktails and lively jazz, this buzzy eaterie serves as a worthy clubhouse for the new Harlem. Superstar chef Marcus Samuelsson (*see p197*) is at his most populist here, drawing on a mix of Southern-fried, East African, Scandinavian and French flavours. At the teardrop bar, Harlem politicos mix with trendy downtowners, swilling cocktails and gorging on rib-sticking food.

Bars

Ginny's Supper Club

310 Malcolm X Boulevard (Lenox Avenue), between 125th & 126th Streets (1-212 421 3821, www.ginnyssupperclub.com). Subway 2, 3 to 125th Street. **Open** 6pm-midnight Thur; 6pm-3am Fri,

Sat; 10.30am & 12.30pm brunch seatings, 6-10pm Sun. **Map** p195 C5 **❽**
This sprawling basement lounge is modelled after the Harlem speakeasies of the '20s. The menu, eclectic cocktails and a steady line-up of live music all revive the sophisticated supper club experience.

Park 112

2080 Fredrick Douglass Boulevard (Eighth Avenue), at 112th Street (1-646 524 6610, www.thepark112.com). Subway B, C to 110th Street-Cathedral Parkway. **Open** 5.30pm-midnight Tue, Wed; 5.30pm-1am Thur; 5.30pm-2am Fri; noon-4pm, 5.30pm-2am Sat; 11am-11pm Sun. **Map** p195 B6 **❾**
Styled with illuminated communal tables and brown-leather banquettes, this 90-seat restaurant and bar is equipped with a self-serve Enomatic wine machine. In addition to the 30-bottle wine list, you'll find global fare from Aquavit alum Kingsley John. Note that the kitchen closes at 11pm most weekdays (1am on Fridays and Saturdays).

Shrine

2271 Adam Clayton Powell Jr Boulevard (Seventh Avenue), between 133rd & 134th Streets (1-212 690 7807, www.shrinenyc.com). Subway B, C, 2, 3 to 135th Street. **Open** 4pm-4am daily. **No credit cards**. **Map** p195 B4 **❿**
Playfully adapting a sign left over from the previous tenants (the Black United Foundation), the Shrine advertises itself as a 'Black United Fun Plaza'. The interior is tricked out with African art and vintage album covers, and actual vinyl adorns the ceiling. Nightly performances might feature indie rock, jazz, reggae or DJ sets. The cocktail menu aspires to similar diversity with wittily named tipples like the rum-based Afro Trip.

Harlem Haberdashery.

Shops & Services

★ Harlem Haberdashery
245 Malcolm X Boulevard (Lenox Avenue), between 122nd & 123rd Streets (1-646 707 0070, www. harlemhaberdashery.com). Subway 2, 3 to 125th Street. **Open** 11.30am-9pm Mon-Sat. **Map** p195 B5 ⓫ Fashion

File this under 'If it's good enough for Jay Z'. Harlem Haberdashery was founded by the folks behind clothing label 5001 Flavors, which dressed the rapper for his 'Empire State of Mind' video. In addition to locally made urban-meets-preppy clothes for men and women, there are high-top Android Homme sneakers, graphic T-shirts and custom-tailored suits. Fun fact: the boutique is housed in a brownstone where Malcolm X once lived.

Trunk Show Designer Consignment
275-277 W 113th Street, between Adam Clayton Powell Jr Boulevard (Seventh Avenue) & Frederick Douglass Boulevard (Eighth Avenue) (1-212 662 0009, www.trunkshowconsignment.com). Subway B, C to 110th Street-Cathedral Parkway. **Open** 1-8.30pm Tue-Fri; 1-7.30pm Sat; noon-6.30pm Sun. **Map** p195 B6 ⓬ Fashion

Modelling agent Heather Jones graduated from hosting oversubscribed pop-up trunk shows to co-opening this small Harlem storefront. Men's and women's threads and accessories range from edgier brands (Margiela, Rick Owens) to Madison Avenue labels (Gucci, Chanel, Céline), with in-season items marked down between 20% and 70%. The shop sometimes keeps erratic hours, so call before making a special trip.

EAST HARLEM
Subway 6 to 110th Street or 116th Street.
East of Fifth Avenue is **East Harlem**, commonly called Spanish Harlem but also known to its primarily Puerto Rican residents as El Barrio. The traditional southern boundary with the Upper East Side is 96th Street, but is becoming increasingly blurred as gentrification creeps northward. Its main east–west cross street, East 116th Street, shows signs of a recent influx of Mexican immigrants. The modest **Graffiti Hall of Fame** (106th Street, between Madison & Park Avenues) celebrates old- and new-school taggers in a schoolyard. Be sure to check out the nearby **El Museo del Barrio** (*see p185*), too.

Bars

For bars on the border of the Upper East Side and East Harlem, *see p190*.

Camaradas el Barrio
2241 First Avenue, at 115th Street (1-212 348 2703, www.camaradaselbarrio.com). Subway 6

to 116th Street. **Open** 3pm-1am Mon-Wed, Sun; 3pm-2am Thur-Sat. **Map** p195 D6 ⓭
Owner Orlando Plaza pays tribute to his Puerto Rican heritage at this lively bar, eatery and nightspot. The look is downtown chic: exposed brick, local art on the walls and rough-hewn wooden benches. Grab a seat and sample 'Puerto Rican pub fare' like alcapurrias (yucca and ground beef fritters) or empanadas, or kick back over a pitcher of sangria and take in some live salsa or jazz.

HAMILTON HEIGHTS
Subway A, B, C, D, 1 to 145th Street; 1 to 137th Street.

Named after Alexander Hamilton, who owned an estate and a farm here, **Hamilton Heights** extends from 125th Street to the Trinity Cemetery at 155th Street, between Riverside Drive and St Nicholas Avenue. Hamilton's 1802 Federal-style house, the **Grange**, now a national memorial, was moved from 287 Convent Avenue around the corner to St Nicholas Park.

The neighbourhood developed after the West Side elevated train was built in the late 19th century; it's notable for the elegant turn-of-the-20th-century row houses in the **Hamilton Heights Historic District**, centred on the side streets off scenic **Convent Avenue** between 140th and 145th Streets – just beyond the Gothic Revival-style campus of the **City College of New York** (Convent Avenue, from 135th to 140th Streets).

Sights & Museums

FREE Hamilton Grange National Memorial
St Nicholas Park, 414 W 141st Street, near Convent Avenue (1-646 548 2310, www.nps.gov/hagr). Subway A, B, C, D to 145th Street. **Open** *Visitor centre* 9am-5pm Wed-Sun. *Tours* 10am, 11am, 2pm, 4pm. **Admission** free. **Map** p195 B4 ⓮
The Federal-style estate of America's first Secretary of the Treasury was completed two years before he was shot in a duel with Vice President Aaron Burr. Restored period rooms include Hamilton's study and the parlour, with his daughter's pianoforte. A short film about the founding father's life is shown in the visitor centre.

Restaurants & Cafés

Grange Bar & Eatery
1635 Amsterdam Avenue, at 141st Street (1-212 491 1635, www.thegrangebarnyc.com). Subway A, B, C, D to 145th Street; 1 to 137th Street-City College. **Open** 11.30am-4am Mon-Fri; 10.30am-4am Sat, Sun. **Main courses** $13-$25. **Map** p195 A4 ⓯ American

EXPLORE

Grange Bar & Eatery. See p199.

Harlem goes back to its rural roots at this locavore bistro and bar, outfitted with Mason jars, white-oak floors and chandeliers. Aric Sassi oversees a comfort-food menu rooted in seasonal produce; having scoured nearby farms, the chef dispatches dishes such as seared crab cakes with celery-parsnip slaw and a roast-beet salad with lime yoghurt, almonds and goat's cheese croutons. At the 40ft-long butcher-block bar, cocktails designed by Dead Rabbit head bartender Jack McGarry include the Grange Collins (gin, pomegranate liqueur, basil, lemon juice and soda).

Washington Heights & Inwood

Subway A, C, 1 to 168th Street-Washington Heights; A to 190th Street; C to 163rd Street-Amsterdam Avenue; 1 to 157th Street or 191st Street.

The area from West 155th Street to Dyckman (200th) Street is called **Washington Heights**; venture north of that and you're in Inwood, Manhattan's northernmost neighbourhood, where the Harlem and Hudson Rivers converge. An ever-growing number of artists, musicians and young families are relocating to these parts, attracted by the spacious pre-war buildings, big parks, hilly streets and (comparatively) low rents.

Washington Heights' main attraction is the **Morris-Jumel Mansion**, a stunning Palladian-style house that served as a swanky headquarters for George Washington during the autumn of 1776. But the small **Hispanic Society of America**, featuring a surprising collection of masterworks, is an overlooked gem.

Since the 1920s, waves of immigrants have settled in Washington Heights. In the post-World War II era, many German-Jewish refugees (among them Henry Kissinger and Dr Ruth Westheimer) moved to the western edge of the district. Broadway was once home to a small Greek population – opera singer Maria Callas lived here in her youth. But in the last few decades, the southern and eastern parts of the area have become predominantly Spanish-speaking due to a large population of Dominican settlers.

A trek along Fort Washington Avenue, from about 173rd Street to **Fort Tryon Park**, puts you in the heart of **Hudson Heights** – the posh area of Washington Heights. Start at the **George Washington Bridge**, the city's only bridge across the Hudson River. A pedestrian walkway (also used by cyclists) commands dazzling Manhattan views. Under the bridge on the New York side is a diminutive lighthouse. To see it up close, look for the footpath on the west side of Henry Hudson Parkway below 181st Street, which leads down to the riverside Fort Washington Park and the Hudson River Greenway, a popular route for walkers, joggers and cyclists.

North of the bridge is the beautiful Fort Tryon Park; at the park's northern edge is the **Cloisters**, a museum built in 1938 using segments of five medieval cloisters. It houses the Metropolitan Museum of Art's medieval art collection.

Inwood stretches from Dyckman Street up to 218th Street, the last residential block in Manhattan. Dyckman buzzes with street life from river to river, but, north of that, the island narrows considerably and the parks along the western shoreline culminate in the seclusion of **Inwood Hill Park**, another Frederick Law Olmsted legacy. Some believe that this is the location of the legendary 1626 transaction between Peter Minuit and the Native American Lenapes for the purchase of a strip of land called Manahatta – a plaque at the south-west corner of the ballpark near 214th Street marks the purported spot. The 196-acre refuge contains the island's last swathes of virgin forest and salt marsh. Today, you can hike over the hilly terrain, liberally scattered with massive glacier-deposited boulders (called erratics) and picture Manhattan as it was before development.

Sights & Museums

★ The Cloisters
Fort Tryon Park, Fort Washington Avenue, at Margaret Corbin Plaza (1-212 923 3700, www.metmuseum.org). Subway A to 190th Street, then 10min walk. **Open** *Mar-Oct* 10am-5.15pm daily. *Nov-Feb* 10am-4.45pm daily. **Admission** *Suggested donation* (incl same-day admission to Metropolitan Museum of Art) $25; $12-$17 reductions; free under-12s. **Map** p403 B3

EXPLORE

Set in a lovely park overlooking the Hudson River, the Cloisters houses the Metropolitan Museum's medieval art and architecture collections. A path winds through parkland to a castle that seems to date from the Middle Ages; in fact it was built in the 1930s using pieces from five medieval French cloisters, shipped from Europe by the Rockefeller clan. Highlights include the impressive limestone apse of the 12th-century Fuentidueña Chapel, the Unicorn Tapestries and the *Annunciation* triptych by Robert Campin.

FREE Hispanic Society of America

Audubon Terrace, Broadway, between 155th & 156th Streets (1-212 926 2234, www.hispanic society.org). Subway 1 to 157th Street. **Open** 10am-4.30pm Tue-Sat; 1-4pm Sun. **Admission** free. **Map** p195 B9

Though few people seem aware of it, the Hispanic Society boasts the largest assemblage of Spanish art and manuscripts outside Spain. Goya's masterful *Duchess of Alba* greets you as you enter, and several haunting El Greco portraits are on the second floor. The collection is dominated by religious artefacts, including 16th-century tombs from the monastery of San Francisco in Cuéllar, Spain. Also among its holdings are decorative art objects and thousands of black and white photographs that document life in Spain and Latin America from the mid 19th century to the present. One highlight is Valencian painter Joaquín Sorolla y Bastida's *Vision of Spain*, comprising 14 monumental oils commissioned by the Society in 1911.

Morris-Jumel Mansion

65 Jumel Terrace, between 160th & 162nd Streets (1-212 923 8008, www.morrisjumel.org). Subway C to 163rd Street-Amsterdam Avenue. **Open** 10am-4pm Tue-Fri; 10am-5pm Sat, Sun. **Admission** $5; $4 reductions; free under-12s. **Map** p195 C8 ⓱

Constructed in 1765, Manhattan's only surviving pre-Revolutionary pile was originally built for British governor Roger Morris but later served as General Washington's headquarters in the early months of the Revolutionary War. Later, an elderly Aaron Burr lived here after marrying widow Eliza Brown Jumel in 1833. (They divorced a year later.) The restored interior features many of the 19th-century French decorations of which Eliza was so fond, and a colonial-era kitchen with the original hearth. The handsome Palladian-style villa offers fantastic views. While you're here, check out its former driveway, Sylvan Terrace, which has the longest continuous stretch (one block in total) of old wooden houses in all of Manhattan.

Restaurants & Cafés

$ Taszo Espresso Bar

5 Edward M Morgan Place, between 157th & 158th Streets (1-212 694 8770, www.taszo.com). Subway 1 to 157th Street. **Open** 7am-10pm Mon-Fri; 8am-10pm Sat, Sun. **Main courses** $8-$17. **Map** p195 A2 ⓲ **Café**

A laid-back café where you can accompany your Brooklyn Roasting Company java with cult baked goods such as Danny Macaroons and Balthazar Bakery pastries, or light eats like house-made panini and frittatas. Alternatively, pair a craft beer or a glass of wine with cheese from Greenwich Village institution Murray's. All this, plus evening sets by local musicians (jazz, folk, singer-songwriters), draws an eclectic crowd that often spills out on to the sidewalk.

EXPLORE

The Cloisters.

Brooklyn

Not long ago, many Manhattanites baulked at the idea of crossing the East River for a day or night out. Times sure have changed. Not only is the second borough a destination in its own right, with a thriving cultural and food scene, but 'Brooklyn' has also become shorthand for a particular brand of indie cool, recognised the world over. Popular areas such as Williamsburg, known for its nightlife, and Dumbo, gateway to the gorgeous Brooklyn Bridge Park, are easily accessible – even by foot.

Settled by the Dutch in the early 17th century, it was America's third largest municipality until its amalgamation with the four other boroughs that created New York City in 1898. Its many brownstones are a testament to a large and wealthy merchant class that made its money from the shipping trade. By the end of the 19th century, Brooklyn had become so prosperous, and its view of itself so grandiloquent, it built copies of the Arc de Triomphe (in Grand Army Plaza) and the Champs-Elysées (Eastern Parkway), and a greensward (Prospect Park) to rival Central Park.

Green-Wood Cemetery.

Don't Miss

1 Brooklyn Bridge Approach the borough on foot for spectacular panoramas (p205).

2 Semilla A tasting menu worth the trek (p220).

3 Vinegar Hill House A tucked-away gem in a time-warp street (p208).

4 Brooklyn Museum The second borough's answer to the Met (p214).

5 Green-Wood Cemetery Where the great, the good and the bad are buried (p214).

Brooklyn Heights Promenade.

EXPLORE

BROOKLYN HEIGHTS, DOWNTOWN & DUMBO

Brooklyn Heights – Subway A, C, F to Jay Street-Borough Hall; A, C, G to Hoyt-Schermerhorn; M, R to Court Street; 2, 3, 4, 5 to Borough Hall. Dumbo – Subway to A, C to High Street; F to York Street.

Home to well-to-do families and professionals lured by its proximity to Wall Street, **Brooklyn Heights** is where you'll find the idyllic leafy, brownstone-lined streets of Brooklyn legend. Thanks to the area's historic district status, it has many Greek Revival and Italianate row houses dating from the 1820s. Take a stroll down the gorgeous tree-lined streets – try Cranberry, Hicks, Pierrepont and Willow – to see the area at its best.

Given its serenity and easy access to Manhattan, it's not surprising that Brooklyn Heights has been home to numerous illustrious (and struggling) writers. Walt Whitman printed the first edition of *Leaves of Grass* at 98 Cranberry Street (in a building since demolished); Truman Capote wrote *Breakfast at Tiffany's* at 70 Willow Street; and Thomas Wolfe penned *Of Times and the River* at 5 Montague Terrace.

Henry and Montague Streets are the prime strips for shops, restaurants and bars. At the end of Montague, the **Brooklyn Heights Promenade** offers spectacular waterfront views of lower Manhattan, New York Harbor and the nearby **Brooklyn Bridge**, a marvel of 19th-century engineering.

In the other direction, Downtown Brooklyn's grand **Borough Hall** (209 Joralemon Street, at Court Street), the seat of local government, stands as a monument to Brooklyn's past as an independent municipality. Completed in 1851 but only later crowned with a Victorian cupola, the Greek Revival edifice was renovated in the late 1980s. The building is linked to the **New York State Supreme Court** (360 Adams Street,

between Joralemon Street & Tech Place) by **Cadman Plaza** (from Prospect Street to Tech Place, between Cadman Plaza East & Cadman Plaza West).

By the end of the 19th century, **Dumbo** (Down Under the Manhattan Bridge Overpass) was a thriving industrial district; all kinds of manufacturers, including Brillo and Benjamin Moore, were based here, leaving behind a fine collection of factory buildings and warehouses; the most famous of these, the **Eskimo Pie Building** (100 Bridge Street, at York Street), with its embellished façade, was actually built for the Thomson Meter Company in 1908-09.

In the 1970s and '80s, these warehouses were colonised by artists seeking cheap live/work spaces. But playing out a familiar New York migration pattern, the area is now bursting with million-dollar apartments and high-end design shops. The spectacular views – taking in the Statue of Liberty, the lower Manhattan skyline and the Brooklyn and Manhattan Bridges – remain the same. The best vantage point is below the Brooklyn Bridge at the **Fulton Ferry Landing**, which juts out over the East River at Old Fulton and Water Streets. It was here that General George Washington and his troops beat a hasty retreat by boat from the Battle of Brooklyn in 1776. It's now a stop on the East River Ferry service (*see p375*), which links to Manhattan and Queens. Along the same pier is the **Brooklyn Ice Cream Factory** (Fulton Ferry Landing,

IN THE KNOW LOVE LOCKS

Wondering why there are padlocks scattered on the fence on the Brooklyn Bridge? Couples attach them and throw the keys in the river as a symbol of everlasting love – until Department of Transportation workers cut them off, that is.

1 Water Street, 1-718 246 3963, closed Mon Dec-Mar), located in a 1920s fireboat house. Next door, docked at the pier, is one of the borough's great cultural jewels: **Bargemusic** (*see p298*), a 100-foot steel barge that was built in 1899 but has staged chamber music concerts since the 1970s.

On both sides of the landing, **Brooklyn Bridge Park** (riverside, from the Manhattan Bridge to Atlantic Avenue) has been undergoing a rolling redesign that includes lawns, freshwater gardens, a water fowl-attracting salt marsh and the Granite Prospect, a set of stairs fashioned out of salvaged granite facing the Manhattan skyline. But the undoubted centrepiece is the vintage merry-go-round known as **Jane's Carousel** which was restored by local artist Jane Walentas over more than two decades and now occupies a Jean Nouvel-designed Plexiglas pavilion in the section of park between Main Street and the Brooklyn Bridge. (For more on the park's family attractions, *see p256*). Along this stretch of riverfront, the post-Civil War coffee warehouses, **Empire Stores**, are being developed into a retail and restaurant complex that should be open by publication of this guide.

The artists who flocked to the area en masse in the 1970s and '80s maintain a presence in the local galleries, most of which support the work of emerging talent. Dumbo is also home to Off Broadway standout, **St Ann's Warehouse** (*see p319*).

Head east on Water or Front Street to discover one of Brooklyn's forgotten neighbourhoods. Once a rough and bawdy patch dotted with bars and brothels frequented by sailors and dockworkers, **Vinegar Hill**, between Bridge Street and the Navy Yard, earned the moniker 'Hell's Half Acre' in the 19th century. Only fragments of the enclave remain (parts of it were designated a historic district in the late 1990s), and it's considerably quieter today. Although inhabited, the isolated strips of early-19th-century row houses and defunct storefronts on Bridge, Hudson and Plymouth Streets, and a stretch of Front Street, have a ghost-town quality, heightened by their juxtaposition with a Con Edison generating station. For refreshment, seek out the enclave's tavern-like **Vinegar Hill House**.

Sights & Museums

★ FREE Brooklyn Bridge

Subway A, C to High Street; J to Chambers Street; 4, 5, 6 to Brooklyn Bridge-City Hall. **Map** p206 D1 ❶
Designed by John Roebling, the Brooklyn Bridge was built in response to the harsh winter of 1867 when the East River froze over, severing connection between Manhattan and what was then the nation's third most populous city. When it opened in 1883, the 5,989ft-long structure was the world's longest bridge, and the first in the world to use steel suspension cables. Every day, 6,600 people walk or bike across the bridge's wide, wood-planked promenade, taking in views of New York Harbor, the Statue of Liberty and the skyscrapers of lower Manhattan.
▶ *You can also walk or bike into Brooklyn across the Manhattan or Williamsburg Bridges.*

Brooklyn Historical Society

128 Pierrepont Street, at Clinton Street, Brooklyn Heights (1-718 222 4111, www.brooklynhistory.org). Subway R to Court Street; 2, 3, 4, 5 to Borough Hall. **Open** *Museum* noon-5pm Wed-Sat. *Gift shop* noon-5pm daily. *Library* 1-5pm Wed-Sat. **Admission** *Suggested donation* $10; $6 reductions; free under-12s, students. **Map** p206 D2 ❷

EXPLORE

Brooklyn Bridge.

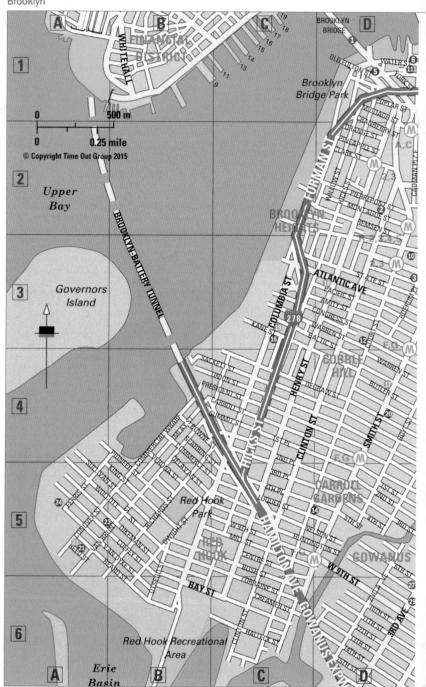

EXPLORE

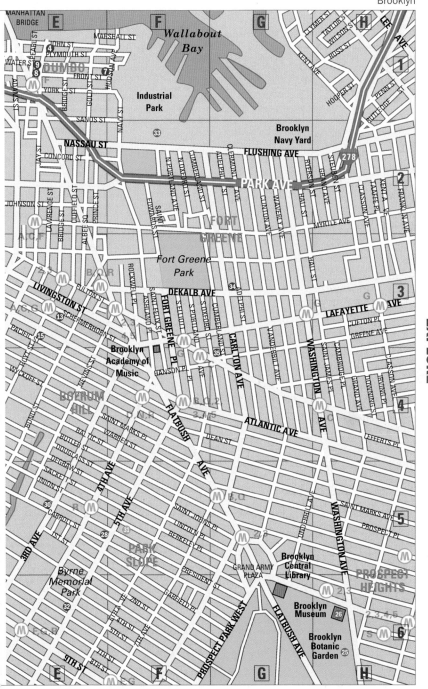

EXPLORE

Founded in 1863, the BHS resides in a landmark Queen Anne-style building. In addition to a major photo and research library – featuring historic maps and newspapers, notable family histories and archives from the area's abolitionist movement – it presents ongoing and temporary exhibitions. 'Brooklyn Abolitionists/In Pursuit of Freedom', on view until winter 2018, examines Kings County's antislavery movement in the 19th century and includes one of the most prized items in the BHS's collection: an original copy of the Emancipation Proclamation, signed by President Lincoln.

New York Transit Museum
Corner of Boerum Place & Schermerhorn Street, Brooklyn Heights (1-718 694 1600, www.mta. info/mta/museum). Subway A, C, G to Hoyt-Schermerhorn; 2, 3, 4, 5 to Borough Hall. **Open** 10am-4pm Tue-Fri; 11am-5pm Sat, Sun. **Admission** $7; $5 reductions; free under-2s; free seniors Wed. **Map** p206 D3 ❸
Located in a historic 1936 IND subway station, this is the largest museum in the United States devoted to urban public transport history. Exhibits explore the social and practical impact of public transport on the development of greater New York; among the highlights is an engrossing walk-through display charting the construction of the city's subway system in the early 1900s, when fearless 'sandhogs' were engaged in dangerous tunnelling. A line-up of turnstiles shows their evolution from the 1894 'ticket chopper' to the current Automatic Fare Card model. But the best part is down another level to a real platform where you can board an exceptional collection of vintage subway and El ('Elevated') cars, some complete with vintage ads.
Other location New York Transit Museum Gallery Annex & Store, Grand Central Terminal, adjacent to stationmaster's office, main concourse (1-212 878 0106; *see p162*).

Restaurants & Cafés

Brooklyn Roasting Company
25 Jay Street, between John & Plymouth Streets, Dumbo (1-718 522 2664, www.brooklynroasting. com). Subway A, C to High Street; F to York Street. **Open** 7am-7pm daily. **Coffee** $1.50-$5.25. **Map** p207 E1 ❹ Café

Supplier of fair-trade, organic beans to many of the borough's best cafés, Brooklyn Roasting Company serves its coffee and espresso drinks in a spacious, industrial-chic on-site café. Kick back on a sofa and savour the aromas wafting from the fuel-efficient roasting machine. You can accompany your brew with baked goods or a sandwich from local purveyors including Fresh Fanatic and Margo Patisserie.
Other location 200 Flushing Avenue, at Washington Avenue, Fort Greene (1-718 858 5500).

Juliana's
19 Old Fulton Street, between Front & Water Streets, Dumbo (1-718 596 6700, www.julianas pizza.com). Subway A, C to High Street; F to York Street. **Open** 11.30am-11pm daily. **Pizzas** $16-$32. **Map** p206 D1 ❺ Pizza
For years, visitors have been making the pilgrimage to famed Dumbo pizza joint Grimaldi's – but they may not be aware that founder Patsy Grimaldi sold the place more than a decade ago. In 2012, he burst out of retirement to reclaim his shop's first location, along with its original coal oven. This time, Grimaldi – who learned to spin dough at age 13 in his Uncle Patsy Lancieri's Harlem institution – named the spot after his mother. At Juliana's, the menu spotlights iconic red-sauce fare, including classic pizzas, such as sausage and broccoli rabe. But he's also mixed in a few nods to modern times: creative pizzas (such as a bagel-like riff with lox and goat's cheese) and a proprietary chocolate-and-raspberry flavour from nearby Brooklyn Ice Cream Factory. Another throwback touch: an antique jukebox plays Patsy's favourite Sinatra tunes.

One Girl Cookies
33 Main Street, at Water Street, Dumbo (1-212 675 4996, www.onegirlcookies.com). Subway A, C to High Street; F to York Street. **Open** 8am-7pm Mon-Fri; 9am-7pm Sat, Sun. **Cookies** $2.75-$4. **Map** p206 D1 ❻ Café
Dawn Casale started baking cookies out of her Greenwich Village apartment in 2000 (hence the name), before hiring chef David Crofton to help. Now married, they run two bakery-cafés. Pair your tea cookies or a whoopie pie with Red Hook-roasted Stumptown coffee, craft beer or wine.
Other locations 68 Dean Street, between Smith Street & Boerum Place, Cobble Hill (1-212 675 4996).

★ Vinegar Hill House
72 Hudson Avenue, between Front & Water Streets, Dumbo (1-718 522 1018, www.vinegarhillhouse. com). Subway A, C to High Street; F to York Street. **Open** 6-11pm Mon-Thur; 6-11.30pm Fri; 10.30am-3.30pm, 6-11.30pm Sat; 10.30am-3.30pm, 5.30-11pm Sun. **Main courses** $15-$29. **Map** p207 E1 ❼ American
As it's hidden in a residential street in the forgotten namesake neighbourhood (now essentially part of Dumbo), tracking down Vinegar Hill House

Modern Anthology.

engenders a treasure-hunt thrill. In the cosy, tavern-like space, the daily-changing menu focuses on seasonal comfort foods. In the warmer months, linger over brunch in the secluded back garden.

Shops & Services

Egg
72 Jay Street, between Front & Water Streets, Dumbo (1-347 356 4097, www.egg-baby.com). Subway A, C to High Street; F to York Street. **Open** 10am-6pm Mon-Sat; 11am-5pm Sun. **Map** p207 E1 ❾ **Children**
Set in the old HQ of the Grand Union Tea Company, designer Susan Lazar's NYC store has a retro garment-factory vibe. Among her seasonally changing creations for babies and kids up to age eight, you might find striped infant bodysuits, print dresses for girls, and peacoats for both genders.
Other location 104 Franklin Street, between West Broadway & Church Street, Tribeca (1-646 780 1920).

★ Modern Anthology
68 Jay Street, between Front & Water Streets, Dumbo (1-718 522 3020, www.modernanthology. com). Subway A, C to High Street; F to York Street. **Open** 11am-7pm Mon-Sat; noon-6pm Sun. **Map** p207 E1 ❾ **Fashion/homewares**
Design gurus Becka Citron and John Marsala, who helped create the *Man Caves* TV series, are behind this one-stop lifestyle shop that brings together vintage and contemporary homewares, clothing, accessories and grooming products. Understatedly stylish dudes can update their wardrobes with shirts and sweaters from New York designers Ernest Alexander and Todd Snyder, USA-crafted jeans from Raleigh Denim and footwear by Oak Street Bootmakers, among other labels. Hip home items include the Air, Land and Sea collection of blankets

in collaboration with Faribault Woolen Mills, featuring retro images inspired by technical illustrations in classic Haynes owners' manuals. And what bachelor pad is complete without a stack of vintage issues of *Playboy* and barware?

Neiman Marcus Last Call
210 Joralemon Street, at Court Street, Downtown Brooklyn (1-929 324 3150, www.lastcall.com). Subway A, C, F, R to Jay Street-MetroTech; 2, 3 to Borough Hall. **Open** 10am-8pm Mon-Sat; 10am-8pm Sat; 11am-7pm Sun. **Map** p206 D3 ❿ **Fashion/homewares**
The first NYC location of the Neiman Marcus discount spinoff opened in winter 2014. While the swanky department store chain has yet to open its full-price Manhattan outpost (it's tipped for 2018), you can scoop up deals here on brands like Alice + Olivia, Diane von Furstenberg, Michael Kors and Vince, among others.

Powerhouse Arena
37 Main Street, between Front & Water Streets, Dumbo (1-718 666 3049, www.powerhousearena. com). Subway A, C to High Street; F to York Street. **Open** 10am-7pm Mon-Wed; 10am-8pm Thur, Fri; 11am-8pm Sat; 11am-7pm Sun (extended hours in summer). **Map** p206 D1 ⓫ **Books & music**
Also serving as a gallery and performance space, the Powerhouse Arena is the cavernous retail arm of Powerhouse Books, which produces coffee-table tomes on such diverse subjects as New York laundromats, celebrity dogs and the Brooklyn Navy Yard.
Other location Powerhouse on 8th, 1111 Eighth Avenue, between 11th & 12th Streets, South Slope (1-718 801 8375).

BOERUM HILL, CARROLL GARDENS & COBBLE HILL

Subway A, C, F to Jay Street-MetroTech; F, G to Bergen Street, Carroll Street; 2, 3, 4, 5 to Borough Hall.

These blurred-boundaried 'hoods, which go by the convenient if annoying real estate agents' contraction of BoCoCa, are a prime example of gentrification at work. Gone are the bodegas and cheap shoe shops along the stretch of Smith Street that runs from Atlantic Avenue to the Carroll Street subway stop; it's now lined with restaurants and upscale shops. The mile-long stretch of Atlantic Avenue between Henry and Nevins Streets, most of which falls under **Boerum Hill**, was once crowded with Middle Eastern restaurants and markets; one remaining stalwart is the **Sahadi Importing Company** (no.187, between Clinton & Court Streets, Cobble Hill, 1-718 624 4550, closed Sun), a neighbourhood institution that sells olives, spices, cheeses, nuts and other gourmet treats. These days, you'll find

EXPLORE

a slew of antique and modern furniture stores on the strip, including **City Foundry** (nos.365 & 367, between Bond & Hoyt Streets, Boerum Hill; 1-718 923 1786, www.cityfoundry.com), which specialises in midcentury design and industrial-style pieces. Clothing stores have also moved in, including an outpost of **Barneys New York** (no.194; *see p183*).

West of Smith Street, **Cobble Hill** has a palpable small-town feel. Here, **Court Street** is dotted with cafés and shops. Walk over the Brooklyn-Queens Expressway to the industrial waterfront and the excellent Thai spot **Pok Pok NY**.

Further south, you'll cross into the still predominantly Italian-American **Carroll Gardens**. Pick up a prosciutto loaf from **Caputo Bakery** (329 Court Street, between Sackett & Union Streets, 1-718 875 6871) or an aged *soppressata* salami from **G Esposito & Sons** (357 Court Street, between President & Union Streets, 1-718 875 6863); then relax in **Carroll Park** (from President to Carroll Streets, between Court & Smith Streets) and watch the old-timers play *bocce* (lawn bowls).

Restaurants & Cafés

★ Blue Marble Ice Cream

196 Court Street, between Bergen & Warren Streets, Cobble Hill (1-718 858 0408, www.bluemarbleicecream.com). Subway F, G to Bergen Street. **Open** varies by season; usually noon-11pm daily. **Ice-cream** $4-$8. **Map** p206 D3 ⓬ **Ice-cream**
With 19 rotating seasonal flavours, including sweet-tart strawberry, maple-toffee popcorn and sea salt caramel, Blue Marble is beloved by locals of all ages. Produced in NYC's only certified-organic ice-cream plant, it's a cut above standard scoops. The shop also sells superior La Colombe coffee.
Other location 186 Underhill Avenue, between St John's & Sterling Places, Brooklyn Heights (1-718 399 6926).

★ Chef's Table at Brooklyn Fare

200 Schermerhorn Street, at Hoyt Street, Boerum Hill (1-718 243 0050, www.brooklynfare.com/chefs-table). Subway A, C, G to Hoyt-Schermerhorn; B, N, Q, R to DeKalb Avenue; 2, 3 to Hoyt Street; 2, 3, 4, 5 to Nevins Street. **Open** *Seatings* 7pm, 7.45pm Tue, Wed; 6pm, 6.45pm, 9.30pm, 9.55pm Thur-Sat. **Prix fixe** $255. **Map** p207 E3 ⓭ **Eclectic**
Scoring a place at chef César Ramirez's 18-seat restaurant within the Brooklyn Fare supermarket takes determination: reservations are only taken on Mondays at 10.30am, six weeks before your desired date. But the luxurious set dinner of approximately 15 courses is among the best small-plate cuisine in New York, and the dinner-party vibe is convivial: diners perch on stools around a prep table. The menu changes weekly, but might include such delicacies as a Kumamoto oyster reclining on crème fraîche and yuzu gelée or halibut served in a miraculous broth of dashi and summer truffles.

Frankies 457 Spuntino

457 Court Street, between Lucquer Street & 4th Place, Carroll Gardens (1-718 403 0033, www.frankiesspuntino.com). Subway F, G to Carroll Street. **Open** 11am-11pm Mon-Thur, Sun; 11am-midnight Fri, Sat. **Main courses** $13-$19. **Map** p206 C5 ⓮ **Italian**
This casual spuntino was an instant classic when it debuted in Carroll Gardens in 2004. The mavericks behind the place – collectively referred to as 'the Franks' Castronovo and Falcinelli – went on to become neighbourhood pillars, opening German-leaning steakhouse Prime Meats down the block and a coffee shop, Café Pedlar, in Cobble Hill. But their flagship remains as alluring as ever, turning out an impressive selection of cheeses, antipasti and cured meats, distinctive salads and exceptional pastas to a mostly local crowd. Cavatelli with hot sausage and browned sage butter is a staple, as are the flawless meatballs – feather-light orbs stuffed into a sandwich or served solo.
Other location Frankies 570 Spuntino, 570 Hudson Street, at 11th Street, West Village (1-212 924 0818).

Mile End Deli

97A Hoyt Street, between Atlantic Avenue and Pacific Street, Boerum Hill (1-718 852 7510, www.mileenddeli.com). Subway A, C, G to Hoyt-Schermerhorn; 2, 3 to Hoyt Street. **Open** 5.30-10pm Mon-Fri; noon-10pm Sat, Sun. **Sandwiches** $11-$24. **Map** p207 E3 ⓯ **Deli**
New Yorkers have pastrami, Montrealers have smoked meat – luscious brisket that's been dry-rubbed, cured, smoked, steamed and hand cut, resulting in flavourful, delicious slices bound for mustard-slathered rye. This Montreal-style deli from Québécois Noah Bernamoff and his wife, Rae Cohen, serves the sandwiches in old-school fashion, along with other regional specialities – like the excellent poutine (including a smoked-meat riff), and, at brunch, a killer hash.
Other location 53 Bond Street, between Bowery & Lafayette Street, East Village (1-212 529 2990).

★ Pok Pok NY

117 Columbia Street, at Kane Street, Cobble Hill (1-718 923 9322, www.pokpokny.com). Subway F, G to Bergen Street. **Open** 5.30-10.30pm daily. **Main courses** $10-$21. **Map** p206 C3 ⓰ **Thai**
James Beard Award-winning chef Andy Ricker's Brooklyn restaurant replicates the indigenous dives of Chiang Mai with colourful oilcloths on the tables and second-hand seats in the spartan space. But what separates Pok Pok from other cultish Thai restaurants is the curatorial role of its minutiae-mad chef. Ricker highlights a host of surprisingly mild

northern dishes, including a delicious Burmese-inflected sweet-and-sour pork curry, *kaeng hung leh*. His version of *khao soi* – chicken noodle soup delicately spiced with yellow curry and topped with fried noodles for crunch – is accompanied with raw shallots and pickled mustard greens.

Bars

Clover Club

210 Smith Street, between Baltic & Butler Streets, Cobble Hill (1-718 855 7939, www.cloverdubny. com). Subway F, G to Bergen Street. **Open** 4pm-2am Mon-Thur; 4pm-4am Fri; 10.30am-4am Sat; 10.30am-1am Sun. **Map** p206 D4 ⓱

Classic cocktails are the signature tipples at Julie Reiner's Victorian-styled cocktail parlour. Sours, fizzes, mules, punches and cobblers all get their due at the 19th-century mahogany bar. Highbrow snacks (fried oysters, steak tartare) accompany drinks like the eponymous Clover Club (with gin, raspberry syrup, egg whites, dry vermouth and lemon juice).

Long Island Bar

110 Atlantic Avenue, at Henry Street, Cobble Hill (1-718 625 8908). Subway F, G to Bergen Street;

2, 3, 4, 5 to Borough Hall. **Open** 5.30pm-midnight Mon-Thur; 5.30pm-2am Fri, Sat; 11am-midnight Sun. **Map** p206 D3 ⓲

A revivalist spirit is at the core of this retro-fitted bar from cocktail vet Toby Cecchini, which was formerly a midcentury greasy spoon. The menu swaps the *tortas* that once powered neighbourhood blue-collars for Cecchini's fine-tuned list of six bedrock quaffs. Here you'll find a biting but balanced rye-and-Campari Boulevardier and a tart gimlet, given a fiery kick from ginger grated into the lime cordial. The iconic signage and old-line interior – terrazzo floors, Formica walls – have been preserved with an almost religious reverence, down to the faded cigarette burns that still cheetah-spot the gleaming art deco bar.

Whiskey Soda Lounge NY

115 Columbia Street, at Kane Street, Cobble Hill (1-718 797 4120, www.whiskeysodalounge-ny. com). Subway F, G to Bergen Street. **Open** 5.30-10.30pm Wed, Thur, Sun; 5.30pm-midnight Fri, Sat. **Map** p206 C3 ⓳

Andy Ricker's Thai canteen was conceived as a spill-over spot for Pok Pok NY hopefuls, but the boozier kid bro is a destination in its own right, offering a

EXPLORE

Long Island Bar.

highlight reel of *ahaan kap klaem* (Thai drinking food) and smartly tweaked cocktails. Not surprisingly, whiskey – commonly drunk with fizzy water in Thailand – is front and centre. There's a 30-plus roster of American slugs, as well as selections from Japan, Ireland and Canada. The low-ceilinged room is sparse – wood-panelled walls, drooping Christmas lights – but dashed with poppy touches of Bangkok-in-Brooklyn kitsch.

Shops & Services

By Brooklyn
261 Smith Street, between DeGraw & Douglass Streets, Carroll Gardens (1-718 643 0606, www. bybrooklyn.com). Subway F, G to Carroll Street. **Open** 11am-7pm Mon-Wed, Sun; 11am-8pm Thur-Sat. **Map** p206 D4 ② **Gifts & souvenirs**
Gaia DiLoreto's modern-day general store offers an array of New York-made goods, including chocolate, jams and pickles, soaps, T-shirts, jewellery, housewares, accessories and cookbooks by Brooklyn authors. Look out for Maptote borough-specific bags and Brooklyn Slate Co's burlap-wrapped reclaimed slate cheese boards.
Other location 142 Grand Street, between Bedford & Berry Streets, Williamsburg.

RED HOOK
Subway F, G to Smith-9th Streets, then B61 bus.

To the south-west of Carroll Gardens, beyond the Brooklyn-Queens Expressway, the formerly rough-and-tumble industrial locale of **Red Hook** has long avoided urban renewal. In recent years, however, the arrival of gourmet mega-grocer Fairway, Swedish furniture superstore IKEA and several new restaurants have served notice that gentrification is moving in.

Luckily for its protective residents, the Hook still feels secluded, tucked away on a peninsula. While the area continues to evolve, its time-warp charm is still evident, and its decaying piers make a moody backdrop for empty warehouses and trucks clattering over cobblestone streets. The lack of public transport has thus far prevented it from becoming overdeveloped. From the Smith-9th Streets subway stop, it's either a half-hour walk south or a transfer to the B61 bus, although the **New York Water Taxi** (*see p376*) has improved the situation with its IKEA express shuttle from downtown Manhattan.

The area offers singular views of the Statue of Liberty and New York Harbor from **Valentino Pier**, and has an eclectic selection of bars, eateries and artists' studios. To see local creative output, seek out **Kentler International Drawing Space** (353 Van Brunt Street, between Wolcott & Dikeman Streets, 1-718 875 2098, www.kentler gallery.org, closed Mon-Wed & Jan, Aug) or check

the website of **Brooklyn Waterfront Artists Coalition** (499 Van Brunt Street, at Beard Street Pier, 1-718 596 2506, www.bwac.org) for details of its large group shows at weekends in spring, summer and autumn.

Restaurants & Cafés

Brooklyn Crab
24 Reed Street, between Conover & Van Brunt Streets (1-718 643 2722, www.brooklyncrab.com). Subway F, G to Smith-9th Streets, then B61 bus. **Open** *Mid Mar-mid Oct* 11.30am-10pm Mon-Thur, Sun; 11.30am-11pm Fri, Sat. *Mid Oct-mid Mar* 11.30am-10pm Wed, Thur, Sun; 11.30am-11pm Fri, Sat. **Main courses** $13-$49. **Map** p206 A5 ④ **Seafood**
Channelling Maine's minigolf clam shacks, this hulking 250-seat spot brings games and seaside flavours to Red Hook's waterfront. Elevated on stilts, the three-storey stand-alone restaurant is done up with wharf-themed flourishes: lobster traps, fishing rods and a mounted shark's head. Gather friends for a round of minigolf, shuffleboard or cornhole (bean-bag toss) outdoors, then grab a picnic table and dig into simple coastal fare, such as peel-and-eat shrimp, and steam pots brimming with crabs and lobster. Drinkers can sip margaritas and piña coladas or split a mixed bucket of five beers on the open-air roof deck, with views of New York's Upper Bay.

Bars

★ Sunny's Bar
253 Conover Street, between Beard & Reed Streets (1-718 625 8211, www.sunnysredhook.com). Subway F, G to Smith-9th Streets, then B61 bus. **Open** 8pm-4am Wed-Fri; 4pm-4am Sat; 4pm-11pm Sun (extended hrs in summer). **No credit cards.** **Map** p206 A5 ②
Fans raised $100,000 after Superstorm Sandy to revive this waterfront bar for a reason: there's nothing else like it in town. The time-warp watering hole has been passed down in the Balzano family since 1890. A casual, hip (but not hipster) crowd tap their

toes to bluegrass jamborees every Saturday at 10pm (bring an instrument and join in!), and other nights feature everything from sultry jazz singers to accordion players. But the biggest draw is the Old World vibe, with a hodge podge of folk art (think bedpan banjos), knick-knacks from the 1940s, dim lighting and a perfect location just off New York Harbor.

Shops & Services

Erie Basin

388 Van Brunt Street, at Dikeman Street (1-718 554 6147, www.eriebasin.com). Subway F, G to Smith-9th Streets, then B61 bus. **Open** varies seasonally; usually by appointment Mon, Tue; noon-6pm Wed-Sat. **Map** p206 B5 ❷ **Accessories**
For a one-of-a-kind keepsake, check out Russell Whitmore's finely honed collection of jewellery dating from the 18th century to the 1940s. The striking stock spans everything from unusual *fin de siède* earrings, lockets and brooches to art deco cocktail rings; vintage engagement and wedding rings are a speciality. Whitmore often incorporates antique gems in his EB line of fine jewellery, which is also available in the shop, alongside a selection of furniture and decorative objects.

Steve's Authentic Key Lime Pie

185 Van Dyke Street, at Ferris Street (1-718 858 5333, www.stevesauthentic.com). Subway F, G to Smith-9th Streets, then B61 bus. **Open** varies; usually 11am-5pm Fri-Sun. **Map** p206 A5 ❷
Food & drink
An authentic Florida dessert in Brooklyn? Miami transplant and Key Lime pie purist Steve Tarpin and his crew make small-batch treats using freshly squeezed citrus at this quirky Red Hook institution. In the orange-hued bakery, you can buy the signature graham-cracker-crusted pies (in ten-inch, eight-inch or single-serving four-inch sizes), filled with a condensed-milk custard laced with zesty lime juice. Also available is the Swingle, a frozen tartlet on a stick, dipped in dark Belgian chocolate.

PARK SLOPE, GOWANUS & PROSPECT HEIGHTS

Park Slope & Gowanus – Subway F to 7th Avenue or 15th Street-Prospect Park; F, G to Fourth Avenue-9th Street; R to Union Street. Prospect Heights – Subway B, Q, Franklin Avenue S to Prospect Park; 2, 3 to Eastern Parkway-Brooklyn Museum or Grand Army Plaza; R to 25th Street.

Bustling with parents pushing baby strollers and herding lively children, **Park Slope** houses hip young families in Victorian brownstones and feeds them organically from the nation's oldest working food co-operative (only open to members). The neighbourhood's intellectual, progressive and lefty political heritage is palpable. Famous residents include novelist Paul Auster and actors Maggie Gyllenhaal, Peter Sarsgaard and Patrick Stewart.

Fifth Avenue is Park Slope's strip for restaurants, bars and shops, but recently interest has shifted west to **Gowanus**, the neighbourhood hugging the canal of the same name. It might seem baffling that anyone would want to build glitzy condos or big retail shops near a polluted waterway, but that's precisely what's happening. The canal was named a Superfund site in 2010, and the city and the Environmental Protection Agency are expected to work on clean-up for at least the next decade. That hasn't stopped businesses from moving in: all-purpose performance hub the **Bell House** (*see p285*) was among the first hotspots in the area, joined in 2014 by the eccentric **Morbid Anatomy Museum**. The arrival of upscale supermarket Whole Foods at the corner of Third Avenue and 3rd Street is a sure signal of rising property prices.

The western edge of Prospect Park is a section of the **Park Slope Historic District**. Brownstones and several fine examples of Romanesque Revival and Queen Anne residences grace these streets. Particularly charming are the brick edifices that line Carroll Street, Montgomery Place and Berkeley Place. Fans of writer-director Noah Baumbach, who grew up in these parts, may recognise the locale from 2005 hit *The Squid and the Whale*, much of which was set here.

Central Park may be bigger and far more famous, but **Prospect Park** (main entrance at Grand Army Plaza, Prospect Heights, 1-718 965 8999, www.prospectpark.org) has a more rustic quality. This masterpiece, which designers Frederick Law Olmsted and Calvert Vaux said was more in line with their vision than Central Park, is a great spot for birdwatching, especially with a little guidance from the **Prospect Park Audubon Center** at the Boathouse. You can pretend you've left the city altogether by hiking along the paths of the **Ravine District** (park entrances on Prospect Park West, at 3rd, 9th & 15th Streets), a landscape of dense woods, waterfalls and stone bridges in the park's centre.

Children enjoy riding the hand-carved horses at the antique carousel (Flatbush Avenue, at Empire Boulevard) and seeing real animals in the **Prospect Park Zoo** (park entrance on Flatbush Avenue, near Ocean Avenue, Prospect Heights, 1-718 399 7339, www.prospectpark zoo.com). For more on the park's family attractions, *see p256*. A 15-minute walk from Prospect Park is the verdant necropolis of **Green-Wood Cemetery**.

Near the main entrance to Prospect Park sits the massive Civil War memorial arch at **Grand Army Plaza** (intersection of Flatbush Avenue, Eastern Parkway & Prospect Park West) and the imposing art deco central branch of the

EXPLORE

Brooklyn Botanic Garden.

Brooklyn Public Library (10 Grand Army Plaza, Prospect Heights, 1-718 230 2100, www. bklynpubliclibrary.org). Around the corner are the tranquil **Brooklyn Botanic Garden** and the **Brooklyn Museum**.

To the north is the borough's biggest and most prominent new development, the much-delayed and rebranded 22-acre Pacific Park complex (formerly Atlantic Yards) on the edge of Downtown Brooklyn. While most of the residential buildings are still under construction, the **Barclays Center** (*see p282*), a major concert venue and the home of the (rechristened) Brooklyn Nets, opened in 2012.

Sights & Museums

Brooklyn Botanic Garden

990 Washington Avenue, at Eastern Parkway, Prospect Heights (1-718 623 7200, www.bbg.org). Subway B, Q, Franklin Avenue S to Prospect Park; 2, 3 to Eastern Parkway-Brooklyn Museum. **Open** *Mar-Oct* 8am-6pm Tue-Fri; 10am-6pm Sat, Sun. *Nov-Feb* 8am-4.30pm Tue-Fri; 10am-4.30pm Sat, Sun. **Admission** $12; $6 reductions; free under-12s. Free Tue; 10am-noon Sat. **Map** p207 H6 **㉕**
This 52-acre haven of luscious greenery was founded in 1910. In spring, when Sakura Matsuri, the annual Cherry Blossom Festival, takes place, prize buds and Japanese culture are in full bloom. Linger in serene spots like the Japanese Hill-and-Pond Garden, the first Japanese-inspired garden built in the US, and the Shakespeare Garden, brimming with plants mentioned in the Bard's works. Start your stroll at the eco-friendly visitor centre – it has a green roof filled with 45,000 plants.

★ Brooklyn Museum

200 Eastern Parkway, at Washington Avenue, Prospect Heights (1-718 638 5000, www.brooklyn museum.org). Subway 2, 3 to Eastern Parkway-Brooklyn Museum. **Open** 11am-6pm Wed, Fri-Sun; 11am-10pm Thur. Open 11am-11pm 1st Sat of mth (except Sept). **Admission** *Suggested donation* $16; $10 reductions; free under-20s. Free 5-11pm 1st Sat of mth (except Sept). **Map** p207 H6 **㉖**
Among the many assets of Brooklyn's premier institution are the third-floor Egyptian galleries; highlights include the Mummy Chamber, an installation of 170 objects, including human and animal mummies. Also on this level, works by Cézanne, Monet and Degas, part of an impressive European art collection, are displayed in the museum's skylighted Beaux-Arts Court. The Elizabeth A Sackler Center for Feminist Art on the fourth floor is dominated by Judy Chicago's monumental mixed-media installation, *The Dinner Party*. The fifth floor is mainly devoted to American works, including Albert Bierstadt's immense *A Storm in the Rocky Mountains, Mt Rosalie*, and the Visible Storage-Study Center, where paintings, furniture and other objects are intriguingly juxtaposed. It's always worth checking the varied schedule of temporary shows, and the institution is also home to Michelin-starred restaurant Saul.

★ FREE Green-Wood Cemetery

Fifth Avenue, at 25th Street, Sunset Park (1-718 210 3080, www.green-wood.com). Subway R to 25th Street. **Open** varies by season; usually 8am-6pm daily. **Admission** free. **Map** p404 S13
Filled with Victorian mausoleums, cherubs and gargoyles, hills and ponds, this lush 478-acre landscape is the resting place of some half-million New Yorkers, among them Jean-Michel Basquiat, Leonard Bernstein, Boss Tweed and Horace Greeley.

Morbid Anatomy Museum

424A Third Avenue, at 7th Street, Gowanus (1-347 799 1017, www.morbidanatomymuseum. org). Subway F, G, R to Fourth Avenue-9th Street. **Open** noon-6pm Mon, Wed-Sun. **Admission** $8; $6 reductions; free under-12s. **Map** p206 D6 **㉗**
Graphic designer Joanna Ebenstein opened her Morbid Anatomy Library – a mishmash of taxidermied animals, medical artifacts, creepy gewgaws and tomes on everything from sideshow freaks to medical

art – in 2008. Thanks to support from the Brooklyn Arts Council, it has expanded into a three-storey museum and hub for those who, like Ebenstein, are interested in the 'intersection of death and beauty'. On the second level, changing exhibitions explore such offbeat subjects as eccentric private collections (antique dental models, 19th-century erotic paintings and a two-headed kitten, for example), and the dark stage arts of early 20th-century magician Howard Thurston. On the ground floor, the museum shop sells macabre souvenirs such as antique mourning jewellery made from real hair, an artist-made wax moulage depicting a syphilitic mouth and taxidermied critters in whimsical anthropomorphic poses. Lectures, workshops – including highly popular taxidermy classes – and other events are held in the 'cellar'.

Restaurants & Cafés

Al di là

248 Fifth Avenue, at Carroll Street, Park Slope (1-718 783 4565, www.aldilatrattoria.com). Subway R to Union Street. **Open** noon-3pm, 6-10.30pm Mon-Thur; noon-3pm, 6-11pm Fri; 11am-3.30pm, 5.30-11pm Sat; 11am-3.30pm, 5-10pm Sun. **Main courses** $10-$27. **Map** p207 E5 ㉘ **Italian**

A fixture on the Slope's Fifth Avenue for more than a decade, this convivial, no-reservations restaurant is still wildly popular. Affable owner Emiliano Coppa orchestrates the inevitable wait with panache. Coppa's wife, co-owner and chef, Anna Klinger, produces northern Italian dishes with a Venetian slant. It would be hard to better her braised rabbit with black olives atop polenta, and even simple pastas, such as house-made tagliatelle *al ragù*, are superb. The full menu is also served in the restaurant's bar, which has a separate entrance around the corner on Carroll Street.

IN THE KNOW ARTY PARTY

On the first Saturday of each month, the **Brooklyn Museum** stays open until 11pm and puts on music and dance performances, talks, workshops, films and more. Admission is waived from 5pm until closing, but it's a good idea to get there early since events are free but ticketed on a first-come, first-served basis.

★ Four & Twenty Blackbirds

439 Third Avenue, at 8th Street, Gowanus (1-718 499 2917, www.birdsblack.com). Subway F, G, R to Fourth Ave-9th Street. **Open** 8am-8pm Mon-Fri; 9am-8pm Sat; 10am-7pm Sun. **Pie** $5.25/ slice. **Map** p206 D6 ㉙ **Café**

Emily and Melissa Elsen, the South Dakota-reared sisters who opened cult bakery Four & Twenty Blackbirds, learned pie-baking from their grandma, and her expert instruction is evident in varieties like lemon chess, salted caramel apple and the rich chocolate-and-custard Black Bottom Oat. Settle in at one of this homey space's communal tables and savour a slice.

Other location Brooklyn Public Library, 10 Grand Army Plaza, Prospect Heights (1-718 230 2210).

The Pines

284 Third Avenue, between Carroll & President Streets, Gowanus (1-718 596 6560, www.the pinesbrooklyn.com). Subway R to Union Street. **Open** 6-10pm Mon, Sun; 6-11pm Tue-Sat. **Main courses** $20-$36. **Map** p207 E5 ㉚ **American**

EXPLORE

Morbid Anatomy Museum.

With folding chairs and peeling tin walls, the Pines may seem an unlikely setting for ambitious fare from John Poiarkoff (previously at MoMA's fine-dining spot, the Modern). A meal might begin with torn hunks of craggy semolina bread, plated among rosettes of locally cured beef bresaola and a purée of fermented tangerine. Rich, gamey lamb neck is paired with butter-drenched kasha, fava beans and a sauce made with mentholy hyssop – a crafty surrogate for traditional mint jelly. The seasonal trellised backyard (open May-Oct) has it own dedicated menu of fire-licked dishes prepared on an open wood grill.

Bars

Union Hall
702 Union Street, between Fifth & Sixth Avenues, Park Slope (1-718 638 4400, www.unionhallny. com). Subway R to Union Street. **Open** 4pm-4am Mon-Fri; 1pm-4am Sat, Sun. **Map** p207 F5 ㉛
Upstairs at Union Hall, couples chomp on mini burgers and sip microbrews in the gentlemen's club anteroom (decorated with Soviet-era globes, paintings of fez-capped men, fireplaces) – before battling it out on the clay bocce courts. Downstairs, in the taxidermy-filled basement, the stage hosts bands, comedians and offbeat events.

Shops & Services

Brooklyn Superhero Supply Company
372 Fifth Avenue, between 5th & 6th Streets, (1-718 499 9884, www.superherosupplies.com). Subway F, G, R to Fourth Ave-9th Street. **Open** varies; usually 11am-5pm daily (call before visiting). **Map** p206 E6 ㉜ **Gifts & souvenirs**
To unleash your inner superhero, stop by this purveyor of capes, X-ray goggles, truth serum and gallon tins of Immortality. Just be sure you adhere to the Vow of Heroism you must recite before your purchases are handed over. Proceeds benefit the 826NYC kids' writing centre behind a concealed door in the back of the store, so you can feel super about that, too.

FORT GREENE

Subway B, Q, R to DeKalb Avenue; B, D, N, Q, R, 2, 3, 4, 5 to Atlantic Avenue-Barclays Center; C to Lafayette Avenue; G to Fulton Street or Clinton-Washington Avenues.

With its stately Victorian brownstones and other grand buildings, Fort Greene has undergone a major revival over the past two decades. It has long been a centre of African-American life and business – Spike Lee, Branford Marsalis and Chris Rock have all lived here. **Fort Greene Park** (from Myrtle to DeKalb Avenues, between St Edwards Street & Washington Park) was conceived in 1846 at the behest of poet Walt

Whitman (then editor of the *Brooklyn Daily Eagle*); its masterplan was fully realised by Olmsted and Vaux in 1867. At the centre of the park stands the Prison Ship Martyrs Monument, erected in 1909 (from a design by Stanford White) in memory of 11,000 American prisoners who died on squalid British ships that were anchored nearby during the Revolutionary War.

Despite its name, the 34-floor **Williamsburgh Savings Bank**, at the corner of Atlantic and Flatbush Avenues, is in Fort Greene, not Williamsburg. The 512-foot-high structure was long the tallest in Brooklyn and, with its four-sided clocktower, one of the most recognisable features of its skyline. The 1927 building has been renamed One Hanson Place, and converted into (what else?) luxury condominiums.

Every Saturday from April to November, New Yorkers from across the five boroughs hit the **Brooklyn Flea** (*see p35* **Flea Season**) in the yard of a public high school on Lafayette Avenue between Clermont & Vanderbilt Avenues. The combination of antiques, vintage clothes, indie crafts and food has proved so popular it's sparked several spin-offs and other markets across the city.

Though originally founded in Brooklyn Heights, the **Brooklyn Academy of Music** (*see p305*) moved to its current site on Fort Greene's southern border in 1901. America's oldest operating performing arts centre, BAM was the home of the Metropolitan Opera until 1921; today, it's at the centre of a growing cultural district that also includes the **Polonsky Shakespeare Center** (*see p319*). Almost as famous is the cheesecake at nearby **Junior's Restaurant** (386 Flatbush Avenue, at DeKalb Avenue, 1-718 852 5257).

In addition to some funky shops, a slew of restaurants can be found on or near **DeKalb Avenue**, including South African institution **Madiba Restaurant**.

Sights & Museums

FREE BLDG 92
63 Flushing Avenue, at Carlton Avenue (1-718 907 5992, www.bldg92.org). Subway A, C to High Street; F to York Street; G to Clinton-Washington Avenues. **Open** noon-6pm Wed-Sun. **Admission** free. **Map** p207 F2 ㉝
The public gateway to the Brooklyn Navy Yard, this small museum chronicles the mighty history of the former shipbuilding centre – which, at its peak during World War II, employed more than 70,000 people. Exhibits examine the yard's origins and significance throughout history, but the institution also illuminates its new role as a modern manufacturing hub with businesses that include an urban farm, furniture makers and a distillery. The premises also has a café (reopening early 2016) and rotating exhibitions, and offers weekend bus, bike and factory tours.

Restaurants & Cafés

Madiba Restaurant

*195 DeKalb Avenue, between Carlton Avenue &
Adelphi Street (1-718 855 9190, www.madiba
restaurant.com). Subway C to Lafayette Avenue;
C, G to Clinton-Washington Avenues.* **Open**
11am-11pm Mon-Thur, Sun; 11am-midnight Fri,
Sat. **Main courses** $13-$25. **Map** p207 G3 ❸
South African

Brooklyn's first South African eaterie honours the
spirit of the late Nelson Mandela – Madiba is his clan
name. Wooden chairs and folk art grace the convivial, high-ceilinged space, and live music ranges from
Afrobeat to Afropop. The menu features fragrant
curries and stews, as well as offbeat eats like thin,
pleasantly gamey ostrich carpaccio. The safari platter, loaded with cured, salted and dried beef tenderloin, is a presidential feast.

Other location 46 W 116th Street, between Fifth
Avenue & Malcolm X Boulevard (Lenox Avenue)
(1-646 738 3043, www.madibaharlem.com)

No. 7

*7 Greene Avenue, between Cumberland & Fulton
Streets (1-718 522 6370, www.no7restaurant.com).
Subway C to Lafayette Avenue; C, G to Clinton-
Washington Avenues.* **Open** 5-11pm Tue-Fri;
noon-3pm, 5-11pm Sat; noon-3pm, 4-9pm Sun.
Main courses $19-$24. **Map** p207 G4 ❸ **Eclectic**
Given the constraints of No. 7's tiny kitchen, chef
Tyler Kord's eclectic cuisine – influenced by Asian
and eastern European flavours, among others – is
impressively bold. The menu changes frequently
but might include such cross-cultural hybrids as
crisp broccoli tempura with black-bean purée, or
fish tacos with pickled strawberries, hot mayonnaise
and cheddar.

WILLIAMSBURG, GREENPOINT & BUSHWICK

*Williamsburg – Subway G to Metropolitan
Avenue; J, M, Z to Marcy Avenue; L to Bedford
Avenue or Lorimer Street. Greenpoint – Subway
G to Greenpoint Avenue or Nassau Avenue.
Bushwick – Subway L to Jefferson Street or
Morgan Avenue.*

With a thriving music scene and an abundance of
laid-back bars, small galleries and independent
shops, **Williamsburg** – or 'Billyburg' as it's
affectionately known – channels the East Village
(just one stop away on the L train) in its heyday.
But the area teeters on the brink of (or, some
argue, has already fallen into) hipster cliché.

Long before the trendsetters invaded,
Williamsburg's waterfront location had made
it ideal for industry. When the Erie Canal linked
the Atlantic Ocean to the Great Lakes in 1825, the
area became a bustling port. Companies such as
Pfizer and Domino Sugar started here, but
businesses had begun to abandon the area's
huge industrial spaces by the late 20th century.
The Domino refinery closed in 2004, and is
currently being developed into apartments.

Bedford Avenue is the neighbourhood's
main thoroughfare. By day, the epicentre of
the strip is the **Bedford MiniMall** (no.218,
between North 4th & North 5th Streets) – you
won't find a Gap or Starbucks here, but you can
browse an exceptionally edited selection of titles
at **Spoonbill & Sugartown, Booksellers**
(1-718 387-7322, www.spoonbillbooks.com)
and snack on old-fashioned snocones or candy
from **Handsome Dan's** (1-347 889 6683,
www.handsomedansstand.com). The area has
a constantly shifting array of cafés and eateries;
south of the Williamsburg Bridge on Broadway,
Marlow & Sons was a pioneer in the kind of
rustic aesthetic and farm-to-table fare that's
become the norm in Kings County. Nearby, New
York institution **Peter Luger** grills what most
carnivores consider to be the best steak in the city.

You'll find chic shops dotted around the area,
and the 'hood has more than 25 art galleries,
which stay open late on the second Friday of
every month. Pick up the free gallery guide
Wagmag at local shops and cafés or visit
www.wagmag.org for listings. However,
Billyburg is better known for its music scene.
Local rock bands and touring indie darlings
play at **Music Hall of Williamsburg**,
Pete's Candy Store and **Knitting Factory
Brooklyn** (for all, *see p288*).

Those with a nostalgic bent will enjoy quirky
repository of NYC ephemera **City Reliquary**.
Another local gem is the **Brooklyn Brewery**
(79 North 11th Street, between Berry Street &
Wythe Avenue, 1-718 486 7422, www.brooklyn
brewery.com), housed in a former ironworks.
The tasting room is open from Friday to Sunday,
but visit during the happy 'hour' (6-11pm Fri)
for $5 drafts. You can take a tour on Saturdays
(hourly 1-5pm).

With Williamsburg approaching hipster
saturation point and rents rising accordingly,
many of its young, creative residents seek
cheaper digs nearby – which usually starts the
gentrification cycle over again. **Greenpoint**,
Williamsburg's northern neighbour, has been
quietly undergoing a transformation of its own
in the past decade. The former Polish stronghold's
cachet recently rose even further as the setting
of HBO's *Girls*. WNYC Transmitter Park – a 1.6-
acre waterfront green space between Greenpoint
Avenue and Kent Street that was once the site of
the local public radio station's AM transmitter
towers – offers a stellar view of the Manhattan
skyline. Young, wealthy residents are moving into
the neighbourhood in droves, leading to inevitable
tensions between old and new denizens.

EXPLORE

Brooklyn

Bushwick has also attracted a creative demographic to its industrial spaces. In late spring, the annual **Bushwick Open Studios** (www.artsinbushwick.org) gives you a glimpse inside hundreds of artists' work spaces, but you'll also see plenty of street art in the vicinity of the Morgan Avenue subway stop. Bounded by Bushwick Avenue to the north-west and Broadway to the south-west, this traditionally Latino neighbourhood has begun to sprout coffee shops, bars and vintage stores over the past several years, not to mention restaurants, such as acclaimed locavore eaterie **Roberta's**.

Sights & Museums

City Reliquary
370 Metropolitan Avenue, at Havemeyer Street, Williamsburg (1-718 782 4842, www.cityreliquary. org). Subway G to Metropolitan Avenue; L to Lorimer Street. **Open** noon-6pm Thur-Sun. **Admission** $5; $4 reductions; free-under-12s. **Map** p219 B3 ⊕
This not-for-profit mini-museum of New York history is crammed with fascinating Gotham ephemera. The collection includes memorabilia from both NYC World's Fairs, a shrine to the Brooklyn Dodgers' Jackie Robinson, hundreds of Lady Liberty figurines and such anachronisms as subway tokens and seltzer bottles. Other idiosyncratic relics include a vintage barber-shop diorama furnished with a chair from Barber Hall of Famer Antonio Nobile's Bay Ridge, Brooklyn, shop, and a transplanted Chinatown newsstand.

Restaurants & Cafés

Allswell
124 Bedford Avenue, at North 10th Street, Williamsburg (1-347 799 2743, www.allswell nyc.com). Subway L to Bedford Avenue. **Open** 10am-2am Mon-Thur; 10am-4am Fri; 9am-4am Sat; 9am-2am Sun. **Main courses** $14-$36. **Map** p219 B3 ⊕ **American**
Chef-owner Nate Smith, who earned his gastropub stripes at the Spotted Pig, broke out on his own with this laid-back Williamsburg tavern. The 47-seat space is done up with a reclaimed pine bar, vintage wallpaper in different patterns and brass-hunting-horn chandeliers with matching sconces. The fequently changing menu includes chefly bar grub (like oysters or meat pies) and heartier dishes (such as roasted lamb or sirloin flap steak with seasonal vegetables). The drinks list takes a locavore slant with small-production wines and craft beers on tap, plus a selection of market-driven cocktails.

BrisketTown
359 Bedford Avenue, between South 4th & 5th Streets, Williamsburg (1-718 701 8909, http:// delaneybbq.com). Subway L to Bedford Avenue.
Open 5-11pm Wed-Fri; noon-11pm Sat, Sun (extended hrs in summer; call or see website). **Main courses** $7-$20. **Map** p219 A3 ⊕ **American barbecue**
New Jersey-born Daniel Delaney – a former journalist – might not seem like an obvious poster child for purist Texan 'cue. But the Yankee is turning out some seriously crave-worthy meat. Delaney takes the traditionalist route, coating chunks of heritage beef in salt and pepper before smoking them over oak-fuelled fire for 16 hours. That deep-pink brisket, along with remarkably tender pork ribs, draws Williamsburg's jeans-and-plaid set, who tuck in while indie tunes jangle over the speakers.

Glasserie
95 Commercial Street, between Box Street & Manhattan Avenue, Greenpoint (1-718 389 0640, www.glasserienyc.com). Subway G to Greenpoint Avenue. **Open** 5.30-11pm Mon-Thur; 5.30pm-midnight Fri; 10am-5pm, 5.30pm-midnight Sat; 10am-5pm, 5.30-11pm Sun. **Shared plates** $18-$24. **Map** p219 B1 ⊕ **Eclectic**
In an old industrial glass factory, chef Eldad Shem Tov (Alain Ducasse, Per Se, wd~50) brings a touch of the breezy Mediterranean coast to the gritty Greenpoint waterfront. The menu, a mix of small and large plates, spans Spain, Greece and the Middle East, in dishes such as squash katif pastry, served with fresh ricotta and okra, or grilled squid in an heirloom tomato stew. At brunch, the best way to sample everything is by ordering the meze feast of ten small dishes. The whitewashed brick walls of the rustic interior are hung with framed catalogue prints from the erstwhile factory and the loading dock has been transformed into a small terrace.

Marlow & Sons
81 Broadway, between Berry Street & Wythe Avenue, Williamsburg (1-718 384 1441, www.marlowandsons.com). Subway J, M, Z to Marcy Avenue. **Open** 8am-midnight daily. **Main courses** $20-$30. **Map** p219 A4 ⊕ **American creative**
In this charming oyster bar, restaurant and café, diners wolf down meze, market-fresh salads and succulent brick chicken. In the back, a shucker cracks open the catch of the day, while the bartender mixes the kind of potent drinks that helped to make the owners' earlier ventures (including the next-door Diner, a tricked-out 1920s dining car) successes.

Mast Brothers Chocolate Brew Bar
105A North 3rd Street, between Berry Street & Wythe Avenue (1-718 388 2625, www.mast brothers.com). Subway L to Bedford Avenue. **Open** 10am-7pm Mon-Sat; 10am-5pm Sun. **Chocolate drinks** $4-$5. **Map** p219 A3 ⊕ **Café**
Revisiting chocolate's history as a bitter sipper, Michael and Rick Mast are brewing cocoa beans into

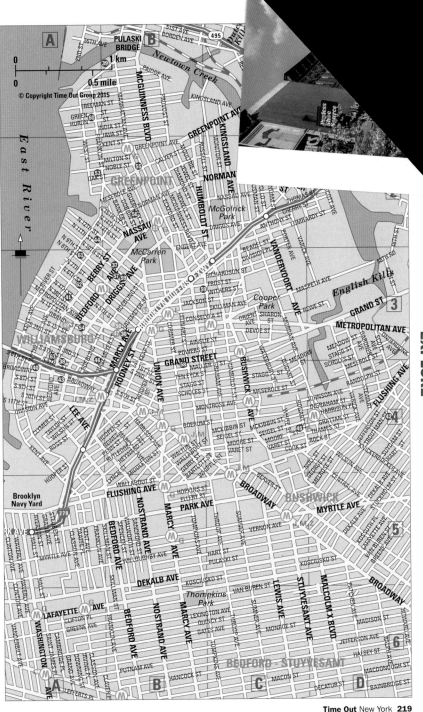

Bushwick. *See p218.*

beverages in the small, subway-tiled space where they first started their company in 2007 (the factory and shop are now at no.111). Inside a renovated 1800s spice factory, baristas scoop and grind globally sourced, house-roasted beans for hot pour-overs and cold brews, including six single origin hot chocolates (Peru, Brazil, Madagascar) to be taken 'red' – as opposed to coffee's 'black' – or slightly sweetened with milk and sugar.

Northeast Kingdom

18 Wyckoff Avenue, at Troutman Street, Bushwick (1-718 386 3864, www.north-eastkingdom.com). Subway L to Jefferson Street. **Open** 11.30am-2.30pm, 6-11pm Mon-Wed; 11.30am-2.30pm, 6-11.30pm Thur; 11.30am-2.30pm, 6pm-midnight Fri; 11am-3pm, 6pm-midnight Sat; 11am-3pm, 6-11pm Sun. **Main courses** $15-$30. **Map** p219 D4 ❷ **American**

The mood inside this 28-seat eatery is half cabin in the woods (wide-plank wood floors, clunky butcher-block tables) and half Grandma's living room (quaint sconces). In keeping with the country vibe, the kitchen uses meat and produce from local farms and foraged ingredients. The seasonal menu features such elevated fare as Hudson Valley foie gras and Rhode Island scallops alongside classics like an excellent burger.

★ Peter Luger

178 Broadway, at Driggs Avenue, Williamsburg (1-718 387 7400, www.peterluger.com). Subway J, M, Z to Marcy Avenue. **Open** 11.45am-9.45pm Mon-Thur; 11.45am-10.45pm Fri, Sat; 12.45-9.45pm Sun. **Steaks** $49-$199. **No credit cards.** **Map** p219 A4 ❸ **Steakhouse**

At Luger's old-school steakhouse, the menu is limited, but the porterhouse is justly famed. Choose from various sizes, from a small single steak to 'steak for four'. Although a slew of Luger copycats have prospered over the years, none has captured the elusive charm of this stucco-walled, beer hall-style eaterie, with worn wooden floors and tables, and waiters in waistcoats and bow ties.

Reynard

Wythe Hotel, 80 Wythe Avenue, at North 11th Street, Williamsburg (1-718 460 8004, www.wythehotel.com). Subway L to Bedford Avenue. **Open** 7am-4pm, 5.30pm-midnight daily. **Main courses** $20-$30. **Map** p219 A2 ❹ **American creative**

The Wythe's sprawling restaurant is a Balthazar for Brooklyn, urbane and ambitious, mature and low-key. Its chef, Sean Rembold, serves casual breakfast and lunch to a drop-in crowd, including a terrifically earthy grass-fed burger. His menu, which changes often – sometimes daily – becomes much more serious at night. There's no fanfare at any time to his spare list of dishes, no trendy buzzwords, barely any descriptions at all. Rembold's thoughtful food, portioned to satisfy and priced to move, mostly speaks for itself.

★ Roberta's

261 Moore Street, between Bogart & White Streets, Bushwick (1-718 417 1118, www.robertaspizza.com). Subway L to Morgan Avenue. **Open** 11am-midnight Mon-Fri; 10am-midnight Sat, Sun. **Pizzas** $9-$16. **Map** p219 C4 ❺ **Italian**

This sprawling hangout has become the unofficial meeting place for Brooklyn's sustainable-food movement. Opened in 2008 by a trio of friends, Roberta's has its own on-site garden that provides some of the ingredients for its locally sourced dishes. The pizzas – like the Cheesus Christ, topped with mozzarella, taleggio, parmesan, black pepper and cream – are among Brooklyn's finest. Blanca, a sleek spot in the back, showcases chef Carlo Mirarchi's acclaimed evening-only tasting menu (6-9pm Wed-Fri; 5-8pm Sat; $195).

★ Semilla

160 Havemeyer Street, between South 2nd & 3rd Streets, Williamsburg (1-718 782 3474, www.semillabk.com). Subway J, Z, M to Marcy Avenue. **Open** 6-11pm Tue-Sat. **Prix fixe** $75. **Map** p219 A3 ❻ **American creative**

Unlike more navel-gazing chefs, José Ramírez-Ruiz and Pamela Yung don't let dishes marinate on their menu long enough to become signatures. Instead, the partners, in both life and the kitchen, offer a vegetable-forward, eight-to-ten-course meal that changes weekly, sometimes daily. Their cooking is as high-flying as it is rootsy, offset by genuinely warm service. The chefs personally deliver dishes to diners at the stark, 18-seat ashwood counter in the intimate space. Standouts on a recent visit included ribbons of potent grilled celeriac nestled on a swathe of rich, creamy cheddar cheese, then given a tableside slickening of warm, malty celery soup, stirred with Evil Twin Brewing's cardamom-coffee Turkish Delight ale and speckled with crunchy nibs of puffed quinoa. But the dish of the night plaudit has to go to Yung's spectacular porridge sourdough, supremely moist and nutty and served with Cowbella butter and tangy buttermilk.

Bars

Boobie Trap

308 Bleecker Street, between Irving & Wyckoff Avenues, Bushwick (1-347 240 9105, www. boobietrapbrooklyn.com). Subway L, M to Myrtle-Wyckoff Avenues. **Open** noon-4am Mon-Sat; noon-midnight Sun.

Lady lumps abound at this brazen, retro-kitted dive, done up with hot-pink lights and heaps of B-movie camp. The bathroom ceiling is tiled with rubber knockers lit by a chandelier of Barbies, the gold zebra-printed walls are nailed with '90s troll dolls and plastic dinosaurs, and a neon sign boldly proclaims 'fuck off' from behind the bar. But hidden beneath the kitsch is a surprisingly respectable neighbourhood hangout. While you'll find big-name domestic cans like Bud and Blue Moon at the bar, two draft lines sprouting from a naked mannequin pour one light (Pacífico) and one dark (Negra Modelo) brew. Smoked meats, including tender, braised chicken with a mesquite bite, and sides like Cajun macaroni and cheese, are doled out in carboard boats on plastic cafeteria trays.

Commodore

366 Metropolitan Avenue, at Havemeyer Street, Williamsburg (1-718 218 7632). Subway J, M, Z to Marcy Avenue; L to Bedford Avenue. **Open** 4pm-4am Mon-Fri; 11am-4am Sat, Sun. **Map** p219 B3 ⓐ

With its old arcade games, cheap Schaefer in a can and stereo pumping out the *Knight Rider* theme song, this Williamsburg gastrodive offers some of the city's best cheap-ass bar eats. The 'hot fish' sandwich, for one, is a fresh, flaky, cayenne-rubbed catfish fillet poking out of both sides of a butter-griddled sesame-seed roll. You'll be thankful it's available after a few rounds of the Commodore's house drink – a slushy, frozen piña colada.

Dirck the Norseman

7 North 15th Street, at Franklin Street, Greenpoint (1-718 389 2940, www.dirckthenorseman.com). Subway G to Nassau Avenue. **Open** 5pm-2am Mon-Fri; noon-2am Sat, Sun. **Map** p219 B2 ⓐ

You can't throw a bottle cap without hitting a beer bar in Brooklyn, but this Greenpoint suds depot from brew guru Ed Raven – the man behind bottle emporium Brouwerij Lane and beer importer Ravenbrands – one-ups the competition by crafting its beers on-site. Inspired by the Scandinavian shipbuilder who first settled the neighbourhood in 1645, the mighty Germanic hall boasts a solid, selective line-up of Deutsch-proud beers (Jever, Gaffel), but the must-order is one of the nine proprietary blends cooked up by brewmaster Chris Prout under the imprint Greenpoint Beer & Ale Co. *Photo p222.*

Boobie Trap.

Dirck the Norseman. *See p221.*

Maison Premiere

298 Bedford Avenue, between Grand & South 1st Streets, Williamsburg (1-347 335 0446, www.maisonpremiere.com). Subway L to Bedford Avenue. **Open** *4pm-2am Mon-Wed; 4pm-4am Thur, Fri; 11am-4am Sat; 11am-2am Sun.* **Map** p219 A3 ④⑨
Most of NYC's New Orleans-inspired watering holes choose debauched Bourbon Street as their muse, but this gorgeous salon embraces the romance found in the Crescent City's historic haunts. Belly up to the oval, marble-topped bar and get familiar with the twin pleasures of oysters and absinthe: two French Quarter staples with plenty of appeal in Brooklyn. The mythical anise-flavoured liqueur appears in 27 international varieties, in addition to a trim list of cerebral cocktails.

Spuyten Duyvil

359 Metropolitan Avenue, at Havermeyer Street, Williamsburg (1-718 963 4140, www.spuyten duyvilnyc.com). Subway L to Bedford Avenue; G to Metropolitan Avenue. **Open** *5pm-2am Mon-Thur; 5pm-4am Fri; noon-4am Sat; noon-2am Sun.* **Map** p219 B3 ⑤⓪
Don't arrive thirsty. It takes at least ten minutes to choose from roughly 150 quaffs, a list that impresses even microbrew mavens. Most selections are middle-European regionals, and bartenders are eager to explain the differences among them. The cosy interior is chock-full of flea market finds, most of which are for sale. There's also a tasty bar menu of smoked meats, pâtés, cheeses and terrines.

Tørst

615 Manhattan Avenue, between Driggs & Nassau Avenues, Greenpoint (1-718 389 6034). Subway G to Nassau Avenue. **Open** *noon-midnight Mon-Wed, Sun; noon-2am Thur; noon-3am Fri-Sat.* **Map** p219 B2 ⑤①
Danish for 'thirst', Tørst is helmed by legendary 'gypsy brewer' Jeppe Jarnit-Bjergsø and chef Daniel Burns, formerly of Noma in Copenhagen. These warriors are laying waste to tired ideas of what a great taproom should be, with a minimalist space that looks like a modernist log cabin, and rare brews from throughout Europe and North America. The ever-changing, 21-tap draft menu can move faster than a Swedish vallhund, but usually includes selections from Jarnit-Bjergsø's own Evil Twin Brewing. More than 100 bottled beers are also available. Tørst has more in common with a high-end wine bar than with your average local watering hole – well-heeled locals and pilgrimaging brew buffs quietly sip from designer wineglasses at the sleek white marble counter. Luksus, the restaurant hidden away in the back room, offers a tasting menu for $95 from 6.30pm to midnight Tuesday through Saturday.

Union Pool

484 Union Avenue, at Meeker Avenue, Williamsburg (1-718 609 0484, www.union-pool.com). Subway L to Lorimer Street; G to Metropolitan Avenue. **Open** *5pm-4am Mon-Fri; 1pm-4am Sat, Sun.* **Map** p219 B3 ⑤②
This former pool-supply outlet now supplies booze to scruffy Williamsburgers, who pack the tin-walled main room's half-moon booths and snap saucy photo-kiosk pics. Bands strum away on the adjacent stage, while the spacious courtyard and outdoor bar is popular during the warmer months.
▶ *For more on the entertainment at Union Pool, see p290.*

Shops & Services

Academy Record Annex

85 Oak Street, between Franklin & West Streets, Greenpoint (1-718 218 8200, www.academyannex. tumblr.com). Subway G to Greenpoint Avenue. **Open** *noon-8pm daily.* **Map** p219 A2 ⑤③ **Books & music**
See p223 **On the Record.**

Bird

203 Grand Street, between Bedford & Driggs Avenues, Williamsburg (1-718 388 1655, www.shopbird.com). Subway L to Bedford Avenue. **Open** *11am-8pm Mon, Fri; noon-8pm Tue-Thur; 11am-7pm Sat, Sun.* **Map** p219 A3 ⑤④ **Fashion**
A former assistant buyer at Barneys, Jen Mankins opened her first Bird boutique in Park Slope in 1999. Now fashion-forward Brooklyn (and Manhattan) residents flock to three locations for up-and-coming local and international designers. The spacious LEED-certified green Williamsburg store stocks clothing and accessories for men and women. Rubbing shoulders on the racks are eclectic pieces by well-known and not-so-familiar

names such as Acne, Isabel Marant, A Détacher, Tsumori Chisato and Black Crane.
Other locations 220 Smith Street, at Butler Street, Cobble Hill (1-718 797 3774); 316 Fifth Avenue, between 2nd & 3rd Streets, Park Slope (1-718 768 4940).

Captured Tracks
195 Calyer Street, between Manhattan Avenue & Leonard Street, Greenpoint (1-718 609 0871, www.capturedtracks.com). Subway G to Greenpoint Avenue or Nassau Avenue. **Open** *noon-8pm daily.* **Map** p219 B2 ⑮ **Books & music**
See below **On the Record**.

Co-Op 87 Records
87 Guernsey Street, between Nassau & Norman Avenues, Greenpoint (1-347 294 4629, www. coop87records.tumblr.com). Subway G to Nassau Avenue. **Open** 11am-9pm daily. **Map** p219 B2 ⑯ **Books & music**
See below **On the Record**.

Earwax
167 North 9th Street, between Bedford & Driggs Avenues, Williamsburg (1-718 486 3771, www.earwax records.net). Subway L to Bedford Avenue. **Open** 11am-9pm daily. **Map** p219 B3 ⑰ **Books & music**
See below **On the Record**.

ON THE RECORD
Embark on a crate-digging crawl of Williamsburg and Greenpoint.

Record stores have been springing up in already crate-digger-friendly North Brooklyn, making it a prime place for casual music lovers and serious vinyl collectors to spend an afternoon. In late 2013, revered UK indie retailer **Rough Trade** (see *p224*) opened its first Stateside outpost in a 15,000-square-foot Williamsburg warehouse, complete with in-house café. In addition to tens of thousands of all-new titles – roughly half of them vinyl and half CDs – the megastore sells music books, magazines and equipment, curates rotating art installations, and hosts gigs both ticketed and free from the likes of Television, Sky Ferreira and Beach Fossils (for schedule and tickets, see www.roughtradenyc.com).

Rough Trade joined old timers like **Earwax** (see *above*), which opened in 1991 (elsewhere in the 'hood). The selection spans genres and decades, from buzzy indie pop to funk, psychedelic and world music, and the insanely knowledgeable staff can be counted on to provide some tuneful inspiration.

Just a few blocks north, Greenpoint is drawing record stores with cheaper rents than its gentrified neighbour. A recent addition to the growing LP nexus is the **Academy Record Annex** (see *p222*), which moved from its long-time home in Williamsburg to its current sunny digs by the Greenpoint waterfront. Expect serious buyers, reasonable prices and a massive collection of punk, rock 'n' roll, jazz, soul and experimental records. Another local standby is the welcoming **Permanent Records** (see *p224*), with amiable folks behind the counter, a listening station and thousands of hand-picked, mostly second-hand records and CDs, some of which go for as little as a dollar.

Rough Trade.

Nearby is **Co-Op 87 Records** (see *above*), launched by the folks behind the valuable Kemado and Mexican Summer labels, whose offices are housed upstairs. The diminutive shop packs a punch with meticulously curated collector pieces, bootlegs and other rarities, from avant-garde electronica to classic rock. Trendsetting label **Captured Tracks** (see *above*) also has its eponymous flagship in Greenpoint; in addition to stocking an ever-changing trove of vinyl, there are lots of cassettes, art books, vintage recording equipment and curation booths from local musicians. Don't be surprised to find yourself browsing alongside artists from the top-shelf Captured Tracks roster, such as DIIV's Zachary Cole Smith and Canadian troubadour Mac DeMarco.

EXPLORE

Grand Street Bakery

602 Grand Street, between Leonard & Lorimer Streets, Williamsburg (1-718 387 2390, www. grandstbakery.com). **Open** noon-8pm daily. **Map** p219 B4 ⑱

Despite the signage, Grand Street Bakery doesn't sell bread and pastries. It's stocked with clothing and accessories dating from the 1960s to the '90s, almost exclusively made in the US. Many of the shop's original fixtures – including metal baking racks that hold stacks of Levi's 501s – remain intact. Former Urban Outfitters vintage buyer Neal Mello and his girlfriend, Cyd Mullen, scour the country for classic Americana garb, such as ladies' fisherman knit sweaters and denim overalls. Guys' buys include Pendleton plaid wool shirts and denim jackets.

Myths of Creation

421 Graham Avenue between Frost & Withers Streets, Williamsburg (1-718 389 3036, www. mythsofcreation.com). Subway L to Graham Avenue. **Open** noon-8pm daily. **Map** p219 C3 ⑲ **Fashion/accessories**

Bartender Xenia Viray aimed to open a store that boasted similar styles you'd find on the racks at Anthropologie – but for a fraction of the price. Succulents planted in vintage beer cans and distressed mirrors lend a homey vibe to this off-kilter joint, where you can score chic and affordable women's clothing by English Factory and FRNCH, high-waisted Just Black jeans for a mere $60 and handmade jewellery by Laila K Lott and Pigeon Dynamite. Viray's quirky aesthetic – think collectable shopping bags inspired by vintage airline messengers and a kitschy 'bunnies eating pizza' greeting card collection by Jessamy Dipper – adds to this shop's indie charm.

Permanent Records

181 Franklin Street, between Green & Huron Streets, Greenpoint (1-718 383 4083, www. permanentrecords.info). Subway G to Greenpoint Avenue. **Open** noon-7pm daily. **Map** p219 A1 ⑳ **Books & music**

See p223 **On the Record**.

Rough Trade

64 North 9th Street, between Kent & Wythe Avenues, Williamsburg (1-718 388 4111, www. roughtrade.com). Subway L to Bedford Avenue. **Open** 11am-11pm Mon-Sat; 11am-9pm Sun. **Map** p219 A3 ㉑ **Books & music**

See p223 **On the Record**.

Space Ninety 8

98 North 6th Street, between Berry Street & Wythe Avenue (1-718 599 0209, www.spaceninety8.com). Subway L to Bedford Avenue. **Open** 11am-10pm Mon-Fri; 10am-10pm Sat; 11am-9pm Sun. **Map** p219 A3 ㉒ **Fashion/books & music/homewares**

Following Urban Outfitters' Space 15 Twenty in Los Angeles, Space Ninety 8 brought the company's address-as-name brand extension to Brooklyn. The multi-floor market features products you'd find at any Urban Outfitters (moderately priced men's and women's clothing, jewellery, home-decor goods), plus an expanded record shop and a gallery space that features pop-up shops. The Market Space on the first floor, is home to handcrafted, one-of-a-kind pieces – many created in New York. And when you need to take a break from all the shopping, there's the Gorbals, a restaurant and bar from *Top Chef* winner Ilan Hall that occupies part of the third floor and the rooftop.

Swords-Smith

98 South 4th Street, between Bedford Avenue & Berry Street, Williamsburg (1-347 599 2969, www.swords-smith.com). Subway L to Bedford Avenue; J, M, Z to Marcy Avenue. **Open** noon-8pm Mon-Fri; 11am-8pm Sat; noon-7pm Sun. **Map** p219 A3 ㉓ **Fashion**

Fashion vets Briana Swords (a former womenswear designer for Levi Strauss) and R Smith (a graphic designer whose credits include *Vogue*) are behind this boutique for men and women. The duo offers a carefully curated collection of clothing and accessories from more than 80 up-and-coming designers in the skylighted, minimalist space. Labels are sourced from around the world and include Soulland and Henrik Vibskov (from Copenhagen), Samuji (Helsinki), and New York's own Lucio Castro and Samantha Pleet. Unusual prints and strong silhouettes appeal to creative dressers.

CONEY ISLAND & BRIGHTON BEACH

Subway B, Q to Brighton Beach; D, F, N, Q to Coney Island-Stillwell Avenue; F to Neptune Avenue; F, Q to West 8th Street-NY Aquarium.

Combining old-time fairground attractions, new amusement park rides and traditional seaside pleasures against a gritty urban backdrop, Coney Island is a strange hybrid undergoing a revitalisation plan that also includes improvements to the surrounding residential neighbourhood. In its heyday, from the turn of the century until World War II, Coney Island was New York City's playground, drawing millions each year to its seaside amusement parks Dreamland, Luna Park and Steeplechase Park. The first two were destroyed by fire (Dreamland in 1911 and Luna Park in 1944) and not rebuilt, while Steeplechase Park staggered on until 1964. Astroland was built in 1962 in the euphoria of the World's Fair, went up in flames in 1975 and was rebuilt, only to shutter in 2008.

A year later, the city commissioned a new incarnation of **Luna Park** (1000 Surf Avenue, at W 10th Street, 1-718 373 5862, www.lunapark nyc.com, open Apr-Oct) that will eventually form the core of a 27-acre amusement district. Opening in 2010, it now has more than 40 attractions, including the new Thunderbolt Coney Island's first custom-built rollercoaster since the **Cyclone** opened in 1927. That whiplash-inducing ride is still going strong, along with the 1918 **Deno's Wonder Wheel** – both are protected landmarks.

Nostalgic visitors will enjoy a stroll along the three-mile-long boardwalk, lined with corny carnival games and souvenir shops. The iconic 1939 **Parachute Jump** has been restored and is illuminated at night. Non-profit arts organisation Coney Island USA keeps the torch burning for 20th-century-style attractions at its **Coney Island Museum** with seasonal circus sideshows, as well as kitsch summer spectacle the **Mermaid Parade** (*see p35*). The local baseball team, **Brooklyn Cyclones**, play at the seaside **MCU Park**.

Walk left along the boardwalk from Coney Island and you'll reach **Brighton Beach**, New York's Little Odessa. Groups of Russian expats (the big hair and garish fashion can be jaw-dropping) crowd semi-outdoor eateries such as **Tatiana** (3152 Brighton 6th Street, at the Boardwalk, 1-718 891 5151) – on weekend nights, it morphs into a glitzy club.

Sights & Museums

Coney Island Museum

1208 Surf Avenue, at 12th Street, Coney Island (1-718 372 5159, www.coneyisland.com). Subway D, F, N, Q to Coney Island-Stillwell Avenue. **Open** *Museum June-Aug* noon-7pm Wed-Sun. *Sept-May* noon-6pm Sat, Sun. *Shows* vary. **Admission** *Museum* $5; $3 reductions. *Shows* $10-$15; $5 reductions.

Housed in a 1917 building, the Coney Island Museum acts as both a repository of the district's past and the focus of its current alternative culture. Exhibitions include Coney Island-inspired work by local artists and artefacts from the permanent collection such as fun house mirrors and antique postcards. From Easter to the end of September, its venue, Sideshows by the Seashore, showcases the freaky talents of 'human blockhead', fire-eater and juggler Ray Valenz, and multi-talented sword swallower Betty Bloomerz, among others, while Burlesque at the Beach slinks on to the stage on summer Friday and Saturday nights (see website for the schedule).

Restaurants & Cafés

Nathan's Famous

1310 Surf Avenue, at Stillwell Avenue, Coney Island (1-718 333 2202, www.nathansfamous. com). Subway D, F, N, Q to Coney Island-Stillwell Avenue. **Open** 9am-midnight Mon-Thur, Sun; 9am-1am Fri, Sat. **Hot dogs** $3.50-$4. **American** Opened in 1916, the famed frank joint has retained its subway tiles and iconic signage, as well as staples like crinkle-cut fries and thick-battered corn dogs. But there's one shiny 'new' addition: a curbside clam bar, a revival of the restaurant's 1950s raw bar. East Coast oysters and littlenecks are shucked over a mountain of ice, served with chowder crackers, lemon wedges, sinus-clearing horseradish and cocktail sauce.

EXPLORE

Nathan's Famous.

Queens

While Queens is the point of arrival for visitors flying into JFK or La Guardia airports, the borough hasn't traditionally been on most tourists' must-see list. Now, however, cultural institutions, such as MoMA PS1, the Museum of the Moving Image and the revamped Queens Museum are drawing both out-of-towners and Manhattanites across the Ed Koch Queensboro Bridge, while the rising Ridgewood neighbourhood on the border with hip Bushwick has been christened Quooklyn.

Queens is an increasingly popular gastronomic destination. It's one of the country's most diverse urban areas, with almost half its residents hailing from outside the US. Not for nothing is the elevated 7 subway line that serves these parts nicknamed the 'International Express'. Astoria is home to Greek tavernas and Brazilian *churrascarias*; Jackson Heights has Indian, Thai and South American eateries; and Flushing has the city's second largest Chinatown.

Bohemian Hall & Beer Garden

Don't Miss

1 **MoMA PS1** Adventurous shows and food, plus some of the best parties in the city (p228).

2 **Mu Ramen** Much more than the titular cult bowl (p230).

3 **Noguchi Museum** A serene sanctuary in industrial Queens (p232).

4 **Bohemian Hall & Beer Garden** Beer bars have returned to the borough, but this is the original (p234).

5 **Spicy & Tasty** If you like it hot, head to Flushing's Chinatown (p237).

LONG ISLAND CITY

Subway E, M to Court Square-23rd Street;
G to Court Square or 21st Street; 7 to Vernon
Boulevard-Jackson Avenue or Court Square.

Just across the East River from Manhattan, Long Island City has seen a rapid transformation over the past decade, with shiny modern apartment towers replacing swathes of industrial wasteland. Fronting the main stretch of residential riverside development, **Gantry Plaza State Park** (48th Avenue, at Center Boulevard) commands an impressive panorama of midtown. The 12-acre park takes its name from the hulking industrial gantries that still stand watch over the piers and were used to haul cargo from rail barges. Deckchairs offer direct views of the United Nations across the East River.

Vernon Avenue is the neighbourhood's prime restaurant, retail and bar hub. The cultural jewel is the progressive art institution **MoMA PS1**. In summer months, its courtyard becomes a dance-music hub when it hosts the hugely popular Saturday-afternoon **Warm Up** parties (*see p280*). Other notable art spaces include **SculptureCenter**, housed in a dramatic industrial space, and the **Fisher Landau Center for Art** (38-27 30th Street, between 38th and 39th Avenues, 1-718 937 0727, www. flcart.org; closed Tue, Wed), which showcases the 1,500-piece contemporary art collection of Emily Fisher Landau. A well-preserved block of 19th-century houses constitutes the **Hunter's Point Historic District** (45th Avenue, between 21st & 23rd Streets).

IN THE KNOW
WHERE THE ACTION IS

Broadway Danny Rose (1984) and *Do the Right Thing* (1989) are among the movies shot at **Long Island City's Silvercup Studios** (42-22 22nd Street, between 43rd & 44th Avenues, www.silvercupstudios.com), a former bread factory in an industrial section by the Ed Koch Queensboro Bridge. The studios have also been home to some of the most iconic New York-set (and New Jersey-set) TV shows: *Sex and the City* (the series and both movies), *The Sopranos* and *Girls*. While you're in the neighbourhood, look out for its massive retro sign, which featured in the rooftop fight scene of 1986 flick *Highlander*.

Sights & Museums

For the **Noguchi Museum**, *see p232.*

★ MoMA PS1

22-25 Jackson Avenue, at 46th Avenue (1-718 784 2084, www.momaps1.org). Subway E, M to Court Square-23rd Street; G to 21st Street; 7 to Court Square. **Open** noon-6pm Mon, Thur-Sun. **Admission** $10; $5 reductions; free under-16s. **Map** p229 A5 ❶
MoMA PS1 mounts cutting-edge shows in a distinctive Romanesque Revival building (formerly a public school, hence the name). The contemporary art centre became an affiliate of MoMA in 1999, and the

Long Island City.

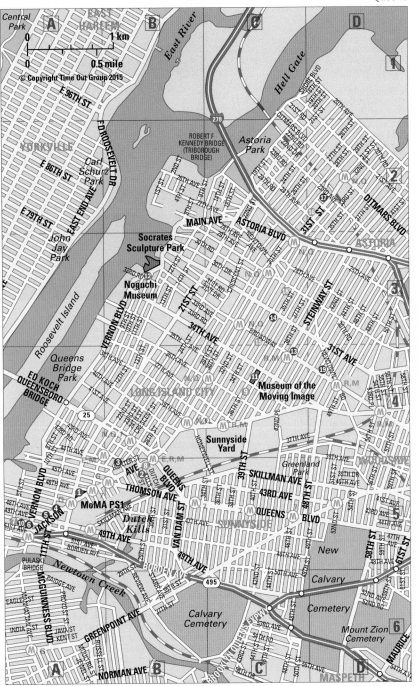

EXPLORE

Central Park
EAST HARLEM

0 ____ 1 km
0 ____ 0.5 mile
© Copyright Time Out Group 2015

East River

Hell Gate

SHORE BLVD
DITMARS BLVD
ASTORIA BLVD

E 96TH ST
YORKVILLE
E 86TH ST
Carl Schurz Park
E 79TH ST
John Jay Park
EAST END AVE
ED ROOSEVELT DR

278
ROBERT F KENNEDY BRIDGE (TRIBOROUGH BRIDGE)

Astoria Park

DITMARS BLVD
ASTORIA

MAIN AVE
ASTORIA BLVD

Socrates Sculpture Park

Noguchi Museum
VERNON BLVD
21ST ST
34TH AVE

STEINWAY ST
31ST AVE

Roosevelt Island

Queens Bridge Park

ED KOCH QUEENSBORO BRIDGE

25

LONG ISLAND CITY

Museum of the Moving Image

BROADWAY

Sunnyside Yard

HONEYWELL ST
QUEENS BLVD
39TH ST

Greenland Park

SKILLMAN AVE
43RD AVE

WOODSIDE

VERNON BLVD
MoMA PS1
THOMSON AVE
Dutch Kills
49TH AVE
JACKSON AVE
VAN DAM ST

QUEENS BLVD
SUNNYSIDE

58TH ST
61ST ST

PULASKI BRIDGE
Newtown Creek
PAIDGE AVE

495

New Calvary Cemetery

MCGUINNESS BLVD
GREENPOINT AVE

NORMAN AVE

Calvary Cemetery

BROOKLYN-QUEENS EXPRESSWAY

Mount Zion Cemetery

MAURICE

MASPETH

two institutions sometimes stage collaborative exhibitions, such as the quinquennial Greater New York. The DJed summer Warm Up parties are a fixture of the dance-music scene and on-site eatery M Wells Dinette is a foodie destination.

★ SculptureCenter

44-19 Purves Street, at Jackson Avenue (1-718 361 1750, www.sculpture-center.org). Subway E, M to Court Square-23rd Street; G, 7 to Court Square. **Open** 11am-6pm Mon, Thur-Sun. **Admission** *Suggested donation* $5; $3 reductions. **Map** p229 B5 ❷

One of the best places to see sculpture by blossoming and mid-career artists, this non-profit space is known for its broad definition of the discipline. Housed in an impressive former trolley-repair shop that was reimagined by acclaimed architect Maya Lin in 2002, the SculptureCenter has increased exhibition space thanks to a 2014 expansion by Andrew Berman – designer of the AIA Center for Architecture, no less.

Restaurants & Cafés

M Wells Steakhouse

43-15 Crescent Street, between 43rd Avenue & 44th Drive (1-718 786 9060, www.magasinwells.com). Subway N, Q, 7 to Queensboro Plaza. **Open** 5.30-11.30pm Mon, Wed-Sat; 5.30-10.30pm Sun. **Main courses** $17-$75. **Map** p229 B5 ❸ Steakhouse/eclectic

At Hugue Dufour and Sarah Obraitis's cool spin on a classic steakhouse, hipsters mingle with families in a former auto-body shop to get their fill of pork chops, shellfish, Flintstones-worthy bone-in hamburgers and, of course, smoky steaks cooked over a wood fire. The quirky power couple also offer creative cuisine at M Wells Dinette, inside MoMA PS1, where schoolroom-themed decor pays homage to the building's roots.

★ Mu Ramen

12-09 Jackson Avenue, between 47th Road & 48th Avenue (1-917 868 8903, www.muramennyc.com). Subway G to 21st Street; 7 to Vernon Boulevard-Jackson Avenue. **Open** 5.30-10pm Mon-Sat. **Ramen** $15-$18. **No credit cards**. **Map** p229 A5 ❹ Japanese

Born from a pop-up, which operated out of a bagel shop and then owner Joshua Smookler's apartment, this permanent location opened to meet high demand. In addition to the signature bowl, built on a beef broth made with oxtail and bone marrow, and given extra-meaty oomph from melting cubes of brisket, the *tebasaki gyoza*, a deboned chicken wing crammed with creamy foie gras, soft brioche and quince compote, makes Mu destination-worthy.

Sweetleaf

10-93 Jackson Avenue, at 11th Street (1-917 832 6726, www.sweetleaflic.com). Subway 7 to Vernon

M Wells Steakhouse.

Boulevard-Jackson Avenue. **Open** 7am-7pm Mon-Fri; 8am-7pm Sat, Sun. **Coffee** $2.50-$4.75. **No credit cards**. **Map** p229 A5 ❺ Café

Long Island City's first speciality coffee shop opened in 2008 in this quaint, tin-ceilinged, antique-furnished space. There are now three locations serving direct-trade coffee, house-made pastries and artisan espresso. Get a tasty caffeine blast with Rocket Fuel – cold-brewed iced coffee sweetened with maple syrup and milk. The larger Queens location, in a high-rise near the waterfront, also offers cocktails in the evening.

Other locations 4615 Center Boulevard, between 46th & 47th Avenues, Long Island City (1-347 527 1038); 135 Kent Avenue, between North Fifth & North Sixth Streets, Williamsburg, Brooklyn (1-347 725 4862).

Tournesol

50-12 Vernon Boulevard, between 50th & 51st Avenues (1-718 472 4355, www.tournesolnyc.com). Subway 7 to Vernon Boulevard-Jackson Avenue. **Open** 5.30-11pm Mon; 11.30am-3pm, 5.30-11pm Tue-Thur; 11.30am-3pm, 5.30-11.30pm Fri; 11am-3.30pm, 5.30-11.30pm Sat; 11am-3.30pm, 5-10pm Sun. **Main courses** $16-$22. **No credit cards** (except AmEx). **Map** p229 A5 ❻ French

While Tournesol is a local favourite for steak frites and *magret de canard*, it's worth making a journey here for beautifully executed south-western French cuisine at prices you'd be hard-pressed to find across the East River. Squeeze into one of the red banquettes in the intimate one-room dining space

EXPLORE

outfitted with white tin ceilings and local artwork, and split an appetiser of the obscenely good house-made foie gras terrine.

Bars

Alewife

5-14 51st Avenue, between Vernon Boulevard & 5th Street (1-718 937 7494, www.alewifenyc. com). Subway 7 to Vernon Boulevard-Jackson Avenue. **Open** 4pm-1am Mon-Thur; 4pm-3am Fri; 11am-3am Sat; 11am-1am Sun. **Map** p229 A5 **7**

A serious craft-beer selection is the draw at this bi-level beer hall, which comes from a team of hops zealots with ties to Alewife Baltimore and the cultish Lord Hobo in Cambridge, MA. It's a generic-looking gastropub, and we could do without the poppy soundtrack and truffle oil on our fries. But the owners come through where it counts, curating a balanced and worldly beer list (28 taps and casks and 100-plus bottles) that can go toe-to-toe with the most pedigreed suds haunts.

Dutch Kills

27-24 Jackson Avenue, at Dutch Kills Street (1-718 383 2724, www.dutchkillsbar.com). Subway E, M, R to Queens Plaza. **Open** 5pm-2am daily. **Map** p229 B5 **8**

What separates Dutch Kills from NYC's other mixology temples modelled after vintage saloons is the abundance of elbow room. Settle into one of the deep, dark-wood booths in the front, or perch at the bar. Cocktails are mostly classic, with prices slightly lower than in similar establishments in Manhattan.

Garden at Studio Square

35-33 36th Street, between 35th & 36th Avenues (1-718 383 1001, www.studiosquarebeergarden. com). Subway M, R to 36th Street; N, Q to 36th Avenue. **Open** 3pm-4am Mon-Thur; noon-4am Fri-Sun. **Map** p229 D4 **9**

A contemporary interpretation of a classic beer garden, Studio Square's grand cobblestoned court-yard is lined with communal picnic tables. Modern fire pits keep out evening chills, but there is also an indoor bar. The 20-strong suds list includes European classics and American microbrews. Basic pub grub is supplemented with trad specialities like kielbasa and pretzels, and the party-hearty ambi-ence is fuelled by DJs and bands.

Shops & Services

Elska

5-35 51st Avenue, between Vernon Boulevard & 5th Street (1-718 361 5650, www.elskashop.com). Subway 7 to Vernon Boulevard-Jackson Avenue. **Open** 11am-7pm Tue-Sat; 11am-5pm Sun. **Map** p229 A5 **10** Fashion/homewares

Scandinavian style aficionados Rebekah Witzke and Jillian Tangen combine a Nordic aesthetic with a New York sensibility at their lifestyle boutique (formerly LIC Living). In addition to under-the-radar women's clothing lines, you'll find accessories for both guys and gals, home items and gifts. The highly appealing mix brings together the likes of cool Danish goose-feather lamps (using a food-industry byproduct), original signed prints by Norwegian artist Elise Stalder, and Upstate Stock candles made in Schenectady, New York.

EXPLORE

Elska.

ASTORIA

Subway R, M to Steinway Street; N, Q to Broadway, 30th Avenue, 36th Avenue or Astoria-Ditmars Boulevard.

A lively, traditionally Greek and Italian neighbourhood, Astoria has over the last few decades seen an influx of Brazilians, Bangladeshis, Eastern Europeans, Colombians and Egyptians. Gentrification has also moved in. A 15-minute downhill hike from Broadway subway station towards Manhattan brings you to the **Noguchi Museum**, which was created by the visionary sculptor. Nearby lies the **Socrates Sculpture Park** (Broadway, at Vernon Boulevard, www.socratessculpturepark.org), a riverfront art space in an industrial setting with great views of Manhattan.

In the early days of cinema, Astoria was a major celluloid hub. Taking advantage of its proximity to talent-laden Broadway, Famous Players-Lasky (later Paramount Pictures) opened its first studios in the neighbourhood in 1920. Portions of Valentino's blockbuster *The Sheikh* (1921) were filmed there, and the studio produced the Marx Brothers' *The Cocoanuts* (1929) and *Animal Crackers* (1930) before Paramount moved its operations west. After years of neglect, the studios were declared a National Historic Landmark in 1976, and, in 1982, developer George S Kaufman bought the site and created **Kaufman Astoria Studios** (34-12 36th Street, between 34th & 35th Avenues, www.kaufmanastoria. com). Scenes for numerous films, including *Birdman* (2014) and *The Bourne Legacy* (2012), were shot there, and the studios are also home to TV shows *Saturday Night Live*, *Nurse Jackie* and *Sesame Street*, among others. The **Museum of the Moving Image** is across the street.

Still New York's Greek-American stronghold, Astoria is well known for Hellenic eateries and cafés. You can puff on a shisha – a (legal) hookah pipe – with a thick Turkish coffee in the cafés of 'Little Egypt' along Steinway Street, between 28th Avenue and Astoria Boulevard. At the end of the N and Q subway lines (Astoria-Ditmars Boulevard), walk west to **Astoria Park** (from Astoria Park South to Ditmars Boulevard, between Shore Boulevard & 19th Street) for its dramatic views of two bridges: the Robert F Kennedy Bridge (formerly the Triborough), Robert Moses's automotive labyrinth connecting Queens, the Bronx and Manhattan; and the 1916 Hell Gate Bridge, a steel single-arch tour de force and template for the Sydney Harbour Bridge. On the area's north-east fringes, you can tour the still-thriving red-brick 1871 piano factory **Steinway & Sons** (1 Steinway Place, between 19th Avenue & 38th Street, 1-718 721 2600, tours@steinway. com). The weekly tour, conducted on Tuesday

mornings from September through June, is free, but reservations are required (and it books up months in advance).

Sights & Museums

Museum of the Moving Image

36-01 35th Avenue, at 36th Street (1-718 777 6888, www.movingimage.us). Subway R, M to Steinway Street; N, Q to 36th Avenue. **Open** *Galleries* 10.30am-5pm Wed, Thur; 10.30am-8pm Fri; 11.30am-7pm Sat, Sun. **Admission** $12; $6-$9 reductions; free under-3s. Free 4-8pm Fri. **Map** p229 C4 🔟

The Museum of the Moving Image reopened in 2011 after a major renovation that doubled its size and made it one of the foremost museums in the world dedicated to TV, film and video. The institution's collection, galleries and state-of-the-art screening facilities are housed on the campus of Kaufman Astoria Studios. On the second and third floors, the core exhibition, 'Behind the Screen', contains approximately 1,400 artefacts – including the super creepy stunt doll used in *The Exorcist*, with full head-rotating capabilities, and the (surprisingly small) model of the Tyrell Corporation building from *Blade Runner*, alongside interactive displays. A new gallery devoted to Muppets creator Jim Henson is expected to open in late 2015.

★ Noguchi Museum

9-01 33rd Road, at Vernon Boulevard (1-718 204 7088, www.noguchi.org). Subway N, Q to Broadway, then 15min walk or Q104 bus to 11th Street; 7 to Vernon Boulevard-Jackson Avenue, then Q103 bus to 10th Street. **Open** 10am-5pm Wed-Fri; 11am-6pm Sat, Sun. **Admission** $10; $5 reductions; free under-12s. Free 1st Fri of the mth. No pushchairs/strollers. **Map** p229 B3 🔟

When Japanese-American sculptor and designer Isamu Noguchi (1904-88) opened his Queens museum in 1985, he became the first living artist in the US to establish such an institution. The Noguchi Museum occupies a former photo-engraving plant across the street from the studio he had occupied since the 1960s; its location allowed him to be close to stone and metal suppliers along Vernon Boulevard. Noguchi designed the entire building to be a meditative oasis amid its gritty, industrial setting. Eleven galleries, spread over two floors, are filled with his sculptures, as well as drawn, painted and collaged studies, architectural models, and stage and furniture designs. The serene garden features a minimalist fountain and such works as his megalithic 1978 *Core (Cored Sculpture)* carved from vocanic basalt. *Photo p234.*

Restaurants & Cafés

$ The Queens Kickshaw

40-17 Broadway, between Steinway & 41st Streets (1-718 777 0913, www.thequeenskickshaw.com).

RIDGEWOOD ON THE RISE

The nabe is having a moment, with the food-and-drink scene to prove it.

Buzzy cocktail bars. Craft breweries. Locally sourced food. The newest up-and-coming nabe has all the hallmarks of hip Brooklyn – except the zip code. Ridgewood, Queens, a residential tract of land north-east of Bushwick, off the L and M trains, has been jokingly dubbed Quooklyn. (Queens plus Brooklyn, get it?) We understand why. Here are the places that should be on your radar before the rest of the world catches on.

BIERLEICHEN

Adam Collison, who also owns the Drink in Williamsburg (www.thedrinkbrooklyn.com) and the Bounty in Greenpoint (www.thebounty brooklyn.com), was gearing up to open this restaurant and beer garden as this guide went to press. The Bavarian-inspired space will serve mostly German drafts, as well as house-made pretzels, *sauerbraten* and both meat and veggie sausages. *582 Seneca Avenue, between Grove & Menahan Streets (no phone yet).*

BRIDGE AND TUNNEL BREWERY

Consider 'bridge-and-tunnel' an insult no more. Rich Castagna is bringing his one-man operation from Maspeth and plans to be open by midsummer 2015. Expect a tasting room, with growler and pint pours on-site. *1535 Decatur Street, between Irving & Wyckoff Avenues (1-347 392 8593, www.bridgeandtunnelbrewery.com).*

HOUDINI KITCHEN LABORATORY

Located in an old brewery with a hidden entrance, Houdini has the trappings of a hip Brooklyn haunt. But what keeps the place bustling is the Neapolitan-style pizza with local toppings straight from a brick oven. *15-63 Decatur Street, at Wyckoff Avenue (1-718 456 3770).*

JULIA'S BEER & WINE BAR

This cosy space, from the duo behind Ridgewood fave Norma's (www.cafenormas. com), hosts wine tastings and drink-and-draw workshops. Visitors can sip organic vino and local beers (including a wide range of products from nearby Finback Brewery) and munch on small plates, surrounded by pearl-strung chandeliers and local art. *818 Woodward Avenue, between Cornelia Street & Putnam Avenue (1-917 909 1314).*

THE KEEP

Since opening on Halloween 2014, the eclectic, antique-filled space has hosted all manner of events: magic shows, burlesque performances, film-noir nights and more. A café and vintage shop by day and cocktail bar by night, the Keep also serves small plates for brunch and dinner. Oh, and there's backgammon. *205 Cypress Avenue, between Starr Street & Willoughby Avenue (1-718 381 0400, www.thekeepny.com).*

EXPLORE

The Keep.

Noguchi Museum. *See p232.*

Subway M, R to Steinway Street. **Open** 7.30am-midnight Mon-Wed; 7.30am-1am Thur, Fri; 9am-1am Sat; 9am-midnight Sun. **Sandwiches** $9-$11. **Map** p229 C4 🔞 **Café**

Serious java draws caffeine fiends to this airy café, which also specialises in grilled-cheese sandwiches. While the pedigreed beans – from Counter Culture Coffee – are brewed with Hario V60 drip cones and a La Marzocco Strada espresso machine, there's no coffee-snob attitude here. Fancy grilled-cheese choices include a weekend-morning offering of soft egg folded with ricotta, a gruyère crisp and maple hot sauce between thick, buttery slices of brioche.

Zenon Taverna

34-10 31st Avenue, at 34th Street (1-718 956 0133, www.zenontaverna.com). Subway N, Q to Broadway. **Open** noon-11pm daily. **Main courses** $16-$30. **No credit cards.** **Map** p229 C3 🔞 **Greek**

The faux-stone entryway and murals of ancient ruins don't detract from the Mediterranean charm of this humble place that's been serving Greek and Cypriot food for more than 25 years. Specials rotate daily, embracing all the classics – stuffed grape leaves, *keftedes* (Cypriot meatballs), *spanakopita* (spinach pie) – and less ubiquitous dishes such as rabbit stew and plump *loukaniko* (pork sausages). Filling sweets, such as *galaktopoureko* (syrupy layers of filo baked with custard cream), merit a taste.

Bars

Astoria Bier and Cheese

34-14 Broadway, between 34th & 35th Streets (1-718 545 5588, www.astoriabierandcheese.com). Subway M, R to Steinway Street; N, Q to Broadway. **Open** noon-11pm Mon-Thur; noon-midnight Fri, Sat; noon-10pm Sun. **Map** p229 C3 🔞

Manhattan's hybrid bar-shop trend has crossed the bridge with this quirky curds-and-brew haven. At the marble bar, grab one of the ten seasonal, mostly local drafts, including selections from the borough's own Finback brewery. There are close to 300 bottles and cans – organised by style and offered in mix-and-match six packs – that can be purchased to go or opened on-site for a $2 corking fee. Fromage buff Mike Fisher (a Bedford Cheese Shop vet) culls close to 80 selections for the refrigerated case, some of which are worked into a sit-down menu that includes a selection of grilled cheese melts.

Other location 5-11 Ditmars Boulevard, between 35th and 36th Streets, Astoria (1-718 255 6982).

★ Bohemian Hall & Beer Garden

29-19 24th Avenue, between 29th & 31st Streets (1-718 274 4925, www.bohemianhall.com). Subway N, Q to Astoria Boulevard. **Open** 5pm-midnight Mon-Thur; 5pm-3am Fri; noon-3am Sat; noon-midnight Sun. **Map** p229 D2 🔞

This authentic Czech beer garden features plenty of mingle-friendly picnic tables, where you can sample cheap, robust platters of sausage, goulash and other specialities alongside 16 mainly European drafts. Though the huge, linden-canopied garden is open year-round (in winter, the area is tented and heated), summer is prime time to visit.

Bonnie

29-12 23rd Avenue, between 29th & 31st Streets (1-718 274 2105, www.thebonnie.com). Subway N, Q to Ditmars Boulevard. **Open** 3pm-4am Mon-Fri; 10.30am-4am Sat, Sun. **Map** p229 D2 🔞

Astorians were buzzing about this cocktail bar and eaterie months before its opening. Not only is it beautiful, with its brick walls and two spacious bars, but its locally focused menu (highlighting goods from nearby farms, butchers and breweries) isn't too shabby either, with notable picks including a roasted carrot sandwich. The cocktail menu offers a few throwbacks, such as a selection of cobblers, and twists on classics like the dirty pickle martini.

Sweet Afton

*30-09 34th Street, between 30th & 31st Avenues
(1-718 777 2570, www.sweetaftonbar.com).
Subway N, Q to 30th Avenue.* **Open** 4pm-4am
Mon-Fri; 10.30am-4am Sat, Sun. **Map** p229 C3 ⑮
Sweet Afton combines an industrial feel – lots of
concrete and massive beams – with the dark-wood
cosiness of an Irish pub. The smartly curated array
of reasonably priced suds includes strong selections
from craft breweries like Sixpoint, Allagash and
Smuttynose, but the bartender will happily mix
a cocktail. The satisfying food menu includes the
beer-battered McClure's pickles – an epic bar snack.

Shops & Services

Long Island City Kleaners

*45-03 Broadway, between 45th & 46th Streets
(1-718 606 0540, www.licknyc.com). Subway
M, R to 46th Street.* **Open** 11am-8pm Mon-Sat;
noon-6pm Sun. **Map** p229 D4 ⑲ **Fashion**
This concept store evokes gritty NYC storefronts
from the 1980s that posed as dry cleaners but hosted
illegal activities. There's nothing sketchy about it,
though – in the repurposed space you'll find T-shirts
hanging on the racks in dry-cleaning bags, skating
goods and footwear, including the Nike SB range.

JACKSON HEIGHTS

*Subway E, F, M, R to Jackson Heights-Roosevelt
Avenue; 7 to 74th Street-Broadway.*

Dizzying even by Queens standards, Jackson
Heights' multiculturalism gives it an energy
all its own. Little India greets you with a cluster
of small shops on 74th Street between 37th
Road and 37th Avenue, selling Indian music,
Bollywood DVDs, saris and glitzy jewellery.
But the main appeal for visitors is culinary.
The unofficial HQ of the Indian expat community,
Jackson Diner serves sumptuous curries.
Along with neighbouring Elmhurst and
Woodside, Jackson Heights has also welcomed
waves of Latin American and South-east Asian
immigrants. Fresh, meaty tacos – think broiled
beef and steamed tongue – give **Taqueria
Coatzingo** (76-05 Roosevelt Avenue, between
76th & 77th Streets, 1-718 424 1977) an edge
over the other tempting holes-in-the-wall under
the 7 train track.

Restaurants & Cafés

$ Jackson Diner

*37-47 74th Street, between 37th Avenue & 37th
Road (1-718 672 1232, www.jacksondiner.com).
Subway E, F, M, R to Jackson Heights-Roosevelt
Avenue; 7 to 74th Street-Broadway.* **Open**
11.30am-10pm daily. **Main courses** $11-$24.
Map p406 Y5 **Indian**

Harried waiters and Formica-topped tables evoke
a diner experience at this weekend meet-and-eat
headquarters for New York's Indian expat community. Watch Hindi soaps on Zee TV while enjoying
samosa chat topped with chickpeas, yoghurt, onion,
tomato, and a sweet-spicy mix of tamarind and mint
chutneys. Specials such as murgh tikka makhan-
wala, tender pieces of marinated chicken simmered
in curry and cream, are fiery and flavourful.
Other locations 256-01 Hillside Avenue, at 256th
Street, Floral Park (1-718 343 7400); 72 University
Place, between 10th & 11th Streets, East Village
(1-212 466 0820).

★ $ Sripraphai

*64-13 39th Avenue, between 64th & 65th Streets
(1-718 899 9599, www.sripraphairestaurant.com).
Subway 7 to 61st Street-Woodside.* **Open** 11.30am-
9.30pm Mon, Tue, Thur-Sun. **Main courses**
$9-$18. **No credit cards. Map** p229 Y5 **Thai**
Woodside's destination eatery offers distinctive,
traditional dishes such as catfish salad or green
curry with beef: a thick, piquant broth filled out
with roasted Thai aubergine. The dining areas,
which sprawl over two levels and a garden (open in
summer), are packed with Manhattanites who can be
seen eyeing the plates enjoyed by the Thai regulars,
mentally filing away what to order the next time.

FLUSHING

*Subway 7 to Flushing-Main Street, 103rd Street-
Corona Plaza, 111th Street or Mets-Willets Point.*

Egalitarian Dutchmen staked their claim to
'Vlissingen' in the 1600s and were shortly joined
by pacifist Friends, or Quakers, seeking religious
freedom in the New World. The plain wooden
Old Quaker Meeting House (137-16 Northern
Boulevard, between Main & Union Streets), built
in 1694, creates a startling juxtaposition to the
predominantly Chinese businesses that surround
its weathered wooden walls. **Flushing Town
Hall** (137-35 Northern Boulevard, at Linden Place,
1-718 463 7700, www.flushingtownhall.org),
built during the Civil War in the highly fanciful
Romanesque Revival style, showcases local
arts groups, and hosts jazz and chamber music
concerts. A short walk away, the 1854 landmark
St George's Church (135-32 38th Avenue,
between Main & Prince Streets, 1-718 359 1171,
www.saintgeorgesflushing.org) contains two
examples of Queens-made Tiffany stained glass.
    However, most non-locals come to these
parts for the restaurants and dumpling stalls.
Flushing's sprawling **Chinatown** has a more
affluent demographic than its Manhattan
counterpart – a case in point is the gleaming
New World Mall (136-20 Roosevelt Avenue,
at Main Street, 1-718 353 0551, www.newworld
mallny.com) and its opulent third-floor dim sum

EXPLORE

palace, **Grand Restaurant** (1-718 321 8258). Downstairs, at the spacious **Jmart** supermarket, peruse such exotic produce as the formidably prickled durian and the elusive mangosteen, or gawk at buckets full of live eels and frogs.

The most visited site in Queens is rambling **Flushing Meadows Corona Park** (from 111th Street to Van Wyck Expressway, between Flushing Bay & Grand Central Parkway, 1-718 760 6565, www.nycgovparks.org), where the 1939-40 and 1964-65 World's Fairs were held. Larger than Central Park, it's home to the **Queens Zoo** (1-718 271 1500, www.queenszoo.com); **Queens Theatre in the Park** (1-718 760 0064,

www.queenstheatre.org), an indoor amphitheatre designed by Philip Johnson; the **New York Hall of Science** (*see p254*), an acclaimed interactive museum; the **Queens Botanical Garden**, a 39-acre cavalcade of greenery; and the recently expanded **Queens Museum**. Also here are **Citi Field** (Roosevelt Avenue, near 126th Street, 1-718 507 8499, www.newyork.mets.mlb.com), the home of the Mets baseball team, and the **USTA (United States Tennis Association) National Tennis Center**. The US Open (*see p37*) raises an almighty racket at summer's end, but the general public can play here the other 11 months of the year.

ROCK ROCK ROCKAWAY BEACH

The urban surf hub is a summertime hotspot.

Situated on a long peninsula, the 170-acre **Rockaway Beach**, popular with local surfers, has become a hip summer destination. Part of its appeal is that it's an easy, if lengthy, subway ride from Manhattan: take the A train to Broad Channel, then transfer to the S.

We recommend getting off at Beach 98 Street so you can swing by the superb seasonal **Rockaway Taco** (95-19 Rockaway Beach Boulevard, at Beach 96 Street, 1-347 213 7466) for fish, *carne*, chorizo or tofu tacos ($3.50 each) before hitting the sand.

Once you've had enough sun and surf, head to beloved dive **Connolly's** (155 Beach 95th Street, between Rockaway Beach Boulevard and Shore Front Parkway, 1-718 474 2374) for one of the bar's (in)famous frozen piña coladas. Or, for something a little more sophisticated, stop by **Sayra's Wine Bar** (91-11 Rockaway Beach Boulevard, between Beach 91st & 92nd Streets, 1-347 619 8009), the brainchild of local surfer Rashida Jackson and artist Patrick Flibotte. The 28-seat shoreside drinkery showcases vino from around the world, alongside tapas including smoked-paprika-rosemary chips, olives and barbecue pulled-pork sandwiches. Out back is a 1,200-square-foot garden fitted with beach rocks and wooden picnic tables.

Those looking to make a night of it should try hipster haven **Playland Motel** (97-20 Rockaway Beach Boulevard, between Beach 97th & 98th Streets, 1-347 954 9063, www.playlandmotel.com). The restaurant, bar, late-night club, outdoor hangout, pizzeria and, yes, hotel (there are 12 creatively decorated rooms) is an arty-yet-casual oasis that attracts both fashion-conscious clubbers and weathered locals.

Sayra's Wine Bar.

Queens Museum.

Sights & Museums

Louis Armstrong House

34-56 107th Street, between 34th & 37th Avenues, Corona (1-718 478 8274, www.louisarmstrong house.org). Subway 7 to 103rd Street-Corona Plaza. **Open** 10am-5pm Tue-Fri; noon-5pm Sat, Sun. *Tours* hourly (last tour 4pm). **Admission** $10; $6-$7 reductions; free under-4s.

Pilgrims to the two-storey house where 'Satchmo' lived from 1943 until his death in 1971 will find a shrine to the revolutionary trumpet player – as well as his wife's passion for wallpaper. Her decorative attentions extended to the interiors of cupboards, closets and even bathroom cabinets. The 40-minute guided tour is enhanced by audiotapes of Armstrong that give much insight into the tranquil domesticity he sought in the then suburban neighbourhood. Among the artefacts on display are a detailed life mask of the great musician and the gold-plated horn given to him by King George V in 1933.

Queens Museum

New York City Building, Flushing Meadows Corona Park (1-718 592 9700, www.queensmuseum.org). Subway 7 to Mets-Willets Point, then 15min walk. **Open** noon-6pm Wed-Sun. **Admission** *Suggested donation* $8; $4 reductions; free under-12s.

Facing the Unisphere, the 140ft stainless-steel globe created for the 1964 World's Fair, in Flushing Meadows Corona Park, the Queens Museum occupies the former New York City Building, a Gotham-themed pavilion built for the earlier World's Fair in 1939. In the 1940s, the structure was the first home of the United Nations. During the 1964 World's Fair, the New York City Building showcased the Panorama of the City of New York, a 9,335sq ft scale model of the city dreamed up by powerful urban planner Robert Moses. Still on display in the museum, it includes every one of the 895,000 buildings constructed before 1992. In autumn 2013, the Museum wrapped up an expansion-cum-renovation project that doubled its size. The centrepiece of the 50,000sq ft addition, which used to house an ice-rink, is an airy atrium. The extra space accommodates nine studios for local artists, a café and the World's Fair Visible Storage and Gallery, where more than 900 artefacts from the 1939 and 1964 fairs are on display. If you want to take home a souvenir of your own, original World's Fair memorabilia is sold in the museum shop.

Restaurants & Cafés

★ $ Fu Run

40-09 Prince Street, between Roosevelt Avenue and 40th Road (1-718 321 1363, www.furunflushing. com). Subway 7 to Flushing-Main Street. **Open** 11.30am-midnight daily. **Main courses** $10-$25. **Chinese**

Thanks to a change in immigration patterns, Flushing has seen an increase in Northern Chinese restaurants like Fu Run, whose owners are from Dongbei (what was once known as Manchuria). They call their justly celebrated dish the 'Muslim lamb chop', but it's more like a half rack of ribs: a platter of bone-in, fatty meat is braised, then battered and deep-fried, the whole juicy slab blanketed with cumin seeds, chilli powder and flakes, and black and white sesame seeds.

★ $ Spicy & Tasty

39-07 Prince Street, between Roosevelt & 39th Avenues (1-718 359 1601, www.spicyandtasty.com). Subway 7 to Flushing-Main Street. **Open** 11.30am-10.30pm Mon-Thur, Sun; 11.30am-11pm Fri, Sat. **Main courses** $11-$26. **No credit cards. Chinese**

Any serious trip to Flushing for spicy Szechuan food should begin here. Revered by in-the-know regulars, this brightly lit eaterie serves plates of peppercorn-laden pork and lamb swimming in a chilli sauce that's sure to set even the most seasoned palate aflame. Stock up on cold-bar options, like zesty sesame noodles, crunchy chopped cucumbers and smooth, delicate tofu – you'll need the relief. Service is speedy and mercifully attentive to water requests.

The Bronx

The only NYC borough that's physically attached to the mainland of America, the Bronx seems remote to most visitors – and, indeed, many New Yorkers. Part of this perceived distance is due to the South Bronx's lingering reputation for urban strife, which was at its height in the 1970s. But there's more to the boogie-down borough than gritty cityscapes. In addition to its two best-known visitor attractions, Yankee Stadium and the Bronx Zoo, the area offers striking art deco architecture on the Grand Concourse, an up-and-coming art scene, old-school Italian eateries on Arthur Avenue and some of the most exquisite gardens in the city.

Visitors should note that although many parts of the Bronx are safe to explore, others, such as sections of the South Bronx and the northern swathe of the Grand Concourse, are still rough around the edges.

EXPLORE

Wave Hill.

Don't Miss

1 Grand Concourse A fascinating parade of (somewhat faded) art deco architecture (p241).

2 New York Botanical Garden The sprawling green space is an all-seasons oasis p243).

3 Mike's Deli Taste the 'real Little Italy' at this Arthur Avenue original (p244).

4 Bronx Beer Hall For brewed-in-the-borough suds (p244).

5 Wave Hill Lush gardens with stunning Hudson River views (p245).

EXPLORE

THE SOUTH BRONX

*Subway 4 to 161st Street-Yankee Stadium;
6 to Hunts Point Avenue or 138th Street-
Third Avenue.*

In the 1960s and '70s, the **South Bronx** was so
ravaged by post-war 'white flight' and community
displacement from the construction of the Cross
Bronx Expressway that the neighbourhood
became virtually synonymous with urban blight.
Crime was rampant and arson became widespread,
as landlords discovered that renovating decayed
property was far less lucrative than simply
burning it down to collect insurance. During a
World Series game at Yankee Stadium in 1977, TV
cameras caught a building on fire just blocks away.
'Ladies and gentlemen,' commentator Howard
Cosell told the world, 'the Bronx is burning.'

These days, the South Bronx is rising from
the ashes. In 2006, the South Bronx Initiative was
formed to revitalise the area, while eco-sensitive
outfits such as Sustainable South Bronx (www.
ssbx.org) have helped to transform vacant lots
into green spaces such as **Barretto Point Park**
(between Tiffany & Barretto Streets) and **Hunts
Point Riverside Park** (at the foot of Lafayette
Avenue on the Bronx River). In 2005, Hunts Point
became home to the city's **Fulton Fish Market**
(1-718 378 2356, www.newfultonfishmarket.com),
which moved from the site it had occupied for 180
years at South Street Seaport to a 400,000-square
foot modern facility that is the largest consortium
of seafood retailers in America.

Unsurprisingly, the rejuvenated area has also
seen an influx of young professional refugees

**IN THE KNOW
THE BRONX CULTURE TROLLEY**

To check out the South Bronx's burgeoning
art scene, hop on the free **Bronx Culture
Trolley** (www.bronxarts.org), which stops
at about a half-dozen venues on the first
Wednesday of each month, except
September and January.

from overpriced Manhattan and Brooklyn: new
condos are sprouting up, old warehouses are
being redeveloped, once-crumbling tenements
are being refurbished and, inevitably, chain
stores are moving in. Young families have been
snapping up the renovated townhouses on
Alexander Avenue and furnishing them from the
thoroughfare's antiques stores, while industrial
lofts on Bruckner Boulevard have become homes
to creatives. Yet despite developers' hopes for
'SoBro', the area has not quite turned into the
Next Big Thing. Yet.

Hunts Point is also becoming a creative
live-work hub. In 1994, a group of artists and
community leaders converted an industrial
building into the **Point** (940 Garrison Avenue,
at Manida Street, 1-718 542 4139, www.thepoint.
org, closed Sat, Sun), an arts-based community
development centre with a much-used
performance space and gallery, studios for dance,
theatre and photography, an environmental
advocacy group, and lively summer and after-
school workshops for neighbourhood children.
Another artistic South Bronx hotbed is

Yankee Stadium.

simmering further south-west in **Mott Haven**. Here, **Longwood Art Gallery @ Hostos** (450 Grand Concourse, at 149th Street, 1-718 518 6728, www.bronxarts.org/lag.asp), the creation of the Bronx Council on the Arts, mounts top-notch exhibits in a variety of media.

Of course, the vast majority of visitors to the South Bronx are just stopping long enough to take in a baseball game at **Yankee Stadium**, where some of baseball's most famous legends, from Babe Ruth to Derek Jeter, have made history.

Sights & Museums

Yankee Stadium
River Avenue, at 161st Street (1-718 293 6000, www.yankees.com). Subway B, D, 4 to 161st Street-Yankee Stadium.
In 2009, the Yankees vacated the fabled 'House that Ruth Built' and moved into their new $1.3-billion stadium across the street. Monument Park, an open-air museum behind centre field that celebrates the exploits of past Yankee heroes, can be visited as part of a tour ($25, $23 reductions, $20 booked online, free under-3s; 1-646 977 8687), along with the New York Yankees Museum, the dugout, and – when the Yankees are on the road – the clubhouse.

Restaurants & Cafés

Mo Gridder's BBQ
565 Hunts Point Avenue, between Oak Point & Randall Avenues (1-718 991 3046). Subway 6 to Hunts Point Avenue. **Open** 11am-4pm Mon-Sat. **Main courses** $5-$18. **Barbecue**
On the lot of the Hunts Point Auto Sales & Service Station, surrounded by junked car yards and auto parts stores, Mo Gridder's BBQ operates out of a red Wells Cargo trailer that sports a serious-looking smoker on its open back half. If you're here for auto issues, get the oil change and ribs special for $35. Otherwise, park yourself at a picnic table for the sauce-shellacked ribs and barbecue chicken that's nicely charred on the outside and juicy on the inside. Sides like potato salad and collard greens are less stellar, but decent enough.

Bars

Mott Haven Bar & Grill
1 Bruckner Boulevard, at Third Avenue (1-718 665 2001, http://motthavenbar.com). Subway 6 to Third Avenue-138th Street. **Open** 11am-midnight daily.
This popular neighbourhood hangout has eight beers on tap, including Bronx Brewery Pale Ale, plus a wide range of bottled craft beers, and an eclectic menu of bar snacks, sandwiches and burgers. The local cultural hub also serves as a gallery spotlighting local talent.

THE GRAND CONCOURSE

Subway B, D to 167th Street; B, D, 4 to Kingsbridge Road; 4 to 161st Street-Yankee Stadium.

A few blocks east of Yankee Stadium runs the four-and-a-half-mile **Grand Concourse**, which begins at 138th Street in the South Bronx and ends at Mosholu Parkway just shy of **Van Cortlandt Park** (*see p244*). Once the most prestigious drag in the Bronx, the Grand Boulevard and Concourse (to give the artery's grandiose official title) is still a must for lovers of art deco. Engineer Louis Risse designed the boulevard in 1892, modelling it on Paris's Champs-Elysées, and it opened to traffic in 1909. Following the arrival of a new subway line nearly a decade later, rapid development along the Concourse began in the deco style so popular in the 1920s and '30s.

Starting at 161st Street and heading south, look for the permanent street plaques that make up the **Bronx Walk of Fame**, honouring famous Bronxites from Stanley Kubrick and Tony Orlando to Colin Powell and hip hop 'godfather' Afrika Bambaataa. Heading north, the buildings date mostly from the 1920s to the early '40s, and constitute the country's largest concentration of art deco housing outside Miami Beach. Erected in 1937 at the corner of 161st Street, **888 Grand Concourse** has a large concave entrance of gilded mosaic and is topped by a curvy metallic marquee. Inside, the mirrored lobby's central fountain and sunburst-patterned floor could rival those of any hotel on Miami's Ocean Drive. On the south side of **Joyce Kilmer Park**, at 161st Street, is the elegant white-marble Lorelei Fountain, built in 1893 in Germany in homage to Heinrich Heine, who wrote the poem entitled 'Lorelei'. This was intended as the original entrance to the Concourse before it was extended south. The grandest building on the Concourse is the landmark **Andrew Freedman Home** (no.1125, between McClellan & E 165th Street), a 1924 French-inspired limestone palazzo between McClennan and 166th Streets. Freedman, a millionaire subway contractor, left the bulk of his $7 million fortune with instructions to build a poorhouse for the rich – that is, those who had lost their fortunes and were suffering an impecunious old age. In 2012, it was reborn as a 1920s-inspired B&B (1-718 588 8200, www.andrewfreedman complex.com), part of a local hospitality-training scheme, and a venue for arts events and exhibitions. The Family Preservation Center (FPC), a community-based social service agency, occupies the lower level. Across the street, the **Bronx Museum of the Arts**, established in 1971 in a former synagogue, stages socially conscious, contemporary exhibitions.

A few blocks north, at **1150 Grand Concourse**, at McClellan Place, is a 1937

Bronx Zoo.

art deco apartment block commonly referred to as the 'Fish Building' because of the colourful marine-themed mosaic flanking its doors; pause inside the restored lobby for a glimpse of its two large murals depicting pastoral scenes. Near the intersection of Fordham Road, keep an eye out for the Italian rococo exterior of the **Paradise Theater** (2403 Grand Concourse, at 187th Street). Once the largest cinema in the city, it's now occupied by a religious organisation. Just north is the ten-storey **Emigrant Savings Bank**, at 2526 Grand Concourse, worth ducking into for a glimpse of five striking murals by the artist Angelo Manganti, depicting scenes of the Bronx's past.

Further north to Kingsbridge Road lies the **Edgar Allan Poe Cottage**, a small wooden farmhouse where the writer lived from 1846 to 1849. It was moved to the Grand Concourse from its original spot on Fordham Road in 1913.

Sights & Museums

FREE ★ Bronx Museum of the Arts
1040 Grand Concourse, at 165th Street (1-718 681 6000, www.bronxmuseum.org). Subway B, D to 167th Street; 4 to 161st Street-Yankee Stadium. **Open** 11am-6pm Thur, Sat, Sun; 11am-8pm Fri. **Admission** free.
Featuring more than 1,000 works, this multicultural art museum shines a spotlight on 20th- and 21st-century artists who are either Bronx-based or of African, Asian or Latino ancestry.

Edgar Allan Poe Cottage
2640 Grand Concourse, at Kingsbridge Road (1-718 881 8900, www.bronxhistoricalsociety.org/ poecottage). Subway B, D, 4 to Kingsbridge Road. **Open** 10am-3pm Thur, Fri; 10am-4pm Sat; 1-5pm Sun. **Admission** $5; $3 reductions.
Pay homage to Poe in the house where he spent the last three years of his life and wrote such literary marvels as *Annabel Lee* and *The Bells*. After a major renovation, the cottage has been restored with period furnishings, including the author's rocking chair, and a new visitors' centre complete with a sloping shingle roof designed to resemble the wings of the bird from Poe's narrative poem *The Raven*.

BELMONT & BRONX PARK

Subway B, D, 4 to Fordham Road, then Bx12 bus to Arthur Avenue.

Settled in the late 19th century by Italian immigrants hired to landscape nearby Bronx Zoo, close-knit **Belmont** is centred on Arthur Avenue, lined with delis, bakeries, restaurants and stores selling T-shirts proclaiming the locale to be New York's 'real Little Italy'. Still celebrating Mass in Italian, neoclassical **Our Lady of Mt Carmel Church** (627 E 187th Street, at Hughes Avenue, 1-718 295 3770) has been serving the community for more than a century. Aspects of Italian-American history and culture are highlighted in the modest, changing exhibits at the **Enrico Fermi Cultural Center** (in the Belmont Branch

Library, 610 E 186th Street, between Arthur & Hughes Avenues, 1-718 933 6410, closed Sun).

Food, however, is the main reason to visit. **Arthur Avenue Retail Market** (2344 Arthur Avenue, between Crescent Avenue & E 186th Street) is a covered market built in the 1940s when Mayor Fiorello La Guardia campaigned to get the pushcarts off the street. Inside, you'll find **Mike's Deli**, where you can order enormous sandwiches bursting with Italian cold cuts. For a full meal, try old-school red-sauce joints such as **Mario's**, featured in several *Sopranos* episodes and Mario Puzo's novel *The Godfather*, or bare-bones canteen **Dominick's**.

Belmont is within easy walking distance of **Bronx Park**, home to two of the borough's most celebrated attractions. Make your way east along 187th Street, then south along Southern Boulevard, and you'll come to the **Bronx Zoo**. Opened in 1899 by Theodore Roosevelt, at 265 acres it's the largest urban zoo in the US. A 15-minute walk north of the zoo – and still in Bronx Park – brings you to the serene 250 acres of the **New York Botanical Garden**, which offers respite from cars and concrete in the form of 50 different gardens.

Sights & Museums

Bronx Zoo/Wildlife Conservation Society

Bronx River Parkway, at Fordham Road (1-718 367 1010, www.bronxzoo.com). Subway 2, 5 to E Tremont/W Farms Square, then walk to the zoo's Asia entrance; or Metro-North (Harlem Line local) from Grand Central Terminal to Fordham, then take the Bx9 bus to 183rd Street & Southern Boulevard. **Open** *Apr-Oct* 10am-5pm Mon-Fri; 10am-5.30pm Sat, Sun. *Nov-Mar* 10am-4.30pm daily. **Admission** $20; $13-$18 reductions; pay what you wish Wed. Some rides & exhibitions cost extra.

The Bronx Zoo shuns cages in favour of indoor and outdoor environments that mimic natural habitats. More than 60,000 creatures, from more than 600 species, live here. Home for monkeys, leopards and tapirs is inside the lush, steamy Jungle World, a recreation of an Asian rainforest inside a 37,000sq ft building, while lions, giraffes, zebras and other animals roam the African Plains. The popular Congo Gorilla Forest has turned 6.5 acres into a dramatic central African rainforest habitat. A glass-enclosed tunnel winds through the forest, allowing visitors to get close to the dozens of primate families in residence, including majestic western lowland gorillas. Tiger Mountain is populated by Siberian tigers, while the Himalayan Highlands features snow leopards and red pandas.
▶ *For other zoos, see p175, p213 and p236.*

★ New York Botanical Garden

Bronx River Parkway, at Fordham Road (1-718 817 8700, www.nybg.org). Subway B, D, 4 to Bedford Park Boulevard, then Bx26 bus to the garden's Mosholu Gate; or Metro-North (Harlem Line local) from Grand Central Terminal to Botanical Garden. **Open** *Jan, Feb* 10am-5pm Tue-Sun. *Mar-Dec* 10am-6pm Tue-Sun. **Admission** $20-$25; $8-$22 reductions. *Grounds only* $13; $3-$6 reductions; grounds free Wed, 9-10am Sat.

The serene 250 acres comprise 50 gardens and plant collections, including the Rockefeller Rose Garden, the Everett Children's Adventure Garden and the last 50 original acres of a forest that once covered the whole city area. In spring, clusters of lilac, cherry, magnolia and crab apple trees burst into bloom; in autumn you'll see vivid foliage in the oak and maple groves. The Azalea Garden features around 3,000 vivid azaleas and rhododendrons. The Enid A Haupt Conservatory – the nation's largest greenhouse, built in 1902 – contains the World of Plants, a series of environmental galleries that take you on an eco-tour through tropical rainforests, deserts and a palm tree oasis.

Restaurants & Cafés

Dominick's

2335 Arthur Avenue, between Crescent Avenue & E 186th Street (1-718 733 2807). Subway B, D, 4 to Fordham Road, then Bx12 bus to Arthur Avenue. **Open** noon-10pm Mon, Wed, Thur, Sat;

New York Botanical Garden.

Arthur Avenue retail market
See p245.

noon-11pm Fri; 1-9pm Sun. **Main courses** $15-$42. **No credit cards**. Italian
At Charlie DiPaolo's pinewood dining room – one of the most popular on Arthur Avenue – neighbourhood folks, out-of-towners and tracksuited wiseguys feast at long, crowded tables on massive platters of veal *parmigiana*, steaming bowls of mussels marinara and linguine with white clam sauce. There's no written menu, but you can trust your waiter's advice.

Mario's
2342 Arthur Avenue, between Crescent Avenue & E 186th Street (1-718 584 1188, www.marios restarthurave.com). Subway B, D, 4 to Fordham Road, then Bx12 bus to Arthur Avenue. **Open** noon-9pm Tue-Thur, Sun; noon-10pm Fri, Sat. **Main courses** $13.75-$35. Italian
The Migliucci family has stayed in business since 1919 by pleasing the customer; if you don't see what you want on the menu, feel free to ask for embellishments or modifications to the Neapolitan-inspired cuisine. Do as the regulars do and order the signature gnocchi, which arrive perfectly light and plump with a deliciously savoury and tangy sauce. For something more hearty, try the *saltimbocca alla romana* (veal braised in Marsala wine and served over spinach sautéed with prosciutto), or the generous lobster-tail *oreganata*, accompanied by a baked clam.

★ Mike's Deli
Arthur Avenue Retail Market, 2344 Arthur Avenue, between Crescent Avenue & E 186th Street (1-718 295 5033, www.arthuravenue.com). Subway B, D, 4 to Fordham Road, then Bx12 bus to Arthur Avenue. **Open** 7am-6pm Mon-Wed; 7am-9pm Thur-Sat; 10am-6pm Sun. **Sandwiches** $6.50-$13. Café/deli

This venerable delicatessen, butcher and café may leave you paralysed with indecision: the glossy menu lists more than 50 sandwiches, plus platters, pastas, soups, salads, stromboli (a kind of cheese turnover) and sides. Try the Yankee Stadium Big Boy hero sandwich, filled with prosciutto, soppressata, mozzarella, capicola, mortadella, peppers and lettuce.

Bars

★ Bronx Beer Hall
2344 Arthur Avenue, between Crescent Avenue & E 186th Street (1-347 396 0555, www.the bronxbeerhall.com). **Open** 11am-3am Mon-Sat; 11am-9pm Sun.
Surrounded by the cigar makers and meat and cheese counters of the septuagenarian Arthur Avenue Market, patrons can sit at BBH's rustic wooden bar and imbibe one of five New York State choices on draft – there's a particular emphasis on the borough's own Jonas Bronck's Beer Co. Try the brewery's New York Chocolate Egg Cream Stout, a bi-borough creation made with Brooklyn's Fox's U-bet chocolate syrup, or another local favourite, City Island Beer Company's balanced pale ale. Mike's Deli supplies the grub, like cheese boards and sausages served with bread and sides such as hot peppers.

RIVERDALE & VAN CORTLANDT PARK
Subway D to Norwood-205th Street; 1 to 242nd Street-Van Cortlandt Park.

Riverdale, along the north-west coast of the Bronx, reflects the borough's suburban past; its huge homes perch on narrow, winding streets that meander towards the Hudson river. The only one you can actually visit is **Wave Hill**, an 1843 stone mansion set on a former private estate that has beautiful gardens and a gallery. In the nearby 1,146-acre **Van Cortlandt Park** (entrance on Broadway, at 242nd Street), you can hike through a 100-year-old forest, play golf on the nation's first municipal course or ride horses hired from stables set within the park.

The oldest building in the Bronx is **Van Cortlandt House Museum**, a 1749 Georgian building that was commandeered by both sides during the Revolutionary War. Abutting the park is **Woodlawn Cemetery**, the resting place for such notable souls as Herman Melville, Duke Ellington, Miles Davis, FW Woolworth and Fiorello La Guardia. To help you to pay your respects, maps are available at the entrance at Webster Avenue and E 233rd Street. About five blocks south on Bainbridge Avenue, history buffs will also enjoy the **Museum of Bronx History**, set in a 1758 stone farmhouse.

Sights & Museums

Museum of Bronx History
Valentine-Varian House, 3266 Bainbridge Avenue, between Van Cortlandt Avenue East & 208th Street (1-718 881 8900, www.bronxhistoricalsociety.org/ museumofbronxhistory.html). Subway D to Norwood-205th Street. **Open** 10am-4pm Sat; 1-5pm Sun. **Admission** $5; $3 reductions.
Operated by the Bronx County Historical Society, the museum displays its collection of documents and photos in the Valentine-Varian House, a Federal-style fieldstone residence built in 1758.
▶ *The society also offers historical tours of the Bronx neighbourhoods.*

Van Cortlandt House Museum
Van Cortlandt Park, entrance on Broadway, at 246th Street (1-718 543 3344, www.vchm.org). Subway 1 to 242nd Street-Van Cortlandt Park. **Open** 10am-4pm Tue-Fri; 11am-4pm Sat, Sun (hrs may vary; call before visiting). **Admission** $5; $3 reductions; free under-12s; pay what you wish Wed.
A one-time wheat plantation that has since been turned into a colonial museum, Van Cortlandt House

was alternately used as headquarters by George Washington and British General Sir William Howe during the Revolutionary War.

★ Wave Hill
W 249th Street, at Independence Avenue (1-718 549 3200, www.wavehill.org). Metro-North (Hudson Line local) from Grand Central Terminal to Riverdale. **Open** *Mid Mar-Oct* 9am-5.30pm Tue-Sun. *Nov-mid Mar* 9am-4.30pm Tue-Sun. **Admission** $8; $2-$4 reductions; free under-6s. Free Tue, 9am-noon Sat.
Laze around in 28 lush acres overlooking the Hudson River at Wave Hill, the setting of a Georgian Revival house that was home at various times to Mark Twain, Teddy Roosevelt and conductor Arturo Toscanini. Now open to the public, the grounds contain exquisite cultivated gardens and woodlands commanding excellent views of the river. The small on-site gallery hosts intriguing contemporary art shows inspired by nature, and the property is also a venue for concerts and other events.

PELHAM BAY PARK
Subway 6 to Pelham Bay Park.

Pelham Bay Park, in the borough's north-eastern corner, is NYC's largest park. Take a car or a bike if you want to explore the 2,765 acres; pick up a map at the Ranger Nature Center, near the entrance on Bruckner Boulevard at Wilkinson Avenue. The **Bartow-Pell Mansion Museum**, in the park's south-eastern quarter, overlooks Long Island Sound. The park's 13 miles of coastline skirt the Hutchinson river to the west and the Long Island Sound and Eastchester Bay to the east. In summer, locals hit sandy **Orchard Beach**; set up in the 1930s, this 'Riviera of New York' is that rare beast – a Robert Moses creation not universally lamented.

Sights & Museums

Bartow-Pell Mansion Museum
895 Shore Road North, at Pelham Bay Park (1-718 885 1461, www.bartowpellmansionmuseum.org). Subway 6 to Pelham Bay Park, then Bee-Line bus 45 (ask driver to stop at Bartow-Pell Mansion). **Open** noon-4pm Wed, Sat, Sun. **Admission** $5; $3 reductions; free under-6s.
The origins of this impressive property, which has been a museum since 1946, date from 1654, when Thomas Pell bought the land from the Siwonay Indians. It was Robert Bartow, publisher and Pell descendant, who added the 1842 Greek Revival stone mansion, which faces a reflecting pool ringed by gardens.
▶ *Just east of Pelham Bay Park lies City Island (see p326), a rustic fishing village with a New England feel.*

IN THE KNOW HIP HOP HISTORY

DJ Kool Herc's old digs at 1520 Sedgwick Avenue in the West Bronx is the acknowledged birthplace of hip hop, but the area in and around the Bronx River Houses (174th Street, between Bronx River & Harrod Avenue) is where Afrika Bambaataa and his Universal Zulu Nation developed it into a phenomenon.

EXPLORE

Staten Island

With a largely suburban vibe, abundant parkland and beaches, New York's third largest – but least-populated – borough feels removed from the rest of the city. And, physically, it is. To visitors, Staten Island is best known for its ferry – the locals' sole public-transport link with Manhattan happens to pass by Lady Liberty. If you decide to embark on this free mini cruise, it's worth taking time to stroll along the Esplanade or venture further to explore historic structures and sprawling green spaces.

The island took a battering from 2012's Hurricane Sandy, suffering more than half of the city's total fatalities, but $600,000 in state funds were allocated towards rebuilding homes in early 2015. Combined with plans for a massive retail complex near the ferry terminal, anchored by the world's tallest Ferris wheel, SI's fortunes seem to be on the rise.

Fort Wadsworth.

Don't Miss

1 Alice Austen House Exquisite photographs and views (p248).

2 Fort Wadsworth An impressive panorama from one of the nation's oldest military sites (p248).

3 Greenbelt Go wild in suburban SI (p248).

4 Snug Harbor Quirky collections and gardens in a picturesque old sailors' home (p248).

5 Killmeyer's Old Bavaria Inn Raise a stein at this German hold-out (p249).

Staten Island became one of the five boroughs in 1898, but remained a backwater until 1964, when the Verrazano-Narrows Bridge joined the island to Bay Ridge in Brooklyn. Many say that's when small-town Staten Island truly vanished.

Still, many quaint aspects remain – not least the free **Staten Island Ferry** (1-718 727 2508, www.nyc.gov/dot), which runs between the Financial District's Whitehall Terminal (4 South Street, at Whitehall Street) and the island's St George Terminal, where you can catch the buses noted in this chapter. The crossing takes 25 minutes. When you alight, head right along the **Esplanade**, with its stirring views of lower Manhattan across the harbour, to pay your respects at *Postcards*, a memorial to the 274 Staten Islanders lost on 9/11. The fibreglass wings of the sculpture frame the spot where the Twin Towers used to stand.

Also near the terminal is the small **Staten Island Museum** (75 Stuyvesant Place, at Wall Street, 1-718 727 1135, www.statenisland museum.org). The institution is expanding with a second location in an august Greek Revival building on the campus of the Snug Harbor Cultural Center. In September 2015, the new museum will open with four exhibitions linked to Staten Island's history.

Sights & Museums

Alice Austen House
2 Hylan Boulevard, between Bay & Edgewater Streets (1-718 816 4506, www.aliceausten.org). S51 bus to Hylan Boulevard. **Open** *Mar-Dec* 11am-5pm Tue-Sun. Closed Jan, Feb. **Admission** suggested donation $3.
The beautiful photographs of Alice Austen (1866-1952) are the highlight at this 17th-century cottage – it contains 3,000 of her glass negative images. The restored house and grounds often host concerts and events, and offer breathtaking harbour views.

Conference House (Billopp House)
7455 Hylan Boulevard, at Satterlee Street (1-718 984 6046, www.conferencehouse.org). S78 bus to Craig Avenue & Hylan Boulevard. **Open** *Apr-mid Dec* 1-4pm Fri-Sun. Closed Jan-Mar. **Admission** $4; reductions free-$3.
In 1776, Britain's Lord Howe parlayed with John Adams and Benjamin Franklin in this 17th-century house, trying to forestall the American Revolution. Tours point out 18th-century furnishings, decor and daily objects. The lovely grounds command a terrific view over Raritan Bay, and provide a picturesque setting for free concerts and events.

FREE Fort Wadsworth
210 New York Avenue, on the east end of Bay Street (1-718 354 4500, www.nyharborparks.org). S51 bus to Fort Wadsworth. **Open** dawn-dusk daily. **Admission** free.

Explore the fortifications that guarded NYC for almost 200 years. The site was occupied by a blockhouse as far back as the 17th century.

FREE Greenbelt
Greenbelt Nature Center *700 Rockland Avenue, at Brielle Avenue (1-718 351 3450, www.sigreenbelt.org). S61 bus to Forest Hill Road/Rockland Avenue.* **Open** *Apr-Oct* 10am-5pm Tue-Sun. *Nov-Mar* 11am-5pm Wed-Sun. **Admission** free.
High Rock Park *200 Nevada Avenue, at Rockland Avenue. S62 bus to Manor Road, then S54 bus to Nevada Avenue.* **Open** dawn-dusk daily.
With 2,800 acres of open space, the Greenbelt offers 35 miles of trails through parks and woodland. Start your expedition at the Nature Center, where you can pick up a copy of the trail map (also on the website). A mile away, at the 90-acre High Rock Park, visitors can hike the mile-long Swamp Trail, climb Todt Hill or walk through forests, meadows and wetlands.

Jacques Marchais Museum of Tibetan Art
338 Lighthouse Avenue, off Richmond Road (1-718 987 3500, www.tibetanmuseum.org). S74 bus to Lighthouse Avenue. **Open** *Apr-Dec* 1-5pm Wed-Sun. *Feb, Mar* 1-5pm Fri-Sun. Closed Jan. **Admission** $6; $4 reductions; free under-6s.
This tiny museum contains a formidable Buddhist altar, tranquil meditation gardens and an extensive collection of Tibetan art and artefacts.

★ Snug Harbor Cultural Center & Botanical Garden
1000 Richmond Terrace, between Snug Harbor Road & Tysen Avenue (1-718 448 2500, www.snug-harbor.org). S40 bus to Richmond Terrace/Sailors SH Gate. **Open** *Grounds* dawn-dusk daily.
Stately Greek Revival structures form the nucleus of this former sailors' retirement home. Dating from 1833, the centre has been restored and converted into an arts complex that includes one of the city's oldest concert halls. In addition to the listings below, the Staten Island Children's Museum (1-718 273 2060, www.statenislandkids.org, closed Mon) and Art Lab (1-718 447 8667, www.artlabsi.com), a non-profit art school, are also based here.

IN THE KNOW
THE STATEN ISLAND RAILWAY

Although it isn't connected to any of the city's other subway lines, the Staten Island Railway (SIR) does accept the MetroCard. The railway has one line, which runs from St George to Tottenville on the southern tip of the island.

WHEEL OF FORTUNE

The most overlooked borough gets a destination attraction of its own.

New York City is building a brand-new landmark, but it's not a skyscraper or a monumental statue. At press time, construction was due to start on the New York Wheel on Staten Island's North Shore. This isn't your average carnival Ferris wheel. Once complete in 2017, it will tower at an impressive 630 feet – almost 200 feet higher than the London Eye, which was the inspiration for the project. The wheel will be able to carry up to 1,440 passengers in its 36 pod-like capsules for each 38-minute rotation, offering unobstructed views of New York Harbor, lower Manhattan, the Statue of Liberty and the Verrazano-Narrows Bridge.

'We're expecting to target and achieve about four million visitors per year,' says Richard A Marin, New York Wheel CEO and president, citing the two million visitors who already ride the Staten Island Ferry annually – the wheel will be in walking distance from the St George Ferry Terminal. Currently, many of those tourists don't explore the island, though they have to disembark before heading back to Manhattan. Further boosting the borough's attractions is NYC's first outlet mall. Expected to open in 2016, Empire Outlets (www.empireoutletsnyc.com) will feature around 100 high-end retailers, including discount department store Nordstrom Rack, plus restaurants and a 190-room hotel.

Newhouse Center for Contemporary Art
1-718 425 3524, www.snug-harbor.org/newhouse. **Open** 10am-5pm Tue-Sun. **Admission** $5; $4 reductions; free under-12s. **No credit cards.**
Staten Island's premier venue for contemporary art holds several annual exhibitions from leading international sculptors, painters and mixed-media artists.
Noble Maritime Collection *1-718 447 6490, www.noblemaritime.org.* **Open** 1-5pm Thur-Sun. **Admission** Pay what you wish.
This museum is dedicated to the artist-seaman John A Noble, who had a 'floating studio' moored in the Kill van Kull, between Staten Island and New Jersey. As well as his maritime-themed paintings, Noble's houseboat is on display, restored to its appearance when the artist was featured in *National Geographic* magazine in 1954. Upstairs is a recreated dormitory room of the former Sailors' Snug Harbor, circa 1900.
Staten Island Botanical Garden *1-718 448 2500, www.snug-harbor.org.* **Open** 10am-5pm Tue-Sun. **Admission** *Chinese Scholar's Garden* $5; $4 reductions; free under-12s. *Grounds & other gardens* free.
Stroll through more than 13 themed gardens, including the traditional Chinese Scholar's Garden, with its pavilions, meandering paths and delicate footbridges, and the medieval-style children's Secret Garden, complete with a 38ft-high castle and a maze.

Restaurants & Cafés

Beso
11 Schuyler Street, between Richmond Terrace & Stuyvesant Place (1-718 816 8162, www.beso nyc.com). **Open** 11.30am-11pm Mon-Thur; 11.30am-midnight Fri, Sat; noon-10pm Sun. **Main courses** $21-$26. **Spanish**

Although Beso is billed as a Spanish tapas bar, the menu at this little spot right by the ferry terminal goes far beyond Iberia (by way of Cuba, Mexico and Puerto Rico, for starters). Grab a fruity-sweet glass of tequila-spiked sangria and go straight for the Prince Edward Island mussels sautéed with garlic and brandy; or the Bistec Cubano – skirt steak marinated in sherry with herbs and garlic and served with ginger-mojito sauce, fried plantains and Cuban salad.

Trattoria Romana
1476 Hylan Boulevard, at Benton Avenue (1-718 980 3113, www.trattoriaromanasi.com). Staten Island Railway to Old Town. **Open** noon-10pm Mon-Thur; noon-11.30pm Fri, Sat; 1-9.30pm Sun. **Main courses** $17-$38. **Italian**
This casually elegant eaterie owes its popularity to the constant presence of chef-owner Vittorio Asoli as well as to the wood-burning brick oven that cooks everything from pizza to portobellos. The *saltimbocca alla romana* is a classic done right – tender veal scaloppine topped with salty prosciutto and accented with butter and sage.

Bars

Killmeyer's Old Bavaria Inn
4254 Arthur Kill Road, at Sharrotts Road (1-718 984 1202, www.killmeyers.com). S74 bus to Arthur Kill Road/Sharrotts Road. **Open** 11am-midnight Mon-Thur; 11am-2am Fri, Sat; noon-midnight Sun.
Semi-industrial Arthur Kill Road is home to this Bavarian beer garden. Sit outside and enjoy any of nearly 200 beers, plus sauerbraten, spicy goulash and potato pancakes.

EXPLORE

RADIO CITY
MUSIC HALL
Music Hall RADIO C
RON WHITE OCTOBER 3 RON WHITE

Arts & Entertainment

Children

The crowded and fast-paced metropolis may not seem like the world's most child-friendly place at first glance, but its 21st-century baby boom has given rise to myriad cultural, culinary and just plain fun offerings for families. Such icons as the Statue of Liberty and the American Museum of Natural History are not to be missed, but they are just the beginning. Among the most frequented corners of the city are its green spaces and playgrounds – seek one out when you're in need of a breather from the city's constant buzz. And for the latest child-centric events, visit www.timeout.com/newyorkkids.

SIGHTSEEING & ENTERTAINMENT

Animals & nature

Bronx Zoo
For listings, see p252.
Step aboard the Wild Asia Monorail (open May-Oct, admission $5), which tours 38 acres of exhibits housing flamingos, zebras, poison dart frogs, red pandas and more. Madagascar! is a permanent home to exotic animals from the lush island nation off the eastern coast of Africa. Among its residents are lemurs, giant crocodiles, geckos, radiated tortoises and, coolest (and grossest) of all, hissing cockroaches.
▶ *There are also zoos in Central Park (see p175), Brooklyn (see p213) and Queens (see p236).*

New York Aquarium
602 Surf Avenue, at West 8th Street, Coney Island, Brooklyn (1-718 265 3474, www.nyaquarium. com). Subway D, N, Q to Coney Island-Stillwell Avenue; F, Q to W 8th Street-NY Aquarium. **Open** *Sept-May* 10am-4.30pm daily. *June-Aug* 10am-6pm daily. **Admission** $12; free under-3s. Pay what you wish after 3pm Fri.
Get an up-close look at aquatic animals of all shapes and sizes, from Technicolor tropical fish and coral to black-footed penguins and pacific walrus. In the Conservation Hall, kids can stick their hands in a touch tank to hold small marine creatures, and see penguin, otter and walrus feedings throughout the day. At time of writing, the aquarium was still partially under construction due to damage caused by Hurricane Sandy, but 2016 should see the opening of its much-anticipated exhibit 'Ocean Wonders: Sharks!', which will be home to 25 species of sharks and rays as well as other marine wildlife.

Museums

Blasting the stuffy cliché, many of Manhattan's most venerable institutions are extremely child-friendly. The **DiMenna Children's History Museum** inside the **New-York Historical Society** (*see p171*) engages kids with New York's past by looking at the childhoods of various residents, some famous (Alexander Hamilton), others anonymous (child newspaper sellers in the early 20th century). For years, workshops for kids of all ages have been offered at many top institutions, including the **Museum of Modern Art** (*see p157*), the **Metropolitan Museum of Art** (*see p185*), the **Rubin Museum** (*see p128*) and the **Museum of Arts and Design** (*see p171*); check their websites for schedules. The Met, with its mummies and Temple of Dendur, a real ancient Egyptian temple, is a particular hit with children, as long as you don't try to tackle too much of the massive collection.

Even very young kids love exploring the **American Museum of Natural History** (*see p170*). The Fossil Halls are home to the museum's huge, beloved dinosaurs – most reconstructed from actual fossils – and the myriad wildlife dioramas are a fascinating (and astonishingly lifelike) peek at the world's fauna. Firefighter wannabes will enjoy the **New York City Fire Museum** (*see p68*), housed in a historic fire station; kids can check out uniforms and equipment from the late 18th century to the present, including a hand-pumped fire engine. The highlight at the aircraft carrier-turned-attraction **Intrepid Sea, Air & Space Museum** (*see p153*) is the Space Shuttle Pavilion, housing the *Enterprise*, an original prototype. With 30-plus interactive exhibits, the new **Museum of Mathematics (MoMath)** (*see p138*) will probably win round those who claim to hate the subject.

In the boroughs, the excellent core exhibition 'Behind the Screen' at the **Museum of the Moving Image** (*see p232*), outfitted with state-of-the-art movie-making stations, makes it worth the trek to Astoria, Queens. Children and adults will be fascinated by the amazing scale-model Panorama of the City of New York at the **Queens Museum** (*see p237*), while youngsters can pretend to drive a real bus and board vintage subway cars at Brooklyn's **New York Transit Museum** (*see p208*).

Brooklyn Children's Museum

145 Brooklyn Avenue, at St Marks Avenue, Crown Heights, Brooklyn (1-718 735 4400, www.brooklynkids.org). Subway A, C to Nostrand Avenue; C to Kingston-Throop Avenues; 3 to Kingston Avenue. **Open** 10am-5pm Tue-Sun; 10am-7pm 3rd Thur of each mth. **Admission** $9; free under-1s, seniors; free 3-5pm Thur (4-7pm 3rd Thur of each month). **Map** p404 V11.
The city's oldest museum for kids is also one of its best after a major renovation in 2008. The star

attraction, 'World Brooklyn', is an interactive maze of small mom-and-pop shops based on real-world Brooklyn businesses. 'Neighborhood Nature' puts the spotlight on the borough's diverse ecosystems with a collection of pond critters in terrariums and a tide-pool touch tank. Under-fives will delight in 'Totally Tots', a sun-drenched play space with a water station, a sand zone, and a special hub for babies aged 18 months and under.

★ Children's Museum of Manhattan

212 W 83rd Street, between Amsterdam Avenue & Broadway, Upper West Side (1-212 721 1234, www.cmom.org). Subway B, C to 81st Street-Museum of Natural History; 1 to 86th Street. **Open** 10am-5pm Tue-Fri, Sun; 10am-7pm Sat. **Admission** $11; $7 reductions; free under-1s. **Map** p399 C19.
An essential stop on every Upper West Side child's social agenda, this museum customises its themed exhibits by age group. 'PlayWorks', an imaginative play environment, is for babies and toddlers up to four; 'Adventures with Dora and Diego', a bilingual playspace that transports visitors to some of the Nickelodeon TV show's settings, is for ages two to six. 'EatSleepPlay: Building Health Every Day', for all ages, is an interactive exhibit that gives families strategies for taking up a more healthy lifestyle.

Children's Museum of the Arts

103 Charlton Street, between Greenwich & Hudson Streets, Soho (1-212 274 0986, www.cmany.org). Subway A, B, C, D, E, F, M to W 4th Street; C, E to Spring Street; 1 to Houston Street. **Open** noon-5pm Mon, Wed; noon-6pm Thur, Fri; 10am-5pm Sat, Sun. **Admission** $11; free under-1s; pay what you wish 4-6pm Thur. **Map** p397 E30.

ARTS & ENTERTAINMENT

New York Aquarium.

Children's Museum of the Arts.
See p253.

This creativity-inspiring mainstay focuses on teaching, creating, collecting and exhibiting kids' artwork. Engaging temporary exhibits in the 10,000sq ft space are juxtaposed with works from the museum's collection of more than 2,000 pieces of children's art. For kids, the most exciting aspects of the museum are its hands-on art workshops, clay lab and interactive media lab, plus the ball pit for letting off steam.

★ New York Hall of Science

47-01 111th Street, at 47th Avenue, Flushing Meadows Corona Park, Queens (1-718 699 0005, www.nysci.org). Subway 7 to 111th Street. **Open** *Sept-Mar* 9.30am-5pm Tue-Fri; 10am-6pm Sat, Sun. *Apr-Aug* 9.30am-5pm Mon-Fri; 10am-6pm Sat, Sun. **Admission** $15; $12 reductions. *Sept-June* free 2-5pm Fri; 10-11am Sun. *Science playground* (open Mar-Nov) extra $5. *Rocket Park Mini Golf* extra $6; $5 reductions.

Housed in a 1964 World's Fair pavilion and flanked by rockets from the US space programme, this museum has always been worth a trek for its discovery-based interactive displays. Kids can get their hands on microscopes in the 'Hidden Kingdoms' exhibit, or try everything from block printing to soap making as part of the Little Makers series. From March

through November, the 30,000sq ft outdoor Science Playground teaches children the principles of balance, gravity and energy, while a mini-golf course in Rocket Park lets families play outdoors surrounded by refurbished rockets that date from the 1960s space race.

★ FREE Sony Wonder Technology Lab

Sony Plaza, 56th Street & Madison Avenue, Midtown East (1-212 833 8100, www.sony wondertechlab.com). Subway E, M to Fifth Avenue-53rd Street; N, Q, R to Lexington Avenue-59th Street; 4, 5, 6 to 59th Street. **Open** 9.30am-5.30pm Tue-Sat. **Admission** free (advance reservations required). **Map** p399 E22.

Techies and video-game aficionados of all ages will enjoy Sony's cutting-edge, mind-expanding exhibits – and, even better, admission is free (you just need to reserve your slot at least seven days ahead). 'Dance Motion Capture' lets youngsters see their moves performed by their favourite Sony animated characters in real time. Kids can learn how robots sense and behave in the 'Robot Zone' or perform a mock open-heart operation in 'Virtual Surgery'. SWTL offers weekly children's screenings and family workshops featuring science and technology, too.

Performing arts

Broadway is packed with excellent, if pricey, family fare, from long-runners like *The Lion King* and *Wicked* to London import *Matilda*, based on the book by Roald Dahl. *The Nutcracker* (*see p305* **David H Koch Theater**) is an annual Christmas family tradition. In summer, **Madison Square Park** (*see p136*) hosts regular children's concerts, and warm-weather events such as the **River to River Festival** (*see p35*) and **SummerStage** (*see p33*) always include music and theatre tailored to little ones.

Carnegie Hall Family Concerts

For listings, see p396. **Tickets** $10-$22.
Even children who solemnly profess to hate classical music are usually impressed by a visit to Carnegie Hall. The Family Concert series builds on that, featuring first-rate classical, world music and jazz performers, plus a pre-concert workshop an hour before the show. Recommended for ages five to 12.

Just Kidding at Symphony Space

For listings, see p302. **Shows** *Oct-Apr* Sat (times vary). **Tickets** $9-$26.
Tell your munchkins to forgo their weekly dose of cartoons. In Manhattan, children can spend most Saturday mornings (and select Sunday mornings) grooving to live concerts or watching theatre, dance or a puppet show. Symphony Space's Just Kidding series features both local and nationally recognised talent, from kid rockers and bluegrass bands to hip hop storytellers and NYC star Gustaver Yellowgold.

★ New Victory Theater
209 W 42nd Street, between Seventh & Eighth Avenues, Theater District (1-646 223 3010, www.newvictory.org). Subway N, Q, R, S, 1, 2, 3, 7 to 42nd Street-Times Square. **Box office** 11am-5pm Mon, Sun; noon-7pm Tue-Sat. **Tickets** $15-$43. **Map** p398 D24.
New York's only full-scale young people's theatre. Recent shows have included the joyous urban acrobatics of Quebecois circus troupe Flip Fabrique, and a concert for under-age rockers by Justin Roberts and the Not Ready for Naptime Players. Shows often sell out well in advance, so buy tickets well ahead.

Puppetworks
338 Sixth Avenue, at 4th Street, Park Slope, Brooklyn (1-718 965 3391, www.puppetworks.org). Subway F to Seventh Avenue. **Shows** 12.30pm, 2.30pm Sat, Sun. **Tickets** $10; $9 under-12s. **No credit cards. Map** p404 T11.

The Brooklyn company puts on musicals adapted from fairy tales and children's stories that feature a cast of marionettes operated by puppeteers (the voice and music track is pre-recorded). The company also demonstrates how the puppets work at the beginning of each performance.

★ TADA! Youth Theater
15 West 28th Street, between Broadway & Fifth Avenue, Flatiron District (1-212 252 1619, www.tadatheater.com). Subway N, R to 28th Street. **Shows** Jan-Feb, Apr-May, July. **Tickets** $20-$25; $10-$15 under-16s. **Map** p398 E26.
Offering everything from adaptations of the classics to enchanting new fairy tales for families, TADA! professionally produces original musicals performed by kids from eight to 18. The space regularly offers opportunities for visitors to learn a song and dance after the show. Best of all, the whole family can see a play for less than the price of a single Broadway ticket.

Vital Theatre Company
McGinn/Cazale Theatre, 4th floor, 2162 Broadway, at 76th Street, Upper West Side (1-212 579 0528, www.vitaltheatre.org). Subway 1 to 79th Street; 2, 3 to 72nd Street. **Shows** vary. **Tickets** $30-$40. **Map** p399 C19.
Founded in 1999, Vital has produced a series of original theatrical hits for kids, the biggest of which frequently return to the Upper West Side after going on tour. Among the most popular are family favourite *Pinkalicious*, about a girl who comes down with a case of 'pinkititis', and *Fancy Nancy*, which is often reprised in a Christmas show.

ARTS & ENTERTAINMENT

High Line. *See p256.*

PARKS

Most New Yorkers don't have their own backyard – instead, they run around and relax in parks. Spend an afternoon exploring quirky landmarks, going kayaking, riding on old-fashioned carousels and joining other activities within these beautiful green spaces.

Battery Park City Parks

Hudson River, between Chambers Street & Battery Place, Financial District (1-212 267 9700, www. bpcparks.org). Subway A, C, 1, 2, 3 to Chambers Street; 1 to Rector Street. **Open** 6am-1am daily. **Map** p396 D32.

Besides watching the boats along the Hudson, kids can explore Teardrop Park, a hidden urban oasis with an enormous slide, and Nelson A Rockefeller Park, with an open field for Frisbee and lazing, plus a playground with a unique pedal carousel and a charming duck pond. Don't miss Pier 25, just north of BPC: there's a playground, a mini-golf course and snack bar, an Astroturf area and a skate park.

Brooklyn Bridge Park

Riverside, from the Manhattan Bridge, Dumbo, to Atlantic Avenue, Brooklyn Heights (1-718 802 0603, www.brooklynbridgepark.org). Subway A, C to High Street; F to York Street; 2, 3 to Clark Street. **Open** 6am-1am (playgrounds dawn-dusk) daily. **Map** p404 S9.

Get a whole new view of the Brooklyn Bridge and the Statue of Liberty from a kayak on the East River. The Brooklyn Bridge Park Boathouse (Pier 2, 1-718 222 9939, www.bbpboathouse.org) offers free, 20-minute kayaking trips from June through August (see website for details). Show up and they'll outfit you with a life vest, give you a kayaking crash course and send you on your way. All paddling is done in a protected embayment under supervision of the boathouse staff. Single kayaks are available for adults and teens ages 14 and up with a parent or guardian present; younger kids can ride along with an adult in a double. The park also has a beach, sporting facilities, several playgrounds and an array of food vendors, including locally made Ample Hills Creamery ice-cream at Pier 5. But the jewel of the park is Jane's Carousel (Dock Street, at the East River, www.janescarousel.com; $2), which takes its name from Jane Walentas, who spent nearly 25 years lovingly restoring the 1922 spinner's 48 hand-painted horses, scenery panels and crests.

★ High Line

For listings, see p123.

The 1.45-mile-long elevated park features not only public art, colourful plants and amazing views of the Hudson River, but also offers free programming for families. In July and August, tykes up to age three will love Lawn Time, featuring readings by different storytellers each week. Wild Wednesday (ages four and above) offers nature-related crafts and activities, and Arty Hours lets kids explore their creativity through hands-on art projects. See www.thehigh-line.org for information. *Photo p255.*

★ Prospect Park

Prospect Park West to Flatbush Avenue, between Prospect Park Southwest & Ocean Avenue (1-718 965 8951, www.prospectpark.org). Subway B, Q, Franklin Ave S to Prospect Park; F, G to 15th Street-Prospect Park; 2, 3 to Grand Army Plaza. **Open** 5am-1am daily (hours for attractions vary). **Map** p404 U11-U13.

Trade urban exploration for an afternoon in what many consider the city's most beautiful park. A slew of activities is available: summer performances, horseback riding, boating and bike paths, among others. In addition to the Prospect Park Zoo, the park's Audubon Center offers live animal presentations, woodland tours and birdwatching walks. The carousel ($2 per ride) features 53 magnificent horses, a giraffe, a deer, a lion and two dragon-pulled chariots. Other essential family stops include the LeFrak Center at Lakeside for seasonal ice skating and the Lefferts Historic House, an 18th-century working garden and homestead stocked with traditional toys and games, which offers activities like butter churning and candle making.

RESTAURANTS & CAFÉS

★ Alice's Teacup

102 W 73rd Street, at Columbus Avenue, Upper West Side (1-212 799 6361, www. alicesteacup.com). Subway B, C to 72nd Street. **Open** 8am-8pm daily. **Main courses** $10-$14. **Map** p399 C20.

Adored by Alice aficionados, this magical spot offers much more than tea (though the three-tiered version, comprising an assortment of sandwiches, scones and desserts, truly is a treat). The brunch menu is fit for royalty, with Alice's Curious French Toast (drenched in fruit coulis, crème anglaise and syrup) and scones in scrumptious flavours like blueberry and pumpkin. And at a little shop in the front of the eaterie, you can outfit your fairy princess in training with a pair of bright, glittery wings.

Other locations 156 E 64th Street, at Lexington Avenue, Upper East Side (1-212 486 9200); 220 E 81st Street, between Second & Third Avenues, Upper East Side (1-212 734 4832).

Cowgirl

519 Hudson Street, at 10th Street, West Village (1-212 633 1133, www.cowgirlnyc.com). Subway 1 to Christopher Street-Sheridan Square. **Open** 11am-11pm Mon-Thur; 11am-midnight Fri; 10am-midnight Sat; 10am-11pm Sun. **Main courses** $12-$21; $6-$7 children's menu. **Map** p397 D28.

CENTRAL PARK SEVEN

An essential family guide to Manhattan's garden of delights.

1 BELVEDERE CASTLE
Little visitors can climb up to three viewing platforms at the classic fairy tale-like folly (mid-park at 79th Street) overlooking the Turtle Pond. Between 10am and 5pm daily, budding naturalists can borrow nature kits equipped with binoculars and field guides with which to explore the castle's dominion.

2 CAROUSEL
Central Park's classic merry-go-round (mid-park at 64th Street, open daily Apr-Oct, call 1-212 439 6900 for out-of-season hours; $3 per ride), was built in 1908. It's the fourth carousel on the site since 1871 (the first was operated by a mule or horse hidden under the floorboards). Found in a Coney Island warehouse, the current model belts out pop organ music for riders of its 57 steeds.

3 CENTRAL PARK ZOO
In the southern stretch of the park, the zoo (*see p175*) offers kids the magical opportunity to see exotic animals like penguins and snow leopards without leaving the city boundaries. Synchronise your visit with the sea lion and penguin feedings. The creation of a snow leopard habitat has added a breathtaking endangered animal to the zoo's menagerie. The Tisch Children's Zoo houses species that enjoy being petted – and fed – such as alpacas, sheep and goats.

4 CONSERVATORY WATER
From April through October, you can rent a remote-controlled vessel ($11/30mins, 1-917 522 0054) at this mecca for model-yacht racers near the 72nd Street and Fifth Avenue entrance ot the park. Kids can't resist climbing on the bronze rendering of Lewis Carroll's Alice, the Mad Hatter and the White Rabbit north of the pond, while the Hans Christian Andersen statue is a gathering point for free summer storytelling sessions (early June-late Sept 11am-noon Sat, www.hcastorycenter.org).

5 HECKSCHER PLAYGROUND
There are 21 playgrounds in Central park, but the Heckscher, in the south-west corner, is the largest, sprawling over more than an acre and a half. It has an up-to-date adventure area, a water feature and handy restrooms.

6 SWEDISH COTTAGE MARIONETTE THEATER
Tucked just inside the western boundary of the park at 81st Street is a curiously incongruous old wooden structure. Designed as a schoolhouse, the building was Sweden's entry in the 1876 Centennial Exposition in Philadelphia (it was moved to NYC a year later). Inside is one of the best-kept secrets in town: a tiny marionette theatre with regular shows. It's best to book tickets in advance (1-212 988 9093, www.cityparksfoundation.org).

7 TRUMP RINK & VICTORIAN GARDENS
Skating amid snowy trees at this popular rink (mid-park at 62nd Street, 1-212 439 6900, www.wollmanskatingrink.com; open late Oct-Mar) is a New York tradition. In summer, the site hosts Victorian Gardens (1-212 982 2229, www.victoriangardensnyc.com), a quaint amusement park for younger children. It's hardly white-knuckle stuff, but the revolving swing ride will satisfy little thrill-seekers.

ARTS & ENTERTAINMENT

Central Park Zoo.

This neighbourhood favourite is one of those rare spots that appeals to both adults and children. Parents can unwind with a pitcher of margaritas amid the charming 1950s-era ranch decor. The whimsical setting, along with a small old-time candy shop and plenty of crayons, means the whole crowd will remain buoyant while waiting for rib-sticking fare such as quesadillas, pulled-pork sandwiches and gooey mac and cheese. For dessert, share the super-rich Bark Brownie Sundae – dark chocolate brownie, vanilla ice cream, hot fudge sauce and whipped cream.
Other location Cowgirl Sea-Horse, 259 Front Street, at Dover Street, Financial District (1-212 608 7873, www.cowgirlseahorse.com).

Crema

111 W 17th Street, between Sixth & Seventh Avenues, Chelsea (1-212 691 4477, www.crema restaurante.com). Subway F, M, 1, 2, 3 to 14th Street; L to Sixth Avenue. **Open** noon-10.30pm Mon-Wed; noon-11pm Thur; noon-midnight Fri; 11.30am-midnight Sat; 11.30am-10pm Sun. **Main courses** $14-$28. **Map** p397 D27.
Among the many child-friendly items on the menu at Julieta Ballesteros's upscale Mexican restaurant are quesadillas filled with chihuahua cheese and shrimp, grilled-steak tacos and sides such as seasonal rice or *granielote* (corn kernels with cream). Tropical-flavoured lemonade, ice-cream and sorbet round out the à la carte offerings.

★ Ditch Plains

29 Bedford Street, at Downing Street, Greenwich Village (1-212 633 0202, www.ditch-plains.com).

Subway A, B, C, D, E, F, M to W 4th Street; 1 to Houston Street. **Open** 11am-2am daily. **Main courses** $8-$28; $5-$12 children's menu. **Map** p397 D29.
This New England-style fish shack, named after chef-owner Marc Murphy's favourite surfing spot in Montauk, Long Island, is sophisticated and sleek: there are no seaside knick-knacks here. It's perfect for families at all times of day, as it excels at simple but upscale fare such as the lobster roll (served with a side of sweet-potato chips), calamari and soft tacos. The place offers kids a stellar menu of their own, packed with an array of hot dogs and health-conscious treats like whole-wheat quesadillas.

S'MAC

345 E 12th Street, between First & Second Avenues, East Village (1-212 358 7912, www.smacnyc.com). Subway L to First Avenue. **Open** 11am-11pm Mon-Thur, Sun; 11am-1am Fri, Sat. **Main courses** $8-$20. **Map** p397 F28.
A dozen varieties of mac and cheese range from simple all-American (mild enough for picky types) to a more complex dish with brie, roasted figs and shiitake mushrooms, or mac and manchego with fennel and shallots. There's a size for everyone: 'nosh' (great for kids), 'major munch' (a hearty adult serving), 'mongo' (if you want leftovers to take with you) and 'partay' (which serves eight to 12). Children are offered a regular bowl in lieu of the sizzling skillet in which meals are typically served.
Other location 157 E 33rd Street, between Lexington & Third Avenues, Midtown East (1-212 383 3900).

Jane's Carousel, Brooklyn Bridge Park. See p256.

Film

Even if this is your first visit to NYC, chances are the cityscape will feel familiar. Every corner of the metropolis has been immortalised on celluloid, whether it's Woody Allen's vision of the Upper East Side, Martin Scorsese's midtown street scenes or Spike Lee's take on Bedford-Stuyvesant. It's easy to feel as if you've walked on to a massive movie set, especially when photogenic landmarks such as the Empire State Building pan into view. You might even stumble upon an actual shoot – the thriving local film industry is based in Queens. When it comes to going to the pictures, cinephiles are in their element. There are superb indie screens throughout the city, from Harlem to Brooklyn, not to mention excellent programmes in cultural institutions and star-studded annual events like the New York Film Festival.

CINEMAS

Few cities offer the film-lover as many options as New York. If you insist, you can check out the blockbusters at the multiplexes on 42nd Street and dotted throughout the city. But Gotham's gems are its arthouses, museums and other film institutions. For current movie listings, consult *Time Out New York* magazine or www.timeout. com/newyork.

Angelika Film Center

18 W Houston Street, at Mercer Street, Greenwich Village (1-212 995 2570, www.angelikafilmcenter. com). Subway B, D, F, M to Broadway-Lafayette Street; N, R to Prince Street; 6 to Bleecker Street. **Tickets** $14.50; $11.75 reductions. **Map** p397 E29.
When it opened in 1989, the Angelika immediately became a player in the then-booming Amerindie scene, and the six-screen cinema still puts the emphasis on edgier fare, both domestic and foreign. The complex is packed at weekends, so come extra early or visit the website to buy advance tickets.

Anthology Film Archives

32 Second Avenue, at 2nd Street, East Village (1-212 505 5181, www.anthologyfilmarchives.org). Subway F to Lower East Side-Second Avenue;

6 to Bleecker Street. **Tickets** $10; $8 reductions. **Map** p397 F29.
This red-brick building feels a bit like a fortress – and, in a sense, it is one, protecting the legacy of NYC's fiercest film experimenters. Dedicated to the preservation, study and exhibition of independent, avant-garde and artist-made work, Anthology houses two screens and a film museum.

BAM Rose Cinemas

Brooklyn Academy of Music, 30 Lafayette Avenue, between Ashland Place & St Felix Street, Fort Greene, Brooklyn (1-718 636 4100, www.bam.org). Subway B, D, N, Q, R, 2, 3, 4, 5 to Atlantic Avenue-Barclays Center; C to Lafayette Avenue; G to Fulton Street. **Tickets** $13; $9 reductions. **Map** p404 T10.
Brooklyn's premier art-film venue does double duty as a rep house for well-programmed classics on 35mm and as a first-run multiplex for indie films. June's annual BAMcinemaFest is an excellent showcase of new American work.

Cinema Village

22 E 12th Street, between Fifth Avenue & University Place, Greenwich Village (1-212 924 3363, www.cinemavillage.com). Subway L, N, Q, R, 4, 5, 6 to 14th Street-Union Square. **Tickets** $12; $8 reductions. **Map** p397 E28.

A classic cinema that charmed Noah Baumbach long before he made *The Squid and the Whale*, this three-screener specialises in indie flicks, cutting-edge documentaries and foreign films.

★ Film Forum

209 W Houston Street, between Sixth Avenue & Varick Street, Soho (1-212 727 8110, www.film forum.org). Subway 1 to Houston Street. **Tickets** $13; $7.50 reductions. **No credit cards** (except for online purchases). **Map** p397 D29.

The city's leading tastemaking venue for independent new releases and classic movies, Film Forum is programmed by festival-scouring staff who take their duties as seriously as a Kurosawa samurai. Born in 1970 as a makeshift screening space with folding chairs, Film Forum is still one of the few nonprofit cinemas in the United States – but thankfully its three screens are now furnished with comfortable seats.

★ IFC Center

323 Sixth Avenue, at W 3rd Street, Greenwich Village (1-212 924 7771, www.ifccenter.com). Subway A, B, C, D, E, F, M to W 4th Street. **Tickets** $14; $9-$10 reductions. **Map** p397 D29.

In 2005, the long-darkened 1930s Waverly was reborn as a five-screen arthouse cinema, showing the latest indie hits, along with choice midnight cult items and occasional foreign classics. You may come face to face with the directors or the actors on the screen, as many introduce their work on opening night and stick around for post-screening Q&As.

Landmark Sunshine Cinema

143 E Houston Street, between First & Second Avenues, East Village (1-212 260 7289, www. landmarktheatres.com). Subway F to Lower East Side-Second Avenue. **Tickets** $13.50; $10-$11 reductions. **Map** p397 F29.

Once a renowned Yiddish theatre, this comfortable, date-friendly venue has snazz and chutzpah to spare. Intimate auditoriums and excellent sound are a beautiful complement to the indie films; it also hosts New York's most consistently excellent midnight series on Fridays and Saturdays.

Leonard Nimoy Thalia

Symphony Space, 2537 Broadway, at 95th Street, Upper West Side (1-212 864 5400, www. symphonyspace.org). Subway 1, 2, 3 to 96th Street. **Tickets** $14; $12 reductions. **Map** p400 C17.

The famed Thalia arthouse, which featured in *Annie Hall* (when it was screening *The Sorrow and the Pity*), has since undergone an upgrade. The cinematic fare at the Symphony Space theatre is an eclectic mix of international, arthouse and documentary films, plus HD screenings of plays and operas.

Maysles Cinema

343 Malcolm X Boulevard (Lenox Avenue), between 127th & 128th Streets, Harlem (1-212 537 6843, www.maysles.org). Subway A, B, C, D, 2, 3 to 125th Street. **Tickets** Suggested donation $10. **Map** p401 D13.

An intimate screening venue, run by *cinema vérité* legend Albert Maysles and his extended family. Socially conscious documentaries, naturally, make up the bulk of the programming, but you're also likely to catch funky series of hip hop and jazz films, critics presenting personal esoteric favourites and plenty of uptown-centric flicks.

★ Nitehawk Cinema

136 Metropolitan Avenue, between Berry Street & Wythe Avenue, Williamsburg, Brooklyn (1-718 384 3980, www.nitehawkcinema.com). Subway L to Bedford Avenue. **Tickets** $11; $9 reductions. **Map** p405 U8.

At this cinema-restaurant-bar hybrid, you can have dinner and see a movie at the same time. Seats are arranged in pairs with tables, and viewers order from a menu created by chef Michael Franey. Just write down your order at any point during the movie on a piece of paper for a server to pick up. The comfort food available includes a tasty burger, but the real highlights are the fancy variations on concession-stand staples, like popcorn tossed with truffle butter. Best of all, you can sip cocktails, beer or wine in your seat. *Photo p262.*

Cinema Village. See p259.

ESSENTIAL NEW YORK FILMS

Six celluloid visions of the great metropolis.

Do the Right Thing.

DOG DAY AFTERNOON SIDNEY LUMET (1975)

Al Pacino heads a stellar cast in this tense, moving tale of a first-time crook whose plan to rob a Brooklyn bank goes awry. The film brims with distinctly New York characters: John Cazale as a spaced-out partner in crime; Chris Sarandon as a fragile transsexual; and Charles Durning as a frazzled detective.

DO THE RIGHT THING SPIKE LEE (1989)

Outraged by the 1986 Howard Beach incident, where a man died in a racially motivated incident, Lee responded with a 360-degree look at what can happen when New York's melting pot boils over. The film doubles as a vivid portrait of his native Brooklyn, where every stoop philosopher, nosy matriarch and beat-box-loving B-boy gets his or her moment in the spotlight.

MANHATTAN WOODY ALLEN (1979)

Allen's love sonnet to his home city frames an edgy social comedy. The movie reminds you what a gorgeous sight the island really is from the moment the Gershwin-scored opening montage kicks in: the fish markets and basketball courts; the Fifth Avenue boutiques and Broadway theatres; the high-rise dwellers and lowlifes.

ROSEMARY'S BABY ROMAN POLANSKI (1968)

This realistic supernatural drama was a transfusion of thick, urbane blood to the dated horror genre, and much of its revolutionary impact should be credited to the city of New York itself. A young couple, played by Mia Farrow and John Cassavetes, moves into the Dakota Building – as much of a Gothic pile as any Transylvanian mansion.

SWEET SMELL OF SUCCESS ALEXANDER MACKENDRICK (1957)

This adaptation of a novella about a megalomaniacal gossip columnist (Burt Lancaster) – based on newspaperman Walter Winchell – and a parasitic press agent (Tony Curtis) encapsulates what once went down in the booths of the 21 Club.

TAXI DRIVER MARTIN SCORSESE (1976)

'You talking to me?' Cracked hero Travis Bickle (Robert De Niro) cruises through Greenwich Village and Hell's Kitchen in his taxi. The story may be all in his head: a deranged man's dream of vanilla romance with Cybill Shepherd, unchecked fury at political impotence and the compulsive urge to right every wrong, no matter how slight.

Nitehawk Cinema.
See p260.

Paris Theatre

4 W 58th Street, between Fifth & Sixth Avenues, Midtown (1-212 688 3800, www.theparistheatre. com). Subway N, Q, R to Fifth Avenue-59th Street. **Tickets** *$14.50; $11.75 reductions.* **Map** *p399 E22.*
The elegant, single-screen Paris is one of the oldest continually operating movie houses in the country (it was founded in 1948). Its tiny lobby, plush carpets and seats, and a romantic balcony level have plenty of retro appeal.

Quad Cinema

34 W 13th Street, between Fifth & Sixth Avenues, Greenwich Village (1-212 255 8800, www.quad cinema.com). Subway F, M to 14th Street; L to Sixth Avenue. **Tickets** *$13; $8 reductions.* **Map** *p397 E28.*
Characterised by a cosy, old-school arthouse feel and plenty of homo-friendly film programming, this small four-screen cinema shows new indie flicks, social-issue docs and second-run features you want to catch on the big screen one last time.

IN THE KNOW ALFRESCO FILMS

Each summer, outdoor film series return to city parks, including Bryant Park (www.bryantpark.org) and Central Park (see pp175-176). Arrive early to claim a prime patch of grass in front of the big screen. From May through August, **Rooftop Films** (www.rooftopfilms.com) shows new independent films against an urban backdrop at more than 40 locations.

★ Ziegfeld Theater

141 W 54th Street, between Sixth & Seventh Avenues, Midtown (1-212 307 1862, www. bowtiecinemas.com). Subway B, D, E to Seventh Avenue; F, N, Q, R to 57th Street; 1 to 50th Street. **Tickets** *$15; $11.50 reductions.* **Map** *p399 D22.*
Despite its Jazz Age moniker, this movie palace actually opened in 1969; since then, its red carpets and gilded staircases have served as a last stand against stadium-seated sameness. Temporarily endangered but saved by Bow Tie Cinemas, the largest single-screen theatre in the city seats 1,162 citizens under a vast ceiling of chandeliers, harking back to when a night at the pictures was an aspirational experience. Even the plush ladies' powder room exudes Holly Golightly class.

OTHER INSTITUTIONS

★ Film Society of Lincoln Center

144 & 165 W 65th Street, between Broadway & Amsterdam Avenue, Upper West Side (1-212 875 5600, www.filmlinc.com). Subway 1 to 66th Street-Lincoln Center. **Tickets** *$14; $8-$10 reductions.* **Map** *p399 C21.*
Founded in 1969, the FSLC hosts the prestigious New York Film Festival, among other annual fests, in addition to presenting diverse programming throughout the year. Series are usually thematic, with an international perspective, or focused on a single auteur. The $40-million Elinor Bunin Munroe Film Center houses two plush cinemas that host frequent post-screening Q&As. Between these state-of-the-art screens and the operational Walter Reade Theater across the street, a small multiplex has been born. The Bunin also houses a café, Indie Food and Wine.

Museum of Modern Art

For listings, see p157. **Tickets** free with museum admission; $12; $8-$10 reductions; free under-17s.
Renowned for its superb programming of art films and experimental work, MoMA draws from a vast vault. You have to buy tickets in person at the museum at the lobby desk or the film desk (see www.moma.org or call 1-212 708 9480 for more information). Note that while museum admission includes the day's film programme, a film ticket doesn't include admission to the museum galleries – although it can be applied towards the cost within 30 days.

Museum of the Moving Image

For listings, see p232. **Tickets** $12; $6-$9 reductions.
Like the rest of this Queens institution housed in the Astoria Studios complex, the museum's cinema has received a magnificent renovation, resulting in a state-of-the-art 267-seat cinema. Expect excellent prints and screenings of the classics.

FOREIGN-LANGUAGE SPECIALISTS

You can catch the latest foreign-language flicks at art and revival houses, but there is a wealth of specialist venues as well, including the **French Institute Alliance Française** (22 E 60th Street, 1-212 355 6100, www.fiaf.org), the **Japan Society** (*see p162*) and **Scandinavia House** (*see p164*). The **Asia Society & Museum** (*see p180*) screens works from Asian countries plus Asian-American productions.

FILM FESTIVALS

From late September to mid October, the Film Society of Lincoln Center hosts the **New York Film Festival** (1-212 875 5050, www.film linc.com), more than two weeks packed with premières, features and short flicks from around the globe. Together with Lincoln Center's *Film Comment* magazine, the FSLC also offers the popular **Film Comment Selects**, showcasing films that have yet to be distributed in the United States.

January brings the annual **New York Jewish Film Festival** (www.nyjff.org) to Lincoln Center's Walter Reade Theater (*see p262*). In early March, the **New York International Children's Film Festival** (1-212 349 0330, www.gkids.com) kicks off three to four weeks of anime, shorts and features made for kids and teens.

Each spring, the Museum of Modern Art and the Film Society of Lincoln Center sponsor the highly regarded **New Directors/New Films** series, presenting works by on-the-cusp filmmakers. And in April, Robert De Niro's **Tribeca Film Festival** (1-212 941 2400, www.tribecafilm.com) draws more than 400,000 fans to screenings of independent movies and other events.

It's followed by the **New York Lesbian & Gay Film Festival** (1-646 290 8136, www.newfest.org) in summer. The season also brings several outdoor film festivals (*see p262* **In the Know**).

Tribeca Film Festival.

ARTS & ENTERTAINMENT

Gay & Lesbian

Ever since the 1969 Stonewall riots gave birth to the modern gay rights movement, New York has been a beacon for LGBT folks from all corners of the globe. The constant influx of new blood keeps the city's queer scene vital, from buzzing bars to activist events and cutting-edge performances. Even as gay culture permeates the mainstream in our post-*Will & Grace* world, NYC remains a bastion of the wonderfully weird and uniquely queer. The scene is also remarkably accessible, with two primary, highly walkable gaybourhoods: the Village, which is home to the Stonewall Inn (now a National Historic Landmark), as well as other decades-old bars clustered around Christopher Street, and Hell's Kitchen, a modern gay playground, packed with bars, restaurants and shops. Yet the East Village, Williamsburg in Brooklyn and Jackson Heights in Queens all have thriving communities too, just a subway ride away.

THE QUEER CALENDAR

NYC Pride, New York's biggest queer event, takes place the last week of June, bringing with it a whirl of parties and performances. Capping the weekend, the **NYC LGBT Pride March**, which takes five hours to wind down Fifth Avenue from midtown to the West Village, draws millions of spectators and participants. **Urban Bear Weekend** in May and **Black Party Weekend** in March also draw hordes to NYC, visibly upping the gay quotient around town. Film fans might like the offerings at summer's **NewFest** (www.newfest.org). As the temperature soars, the social scene extends to scenic **Fire Island**, home to the neighbouring beach resorts of Cherry Grove and the Pines (about a 90-minute train and ferry ride from Manhattan). Autumn in gay New York kicks off with the **Bushwig** festival, in which north Brooklyn's thriving drag scene celebrates itself, and **Halloween** is a major to-do, with bars and clubs packed with costumed revellers. Culture buffs can check out summer's annual **Hot!** festival of lesbian and gay arts at Dixon Place, offering a wide variety of queer art, theatre, dance and comedy events.

INFORMATION, MEDIA & CULTURE

There is one gay-specific bookstore in New York, the Bureau of General Services – Queer Division, which is located inside the city's **LGBT Community Center**. In addition, **Bluestockings** has a good selection of queer and feminist works, while most major bookstores have large LGBT sections.

To find out what's going on, refer to *Time Out New York* magazine or www.timeout.com/newyork. Also popular is the gay entertainment magazine *Next* (www.nextmagazine.com), which offers extensive boy-centric information on bars, clubs, restaurants and events. The monthly *Go!* (www.gomag.com), 'a cultural road map for the city girl', gives the lowdown on the lesbian nightlife and travel scene. *Gay City News* (www.gaycitynews.com) provides feisty political coverage with an activist slant. All are free and widely available (look out for copies in street boxes, gay and lesbian bars and stores). A number of popular gay blogs and websites are also based in the city, and feature attitude-filled thoughts on the queer scene.

Among the best sites are sexy and occasionally gossipy Queerty (www.queerty.com), news-focused Joe.My.God (www.joemygod.com) and the wide-ranging Towleroad (www.towleroad.com).

Bluestockings

172 Allen Street, between Rivington & Stanton Streets, Lower East Side (1-212 777 6028, www.bluestockings.com). Subway F to Lower East Side-Second Avenue. **Open** 11am-11pm daily. **Map** p397 F29.

This radical bookstore, fair-trade café and activist resource centre stocks LGBT literature and regularly hosts queer events (often with a feminist slant), including dyke knitting circles, trans-politics forums and women's open-mic nights.

★ Lesbian, Gay, Bisexual & Transgender Community Center

208 W 13th Street, between Seventh & Eighth Avenues, West Village (1-212 620 7310, www.gaycenter.org). Subway A, C, E, 1, 2, 3 to 14th Street; L to Eighth Avenue. **Open** 9am-10pm Mon-Sat; 9am-9pm Sun. **Map** p397 D27.

Founded in 1983, the Center provides information and a gay support network. As well as being a friendly resource that offers guidance to gay tourists, it is used as a venue by more than 300 groups. The public programming at the Center includes everything from book signings to dance parties. It is also home to the Bureau of General Services – Queer Division, the city's only LGBT bookstore, the National Archive of Lesbian, Gay, Bisexual and Transgender History and the

Pat Parker/Vito Russo Library. In 2014, a major renovation brought a new café and cyber centre.

Lesbian Herstory Archives

484 14th Street, between Eighth Avenue & Prospect Park West, Park Slope, Brooklyn (1-718 768 3953, www.lesbianherstoryarchives.org). Subway F to 15th Street-Prospect Park. **Open** varies; see website calendar. **Map** p404 T12.

The Herstory Archives contain more than 20,000 books (cultural theory, fiction, poetry, plays), 1,600 periodicals, 600 films and videos and

ARTS & ENTERTAINMENT

NYC Pride.

ARTS & ENTERTAINMENT

IN THE KNOW
NOT-SO-SQUARE DANCING

If throbbing house music isn't your style, one alternative to a club is the **Big Apple Ranch**, a lively gay and lesbian country and western bash held every Saturday night at a Garment District dance studio (4th Floor, 25 W 31st street, between Broadway and Fifth Avenue, www.bigappleranch.com). Admission is $10 and an 8pm lesson is followed by the party at 9pm – offering a chance to don your chaps and do-si-do. followed by the party at 9pm – offering a chance to don your chaps and do-si-do.

assorted memorabilia. The cosy brownstone also hosts screenings, readings and social gatherings, plus an open house in June (during Brooklyn Pride) and December.

★ Leslie-Lohman Museum of Gay & Lesbian Art

26 Wooster Street, between Canal & Grand Streets, Soho (1-212 431 2609, www.leslielohman.org). Subway A, C, E to Canal Street. **Open** noon-6pm Tue, Wed, Fri-Sun; noon-8pm Thur. **Admission** free. **Map** p397 E30.

Formerly the Leslie-Lohman Gay Art Foundation, this institution was granted museum status by the state of New York in 2011. Founded in 1990 by Fritz Lohman and Charles Leslie, the museum seeks to preserve and highlight the contributions of LGBT artists throughout history and up to the present. In addition to changing exhibitions, it has a large permanent collection and library, and hosts regular book signings, panel discussions and low-key parties.

WHERE TO STAY

While you'd be hard-pressed to find a gay-unfriendly hotel in New York, the following establishments are either exclusively gay or geared towards a queer clientele.

Chelsea Mews Guest House

344 W 15th Street, between Eighth & Ninth Avenues, Chelsea (1-212 255 9174, www. chelseamewsguesthouse.com). Subway A, C, E to 14th Street; L to Eighth Avenue. **Rooms** 8. **No credit cards. Map** p397 C27.

Built in 1840, this clothing-optional guesthouse caters to gay men. The rooms are comfortable and well furnished and, in most cases, share a bathroom. Bicycle tours and coffee are complimentary – as is access to a songbird aviary! An on-site massage therapist and soothing Tempur-Pedic beds in every room help to ensure a relaxing stay. New

arrivals take note: there's no sign out front, so keep your eye on the building numbers.

★ Chelsea Pines Inn

317 W 14th Street, between Eighth & Ninth Avenues, Chelsea (1-212 929 1023, www.chelsea pinesinn.com). Subway A, C, E to 14th Street; L to Eighth Avenue. **Rooms** 23. **Map** p397 C27.

On the border of Chelsea and the West Village, Chelsea Pines welcomes gay guests of all persuasions. The rooms are clean and comfortable, with classic-film themes; all have private bathrooms, and are equipped with an iPhone/iPad docking station, a TV with satellite channels, a refrigerator and free Wi-Fi. Complimentary breakfast is offered daily.

Colonial House Inn

318 W 22nd Street, between Eighth & Ninth Avenues, Chelsea (1-212 243 9669, 1-800 689 3779, www.colonialhouseinn.com). Subway C, E to 23rd Street. **Rooms** 22 **Map** p398 C26.

This beautifully renovated 1850s townhouse sits on a quiet street in Chelsea. The hotel was founded by late dance-music legend Mel Cheren, and is still run by (and primarily for) gay men; it's a great place to stay, even if some of the cheaper rooms are a bit snug. Bonuses include fireplaces in three of the deluxe rooms and a rooftop deck (nude sunbathing is allowed).

Incentra Village House

32 Eighth Avenue, between Jane & W 12th Streets, West Village (1-212 206 0007, www.incentra village.com). Subway A, C, E to 14th Street; L to Eighth Avenue. **Rooms** 11. **Map** p397 D28.

Two cute 1841 townhouses in the Village make up this nicely restored and gay-run guesthouse. The spacious rooms have private bathrooms and kitchenettes; some also have fireplaces. A 1939 Steinway baby grand graces the parlour and sets a tone of easy sophistication.

OUT Hotel

510 W 42nd Street, between Tenth & Eleventh Avenues, Midtown (1-212 947 2999, www.the outnyc.com). Subway A, C, E to 42nd Street-Port Authority. **Rooms** 103. **Map** p398 C24.

This all-gay megacomplex in a converted motel is located just a few blocks from Times Square and the Theater District, and in convenient proximity to the Hell's Kitchen strip of gay bars. But there's actually no need to leave – in addition to a gym, a spa and an unremarkable but serviceable restaurant, the OUT houses the XL nightclub, Rosebud cocktail bar and 42West cabaret space. Rooms are arranged around three courtyards, and despite a few style statements, the monochrome room decor is on the spare side. The quad rooms, with four curtained cubby-bunks that are reminiscent of sleeper compartments – upgraded with double beds and TVs – are a budget option for groups. *Photo p268.*

BUSHWIGGIN' OUT

A new breed of drag stars is making waves – especially in north Brooklyn.

Lady Bunny. RuPaul. Bianca Del Rio. New York has served as an incubator for some of the most beloved and influential drag stars of all time. So it's no surprise that a new breed of cross-dressing performer is emerging here. Arty, punkish and occasionally hirsute gender-benders are making a splash in north Brooklyn.

The new generation of drag queens on the rise in Bushwick eschews old-school girlie glamour in favour of a more rock 'n' roll aesthetic, which sometimes includes beards, shaved heads and other unfemme choices. They were drawn to the neighbourhood by the ever-enticing cheap rent. 'In the '90s, it was the East Village drag scene that was kind of pushing boundaries, making drag more of an art form,' says scene queen Simon Leahy. 'And now it's Bushwick, because all the young, broke artists live here.'

Much of the neo-drag action is focused on the House of Bushwig collective, which hosts an annual **Bushwig** fête each September. Organised by Leahy (aka Babes Trust) and Horrorchata, the multi-day party serves as a showcase for alt-drag stars including Untitled Queen, Merrie Cherry and Hamm Samwich. Even the Manhattan establishment has taken notice: drag pioneers Lady Bunny and Linda Simpson have made appearances at Bushwig, and *RuPaul's Drag Race* alum Milk has performed at the fest.

But the Bushwick drag scene (which spills into nearby Greenpoint and Williamsburg) isn't confined to one weekend a year. These radical queens regularly host and perform at Brooklyn venues like **One Last Shag** (348 Franklin Avenue, between Greene & Lexington Avenues, Bedford-Stuyvesant, 1-718 398 2472, www.onelastshag.com), **This n That** (see p272) and **LoveGun** (see p272). You'll even occasionally find them on the other side of the river at downtown boîtes like **Eastern Bloc** (see p269). Subscribe to newsletters from Gayletter (www.gayletter.com) and the Culture Whore (www.theculturewhore.com) for up-to-the-minute updates on where you can find these artists, who, as Leahy puts it, 'want to showcase that there's more to drag than just lip-synching to Britney songs'.

Bushwig.

ARTS & ENTERTAINMENT

OUT Hotel. See p266.

RESTAURANTS & CAFES

The sight of same-sex couples holding hands across a candlelit table is a pretty commonplace one in New York City. But if you want to increase the chances of being part of the majority when you dine, check out the following gay-friendly places.

Bamboo 52

344 W 52nd Street, between Eighth & Ninth Avenues, Hell's Kitchen (1-212 315 2777, www.bamboo52nyc.com). Subway C, E to 50th Street. **Open** 11am-2am Mon-Fri; 4pm-2am Sat, Sun. **Sushi rolls** $7-$16. **Map** p398 C23.

This sushi restaurant (with a bamboo garden to boot) feels more like a gay bar with an extended raw fish menu. There's loungey seating (patrons nestle on low banquettes and nibble off knee-high tables), a DJ and free-flowing drinks. The fun menu features such unorthodox combinations as buffalo chicken speciality rolls and a spicy sushi sandwich – a tasty triangle of seasoned rice layered with spicy tuna, avocado, eel and American cheese.

Elmo

156 Seventh Avenue, between 19th & 20th Streets, Chelsea (1-212 337 8000, www.elmorestaurant. com). Subway 1 to 18th Street. **Open** 11am-11pm Mon, Tue; 11am-midnight Wed; 11am-1am Thur, Fri; 10am-1am Sat; 10am-10pm Sun. **Main courses** $16-$24. **Map** p397 D27.

The main attraction at this spacious, brightly decorated eaterie is the good, reasonably priced, seasonally changing American comfort food. Then there's the bar, which provides a view of the dining room jammed with guys in clingy tank tops. During warmer months, the sidewalk café is constantly bustling.

★ Empanada Mama

763 Ninth Avenue, between 51st & 52nd Streets, Hell's Kitchen (1-212 698 9008, www.empmama nyc.com). Subway C, E to 50th Street. **Open** 24hrs daily. **Empanadas** $3-$3.50. **Map** p398 C23.

Massive flavours are crammed into tiny packages at this cute spot, right in the middle of the Hell's Kitchen's boy-bar crawl. Savoury and sweet empanadas (both flour and corn varieties) make great on-the-go snacks, or combine several for a full meal. The joint tends to be packed from dinner time until the wee hours.

Rocking Horse Café

182 Eighth Avenue, between 19th & 20th Streets, Chelsea (1-212 463 9511, www.rockinghorsecafe. com). Subway C, E to 23rd Street. **Open** noon-4.30pm, 5-11pm Mon-Thur; noon-4.30pm, 5pm-midnight Fri; 11am-4.30pm, 5pm-midnight Sat; 11am-11pm Sun. **Main courses** $17-$25. **Map** p397 D27.

Eclectic Mexican cuisine is what originally established the Rocking Horse Café as a unique place to eat in Chelsea, but the bar now holds a distinguished reputation for its tongue-numbingly stiff frozen margaritas (the Two Fruit version features prickly pear and mango).

Superfine

126 Front Street, between Jay & Pearl Streets, Dumbo, Brooklyn (1-718 243 9005, www. superfine.nyc). Subway A, C to High Street; F to York Street. **Open** 11.30am-3pm, 6-11pm

Tue-Sat; 11.30am-3pm, 6-10pm Sun. **Main courses** $18-$36. **Map** p405 T9.
Owned by a couple of super-cool lesbians, this eaterie, bar and gallery serves Mediterranean cuisine in a massive, hip space. The mellow vibe and pool table draw a mixed local crowd. The Sunday brunch is justifiably popular.

Vynl
754 Ninth Avenue, between 50th & 51st Streets, Hell's Kitchen (1-212 974 2003, www.vynl-nyc. com). Subway C, E to 50th Street. **Open** 11am-11pm Mon, Tue; 11am-midnight Wed, Thur; 11am-1am Fri; 10am-1am Sat; 10am-11pm Sun. **Main courses** $16-$22. **Map** p398 C23.
This pop music-themed eaterie is a big hit with the boys – old albums adorn the walls above the cosy booths and mirrorballs are shoved into every available space. Menu items are an odd mishmash of comfort food (burgers, turkey meatloaf) and Asian cuisine (massaman curry, pad thai). Cocktails are named after pop icons and the vibe is all-around fun.

BARS & CLUBS

'It ain't what it used to be,' grumble veterans of New York's gay nightlife. And they're right. The after-hours scene is continually morphing – sometimes for the better, sometimes not. Club nights such as **Viva Saturdays** at **Stage 48** (605 W 48th Street, between Eleventh & Twelfth Avenues, www.vivasaturdays.com) draw crowds of hot guys looking to dance to tunes from big-name DJs and even the occasional slumming pop star. But for serious dance music fans, the real action is at smaller venues. The basement disco at

the **Monster** features reliably sweaty (in a good way) parties most nights, and MEN's JD Samson hosts **Scissor Sundays** at the **Rusty Knot** (425 West Street, West Village, 1-212 645 5668), a top-notch tea dance that assembles an eclectic crowd.

East Village

Cock
29 Second Avenue, between 2nd & 3rd Streets (no phone, www.thecockbar.com). Subway F to Lower East Side-Second Avenue. **Open** 11pm-4am daily. **Admission** free-$10. **No credit cards**. **Map** p397 F29.
This grungy hole-in-the-wall still holds the title of New York's sleaziest gay hangout, but nowadays it's hit-and-miss. At weekends, it's a packed grind-fest, but on other nights the place can often be depressingly under-populated. It's best to go very late when the cruising is at its peak.

Eastern Bloc
505 E 6th Street, between Avenues A & B (1-212 777 2555, www.easternblocnyc.com). Subway F to Lower East Side-Second Avenue. **Open** 7pm-4am daily. **No credit cards**. **Map** p397 G28.
This cool little space has mostly shed its commie revolutionary decor for a funky living-room feel. The bartenders are cuties, and there are nightly themes, DJs and happy hours to get the ball rolling.

★ Nowhere
322 E 14th Street, at First Avenue (1-212 477 4744, www.nowherebarnyc.com). Subway L to First Avenue. **Open** 3pm-4am daily. **No credit cards**. **Map** p397 F27.

ARTS & ENTERTAINMENT

Cock.

ARTS & ENTERTAINMENT

Low ceilings and dim lighting create a speakeasy vibe at this subterranean bar. It attracts everyone from young lesbians to bears, thanks to an entertaining line-up of theme nights. Tuesdays are especially fun, when DJ Damian's long-running Buddies party takes over. The pool table is another big draw.

West Village

★ Cubbyhole
281 W 12th Street, between 4th Street & Greenwich Avenue (1-212 243 9041, www.cubbyholebar.com). Subway A, C, E to 14th Street; L to Eighth Avenue. **Open** 4pm-4am Mon-Fri; 2pm-4am Sat, Sun. **No credit cards. Map** p397 E28.
This minuscule spot is filled with flirtatious girls (and their dyke-friendly boy pals), with the standard Melissa Etheridge or kd lang soundtrack blaring. Chinese lanterns, tissue-paper fish and old holiday decorations emphasise the festive, homespun charm.

Henrietta Hudson
438 Hudson Street, at Morton Street (1-212 924 3347, www.henriettahudson.com). Subway 1 to Houston Street. **Open** 5pm-2am Mon, Tue; 4pm-4am Wed-Fri; 2pm-4am Sat; 2pm-2am Sun. **Admission** free-$10. **Map** p403 D29.
A much-loved lesbian hangout, this glam lounge is slightly off the beaten path, and attracts women from all over the city and the 'burbs. Every night is different, with hip hop, pop, rock and live shows among the musical offerings.

The Monster
80 Grove Street, at Sheridan Square (1-212 924 3558, www.manhattan-monster.com). Subway 1 to Christopher Street-Sheridan Square. **Open** 4pm-4am Mon-Fri; 2pm-4am Sat, Sun. **No credit cards. Map** p397 D28.
Upstairs, locals gather to sing showtunes in the piano lounge, which is adorned with strings of lights and rainbow paraphernalia. The downstairs dancefloor attracts surprisingly serious DJs on weekends, and it's always packed with a cute, sweaty crowd.

Rockbar
185 Christopher Street, at Weehawken Street (1-212 675 1864, www.rockbarnyc.com). Subway 1 to Christopher Street-Sheridan Square. **Open** 4pm-2am Mon-Thur; 4pm-4am Fri; 2pm-4am Sat; 2pm-2am Sun. **Map** p397 C29.
A burly, bearish crowd tends to congregate at this far-west dive with a rock 'n' roll theme. Various events include dance parties, game nights, comedy showcases and musical performances.

Stonewall Inn
53 Christopher Street, at Waverly Place (1-212 488 2705, www.thestonewallinnnyc.com). Subway 1 to Christopher Street-Sheridan Square. **Open** 2pm-4am daily. **Map** p397 D28.
This gay landmark is the site of the 1969 gay rebellion against police harassment (though back then it also included the building next door). Special

Atlas Social Club.

XL Nightclub. See p272.

nights range from dance soirées and drag shows to burlesque performances and bingo gatherings.
► *While you're here, check out George Segal's sculptures in nearby Christopher Park; see p119.*

Chelsea & Flatiron District

Barracuda
275 W 22nd Street, between Seventh & Eighth Avenues (1-212 645 8613, www.facebook.com/ barracudalounge). Subway C, E, 1 to 23rd Street. **Open** 4pm-4am daily. **No credit cards.** **Map** p398 D26.
This much beloved, slightly divey Chelsea institution is one of the most reliably bustling spots in the neighbourhood. Some of the city's most talented drag queens perform here nightly. Drinks are on the pricey side, but you'll often get a great show with no cover, so it balances out.

★ Eagle
554 W 28th Street, at Eleventh Avenue (1-646 473 1866, www.eaglenyc.com). Subway C, E to 23rd Street. **Open** 10pm-3am Mon; 10pm-4am Tue-Sat; 4pm-4am Sun. **No credit cards.** **Map** p398 C26.
You don't have to be a kinky leather daddy to enjoy this manly spot, but it definitely doesn't hurt. The fetish bar is home to an array of beer blasts, footworship fêtes and leather soirées, plus simple pool playing and cruising nights. Thursdays are gear night, so be sure to dress the part or you might not get past the doorman. In summer, the rooftop is a surprising oasis.

G Lounge
225 W 19th Street, at Seventh Avenue (1-212 929 1085, www.glounge.com). Subway 1 to 18th Street. **Open** 4pm-4am daily. **Map** p397 D27.

The neighbourhood's original slick boy lounge – a moodily lit cave with a cool brick-and-glass arched entrance – wouldn't look out of place in a boutique hotel. It's a favourite after-work cocktail spot, where a roster of DJs stays on top of the mood.

Gym Sports Bar
167 Eighth Avenue, between 18th & 19th Streets (1-212 337 2439, www.gymsportsbar.com). Subway A, C, E to 14th Street; L to Eighth Avenue. **Open** 4pm-2am Mon-Thur; 4pm-4am Fri; 1pm-4am Sat; 1pm-2am Sun. **Map** p397 D27.
This popular spot is all about games – of the actual sporting variety. Catch theme parties that revolve around gay sports leagues, play at the pool tables and video games, or watch the pro events – from rodeo competitions to figure skating – on big-screen TVs.

Hell's Kitchen & Theater District

Atlas Social Club
753 Ninth Avenue, between 50th & 51st Streets (1-212 762 8527, www.atlassocialclub.com). Subway C, E to 50th Street. **Open** 4pm-4am daily. **Map** p398 C23.
This drinkery, designed to look like a cross between an old-school athletic club and a speakeasy, is one of the more relaxed options on the HK strip – at least when it's not packed to the gills, which it can be at weekends. Be sure to check out the bathrooms, which are brightly papered with vintage beefcake and sports magazines.

Boxers HK
742 Ninth Avenue, between 50th & 51st Streets (1-212 951 1518, www.boxersnyc.com). Subway C, E to 50th Street. **Open** 4pm-2am Mon-Wed; 4pm-4am Thur, Fri; 1pm-4am Sat; 1pm-2am Sun. **Map** p398 C23.

The second location of this local gay sports bar chainlet is a massive three-level funhouse packed with polo-shirted HK boys and happy hour commuters on their way to the nearby Port Authority Bus Terminal. Cheap beer is on tap, machines churn out frozen drinks and it's all served by hunky (and usually topless) bartenders and waiters. In the summer months, the roof deck is one of the prettiest spots in the neighbourhood.

Other location 37 W 20th Street, between Fifth & Sixth Avenues, Chelsea (1-212 255 5082).

Flaming Saddles

793 Ninth Avenue, at 53rd Street (1-212 713 0481, www.flamingsaddles.com). Subway C, E to 50th Street. **Open** 3pm-4am Mon-Fri, Sun; noon-4am Sat, Sun. **No credit cards. Map** p399 C23.

City boys can party honky-tonk-style at this country and western gay bar. It's outfitted to look like a Wild West bordello, with red velvet drapes, antler sconces and rococo wallpaper. Performances by bartenders dancing in cowboy boots add to the raucous vibe.

Industry

355 W 52nd Street, between Eighth & Ninth Avenues (1-646 476 2747, www.industrybar.com). Subway C, E to 50th Street. **Open** 4pm-4am daily. **No credit cards. Map** p399 C23.

Pretty boys flock to this appropriately named garage-like industrial-chic boite, which has a stage for regular drag shows and other performances, a pool table, and couches for lounging. DJs spin nightly to a sexy, fashionable crowd.

Therapy

348 W 52nd Street, between Eighth & Ninth Avenues (1-212 397 1700, www.therapy-nyc.com). Subway C, E to 50th Street. **Open** 5pm-2am Mon-Wed, Sun; 5pm-4am Thur-Sat. **Map** p398 C23.

Therapy is just what your analyst ordered. The dramatic two-level space hosts comedy and musical performances, there are some clever cocktails (including the Freudian Sip) and a crowd of well-scrubbed boys. You'll find good food and a cosy fireplace to boot.

IN THE KNOW MOVIE NIGHT

Once a week, the ever-bubbly green-topped drag queen Hedda Lettuce takes over the **Chelsea Bow Tie Cinema** (260 W 23rd Street, between Seventh & Eighth Avenues, 1-212 691 5519, www.bowtiecinemas. com) to provide a comedic fluffing before a (typically) campy flick. Past screenings have included Zsa Zsa Gabor vehicle *Queen of Outer Space*, horror classic *Carrie* and goofy '80s comedy *Elvira, Mistress of the Dark*.

XL Nightclub

516 W 42nd Street, between Tenth & Eleventh Avenues (1-212 239 2999, www.xlnightclub.com). Subway A, C, E to 42nd Street-Port Authority. **Open** varies. **Admission** varies. **Map** p398 C24.

Part of the OUT Hotel complex, the cavernous XL has a giant dancefloor, a handful of VIP areas and a large stage backed by an LED wall. The scene varies widely depending on the event, so check out the website before you approach the velvet rope. *Photo p271.*

Brooklyn

Ginger's Bar

363 Fifth Avenue, between 5th & 6th Streets, Park Slope (1-718 788 0924, www.gingersbarbklyn. com). Subway F, R to Fourth Avenue-9th Street. **Open** 5pm-4am Mon-Fri; 2pm-4am Sat, Sun. **No credit cards. Map** p404 T11.

The front room of Ginger's, with its dark-wood bar, looks out on to a bustling street. The back, with an always-busy pool table, evokes a rec room, while the patio feels like a friend's yard. This local hangout is full of all sorts of dykes, many with their dogs – or favourite gay boys – in tow.

LoveGun

617 Grand Street, between Leonard & Lorimer Streets, Williamsburg (1-718 388 3441, www. lovegunnyc.com). Subway G to Metropolitan Avenue; L to Lorimer Street. **Open** 9pm-2am Mon-Wed; 9pm-4am Thur-Sat. **Map** p405 V8.

The guys behind the popular Manhattan drinkery Atlas Social Club brought their act to Williamsburg with this sleek bar that hosts a variety of DJs, theme nights and performances. There's rarely a cover charge, but check its Facebook or Twitter page as some special events are ticketed.

Metropolitan

559 Lorimer Street, at Metropolitan Avenue, Williamsburg (1-718 599 4444, www.metropolitan barny.com). Subway G to Metropolitan Avenue; L to Lorimer Street. **Open** 3pm-4am daily. **Map** p405 V8.

Some Williamsburg spots are a little pretentious, but not this refreshingly unfancy bar, which resembles a 1960s ski lodge, complete with a brick fireplace. Guys dominate, but there's always a female contingent, and even some straight folks. There are weekend barbecues on the patio in summer.

★ This n' That (TNT)

108 North 6th Street, between Berry Street & Wythe Avenue, Williamsburg (1-718 599 5959, www. thisnthatbrooklyn.com). Subway L to Bedford Avenue. **Open** 4pm-4am daily. **Map** p405 U7.

This cavernous boite is parked in the middle of the most hipstery block of the city's most hipstery neighbourhood. Still, most nights you'll find a surprisingly unpretentious crowd here, enjoying various parties (trivia, movie nights, sweaty dance fests).

Nightlife

After a few touch-and-go years when New York relinquished the clubbing crown to European cities such as Berlin and London, Gotham has got its groove back. The nightlife scene has survived such buzz-killing trends as 5am sober raves, bottle service, Mayor Giuliani and celebrity iPod DJs. New clubs and roving parties – especially in Brooklyn – are revitalising the after-dark landscape.

Hot on the heels of the new Barclays Center, a revamped movie palace, the Kings Theatre, debuted in 2015 as Brooklyn's second-biggest concert venue. For smaller rock gigs, hit the Lower East Side or Williamsburg; the latter is the epicentre of the indie rock scene.

Comedy, meanwhile, is enjoying a moment, with thriving venues across the city. Many of the best weekly shows are free, which makes going out for a few laughs an inexpensive night on the town.

Clubs

Hallowed halls such as Studio 54, Paradise Garage, Limelight and Area are embedded in nightlife's collective consciousness as near-mythic ideals, but today's scene is the strongest it's been in years. This is largely thanks to a burst of nomadic shindigs, often held in out-of-the-way warehouses, lofts and converted whatever-you-can-finds that have sent the energy of NYC nightlife where it belongs: underground. In addition to the parties listed below, look out for Dope Jams' Celebrate Life, Wolf+Lamb, the Freak Show, BangOn!, Bespoke Musik and the Loft (one of the all-time-greats, which has been running since 1970). A visit to www.timeout.com/newyork will always help to clue you in.

Many music venues, including **Baby's All Right**, the **Bell House**, **Brooklyn Bowl** and **Le Poisson Rouge**, also host DJ sets. *See p282-294.*

DANCE CLUBS

FREE Le Bain

The Standard, 444 W 13th Street, at Washington Street, Meatpacking District (1-212 645 4646, www.standardhotels.com). Subway A, C, E to 14th Street; L to Eighth Avenue. **Open** 10pm-4am Wed-Fri; 2pm-4am Sat; 2pm-3am Sun. **Admission** free. **Map** p397 C27.

Although an EDM-driven club scene is filling bigger and bigger venues, for a more intimate night out, head to this penthouse club and terrace atop the Standard hotel. The swanky space offers spectacular Hudson River views from floor-to-ceiling windows and a spacious rooftop with artificial grass and a hot tub in the summer. And you can get within hugging distance of underground superstars that have included disco daddy Dimitri from Paris, deep-house kingpin Marques Wyatt and the aurally anarchic DJ Harvey.

Cielo.

Bossa Nova Civic Club

1271 Myrtle Avenue, at Hart Street, Bushwick, Brooklyn (1-718 443 1271, www.bossanova civicclub.com). Subway J to Kosciuszko Street; M to Central Avenue. **Open** 5pm-4am daily. **Admission** free-$10. **Map** p405 W9.

This 'tropical fantasy dance club' is yet another entry in the thriving Bushwick scene, but the newly renovated space has the edge over its competitors with a legitimate sound system and consistently hot line-ups of under-underground house and techno DJs. Since opening in 2012, the nightspot has made a big name for itself in the community, curating its own stage at Sustain-Release (an upstate New York microfestival from Aurora Halal of Mutual Dreaming) and hosting original techno pioneer Adam X on his *Irreformable* album tour.

★ Cameo

93 North 6th Street, between Berry Street & Wythe Avenue, Williamsburg, Brooklyn (1-718 302 1180, www.cameony.com). Subway L to Bedford Avenue. **Open** varies; usually 8pm- midnight Mon-Thur, Sun; 8pm-4am Fri, Sat. **Admission** free-$20. **Map** p405 U7.

To enter this two-floor nightclub and performance space, you'll need to walk through Caribbean restaurant Jify's. The space isn't huge, but what it lacks in size it makes up for in creative bookings. When not hosting alternative comedy nights or up-and-coming indie rock bands, Cameo presents carefully curated and eclectic electronic artist performances that go late into the night (or early into the morning). Big-name guests are known to drop by as well – Nicolas Jaar and Jacques Greene have played to a still-jam-packed house at 6am after tweeting their announcement hours before.

Cielo

18 Little W 12th Street, at Ninth Avenue, Meatpacking District (1-212 645 5700, www. cielodub.com). Subway A, C, E to 14th Street; L to Eighth Avenue. **Open** 10pm-4am Mon, Wed-Sat. **Admission** free-$25. **Map** p397 C28.

You'd never guess from all the Kardashian wannabes hanging out in the neighbourhood that the attitude at this longstanding, exclusive club is close to zero – at least once you get past the bouncers on the door and the mandatory coat check in winter. On the sunken dancefloor, hip-to-hip crowds gyrate to deep beats from top DJs, including NYC old-schoolers François K, Tedd Patterson and Louie Vega. Cielo, which features a crystal-clear sound system (by the legendary Funktion One), has won a bevy of 'best club' awards. Cielo was the mini Manhattan blueprint for Brooklyn's Output and is owned and operated by the same team.

★ Good Room

98 Meserole Avenue, between Lorimer Street & Metropolitan Avenue, Greenpoint, Brooklyn

Output.

ARTS & ENTERTAINMENT

(1-718 349 2373, www.goodroombk.com). Subway G to Nassau Avenue. **Open** 10pm-4am Wed-Sat. **Admission** free-$20. **Map** p405 V7.

Located in the home of former glitzy Polish venue Club Europa, Good Room was reinvented by nightlife impresario Steve Lewis in autumn 2014. The main room was designed with the DJ in mind with a centrally placed booth and solid sound system, ample dancefloor and small raised stage for performances. Another room houses the massive square bar, where friendly bartenders mix surprisingly reasonably priced drinks. A third, smaller room – 'the Bad Room' – contains a massive wall of vinyl and another DJ set-up for separate tunes. If you don't want to deal with the hassle (or cost) of Williamsburg's megaclubs, Good Room is the perfect antidote.

Marquee

289 Tenth Avenue, between 26th & 27th Streets, Chelsea (1-646 473 0202, www.marqueeny.com). Subway C, E to 23rd Street. **Open** 11pm-4am Wed, Fri-Sat. **Admission** varies. **Map** p398 C26.

After shutting down for major renovation, this onetime models-and-bottles club has re-emerged…as a models-and-bottles club! In fairness, Marquee 2.0 is an entirely different – and far better – beast than it was in its original incarnation, with more open space, all manner of disco lights and enough razzle-dazzle to make your head spin. Most importantly, the Friday-night bookings have been taken over by NYC disc-jockey power couple Sleepy & Boo, who have been bringing in the world's house-and-techno elite – Slam, Marco Carola, Damian Lazarus, the Martinez Brothers and the like – to work their four-to-the-floor magic.

Nublu

62 Avenue C, between E 4th Street & E 5th Street, East Village (no phone, www.nublu.net). Subway F to Lower East Side-Second Avenue. **Open** 8pm-4am daily. **Admission** $10. **Map** p397 G28.

Since Swedish-Turkish promoter Ilhan Ersahin opened Nublu in 2002, the club has evolved from a late-night hangout and jam session spot for musicians to a club and small performance space that hosts bands and DJs of all stripes. At the nexus of funk, soul, bossa nova and instrumental hip hop, the bar also holds acts in its orbit such as In Flagranti, Brazilian Girls, Norah Jones, Forro in the Dark and Kudu, as well as record label Wax Poetic. The club also has its own record label and throws Nublu Jazz Festivals in NYC, São Paolo and Istanbul.

Output

74 Wythe Avenue, at North 12th Street, Williamsburg (no phone, www.outputclub.com). Subway L to Bedford Avenue. **Open** 10pm-4am Wed, Thur; 10pm-6am Fri, Sat. **Admission** varies. **Map** p405 U7.

With the opening of Output in early 2013, New York nightlife's centre of gravity continued its eastward push into Brooklyn. Akin in ethos to such underground music headquarters as Berlin's Berghain/Panorama Bar complex or London's Fabric, the club boasts a warehouse-party vibe and a killer sound system. The place is deceptively massive, with a two-floored main room, the smaller Panther Room next door complete with a grand staircase and fireplace, the intimate Stilton House (which occasionally serves food) and two rooftop smoking patios.

NYC CLUB RULES

TONY nightlife editor Christopher Tarantino shares his top ten tips.

DO YOUR HOMEWORK
Check addresses, pre-arrange transport and set meeting points in case you get separated from your friends.

FACEBOOK IS YOUR FRIEND
Club websites/event pages often don't list set start or end times, so check the DJ's page.

KNOW WHERE YOU'RE GOING
Don't expect to find out the address of your 'secret location' warehouse party until the very last minute (keep checking Facebook). Once you have it, text it to yourself or save a screenshot of a map of it.

AVOID THE QUEUE
If you do manage to find out when the headliner is on, arrive an hour or two early if you don't want to wait in a massive line.

BEWARE FREE DRINKS
There's a reason clubs offer very early open bars – because no one's there. Literally no one. If you really want free drinks, by all means, go for it – but just remember, you'll be stuck there all night.

PACK EAR PLUGS
Never mind about looking silly – there actually are times where the music is too loud. If you forget 'em, you can quickly fashion a pair of 'Ghetto Plugs' (patent pending) by balling up a small piece of bar napkin for each ear.

GET PAST THE DOOR
Godlike bouncers are a thing of the past, but there are still rules. First off, be nice. Leave your attitude at home, along with sports jerseys, hats and tacky 'rave gear'. And don't arrive at the clubs listed here wearing a shiny designer shirt drenched in Drakkar Noir.

KEEP AN EYE ON YOUR TAB
Big clubs can be fun, but never forget, they are there to make money. Ask about hidden policies, such as 20-25% automatic gratuity on bar tabs. Or just use good ol' fashioned cash.

DON'T LOSE YOUR COAT
If you're travelling with a mobile phone, take a photo of your coat-check ticket in case it goes astray. While you can sometimes avoid a mandatory coat check just by asking, bear in mind some clubs employ 'coat sweep teams' for outerwear stashed behind trash cans.

BRING A FLASK
Clubs may stay open later, but booze usually ends at 4am. Plan accordingly. As a rule of thumb, larger clubs will search you but smaller ones and warehouse parties generally won't.

Santos Party House.

Verboten.

Confusingly, only certain rooms are open each night. Top-shelf DJs (both international hotshots and local heroes) of every single dance-music genre play to packed crowds, spinning the kind of left-field house, techno and bass music you rarely hear in commercially oriented spots. Be sure and head to the rooftop bar – the view of the Manhattan skyline is a stunner.

Pacha

618 W 46th Street, between Eleventh & Twelfth Avenues, Hell's Kitchen (1-212 209 7500, www. pachanyc.com). Subway C, E to 50th Street. **Open** 10pm-6am Fri; 10pm-8am Sat. **Admission** $19-$100. **Map** p398 B23.

The worldwide glam-club chain Pacha, with outposts in nightlife capitals such as Ibiza, London and Buenos Aires, hit the US market back in 2005 with this swanky joint helmed by superstar spinner Erick Morillo. The spot attracts heavyweights ranging from local hero Danny Tenaglia to international crowd-pleasers such as Fedde Le Grande and Benny Benassi. Like most big clubs, it pays to check the line-up in advance if you're into more underground beats as opposed to the main room house usually on offer here.

Santos Party House

96 Lafayette Street, between Walker & White Streets, Tribeca (1-212 584 5492, www.santos partyhouse.com). Subway J, N, Q, Z, 6 to Canal Street. **Open** varies. **Admission** $5-$35. **Map** p396 E31.

Launched by a team that includes rocker Andrew WK, Santos Party House – two black, square rooms done out in a bare-bones, generic club style – was initially hailed as a scene game-changer. While those high expectations initially panned out, they eventually flagged. It is still a solid choice, though, particularly when Danny Krivit takes over the spot for the soulful house- and classics-oriented 718 Sessions (www.dannykrivit.net).

★ Verboten

54 North 11th Street, between Kent & Wythe Avenues, Williamsburg (1-347 223 4732, www. verbotennewyork.com). Subway L to Bedford Avenue. **Open** varies. **Admission** $20-$30. **Map** p405 U7.

After more than a decade of hosting top-shelf one-offs around the city, the Verboten crew opened this long-awaited club (capacity 750) for house, techno and bass music, plus live gigs, just around the corner from Output. The modern-industrial main room features an expansive dancefloor and Martin Audio sound system, while the side Cabaret Room serves as a showcase for smaller DJs and a sometime restaurant and lounge. Trouble & Bass, Bespoke Musik, Push the Night and PopGun all join Verboten in curatorial duties, and Carl Craig, Guy Gerber, Matthew Dear, Davide Squillace, Ida Engberg, Matt Tolfrey and Lee Curtiss are among the notables claiming residencies.

Webster Hall

125 E 11th Street, at Third Avenue, East Village (1-212 353 1600, www.websterhall.com). Subway L to Third Avenue; L, N, Q, R, 4, 5, 6 to 14th Street-Union Square. **Open** 10pm-4am Thur-Sat. **Admission** free-$30. **Map** p397 F28.

IN THE KNOW
LIVE FROM NEW YORK...

Seminal NYC comedy-sketch show *Saturday Night Live* turned 40 in spring 2015. To try to score tickets to the dress rehearsal (8pm) or live show (11.30pm) taping, check the website (www.nbc.com/snl) in August for information – they're assigned by lottery each autumn. Alternatively, try the standby lottery on the day. Line up by 7am (but to have a chance, you'll need to get there much earlier) under the NBC Studio marquee (on the 48th Street side of 30 Rockefeller Plaza). You must be over 16 with photo ID.

NYC's self-proclaimed 'first nightclub' isn't exactly on clubland's A-list, due to a populist DJ selection, a loose door policy and a young crowd that favours muscle shirts and gelled hair. But, hey, it's been open, on and off, since 1866, so it must be doing something right. Friday night's Girls & Boys bash attracts music makers of the stature of Grandmaster Flash and dubstep duo Nero. And the place gets bonus points as a venue without a bad sightline in the house.

BURLESQUE CLUBS

New York's burlesque scene is a winking throwback to the days when the tease was as important as the strip. Much of the scene tends to revolve around specific revues rather than dedicated venues; good bets include shows produced by **Dances of Vice** (www.dances ofvice.com), **Wasabassco Burlesque** (www. wasabassco.com), **Thirsty Girl Productions** (www.thirstygirlproductions.com), **Angie Pontani** of the World Famous Pontani Sisters (www.angiepontani.com) and **Calamity Chang**, 'the Asian Sexation' (www.calamitychang.com).

Duane Park
308 Bowery, between Bleecker & E Houston Streets, East Village (1-212 732 5555, www.duaneparknyc. com). Subway F to Lower East Side-Second Avenue; 6 to Astor Place. **Shows** 8pm Tue; 9pm Wed, Thur; 9.30pm Fri; 7.45pm, 10.30pm Sat. **Admission** varies. **Map** p397 F29.
What was the Bowery Poetry Club now operates as Southern-inflected supper club Duane Park, though Bowery Poetry (www.bowerypoetry.com) still holds events on Sundays and Mondays. Get dinner and a show – burlesque, jazz, vaudeville or magic – in decadent surroundings featuring crystal chandeliers and Corinthian-topped columns.

FREE Nurse Bettie
106 Norfolk Street, between Delancey & Rivington Streets, Lower East Side (1-212 477 7515,

Webster Hall. See p277.

www.nursebettie.com). Subway F to Delancey Street; J, Z to Delancey-Essex Streets. **Open** 6pm-4am daily. **Admission** free. **Map** p397 G30.
The '50s-pin-up-inspired venue – named after Bettie Page, one of the 20th century's premier hotsy-totsies – is a natural setting for burlesque. Weekly shows include Spanking of the Lower East Side, produced by Calamity Chang, which usually includes six or seven acts, as well as pre-show go-go dancers. Prepare to get up close and personal in the intimate space.

★ Slipper Room

167 Orchard Street, at Stanton Street, Lower East Side (1-212 253 7246, www.slipperroom.com). Subway F to Lower East Side-Second Avenue. **Shows** vary Mon, Sun; 8pm Tue; 8pm, 10pm Wed, Thur; 10pm, midnight Fri, Sat. **Admission** $10-$20. **Map** p397 F29.
After being rebuilt from the ground up (which took a little more than two years), the Slipper Room reopened with a better sound system, new lighting and a mezzanine, among other swank touches, and reclaimed its place as the city's premier burlesque venue. Among the jam-packed weekly schedule are such long-running shows as Mr. Choade's Upstairs Downstairs (which began in 1999). *Photo p280.*

DANCE PARTIES

New York has a number of regular, peripatetic, season-specific and often long-running bashes. Check the websites listed for dates and locations.

Blkmarket Membership

www.blkmarketmembership.com.
Competing with the Bunker for the unofficial title of NYC's best techno party, the Blkmarket crew hosts bashes in the city's established clubs as well as out-of-the-way warehouse spaces.

The Bunker

www.thebunkerny.com.
Before the Bunker, there were very few nights in New York devoted to envelope-pushing electronic dance music; now, we've got oodles of 'em. Coincidence? We think not – the party blazed the trail, and it's done so with an uncompromising attitude, paying little heed to commercial trends and concentrating on sheer quality. Big guns from such labels as Spectral Sound and Kompakt regularly pack spaces such as Output (*see p275*), and the bash is busier than ever despite running for more than a decade.

★ Fixed

www.fixednyc.com.
This roving party, thrown by Dave P and JDH, has been running since 2004, but definitely does not look its age. Fixed has outlasted many venues and even more expectations simply by booking the best electronic talent, unbound by genre. It doesn't hurt that

the hosts are also terrific DJs themselves, who know exactly what an opening slot should sound like and rarely miss their mark.

Let's Play House

www.lphnyc.com.
Founded in 2009, this roving party and record label was started by Nik Mercer and DJ Jacques Renault. Their ubiquitous logo, plastered on their many 12in releases (yes, actual vinyl!), has come to signify local quality and, like their party, is devoted to oddball aurals of the disco, techno and – as the name implies – house persuasions.

★ Mister Saturday Night/Mister Sunday

www.mistersaturdaynight.com.
Two of clubland's stalwart DJs, Justin Carter and Eamon Harkin, have pooled their years of experience to throw the friendliest of parties in venues ranging from intimate loft spaces and raw warehouses to tree-shaded meadows. The music runs the gamut too – deep disco, jacking house and outer-fringes dubstep and techno – with some of the underground's top names stopping by for a date on the decks. A truly all-inclusive affair where even children (gasp!) are welcome, yet it somehow never threatens to feel like a Club Gymboree.

Mutual Dreaming

www.aurorahalal.com/mutualdreaming.
While its spiritual and physical home, 285 Kent, may be gone (rest in power), Mutual Dreaming continues to let its freak flag fly. The reliably experimental audio-visual electronic party returned to Brooklyn after taking a short break to organise the intimate Sustain-Release festival in upstate New York, which we hope will be an annual fixture.

No Ordinary Monkey

www.noordinarymonkey.com.
Golf Channel's Phil South and Ghost Note's Anton Esteban have been throwing their NOM parties since 2005 and never disappoint. If you enjoy digging for the rare forgotten records of yesteryear (or just listening to them), you can do no better than South, Esteban and frequent collaborator Justin Van Der Volgen (Keep it Cheap). The organisers raised the bar further with their triumphant 2015 New Year's Eve party featuring a live, reformed Joubert Singers performing their '70s underground gospel-disco smash 'Stand on the Word'.

ReSolute

www.resolutenyc.com.
ReSolute makes up the third side of the isosceles techno triangle of NYC (the other two being Blkmarket Membership and The Bunker). It's a fiercely underground affair, which has been bringing the deeper and darker sides of international DJs to town whenever, wherever and however they can since 2007.

Slipper Room. *See p279.*

Tiki Disco

www.tikidisco.com.

Tiki Disco is an all-inclusive and incredibly popular party, which began in 2009 as a bi-weekly Sunday afternoon summer soirée in the backyard of Bushwick pizza joint Roberta's. Since then, it has moved venues multiple times, as well as morphing into a semi-year-round fixture hosting events on the boardwalk at Rockaway Beach at Ripper's (complete with free round-trip transport), evening parties on boats and other one-offs. If you want to listen to disco and house classics interspersed with Lionel Richie tunes, in the company of more hipsters than you can shake a stick at, DJs Andy Pry, Lloydski and edit master Eli Escobar have got you covered.

★ Warm Up

MoMA PS1 (for listings, see p228). **Open** *July, Aug* noon-9pm Sat. **Admission** call or see website. **Map** p406 V5.

Since 1997, PS1's courtyard has played host to one of the most anticipated, resolutely underground clubbing events in the city. Thousands of dance-music fanatics and alt-rock enthusiasts make the pilgrimage to Long Island City on summer Saturdays to drink and dance. The sounds range from spiritually inclined soul to full-bore techno or dubstep, sometimes on the same day. Each season brings massive, Burning Man-worthy site-specific outdoor art, plus installations inside the museum that rotate during the course of the festival. There are lots of delicious local food stands as well.

Comedy

New York is one of the greatest cities in the world for comedy. On top of scheduled shows at the best venues, anyone from Chris Rock to Whitney Cummings and Gilbert Gottfried could drop by unannounced.

★ Carolines on Broadway

1626 Broadway, between 49th & 50th Streets, Theater District (1-212 757 4100, www.carolines. com). Subway N, Q, R to 49th Street; 1 to 50th Street. **Shows** vary. **Admission** varies (2-drink min). **Map** p398 D23.

Even comics who are regulars at the city's other stand-up rooms have to work extra hard to get stage time at this venerable institution. Carolines is the best place to see marquee names, including sitcom-ready stars, familiar faces from the '80s comedy boom, Friars Club-style spritzers and cable-special ravers. You'll never see anything less than professional here.

★ Comedy Cellar

117 MacDougal Street, between Bleecker & 3rd Streets, Greenwich Village (1-212 254 3480, www. comedycellar.com). Subway A, B, C, D, E, F, M to W 4th Street. **Shows** 7.30pm, 9.30pm, 11.15pm Mon, Tue; 8pm, 9.45pm, 11.30pm Wed; 7.45pm, 9.30pm, 11.30pm Thur; 7pm, 8.45pm, 10.30pm, 12.15am Fri, Sat; 8pm, 9.45pm, 11pm Sun. **Admission** $14-$24 (2-item min). **Map** p397 E29.

Claustrophobes, beware: it gets crowded down here, especially at weekends, thanks to the immense popularity of this Village standby. Big names from Louis CK to Aziz Ansari will just drop by for a set, and on any given night you can expect to see local greats whose acts are more X-rated than at other clubs (and who will distract you from your bachelorette-partying neighbours).

Other location Comedy Cellar at the Village Underground, 130 W 3rd Street, between Sixth Avenue & Macdougal Street, Greenwich Village (1-212 254 3480).

Creek & the Cave
10-93 Jackson Avenue, at 11th Street, Long Island City, Queens (1-718 706 8783, www.creeklic.com). Subway 7 to Vernon Boulevard-Jackson Avenue. **Shows** daily, times vary. **Admission** free-$5. **Map** p406 V5.

This burgeoning, multi-level comedy palace in Long Island City is the gem of the Queens comedy scene. Owner Rebecca Trent programmes shows seven nights a week, and at times you can catch up to five free shows on a busy weekend night. Among its features: cheap, serviceable Mexican food, a ramshackle theatre hosting larger events, a smaller space downstairs for intimate stand-up or storytelling and a bar with adjoining patio for pre- or post-show chilling.

Dangerfield's
1118 First Avenue, between 61st & 62nd Streets, Upper East Side (1-212 593 1650, www. dangerfields.com). Subway N, Q, R to Lexington Avenue-59th Street; 4, 5, 6 to 59th Street. **Shows** 8.30pm Mon-Thur, Sun; 8.30pm, 10.30pm, 12.30am Fri; 8pm, 10.30pm, 12.30am Sat. **Admission** $20 (2-item min). **Map** p399 F22.

The decor and gentility of the city's oldest comedy club are throwbacks to the era of its founder, the late great Rodney Dangerfield, who established it in 1969. Instead of putting eight to ten comics in a showcase, on weekends Dangerfield's gives three or four the opportunity to settle into longer acts.

Gotham Comedy Club
208 W 23rd Street, between Seventh & Eighth Avenues, Chelsea (1-212 367 9000, www.gotham comedyclub.com). Subway F, M, N, R to 23rd Street. **Shows** vary. **Admission** varies (2-drink min). **Map** p398 D26.

Chris Mazzilli's vision for his club involves elegant surroundings, professional behaviour and mutual respect. That's why the talents he fosters, such as Jim Gaffigan, Tom Papa and Ted Alexandro, keep coming back here after they've found national fame.

Greenwich Village Comedy Club
99 MacDougal Street, between Bleecker Street & Minetta Lane, Greenwich Village (1-212 777 5233, www.greenwichvillagecomedyclub.com). Subway A, B, C, D, E, F, M to W 4th Street. **Shows** 9.45pm Mon, Sun; 7.30pm, 9.45pm Tue-Thur; 8pm, 9.45pm, 11.45pm Fri; 6pm, 8.30pm, 10.30pm, 12.30am Sat. **Admission** $15-$20 (2-drink min). **Map** p397 E29.

Al Martin, the longtime owner of both the New York Comedy Club and Broadway Comedy Club, follows the same basic tenets of those ventures in this intimate basement space below an Indian restaurant. Though a few pillars in the 60-seat venue interfere with sightlines, the pub grub, extensive cocktail selection and long list of stars who just might do a spot while passing through town draw crowds every night.

Magnet Theater
254 W 29th Street, between Seventh & Eighth Avenues, Chelsea (1-212 244 8824, www. magnettheater.com). Subway A, C, E to 34th Street-Penn Station; 1 to 28th Street. **Shows** vary. **Admission** free-$20. **Map** p398 D25.

This comedy theatre exudes a distinctly Chicago vibe, from its DIY aesthetic to its performers, some of whom are from the Windy City. Even the local players here prefer theatrical to premise-based improvisation, and their shows give the impression they're not just seeking fame or commercial exposure, but pursue the craft simply for the joy of being on stage.

Peoples Improv Theater
123 E 24th Street, between Park & Lexington Avenues, Flatiron District (1-212 563 7488, www.thepit-nyc.com). Subway 6 to 23rd Street. **Shows** daily, times vary. **Admission** free-$20. **Map** p398 E26.

After inhabiting a black box in Chelsea for eight years, the PIT leapt across town into the former Algonquin Theatre. The improv and sketch venue has a beautiful proscenium stage, an additional basement space for experimental shows or stand-up, and an elegant (if cluttered) full-service bar.

★ The Stand
239 Third Avenue, between 19th & 20th Streets, Gramercy Park (1-212 677 2600, www.thestand nyc.com). Subway L, N, Q, R, 4, 5, 6 to 14th Street-Union Square. **Open** 11.30am-midnight Mon-Tue, Sun; 11.30am-2am Wed-Sat. **Shows** 8pm Mon-Thur; 8pm, 10pm, midnight Fri, Sat; 8pm, 10pm Sun. **Admission** $5-$40. **Map** p397 F27.

ARTS & ENTERTAINMENT

Hotel Chantelle's Seth Levine turns out comfort-food spins – such as cheeseburger pot stickers and duck-topped pizzas – at this comedy club-restaurant hybrid. After dinner, head downstairs to the club, where you can sip cocktails while acts like Judah Friedlander and Artie Lange supply the belly laughs. Test your stand-up knowledge by trying to name all the comedians on the wallpaper in the bathroom.

Stand-up New York
236 W 78th Street, at Broadway, Upper West Side (1-212 595 0850, www.standupny.com). Subway 1 to 79th Street. **Shows** 8pm, 10.15pm Mon-Thur, Sun; 7pm, 9pm, 11pm Fri; 5pm, 8pm, 10pm, 11.30pm Sat. **Admission** $15-$20 (2-drink min). **Map** p399 C19.

After some managerial shifts, this musty uptown spot has begun to garner attention again. The line-ups (including stalwart club denizens such as Jay Oakerson and Godfrey) keep things pretty simple, but there's almost always one performer on the bill that makes it worth the trip.

Tribeca Comedy Lounge
22 Warren Street, between Broadway & Church Street, Tribeca (1-646 504 5653, www.tribeca comedylounge.com). Subway A, C, 1, 2, 3 to Chambers Street; N, R to City Hall. **Shows** 8pm Tue-Thur; 8pm, 10pm Fri, Sat. **Admission** $25 (2-drink min). **Map** p396 E32.

The atmosphere in this spot – not to be confused with the space's previous occupant, the Tribeca Comedy Club – is a congenial one. The brick walls and makeshift stage remind you that you're in a basement, but the doting waitstaff, haute Italian menu from Brick NYC upstairs and roomy layout will please fans of creature comforts. Adam Strauss, the owner-booker and a burgeoning comic, makes sure that his programming is packed with young, funny next-wave talent while also saving stage time for himself.
▶ *The club has also expanded to nearby Dark Horse Comedy Club (17 Murray Street, between Broadway & Church Street, 1-646 504 5653, www.darkhorsecomedyclub.com).*

★ Upright Citizens Brigade Theatre
307 W 26th Street, at Eighth Avenue, Chelsea (1-212 366 9176, www.ucbtheatre.com). Subway C, E to 23rd Street; 1 to 28th Street. **Shows** daily, times vary. **Admission** free-$10. **No credit cards. Map** p398 D26.

The most visible catalyst in New York's current alternative comedy boom. The improv troupes and sketch groups here are some of the best in the city. Stars of *Saturday Night Live* and writers for late-night talk-shows gather on Sunday nights to wow crowds in the long-running ASSSSCAT 3000. Other premier teams include the Stepfathers (Friday) and the Curfew (Saturday). Arrive early for a good seat – the venue has challenging sightlines.

The newer UCBEast (153 E Third Street, East Village, 1-212 366 9231) brings the same sort of cheap, raw and rowdy shows featured on the West Side, though this space focuses as much on sketch and stand-up as it does improv.

Music
ROCK, POP & SOUL
Not only are venues offering increasingly eclectic fare, but gigs are also busting out of their usual club and concert hall confines: the **City Winery** crushes and ferments grapes as well as staging shows, while bowling alley-music venue hybrid **Brooklyn Bowl** hosts a smattering of high-profile acts as well as regular dance parties.

INFORMATION & TICKETS
Tickets are usually available from clubs in advance and at the door, but bear in mind that if you purchase your ticket on-site you may have to pay cash. For larger events, buy online through the venue's website or via **Ticketmaster** (www.ticketmaster.com, 1-800 745 3000) or **TicketWeb** (www.ticketweb.com). Phone ahead for information and show times, which can change without notice.

Major arenas

★ Barclays Center
620 Atlantic Avenue, at Flatbush Avenue, Prospect Heights, Brooklyn (1-917 618 6100, www.barclays center.com) Subway B, D, N, Q, R, 2, 3, 4, 5 to Atlantic Avenue-Barclays Center. **Box office** noon-6pm Mon-Fri; noon-2pm Sat (varies on event days). **Tickets** vary. **Map** p404 T10.
The city's newest arena, home of the rechristened Brooklyn Nets basketball team, opened in autumn 2012 with a series of concerts by native son and Nets investor Jay Z. Despite its short life, the arena has already proven to be a success. The staff is efficient and amiable, the acoustics are excellent, and there's a top-notch view from nearly every one of the 19,000 seats. But, most importantly, the venue has attracted an unexpectedly cool list of acts, with artists as diverse as the Weeknd, black sabbath and Luke Bryan gracing its stage.

★ Madison Square Garden
Seventh Avenue, between 31st & 33rd Streets, Garment District (1-212 465 6741, www.the garden.com). Subway A, C, E, 1, 2, 3 to 34th Street-Penn Station. **Box office** 10am-6pm Mon-Sat (plus 1hr after show starts). **Tickets** vary. **Map** p398 D25.
Some of music's biggest acts – Lady Gaga, Eric Clapton, Rush – come out to play at the world's most famous basketball arena, home to the Knicks and also hockey's Rangers. Whether you'll actually be able to

get a look at them depends on your seat number or the quality of your binoculars. While it is undoubtedly a part of the fabric of New York, the storied venue is too vast for a rich concert experience, but it has been improved by a major renovation. The three-year revamp brought new seating and food from top New York City chefs, among other improvements, while respecting the Garden's history. The striking circular ceiling has been restored, while the north and south corridors on the entry level have been returned to their original appearance; attendees can also choose to peer down from newly installed Chase Bridge seats that hover above the action.

Venues

★ Apollo Theater
253 W 125th Street, between Adam Clayton Powell Jr Boulevard (Seventh Avenue) & Frederick Douglass Boulevard (Eighth Avenue), Harlem (1-212 531 5300, www.apollotheater.org). Subway A, B, C, D, 1 to 125th Street. **Box office** 10am-6pm Mon-Fri; noon-5pm Sat. **Tickets** vary. **Map** p401 D13.
This 100-year-old former burlesque theatre has been a hub for African-American artists for decades, and launched the careers of Ella Fitzgerald and D'Angelo, among many others. The now-legendary Amateur Night showcase has been running since 1934. The venue, known for jazz, R&B and soul, mixes veteran talents such as Dianne Reeves with younger artists like Janelle Monae and Sam Smith.

★ Baby's All Right
146 Broadway, at Bedford Avenue, Williamsburg, Brooklyn (1-718 599 5800, www.babysallright. com). Subway J, M, Z to Marcy Avenue. **Open** 5pm-4am Mon-Fri; noon-4am Sat, Sun. **Shows** vary. **Tickets** free-$20. **Map** p405 U8.
This eatery, bar and stage, located on a happening little Williamsburg strip, is well on its way to becoming a local musical institution with its lively schedule of au courant acts and DJs that range from experimental (Pharmakon) to the voguish (Ariel Pink). The buzzy spot always seems to have something interesting on deck: it's not unusual to find three bills crammed into the same night.

Barbès
376 9th Street, between Sixth & Seventh Avenues, Park Slope, Brooklyn (1-347 422 0248, www.barbes brooklyn.com). Subway F to Seventh Avenue. **Open** 5pm-2am Mon-Thur; 2pm-4am Fri, Sat; 2pm-2am Sun. **Tickets** *suggested donation* $10. **Map** p404 T11.
Show up early if you want to get into Park Slope's global-bohemian club – it's tiny. Run by musically inclined French expats, this *boîte* brings in traditional swing and jazz of more daring stripes: depending on the night, you could catch Colombian, Brazilian, African or French music or acts that often defy categorisation.

Madison Square Garden.

BEST WEEKLY COMEDY SHOWS

Time Out's top five long-running laugh fests.

When you're on a mission to see great comedy in New York, it can be tough to know where to start. But you know what's a sign of a good comedy show? Longevity. When a show brings audiences back week after week, you know it's really worth your time. It also doesn't hurt when they attract surprise special guests such as Chris Rock, Louis CK or Michael Che, of course – which many of the weekly shows on our list do on a regular basis. Even better, they're all cheap or free.

ASSSSCAT 3000
One of the city's most popular comedy nights sees NYC's long-form improv royalty (think folks from *Saturday Night Live* and some adored Upright Citizens Brigade regulars) play pick-up-game-style in this famous long-running show.
Upright Citizens Brigade Theater (see p282), Sunday.

COMEDY AS A SECOND LANGUAGE
Started by *Time Out New York* favourite Sean Patton, this weekly show takes place in the back of an East Village dive bar, but don't be deceived by appearances: not only is it home to some of the best up-and-coming comics, but some of the biggest names in stand-up – Louis CK, Bonnie McFarlane and Murderfist – have also dropped by.
Lit Lounge, 93 Second Avenue, between 5th & 6th Streets (1-212 777 7987, www.litloungenyc.com), Thursday.

FRANTIC!
Key to a great weekly show is great regulars, and the Stand's ever-popular free show, hosted by Aaron Berg, has this in spades: the likes of Judah Friedlander and Aparna Nancherla are often on hand to supply the belly laughs.
The Stand (see p281), Mondays.

GANDHI, IS THAT YOU?
Brendan Fitzgibbons and Lance Weiss welcome comedy fans into this Lower East Side bar's basement for this friendly stand-up show. So friendly, in fact, that famous comedians including Jim Gaffigan and Todd Barry are known to stop by and try out new material.
Lucky Jack's, 129 Orchard Street, between Delancey & Rivington Streets, Lower East Side (1-212 477 6555, www.luckyjacksnyc.com), Wednesday.

WHIPLASH
This wildly popular show, hosted by Leo Allen, is known for always featuring the city's best rising comedians. But it's the surprise VIPs (name-check: Chris Rock, Louis CK and David Cross) who keep audiences hooked.
Upright Citizens Brigade Theater (see p282), Monday.

Comedy as a Second Language.

★ Beacon Theatre

2124 Broadway, between 74th & 75th Streets, Upper West Side (1-212 465 6500, www. beacontheatrenyc.com). Subway 1, 2, 3 to 72nd Street. **Box office** 11am-7pm Mon-Sat (varies on event days). **Tickets** vary. **Map** p399 C20.

This spacious former vaudeville theatre hosts a variety of popular acts, from comedian John Oliver to indie-folk artist Sufjan Stevens. While the vastness can be daunting to performers and audience alike, the baroque, gilded interior and uptown location make you feel as though you're having a real night out on the town.

Bell House

149 7th Street, between Second & Third Avenues, Gowanus, Brooklyn (1-718 643 6510, www.thebell houseny.com). Subway F, G, R to Fourth Avenue-9th Street. **Shows** vary. **Tickets** free-$27. **Map** p404 S11.

This pioneering venue offers a plethora of cool events each week, including concerts, nerdy lectures and dance parties. In addition to gigs by the likes of Mission of Burma, regular fixtures on the schedule include off-the-cuff storytelling slam the Moth, trivia show Ask Me Another and the Rub, a funky long-running affair tossed by DJs Ayres and Eleven.

Best Buy Theater

1515 Broadway, at 44th Street, Theater District (1-212 930 1950, www.bestbuytheater.com). Subway N, Q, R, S, 1, 2, 3, 7 to 42nd Street-Times Square. **Box office** noon-6pm Mon-Sat. **Tickets** $20-$70. **Map** p398 D24.

This large, corporate club begs for character but finds redemption in its creature comforts. The sound and sightlines are both good, and there's even edible food. Those who wish to look into a musician's eyes can stand in the ample front section; foot-weary fans can sit in the cinema-like section at the back. It's a comfortable place to see a well-known band that hasn't (yet) reached stadium-filling fame.

★ Bowery Ballroom

6 Delancey Street, between Bowery & Chrystie Street, Lower East Side (1-212 533 2111, www.bowery ballroom.com). Subway B, D to Grand Street; J, Z to Bowery; 6 to Spring Street. **Box office** at Mercury Lounge *(see p288).* **Tickets** $15-$35. **Map** p397 F30.

Bowery Ballroom is probably the best venue in the city for seeing indie bands, either on the way up or holding their own. But it also brings in a diverse range of artists from home and abroad, and you can expect a clear view and bright sound from any spot in the venue. The spacious downstairs lounge is a great place to hang out between sets.

Brooklyn Bowl

61 Wythe Avenue, between North 11th & 12th Streets, Williamsburg, Brooklyn (1-718 963 3369, www. brooklynbowl.com). Subway L to Bedford Avenue. **Shows** vary. **Tickets** $5-$25. **Map** p405 U7.

This bowling alley and music venue fully embraces the mania for local nostalgia. The place takes its design cues from Coney Island with old freak-show posters and carnival-game relics, and all the beer sold inside is made in the borough. The 600-capacity concert space hosts a smattering of high-profile acts (Trey Anastasio Band, Robert Plant) as well as regular DJ nights and dance-offs.

Cake Shop

152 Ludlow Street, between Rivington & Stanton Streets, Lower East Side (1-212 253 0036, www. cake-shop.com). Subway F to Lower East Side-Second Avenue. **Open** *Café* 9am-2am daily. *Bar* 5pm-2am Mon-Thur, Sun; 5pm-4am Fri-Sat. **Tickets** free-$12. **Map** p397 G29.

It can be difficult to see the stage in this narrow, stuffy basement space, but Cake Shop gets big points for its keen indie and underground-rock bookings, which are among the best and most adventurous in the city. The venue lives up to its name, selling vegan pastries and coffee upstairs, as well as a curated selection of mostly local records. *Photo p286.*

City Winery

155 Varick Street, at Vandam Street, Tribeca (1-212 608 0555, www.citywinery.com). Subway 1 to Houston Street. **Open** 11.30am-3pm, 5pm-midnight Mon-Fri, Sun; 5pm-midnight Sat. **Box office** 11am-6pm Mon-Fri. **Tickets** vary. **Map** p397 D30.

Unabashedly grown-up and yuppie-friendly, this slick, spacious club launched by oenophile Michael Dorf is New York's only fully functioning winery – as well as a 300-seat concert space. Acts tend to be on the quiet side – this is, after all, a wine bar – but that doesn't mean the shows lack bite. Younger singer-songwriters such as Laura Marling and Keren Ann have appeared, but the place is dominated by older artists (Mott the Hoople's Ian Hunter, the Doors' Robby Krieger).

▶ *Michael Dorf was also the founder of the Knitting Factory; see p288.*

Gramercy Theatre

127 E 23rd Street, between Park & Lexington Avenues, Gramercy Park (1-212 614 6932, www. thegramercytheatre.com). Subway N, R, 6 to 23rd Street. **Box office** noon-6.30pm Mon-Fri; 1-5pm Sat. **Tickets** $10-$50. **Map** p398 E26.

The Gramercy Theatre looks exactly like what it is, a run-down former cinema; yet it has a decent sound system and good sightlines. Concert-goers can lounge in raised seats on the top level or get closer to the stage. Bookings have included such Baby Boom underdogs as Loudon Wainwright III and Todd Rundgren, and the occasional hip hop show, but tilt towards niche metal and emo.

Hammerstein Ballroom

Manhattan Center, 311 W 34th Street, between Eighth & Ninth Avenues, Garment District

ARTS & ENTERTAINMENT

Cake Shop. See p285.

(1-212 279 7740, Ticketmaster 1-800 745 3000, www.mcstudios.com). Subway A, C, E to 34th Street-Penn Station. **Tickets** vary. **Map** p398 C25. Queues can wind across the block, drinks prices are high, and those seated in the balcony should bring binoculars. Still, this cavernous space regularly draws big performers in the limbo between club and arena shows, and it's ideal for theatrical blowouts; Beck, Nick Cave and Ryan Adams have all packed the house.

Highline Ballroom
431 W 16th Street, between Ninth & Tenth Avenues, Chelsea (1-212 414 5994, www.highline ballroom.com). Subway A, C, E to 14th Street; L to Eighth Avenue. **Box office** 11am-end of show. **Tickets** free-$100 ($10 food/drink min at tables). **Map** p397 C27.
This West Side club is LA-slick and bland, in a corporate sense, but it has a lot to recommend it: the sound is top-of-the-heap and sightlines are pretty good. The bookings are also impressive, ranging from pop heatseekers such as Tinashe and Tove Lo, to singer-songwriter pop, world music and burlesque.

Irving Plaza
17 Irving Place, at 15th Street, Gramercy & Flatiron (1-212 777 6800, www.irvingplaza.com). Subway L, N, Q, R, 4, 5, 6 to 14th Street-Union Square. **Box office** noon-6.30pm Mon-Fri; 2hrs before shows Sat, Sun. **Tickets** $15-$75. **Map** p397 E27.
This midsize rock venue has served as a Democratic Party lecture hall (in the 19th century), a Yiddish theatre and a burlesque house (Gypsy Rose Lee made an appearance). It's a great place to see big stars keeping a low profile (Foo Fighters and Paul McCartney, for starters) and medium heavies on their way up.

★ Joe's Pub
Public Theater, 425 Lafayette Street, between Astor Place & E 4th Street, East Village (1-212 967 7555, www.joespub.com). Subway N, R to 8th Street-NYU; 6 to Astor Place. **Box office** 2-7pm Mon-Sat; 2-6pm Sun. **Tickets** ($12 food or 2-drink min) $12-$50. **Map** p397 E28.
One of the city's premier small spots for sit-down audiences, Joe's Pub brings in impeccable talent of all genres and origins. While some well-established names play here, Joe's also lends its stage to up-and-comers (this is where Amy Winehouse made her debut in the United States), drag acts and cabaret performers (Justin Vivian Bond is a mainstay). The food menu – a mix of snacks, shareable plates and main courses – has been revitalised by hot chef Andrew Carmellini.

Kings Theatre
1027 Flatbush Avenue between Duryea Place & Tilden Avenue, East Flatbush, Brooklyn (Ticketmaster 1-800 745 3000, www.kingstheatre.com). Subway B, Q, 2, 5 to Church Avenue. **Box office** noon-5pm Mon-Sat. **Tickets** vary. **Map** p404 U13.
See p287 **Return of the Kings.**

RETURN OF THE KINGS

A revamped gilded show palace is attracting rock and pop royalty.

Before BAM or the Barclays Center, Brooklyn's crown cultural jewel was a gilded movie palace called the **Kings Theatre** (*see p286*). Now, after a two-year, $93 million restoration, the venue is back. Built in 1929 to show films and vaudeville acts, the East Flatbush theatre fell into decline in the 1950s as multiplex cinemas gained popularity. It closed in 1977, and although a variety of proposals to revitalise the venue emerged, the longer it sat vacant, the more costly restoration became. Lacking sufficient funding or political will, the theatre sat empty and unused for 37 years.

In 2008, the New York City Economic Development Corporation and then Borough President Marty Markowitz issued a request for proposals to revive the facility. The ACE Theatrical Group was chosen in 2010, partnering with the city, the state, Goldman Sachs Urban Investment Group and private investors to foot the bill. When work began in 2013, the theatre's once majestic ceiling had fallen in. Walls, carpets and seats were covered in mould. Chandeliers had been stolen, and gargoyles had been decapitated.

'In a lot of ways, it's almost like a giant sculpture,' says executive director Matthew Wolf. And like restoring a piece of art, no detail has been overlooked. It took five months to rid the venue of mould and asbestos, and experts analysed paint chips to determine the original colours – a six-month project in itself.

To recreate the intricacy of the ceilings and gargoyles, moulds were cast from parts that remained intact and then used to restore the plaster in places where it had fallen or eroded. The theatre still boasts the original marble and American-walnut wood, but the seats have been replaced with replicas of the originals (the new ones are wider).

The Kings Theatre is now Brooklyn's second-biggest concert space (after Barclays), and its stellar line-ups so far reflect the diversity of the borough. Opening night featured Diana Ross; since then, bookings have included salsa singer Gilberto Santa Rosa, folk-rock legends Crosby Stills & Nash and indie-rock staples such as Spoon and Pixies.

ARTS & ENTERTAINMENT

Radio City Music Hall.

Knitting Factory Brooklyn

361 Metropolitan Avenue, at Havemeyer Street,
Williamsburg, Brooklyn (1-347 529 6696, www.
knittingfactory.com). Subway L to Lorimer Street;
G to Metropolitan Avenue. **Open** 5pm-3.30am
Mon-Fri; 3pm-3.30am Sat, Sun. **Tickets** free-$25.
Map p405 U8.
Once a downtown Manhattan incubator of experimental music (of both the jazz and the indie-rock
variety), Knitting Factory now has outposts across
the country. Its New York base, which relocated to
Williamsburg, is a professional, well-managed club,
with a happening front-room bar, and solid indie-
rock and hip hop bills (Screaming Females, Why?)
designed to suit its hipster clientele.
▶ *For Knitting Factory founder Michael Dorf's*
latest venture, see p285 City Winery.

Living Room

134 Metropolitan Avenue, between Berry Street
& Wythe Avenue, Williamsburg, Brooklyn (1-718
782-6600, www.livingroomny.com). Subway L to
Bedford Avenue. **Shows** vary. **Tickets** free-$35.
Map p405 U8.
The venerable, roots-centric LES haunt moved
across the river to a new Williamsburg location in
2014. It's made the transition intact: the new spot
features the same top-notch singer-songwriter, bluegrass and Americana fare.

Mercury Lounge

217 E Houston Street, between Essex & Ludlow
Streets, Lower East Side (1-212 260 4700, www.
mercuryloungenyc.com). Subway F to Lower East
Side-Second Avenue. **Box office** noon-6pm Tue-
Sat. **Tickets** $8-$20. **Map** p397 G29.
The unassuming, boxy Mercury Lounge is an old
standby, with solid sound and sightlines (and a
cramped bar in the front room). There are four-
band bills most nights, although they can seem
stylistically haphazard and set times are often later
than advertised. (It's a good rule of thumb to show
up half an hour later than you think you should.)
Some of the bigger shows sell out in advance, and the
club thrives during autumn's CMJ Music Marathon;
young hopefuls from years gone by include
Mumford & Sons.

★ Music Hall of Williamsburg

66 North 6th Street, between Kent & Wythe
Avenues, Williamsburg, Brooklyn (1-718 486
5400, www.musichallofwilliamsburg.com).
Subway L to Bedford Avenue. **Box office**
11am-6pm Sat. **Tickets** $15-$35. **Map** p405 U7.
When, in 2007, the local promoter Bowery
Presents found itself in need of a Williamsburg
outpost, it gave the former Northsix a facelift and
took over the bookings. It's basically a Bowery
Ballroom in Brooklyn – and bands such as Swans,
They Might Be Giants and José González head-
line, often on the day after they've played Bowery
Ballroom or Terminal 5.

★ FREE Pete's Candy Store

709 Lorimer Street, between Frost & Richardson
Streets, Williamsburg, Brooklyn (1-718 302 3770,
www.petescandystore.com). Subway L to Lorimer
Street. **Open** 5pm-2am Mon-Wed; 5pm-4am Thur;
3.30pm-4am Fri, Sat; 3.30pm-2am Sun. **Admission**
free. **Map** p405 V7.
An overlooked gem tucked away in an old candy
shop, Pete's is beautifully ramshackle, tiny and
almost always free. The performers are generally
unknown and crowds can be thin, but it can be a
charming place to catch a singer-songwriter testing
out new material.

Pianos

158 Ludlow Street, between Rivington & Stanton Streets, Lower East Side (1-212 505 3733, www. pianosnyc.com). Subway F to Delancey Street; J, M, Z to Delancey-Essex Streets. **Open** 2pm-4am daily. **Admission** free-$10. **Map** p397 G29.

In recent years, a lot of the cooler bookings have moved down the block to venues such as Cake Shop or to Brooklyn. But while the sound is often lousy and the room can get uncomfortably mobbed, there are always good reasons to go back to Pianos – very often the under-the-radar, emerging rock bands that make local music scenes tick.

★ Le Poisson Rouge

158 Bleecker Street, at Thompson Street, Greenwich Village (1-212 505 3474, www.lepoissonrouge. com). Subway A, B, C, D, E, F, M to W 4th Street. **Open** 5pm-2am Mon-Wed, Sun; 5pm-4am Thur-Sat. **Box office** 5pm-close daily. **Tickets** free-$30. **Map** p397 E29.

Tucked into the basement of the long-gone Village Gate – a legendary performance space that hosted everyone from Miles Davis to Jimi Hendrix – Le Poisson Rouge was opened in 2008 by a group of young music enthusiasts with ties to both the classical and the indie rock worlds. The cabaret space's booking policy reflects both camps, often on a single bill. No other joint in town books such a wide range of great music, whether from a feverish Saharan guitarist (Bombino), noisy indie luminaries (Lightning Bolt) or young classical stars (pianist Simone Dinnerstein).

★ Radio City Music Hall

1260 Sixth Avenue, at 50th Street, Midtown (1-212 247 4777, www.radiocity.com). Subway B, D, F, M to 47th-50th Streets-Rockefeller Center. **Box office** 10am-6pm daily. **Tickets** vary. **Map** p398 D23.

Few rooms scream 'New York City!' more than this gilded hall, which in recent years has drawn The xx, Dave Chappelle and Leonard Cohen as headliners. The greatest challenge for any performer is to not be upstaged by the awe-inspiring art deco surroundings, although those same surroundings lend historic heft to even the flimsiest showing. Bookings are all over the map; expect everything from seasonal staples like the Rockettes to lectures from the Dalai Lama.

★ Rockwood Music Hall

196 Allen Street, between E Houston & Stanton Streets, Lower East Side (1-212 477 4155, www. rockwoodmusichall.com). Subway F to Lower East Side-Second Avenue. **Open** 6pm-3am Mon-Fri; 3pm-3am Sat, Sun. **Tickets** free-$20 (1-drink min per set). **Map** p397 F29.

The cramped quarters are part of this club's appeal: there are no bad seats (or standing spots) in the house. You can catch multiple acts every night of the week on three separate stages, and it's likely that many of those performers will soon be appearing in much bigger halls. Multi-genre polymath Gabriel Kahane is a regular, as is bluegrass great Michael Daves.

★ Saint Vitus

1120 Manhattan Avenue, between Box and Clay Streets, Greenpoint, Brooklyn (no phone, www. saintvitusbar.com). Subway G to Greenpoint Avenue. **Open** 6pm-4am Mon-Sat; 6pm-midnight Sun. **Shows** vary. **Tickets** free-$25. **Map** p405 U6.

Once a mainstay of NYC's downtown scene, true rock 'n' roll clubs feel like a dying breed in the post-Giuliani era. But this Greenpoint drinkery – moodily decorated with all-black walls and dead roses hanging above the bar – reinvigorates the tradition with a Brooklyn twist. Metal heads and rockers will be delighted to find both legendary groups (Pentagram) and local up-and-comers (Sannhet) taking to the stage.

FREE Sidewalk Café

94 Avenue A, at 6th Street, East Village (1-212 473 7373, www.sidewalkny.com). Subway 6 to Astor Place. **Open** 11am-3am Mon-Thur; 11am-4am Fri, Sat; 11am-2am Sun. **Shows** usually 7pm daily. **Admission** free (2-drink min). **Map** p397 G28.

Despite its cramped, awkward layout, the Sidewalk Café is the focal point of the city's anti-folk scene – although that category means just about anything from piano pop to wry folk. Nellie McKay, Regina Spektor and the Moldy Peaches all started here.

SOB's

204 Varick Street, at Houston Street, Tribeca (1-212 243 4940, www.sobs.com). Subway 1 to Houston Street. **Box office** 11am-6pm Mon-Fri. **Tickets** $10-$40. **Map** p397 D29.

The titular Sounds of Brazil (SOB, geddit?) are just some of the many global genres that keep this venue hopping. Soul, hip hop, reggae and Latin beats figure in the mix, with Raekwon, Schoolboy Q and

Eddie Palmieri each appearing of late. The drinks are expensive, but the sharp-looking clientele don't seem to mind.

Terminal 5
610 W 56th Street, between 11th & 12th Avenues, Hell's Kitchen (1-212 582 6600, www.terminal 5nyc.com). Subway A, B, C, D, 1 to 59th Street-Columbus Circle. **Box office** at Mercury Lounge *(see p288).* **Tickets** $15-$90. **Map** p399 C22.
This three-floor, 3,000-capacity venue is part of the Bowery Presents empire. Bookings include bands that only a short time ago were playing in the smaller Bowery confines (Toro Y Moi), plus bigger stars (Cold War Kids) and veterans with their loyal fan bases (Marilyn Manson, Mazzy Star). It's great for dancey acts (Chromeo, Matt & Kim), but be warned: sightlines from the T5 balconies are among the worst in the city.

Town Hall
123 W 43rd Street, between Sixth Avenue & Broadway, Theater District (1-212 840 2824, www. thetownhall.org). Subway B, D, F, M to 42nd Street-Bryant Park; N, Q, R, S, 1, 2, 3, 7 to 42nd Street-Times Square; 7 to Fifth Avenue. **Box office** noon-6pm Mon-Sat. **Tickets** vary. **Map** p398 D24.
Acoustics at the 1921 'people's auditorium' are superb, and there's no doubting the gravitas of the surroundings – the building was designed by illustrious architects McKim, Mead & White as a meeting house for a suffragist organisation. Band of Horses, Sharon Van Etten and Joe Jackson have performed here, and smart indie songwriters such as the Magnetic Fields have set up shop for a number of nights.

Union Hall
For listings, *see p216.* **Tickets** free-$15.
The spacious main floor of this Brooklyn bar has a garden, food service and a bocce ball court. Tucked in the basement is a comfortable space dominated by the more delicate side of indie rock, with infrequent sets by indie comics such as Mike Birbiglia and Eugene Mirman.

Union Pool
For listings, *see p222.* **Tickets** free-$15.
Wind through the kitschy backyard space of this modest but super-cool Williamsburg bar (which featured in the movie *Nick and Norah's Infinite Playlist*) and you'll find yourself back indoors, facing a small stage. Local stars check in from time to time (members of Yeah Yeah Yeahs have showed off their side projects here), but it's dominated by well-plucked smaller indie acts. For a rowdy, amusing Monday night, check out Reverend Vince Anderson and his Love Choir.

Webster Hall
For listings, *see p277.*
A great-sounding alternative for bands (and fans) who've had their fill of the comparably sized Irving Plaza, Webster Hall is booked by Bowery Presents, the folks who run Bowery Ballroom and Mercury Lounge, among other venues. Expect to find high-calibre indie acts (Modest Mouse, Patti Smith, Noel Gallagher), but be sure to arrive early if you want a decent view. A smaller space downstairs, the Studio at Webster Hall, hosts cheaper shows, mainly by local bands.

WORLD, COUNTRY & ROOTS
Among the cornucopia of live entertainment programmes at the **Brooklyn Academy of Music** *(p295),* the **BAMcafé** above the lobby comes to life on weekend nights with world music and other genres. Other venues featuring acts defined by these styles include **Barbès** *(p283),* **BB King Blues Club & Grill** *(p292),* **Nublu** *(p275)* and **SOB's** *(p289).*

Hill Country
For listings, *see p140.* **Tickets** free-$35.
Get a taste of Texas and an earful of unpretentious roots, rockabilly and country music at this well-regarded BBQ, which usually offers live entertainment with no cover. The mixture of Austin-derived Southern chow and twangy music has been so successful the venue opened a second spot in Brooklyn.

JAZZ, BLUES & EXPERIMENTAL
Ever since Duke Ellington urged folks to take the A train up to Harlem, New York has been a hotbed of improvisational talent. While Harlem is no longer the centre of the jazz scene, you can soak up the vibe at clubs in the Village that once provided a platform for the virtuoso experimentations of Miles Davis, John Coltrane and Thelonious Monk. Boundaries are still being pushed in eclectic avant-garde venues such as **Roulette**, **Spectrum** (for both, *see p300*) and the **Stone**. For well-known jazz joints such as the **Village Vanguard** and **Birdland**, booking ahead is recommended.

55 Bar
55 Christopher Street, between Seventh Avenue South & Waverly Place, West Village (1-212 929 9883, www.55bar.com). Subway 1 to Christopher Street-Sheridan Square. **Open** 3pm-4am daily. **Tickets** free-$10 (2-drink min). **No credit cards**. **Map** p397 D28.
This tiny Prohibition-era dive is one of New York's most artist-friendly rooms, thanks to its knowledgeable, appreciative audience. You can catch emerging talent almost every night at the free-of-charge early shows; late sets regularly feature established artists such as Mike Stern, Wayne Krantz and David Binney.

92nd Street Y
For listings, *see p298.*
Best known for the series Jazz in July and spring's Lyrics & Lyricists, this multidisciplinary cultural

ESSENTIAL NEW YORK ALBUMS

Want to feel the big city? Listen up.

THE COMPLETE SAVOY & DIAL MASTERS
Charlie Parker (1945-48)
No jazz style more accurately captures New York City's edgy energy and take-no-prisoners attitude than bebop, the cerebral yet visceral style that saxophonist Parker, trumpeter Gillespie and their revolutionary comrades invented in Harlem joints and 52nd Street nightclubs.

NEW YORK DOLLS
New York Dolls (1973)
Loud, snotty and outrageous in their quasi-drag regalia, David Johansen, Johnny Thunders and their raucous cohorts essentially invented shock rock (hello, Kiss!) and glam metal, while also giving punk rock a formative kick in the ass. Johansen is still making waves, but this album cemented his legend for ever.

BOOGIE DOWN PRODUCTIONS
Criminal Minded (1987)
Rapper KRS-One and DJ Scott La Rock may not have invented hip hop, but on this still exhilarating LP the pair created the mould for underworld reportage, gangsta posturing, musical breadth and borough-proud brinksmanship that defines the best in NYC rap.

BERNSTEIN CONDUCTS BERNSTEIN
New York Philharmonic (1961-65)
Leonard Bernstein made front-page news with his New York Philharmonic conducting debut in 1943. This sampling of his New York-inspired music – *West Side Story, On the Town* – is the definitive example of the city firing a composer's imagination.

SUICIDE
Suicide (1977)
Industrial music and techno owe their existence to a confrontational slab of vinyl by caustic vocalist Alan Vega and stolid keyboardist Martin Rev. Misunderstood in its day, Suicide's debut was proclaimed the essential NYC platter by no less an expert than No Wave pioneer Lydia Lunch.

NEW YORK
Lou Reed (1989)
There's no Lou Reed album that couldn't be described as 'essential New York', so acute and unvarnished were his musical chronicles from the Velvet Underground days to the end of his life. But on the album he named for his long-time hometown, Reed leavens his caustic edge with wisdom, insight and grace.

centre also offers cabaret, mainstream jazz and singer-songwriters. The small, handsome theatre provides a fine setting for the sophisticated fare.

BB King Blues Club & Grill

237 W 42nd Street, between Seventh & Eighth Avenues, Theater District (1-212 997 4144, www.bbkingblues.com). Subway A, C, E to 42nd Street-Port Authority; N, Q, R, S, 1, 2, 3, 7 to 42nd Street-Times Square. **Box office** 11am-midnight daily. **Tickets** $12-$150. Food/drink minimum $10. **Map** p398 D24.

BB's Times Square joint hosts one of the most varied music schedules in town. Cover bands and tributes fill the gaps between big-name bookings such as George Clinton and Buddy Guy, but the venue also regularly hosts hip hop and the odd extreme-metal blowout. The best seats are often at the dinner tables in front, but the menu prices are steep (and watch out for drink minimums).

Birdland

315 W 44th Street, between Eighth & Ninth Avenues, Theater District (1-212 581 3080, www. birdlandjazz.com). Subway A, C, E to 42nd Street-Port Authority. **Open** 5pm-1am daily. **Tickets** $20-$50 ($10 food/drink min). **Map** p398 C24.

The flagship venue for midtown's jazz resurgence, Birdland takes its place among the neon lights of Times Square seriously. That means it's a haven for great jazz musicians (Joe Lovano, Kurt Elling) as well as performers like John Pizzarelli, and Broadway cabaret night Jim Caruso's Cast Party. The club is also notable for its roster of bands-in-residence. Sundays belong to the Arturo O'Farrill Afro Latin Jazz Orchestra.

Blue Note

131 W 3rd Street, between MacDougal Street & Sixth Avenue, Greenwich Village (1-212 475 8592, www.bluenote.net). Subway A, B, C, D, E, F, M to W 4th Street. **Shows** 8pm, 10.30pm Mon-Thur, Sun; 8pm, 10.30pm, 12.30am Fri, Sat. **Tickets** $10-$75 ($5 food/drink min). **Map** p397 E29.

The Blue Note prides itself on being 'the jazz capital of the world'. Bona fide musical titans (Roy Hargrove, Lee Konitz) rub against contemporary heavyweights (the Bad Plus), while the close-set tables in the club get patrons rubbing up against each other. The edgy Friday Late Night Groove series and the Sunday brunches (10.30am-3pm; $35 including show) are the best bargain bets.

★ Carnegie Hall

For listings, *see p296.*

Carnegie Hall means the big time. In recent years, though, the 599-seat, state-of-the-art Zankel Hall has greatly augmented the venue's pop, jazz and world music offerings. Between both halls, the complex has welcomed Bjork, Elvis Costello and Neil Young, among other high-wattage names.

Cornelia Street Café

29 Cornelia Street, between Bleecker & 4th Streets, Greenwich Village (1-212 989 9319, www.cornelia streetcafe.com). Subway A, B, C, D, E, F, M to W 4th Street. **Open** 10am-midnight Mon-Thur, Sun; 10am-1am Fri, Sat. **Shows** 6pm, 8.30pm Mon-Thur, Sun; 6pm, 9pm, 10.30pm Fri, Sat. **Tickets** $8-$15 (sometimes $10 food/drink min). **Map** p397 D29.

Upstairs at the Cornelia Street Café is a cosy eaterie. Downstairs is an even cosier music space hosting adventurous jazz, poetry, world music and folk. Regular mini-festivals spotlight blues and songwriters. Do arrive when the doors open for shows (5.45pm, 8.30pm or 10.15pm) as bookings are only held for 15 minutes after the set starts.

Iridium

1650 Broadway, at 51st Street, Theater District (1-212 582 2121, www.iridiumjazzclub.com). Subway 1 to 50th Street; N, R to 49th Street. **Shows** vary, usually 8.30pm, 10pm daily. **Tickets** $25-$40 ($15 food/drink min). **Map** p398 D23.

Iridium lures upscale crowds with a line-up that's split between household names and those known only to the jazz-savvy. The sightlines and sound system are truly worthy of celebration. Long the site of a Monday-night residency by guitar icon Les Paul, the club now hosts a steady stream of veteran pickers who perform in his honour.

★ Jazz at Lincoln Center

Frederick P Rose Hall, Broadway, at 60th Street, Upper West Side (1-212 258 9800, www.jazz.org). Subway A, B, C, D, 1 to 59th Street-Columbus Circle. **Map** p399 D22.

Rose Theater & the Appel Room *CenterCharge* 1-212 721 6500. **Box office** 10am-6pm Mon-Sat; noon-6pm Sun. **Shows** vary. **Tickets** *Rose Theater* $30-$120. *Appel Room* $55-$65.

Dizzy's Club Coca-Cola *1-212 258 9595.* **Shows** 7.30pm, 9.30pm Mon-Thur, Sun; 7.30pm, 9.30pm, 11.30pm Fri, Sat. **Tickets** $10-$35 ($5-$10 food/drink min).

The jazz arm of Lincoln Center is located several blocks away from the main campus, high atop the Time Warner Center. It includes three rooms: the Rose Theater is a traditional mid-size space, but the crown jewels are the Appel Room and the smaller Dizzy's Club Coca-Cola, with stages that are framed by enormous windows looking on to Columbus Circle and Central Park. The venues feel like a Hollywood cinematographer's vision of a Manhattan jazz club. Some of the best players in the business regularly grace the spot; among them is Wynton Marsalis, Jazz at Lincoln Center's famed artistic director.

Jazz Gallery

5th floor, 1160 Broadway, between 27th & 28th Streets, Flatiron District (1-646 494 3625, www.jazz gallery.org). Subway N, R to 28th Street. **Shows** 8pm, 10pm Thur-Sat. **Tickets** $10-$35. **Map** p398 E26.

Carnegie Hall

This beloved haunt, one of the city's premier incubators for progressive-jazz talent, relocated from its former Soho digs to a gallery-like space near the Flatiron Building. It's a place to witness true works of art from sometimes obscure but always interesting jazzers (Henry Threadgill and Vijay Iyer, to name a couple).

Jazz Standard
116 E 27th Street, between Park Avenue South & Lexington Avenue, Flatiron District (1-212 576 2232, www.jazzstandard.com). Subway 6 to 28th Street. **Shows** 7.30pm, 10pm Mon-Thur; 7.30pm, 10pm, 11.45pm Fri, Sat. **Tickets** $25-$35. **Map** p398 E26.
Renovation was just what the doctor ordered for the jazz den below restaurateur Danny Meyer's Blue Smoke barbecue joint. Now the room's marvellous sound matches its already splendid sightlines. The jazz is of the groovy, hard-swinging variety, featuring such acts as trumpeter Dave Douglas, stick man EJ Strickland and regular Monday-night fixture Mingus Big Band.

Merkin Concert Hall
For listings, *see p299.*
A polished platform for classical and jazz composers, with chamber music, jazz, folk, cabaret and experimental music performers taking the stage at the intimate venue. Popular annual series include the New York Guitar Festival, WNYC's New Sounds Live (part of the Ecstatic Music Festival) and Broadway Close Up.

★ Smalls Jazz Club
183 W 10th Street, between Seventh Avenue South & W 4th Street, West Village (1-212 252 5091, www.smallsjazzclub.com). Subway 1 to Christopher Street-Sheridan Square. **Open** 3pm-4am daily. **Admission** free-$20 (sometimes 1-drink min). **Map** p397 D28.

For those looking for an authentic jazz club experience – rather than the cheesy dinner-club vibe that prevails at some other spots in town – Smalls is a must. The cosy basement space feels like a speakeasy, or more specifically, one of those hole-in-the-wall NYC jazz haunts of yore over which fans obsess. Best of all, the booking skews retro, yet not stubbornly so. You'll hear classic hardbop as well as more adventurous, contemporary approaches.

Smoke
2751 Broadway, between 105th & 106th Streets, Upper West Side (1-212 864 6662, www.smokejazz. com). Subway 1 to 103rd Street. **Shows** 7pm, 9pm, 10.30pm, midnight daily. **Admission** varies ($20 food/drink min). **Map** p400 C16.
Not unlike a swanky living room, Smoke is a classy little joint that acts as a haven for local jazz legends and touring artists looking to play an intimate space. Early in the week, evenings are themed: on Monday, it's big band; Tuesday, organ jazz. On weekends, renowned jazzers hit the stage, relishing the chance to play informal gigs uptown.

★ The Stone
Avenue C, at 2nd Street, East Village (no phone, www.thestonenyc.com). Subway F to Lower East Side-Second Avenue. **Shows** 8pm, 10pm daily. **Admission** $15. **No credit cards.** **Map** p397 G29.
Don't call sax star John Zorn's not-for-profit venture a 'club'. You'll find no food or drinks here, and no nonsense, either: the Stone is an art space dedicated to 'the experimental and the avant-garde'. If you're down for some rigorously adventurous sounds (intense improvisers like Tim Berne and Okkyung Lee, or moonlighting rock mavericks such as Thurston Moore), Zorn has made it easy: no advance sales, and all ages admitted (under-19s get discounts, under-12s free). The bookings are left to different artist-curators each month.

★ Village Vanguard
178 Seventh Avenue South, at Perry Street, West Village (1-212 255 4037, www.villagevanguard. com). Subway A, C, E, 1, 2, 3 to 14th Street; L to Eighth Avenue. **Shows** 8.30pm, 10.30pm daily. **Tickets** $30 (1-drink min). **Map** p397 D28.
Going strong for more than three-quarters of a century, the Village Vanguard is one of New York's legendary jazz centres. History surrounds you: the likes of John Coltrane, Miles Davis and Bill Evans have all grooved in this hallowed basement haunt. Big names – both old and new – continue to fill the schedule here, and the Grammy Award-winning Vanguard Jazz Orchestra has been the Monday-night regular for almost 50 years. Reservations are recommended.

CABARET

In an age of globalism, cabaret is a fundamentally local art: a private party in a cosy club, where music gets stripped down to its bare essence at close range. The intense intimacy of the experience can make it transformative if you're lucky, or awkward if you're not. Expect consistently high-grade entertainment at Manhattan's fanciest venues, the **Café Carlyle** and the more theatre-oriented **54 Below**. Local clubs such as **Don't Tell Mama** and the **Duplex** are cheaper and more casual, but the talent is sometimes entry-level. The **Metropolitan Room** and the **Laurie Beechman Theatre** fall between these two poles, and **Joe's Pub** (*see p286*) attracts many of the wildest and most original alt-cabaret stars, such as Bridget Everett and Taylor Mac.

★ 54 Below
254 W 54th Street, between Broadway & Eighth Avenue, Theater District (1-646 476 3551, www.54below.com). Subway B, D, E to Seventh Avenue; C, E, 1 to 50th Street; R to 57th Street. **Shows** vary. **Admission** $15-$95 ($30 food/drink min). **Map** p399 D22.
This killer supper club below the legendary Studio 54 space offers an evocative speakeasy atmosphere, excellent tech and a calendar stuffed with major talents. The schedule is dominated by big Broadway stars – such as Patti LuPone, Ben Vereen and Marin Mazzie – but there's also room for edgier performers such as Nellie McKay and many rising songwriters.

Café Carlyle
Carlyle, 35 E 76th Street, at Madison Avenue, Upper East Side (1-212 744 1600, www.thecarlyle. com). Subway 6 to 77th Street. **Shows** vary. **Admission** $55-$215 (dinner or $25 food/drink min). **Map** p399 E20.
With its airy murals by Marcel Vertes, this elegant boîte in the Carlyle hotel remains the epitome of New York class, attracting such top-level singers as folk legend Judy Collins, Broadway star Sutton Foster

and soul queen Bettye LaVette. Woody Allen often plays clarinet with Eddie Davis and his New Orleans Jazz Band on Monday nights.
► *Bemelmans Bar, across the hall, has an excellent pianist for those who want to drink in the atmosphere at a somewhat lower price; see p183.*

Don't Tell Mama
343 W 46th Street, between Eighth & Ninth Avenues, Theater District (1-212 757 0788, www. donttellmamanyc.com). Subway A, C, E to 42nd Street-Port Authority. **Open** *Piano bar* 4pm-2am daily. **Shows** vary. **Admission** $10-$25 (2-drink min). *Piano bar* free (2-drink min). **Map** p398 C23.
Showbiz pros and piano-bar buffs adore this dank but homey Theater District stalwart, where acts range from the strictly amateur to potential stars of tomorrow. The line-up may include pop, jazz and musical-theatre singers, as well as comedians and drag artists (including veteran Judy Garland impersonator Tommy Femia).

The Duplex
61 Christopher Street, at Seventh Avenue South, West Village (1-212 255 5438, www.theduplex. com). Subway 1 to Christopher Street-Sheridan Square. **Open** *Piano bar* 9pm-4am daily. **Shows** vary. **Admission** $10-$25 (2-drink min). *Piano bar* free. **Map** p397 D28.
This narrow, brick-lined upstairs room, located in the heart of the West Village, is a chummy testing ground for new talent. The eclectic offerings often come served with a generous dollop of good, old-fashioned camp. The no-cover downstairs piano bar provides an open mic until the wee hours.

Laurie Beechman Theatre
407 W 42nd Street, at Ninth Avenue, Theater District (1-212 695 6909, www.westbankcafe.com). Subway A, C, E to 42nd Street-Port Authority. **Shows** vary. **Admission** $5-$25 ($15-$20 food/ drink min). **Map** p398 C24.
Tucked away beneath the West Bank Café on 42nd Street, the Beechman provides a stage for singers from the worlds of musical theatre and cabaret, including some of the country's most popular drag entertainers. It also hosts occasional comedy shows.

Metropolitan Room
34 W 22nd Street, between Fifth & Sixth Avenues, Flatiron District (1-212 206 0440, www.metropolitanroom.com). Subway F, M, N, R to 23rd Street. **Shows** vary. **Admission** $15-$35 (2-drink min). **Map** p398 E26.
The Metropolitan Room occupies a comfortable middle zone on the city's cabaret spectrum, being less expensive than the fancier supper clubs and more polished than the cheaper spots. Regular performers range from emerging jazz artists to established cabaret acts such as Marilyn Maye, Baby Jane Dexter and Annie Ross.

ARTS & ENTERTAINMENT

Performing Arts

An omnivorous approach to the arts is increasingly common on New York's cultural scene. The city is continuing to enjoy a classical music renaissance, with small genre-crossing venues such as SubCulture in the East Village, Spectrum on the Lower East Side and Brooklyn's Roulette serving as laboratories for exciting new sounds. And change is in the air in the most established quarters as the New York Philharmonic considers a successor to music director Alan Gilbert in advance of an overhaul to its home.

Dance is also stepping beyond traditional boundaries, into venues such as museums, while, in theatre, an Off-Broadway boom has resulted in new spaces including Lincoln Center's Claire Tow Theater, the Polonsky Shakespeare Center and Brooklyn Academy of Music's Richard B Fisher Building, a seven-storey performing arts centre that presents theatre, music and dance. For current cultural listings, check out the weekly *Time Out New York* magazine or www.timeout.com/newyork.

Classical Music & Opera

At the big institutions such as the New York Philharmonic, the Metropolitan Opera and Carnegie Hall, confident artistic leaders such as Alan Gilbert, Peter Gelb and Clive Gillinson are embracing new productions, living composers and innovative approaches to programming. Since Gilbert has announced his departure from the NY Phil, effective in 2017, now is the time to catch his more audacious efforts.

Meanwhile, some of the most exciting work is happening outside of Lincoln Center and Carnegie Hall. New-music groups such as the International Contemporary Ensemble, Alarm Will Sound and So Percussion have grown from promising upstarts to become influential pillars of the artistic community. Genre-blind venues, including **Le Poisson Rouge** (*see p289*), the **Stone** (*see p293*) and **Spectrum**, are happy to give them space to do their thing. These days, it's not rare for a Baroque opera to be followed by a DJ set or for an orchestra to interpret music by Mos Def or Sufjan Stevens. This is the postmodern aesthetic in full bloom and there's no better place to experience it right now than New York.

The standard New York concert season lasts from September to June, but there are plenty of summer events and performances (*see p301* **Everything Under the Sun**). Box office hours may change in summer, so phone ahead or check websites for times.

TICKETS
You can buy tickets directly from most venues, whether by phone, online or at the box office. A surcharge is generally added to tickets not bought in person. For more on tickets, *see p309*.

MAJOR CONCERT HALLS
★ **Brooklyn Academy of Music**
Peter Jay Sharp Building *30 Lafayette Avenue, between Ashland Place & St Felix Street, Fort Greene, Brooklyn.*

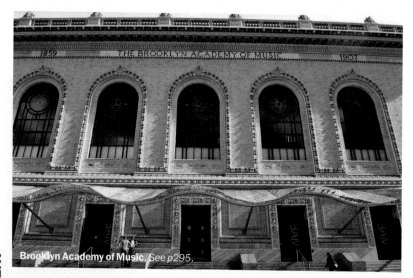

Brooklyn Academy of Music. See p295.

BAM Harvey Theater *651 Fulton Street,*
at Rockwell Place, Fort Greene, Brooklyn.
BAM Richard B Fisher Building
321 Ashland Place, between Ashland Place
& Lafayette Avenue, Fort Greene, Brooklyn.
All *1-718 636 4100, www.bam.org. Subway B,*
D, N, Q, R, 2, 3, 4, 5 to Atlantic Avenue-Barclays
Center; C to Lafayette Avenue; G to Fulton Street.
Box office noon-6pm Mon-Sat (call for summer
hours). *Phone bookings* 10am-6pm Mon-Fri; noon-
6pm Sat; noon-4pm Sun (show days). **Tickets** vary.
Map p404 T10.
America's oldest performing arts academy contin-
ues to present some of the freshest programming
in the city. Every year from September through
December, the Next Wave Festival brings avant-
garde music, dance and theatre to New York. The
nearby BAM Harvey Theater offers a smaller and

more atmospheric setting for multimedia creations
by composers and performers such as Tan Dun,
Meredith Monk and So Percussion. The newest facility, BAM Fisher, has an intimate performance space
and studios.

★ Carnegie Hall

154 W 57th Street, at Seventh Avenue, Midtown
(1-212 247 7800, www.carnegiehall.org). Subway
N, Q, R to 57th Street. **Box office** 11am-6pm Mon-
Sat. *Phone bookings* 8am-8pm Mon-Sat. **Tickets**
vary. **Map** p399 D22.
Artistic director Clive Gillinson continues to put his
stamp on Carnegie Hall. The stars – both soloists and
orchestras – still shine brightly inside this renowned
concert hall in the Isaac Stern Auditorium. But it's
the spunky upstart Zankel Hall that has generated
the most buzz, offering an eclectic mix of classical,
contemporary, jazz, pop and world music. Next
door, the Weill Recital Hall hosts intimate concerts
and chamber music programmes. Keep an eye out
for Ensemble ACJW, which consists of some of
the city's most exciting young musicians and also
performs at the Juilliard School; and the annual
Spring for Music, a festival that features eclectic
programmes from North America's most innovative
regional orchestras.

Lincoln Center

Columbus Avenue, between 62nd & 65th Streets,
Upper West Side (1-212 546 2656, www.lincoln
center.org). Subway 1 to 66th Street-Lincoln Center.
Map p399 C21.
Built in the early 1960s, this massive complex is
the nexus of Manhattan's – in fact, probably the

**IN THE KNOW
LUNCH WITH THE ORCHESTRA**

A variety of free lunchtime concerts are
held around New York by some of the city's
brightest up-and-comers. The early music
series **Midtown Concerts** presides over
St Bartholomew's Church (see *p302*;
www.midtownconcerts.org) every Thursday
at 1.15pm. Downtown, stately sanctuary
Trinity Wall Street (see *p302*) offers gratis
Thursday afternoon recitals in its **Concerts
at One** series (Mar-June, Sept-Dec). Also
look out for **Bach at One** at St Paul's Chapel
(see *p56*) on Wednesdays.

---

whole country's – performing arts scene. The campus has undergone a major revamp, providing new performance facilities as well as more inviting public gathering spaces and restaurants.

Big stars such as conductor Valery Gergiev and pianist Emanuel Ax are Lincoln Center's meat and potatoes. Lately, though, the divide between the flagship Great Performers season and the more audacious, multidisciplinary **Lincoln Center Out of Doors** summer festival (*see p36*) continues to narrow. The **Mostly Mozart Festival**, formerly a moribund four-week summer staple, has been thoroughly reinvented as a showcase of up-and-coming conductors and innovative performers. In autumn, the **White Light Festival** blends high-quality classical performers with world and popular musicians, all of whom angle to tap into the spiritually transcendent qualities of music.

The main entry point for Lincoln Center is from Columbus Avenue, at 65th Street, but the venues that follow are spread out across the square of blocks from 62nd to 66th Streets, between Amsterdam and Columbus Avenues. Tickets to most performances are sold through **CenterCharge** (1-212 721 6500, 10am-9pm daily). There is also a central box office selling discounted tickets to same-day performances at the **David Rubenstein Atrium** (between W 62nd & W 63rd Streets, Broadway & Columbus Avenues). The space is also a venue for frequent free performances (see Lincoln Center's website for details).

Alice Tully Hall

1-212 875 5050. **Box office** 10am-6pm Mon-Sat; noon-6pm Sun. **Tickets** vary.

An 18-month renovation turned the cosy home of the Chamber Music Society of Lincoln Center (www. chambermusicsociety.org) into a world-class, 1,096-seat theatre. A new contemporary foyer with an elegant (if a bit pricey) café is immediately striking, but, more importantly, the revamp also brought dramatic acoustical improvements.

David Geffen (formerly Avery Fisher) Hall

1-212 875 5030. **Box office** 10am-6pm Mon-Sat; noon-6pm Sun. **Tickets** vary.

This handsome, comfortable, 2,700-seat hall is the headquarters of the New York Philharmonic (1-212 875 5656, www.nyphil.org), the country's oldest symphony orchestra (founded in 1842) – and one of its finest. Depending on who you ask, the sound ranges from good to atrocious, but a renovation, partly financed by a $100 million gift from entertainment-industry mogul David Geffen is scheduled for 2019 – hence the name change in autumn 2015. The ongoing Great Performers series (which also takes place at Alice Tully Hall and other Lincoln Center venues) features top international soloists and ensembles.

Metropolitan Opera House

1-212 362 6000, www.metopera.org. **Box office** 10am-8pm Mon-Sat; noon-6pm Sun. **Tickets** $25-$485.

The grandest of the Lincoln Center buildings, the Met is a spectacular place to see and hear opera.

ARTS & ENTERTAINMENT

Lincoln Center.

Merkin Concert Hall.

It hosts the Metropolitan Opera from September to May, with major visiting companies appearing in summer. Audiences are knowledgeable and fiercely devoted, with subscriptions remaining in families for generations. Opera's biggest stars appear here regularly, and music director James Levine has turned the orchestra into a true symphonic force.

The Met had already started becoming more inclusive before current impresario Peter Gelb took the reins in 2006. Now, the company is placing a priority on creating novel theatrical experiences with visionary directors (Robert Lepage, Bartlett Sher, Michael Grandage, David McVicar) and assembling a new company of physically graceful, telegenic stars (Anna Netrebko, Lawrence Brownlee, Sonya Yoncheva, Peter Mattei). Its high-definition movie-screen broadcasts continue to reign supreme outside the opera house. Although most tickets are expensive, a minimum of 100 prime seats (50 of which are reserved for over-65s) are sold for a mere $25 apiece from Monday to Friday, via a same-day lottery conducted through the Met's website, two hours before curtain up.

OTHER VENUES

92nd Street Y
1395 Lexington Avenue, at 92nd Street, Upper East Side (1-212 415 5500, www.92y.org). Subway 6 to 96th Street. **Box office** noon-8pm Mon-Thur, Sun; noon-5pm Fri (call for summer hours). **Tickets** $25-$62. **Map** p400 F17.
The Y has always stood for solidly traditional orchestral, solo and chamber masterpieces. But the organisation also fosters the careers of young musicians and explores European and Jewish-American music traditions, with innovative results. In addition to showcasing several masterclasses (such as pianist Jonathan Biss), the Y has recently lent its stage to Tel Aviv's contemporary Meitar

Ensemble and violinist Jennifer Koh. And in an effort to make its concerts more affordable, discount tickets to premium programmes are available to those age 35 and younger.

★ Bargemusic
Fulton Ferry Landing, between Old Fulton & Water Streets, Dumbo, Brooklyn (1-718 624 4924, www. bargemusic.org). Subway A, C to High Street; F to York Street; 2, 3 to Clark Street. **Tickets** $35; $15-$30 reductions. **No credit cards. Map** p405 S9.
This former coffee bean barge usually presents four chamber concerts a week, set against a panoramic

view of lower Manhattan. It's a magical experience (and the programming has recently grown more ambitious), but be sure to dress warmly in winter. In less chilly months, admire the view from the upper deck during the interval.

Frick Collection

For listings, *see p180*. **Tickets** $40.

Concerts in the Frick Collection's exquisite circular music room are a rare treat, generally featuring both promising debutants and lesser-known but world-class performers. Concerts are broadcast live in the Garden Court, where tickets aren't required.

Gilder Lehrman Hall

The Morgan Library & Museum, 225 Madison Avenue, at 36th Street, Murray Hill (1-212 685 0008, www.themorgan.org). Subway 6 to 33rd Street. **Tickets** vary. **Map** p398 E25.

This elegant, 264-seat gem of a concert hall is a perfect venue for song recitals and chamber groups. The St Luke's Chamber Ensemble was quick to establish a presence here.

Merkin Concert Hall

Kaufman Music Center, 129 W 67th Street, between Amsterdam Avenue & Broadway, Upper West Side (1-212 501 3330, www.kaufman-center. org). Subway 1 to 66th Street-Lincoln Center. **Box office** noon-7pm Mon-Thur, Sun; noon-3pm Fri; 1hr before performance Sat. **Tickets** $10-$60. **Map** p399 C21.

On a side street in the shadow of Lincoln Center, this renovated 449-seat treasure offers a robust

mix of early music and avant-garde programming, plus a healthy amount of jazz, folk and some more eclectic fare. The Ecstatic Music Festival, featuring the latest generation of composers and performers, heats up the space each January through March, while the New York Festival of Song regularly presents outstanding singers in appealingly quirky themed programmes.

Metropolitan Museum of Art

For listings, *see p185*. **Tickets** vary.

When it comes to established virtuosos and revered chamber ensembles, the Met's year-round schedule is rich and full (and ticket prices can be correspondingly high). Under the leadership of Limor Tomer, the museum's programming has recently taken a sharp turn towards genre-flouting performers and intriguing artistic juxtapositions. Performances by Alarm Will Sound and the Estonian Philharmonic

ARTS & ENTERTAINMENT

Bargemusic.

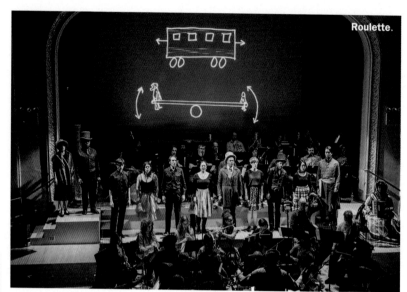

Roulette.

ARTS & ENTERTAINMENT

Chamber Choir have transformed the museum's famous Temple of Dendur into an atmospheric spot in which to hear some mystical music.

▶ *At Christmas and Easter, early music concerts are held in the Fuentidueña Chapel at the Cloisters; see p200.*

★ Miller Theatre at Columbia University

2960 Broadway, at 116th Street, Morningside Heights (1-212 854 7799, www.millertheatre.com). Subway 1 to 116th Street-Columbia University. **Box office** noon-6pm Mon-Fri. **Tickets** $25-$40. **Map** p401 C14.

Columbia University's Miller Theatre is at the forefront of making contemporary classical music sexy in New York City. The credit belongs to former executive director George Steel, who proved that presenting challenging fare in a casual, unaffected setting could attract young audiences – and hang on to them. Director Melissa Smey seems to be continuing the tradition with programmes ranging from early music to contemporary, highlighted by musical upstarts such as Ensemble Signal (and its conductor Brad Lubman).

Roulette

509 Atlantic Avenue, at Third Avenue, Boerum Hill, Brooklyn (1-917 267 0363, www.roulette. org). Subway B, D, N, Q, R, 2, 3, 4, 5 to Atlantic Avenue-Barclays Center. **Box office** 1hr before performance. **Tickets** vary. **Map** p404 T10.

This legendary experimental music institution traded dingy Soho digs for a spectacularly redesigned art deco theatre in Brooklyn. The setting may have changed, but Roulette continues to offer a gold mine of far-out programming that could include anything from a John Cage Musicircus, where the audience is invited to wander through a forest of musical acts all playing at once, to a four-day festival of genre-defying fare from Anthony Braxton.

Spectrum

2nd floor, 121 Ludlow Street, between Delancey & Rivington Streets, Lower East Side (no phone, www.spectrumnyc.com). Subway F to Lower East Side-Second Ave or Delancey Street; J, M, Z to Delancey-Essex Streets. **Tickets** $15; $10 reductions. **No credit cards. Map** p397 G30.

This contemporary-classical laboratory harks back to the days when the city's most innovative work was done in private lofts and similar spaces. Housed in a cosy Lower East Side walk-up, the busy venue relies largely on word of mouth and social media to publicise its ambitious chamber music, progressive jazz and avant-garde rock events.

★ SubCulture

Lower level, 45 Bleecker Street, between Bowery & Lafayette Street, East Village (1-212 553 5470, www.subculturenewyork.com). Subway B, D, F, M to Broadway-Lafayette Street; 6 to Bleecker Street. **Tickets** vary. **Map** p397 F29.

A recent addition to the cultural landscape, this (literally) underground space hosts singer-songwriters, jazz groups and on-stage Q&As, in addition to significant classical programming. A cross between a cabaret venue and a black box theatre, it features raked seating and a standing-room area near a bar. With a

EVERYTHING UNDER THE SUN

When summer arrives, New York's music scene goes outside.

The main fixture on the summer calendar is **SummerStage** (*see p33*), a New York institution that has an ear for every sound under the sun, and also includes theatre, dance and spoken-word performances. Although the main stage is in Central Park, the series brings great world music to parks throughout the five boroughs. Most shows are free, with a handful of benefit concerts covering for them (recent headliners include Beck, Conor Oberst and Counting Crows).

If your tastes veer more towards the classical, the **Metropolitan Opera** (www.metopera.org) and the **New York Philharmonic** (www.nyphil.org) both stage

free concerts in Central Park and other large green spaces in summer.

Not far from Central Park, **Lincoln Center** (*see p296*) has several plazas that come alive with summer performances. The free **Lincoln Center Out of Doors Festival** brings the likes of Roberta Flack and Roseanne Cash to the Damrosch Park Bandshell and, during **Midsummer Night Swing** (*see p35*), you can show off your own moves to live music.

There's also plenty of outdoors action downtown. During the **River to River Festival** (*see p35*), a variety of performers take to waterside stages (Terry Riley and Helado Negro in 2014, for example).

Top: **New York Philharmonic**; middle: **Lincoln Center Out of Doors Festival**; bottom: **River to River Festival**.

ARTS & ENTERTAINMENT

vibe that's casual yet respectful to artists, it has proved an excellent setting for groups such as the Knights, Ensemble ACJW, and even members of the New York Philharmonic (which staged events here during their first-ever contemporary-music Biennial in 2014).

Symphony Space
2537 Broadway, at 95th Streets, Upper West Side (1-212 864 5400, www.symphonyspace.org). Subway 1, 2, 3 to 96th Street. **Box office** 1-6pm Tue-Sun. **Tickets** vary. **Map** p400 C17.
Despite the name, programming at Symphony Space is anything but orchestra-centric: recent seasons have featured sax quartets, Indian classical music, a cappella ensembles and HD opera simulcasts from Europe. The annual Wall to Wall marathons (usually held in spring) provide a full day of music free of charge, all focused on a particular theme (for instance, a composer or period).

Churches

From sacred to secular, a thrilling variety of music is performed in New York's churches. Superb acoustics, out-of-this-world choirs and serene surroundings make these houses of worship particularly attractive venues. A bonus is that some concerts are free or very cheap.

Church of the Ascension
12 W 11th Street, between Fifth & Sixth Avenues, Greenwich Village (1-212 358 1469, tickets 1-212 358 7060, www.voicesofascension.org). Subway N, R to 8th Street-NYU. **Tickets** $10-$75. **Map** p397 E28.
There's a first-rate professional choir, the Voices of Ascension, at this little Village church. Home turf is the best place to hear it.

Church of St Ignatius Loyola
980 Park Avenue, between 83rd & 84th Streets, Upper East Side (1-212 288 2520, www. smssconcerts.org). Subway, 4, 5, 6 to 86th Street. **Tickets** voluntary donation-$85. **Map** p400 E18.

IN THE KNOW
BACKSTAGE PASSES

It's possible to go behind the scenes at several of the city's major concert venues. **Metropolitan Opera Guild Backstage Tours** (1-212 769 7028, $22, $18 reductions) shows you around the famous opera house from October to mid May. A tour of **Carnegie Hall** (1-212 903 9765, $15, $5-$10 reductions, Oct-May) ushers you through what is perhaps the world's most famous concert hall. For $20, you may also watch an open rehearsal of the **New York Philharmonic** (1-212 875 5656, Sept-June).

The 'Sacred Music in a Sacred Space' series is a high point of Upper East Side music culture. Lincoln Center and Carnegie Hall also hold concerts here, capitalising on the fine acoustics and prime location.

Holy Trinity Lutheran Church
65th Street & Central Park West, Upper West Side (1-212 877 6815, www.bachvespersnyc.org). Subway 1 to 66th Street-Lincoln Center. **Tickets** vary. **Map** p399 D21.
The choir, organist and period-instrument chamber orchestra of this church, located near Lincoln Center, perform free concerts of Baroque music every Sunday from October through April as part of the venerable Bach Vespers series.

St Bartholomew's Church
325 Park Avenue, at 51st Street, Midtown East (1-212 378 0248, www.stbarts.org). Subway E, M to Lexington Avenue-53rd Street; 6 to 51st Street. **Tickets** $15-$40. **Map** p398 E23.
This magnificent church hosts the Summer Festival of Sacred Music, one of the city's most ambitious choral music series. It fills the rest of the year with performances by resident ensembles and guests.
▶ *The church also hosts free lunchtime concerts; see p296* **In the Know**.

Trinity Wall Street
89 Broadway, at Wall Street, Financial District (1-212 602 0800, www.trinitywallstreet.org). Subway R, 1 to Rector Street; 4, 5 to Wall Street. **Tickets** vary. **Map** p399 E22.
This historic church has an ambitious music series and is home to one of the city's finest choirs, which regularly performs here and sometimes visits Carnegie Hall and Lincoln Center. At least twice a week, Trinity hosts free lunchtime concerts in both the church and the nearby St Paul's Chapel (209 Broadway, between Fulton and Vesey Streets).

Schools

The **Juilliard School** and the **Manhattan School of Music** are renowned for their talented students, faculty and artists-in-residence, all of whom regularly perform for free or at low cost. Lately, **Mannes College of Music** has made great strides.

Juilliard School
60 Lincoln Center Plaza, W 65th Street, between Amsterdam Avenue & Broadway, Upper West Side (1-212 769 7406, CenterCharge 1-212 721 6500, www.juilliard.edu). Subway 1 to 66th Street-Lincoln Center. **Box office** 11am-6pm Mon-Fri (call for summer hours). **Tickets** free-$30. **Map** p399 C21.
New York City's premier conservatory stages weekly concerts by student soloists, orchestras and chamber ensembles, as well as elaborate opera performances that can rival many professional productions. It's likely

American Opera Projects.

the singers you see here will be making their Met or other opera company debuts within the next few years.

Manhattan School of Music

120 Claremont Avenue, between Broadway & 122nd Street, Morningside Heights (1-917 493 4428, www.msmnyc.edu). Subway 1 to 125th Street. **Box office** 10am-5pm Mon-Fri. **Tickets** free-$30. **Map** p401 B14.

The School offers masterclasses, recitals and off-site concerts by its students and faculty, as well as visiting professionals. The American String Quartet has been in residence here since 1984. Recently, MSM has also become known for performing opera rarities, such as Francesco Cavalli's *La Doridea* and Virgil Thomson's *The Mother of Us All.*

Mannes College of Music

150 W 85th Street, between Columbus & Amsterdam Avenues, Upper West Side (1-212 580 0210 ext 4817, www.mannes.edu). Subway B, C, 1 to 86th Street. **Tickets** usually free. **Map** p400 C18.

In addition to student concerts and faculty recitals, Mannes also mounts its own ambitious, historically themed concert series; the summer is given over to festivals and workshops for instrumentalists. Productions by the Mannes Opera, whose fresh-faced members are drilled by seasoned opera professionals, are a perennial treat.

OPERA COMPANIES

The **Metropolitan Opera** may be the leader of the pack, but it's not the only game in town. Contact the organisations or check their websites for information and prices, schedules and venues.

American Opera Projects

South Oxford Space, 138 S Oxford Street, between Atlantic Avenue & Hanson Place, Fort Greene, Brooklyn (1-718 398 4024, www.operaprojects.org). Subway B, D, N, Q, R, 2, 3, 4, 5 to Atlantic Avenue-Barclays Center; C to Lafayette Avenue; G to Fulton Street. **Tickets** vary (average $20). **Map** p404 T10.

AOP is not so much an opera company as a living, breathing workshop that lets you follow a new work from gestation to completion. Shows, which can be anything from a table reading of a libretto to a complete orchestral production, are staged around the city and beyond.

Amore Opera Company

Connelly Theatre, 220 E 4th Street, between Avenues A & B, Lower East Side (Ovation Tix 1-866 811 4111, www.amoreopera.org). Subway F to Lower East Side-Second Avenue. **Tickets** $20-$40. **Map** p397 G29.

One of two successors to the late, great Amato Opera Company, the Amore has literally inherited the beloved former company's sets and costumes. Many of the cast members have migrated as well to keep the feisty Amato spirit alive. In previous seasons, they have presented US premières of lesser known or forgotten works and, more recently, a family-friendly version of Gilbert and Sullivan's comic opera *H.M.S. Pinafore.*

★ Gotham Chamber Opera

1-212 868 4460, Ticket Central 1-212 279 4200, www.gothamchamberopera.org. **Tickets** $30-$175. **Map** p397 G30.

Although they perform in a variety of venues in the city – such as the Hayden Planetarium for a highly imaginative production of Haydn's *Il Mondo della Luna* – this fine young company often appears at John Jay College's Gerald W Lynch Theater on the Upper West Side. Expect a treasure trove of rarely staged shows (directed by the likes of Mark Morris and Tony-winner Diane Paulus) and new fare.

Dance

With its uptown and downtown divide, New York dance includes both luminous tradition and daring experimentation. While **Lincoln Center** remains the hub for traditional balletic offerings, with annual seasons by American Ballet Theatre and New York City Ballet, the **David H Koch Theater** has opened itself up to modern dance too with Paul Taylor's company each spring. The deeper downtown you travel, the more you will encounter a younger generation – and it's not limited to Manhattan. In Brooklyn, Williamsburg, Bushwick and Bedford-Stuyvesant have sparked a new generation of dancers and choreographers, and Long Island City, Queens, is also pulsing with movement. Increasingly, museums, such as MoMA and the Whitney, are broadening their reach from the visual arts to showcasing dance and performance.

NOTABLE NAMES & EVENTS

The companies of modern dance icons such as Martha Graham, Alvin Ailey, Trisha Brown, Paul Taylor and Mark Morris are still based in the city, alongside a wealth of contemporary choreographers who create works outside the traditional company structure. The downtown performance world is full of singular voices, including Sarah Michelson, Trajal Harrell, Ralph Lemon, Maria Hassabi, Beth Gill and Ann Liv Young, as well as collectives such as AUNTS, a group of young artists who present performances in unlikely places.

Just as museums are giving dance room to branch out, multidisciplinary festivals such as **Crossing the Line** in autumn, presented by the French Institute Alliance Française (22 E 60th Street, between Madison & Park Avenues, 1-212 355 6100, www.fiaf.org), and **Performa** (1-212 366 5700, www.performa-arts.org), a November biennial, showcase the latest developments in dance and performance. Autumn also brings **Fall for Dance** at City Center, which focuses on eclectic mixed bills.

MAJOR VENUES

Baryshnikov Arts Center

450 W 37th Street, between Ninth & Tenth Avenues, Hell's Kitchen (1-646 731 3200, www. bacnyc.org). Subway A, C, E to 34th Street-Penn Station. **Tickets** *free-$35.* **Map** *p398 C25.*
Mikhail Baryshnikov, former artistic director of American Ballet Theatre, is something of an impresario. His home base, on a stark overpass near the Lincoln Tunnel, includes several studios, the Howard Gilman Performance Space – a 136-seat theatre – and superb facilities for rehearsals and workshops. With 238 seats, the Jerome Robbins

Gotham Chamber Opera.
See p303.

Theatre is both intimate and refined. Baryshnikov's background aside, the centre hosts an array of cultural events and operates a robust residency programme; throughout the year, BAC Space artists, who have included Beth Gill, Rashaun Mitchell and Liz Santoro, show works-in-progress.

Brooklyn Academy of Music

For listings, *see p295.*

With its Federal-style columns and carved marble, the 2,100-seat Howard Gilman Opera House is BAM's most regal dance venue, and has showcased the talents of Mark Morris and William Forsythe, as well as the Mariinsky Ballet. The 1904 Harvey Theater hosts contemporary choreographers from New York and Europe. Annual events include the DanceAfrica Festival, held each Memorial Day weekend (late May), and the Next Wave Festival, which features established groups from New York and abroad in autumn.

★ David H Koch Theater

Lincoln Center, 63rd Street & Columbus Avenue, Upper West Side (1-212 870 5570, www.davidkochtheater.com). Subway 1 to 66th Street-Lincoln Center. **Tickets** $10-$200. **Map** p399 C21.

The neoclassical New York City Ballet headlines at this opulent theatre, which Philip Johnson designed to resemble a jewellery box. During its spring, autumn and winter seasons, ballets by George Balanchine are performed by a wonderful crop of dancers including the luminous Sara Mearns; there are also works by Jerome Robbins, Peter Martins (the company's ballet master in chief) and current resident choreographer Justin Peck. The company offers its popular *Nutcracker* from the end of November into the new year. In the early spring, look for performances by the revered Paul Taylor Dance Company, but be sure to check programming: the theater has become a staple for out-of-town ballet troupes.

Joyce Theater

175 Eighth Avenue, at 19th Street, Chelsea (1-212 242 0800, www.joyce.org). Subway A, C, E to 14th Street; 1 to 18th Street; L to Eighth Avenue. **Tickets** $10-$59. **Map** p397 D27.

This intimate space houses one of the finest theatres – we're talking about sightlines – in town. Companies and choreographers that present work here, among them Ballet Hispanico, Pilobolus Dance Theater and Doug Varone, tend to be somewhat traditional. Regional ballet troupes, such as the Houston Ballet or Pacific Northwest Ballet, appear here too. The Joyce hosts dance throughout much of the year – Pilobolus is a summer staple.

Metropolitan Opera House

For listings, *see p297.*

In spring, the majestic space is home to American Ballet Theatre, which presents full-length traditional story ballets, contemporary classics by Frederick Ashton and Antony Tudor, and new works by the company's stellar artist-in-residence, Alexei Ratmansky. The acoustics are wonderful, but the theatre is immense: bring along binoculars or get as reasonably close to the stage as you can afford.

IN THE KNOW HOT TICKETS

Buzzed-about shows, especially those with big stars on the bill, sell out fast. Keep on top of openings by checking sites such as www.playbill.com and www.theatermania.com, as well as www.timeout.com/newyork. All feature the latest news and interviews; Theatermania also has an online booking service and discounted tickets for some shows.

New York City Center

131 W 55th Street, between Sixth & Seventh Avenues, Midtown (1-212 581 1212, www.nycitycenter.org). Subway B, D, E to Seventh Avenue; F, N, Q, R to 57th Street. **Tickets** $10-$150. **Map** p399 D22.

Before Lincoln Center changed the city's cultural geography, this was the home of the American Ballet Theatre, the Joffrey Ballet and the New York City Ballet. Built in 1923, the Moorish Revival building was a Shriners meeting hall before being converted to a performing arts centre two decades later. The lavish decor is golden, as are the companies that perform in the opulent mainstage theatre. Regular events include Alvin Ailey American Dance Theater in December and the popular Fall for Dance festival, in autumn, which features mixed bills for just $15.

OTHER VENUES

Abrons Arts Center

466 Grand Street, at Pitt Street, Lower East Side (1-212 598 0400, www.abronsartscenter.org). Subway B, D to Grand Street; F to Delancey Street; J, M, Z to Delancey-Essex Streets. **Tickets** $15-$35. **Map** p397 G30.

This venue, which has a beautiful proscenium theatre, focuses on a wealth of contemporary dance, courtesy of artistic director Jay Wegman; past artists have included Miguel Gutierrez, Jonah Bokaer, Ann Liv Young and Fitzgerald & Stapleton. In early January, when the Association of Performing Arts Presenters (APAP) comes along, the city is flooded with curators from all over the world. In conjunction, Abrons hosts the American Realness Festival, which features dozens of contemporary artists for marathon-style viewing.

Ailey Citigroup Theater

Joan Weill Center for Dance, 405 W 55th Street, at Ninth Avenue, Hell's Kitchen (1-212 405 9000, www.alvinailey.org). Subway A, B, C, D, 1 to 59th

Street-Columbus Circle; N, Q, R to 57th Street.
Tickets vary. **Map** p399 C22.
The home of Alvin Ailey American Theater contains this flexible downstairs venue; when not in use as rehearsal space by the company or for the home seasons of Ailey II, its junior ensemble, it is rented out to a range of groups of varying quality.

Brooklyn Arts Exchange
421 Fifth Avenue, between 7th & 8th Streets, Park Slope, Brooklyn (1-718 832 0018, www.bax.org). Subway F, G, R to Fourth Avenue-9th Street. **Tickets** $10-$16. **Map** p404 T11.
Brooklyn Arts Exchange holds classes and performances in its intimate theatre; the space hosts more than 50 performance evenings each season. Artists in residence have included choreographers Yasuko Yokoshi, Dean Moss and Jillian Peña; it's a great place to witness the creative process up close.

Center for Performance Research
Unit 1, 361 Manhattan Avenue, at Jackson Street, Williamsburg, Brooklyn (1-718 349 1210, www.cprnyc.org). Subway L to Graham Avenue. **Tickets** $10-$20. **Map** p405 V8.
CPR, founded by choreographers Jonah Bokaer and John Jasperse, represents a new trend of artists taking control of the means of production. It's based in an LEED-certified building with a 40ft by 40ft performance space. Presentations are sporadic.

★ Chocolate Factory Theater
5-49 49th Avenue, at Vernon Boulevard, Long Island City, Queens (1-718 482 7069, www.chocolatefactorytheater.org). Subway G to 21st Street; 7 to Vernon Boulevard-Jackson Avenue. **Tickets** $10-$15. **Map** p406 V5.
Brian Rogers and Sheila Lewandowski founded this 5,000sq ft performance venue in 2005, converting a one-time hardware store into two spaces: a low-ceilinged downstairs room and a loftier, brighter upstairs white box that caters to the interdisciplinary and the avant-garde. Past choreographers include Beth Gill, Jillian Peña, Big Dance Theater and Tere O'Connor. Rogers, an artist in his own right, also presents work here.

★ Danspace Project
St Mark's Church in-the-Bowery, 131 E 10th Street, at Second Avenue, East Village (information 1-212 674 8112, tickets 1-866 811 4111, www.danspaceproject.org). Subway L to Third Avenue; 6 to Astor Place. **Tickets** free-$20. **Map** p397 F28.
A space is only as good as its executive director, and Judy Hussie-Taylor has injected new life into Danspace's programming by creating the Platform series, in which artists curate seasons based on a particular idea. Moreover, the space itself – a high-ceilinged sanctuary – is very handsome. Ticket prices are reasonable, making it easy to take a chance on unknown work.

Dixon Place
161A Chrystie Street, at Delancey Street, Lower East Side (1-212 219 0736, www.dixonplace.org). Subway F to Lower East Side-Second Avenue; J, Z to Bowery. **Tickets** free-$20. **Map** p397 F30.
Ellie Covan started hosting experimental performances in her living room in the mid 1980s; two decades later, this plucky organisation finally opened this state-of-the-art space. Along with a mainstage theatre, there is a cocktail lounge – perfect for post-show discussions. Dixon Place supports emerging artists and works in progress; summer events include the annual Hot! festival of queer arts.

Gibney Dance: Agnes Varis Performing Arts Center
280 Broadway (entrance at 53A Chambers Street), Tribeca (1-646 837 6809, www.gibneydance.org). Subway A, C, J, Z to Chambers Street; R to City Hall; 4, 5, 6 to Brooklyn Bridge-City Hall. **Tickets** free-$20. **Map** p396 E31.
Choreographer and entrepreneur Gina Gibney, who also runs a rehearsal and classroom space at 890 Broadway – the famed building that also houses American Ballet Theatre and Eliot Feld's Ballet Tech – reclaimed the former Dance New Amsterdam, housed in the historic Sun Building, and renovated it to include theatre spaces, studios and rehearsal space. Programming is varied, with an emphasis on contemporary dance and performance.

Harlem Stage at the Gatehouse
150 Convent Avenue, at W 135th Street, Harlem (1-212 281 9240, www.harlemstage.org). Subway 1 to 137th Street-City College. **Tickets** free-$35. **Map** p401 C12.
Performances at this theatre, formerly an operations centre for the Croton Aqueduct water system, celebrate African-American life and culture. Companies that have graced this flexible space, designed by Frederick S Cook and now designated a New York City landmark, include the Bill T Jones/Arnie Zane Dance Company and Kyle Abraham. Each spring, the space hosts the E-Moves Festival.

Jack
505½ Waverly Avenue, between Atlantic Avenue & Fulton Street, Clinton Hill, Brooklyn (no phone, www.jackny.org). Subway C, G to Clinton-Washington Avenues. **Tickets** $10-$25. **Map** p404 U10.
This cosy new arts centre is led by artistic director Alec Duffy, whose mission is to create a cultural hub for cutting-edge theatre, music and dance. Choreographer Stacy Grossfield curates the dance events. Performances have featured such original performers as Greg Zuccolo and Ann Liv Young.

★ The Kitchen
512 W 19th Street, between Tenth & Eleventh Avenues, Chelsea (1-212 255 5793, www.thekitchen.org). Subway A, C, E to 14th Street; L to Eighth

Avenue. **Box office** 2-6pm Tue-Sat; 1hr before performance. **Tickets** free-$25. **Map** p397 C27.

The Kitchen, led by Tim Griffin, offers some of the best experimental dance around: inventive, provocative and rigorous. Some of the artists who have presented work here are the finest in New York, such as Sarah Michelson (who has served as a guest curator for specific programmes), Dean Moss, Ann Liv Young and Jodi Melnick.

La MaMa ETC

74A E 4th Street, between Bowery & Second Avenue, East Village (1-212 475 7710, www. lamama.org). Subway F to Lower East Side-Second Avenue; 6 to Astor Place. **Box office** (at 66 E 4th Street) noon-6pm Mon-Wed; noon-8pm Thur-Sun. **Tickets** $10-$40. **Map** p397 F29.

This experimental theatre hosts the La MaMa Moves dance festival every spring, featuring a variety of up-and-coming artists, and presents international troupes throughout the year. While shows here can be worthwhile, some programming is marginal.

FREE Movement Research at the Judson Church

55 Washington Square South, at Thompson Street, Greenwich Village (1-212 598 0551, www. movementresearch.org). Subway A, B, C, D, E, F, M to W 4th Street. **Tickets** free. **Map** p397 E28.

This free performance series is a great place to check out experimental works and up-and-coming artists. Performances are held roughly every Monday evening at 8pm, from September to June, but it's best to check the website. The group's autumn and spring festivals, which take place in December and May, feature a week-long series of performances held in venues across the city. Movement Research also offers classes and other events around town.

New York Live Arts

219 W 19th Street, between Seventh & Eighth Avenues, Chelsea (1-212 924 0077, www.new yorklivearts.org). Subway 1 to 18th Street. **Box office** 1-9pm Mon-Sat; 1-8pm Sun. **Tickets** free-$65. **Map** p397 D27.

In 2010, the Dance Theater Workshop and the Bill T Jones/Arnie Zane Dance Company merged to form New York Live Arts, which is dedicated to contemporary dance under Mr Jones. The company performs here regularly, along with local and international choreographers.

Performance Space 122

1-212 477 5829, www.ps122.org.

This venue – the public school where *Fame* was shot – is under renovation until summer 2016. In the meantime, Performance Space 122 is presenting work at other spaces (see website for info). Ronald

Harlem Stage at the Gatehouse.

"GO NOW, AND HAVE THE TIME OF YOUR LIFE!"
—NEWSDAY

STOMP

STOMP

ESTABLISHED IN 1994 NYC

ticketmaster® or 800-982-2787

ORPHEUM THEATRE 2ND AVENUE AT 8TH STREET

STOMPONLINE.COM

K Brown and Doug Varone started out here; more recent artists include Maria Hassabi and Ishmael Houston-Jones.

Triskelion Arts'
Muriel Schulman Theater

106 Calyer Street, between Banker Street & Clifford Place, Greenpoint, Brooklyn (1-718 389 3473, www.triskelionarts.org). Subway G to Greenpoint Avenue. **Tickets** $16. **Map** p405 U7.

Abby Bender, who leads her own company Schmantze Theatre – a play on 'dance-theatre' – is the executive director of this space, which recently moved from Williamsburg to Greenpoint. Triskelion is dedicated to offering performances by emerging artists and classes, including hoop dancing and Dancorcism, which is described as a 'one-hour dance party for your soul'.

Theatre

Hugh Jackman, Tom Hanks, Scarlett Johansson and Denzel Washington are among the many boldface names that have shone on Broadway marquees lately. Major musicals tend not to have big stars above the title, but favour the familiar in a different way. In recent years, many of them are adapted from pop-culture sources (such as *Matilda* and *The Lion King*) or are built around existing catalogues of popular songs (such as *Jersey Boys* and *Beautiful – The Carole King Musical*).

TICKETS

Nearly all Broadway and Off Broadway shows are served by one of the city's 24-hour ticketing agencies. For cheap seats, your best bet is one of the Theatre Development Fund's **TKTS** discount booths. For Off-Off Broadway shows or dance events, consider purchasing a $9 ticket (plus $1 service fee) from the TDF. Register at www.tdf.org, where you'll also find a list of eligible shows. For more ticket tips, *see* **In the Know** *p305* and *p310*.

TKTS

Father Duffy Square, Broadway & 47th Street, Theater District (no phone, www.tdf.org). Subway N, Q, R, S, 1, 2, 3, 7 to 42nd Street-Times Square. **Open** *Evening tickets* 3-8pm Mon, Wed-Sun; 2-8pm Tue. *Same-day matinée tickets* 10am-2pm Wed, Thur, Sat; 11am-3pm Sun. **Map** p398 D24.

At Times Square's architecturally striking TKTS base, you can get tickets on the day of the performance for as much as 50% off face value. Although there is often a queue when it opens for business, this has usually dispersed one to two hours later, so it's worth trying your luck an hour or two before the show. The Downtown and Brooklyn branches, which are much less busy, also sell matinée tickets the day before a show (see website for hours). Never buy tickets from anyone who approaches you in the queue as they may have been obtained illegally. You can check what's on the boards at all three locations on the website before setting out. **Other locations** South Street Seaport, corner of Front & John Streets, Financial District; 1 MetroTech Center, corner of Jay Street & Myrtle Avenue Promenade, Downtown Brooklyn.

TKTS.

ARTS & ENTERTAINMENT

Beautiful – The Carole King Musical.

ARTS & ENTERTAINMENT

BROADWAY

Technically speaking, 'Broadway' is the theatre district that surrounds Times Square on either side of Broadway (the actual avenue), between 41st and 54th Streets (plus the Vivian Beaumont Theater, uptown at Lincoln Center). This is where you'll find the grandest theatres in town: wood-panelled, frescoed jewel boxes, mostly built between 1900 and 1930. Officially, 40 of them – those with more than 500 seats – are designated as being part of Broadway. Full-price tickets can easily set you back more than $100; the very best (so-called 'premium') seats can sell for almost $500 at the most popular shows.

The blockbusters are hard to miss, but at any given point, there are also a handful of new plays, as well as serious revivals of classic dramas ranging from Shakespeare to the works of David Mamet. Each season also usually includes several small, artistically adventurous musicals to balance out the rafter-rattlers.

Long-running shows

Straight plays can provide some of Broadway's most stirring experiences, but they're less likely than musicals to enjoy long runs. Check *Time Out New York* magazine or www.timeout.com/newyork for current listings and reviews. (The shows listed here are subject to change.)

Beautiful – The Carole King Musical
Stephen Sondheim Theatre, 124 W 43rd Street, between Broadway & Sixth Avenue, Theater District (Telecharge 1-212 239 6200, www.beautifulonbroadway.com). Subway N, Q, R, S, 1, 2, 3, 7 to 42nd Street-Times Square; B, D, F, M to 42nd Street-Bryant Park. **Box office** 10am-8pm Mon-Sat; noon-6pm Sun. **Tickets** $75-$152. **Map** p398 D24.
Broadway's latest boomer jukebox musical doesn't achieve the comic zip or dramatic force of *Jersey Boys*, but it is an appealing and skilfully built vehicle for Carole King's hit ditties and soulful ballads. Audiences sway and suppress the urge to sing along with hits like 'Will You Love Me Tomorrow,' 'I Feel the Earth Move' and the title song.

★ The Book of Mormon
Eugene O'Neill Theatre, 230 W 49th Street, between Broadway & Eighth Avenue, Theater District (Telecharge 1-212 239 6200, www.bookofmormonbroadway.com). Subway C, E, 1 to 50th Street; N, Q, R, S, 1, 2, 3, 7 to 42nd Street-Times Square; N, R to 49th Street. **Box office** 10am-8pm Mon-Sat; noon-6pm Sun. **Tickets** $99-$477. **Map** p398 D23.
This gleefully obscene and subversive satire may be the funniest show to grace the Great White Way since *The Producers* and *Urinetown*. Writers Trey Parker and Matt Stone of *South Park*, along with composer Robert Lopez (*Avenue Q*), find the perfect blend of sweet and nasty for this tale of mismatched Mormon proselytisers on a mission in Uganda.

★ A Gentleman's Guide to Love and Murder
Walter Kerr Theatre, 219 W 48th Street, between Broadway & Eighth Avenue, Theater District (Telecharge 1-212 239 6200, www.agentlemansguidebroadway.com). Subway N, Q, R to 49th Street; C, E, 1 to 50th Street. **Box office** 10am-8pm Mon-Sat; noon-6pm Sun. **Tickets** $42-$350. **Map** p398 D23.
The king of musical comedy, this Edwardian romp is filled with zany sight gags and the wittiest show tunes in years. Various scions and heirs of the D'Ysquith clan – a gargoylish gallery of twits, snobs

IN THE KNOW CHEAP SEATS

Some of the cheapest tickets on Broadway are known as 'rush' tickets, purchased on the day of a show at a theatre's box office (not all theatres have them). On average, they cost $25. Some venues reserve them for students, while others use a lottery, which is held two hours before the performance.

and prigs, all played by a single actor in a comic tour de force – must fall so that a distant relative can rise to claim his fortune.

Jersey Boys

August Wilson Theatre, 245 W 52nd Street, between Broadway & Eighth Avenue, Theater District (Telecharge 1-212 239 6200, www. jerseyboysinfo.com/broadway). Subway C, E, 1 to 50th Street. **Box office** 10am-8pm Mon-Sat; noon-6pm Sun. **Tickets** $47-$297. **Map** p398 D23.

The Broadway musical does right by the jukebox with this nostalgic behind-the-music tale, presenting the Four Seasons' infectiously energetic 1960s tunes (including 'Walk Like a Man' and 'Big Girls Don't Cry') as they were intended to be performed. Sleek direction by Des McAnuff ensures that Marshall Brickman and Rick Elice's script feels canny instead of canned.

Kinky Boots

Al Hirschfeld Theatre, 302 W 45th Street, between Eighth & Ninth Avenues, Theater District (Telecharge 1-212 239 6200, www.kinkyboots themusical.com). Subway A, C, E to 42nd Street-Port Authority; N, Q, R, S, 1, 2, 3, 7 to 42nd Street-Times Square. **Box office** 10am-8pm Mon-Sat; noon-6pm Sun. **Tickets** $87-$399. **Map** p398 D24.

Harvey Fierstein and Cyndi Lauper's fizzy crowd-pleaser, in which a sassy-dignified drag queen kicks an English shoe factory into gear, feels familiar at every step. But it has been manufactured with solid craftsmanship and care (Lauper is a musical-theatre natural), and is boosted by a heart-strong cast. The overall effect is nigh irresistible.

★ The Lion King

Minskoff Theatre, 200 W 45th Street, between Broadway & Eighth Avenue, Theater District (Ticketmaster 1-866 870 2717, www.lionking.com).

Kinky Boots.

Subway A, C, E to 42nd Street-Port Authority; N, Q, R, S, 1, 2, 3, 7 to 42nd Street-Times Square. **Box office** 10am-8pm Mon-Sat; 11am-7pm Sun. **Tickets** $89-$249. **Map** p398 D24.

Director-designer Julie Taymor surrounds the Disney movie's mythic plot and Elton John-Tim Rice score with African rhythm and music. Through elegant puppetry, Taymor populates the stage with a menagerie of African beasts; her staging has expanded a simple cub into the pride of Broadway.

★ Matilda

Shubert Theatre, 225 W 44th Street, between Broadway & Eighth Avenue, Theater District

Matilda.

(Telecharge 1-212 239 6200, http://us.matildathe musical.com). Subway A, C, E to 42nd Street-Port Authority; N, Q, R, S, 1, 2, 3, 7 to 42nd Street-Times Square. **Box office** 10am-8pm Mon-Sat; noon-6pm Sun. **Tickets** $37-$277. **Map** p398 D24.

Based on Roald Dahl's book about a child prodigy who must outwit horrid parents and a sadistic head-mistress, this English musical delivers mischievous fun while hitting the requisite sentimental notes and smuggling in an anti-authoritarian message. Tim Minchin's cheeky Britpop score and Matthew Warchus's cartoonish staging offer sheer delight.

Wicked

Gershwin Theatre, 222 W 51st Street, between Broadway & Eighth Avenue, Theater District (Ticketmaster 1-800 982 2787, www.wicked themusical.com). Subway C, E, 1 to 50th Street. **Box office** 10am-8pm Mon-Sat; noon-6pm Sun. **Tickets** $62-$242. **Map** p398 D23.

Based on novelist Gregory Maguire's 1995 riff on *The Wizard of Oz, Wicked* is a witty prequel to the classic children's book and movie. The show's combination of pop dynamism and sumptuous spectacle has made it the most popular show on Broadway. Teenage girls, especially, have responded to the story of how a green girl named Elphaba comes to be known as the Wicked Witch of the West.

OFF BROADWAY

As the cost of mounting shows on Broadway continues to soar, many serious playwrights (including major ones such as Edward Albee and Tony Kushner) are opening their shows in the less financially arduous world of Off Broadway, where many of the theatres are not-for-profit enterprises. Venues have between 100 and 499 seats; tickets usually run from $30 to $100. Here, we've listed some reliable long-running shows, plus some of the best theatres and repertory companies.

Long-running shows

★ Avenue Q

New World Stages, 340 W 50th Street, between Eighth & Ninth Avenues, Theater District (Telecharge 1-212 239 6200, www.avenueq.com). Subway C, E, 1 to 50th Street. **Box office** 1-8pm Mon, Thur, Fri; 1-7pm Tue; 10am-8pm Wed, Sat; 10am-7.30pm Sun. **Tickets** $72.50-$126.50. **Map** p398 D23.

After many years, which have included a Broadway run followed by a return to its Off Broadway roots, this sassy and clever puppet musical doesn't show its age. Robert Lopez and Jeff Marx's deft *Sesame Street*-esque novelty tunes about porn and racism still earn their laughs, and *Avenue Q* remains a sly and winning piece of metamusical tomfoolery.

Fuerza Bruta: Wayra.

Blue Man Group

Astor Place Theatre, 434 Lafayette Street, between Astor Place & 4th Street, East Village (1-800 258 3626, www.blueman.com). Subway N, R to 8th Street-NYU; 6 to Astor Place. **Box office** noon-7.45pm daily. **Tickets** $56-$106. **Map** p397 F28.

Three deadpan men with extraterrestrial imaginations (and head-to-toe blue body paint) carry this long-time favourite, which may be the world's most accessible piece of multimedia performance art. A weird, exuberant trip through the trappings of modern culture, the show is as smart as it is ridiculous.

Fuerza Bruta: Wayra

Daryl Roth Theatre, 101 E15th Street, at Union Square East (Telecharge 1-212 239 6200, www. fuerzabrutanyc.com). Subway L, N, Q, R, 4, 5, 6 to 14th Street-Union Square. **Box office** 1-6pm Tue; 1-8pm Wed-Fri; 1-10pm Sat; 1-7pm Sun. **Tickets** $75-$89. **Map** p397 E27.

A set of acts from the granddaddy of immersive theater, *Wayra* is a bona fide thrill ride. Dancers on harnesses sprint perpendicularly along the walls, a

running man smashes through walls of cardboard boxes and – most enchantingly – mysterious women splash and slide along a clear-bottom swimming pool that lowers to within touching distance.

Queen of the Night

Diamond Horseshoe at the Paramount Hotel, 235 W 46th Street, between Broadway & Eighth Avenue, Theater District (1-212 706 7448, www.queenofthenightnyc.com). Subway N, Q,

---

IN THE KNOW
UNDERSTUDY REFUNDS

If you've come to see a particular performer on Broadway, you may be able to cash in your ticket if that star doesn't show up. As a general rule, you are entitled to a refund if the star's name appears above the title of the show. A card on the wall of the lobby will announce any absences that day – go to the box office if you want your money back.

R to 49th Street; C, E, 1 to 50th Street. **Tickets** $150-$475. **Map** p398 D23.

Randy Weiner's deluxe dinner-circus-nightlife experience is set in the gorgeously restored Diamond Horseshoe nightclub. Melding themes from *The Magic Flute* with a swirl of acrobatic stunts and sexy interactive adventures, and accompanied by a dramatically presented feast, it's like a cruise-ship version of Stanley Kubrick's *Eyes Wide Shut*, but in a pleasantly indulgent way.

★ Sleep No More

McKittrick Hotel, 530 W 27th Street, between Tenth & Eleventh Avenues, Chelsea (OvationTix 1-866 811 4111, www.sleepnomorenyc.com). Subway 1 to 28th Street; C, E to 23rd Street. **Tickets** $80-$170. **Map** p398 C26.

A multitude of searing sights awaits at this bedazzling and uncanny installation by the English company Punchdrunk. Your sense of space is blurred as you wend through more than 90 discrete spaces, from a cloistral chapel to a ballroom floor. A Shakespearean can check off allusions to *Macbeth*; others can just revel in the haunted-house vibe.

Repertory companies & venues

59E59 Theaters

59 E 59th Street, between Madison & Park Avenues, Upper East Side (1-212 753 5959, Ticket Central 1-212 279 4200, www.59e59.org). Subway N, Q, R to Lexington Avenue-59th Street; 4, 5, 6 to 59th Street. **Box office** noon-6pm daily. **Tickets** $25-$70. **Map** p399 E22.

This chic, state-of-the-art venue, which comprises an Off Broadway space and two smaller theatres, is chock-a-block with worthy offerings, including intimate music events. It's also where you'll find the annual Brits Off Broadway festival (www.britsoffbroadway.com), which imports some of the UK's best work for brief runs, and its newer offshoot, Americas Off Broadway.

★ Ars Nova

511 W 54th Street, between Tenth & Eleventh Avenues, Hell's Kitchen (1-212 352-3101, OvationTix 1-866 811 4111, www.arsnovanyc. com). Subway C, E, 1 to 50th Street. **Box office** 30mins before show. **Tickets** $15-$50. **Map** p399 C22.

Committed to presenting innovative new theatre, music and comedy, this offbeat space has been a boon to developing artists since it opened in 2002. Along with smart full productions, Ars Nova also presents an eclectic monthly special called Showgasm and the annual ANT Fest for emerging talents.

Atlantic Theater Company

336 W 20th Street, between Eighth & Ninth Avenues, Chelsea (1-212 691 5919, Ticket Central 1-212 279 4200, www.atlantictheater.org). Subway

ARTS & ENTERTAINMENT

Queen of the Night. *See p313.*

RAPPING WITH HAMILTON

A groundbreaking biomusical turns a founding father into a hip hop hero.

'My name is Alexander Hamilton, / And there's a million things I haven't done,' sings composer-lyricist-star Lin-Manuel Miranda early in *Hamilton*. Now the rapping version of the guy on the $10 bill has crossed at least one item off his bucket list: transfer to Broadway. After its stone-cold sold-out run at the Public Theater in early 2015 (and a few tweaks), the best new musical in years has a new home at the Richard Rodgers Theatre (www.richardrodgerstheatre.com).

History ticks to a syncopated beat in this jubilant, overflowingly rich show. And just as syncopation achieves its energising effect by disturbing the expected flow, so Miranda's biomusical on founding father Alexander Hamilton is a rhythm-and-rhyme intervention for American iconography and ideology. This populist throwdown to the way we tell our stories and spin our songs is about the Revolution, and it is a revolution: hip hop grooves stuffed with political critique, heroes of colour taking over the old house and throwing a party.

Miranda based this epic-yet-personal pageant on Ron Chernow's 2004 biography, which clued in the prodigious composer-lyricist to the fact that Hamilton was, as the musical's opening lines have it, 'a bastard, orphan, son of a whore and a / Scotsman, dropped in the middle of a forgotten / Spot in the Caribbean.' Casting himself in the title role, Miranda claims Hamilton for the immigrant dissident.

Despite social challenges, the ambitious and brilliant young Hamilton emigrates north and becomes a successful lawyer, General Washington's go-to aide and one of the Constitution's most eloquent interpreters, all the while starting a family and weathering a sex scandal. Spoiler alert for the historically ignorant: it all crashes in 1804, when Hamilton agrees to a duel with then-Vice President Aaron Burr, a man who has felt scorned and outshined by Hamilton all his professional life.

Those who admired Miranda's Tony-winning *In the Heights* already know his genius for grafting rap, salsa and other pop styles on to Broadway forms, but *Hamilton* kicks it up several notches. Not just for its lyrical virtuosity, but also for its structural elegance and fierce topicality, the piece is a signal achievement, expanding the subgenre of tuneful takes on national identity (including *1776*, *Assassins* and *Bloody Bloody Andrew Jackson*). Even more than that, it offers a template for the fully integrated hip hop musical (also mixing in R&B and indie pop) that repurposes the social and verbal strategies of rap and slam poetry for supposedly off-limits topics. In remixing the past to his own beat, Miranda shows us the future.

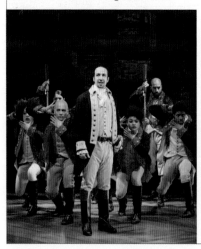

C, E to 23rd Street. **Box office** noon-6pm Tue-Sat. **Tickets** $35-$85. **Map** p397 D27.
Created in 1985 as an offshoot of acting workshops led by playwright David Mamet and actor William H Macy, the dynamic Atlantic Theater Company has presented dozens of new plays, including Steven Sater and Duncan Sheik's rock musical *Spring Awakening*, and Conor McPherson's *The Night Alive*. The Atlantic also has a smaller second stage deep underground at 330 W 16th Street.

★ Brooklyn Academy of Music
For listings, *see p295.*
BAM's beautifully distressed Harvey Theater – along with its grand old opera house in the Peter Jay Sharp Building – is the site of the Next Wave Festival (*see p37*) and other international events. The spring season usually features high-profile productions of classics by the likes of Chekhov and Shakespeare, often shipped over from England with major actors attached.

Classic Stage Company
136 E 13th Street, between Third & Fourth Avenues, East Village (1-212 677 4210, www.classicstage.org). Subway L, N, Q, R, 4, 5, 6 to 14th Street-Union Square. **Box office** noon-6pm Mon-Fri. **Tickets** $15-$125. **Map** p397 F27.
With a purview that runs from medieval mystery plays and Elizabethan standards to early modern drama and original period pieces, Classic Stage Company is committed to making the old new again. Under artistic director Brian Kulick, the company has a knack for attracting major stars, as recent productions of Chekhov plays with Maggie Gyllenhaal and Dianne Wiest attest.

Flea Theater
41 White Street, between Broadway & Church Street, Tribeca (1-212 226 0051, Ovation Tix 1-866 811 4111, www.theflea.org). Subway A, C, E, J, M, N, Q, R, Z, 6 to Canal Street; 1 to Franklin Street. **Box office** noon-6pm Mon-Fri. **Tickets** $15-$70. **Map** p396 E31.
Founded in 1997, this versatile and well-appointed venue has presented avant-garde experimentation and politically provocative satires. A second, basement theatre hosts the Flea's resident young acting company, the Bats. In 2016, the entire organisation is expected to move into a new three-stage complex under construction nearby.

Irish Repertory Theatre
132 W 22nd Street, between Sixth & Seventh Avenues, Chelsea (1-212 727 2737, www.irishrep.org). Subway F, M, 1 to 23rd Street. **Box office** 10am-6pm Mon; 10am-8pm Tue-Fri; 11am-8pm Sat; 11am-6pm Sun. **Tickets** $70. **Map** p398 D26.
Set in a cosily odd, L-shaped venue, the Irish Repertory Theatre puts on compelling shows by Irish and Irish-American playwrights. Fine revivals

of classics by the likes of Oscar Wilde and George Bernard Shaw alternate with Irish-themed musicals and plays by lesser-known modern authors.

Lincoln Center Theater
Lincoln Center, 150 W 65th Street, at Broadway, Upper West Side (Telecharge 1-212 239 6200, www.lct.org). Subway 1 to 66th Street-Lincoln Center. **Box office** 10am-8pm Mon-Sat; noon-6pm Sun. **Tickets** $20-$200. **Map** p399 C21.
The majestic and prestigious Lincoln Center Theater complex has a pair of amphitheatre-style drama venues. Its Broadway house, the 1,080-seat Vivian Beaumont Theater, is home to star-studded and elegant major productions. Downstairs is the 299-seat Mitzi E Newhouse Theater, an Off Broadway space devoted to new work by the upper layer of American playwrights. In an effort to shake off its reputation for stodginess, Lincoln Center launched LCT3, which since 2012 has presented the work of emerging playwrights and directors at the Claire Tow Theater, built on top of the Beaumont.
▶ *For music and festivals at Lincoln Center, see p296 and p36, respectively.*

Manhattan Theatre Club
Samuel J Friedman Theatre, 261 W 47th Street, between Broadway & Eighth Avenue, Theater District (Telecharge 1-212 239 6200, www.manhattantheatreclub.com). Subway N, Q, R, S, 1, 2, 3, 7 to 42nd Street-Times Square. **Box office** noon-6pm Mon; noon-7.30pm Tue, Wed; noon-8.30pm Thur, Fri; 10am-8.30pm Sat; 10am-6pm Sun. **Tickets** $30-$170. **Map** p398 D24.
One of the city's most important non-profit companies, Manhattan Theatre Club spent decades as an Off Broadway outfit before moving into the 622-seat Friedman Theatre in 2003. But it still maintains a smaller space at New York City Center (*see p305*), where it presents some of its best material – such as Lynn Nottage's 2009 Pulitzer Prize winner, *Ruined*. Twentysomethings and teens can sign up for the 30 Under 30 Club to get tickets at both theatres for $30.

New World Stages
340 W 50th Street, between Eighth & Ninth Avenues, Theater District (1-646 871 1730, Telecharge 1-212 239 6200, www.newworldstages.com). Subway C, E, 1 to 50th Street. **Box office** 1-8pm Mon, Thur, Fri; 1-7pm Tue; 10am-8pm Wed, Sat; 10am-7.30pm Sun. **Tickets** $40-$150. **Map** p398 C23.
Formerly a movie multiplex, this centre – one of the last bastions of commercial Off Broadway in New York – boasts a shiny, space-age interior and five stages, presenting everything from family-friendly spectacles (like *Gazillion Bubble Show*) to downsized transfers of Broadway musicals (including the long-running *Avenue Q*).

★ New York Theatre Workshop

79 E 4th Street, between Bowery & Second Avenue, East Village (1-212 460 5475, www.nytw.org). Subway F to Lower East Side-Second Avenue; 6 to Astor Place. **Box office** 5-7.30pm Tue, Wed; 6-8.30pm Thur-Fri; noon-8.30pm Sat; noon-7.30pm Sun. **Tickets** $35-$85. **Map** p397 F29.

Founded in 1979, the New York Theatre Workshop works with emerging directors eager to take on challenging pieces. Besides presenting plays by world-class artists such as Caryl Churchill and Tony Kushner, this company also premièred *Rent*, Jonathan Larson's seminal 1990s musical. The iconoclastic Flemish director Ivo van Hove has made the NYTW his New York pied-à-terre.

Pershing Square Signature Center

480 W 42nd Street, at Tenth Avenue, Hell's Kitchen (1-212 244 7529, www.signaturetheatre.org). Subway A, C, E to 42nd Street-Port Authority. **Box office** 11am-6pm Tue-Sun. **Tickets** $25-$65. **Map** p398 C24.

The award-winning Signature Theatre Company, founded by James Houghton in 1991, focuses on exploring and celebrating playwrights in depth, with whole seasons devoted to works by individual living writers. Over the years, the company has delved into the oeuvres of August Wilson, John Guare, Horton Foote and many more. Special programmes are designed to keep prices low. In 2012, the troupe expanded hugely into a new home – a theatre complex designed by Frank Gehry, with three major spaces and ambitious long-term commission programmes, cementing it as one of the city's key cultural institutions.

★ Playwrights Horizons

416 W 42nd Street, between Ninth & Tenth Avenues, Theater District (1-212 564 1235, Ticket Central 1-212 279 4200, www.playwrights horizons.org). Subway A, C, E to 42nd Street-Port Authority. **Box office** noon-8pm daily. **Tickets** $50-$90. **Map** p398 C24.

More than 300 important contemporary plays have had premières here, including dramas (*Driving Miss Daisy*, *The Heidi Chronicles*) and musicals (Stephen Sondheim's *Assassins* and *Sunday in the Park with George*). More recent seasons have included new works by Edward Albee and Craig Lucas, as well as Bruce Norris's Pulitzer Prize winner *Clybourne Park*.

★ Public Theater

425 Lafayette Street, between Astor Place & 4th Street, East Village (1-212 539 8500, tickets 1-212 967 7555, www.publictheater.org). Subway N, R to 8th Street-NYU; 6 to Astor Place. **Box office** 2-6pm Mon, Sun; 2-7pm Tue-Sat. **Tickets** $15-$95. **Map** p397 F28.

Under the guidance of the civic-minded Oskar Eustis, this local institution – dedicated to producing the work of new American playwrights, but also known for its Shakespeare in the Park productions – has regained its place at the forefront of the Off Broadway world. The ambitious, multicultural programming ranges from new works by major playwrights to the annual Under the Radar festival for emerging artists. The company's home building, a renovated Astor Place landmark, has five stages.

▶ *The building is also home to Joe's Pub, see p286.*

Public Theater.

Roundabout Theatre Company
American Airlines Theatre, 227 W 42rd Street,
between Seventh & Eighth Avenues, Theater
District (1-212 719 1300, www.roundabouttheatre.
org). Subway N, Q, R, S, 1, 2, 3, 7 to 42nd Street-
Times Square. **Box office** 10am-6pm Mon,
Sun; 10am-8pm Tue-Sat. **Tickets** $20-$162.
Map p398 D24.
Devoted mostly to revivals, the Roundabout often
pairs beloved old chestnuts with celebrity casts.
In addition to its Broadway flagship, the company
also mounts shows at Studio 54 (254 W 54th Street,
between Broadway & Eighth Avenue), the Stephen
Sondheim Theatre (124 West 43rd Street, between
Sixth & Seventh Avenues) and Off Broadway's
Laura Pels Theatre (111 W 46th Street, between
Sixth & Seventh Avenues).

St Ann's Warehouse
29 Jay Street, between John & Plymouth Streets,
Dumbo, Brooklyn (1-718 254 8779, www.
stannswarehouse.org). Subway A, C to High Street;
F to York Street. **Box office** 1-6pm Tue-Sat.
Tickets $25-$75. **Map** p405 T9.
The adventurous theatregoer's alternative to
Brooklyn Academy of Music, St Ann's Warehouse
offers a varied line-up of drama and music. The
company is scheduled to move to a converted
space within Brooklyn Bridge Park's 1870s
Tobacco Warehouse in late 2015. Recent shows
have included high-level work by the Wooster
Group, Daniel Kitson and the National Theatre
of Scotland.

Second Stage Theatre
307 W 43rd Street, at Eighth Avenue, Theater
District (1-212 246 4422, www.2st.com). Subway
A, C, E to 42nd Street-Port Authority. **Box office**
10am-6pm Mon-Sat; 10am-3pm Sun. **Tickets** $30-
$125. **Map** p398 D24.
In a beautiful Rem Koolhaas-designed space near
Times Square, Second Stage Theatre specialises in
American playwrights, and hosted the New York
première of Edward Albee's *Peter and Jerry*. It also
provides a stage for serious new musicals, such as
the Pulitzer Prize-winning *Next to Normal*.

**★ FREE Shakespeare in the Park
at the Delacorte Theater**
Enter park at Central Park West, at 81st Street,
and walk east (1-212 539 8750, www.shakespeare
inthepark.org). Subway B, C to 81st Street-
Museum of Natural History. **Tickets** free.
Map p399 D19.
The Delacorte Theater in Central Park is the fair-
weather sister of the Public Theater. When not
producing Shakespeare in the East Village, the
Public offers the best of the Bard outdoors during
Shakespeare in the Park (June-Aug). Free tickets
(two per person) are distributed at the Delacorte at
noon on the day of the performance. Around 8am

is usually a good time to begin waiting, although
the queue can start forming as early as 6am when
big-name stars are on the bill. There is also an online
lottery for tickets.

★ Soho Rep
46 Walker Street, between Broadway & Church
Street, Tribeca (TheaterMania 1-212 352 3101,
www.sohorep.org). Subway A, C, E, N, R, 6 to Canal
Street; 1 to Franklin Street. **Box office** 9am-9pm
Mon-Fri; 10am-9pm Sat, Sun. **Tickets** $35-$50.
Map p396 E31.
A few years ago, this Off-Off mainstay moved to
an Off Broadway contract, but tickets for most
shows have remained cheap. Artistic director Sarah
Benson's programming is diverse and audacious:
recent productions include works by Young Jean
Lee, David Adjmi, Branden Jacobs-Jenkins and the
Nature Theater of Oklahoma.

Theatre for a New Audience
Polonsky Shakespeare Center, 262 Ashland
Place, between Fulton Street & Lafayette Avenue,
Fort Greene, Brooklyn (OvationTix 1-866 811
4111, www.tfana.org). Subway B, D, N, Q, R,
2, 3, 4, 5 to Atlantic Avenue-Barclays Center;
C to Lafayette Avenue; G to Fulton Street.
Box office 1-6pm Tue-Sat. **Tickets** $60-$85.
Map p398 D24.
Founded in 1979, TFANA has grown to become
New York's most prominent classical-theatre com-
pany. Now it has a home of its own: the Polonsky
Shakespeare Center (near BAM, in Brooklyn's
cultural district). This flashy, glass-fronted 299-
seat venue, designed by Hugh Hardy, opened its
doors in 2013 with Julie Taymor's production of *A
Midsummer Night's Dream. Photo p321.*

Theatre Row
410 W 42nd Street, between Ninth & Tenth
Avenues, Theater District (1-212 714 2442,
Telecharge 1-212 239 6200, www.theatrerow.org).
Subway A, C, E to 42nd Street-Port Authority.
Box office noon-6pm daily. **Tickets** $18-$95.
Map p398 C24.
Comprising five main venues of various sizes,
Theatre Row hosts new plays and revivals by scores
of assorted theatre companies. It is also home to the
long-running topical revue *Newsical.*

Vineyard Theatre
108 E 15th Street, at Union Square East, Union
Square (1-212 353 0303, www.vineyardtheatre.
org). Subway L, N, Q, R, 4, 5, 6 to 14th Street-Union
Square. **Box office** 1-6pm Mon-Fri. **Tickets** $45-
$100. **Map** p397 E27.
The Vineyard produces some excellent new plays
and musicals. Past productions have included *The
Scottsboro Boys*, the wittily named *[title of show]*
and the Tony Award-winning *Avenue Q*, all of which
transferred to Broadway.

ARTS & ENTERTAINMENT

See
Boston

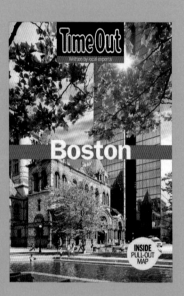

**2015
guidebook
on sale now**

Written by
local experts

like
a
local

OFF-OFF BROADWAY

Technically, the term Off-Off Broadway denotes a show that is presented at a theatre with fewer than 100 seats, usually for less than $25. It's where a lot of inexperienced artists pay their dues, but it's also where some of the most daring writers and performers – who aren't necessarily card-carrying union professionals – create their edgiest work. The **New York International Fringe Festival** (917 745 3397, www.fringenyc. org), held every August, provides a wide opportunity to see the wacky side of the stage, and the **New York Musical Theatre Festival** (www.nymf.org) in September has become an important testing ground for composers and lyricists.

Repertory companies & venues

For multidisciplinary **Dixon Place,** *see p306.*

The Brick
575 Metropolitan Avenue, between Lorimer Street & Union Avenue, Williamsburg, Brooklyn (1-718 285 3863, OvationTix 1-866 811 4111, www.bricktheater.com). Subway G to Metropolitan Avenue; L to Lorimer Street. **Box office** opens 15mins before curtain. **Tickets** $15-$20. **No credit cards. Map** p405 V8.
This spunky, brick-lined venue presents a variety of boundary-pushing work. Its tongue-in-cheek themed summer series have included Moral Values, Hell, Pretentious and Antidepressant Festivals.

★ The Bushwick Starr
207 Starr Street, between Irving & Wyckoff Avenues, Bushwick, Brooklyn (OvationTix 1-866 811 4111, www.thebushwickstarr.org). Subway L to Jefferson Street. **Box office** opens 30mins before curtain. **Tickets** $15-$25. **Map** p405 V8.
As small companies continue to be priced out of Manhattan, everyone's looking to Brooklyn to pick up the slack. This funky black box is one good option: some of the city's fiercest experimental troupes – Half Straddle, the TEAM and others – have made the Starr shine brightly.

HERE
145 Sixth Avenue, between Broome & Spring Streets, Soho (1-212 647 0202, TheaterMania 1-212 352 3101, www.here.org). Subway C, E to Spring Street. **Box office** opens 2hrs before curtain. **Tickets** $20-$50. **Map** p397 E30.
Dedicated to not-for-profit arts enterprises, this theatre complex has been the launch pad for such well-known shows as Eve Ensler's *The Vagina Monologues* and *Arias with a Twist,* drag diva Joey Arias's collaboration with puppeteer extraordinaire Basil Twist. HERE is also involved in numerous multidisciplinary development programmes.

La MaMa ETC
For listings, *see p307.*
Founded by the late Ellen Stewart, La MaMa has been a bastion of the Off-Off scene for more than half a century. The complex has helped to nurture such innovators as Sam Shepard, Charles Ludlam, Lanford Wilson and Ping Chong, and it continues to be an important rung in many rising artists' ladders.

ARTS & ENTERTAINMENT

Theatre for a New Audience. *See p319.*

Escapes & Excursions

Escapes & Excursions

Need a break from the city? New York is well situated for both coastal and countryside getaways, and there are plenty of worthwhile destinations within reach of the five boroughs. Bucolic areas such as New York State's Hudson Valley, north of Manhattan, are little more than an hour away; and although New Jersey is the butt of some unkind jokes, even hardened urbanites concede it has some lovely beaches that can be reached in little more time than it takes to get across town on a bus. What's more, many getaway spots are accessible by public transport, allowing you to avoid the often exorbitant car-rental rates and the heavy summer traffic in and out of town.

Breakneck Ridge.

Hit the Trails

The city's parks are great for a little casual relaxation. But if you're hankering after a real fresh-air escape, set off on one of these day hikes, between one and three hours away. Bring water and snacks: refuelling options are scarce.

BREAKNECK RIDGE

The trek at Breakneck Ridge, in Hudson Highlands State Park, is a favourite of hikers for its accessibility, variety of trails and views of the Hudson Valley and the Catskill Mountains. The trail head is a half-mile walk along the highway from the Cold Spring stop on Metro-North's Hudson line (at weekends, the train stops closer to the trail, at the Breakneck Ridge stop).

You can spend anywhere from two hours to a full day hiking Breakneck, so plan your route in advance. The start of the trail is on the river's eastern bank, atop a tunnel that was drilled out for Route 9D: it's marked with small white paint splotches (called 'blazes' in hiking parlance) on nearby trees. Be warned, though, that Breakneck got its name for a reason. The initial trail ascends

500 feet in just a mile and a half, and gains another 500 feet via a series of dips and rises over the next few miles. If you're not in good shape, you might want to think about an alternative hike. But if you do choose this path, there are plenty of dramatic overlooks where you can stretch out on a rock and take in the majestic Hudson River below.

After the difficult initial climb, Breakneck Ridge offers options for all levels of hikers, and several crossings in the first few miles provide alternative routes back down the slope. Trail information and maps of all the paths, which are clearly marked with different coloured blazes, are available from the New York-New Jersey Trail Conference (1-201 512 9348, www.nynjtc.org); it's strongly recommended that you carry them with you.

Getting there

By train Take the Metro-North Hudson train from Grand Central to the Cold Spring stop, or catch the early train to the Breakneck Ridge stop (Sat & Sun only). Journey time 1hr 15mins; round-trip ticket $28-$37 ($14-$18.50 reductions). Contact the MTA (www.mta.info/mnr) for schedules.

HARRIMAN STATE PARK

Across the Hudson River and south-west of the sprawling campus of West Point lies Harriman State Park, containing more than 200 miles of trails and 31 lakes. It's accessible from stops on the Metro-North Port Jervis line. Of the various trails, our favourite is the **Triangle Trail**. Part

---

IN THE KNOW SLEEPY HOLLOW

South of Cold Spring is the small town of Sleepy Hollow. It's most famous as the putative location for Washington Irving's short story *The Legend of Sleeepy Hollow*, later adapted into a movie by Tim Burton. Irving is buried in the village cemetery.

---

of the White Bar Trail, this is an eight-mile jaunt that begins just past the parking lot at Tuxedo station (which is a little over an hour's journey from Penn Station). The route climbs steadily more than 1,000 feet towards the summit of Parker Cabin Mountain before turning south to offer lovely views of two lakes, Skenonto and Sebago. From there, it heads down steadily, although steeply at times, before ending after roughly five miles at a path marked with red dashes on white. It's a long distance to cover, but the terrain is varied and there are shortcuts. On a hot day, however, the best detour is to take a dip in one of the lakes followed by a nap in the sun.

Getting there

By train Take the Metro-North/NJ Transit Port Jervis train from Penn Station to the Tuxedo stop (with a train switch in Secaucus, NJ). The journey takes 1hr 15mins, and a round-trip ticket costs $27 ($13 reductions). Contact New Jersey

ESCAPES & EXCURSIONS

Harriman State Park

City Island.

Transit (www.njtransit.com) or the MTA (www.mta.info/mnr) for schedules.

OTIS PIKE WILDERNESS

If you're looking for ocean views and a less aggressive hike, consider Fire Island's Otis Pike Wilderness Area. The journey takes 90 minutes on the LIRR from Penn Station to Patchogue, on Long Island, followed by a 45-minute ferry ride south to the Watch Hill Visitor Center, but the pristine beaches and wildlife are worth the effort. The stretch of preserved wilderness from Watch Hill to Smith Point is home to deer, rabbits, foxes and numerous types of seabird, including the piping plover, which nests during the summer. Just be sure you stay out of the plovers' nesting grounds, which are marked with signs, and don't feed any wildlife you see along the way.

Apart from a few sand dunes, **Fire Island** is completely flat; even so, walking on the beaches and sandy paths can be slow going. After traversing the boardwalk leading from the Watch Hill Center, hike along Burma Road, a path that runs across the entire island, and in seven miles you'll arrive at the **Wilderness Visitor Center** (1-631 281 3010, hours vary by season, check www.nps.gov/fiis) at Smith Point.

Getting there

By train/ferry Take the LIRR Montauk train from Penn Station to Patchogue; a round-trip ticket costs $26.50-$36.50 ($18 reductions). Contact the MTA (www.mta.info/lirr) for schedules. The cash-only

Davis Park Ferry (1-631 475 1665, www.davis parkferry.com) from Patchogue to Watch Hill operates mid Mar-Nov, with reduced crossings in spring and autumn, and costs $17 round trip ($11-$16 reductions). Pets and freight cost extra. The journey should take about 2hrs 30mins in total.

Head for the Ocean

CITY ISLAND

It may look like a New England fishing village, but City Island, on the north-west edge of Long Island Sound, is part of the Bronx and accessible by public transport. With a population of fewer than 5,000, it formed the slightly gritty backdrop for films such as *Margot at the Wedding* and *A Bronx Tale*. Yet in its heyday, around World War II, it was home to no fewer than 17 shipyards. Seven America's Cup-winning yachts were built on the island – and, residents note, the Cup was lost in 1983, the very same year they stopped building the boats here. You'll find a room devoted to the island's nautical past at the free **City Island Historical Society & Nautical Museum** (190 Fordham Street, between Minnieford & King Avenues, 1-718 885 0008, www.cityislandmuseum.org, open 1-5pm Sat, Sun). Housed in a quaint former schoolhouse, it's stocked with model ships, Revolutionary War artefacts and tributes to no such local heroes as Ruby Price Dill, the island's first kindergarten teacher.

With seafood spots on practically every corner and boats bobbing in the background, the small community exudes maritime charm. There are still a few sailmakers in the phone book, but City Islanders are far more likely to head into Manhattan for work nowadays.

To the east lies **Hart Island**. The former site of an insane asylum, a missile base and a narcotics rehab centre, today Hart is the public burial ground for the city's unidentifed dead. How's that for a fishy tale?

Eating & drinking

Over on Belden Point are **Johnny's Reef** (2 City Island Avenue, 1-718 885 2086, www. johnnysreefrestaurant.com, open Mar-Nov) and **Tony's Pier Restaurant** (1 City Island Avenue, 1-718 885 1424, www.tonyspier.com); both have outdoor seating. Grab a couple of beers and a basket of fried clams, sit at one of the picnic tables and watch the boats sail by.

Getting there

By subway/bus Take the 6 line to Pelham Bay Park and transfer to the Bx29 bus to City Island.

LONG BRANCH

Although it's not the high-society retreat it was in 1869, when President Ulysses S Grant made it his summer base, this Jersey Shore enclave is in the midst of a revival that has nothing to do with girls with poufed hair or guys with overdeveloped abs. Years after a 1987 fire reduced its amusement pier to a charred skeleton, Jersey boys David and Michael Barry took over the decrepit boardwalk to create **Pier Village**, comprising apartments,

restaurants, shops and a boutique hotel. Nearby, Asbury Park, with its rich rock 'n' roll legacy, is also poised for a comeback.

A day badge to access the pristine **Long Branch beach** costs just $5-$7 for adults (free-$3 reductions), available from the seasonal office at Ocean Boulevard and Melrose Terrace. But, for $25 per day, guests at the **Bungalow** hotel can luxuriate at **Le Club** – an exclusive stretch open from Memorial Day through Labor Day. Lounge under imported palm trees and sip cocktails from the beach club's upscale eaterie **Avenue**. Atop the restaurant is a private pool deck and bar, which morphs into a slick nightclub.

For a grittier seaside vibe, catch the 837 bus from Long Branch Station to **Asbury Park**. Here, continuing redevelopment is bringing indie businesses to the boardwalk opposite the Boss's old stomping ground, the **Stone Pony** (913 Ocean Avenue, at Second Avenue, 1-732 502 0600, www.stoneponyonline.com). Across the street, you can join the pinheads at **Silverball Museum Arcade** (1000 Ocean Avenue, 1-732 774 4994, www.silverballmuseum.com), where collector Rob Ilvento lets the public play on 200 of his prize pinball machines, dating from 1950 to 2013 ($10/hour or $25/day). From the seafront, stroll along Cookman Avenue and browse the strip's vintage and interiors shops.

Eating & drinking

Order the spicy, orange-spiked lobster roll in a brioche bun ($18) at the David Collins-designed beachfront brasserie, **Avenue** (23 Ocean Avenue, at Pier Village, 1-732 759 2900, www.leclub avenue.com), which offers lovely ocean vistas

ESCAPES & EXCURSIONS

Le Club, Long Branch.

Sandy Hook.

ESCAPES & EXCURSIONS

and an outdoor deck. In Asbury Park, get a taste of exotic destinations at **Langosta Lounge** (1000 Ocean Avenue, at Second Avenue, 1-732 455 3275, www.langostalounge.com), where surfer-chef Marilyn Schlossbach's menu is inspired by 'vacation cuisine'.

Hotels

The design of **Bungalow** (50 Laird Street, at Landmark Place, Pier Village, 1-732 229 3700, www.bungalowhotel.net) may have been chronicled in a reality-TV show – *9 by Design*, about Robert and Cortney Novogratz, who juggle work and a large brood – but that doesn't dilute its cool factor. A hand-crafted wood bar by upstate New York artist John Houshmand, a vintage pool table, old board games and a 1960s foosball table encourage hanging out in the lobby. In the 24 guest rooms, whitewashed wood floors and mixed-media works by British artist Ann Carrington evoke the feel of a private beach house.

Getting there

By train Take the North Jersey Coast train from Penn Station to Long Branch. The journey takes around 1hr 30mins and the fare is $15 one way ($6.75 reductions). Contact New Jersey Transit (1-973 275 5555, www.njtransit.com) for schedules. From the station, it's about a 10min walk to Pier Village and the boardwalk, or you can catch a cab.

SANDY HOOK

The first thing you should know about Sandy Hook, New Jersey, is that there's a nudist beach at its north end (Gunnison Beach, at parking lot G). The sights it affords compel boaters with binoculars to anchor close to shore, and there's also a cruisy gay scene – but there's much more to this 1,665-acre natural wonderland than sunbathers in the buff. With all that the expansive Hook has to offer, it's a little like an island getaway on the city's doorstep.

Along with seven miles of dune-backed ocean beach, the **Gateway National Recreation Area** is home to the nation's oldest lighthouse (which you can tour), as well as extensive fortifications from the days when Sandy Hook formed the outer line of defence for New York Harbor.

Elsewhere, natural areas like the **Maritime Holly Forest** attract an astounding variety of birds. In fact, large stretches of beach are closed in summer to allow the endangered piping plover a quiet place to mate. The Audubon Society (www.audubon.org) offers bird walks in the area.

There's even a cool way to get there: hop on the ferry from Manhattan and turn an excursion to the beach into a scenic mini-cruise. Once you

DIA: Beacon.

dock at Fort Hancock, shuttle buses transport you to beaches along the peninsula.

Eating & drinking

Hot dogs and other typical waterside snacks are available from concession stands at the beach areas. Alternatively, picnics are permitted on the beach, so you can bring along goodies for dining alfresco. Guardian Park, at the south end of Fort Hancock, has tables and barbecue grills.

Getting there

By boat The ferry runs from late May through September from E 35th Street at the East River or Pier 11 in the Financial District (east end of Wall Street). Fares are $45 round trip (free-$17 reductions). Contact Sea Streak (1-800 262 8743, www.seastreak. com) for schedules. The ride takes 45 minutes.

IN THE KNOW CASTLE COUP

On the train to Beacon, which runs alongside the Hudson River, keep an eye out for the atmospheric ruins of **Bannerman Castle**, a recreation of a medieval Scottish pile built on tiny Pollepel Island in the early 1900s by an army-surplus heir. Tours are also available via kayak or passenger boat between May and October from Beacon and several other Hudson River locations (see www.bannermancastle.org for details).

Museum Escapes

DIA: BEACON

Take a model example of early 20th-century industrial architecture. Combine it with some of the most ambitious and uncompromising art of the past 50 years. What do you get? One of the finest aesthetic experiences on earth. Indeed, for the more than two dozen artists whose work is on view, and for the visiting public, Dia Art Foundation's outpost in the Hudson Valley is truly a blessing.

The foundation's founders, Heiner Friedrich and his wife Philippa de Menil (an heir to the Schlumberger oil fortune), acquired many of their holdings in the 1960s and '70s. The pair had a taste for the minimal, the conceptual and the monumental, and supported artists with radical ideas about what art was, what it could do and where it should happen. Together with others of their generation, the Dia circle (Robert Smithson, Michael Heizer, Walter De Maria, Donald Judd and Dan Flavin) made it difficult to consider a work of art outside of its context – be it visual, philosophical or historical – ever again. Since 2003, that context has been the Riggio Galleries, a huge museum on a 31-acre tract of land overlooking the Hudson River, as Dia's hugely scaled collection had outgrown even its cavernous former galleries in Chelsea.

An 80-minute train ride from Grand Central Terminal, the 300,000-square foot complex of three brick buildings was erected in 1929 as a box-printing factory for Nabisco. No less than 34,000 square feet of north-facing skylights provide almost all the illumination within. The permanent collection also includes works by such 20th-century luminaries as Louise Bourgeois, Andy Warhol, Sol LeWitt and Joseph Beuys. But what really sets Dia:Beacon apart from other museums is its confounding intimacy. The design of the galleries and gardens by California light-and-space artist Robert Irwin, in collaboration with the Manhattan architectural collective OpenOffice, not only makes this enormous museum feel more like a private house, but it also allows the gallery's curators to draw correspondences between artworks into an elegant and intriguing narrative of connoisseurship.

If you're travelling by car, stop at **Storm King Art Center**, about 14 miles south-west of Beacon on the other side of the Hudson. The gorgeous sculpture park (open April-mid November), features works by Richard Serra, Alexander Calder and Maya Lin, among others.

Further information

Dia: Beacon Riggio Galleries *3 Beekman Street, Beacon, NY (1-845 440 0100, www.diaart.org).* **Open** *Jan-Mar* 11am-4pm Mon, Fri-Sun. *Apr-Oct* 11am-6pm Mon, Thur-Sun (until 8pm Sat June-Aug). *Nov, Dec* 11am-4pm Mon, Thur-Sun. **Admission** $12; $8-$10 reductions; free under-4s.
Storm King Art Center *1 Museum Road, New Windsor, NY (1-845 534 3115, www.stormking. org).* **Open** *Apr-Oct* 10am-5.30pm Wed-Sun.

Nov 10am-4.30pm Wed-Sun. **Admission** $15; $8-$10 reductions; free under-6s.

Getting there

By train Take the Metro-North train from Grand Central Terminal to Beacon station. The journey takes 1hr 20mins, and the round-trip fare is $32-$42.50 (reductions $16-$21). Discount rail and admission packages are available; for details, see 'Deals & Getaways' at www.mta.info/mnr.

COOPERSTOWN

A mecca for baseball devotees, Cooperstown, north of NYC, isn't known for much besides its famous hall of rawhide ephemera, old pine tar-stained lumber and October memories. Happily for those who don't care a lick about America's national pastime, there's more than Major League history to be found at this single-stoplight village (population 2,000) on the shores of Lake Otsego.

The **National Baseball Hall of Fame & Museum** draws around 300,000 visitors a year. The actual hall is exactly what it claims to be: a corridor full of plaques. And as such, it's the museum that's the real diamond here. You'll see everything from Babe Ruth's locker to racist hate mail sent to Jackie Robinson, and the glove worn by Willie Mays when he made his over-the-shoulder catch in the 1954 World Series.

Local shopping is devoted primarily to baseball, so if you're looking for memorabilia or limited-edition collectibles, the **Cooperstown**

Storm King Art Center.

National Baseball Hall of Fame & Museum.

Bat Company (118 Main Street, at Chestnut Street, 1-607 547 2415, closed Sun Jan-Mar) is worth checking out. For a dose of non-sport history, take a walk through the **Christ Episcopal Churchyard Cemetery** (46 River Street, at Church Street, 1-607 547 9555, www.christchurchcooperstown.org), where the Cooper family is buried. A three-minute drive north along Route 80 brings you to the **Fenimore Art Museum**, which displays its fine collection of American art – including folk art and Native American works – in a 1930s mansion on Lake Otsego. Temporary shows have focused on such crowd-pleasing subjects as Modernism and Edward Hopper.

Heading south out of town, the **Brewery Ommegang** (656 County Highway 33, 1-800 544 1800, www.ommegang.com), set on a 136-acre farmstead, brews a half-dozen award-winning Belgian-style ales. You can see how the whole brewing process works on one of the hourly tours, which include a tasting ($5, including souvenir glass).

Eating & drinking

On Cooperstown's Main Street, the **Doubleday Café** (no.93, at Pioneer Street, 1-607 547 5468) provides good American grub, while at his new **Cantina de Salsa** (no.149, at Chestnut Street, 1-607 547 4070, www.alexanderspicnic.com), chef Alex Webster serves creative Mexican fare like sweet plantains with a chipotle-aioli dipping sauce. The local dive, **Cooley's Stone House Tavern** (49 Pioneer Street, at Main Street, 1-607

544 1311), is a beautifully restored tavern and a good spot for a nightcap.

Hotels

At the **Inn at Cooperstown** (16 Chestnut Street, at Main Street, 1-607 547 5756, www.innat cooperstown.com), many of the 18 individually decorated rooms feature four-poster beds, and you can play boardgames by the fire in the cosy parlour.

If you're looking for something a little more swanky, stay at the grand lakeside **Otesaga Resort Hotel** (60 Lake Street, at Pine Boulevard, 1-607 547 9931, www.otesaga.com) and play a round on the par-72 golf course.

Further information

Fenimore Art Museum *5798 Lake Road (State Highway 80) (1-607 547 1400, www.fenimore artmuseum.org).* **Open** *Apr-mid May, mid Oct-Dec* 10am-4pm Tue-Sun. *Mid May-mid Oct* 10am-5pm daily. Closed Jan-Mar. **Admission** $12; $10.50 reductions; free under-12s.
National Baseball Hall of Fame & Museum *25 Main Street, at Fair Street (1-888 425 5633, www.baseballhall.org).* **Open** *June-Aug* 9am-9pm daily. *Sept-May* 9am-5pm daily. **Admission** $23; $12-$15 reductions.

Getting there

By car Take I-87N to I-90 to exit 25A. Take I-88W to exit 24. Follow Route 7 to Route 20W to Route 80S to Cooperstown. The journey takes about 4hrs.

In Context

History

Seeds of the Big Apple.

More than 400 years ago, Henry Hudson, an English explorer in the service of the Dutch East India Company, sailed into New York Harbor, triggering events that would lead to the creation of the most dynamic and ethnically diverse city in the world. A steady flow of settlers, immigrants and fortune-seekers has seen New York evolve with the energy and aspirations of each successive wave of new arrivals. Intertwining cultural legacies have produced the densely layered character of the metropolis, from the wealthy and powerful Anglos who helped to build the city's riches to the fabled tired, poor huddled masses who arrived from far-off lands and faced a tougher struggle. From its beginnings, this forward-looking town has been shaped by a cast of hard-working, ambitious characters, and it continues to be so today.

NATIVE NEW YORKERS

The area's first residents were the indigenous Lenape tribe. They lived among the forests, meadows and farms of the land they called Lenapehoking, pretty much undisturbed by outsiders – until the 16th century, when their idyll was interrupted by European visitors. The first to cast his eyes upon this land was Giovanni da Verrazano in 1524. An Italian explorer commissioned by the French to find a shortcut to the Orient, he found Staten Island instead. Recognising that he was on the wrong track, Verrazano hauled anchor nearly as quickly as he had dropped it, never setting foot on dry land.

Eighty-five years later, Henry Hudson, an Englishman in the service of the Dutch East India Company, found New York Harbor in the same way. After trading with the Lenape, he ventured up the river that now bears his name, thinking it offered a north-west passage to Asia, but halted just south of present-day Albany when its shallowness convinced him it didn't lead to the Pacific. Hudson turned back, and his tales of the lush, river-crossed countryside captured the Dutch imagination. In 1624, the Dutch West India Company sent 110 settlers to establish a trading post here, planting themselves at the southern tip of the island called Mannahata and calling the colony Nieuw (New) Amsterdam. In many battles against the local Lenape, they did their best to drive the natives away from the little company town. But the tribe were immovable.

In 1626, Peter Minuit, New Amsterdam's first governor, thought he had solved the Lenape problem by pulling off the city's very first real-estate rip-off. He made them an offer they couldn't refuse: he 'bought' the island of Manhattan – all 14,000 acres of it – from the Lenape for 60 guilders' worth of goods. Legend famously values the purchase price at $24, but modern historians set the amount closer to $500. It was a slick trick, and one that set a precedent for countless future self-serving business transactions.

The Dutch quickly made the port of New Amsterdam a centre for fur trading. The population didn't grow as fast as the business, however, and the Dutch West India Company had a hard time finding recruits to move to this unknown island an ocean away. The company instead gathered servants, orphans and slaves, and other more unsavoury outcasts such as thieves, drunkards and prostitutes. The population grew to 400 within ten years, but drunkenness, crime and squalor prevailed. If the colony was to thrive, it needed a strong leader. Enter Dutch West India Company director Peter Stuyvesant.

PEG-LEG PETE

A one-legged, puritanical bully with a quick temper, Stuyvesant – or Peg-leg Pete, as he was known – may have been less than popular, but he was the colony's first effective governor. He made peace with the Lenape, formed the first policing force (consisting of nine men), cracked down on debauchery by shutting taverns and

Peter Stuyvesant.

outlawing drinking on Sunday, and established the first school, post office, hospital, prison and poorhouse. Within a decade, the population had quadrupled, and the settlement had become an important trading port.

Lined with canals and windmills, and dotted with gabled farmhouses, New Amsterdam slowly began to resemble its namesake. Newcomers arrived to work in the fur and slave trades, or to farm. Soon, a great variety of languages could be heard in the streets – a fact that made Stuyvesant nervous. In 1654, he attempted to quash immigration by turning away Sephardic Jews who were fleeing the Spanish Inquisition. But, surprisingly for the time, the corporate honchos at the Dutch West India Company reprimanded him for his intolerance and overturned his decision, leading to the establishment of the earliest Jewish community in the New World. It was the first time that the inflexible Stuyvesant was forced to mend his ways. The second time put an end to the 40-year Dutch rule for good.

BRITISH INVASION

In late August 1664, English warships sailed into the harbour, set on taking over the now prosperous colony. To avoid bloodshed and destruction, Stuyvesant surrendered quickly. Soon after, New Amsterdam was renamed New York (after the Duke of York, brother of King Charles II) and Stuyvesant quietly retired to his farm. Unlike Stuyvesant, the English battled with the Lenape; by 1695, those members of the tribe who hadn't been killed off were sent packing upstate, and New York's European population shot up to 3,000. Over the next 35 years, Dutch-style farmhouses and windmills gave way to stately townhouses and monuments to English royals. By 1740, the slave trade had made New York the third-busiest port in the British Empire. The city, now home to more than 11,000 residents, continued to prosper for a quarter-century. But resentment was beginning to build in the colony, fuelled by the ever-heavier burden of British taxation.

Fearing revolution, New York's citizenry fled the city in droves in 1775, causing the population to plummet from 25,000 to just 5,000. The following year, 100 British warships sailed into the harbour of this virtual ghost town, carrying with them an intimidating army of 32,000 men – nearly four times the size of George Washington's militia. Despite the British

presence, Washington organised a reading of the Declaration of Independence, and American patriots tore the statue of King George III from its pedestal. Revolution was inevitable.

The battle for New York officially began on 26 August 1776, and Washington's army sustained heavy losses; nearly a quarter of his men were slaughtered in a two-day period. As Washington retreated, a fire – thought to have been started by patriots – destroyed 493 buildings, including Trinity Church, the city's tallest structure. The British found a scorched city, and a populace living in tents.

The city continued to suffer for seven years. Eventually, of course, Washington's luck turned. As the British forces left, he and his troops marched triumphantly down Broadway to reclaim the city as a part of the newly established United States of America. A week and a half later, on 4 December 1783, the general bade farewell to his dispersing troops at Fraunces Tavern (see p55).

Alexander Hamilton was instrumental in the rebuilding effort. The ultimate self-made man, he was born on the Caribbean island of Nevis in 1755, the illegitimate son of a Scottish nobleman. After the death of his mother, he became an apprentice at a counting house before moving to New York to attend King's College (now Columbia University), but left to volunteer for service. He rose through the ranks and was promoted to lieutenant colonel at age 21 by George Washington. After the war, he laid the groundwork for New York City institutions that remain to this day. He established the Bank of New York, the city's first bank, in 1784. When Washington was inaugurated as the nation's first president in 1789, at Federal Hall on Wall Street, he brought Hamilton on board as the first secretary of the treasury. Thanks to Hamilton's business savvy, trade in stocks and bonds flourished, leading to the establishment in 1792 of what would eventually be known as the New York Stock Exchange.

THE CITY TAKES SHAPE...

New York continued to grow and prosper for the next three decades. Maritime commerce soared, and Robert Fulton's innovative steamboat made its maiden voyage on the Hudson River in 1807. Eleven years later, a group of merchants introduced regularly scheduled shipping (a novel concept at the time) between New York and Liverpool on the

IN CONTEXT

TOP FIVE NYC INVENTIONS

They made it here.

1 TOILET PAPER

In 1857, Joseph C Gayetty began selling packs of 'medicated paper for the water closet' out of his wholesale shop at 41 Ann Street. The paper was made from pure Manila hemp and treated with aloe to assure patrons it was healthier than their old standby: shreds of used newspaper. Best (or worst) of all, each sheet was watermarked with his name.

2 PNEUMATIC RAILWAY

Inventor Alfred Ely Beach unveiled the first air-propelled train (and technically New York's first subway) in 1870. Pushed by a 20-ton fan, the fancy cylindrical car had plush seats and zirconia lamps and cost a quarter to ride. Sadly the Panic of 1873 financial crisis blew away any future for this marvel of 19th-century technology, which ran only one block under Broadway from Warren to Murray Streets.

3 TEDDY BEAR

In 1902, political cartoonists poked fun at President Theodore Roosevelt for refusing to shoot an injured black bear while on a hunt. Inspired by the story, Morris and Rose Michtom, Russian-Jewish candy-store owners from Brooklyn who also sold soft toys, sewed a plush bear and displayed it with the label 'Teddy's bear'. It proved so popular, the couple gave up candy and opened a factory to make the cuddly critters.

Scrabble street sign.

4 SCRABBLE

Out-of-work architect and anagram lover Alfred Mosher Butts conceived this wordy board game in 1931 while living in Jackson Heights, Queens. Hoping to sell the game idea, he made hand-cut tiles and obliged family and friends to help develop the basic rules; the game has since sold more than 150 million copies worldwide. The street sign on Butts' corner on 35th Avenue in Queens now pays homage to his invention with number scores punctuating the letters.

5 REMOTE CONTROL

Nikola Tesla, the Serbian-American New Yorker remembered as the archetypal mad scientist, conceived of a radio-controlled boat back in 1898. The idea was so novel that no one believed such technology could exist – particularly New York's patent officers. Tesla went on to become a hero to future generations of couch surfers – once TV was invented.

Pneumatic Railway.

Black Ball Line. A boom in the maritime trades lured hundreds of European labourers, and the city, which was still entirely crammed in below Houston Street, grew more and more congested. Manhattan real estate became the most expensive in the world.

The first man to tackle the city's congestion problem was Mayor DeWitt Clinton, a protégé of Hamilton. Clinton's dream was to organise the entire island of Manhattan in such a way that it could cope with the eventual population creep northwards. In 1807, he created a commission to map out the foreseeable sprawl. It presented its work four years later, and the destiny of this new city was made manifest: it would be a regular grid of crossing thoroughfares, 12 avenues wide and 155 streets long. Then Clinton overstepped the city's boundaries. In 1811, he presented a plan to build a 363-mile canal linking the Hudson River with Lake Erie. Many of his contemporaries thought it was an impossible task: at the time, the longest canal in the world ran a mere 27 miles. But Clinton pressed on and raised a staggering $6 million for the project.

Work on the Erie Canal began in 1817 and was completed in 1825 – three years ahead of schedule. It shortened the journey between New York City and Buffalo from three weeks to one, and cut the shipping cost per ton from about $100 to $4. Goods, people and money poured into New York, fostering a merchant elite that moved northwards in Manhattan to escape the urban crush. Estates multiplied above Houston Street – all grander and more imposing than their modest colonial forerunners. Once slavery was abolished n New York in 1827, free blacks became an essential part of the workforce. In 1831, the first public transport system began operating, with horse-drawn omnibuses.

...AND SO DO THE SLUMS

As the population multiplied (swelling to 240,000 by 1830 and 700,000 by 1850), so did the city's problems. Tensions bubbled between immigrant newcomers and those who could trace their American lineage back a generation or two. Crime rose and lurid tales filled the 'penny press', the city's proto-tabloids. While wealthy New Yorkers were moving as far 'uptown' as Greenwich Village, the infamous Five Points neighbourhood – the city's first slum – festered in the area now

occupied by City Hall, the courthouses and Chinatown. Built on a fetid drained pond, Five Points became the ramshackle home of poor immigrants and blacks. Brutal gangs with colourful names such as the Forty Thieves, Plug Uglies and Dead Rabbits often met in bloody clashes in the streets, but what finally sent a mass of 100,000 people scurrying from lower Manhattan was an outbreak of cholera in 1832. In just six weeks, 3,513 New Yorkers died.

In 1837, a financial panic left hundreds of Wall Street businesses crumbling. Commerce stagnated at the docks, the real-estate market collapsed, and all but three city banks closed. Some 50,000 New Yorkers lost their jobs, while 200,000 teetered on the edge of poverty. The panic sparked civil unrest and violence. In 1849, a xenophobic mob of 8,000 protesting the performance of an English actor at the Astor Place Opera House was met by a militia that opened fire, killing 22. But the Draft Riots of 1863 were much worse. After a law was passed exempting men from the draft for a $300 fee, the (mostly Irish) poor rose up, forming a 15,000-strong force that rampaged through the city. Fuelled by anger about the Civil War (for which they blamed blacks), the rioters set fire to the Colored Orphan Asylum and vandalised black homes. Blacks were beaten in the streets, and some were lynched. A federal force of 6,000 men was sent to subdue the violence. After four days and at least 100 deaths, peace was finally restored.

ON THE MOVE

Amid the chaos of the mid 19th century, the pace of progress continued unabated. Compared to the major Southern cities, New York emerged nearly unscathed from the Civil War. The population ballooned to two million in the 1880s, and new technologies revolutionised daily life. The elevated railway helped New Yorkers to move into what are now the Upper East and Upper West Sides, while other trains connected the city with upstate New York, New England and the Midwest. By 1871, regional train traffic had grown so much that rail tycoon Cornelius Vanderbilt built the original Grand Central Depot (it was replaced in 1913 by the current Grand Central Terminal).

One ambitious project was inspired by the harsh winter of 1867. The East River froze over, halting ferry traffic between Brooklyn and Manhattan. Brooklyn, by then, had

IN CONTEXT

become the nation's third most populous city, and its politicians and businessmen realised that the boroughs had to be linked. The New York Bridge Company's goal was to build the world's longest bridge, spanning the East River between downtown Manhattan and south-western Brooklyn. Over 16 years (four times longer than projected), 14,000 miles of steel cable were stretched across the 1,595-foot span, while the towers rose a staggering 276 feet above the river. The Brooklyn Bridge opened on 24 May 1883.

THE GREED OF TWEED

As New York recovered from the turmoil of the mid 1800s, William M 'Boss' Tweed began pulling the strings. Using his ample charm, the six-foot, 300-pound bookkeeper, chair-maker and volunteer firefighter became one of the city's most powerful politicians. He had been an alderman and district leader; he had served in the US House of Representatives and as a state senator; and he was a chairman of the Democratic General Committee and leader of Tammany Hall, a political organisation formed by local craftsmen ostensibly to keep the wealthy classes' political clout in check. But even though Tweed opened orphanages, poorhouses and hospitals, his good deeds were overshadowed by his and his cohort's gross embezzlement of city funds. By 1870, members of the 'Tweed Ring' had created a new city charter, granting themselves control of the City Treasury. Using fake leases and inflated bills for city supplies and services, Tweed and his cronies may ultimately have pocketed as much as $200 million.

Tweed was eventually sued by the city for $6 million, and charged with forgery and larceny. He escaped from debtors' prison in 1875, but was captured in Spain a year later and died in 1878. But his greed hurt many. As he was emptying the city's coffers, poverty spread. Then the stock market took a nosedive, factories closed and railways went bankrupt. By 1874, New York estimated its homeless population at 90,000. That winter, *Harper's Weekly* reported, 900 New Yorkers starved to death.

IMMIGRANT DREAMS

In September 1882, a new era dawned brightly when Thomas Alva Edison lit up half a square mile of lower Manhattan with 3,000 electric lamps. One of the newly illuminated offices belonged to financier JP Morgan, who played an essential part in bringing New York's, and America's, economy back to life. By bailing out a number of failing railways, then merging and restructuring them, Morgan jump-started commerce in New York once again. Goods, jobs and businesses returned to the city, and very soon such aggressive businessmen as John D Rockefeller, Andrew Carnegie and Henry Frick wanted a piece of the action. They made New York the HQ of Standard Oil and US Steel, corporations that went on to shape America's economic future.

A shining symbol for less fortunate arrivals also made New York its home around that time. To commemorate the centennial of the Declaration of Independence, the French gave the United States the Statue of Liberty, which was dedicated in 1886. Between 1892 and 1954, the statue ushered more than 12 million immigrants into New York Harbor, and Ellis Island processed many of them. The island had opened as an immigration centre in 1892 with expectations of accommodating 500,000 people annually, but the number peaked at more than a million in 1907. In the 34-building complex, crowds of would-be Americans were herded through examinations, inspections and interrogations. About 98 per cent got through, turning New York into what British playwright Israel Zangwill optimistically called 'the great melting pot where all the races of Europe are melting and reforming'.

Many of these newcomers crowded into dark, squalid tenements on the Lower East Side, while millionaires such as Vanderbilt and Frick constructed huge French-style mansions along Fifth Avenue. Jacob A Riis, a Danish immigrant and police reporter for the *New York Tribune*, made it his business to expose this dichotomy, scouring filthy alleys and overcrowded tenements to research and photograph his 1890 book, *How the Other Half Lives*. Largely as a result of Riis's work, the state passed the Tenement House Act of 1901, calling for drastic housing reforms.

SOARING ASPIRATIONS

On 1 January 1898, the boroughs of Manhattan, Brooklyn, Queens, Staten Island and the Bronx consolidated to form New York City, the largest metropolis in America

IN CONTEXT

Aftermath of the **Triangle Shirtwaist Fire**.

with over three million residents. More and more companies started to move their headquarters to this new city, increasing the demand for office space. With little land left to develop in lower Manhattan, New York embraced the steel revolution and grew steadily skywards. By 1920, New York boasted more than 60 skyscrapers (see p351 **Race to the Top**).

If that weren't enough to demonstrate New Yorkers' unending ambition, the city burrowed below the streets at the same time, starting work on its underground transport system in 1900. The $35-million project took nearly four and a half years to complete. Less than a decade after opening, it was the most heavily travelled subway system in the world, carrying almost a billion passengers on its trains every year.

CHANGING TIMES

By 1909, 30,000 factories were operating in the city, churning out everything from heavy machinery to artificial flowers. Mistrusted, abused and underpaid, factory workers faced impossible quotas, had their pay docked for minor mistakes and were often locked in during working hours. In the end, it took a tragedy to bring about real changes in employment laws. The Triangle Shirtwaist Fire was one of the worst industrial disasters in New York City history. On 25 March 1911, fire broke out on the eighth floor of the ten-storey Greenwich Village building on the corner of Greene Street and Washington Place. The top three floors were occupied by the Triangle Shirtwaist Company and, fed by the fabrics, the

flames spread rapidly up the building. As the roughly 500 garment workers – many of them teenage girls – rushed to escape, they found many of the exits locked. The single flimsy fire escape melted in the heat and fell away from the building. A total of 146 perished. Tried for manslaughter, the factory owners were acquitted, but the fire spurred labour and union organisations to seek major reforms. The Factory Commission of 1911 was established, and spawned the Fire Prevention division of the Fire Department, which enforced the creation of fire escape routes in the workplace. The incident also garnered much-needed support for the Ladies Garment Workers Union.

Between 1910 and 1913, New York City was the site of the largest women's suffrage rallies in the United States. Harriet Stanton Blatch (the daughter of famed suffragette Elizabeth Cady Stanton, and founder of the Equality League of Self-Supporting Women) and Carrie Chapman Catt (the organiser of the New York City Women's Suffrage Party) arranged attention-grabbing demonstrations intended to pressure the state into authorising a referendum on a woman's right to vote. The measure's defeat in 1915 only steeled the suffragettes' resolve. Finally, with the support of Tammany Hall, the law was passed in 1919, challenging the male stranglehold on voting throughout the country. With New York leading the nation, the 19th Amendment was ratified in 1920.

In 1919, as New York welcomed troops home from World War I with a parade, the city also celebrated its emergence on the global stage. It had supplanted London as the investment capital of the world, and had become the centre of publishing, thanks to two men: Joseph Pulitzer and William Randolph Hearst. The New York Times had become the country's most respected newspaper; Broadway was the focal point of American theatre; and Greenwich Village had become an international bohemian nexus, where flamboyant artists, writers and political revolutionaries gathered in galleries and coffeehouses.

The more personal side of the women's movement also found a home in New York City. A nurse and midwife who grew up in a family of 11 children, Margaret Sanger was a fierce advocate of birth control and family planning. She opened the first ever birth-control clinic in Brooklyn on 16 October 1916. Finding this unseemly, the police closed the clinic soon after and imprisoned Sanger for 30 days. She was not deterred, however, and, in 1921, formed the American Birth Control League – the forerunner of the organisation Planned Parenthood – which researched birth control methods and provided gynaecological services.

ALL THAT JAZZ

Forward-thinking women such as Sanger set the tone for an era when women, now a voting political force, were moving beyond the moral conventions of the 19th century. The country ushered in the Jazz Age in 1919 by ratifying the 18th Amendment, which outlawed the distribution and sale of alcoholic beverages. Prohibition turned the city into the epicentre of bootlegging, speakeasies and organised crime. By the early 1920s, New York boasted 32,000 illegal watering holes – twice the number of legal bars before Prohibition.

In 1925, New Yorkers elected the magnetic James J Walker as mayor. A charming ex-songwriter (as well as a speakeasy patron and skirt-chaser), Walker was the perfect match for his city's flashy style and hunger for publicity. Fame flowed in the city's veins: home-run hero Babe Ruth drew a million fans each season to baseball games at the newly built Yankee Stadium, and sharp-tongued Walter Winchell filled his newspaper columns with celebrity titbits and scandals. Alexander Woollcott, Dorothy Parker, Robert Benchley and other writers met up daily to trade witticisms around a table at the Algonquin Hotel; the result, in February 1925, was The New Yorker.

The Harlem Renaissance blossomed at the same time. Writers Langston Hughes, Zora Neale Hurston and James Weldon Johnson transformed the African-American experience into lyrical literary works, and white society flocked to the Cotton Club to see genre-defining musicians such as Bessie Smith, Cab Calloway, Louis Armstrong and Duke Ellington. (Blacks were allowed into the club only if they were performing on the stage, they could not be part of the audience.)

Downtown, Broadway houses were packed with fans of George and Ira Gershwin, Irving Berlin, Cole Porter, Lorenz Hart, Richard Rodgers and Oscar Hammerstein II. Towards the end of the 1920s, New York-born Al Jolson wowed audiences in The Jazz Singer, the first talking picture.

AFTER THE CRASH

The dizzying excitement ended on 29 October 1929, when the stock market crashed. Corruption eroded Mayor Walker's hold on the city: despite a tenure that saw the opening of the Holland Tunnel, the completion of the George Washington Bridge and the construction of the Chrysler and Empire State Buildings, Walker's lustre faded in the growing shadow of graft accusations. He resigned in 1932, when New York, in the depths of the Great Depression, had one million unemployed inhabitants.

In 1934, an unstoppable force named Fiorello La Guardia took office as mayor, rolling up his sleeves to crack down on mobsters, gambling, smut and government corruption. La Guardia was a tough-talking politician known for nearly coming to blows with other city officials; he described himself as 'inconsiderate, arbitrary, authoritative, difficult, complicated, intolerant and somewhat theatrical'. His act played well: he ushered New York into an era of unparalleled prosperity over the course of his three terms. The 'Little Flower', as La Guardia was known, streamlined city government, paid down the debt and updated the transport, hospital, reservoir and sewer systems. New highways made the city more accessible, and North Beach (now La Guardia) Airport became the city's first commercial landing field.

Helping La Guardia to modernise the city was Robert Moses, a hard-nosed visionary who would do much to shape – and in some cases, destroy – New York's landscape. Moses spent 44 years stepping on toes to build expressways, parks, beaches, public housing, bridges and tunnels, creating such landmarks as Lincoln Center, the United Nations complex and the Verrazano-Narrows Bridge, which connected Staten Island to Brooklyn in 1964.

PROTEST AND REFORM

Despite La Guardia's belt-tightening and Moses's renovations, New York began to fall apart financially. When World War II ended, 800,000 industrial jobs disappeared from the city. Factories in need of more space moved to the suburbs, along with nearly five million residents. But more crowding occurred as rural African-Americans and Latinos (primarily Puerto Ricans) flocked to the metropolis in the 1950s and '60s, to meet with ruthless discrimination and a dearth of jobs. Moses's Slum Clearance Committee reduced many neighbourhoods to rubble, forcing out residents in order to build huge, isolating housing projects that became magnets for crime. In 1963, the city also lost Pennsylvania Station, when the Pennsylvania Railroad Company demolished the site over the protests of picketers to make way for a modern station and new sports and entertainment venue Madison Square Garden. It was a wake-up call for New York: architectural changes were hurtling out of control.

But Moses and his wrecking ball couldn't knock over one steadfast West Village woman. Architectural writer and urban-planning critic Jane Jacobs organised local residents when the city unveiled its plan to clear a 14-block tract of her neighbourhood to make space for yet more public housing. Her obstinacy was applauded by many, including an influential councilman named Ed Koch (who would become mayor in 1978). The group fought the plan and won, causing Mayor Robert F Wagner to back down. As a result of Jacobs's efforts in the wake of Pennsylvania Station's demolition, the Landmarks Preservation Commission – the first such group in the US – was established in 1965.

At the dawning of the Age of Aquarius, the city harboured its share of innovative creators. Allen Ginsberg, Jack Kerouac and others gathered in Village coffeehouses to create a new voice for poetry. A folk music scene brewed in tiny clubs around Bleecker Street, showcasing musicians such as Bob Dylan. A former advertising illustrator named Andy Warhol turned images of mass consumerism into deadpan, ironic art statements. And in 1969, the city's long-closeted gay communities came out into the streets, as patrons at the Stonewall Inn on Christopher Street demonstrated against a police raid. The protests, known as the Stonewall riots, gave birth to the modern gay rights movement.

MEAN STREETS

By the early 1970s, deficits had forced heavy cutbacks in city services. The streets were dirty, and subway cars and buildings were scrawled with graffiti; crime skyrocketed as the city's debt deepened to $6 billion. Despite the huge downturn, construction commenced on the World Trade Center; when completed, in 1973, its twin 110-storey towers were the world's tallest buildings. Even as the WTC rose, the city became so desperately overdrawn that Mayor Abraham Beame appealed to the federal government for financial assistance in 1975. Yet President Gerald Ford refused to bail out the city.

Times Square had degenerated into a morass of sex shops and porn theatres, drug use rose and subway use hit an all-time low due to a fear of crime. In 1977, serial killer Son of Sam terrorised the city with six killings, and a blackout one hot August night that same year led to widespread looting and arson. The angst of the time fuelled the punk culture that rose in downtown clubs such as CBGB. At the same time, celebrities, designers and models converged on midtown to disco their nights away at Studio 54.

The Wall Street boom of the 1980s and fiscal petitioning by Mayor Ed Koch brought money flooding back into New York. Gentrification glamorised neighbourhoods such as Soho, Tribeca and the East Village, but deeper societal ills lurked. In 1988, a protest against the city's efforts to impose a strict curfew and displace the homeless from Tompkins Square Park erupted into a violent clash with the police. Crack use became

IN CONTEXT

endemic in the ghettos, homelessness rose and AIDS emerged as a new scourge.

By 1989, citizens were restless for change. They turned to David N Dinkins, electing him as the city's first black mayor. A distinguished, softly spoken man, Dinkins held office for only a single term, marked by a record murder rate, flaring racial tensions in Manhattan's Washington Heights and Brooklyn's Crown Heights and Flatbush neighbourhoods, and the explosion of a bomb in the basement parking garage of the World Trade Center in 1993 that killed six and injured 1,000.

Deeming the polite Dinkins ineffective, New Yorkers voted in former federal prosecutor Rudolph Giuliani. An abrasive leader, Giuliani used bullying tactics to get things done, as his 'quality of life' campaign cracked down on everything from drug dealing and pornography to unsolicited windshield washing. As cases of severe police brutality grabbed the headlines and racial polarisation was palpable, crime plummeted, tourism soared and New York became cleaner and safer than it had been in decades. Times Square was transformed into a family-friendly tourist destination, and the dot-com explosion brought young wannabes to the Flatiron District's Silicon Alley. Giuliani's second term as mayor would close, however, on a devastating tragedy.

21ST-CENTURY TRAUMA

On 11 September 2001, terrorists flew two hijacked passenger jets into the Twin Towers of the World Trade Center, collapsing the entire complex and killing nearly 3,000 people. Amid the trauma, the attack triggered a citywide sense of unity, as New Yorkers did what they could to help their fellow citizens – from feeding emergency crews to cheering on rescue workers en route to Ground Zero.

Two months later, billionaire Michael Bloomberg was elected mayor and took on the daunting task of repairing not only the city's skyline but also its battered economy. The stock market revived, downtown businesses re-emerged and plans for rebuilding the World Trade Center were drawn. True to form, however, New Yorkers debated the future of the site for more than a year until architect Daniel Libeskind was awarded the redevelopment job in 2003. The 9/11 Memorial opened on 11 September 2011 and, in autumn 2013, the WTC's centrepiece

tower, 1 World Trade Center, was officially declared the tallest building in the Western Hemisphere. With the opening of the 9/11 Memorial Museum in spring 2014, and the removal of the barriers surrounding the site, the new World Trade Center finally became fully accessible to the public.

While Mayor Bloomberg ushered in many reforms to make NYC a cleaner, healthier metropolis – from the 2003 smoking ban to a major plan to reduce greenhouse emissions – as his second term neared its end, he became increasingly frustrated that some of his pet proposals hadn't been realised. In the midst of 2008's deepening financial crisis, the mayor proposed a controversial bill to extend the tenure of elected officials from two four-year terms to three. Although it was narrowly passed by the New York City Council in October 2008, many politicos (and citizens) opposed the law change. The encumbent poured a record sum of money into his campaign the following year, winning just 51 per cent of the vote to become the fourth mayor in New York's history to serve a third term. In October 2010, in a remarkable display of chutzpah, Bloomberg voted to restore the two-term limitation. Three years later, the city elected its first Democratic mayor in a generation, Bill de Blasio.

In June 2011, New York celebrated yet another civil rights milestone when it became the largest state in the US to legalise same-sex marriage. A few months later, a group of protesters set up camp in the Financial District's Zuccotti Park, demanding jobs and denouncing the financial industry. Occupy Wall Street demonstrators managed to hold their ground for almost two months until they were forced out by police in November. But the group had already inspired similar movements around the world, spreading the message of the '99 per cent'.

Just before Halloween 2012, the city was rocked by Hurricane Sandy, a disaster without modern precedent that flooded the subway system, plunged lower Manhattan and other parts of the metropolis into darkness and left thousands of New Yorkers homeless. The fallout was still being felt more than a year later; many businesses and landmarks – including the Statue of Liberty and Ellis Island – remained closed for months, others never recovered from the damage.

KEY EVENTS
New York in brief.

1524 Giovanni da Verrazano sails into New York Harbor.
1624 First Dutch settlers establish Nieuw Amsterdam.
1626 Peter Minuit purchases Manhattan for goods worth 60 guilders.
1639 The Broncks settle north of Manhattan.
1646 Village of Breuckelen founded.
1664 Dutch rule ends; Nieuw Amsterdam renamed New York.
1754 King's College (now Columbia University) founded.
1776 Battle for New York begins; fire ravages the city.
1783 George Washington's troops march triumphantly down Broadway.
1784 Alexander Hamilton founds the Bank of New York.
1785 City becomes nation's capital.
1789 President Washington inaugurated at Federal Hall.
1792 New York Stock Exchange opens.
1804 New York becomes country's most populous city, with around 80,000 inhabitants.
1811 Mayor DeWitt Clinton's grid plan for Manhattan introduced.
1827 Slavery officially abolished in New York State.
1851 *The New-York Daily Times* (now *The New York Times*) launched.
1880 Metropolitan Museum of Art opens.
1883 Brooklyn Bridge opens.
1886 Statue of Liberty unveiled.
1891 Carnegie Hall opens.
1892 Ellis Island opens.
1898 The five boroughs are consolidated into the city of New York.
1900 Electric lights replace gas along lower Broadway.
1902 The Fuller (Flatiron) Building becomes the world's first skyscraper.
1904 New York's first subway line opens.
1908 First ball dropped in Times Square to celebrate the new year.
1911 Fire in the Triangle Shirtwaist Company kills 146.

1913 Woolworth Building completed; Grand Central Terminal opens.
1923 The first Yankee Stadium opens.
1929 Stock market crashes; Museum of Modern Art opens.
1931 George Washington Bridge completed; Empire State Building completed; Whitney Museum opens.
1934 Fiorello La Guardia elected mayor.
1939 New York hosts the World's Fair.
1950 United Nations complex finished.
1953 Robert Moses spearheads building of the Cross Bronx Expressway.
1957 Brooklyn Dodgers baseball team move to LA; New York Giants move to San Francisco.
1962 New York Mets debut at the Polo Grounds; Philharmonic Hall, first building in Lincoln Center, opens.
1964 Verrazano-Narrows Bridge completed; World's Fair held in Queens.
1970 First New York City Marathon.
1973 World Trade Center completed.
1975 On verge of bankruptcy, city is snubbed by federal government.
1977 Studio 54 opens; 4,000 arrested during citywide blackout.
1989 David N Dinkins elected city's first black mayor.
1993 Bomb explodes in World Trade Center, killing six and injuring 1,000.
2001 Hijackers fly two jets into World Trade Center, killing nearly 3,000.
2004 Statue of Liberty reopens for first time since 9/11.
2009 Yankees and Mets move into new state-of-the-art stadiums.
2010 Mayor Michael Bloomberg is inaugurated as the fourth mayor in the city's history to serve a third term.
2011 Gay marriage is legalised in New York State; the 9/11 Memorial debuts.
2012 The Barclays Center, home to Brooklyn's first pro sports team since 1957, opens; Hurricane Sandy hits, paralysing the city.
2014 1 World Trade Center, the Western Hemisphere's tallest skyscraper, completed.

IN CONTEXT

Architecture

Tall stories.

TEXT: ERIC P NASH

Manhattan, of course, is synonymous with skyscrapers. Following advances in iron and steel technology in the middle of the 19th century, and the pressing need for space on an already overcrowded island, New York's architects realised that the only way was up. The race to reach the heavens in the early 20th century was supplanted by the minimalist post-war International Style, which saw a rash of towering glass boxes spread across midtown. That race has picked up pace today with a crop of freshly minted cloudbusters.

However, those with an architectural interest and an observant eye will be rewarded by the fascinating mix of styles and unexpected details closer to the ground in virtually every corner of the metropolis, from gargoyles crouching on the façade of an early 20th-century apartment building to extravagant cast-iron decoration adorning a humble warehouse. And it's worth remembering that under New York's gleaming exoskeleton of steel and glass lies the heart of a 17th-century Dutch city.

LOWLAND LEGACY

The Dutch influence is still traceable in the downtown web of narrow, winding lanes. Because the Cartesian grid that rules the city was laid out by the Commissioners Plan in 1811, only a few examples of Dutch architecture remain, mostly off the beaten path. One is the 1785 **Dyckman Farmhouse Museum** (4881 Broadway, at 204th Street, 1-212 304 9422, www.dyckmanfarmhouse. org; closed Mon-Thur) in Inwood, Manhattan's northernmost neighbourhood. Its decorative brickwork and gambrel roof reflect the fashion of the late 18th century. The oldest house still standing in the five boroughs, however, is the **Wyckoff House Museum** (5816 Clarendon Road, at Ralph Avenue, Flatbush, Brooklyn, 1-718 629 5400, www.wyckoffassociation. org; closed Mon Apr-Oct, Mon & Sun Nov-Mar). Erected around 1652, it's a typical Dutch farmhouse with deep eaves and roughly shingled walls.

In Manhattan, the only building left from pre-Revolutionary times is the stately columned and quoined **St Paul's Chapel** (see p56), completed in 1766 (a spire was added in 1796). George Washington, a parishioner here, was officially received in the chapel after his 1789 presidential inauguration. The Enlightenment ideals upon which the nation was founded influenced the church's non-hierarchical layout. **Trinity Church** (see p56) of 1846, one of the first and finest Gothic Revival churches in the country, was designed by Richard Upjohn. Its crocketed, finialed 281-foot spire held sway for decades as the tallest structure in Manhattan.

Holdouts remain from each epoch of the city's architectural history. An outstanding example of Greek Revival from the first half of the 19th century is the 1842 **Federal Hall National Memorial** (see p52), the mighty marble colonnaded structure on the site where George Washington took his oath of office. A larger-than-life statue of Washington by the sculptor John Quincy Adams Ward stands in front. The city's most celebrated blocks of Greek Revival townhouses, built in the 1830s, are known simply as **the Row** (1-13 Washington Square North, between Fifth Avenue & Washington Square West); they're exemplars of the more genteel metropolis of Henry James and Edith Wharton.

Trinity Church

Greek Revival gave way to Renaissance-inspired Beaux Arts architecture, which itself reflected the imperial ambitions of a wealthy young nation during the Gilded Age of the late 19th century. Like Emperor Augustus, who boasted that he had found Rome a city of brick and left it a city of marble, the firm of McKim, Mead & White built noble civic monuments and *palazzi* for the rich. The best-known buildings of the classicist Charles Follen McKim include the main campus of **Columbia University** (see p176), begun in the 1890s, and the austere 1906 **Morgan Library** (see p163), which underwent an interior renovation completed in 2010. His partner, socialite and bon vivant Stanford White (scandalously murdered by his mistress's husband in 1906 on the roof of the original Madison Square Garden, which he himself designed), conceived more festive spaces, such as the **Metropolitan Club** (1 E 60th Street, at Fifth Avenue) and the luxe **Villard Houses** of 1882, now part of the New York Palace Hotel (455 Madison Avenue, between E 50th & E 51st Streets).

Downtown, the old **Alexander Hamilton US Custom House**, which now houses the National Museum of the American Indian (see p52), was built by Cass Gilbert in 1907 and is a symbol of New York Harbor's significance in

Manhattan's growth (before 1913, the city's chief source of revenue was customs duties). Gilbert's domed marble edifice is suitably monumental – its carved figures of the Four Continents are by Daniel Chester French, the sculptor of the Lincoln Memorial in Washington, DC. Another Beaux Arts treasure is Carrère & Hastings' sumptuous white marble **New York Public Library** of 1911 (see p158), built on the site of a former Revolutionary War battleground. The 1913 travertine-lined **Grand Central Terminal** (see p162) remains an elegant transport hub, thanks to preservationists who saved it from the wrecking ball.

VERTICAL REALITY

Cast-iron architecture peaked in the latter half of the 19th century, coinciding with the Civil War. Iron and steel components freed architects from the bulk, weight and cost of stone, and allowed them to build taller structures. Cast-iron columns – cheap to mass-produce – could support enormous weight. The façades of many Soho buildings, with their intricate details of Italianate columns, were manufactured on assembly lines and could be ordered in pieces from catalogues. This led to an aesthetic of uniform building façades, which had a direct impact on later steel skyscrapers and continues to inform the skyline today. To enjoy one of the most telling vistas of skyscraper history, gaze north from the 1859 **Cooper Union Building** (see p100) in the East Village, the oldest steel-beam-framed building in America.

The most visible effect of the move towards cast-iron construction was the way it opened up solid-stone façades to expanses of glass. In fact, window-shopping came into vogue in the 1860s. Mrs Lincoln bought the White House china at the **Haughwout Store** (488-492 Broadway, at Broome Street). The 1857 building's Palladian-style façade recalls Renaissance Venice, but its regular, open fenestration was also a portent of the future. (The cast-iron elevator sign is a relic of the world's first working safety passenger elevator, designed by Elisha Graves Otis in 1852.)

Once engineers perfected steel, which is stronger and lighter than iron, and created the interlocking steel-cage construction that distributed the weight of a building over its entire frame, the sky was the limit. New York has one structure by the great Chicago-based

innovator Louis Sullivan: the 1898 **Bayard-Condict Building** (65-69 Bleecker Street, between Broadway & Lafayette Street). Though only 13 storeys tall, Sullivan's building, covered with richly decorative terracotta, was one of the earliest to have a purely vertical design rather than one that imitated the horizontal styles of the past. Sullivan wrote that a skyscraper 'must be tall, every inch of it tall… From bottom to top, it is a unit without a single dissenting line.'

The 21-storey **Flatiron Building** (see p136), designed by fellow Chicagoan Daniel H Burnham and completed in 1902, is another standout of the era. Its height and modern design combined with traditional masonry decoration was made possible only by its steel-cage construction.

The new century saw a frenzy of skyward construction, resulting in buildings of record-breaking height. When it was built in 1899, the 30-storey, 391-foot **Park Row Building** (15 Park Row, between Ann & Beekman Streets) was the tallest building in the world; by 1931, though, Shreve, Lamb & Harmon's 1,250-foot **Empire State Building** (see p157) had more than tripled its record. (For more on the battle for the city's tallest building, see p351 **Race to the Top**.) Although they were retroactively labelled art deco (such buildings were then simply called 'modern'), the Empire State's setbacks were actually a response to the zoning code of 1916, which required a building's upper storeys to be tapered in order not to block out sunlight and air circulation to the streets. The code engendered some of the city's most fanciful architectural designs, such as the ziggurat-crowned 1926 **Paramount Building** (1501 Broadway, between 43rd & 44th Streets) and the romantically slender spire of the former **Cities Service Building** (70 Pine Street, at Pearl Street), illuminated from within like an enormous rare gem.

OUTSIDE THE BOX

The post-World War II period saw the rise of the International Style, pioneered by such giants as Le Corbusier and Ludwig Mies van der Rohe. The International Style relied on a new set of aesthetics: minimal decoration, clear expression of construction, an honest use of materials and a near-Platonic harmony of proportions. The style's most visible symbol was the all-glass façade, similar to that found

IN CONTEXT

on the sleek slab of the **United Nations Headquarters'** Secretariat Building (see p162).

Designed by Gordon Bunshaft of Skidmore, Owings & Merrill, **Lever House** (390 Park Avenue, between 53rd & 54th Streets) became the city's first all-steel-and-glass structure in 1952. It's almost impossible to imagine the radical vision this glass construction represented on the all-masonry corridor of Park Avenue, because nearly every building since has followed suit. Mies van der Rohe's celebrated bronze-skinned **Seagram Building** (375 Park Avenue, between 52nd & 53rd Streets), which reigns in isolation in its own plaza, is the epitome of the architect's cryptic dicta that 'Less is more' and 'God is in the details'. The detailing on the building is exquisite – the custom-made bolts securing the miniature bronze piers that run the length of the façade must be polished by hand every year to keep them from oxidising and turning green. With this heady combination of grandeur and attention to detail, it's the Rolls-Royce of skyscrapers.

High modernism began to show cracks in its façade during the mid 1960s. By then, New York had built too many such structures in midtown and below. The public had never fully warmed to the undecorated style, and the International Style's sheer arrogance in trying to supplant the traditional city structure didn't endear the movement to anyone. The **MetLife Building** (200 Park Avenue, at 45th Street), originally the Pan Am Building of 1963, was the prime culprit, not so much because of its design (by Walter Gropius of the Bauhaus) but because of its presumptuous location, straddling Park Avenue and looming over Grand Central. There was even a plan to raze Grand Central and construct a twin Pan Am in its place. The International Style had obviously reached the end of its life when Philip Johnson, instrumental in defining the movement with his book The International Style (co-written with Henry-Russell Hitchcock), began disparaging the aesthetic as 'glass-boxitis'.

A different approach was provided by Boston architect Hugh Stubbins's triangle-topped **Citigroup Center** (Lexington Avenue, between 53rd & 54th Streets), which utilised contemporary engineering (the building cantilevers almost magically on high stilts above street level) while harking back to the decorative tops of yesteryear. Sly old Johnson turned the tables on everyone with the heretical Chippendale crown on his Sony Building, originally the **AT&T Building** (350 Madison Avenue, between 55th & 56th Streets), a bold throwback to decoration for its own sake.

Postmodernism provided a theoretical basis for a new wave of buildings that mixed past and present, often taking cues from the environs. Some notable examples include Helmut Jahn's **425 Lexington Avenue** (between 43rd & 44th Streets) of 1988; David Childs's retro diamond-tipped **Worldwide Plaza** (825 Eighth Avenue, between 49th & 50th Streets) of 1989; and the honky-tonk agglomeration of Skidmore, Owings & Merrill's **Bertelsmann Building** (1540 Broadway, between 45th & 46th Streets) of 1990. But even postmodernism became old hat after a while: too many architects relied on fussy fenestration and passive commentary on other styles, and too few were creating vital new building façades.

'Early 21st-century architecture is moving beyond applied symbolism to radical new forms, facilitated by computer-based design methods.'

The electronic spectacle of Times Square (see p151) provided one possible direction for architects. Upon seeing the myriad electric lights of Times Square in 1922, British wit GK Chesterton remarked: 'What a glorious garden of wonder this would be, to anyone who was lucky enough to be unable to read.' The Crossroads of the World continues to be at the cybernetic cutting edge, with the 120-foot-tall, quarter-acre-in-area NASDAQ sign; the real-time stock tickers and jumbo TV screens; and the news ticker wrapping around the original 1904 New York Times HQ, **1 Times Square** (between Broadway & Seventh Avenue).

RACE TO THE TOP

How NYC's architects egged each other onwards and upwards.

For nearly half a century after its 1846 completion, the 281-foot steeple of Richard Upjohn's Gothic Revival **Trinity Church** (*see p56*) reigned in lonely serenity at the foot of Wall Street as the tallest structure in Manhattan. The church was finally topped in 1890 by the since-demolished, 348-foot New York World Building. But it wasn't until the turn of the century that New York's architects started to reach for the skies. So began a mad rush to the top, with building after building capturing the title of the world's tallest.

When it was completed in 1899, the 30-storey, 391-foot **Park Row Building** (15 Park Row, between Ann & Beekman Streets) enjoyed that lofty distinction. However, its record was shattered by the 612-foot Singer Building in 1908 (which, in 1968, became the tallest building ever to be demolished); the 52-storey, 700-foot **Metropolitan Life Tower** (*see p136*) of 1909; and the 793-foot **Woolworth Building** (*see p65*), Cass Gilbert's Gothic 1913 masterpiece.

The Woolworth stood in solitary splendour until skyscraper construction reached a crescendo in the late 1920s, with a famed three-way race. The now largely forgotten **Bank of Manhattan Building** (now known as the Trump Building) at 40 Wall Street was briefly the record-holder, at 71 storeys and 927 feet in 1930. Soon after, William Van Alen, the architect of the **Chrysler Building** (*see p161*), unveiled his secret weapon: a 'vertex', a spire of chrome nickel steel put together inside the dome and raised from within, which brought the building's height to 1,046 feet. But then, 13 months later, Van Alen's homage to the Automobile Age was itself outstripped by Shreve, Lamb & Harmon's 1,250-foot **Empire State Building** (*see p157*). With its broad base, narrow shaft and needled crown, it remains the quintessential skyscraper, and one of the most famous buildings in the world.

Incredibly, there were no challengers for the distinction of New York's – and the world's – tallest building for more than 40 years, until the 110-storey, 1,362- and 1,368-foot Twin

Towers of Minoru Yamasaki's **World Trade Center** were completed in 1973. They were trumped by Chicago's Sears Tower a year later, but remained the city's tallest buildings until 11 September 2001, when the New York crown reverted to the Empire State Building. However, the World Trade Center has since regained the title. In spring 2012, **1 World Trade Center** (*see p59*), designed by David Childs of Skidmore, Owings & Merrill to replace the Twin Towers, overtook the ESB. It has since surpassed the original towers at a height of 1,776 feet, and NYC has beaten the Windy City as home to America's tallest skyscraper.

1 World Trade Center.

CONTEMPORARY VISION

Early 21st-century architecture is moving beyond applied symbolism to radical new forms, facilitated by computer-based design methods. A stellar example is Kohn Pedersen Fox's stainless steel and glass 'vertical campus', the **Baruch College Academic Complex** (55 Lexington Avenue, between 24th & 25th Streets). The phantasmagoric designs that curve and dart in sculptural space are so beyond the timid window-dressing of postmodernism that they deserve a new label.

Frank Gehry's 2007 **IAC Building** (555 W 18th Street, at West Side Highway) is emblematic of the radical reworking of the New York cityscape. The ten-storey, white-glass mirage of a building comprises tilting glass volumes that resemble a fully rigged tall ship. This area of Chelsea, once full of warehouses and industrial buildings, is being transformed by the High Line (see p123). Striking (and not so striking) residential structures are springing up in the blocks alongside it, including Annabelle Selldorf's 19-storey apartment building at 200 Eleventh Avenue and 24th Street, which even has a car elevator. Renzo Piano's new **Whitney Museum of American Art** (see p123) anchors the southern end, while Zaha Hadid's first NYC building, housing curvy, futuristic condos, will soon be unveiled in the northern stretch at 28th Street.

In recent years, Midtown West has become a hotbed of construction. The area's architectural attractions were enhanced in 2006 by Norman Foster's elegant 46-storey crystalline addition to the art deco base of the **Hearst Magazine Building** (300 W 57th Street, at Eighth Avenue). The structure is now a breathtaking combination of old and new, with the massive triangular struts of the tower penetrating the façade of the base and opening up great airy spaces within.

Even as the age of superblock modernism seems to be coming to a close, a new era of green, eco-conscious architecture is emerging. With torqued, glass facets reaching 54 storeys, Cook + Fox's **Bank of America Tower at 1 Bryant Park** (Sixth Avenue, between 42nd & 43rd Streets) has a thermal storage system, daylight dimmers, green roofs and double-wall construction to reduce heat build-up. Renzo Piano's 2007 tower for the **New York Times** at 620 Eighth Avenue (between 40th & 41st Streets) also offers such green amenities as automatic shades that respond to the heat of the sun.

Among the more controversial facelifts of recent years is Brad Cloepfil's renovation of Edward Durell Stone's 1964 modernism meets Venetian palazzo, **2 Columbus Circle**, former home of the Gallery of Modern Art (and now the Museum of Arts & Design, see p171). In the same way that the gallery's collection of mostly figurative painting was seen as reactionary in the face of the abstract art movement, Stone's quotation of a historicist style was laughed into apostasy. But his work is being re-evaluated as a precursor to postmodernism, and many 20th-century architecture enthusiasts lamented the loss of the original façade.

In a reversal of the city's historical pattern of development, there has been significant new construction downtown. The **Blue Building** (105 Norfolk Street, between Delancey & Rivington Streets), Bernard Tschumi's multifaceted, blue glass-walled condominium, is a startling breakaway from the low-rise brick buildings of the Lower East Side. Also noteworthy is the Japanese firm SANAA's **New Museum of Contemporary Art** (see p88); its asymmetrically staggered boxy volumes covered in aluminium mesh shake up the traditional streetfront of the Bowery. A block north, Norman Foster's slender gallery building for **Sperone Westwater** art dealers – complete with a 12- by 20-foot lift that doubles as a moving exhibition space – occupies a narrow gap at 257 Bowery (between Stanton & Houston Streets). On the West Side, the **Urban Glass House** (330 Spring Street, at Washington Street), one of the late Philip Johnson's last designs, sprang up in 2006 amid Tribeca's hulking industrial edifices. The mini-skyscraper is a multiplication of his iconic Glass House in New Canaan, Connecticut. Just south of City Hall, the curled and warped stainless-steel façade of 2011's 76-storey **New York by Gehry** (8 Spruce Street, between Nassau & William Streets) has the unmistakable stamp of its creator.

BEST-LAID PLANS

Some of New York's more ambitious architectural projects have been scaled back in the face of economic realities. The World Trade Center site, conceived by Daniel

Blue Building

Libeskind, saw little progress in the years after 9/11. In 2008, the 16-acre site's overseers, the Port Authority of New York and New Jersey, reported that construction of the 26 interrelated projects was years behind schedule and billions of dollars over the $16 billion budget. However, it seems to be back on track: the 9/11 Memorial Plaza opened in time for the tenth anniversary of the Twin Towers' fall and David Childs's 1,776-foot **1 World Trade Center** (see p59), formerly known as the Freedom Tower, is now the tallest building in the Western Hemisphere. Santiago Calatrava's spectacular plans for a shimmering, subterranean **World Trade Center Transportation Hub**, linking the suburban PATH trains to the subway, no longer feature retractable roof wings, but the ribbed ceiling will still let in the sun with a skylight. Though the station is taking shape, whether it will be completed in 2015 as projected is a matter for speculation.

The transformation of Brooklyn's **Atlantic Yards** into a mega-development started boldly as an architectural site for Frank Gehry and Enrique Norten, but Gehry's design for the Nets' arena was rejected as too expensive. Realised by SHoP Architects, the 19,000-seat **Barclays Center** (see p282), featuring a rust-coloured steel-panelled façade, opened in

autumn 2012, and work started on the first of 15 planned modular residential towers more than a year later. The proposed $1.5 billion renovation of **Lincoln Center** (see p296) was also kept in check, leaving a team of top-notch architects to work with what was already there. Diller Scofidio + Renfro, one of the most creative teams on the scene, turned the travertine marble façade of Alice Tully Hall into a show window, integrating inside and out with glass walls. Billie Tsien and Tod Williams transformed a public atrium between Broadway and Columbus Avenue into a sky-lit space, lined with ferns, moss and flowering vines, for buying tickets and sipping drinks.

Recently, construction has been picking up post-recession momentum. After years of setbacks, Pritzker Prize-winner Jean Nouvel's **53W53** (53 W 53rd Street) is finally rising next to the Museum of Modern Art. The sloped, crystalline structure, with an exoskeleton of irregularly crossing beams, was initially proposed to reach 1,250 feet, but the tower was opposed by activists who feared that its shadow would loom over Central Park and it was rejected by the city's Planning Commission. After 200 feet were snipped off the top, the plan received the green light.

But get ready for the skyscraper on steroids. Christian de Portzamparc's 1,000-foot **One57** and Rafael Viñoly's 1,396-foot **432 Park Avenue** – the tallest residential building in the Western Hemisphere – are making the average midtown building look knee-high in comparison. The graceful if grandiose 28-acre **Hudson Yards** complex, which features 16 new skyscrapers and a park connected to the top of the High Line at West 30th Street, is the largest private real-estate development *ever* in US history. The centrepiece is lead architect William Pedersen's bifurcated 900- and 1,300-foot 30 Hudson Yards tower, designed as a sculptural object to be seen in the round. The only constant in New York is constant change.

To keep up with what's going up, visit the **AIA Center for Architecture** (see p113), the **Skyscraper Museum** (see p61) and the **Storefront for Art and Architecture** (97 Kenmare Street, between Mulberry Street & Cleveland Place, 1-212 431 5795, www.storefrontnews.org, closed Mon & Sun), a non-profit organisation that hosts exhibitions, talks, screenings and more.

IN CONTEXT

Essential Information

Hotels

N ew York's hotel business is booming, with a room-count increase of nearly 25 per cent over the past five years. And despite an average rate of more than $300 a night in the autumn high season, most of them are full year-round. There is now more boutique choice in popular areas like Chelsea, Greenwich Village and the Lower East Side with the arrival of the High Line Hotel, the Marlton and the Ludlow. But perhaps the strongest indication of the economic recovery is a cluster of development on, or around, midtown's West 57th Street, including the glamorous Viceroy New York. Touristy Times Square is also seeing an influx of more stylish options such as citizenM, and it's worth looking to the outer boroughs for competitive pricing – Brooklyn is an increasingly desirable place to stay.

ESSENTIAL INFORMATION

PRICES AND INFORMATION

Accommodation in this chapter has been designated a price band to give you an idea of what you can expect to pay at a given hotel, but note that rates can vary wildly according to the season or room category. As a guide, you can expect to pay $500 or more per night in the deluxe category, $300-$500 for expensive hotels, $150-$300 for moderate properties and under $150 for budget lodgings. Don't forget to factor in 14.75 per cent tax, plus an extra $3.50 per night for most rooms. For gay-oriented hotels and B&Bs, see p266.

FINANCIAL DISTRICT & BATTERY PARK

Expensive

Andaz Wall Street

75 Wall Street, between Water West & Pearl Street, New York, NY 10005 (1-212 590 1234, www. wallstreetandaz.com). Subway 2, 3, 4, 5 to Wall Street. **Rooms** 253. **Map** p396 F33.

The New York outpost of this Hyatt subsidiary occupies the first 17 floors of a former Barclays Bank building. Inside, the vibe is anything but corporate: upon entering the spacious bamboo-panelled lobby-lounge, you're greeted by a free-range 'host', who acts as a combination check-in clerk and concierge. Chic, loft-style rooms are equally casual and user-friendly, with free non-alcoholic drinks and snacks. The restaurant (Dina Rata), bar and spa are welcome attributes in an area with little action at weekends.

Other location 485 Fifth Avenue, at 41st Street, Midtown (1-212 601 1234, www.5th avenue.andaz.com).

Conrad New York

102 North End Avenue, at Vesey Street, New York, NY 10282 (1-212 945 0100, www. conradnewyork.com). Subway A, C, 1, 2, 3 to Chambers Street; E to World Trade Center; R to Cortlandt Street; 2, 3 to Park Place. **Rooms** 88. **Map** p396 D31.

This Hilton offshoot fronts Battery Park City's riverside park. West-facing rooms have Hudson views, but there's also plenty to see within the art-rich property. Sol LeWitt's vivid 100ft by 80ft painting Loopy Doopy (Blue and Purple) graces the dramatic 15-storey, glass-ceilinged, granite-floored lobby, and coolly understated guestrooms are adorned with pieces by the likes of Elizabeth Peyton and Mary Heilmann. Nespresso machines and marble bathrooms with Aromatherapy Associates products are indulgent touches. The rooftop bar (open May-Oct) offers Statue of Liberty views.

TRIBECA & SOHO

Deluxe

★ Crosby Street Hotel

79 Crosby Street, between Prince & Spring Streets, New York, NY 10012 (1-212 226 6400, www.firmdalehotels.com). Subway N, R to Prince Street; 6 to Spring Street. **Rooms** 86. **Map** p397 E30.

In 2009, Britain's hospitality power couple, Tim and Kit Kemp, brought their super-successful Firmdale formula across the Atlantic with the warehouse-style Crosby Street Hotel. Design director Kit's signature style – a fresh, contemporary take on classic English decor characterised by an often audacious mix of patterns, bold colours and judiciously chosen antiques – is instantly recognisable. Other Firmdale imports include a carefully selected art collection, a drawing room, restaurant and bar, a slick, 99-seat screening room and a private garden.

★ Greenwich Hotel

377 Greenwich Street, between Franklin & North Moore Streets, New York, NY 10013 (1-212 941 8900, www.thegreenwichhotel.com). Subway 1 to Franklin Street. **Rooms** 88. **Map** p396 D31.

The design inspiration at this Tribeca retreat, co-owned by Robert De Niro, is as international as the jet-set clientele. Individually decorated rooms combine custom-made English leather seating, Tibetan rugs and gorgeous Moroccan or Carrara-marble-tiled bathrooms, most outfitted with capacious tubs that fill up in a minute flat (bath salts from Nolita spa Red Flower are provided). In the tranquil subterranean spa, the pool is beneath the frame of a 250-year-old Kyoto farmhouse. For dinner, there's no need to rub shoulders with the masses at the always-mobbed house restaurant, Locanda Verde – have your meal delivered to the cloistered courtyard.

▶ *For more on Robert De Niro's Tribeca empire, see p72.*

Expensive

Broome

431 Broome Street, between Broadway & Crosby Street, New York, NY 10013 (1-212 431 2929, www.thebroomenyc.com). Subway 6 to Spring Street. **Rooms** 14. **Map** p397 E30.

The Broome takes the boutique concept to new bijou levels. Set in a five-storey 1825 building and co-owned by four long-time local restaurateurs, it has just 14 rooms, furnished with residential pieces from chic interior stores like Mitchell Gold & Bob Williams and Design Within Reach. Many quarters overlook the open-air interior courtyard, where Moroccan tiles, flower boxes, and classic French café tables create a tranquil setting for the complimentary continental breakfast in warm weather – croissants are baked on-site. With a one-to-one staff-to-room ratio, you can expect personal attention and nice touches like lavender-and-bergamot-infused sheets, free local calls and movies.

James New York

27 Grand Street, at Thompson Street, New York, NY 10013 (1-212 465 2000, 1-888 526 3778, www.jameshotels.com). Subway A, C, E to Canal Street. **Rooms** 114. **Map** p397 D30.

Hotel art displays are usually limited to eye-catching lobby installations or forgettable in-room prints. Not so at the James, where the corridor of each guest floor is dedicated to the work of an individual artist,

Broome.

IN THE KNOW MEET TOMMIE

New hotel chain Tommie (www.tommie hotels.com) arrives in summer 2015. Aimed at millennials, the first property, on the Soho-Tribeca border, features more than 300 cool, compact rooms with multitasking furnishings like flip-down desks and platform beds with built-in storage.

---

selected by a house curator. Although compact, bedrooms make the most of the available space with high ceilings and wall-spanning windows. Natural materials warm up the clean contemporary lines, and bathroom products are courtesy of Intelligent Nutrients. A two-level 'urban garden' (open May-Oct) houses an outdoor bar and eatery. The rooftop bar, Jimmy, opens on to the (tiny) pool.

Soho Grand Hotel
310 West Broadway, between Canal & Grand Streets, New York, NY 10013 (1-212 965 3000, 1-800 965 3000, www.sohogrand.com). Subway A, C, E, 1 to Canal Street. **Rooms** 363. **Map** p397 E30.
The Soho Grand, which pioneered the downtown hotel migration in 1996, is fresh from a revamp. The original designer, Bill Sofield, recently introduced new custom pieces to the elegant brown-and-beige guest rooms, including travel trunk-inspired minibars and natty houndstooth tuxedo chairs. Bathrooms feature charming wallpaper by the late illustrator Saul Steinberg (whose work was a longtime staple of the *New Yorker*) and CO Bigelow products. Endearingly, you can request a goldfish for the duration of your stay. Guests can also borrow old-fashioned bicycles in the warmer months to explore the city; after your exertions, claim a lounger in the hotel's seasonal outdoor bar-eatery the Yard, or hole up with a cocktail by the fireplace in the Club Room, a glamorous year-round lounge.
Other location Tribeca Grand Hotel, 2 Sixth Avenue, between Walker & White Streets, Tribeca (1-212 519 6600, www.tribecagrand.com).

Moderate

Cosmopolitan
95 West Broadway, at Chambers Street, New York, NY 10007 (1-212 566 1900, 1-888 895 9400, www.cosmohotel.com). Subway A, C, 1, 2, 3 to Chambers Street. **Rooms** 131. **Map** p396 E31.
Open continuously since the mid 19th century, the Cosmopolitan has long been a tourist favourite for its address, clean rooms and reasonable rates. At time of writing the hotel was undergoing a rolling, floor-by-floor revamp to upgrade its guest quarters and introduce a bar and restaurant, but it has already added luxurious touches like

Frette linens and room service provided by local comfort-food restaurant Kitchenette. Other convenient facilities include a small gym and a business centre with two Macs that guests can use free of charge (if you don't have your own laptop to take advantage of the complimentary in-room Wi-Fi). A wide range of room configurations is available, including a suite with two queen beds and a sofa bed, ideal for families.

Duane Street Hotel
130 Duane Street, at Church Street, New York, NY 10013 (1-212 964 4600, www.duanestreet hotel.com). Subway A, C, 1, 2, 3 to Chambers Street. **Rooms** 45. **Map** p396 E31.
Opened on a quiet Tribeca street in 2007, this boutique property takes its cues from its well-heeled residential neighbourhood, offering loft-inspired rooms with high ceilings, oversized triple-glazed windows, hardwood floors and a chic, monochrome colour scheme. Free Wi-Fi, L'Occitane products in the slate-tiled bathrooms and complimentary passes to the nearby swanky Equinox gym cement the value-for-money package – a rare commodity in this part of town.

CHINATOWN, LITTLE ITALY & NOLITA

Expensive

Nolitan
30 Kenmare Street, at Elizabeth Street, New York, NY 10012 (1-212 925 2555, www.nolitanhotel. com). Subway J, Z to Bowery; 6 to Spring Street. **Rooms** 57. **Map** p397 F30.
The airy rooms of this boutique hotel feature floor-to-ceiling windows, wooden floors, custom-made walnut beds and Aveda toiletries. The emphasis on keeping it local is reflected in numerous guest perks: the luxuriously laid-back property lends out bikes and skateboards and lays on free local calls and discounts at neighbourhood boutiques. Admire views of Nolita and beyond from the 2,400sq ft roof deck, or your private perch – more than half the guest quarters have balconies.

Budget

Bowery House
220 Bowery, between Prince & Spring Streets, New York, NY 10012 (1-212 837 2373, www. theboweryhouse.com). Subway J, Z to Bowery. **Rooms** 84. **Map** p397 F29.
Two young real-estate developers transformed a 1927 Bowery flophouse into this stylish take on a hostel. Corridors with original wainscotting lead to cubicles (singles are a cosy 35sq ft) with latticework ceilings to allow air circulation, though new quarters with queen beds and street-facing windows have recently been added. It might not be the best bet for light

Bowery House.

sleepers, but the place is hopping with pretty young things attracted to the hip aesthetic and the location. Quarters are decorated with vintage prints and historical photographs, and Egyptian cotton robes are provided. The (gender-segregated) communal bathrooms have rain showerheads and products from local spa Red Flower, while the guest lounge is outfitted with chesterfield sofas and a huge LCD TV.

Sohotel
341 Broome Street, between Elizabeth Street & Bowery, New York, NY 10013 (1-212 226 1482, www.thesohotel.com). Subway J, Z to Bowery; 6 to Spring Street. **Rooms** 98. **Map** p397 F30.
Established as an inn in 1805, but altered considerably since then, this is the oldest hotel in the city. But it's no period piece; a recent renovation put a contemporary spin on the original character with exposed-brick walls, ceiling beams, hardwood floors and subway-tiled showers. The hotel offers perks that place it a rung above similarly priced establishments, including bathroom products courtesy of

CO Bigelow, complimentary morning tea and coffee served in the lobby, free in-room Wi-Fi, and a collection of bars/eateries that includes on-site craft-brew emporium Randolph Beer.

LOWER EAST SIDE
Expensive

Ludlow
180 Ludlow Street, between Houston & Stanton Streets, New York, NY 10001 (1-212 432 1818, www.ludlowhotel.com). Subway F to Lower East Side-Second Avenue. **Rooms** 184. **Map** p397 G29.
Hot on the heels of Sean MacPherson's affordable Village lodging, the Marlton (*see p361*), comes this collaboration with co-owners of the Greenwich Hotel and Pod 39. The newly built red-brick property has an artfully aged interior, but the design is eclectic. An oak-panelled lobby leads to a sprawling living room with a salvaged limestone fireplace and a bar that spills out on to an ivy-clad patio.

Rooms mix classic and contemporary elements: big factory-style windows, rustic ceiling beams, Indo-Portuguese four-poster beds and petrified-wood nightstands. Bathrooms are fitted with brass rain showers or soaking tubs and Martin Margiela robes. The restaurant, Dirty French, is the first foray into Gallic cuisine for the team behind Carbone (see p114).

Moderate

Off Soho Suites Hotel

11 Rivington Street, between Bowery & Chrystie Street, New York, NY 10002 (1-212 979 9808, 1-800 633 7646, www.offsoho.com). Subway B, D to Grand Street; F to Lower East Side-Second Avenue; J, Z to Bowery. **Rooms** 38. **Map** p397 F30. These no-frills suites have become all the more popular in recent years due to the Lower East Side's burgeoning bar and restaurant scene. The rates are a decent value, especially as all have a sitting area and access to a kitchenette. Economy options have two twin beds and a shared kitchen or, if you're travelling in a group, book a deluxe suite – with a queen bed, plus a sleeper sofa in the living area, it can accommodate four. There's also free Wi-Fi, a gym and a handy coin-operated laundry.

EAST VILLAGE

Expensive

Bowery Hotel

335 Bowery, at 3rd Street, New York, NY 10003 (1-212 505 9100, www.theboweryhotel.com). Subway B, D, F, M to Broadway-Lafayette Street; 6 to Bleecker Street. **Rooms** 135. **Map** p397 F29.

This fanciful boutique property from prominent hoteliers Eric Goode and Sean MacPherson is the capstone in the gentrification of the Bowery. Shunning minimalism, they created plush rooms that pair old-world touches (wood-beamed ceilings in some rooms, oriental rugs, marble washstands) with modern amenities (flatscreen TVs with DVD players, complimentary Wi-Fi). The hotel's Italian restaurant, Gemma, which resembles an ancient trattoria, carries on the theme.

▶ *For the hoteliers' flamboyant take on a boarding house, the Jane, see p362.*

Budget

Hotel 17

225 E 17th Street, between Second & Third Avenues, New York, NY 10003 (1-212 475 2845, www.hotel17ny.com). Subway L to Third Avenue; L, N, Q, R, 4, 5, 6 to 14th Street-Union Square. **Rooms** 125. **Map** p397 F27.

Shabby chic is the best way to describe this East Village hotel a few blocks from Union Square. Past the minuscule but well-appointed lobby, the small, classic rooms are characterised by antique woodwork and patterned wallpaper, but with decor updates the hotel is gradually becoming less of a period piece. Bathrooms are generally shared between four rooms, but they're kept immaculately clean. Over the years, the building has been featured in numerous fashion mag layouts and films – including Woody Allen's *Manhattan Murder Mystery* – and has put up Madonna, and, more recently, transsexual downtown diva Amanda Lepore. Who knows who you might bump into on your way to the loo?

Marlton.

GREENWICH VILLAGE
Expensive

Jade Hotel
52 W 13th Street, between Fifth & Sixth Avenues,
New York, NY 10011 (1-212 375 1300, www.
thejadenyc.com). Subway F, M, 1, 2, 3 to 14th
Street; L to Sixth Avenue; L, N, Q, R, 4, 5, 6 to 14th
Street-Union Square. **Rooms** 113. **Map** p397 E27.
With its Georgian-style portico and decorative
brickwork, this new hotel is indistinguishable from
the surrounding pre-war apartment buildings. The
rooms, designed by Andres Escobar in an art deco
style, feature marble-inlaid Macassar ebony desks,
chrome period lamps and champagne satin poufs
– to preserve the period illusion, the TV is hidden

Jane. See p362.

behind a decorative cabinet. The classic black-and-
white tiled bathrooms are stocked with toiletries
from venerable Village pharmacy CO Bigelow.
▶ *A second Jade is tipped to open near midtown's*
Bryant Park in 2016.

Moderate

Marlton
5 W 8th Street, between Fifth and Sixth Avenues,
New York, NY 10011 (1-212 321 0100, www.
marltonhotel.com). Subway A, B, C, D, E, F, M to
W 4th Street; N, R to 8th Street-NYU. **Rooms** 107.
Map p397 E28.
Hip hotelier Sean MacPherson has transformed a
former low-rent lodging into an affordable boutique
hotel. The 1900 building has plenty of local
history – Beat icon Jack Kerouac wrote a couple of
novellas there, and the place put up would-be Andy
Warhol assassin Valerie Solanas – but the lobby's
deceptively lived-in-looking interior, with broken-in
leather armchairs and a coffee bar, has largely been
created from scratch. Measuring a mere 150sq ft
each, the bedrooms are mini versions of a Paris
grand hotel, with gilt-edged velvet headboards,
crown mouldings, and petite marble sinks and Côté
Bastide products in the bathrooms.

Budget

Larchmont Hotel
27 W 11th Street, between Fifth & Sixth Avenues,
New York, NY 10011 (1-212 989 9333, www.
larchmonthotel.com). Subway F, M to 14th Street;
L to Sixth Avenue. **Rooms** 67. **Map** p397 E28.
Housed in a 1910 Beaux Arts building, the
Larchmont is great value for this area. The
basic decor has been spruced up with new IKEA
furniture and flatscreen TVs, but with prices this
reasonable, you can accept less than glossy-mag
style. Except for the en-suite family room, with one
double and one trundle bed, bathrooms are shared,

but all guest quarters come with a washbasin, toiletries, bathrobe and slippers. Continental breakfast is included in the rate and Wi-Fi is thrown in free of charge.

WEST VILLAGE & MEATPACKING DISTRICT
Expensive

Gansevoort Meatpacking NYC
18 Ninth Avenue, at 13th Street, New York, NY 10014 (1-212 206 6700, www.gansevoorthotel group.com). Subway A, C, E to 14th Street; L to Eighth Avenue. **Rooms** 186. **Map** p397 C28.
This Meatpacking District pioneer is known for its rooftop-pool-lounge playgrounds at two NYC locations (the other is on Park Avenue). On summer days, you can soak up the sun, and the Hudson River panorama, on a lounger by the 45ft heated open-air pool. After dark, the wraparound terrace bar becomes a DJed outdoor party with a glittering Manhattan backdrop. The guest quarters feature Studio 54-inspired photography that plays on the hotel's reputation as a party hub, and, in a twist on the minibar, 'glamour bars' with illuminated vanity mirrors and an array of cult cosmetics for purchase. Plush feather-bed layers atop excellent mattresses and marble bathrooms amp up the luxury. The Exhale spa is a dimly lit subterranean sanctuary.
Other location 420 Park Avenue South, at 29th Street, enter on 29th Street, Flatiron District (1-212 317 2900).

Standard, High Line
848 Washington Street, at 13th Street, New York, NY 10014 (1-212 645 4646, www.standard hotels.com). Subway A, C, E to 14th Street; L to Eighth Avenue. **Rooms** 337. **Map** p397 C27.
André Balazs's lauded West Coast mini-chain arrived in New York in 2009. Straddling the High Line, the retro 18-storey structure has been configured to give each room an exhilarating view, either of the river or a midtown cityscape. Quarters are compact (from 230sq ft) but the combination of floor-to-ceiling windows, curving tambour wood panelling and 'peekaboo' bathrooms (with Japanese-style tubs or huge showerheads) give a sense of space. Eating and drinking options include a chop house, a beer garden and a swanky top-floor bar. Nightspot Le Bain (*see p273*) has a massive jacuzzi and 180-degree vistas.
▶ *For more about the High Line, see p123.*
Other location 25 Cooper Square, between 5th & 6th Streets, East Village (1-212 475 5700).

Moderate

★ Jane
113 Jane Street, at West Street, New York, NY 10014 (1-212 924 6700, www.thejanenyc.com).

Subway A, C, E to 14th Street; L to Eighth Avenue. **Rooms** 208. **Map** p397 D28.
Opened in 1907 as the American Seaman's Friend Society Sailors Home, the six-storey landmark was a residential hotel when hoteliers Eric Goode and Sean MacPherson took it over. The Jane's wood-panelled, 50sq ft rooms were inspired by vintage train sleeper compartments: there's a single or bunk bed with built-in storage and brass hooks for hanging up your clothes – but also iPod docks and

High Line Hotel.

wall-mounted flatscreen TVs. Alternatively, opt for a more spacious, wainscotted Captain's Cabin with private facilities – many have terraces or Hudson River views. If entering the hotel feels like stepping on to a film set, there's good reason. Inspiration came from various celluloid sources, including Barton Fink's Hotel Earle for the lobby. *Photo p360.*

CHELSEA
Expensive

High Line Hotel
180 Tenth Avenue, at 20th Street, New York, NY 10011 (1-212 929 3888, www.thehighlinehotel. com). Subway C, E to 23rd Street. **Rooms** 60. **Map** p397 C27.
The railway line-turned-park lends its name to this boutique hotel in the old guest wing of the General Theological Seminary, an imposing 1895 neo-Gothic landmark. Exuding an old-fashioned residential vibe, the 60 rooms feature antique Persian rugs, custom-designed wallpaper and a mix of vintage furnishings and reproductions of pieces sourced by the hotel's design firm, Roman and Williams. Many rooms retain original fireplaces – though these days the eco-friendly property is heated by a geothermal system. Rewired 1930s rotary phones may seem like an antidote to the digital age, but there's also free Wi-Fi and you can connect your smartphone to the Mini Jambox speaker.

Hôtel Americano
518 W 27th Street, between Tenth & Eleventh Avenues, New York, NY 10001 (1-212 216 0000, www.hotel-americano.com). Subway C, E to 23rd Street. **Rooms** 56. **Map** p398 C26.
You won't find any Talavera tiles in Grupo Habita's first property outside Mexico. Mexican architect Enrique Norten's sleek, mesh-encased structure stands alongside the High Line. The minimalist rooms have Japanese-style platform beds, iPads and, in one of several subtle nods to US culture, super-soft denim bathrobes. After a day of gallery-hopping, get an elevated view of the neighbourhood from the rooftop bar and grill, where the petite pool is open from May through September.
▶ *For our picks of Chelsea's galleries, see p130.*

Moderate

Eventi
851 Sixth Avenue, between 29th & 30th Streets, New York, NY 10001 (1-212 564 4567, www. eventihotel.com). Subway B, D, F, M, N, Q, R to 34th Street-Herald Square; N, R to 28th Street. **Rooms** 292. **Map** p398 D25.
This modern 23-floor hotel takes a playful approach to interior design, planting unexpected features in the lobby – a large-scale reproduction of 19th-century British artist Thomas Benjamin Kennington's

Autumn peeks out tantalisingly from behind velvet drapes, for instance. Eventi is managed by Kimpton, which is known for its informal, friendly ethos, flamboyant decor and nice perks like free wine and cheese gatherings in the evening. All of the spacious rooms (which feel even more open thanks to floor-to-ceiling outlooks) have king-size beds, outfitted with dapper gray fabric headboards and Frette linens. Cool marble bathrooms are stocked with CO Bigelow products. There's also an on-site spa.

Budget

Chelsea Lodge
318 W 20th Street, between Eighth & Ninth Avenues, New York, NY 10011 (1-212 243 4499, www.chelsealodge.com). Subway C, E to 23rd Street. **Rooms** 26. **Map** p397 D27.
Situated in a landmark brownstone blocks from the Chelsea gallery district, Chelsea Lodge is a long way from any arcadian idylls. Yet the rustic name is reflected in the mishmash of Americana that adorns the pine panelling of the inn's public spaces, such as rough-hewn duck decoys, cut-out roosters and early 20th-century photos. While all of the mostly tiny wood-floored rooms have TVs, sinks, showers and seasonal air-conditioning, most share toilets, so it's not for everyone. Still, the low prices and undeniable charm mean that it can fill up quickly. For more privacy and space, book one of the four suites down the block at 334 West 20th Street: all are former studio apartments with kitchenettes that sleep up to four people. The two at the back have direct access to the private garden.

FLATIRON DISTRICT & UNION SQUARE
Expensive

★ Ace Hotel New York
20 W 29th Street, at Broadway, New York, NY 10012 (1-212 679 2222, www.acehotel.com). Subway N, R to 28th Street. **Rooms** 265. **Map** p398 E26.
Founded in Seattle by a pair of DJs, this cool chainlet has expanded beyond the States to London and Panama. In its New York digs, the musical influence is clear: select rooms in the 1904 building have functioning turntables, stacks of vinyl and gleaming Gibson guitars. And while you'll pay a hefty amount for the sprawling loft spaces, there are options for those on a smaller budget, fitted with vintage furniture and original art. In the buzzing lobby, the bar is set within a panelled library salvaged from a Madison Avenue apartment and DJs or other performers add to the atmosphere almost every night. Guests can score a table at chef April Bloomfield's popular Breslin Bar & Dining Room (*see p139*) and the John Dory Oyster Bar (*see p141*). There's even an outpost of Opening Ceremony (*see p72*) if you haven't a thing to wear.

ESSENTIAL INFORMATION

★ NoMad Hotel

*1170 Broadway, at 28th Street, New York,
NY 10001 (1-212 796 1500, www.thenomad
hotel.com). Subway N, R to 28th Street.* **Rooms** 168.
Map p398 E26.

Like nearby hipster hub the Ace Hotel, the NoMad
(which shares a developer) is also a self-contained
microcosm encompassing destination dining –
courtesy of Daniel Humm and Will Guidara, of the
Michelin-three-starred Eleven Madison Park (*see
p140*) – and the first stateside outpost of Parisian
concept store Maison Kitsuné. Jacques Garcia,
designer of Paris celeb hangout Hôtel Costes,
transformed the interior of a 1903 New York office
building into this convincing facsimile of a grand
hotel. The chic rooms, furnished with vintage Heriz
rugs and distressed-leather armchairs, are more
personal – Garcia based the design on his old Paris
apartment. Many feature old-fashioned claw-foot
tubs for a scented soak in Côté Bastide bath salts.

GRAMERCY PARK
Deluxe

Gramercy Park Hotel

*2 Lexington Avenue, at 21st Street, New York, NY
10010 (1-212 920 3300, 1-866 784 1300, www.
gramercyparkhotel.com). Subway 6 to 23rd Street.*
Rooms 192. **Map** p398 F26.

Many NYC hotels have exclusive terraces or
gardens, but only one boasts access to the city's most
storied private outdoor space: Gramercy Park. The
hotel's interior resembles a baronial manor occupied
by a rock star, with rustic wooden beams and a
roaring fire in the lobby; a $65 million art collection,
including works by Richard Prince, Damien Hirst
and Andy Warhol; and studded velvet headboards
and mahogany drink cabinets in the bedrooms. Get a
taste of the Eternal City in Maialino, Danny Meyer's
tribute to Roman trattorias.

Budget

★ Carlton Arms Hotel

*160 E 25th Street, at Third Avenue, New York,
NY 10010 (1-212 679 0680, www.carltonarms.
com). Subway 6 to 23rd Street.* **Rooms** 54.
Map p398 F26.

The Carlton Arms Art Project started in the late
1970s, when a small group of creative types brought
fresh paint and new ideas to a run-down shelter.
Today, the site is a bohemian backpackers' paradise
and a live-in gallery – every room, bathroom and
hallway is festooned with outré artwork, including
a couple of early stairwells by Banksy. Eye-popping
themed quarters include the Money Room and a
tribute to the traditional English cottage; new works
are introduced regularly and artists return to restore
their creations. About a third of the rooms have
private bathrooms; the rest are shared.

HERALD SQUARE & GARMENT DISTRICT
Expensive

Refinery Hotel

*63 W 38th Street, between Fifth & Sixth Avenues,
New York, NY 10018 (1-646 664 0310, www.
refineryhotelnewyork.com). Subway B, D, F, M,
N, Q, R to 34th Street-Herald Square; B, D, F, M
to Bryant Park; 7 to Fifth Avenue.* **Rooms** 197.
Map p398 E24.

The Garment District finally has a fittingly
fashionable hotel. Stonehill & Taylor Architects,
the firm behind this 1912 neo-Gothic building's
conversion and design, took inspiration from its
former life as a hat-making hub. In the guest rooms,
furnishings subtly reference the garment industry.
Super-soft bed throws mimic burlap, coffee tables
are modelled on factory carts, and desks are
reproductions of vintage Singer sewing-machine
tables. Luxurious touches like Frette linens and
walk-in showers with room for two offset the
industrial elements. Eating and drinking options
include a sprawling indoor-outdoor rooftop bar/
restaurant and Winnie's Jazz Bar. Named after
the owner of a ladies' tearoom in the building in
the early 20th century, Winnie's offers live music
almost every night.

Moderate

Hotel Metro

*45 W 35th Street, between Fifth & Sixth Avenues,
New York, NY 10001 (1-212 947 2500, www.
hotelmetronyc.com). Subway B, D, F, M, N, Q,
R to 34th Street-Herald Square.* **Rooms** 181.
Map p398 E25.

It may not be trendy, but the Metro is a solid, good-
value hotel that is extremely well maintained. Every
two years, the owners start renovating the rooms,
floor by floor, starting at the top; by the time they're
finished it's almost time to start again. So even 'old'
rooms are virtually new. The stylishly contemporary
quarters feature marble-topped furniture and beige
leather-effect headboards; premier rooms have
luxurious rain showers. Unusually for New York,
the hotel offers 18 family rooms, consisting of
two adjoining bedrooms (one with two beds and a

NoMad Hotel.

table) and a door that closes. Also rare: a generous continental breakfast buffet is offered in the guests' lounge (or take it to the homey adjoining library), outfitted with several large TVs. The rooftop bar (which is open from April to October) has views of the Empire State Building.

THEATER DISTRICT & HELL'S KITCHEN

Deluxe

The Chatwal New York

130 W 44th Street, between Sixth Avenue & Broadway, New York, NY 10036 (1-212 764 6200, www.thechatwalny.com). Subway N, Q, R, S, 1, 2, 3 to 42nd Street-Times Square. **Rooms** 76. **Map** p398 D24.

In a city awash with faux deco and incongruous nods to the style, the Chatwal New York occupies a Stanford White building that has been given a pitch-perfect art deco interior. Hotelier Sant Chatwal entrusted the design of this 1905 Beaux Arts building (formerly the clubhouse for the Lamb's Club, America's first professional theatre organisation) to Thierry Despont, who worked on the centennial restoration of the Statue of Liberty and the interiors of the J Paul Getty Museum in Los Angeles. The glamorous lobby is adorned with murals recalling the hotel's theatrical pedigree – past members of the Lamb's Club include Oscar Hammerstein, Charlie Chaplin, John Wayne and Fred Astaire. The theatrical past is further evoked by black and white photographs in the hotel's restaurant, helmed by Geoffrey Zakarian, which takes its name from the club. The elegant rooms feature vintage Broadway posters as well as hand-tufted Shifman mattresses, 400-thread count Frette linens and custom Asprey toiletries, and 15 rooms have spacious terraces. Unwind in the Elizabeth Arden Red Door Spa, which boasts a small saltwater lap pool.

Expensive

London NYC
151 W 54th Street, between Sixth & Seventh Avenues, New York, NY 10019 (1-866 690 2029, www.thelondonnyc.com). Subway B, D, E to Seventh Avenue. **Rooms** 561. **Map** p399 D22.

This 54-storey high-rise was completely overhauled by the late David Collins and reopened as the London NYC in 2007. The designer's sleek, contemporary-British style pervades the rooms, with attractive signature touches such as limed oak parquet flooring, embossed leather travel trunks at the foot of the beds, hand-woven throws and inventive coffee tables that adjust to dining-table height. But space is perhaps the biggest luxury: guest quarters are a minimum of 500sq ft, either open-plan or divided with mirrored French doors, and bathrooms feature double rain showerheads. Vista suites command views of Central Park. The London is, appropriately, the site of Maze by Gordon Ramsay, Britain's best-known celebrity chef.

citizenM New York.

Moderate

★ 414 Hotel
414 W 46th Street, between Ninth & Tenth Avenues, New York, NY 10036 (1-212 399 0006, www.414hotel.com). Subway A, C, E to 42nd Street-Port Authority. **Rooms** 22. **Map** p398 C23.
Tucked into a residential yet central neighbourhood, this budget boutique hotel is a real find. The place is twice as big as it looks, as it consists of two walk-up buildings separated by a leafy courtyard, which in warmer months is a lovely place to eat your complimentary breakfast. The simple rooms have recently been given a Feng Shui redesign, in a white-and-gold colour palette with eco-friendly paint and natural-fibre carpeting. All are equipped with fridges, flatscreen TVs and iPod docks.

citizenM New York
218 W 50th Street, between Broadway & Eighth Avenue, New York, NY 10019 (1-212 461 3638, www.citizenm.com). Subway C, E to 50th Street; N, Q, R to 49th Street; 1 to 50th Street. **Rooms** 230. **Map** p398 D23.
The fast-growing citizenM brand aims to democratise the luxury-hotel experience. With rates starting at less than $200 a night, guests can can kick back on a $10,000 Vitra armchair in the eclectic lobby and admire the 26-foot-tall installation *Walking in Times Square* by Julian Opie. Catering to a time-zone-crossing, tech-savvy clientele (the M stands for 'mobile'), the Amsterdam-based company has devised a new model informed by its founders' travel frustrations, cutting high-overhead amenities like room service in the process. The 24-hour canteenM dispenses cocktails (until 2am), coffee, all-day breakfast and other dishes. The compact rooms focus on the essentials: an extra-large king-size bed and a powerful rain shower (in a cool cubicle with coloured ceiling lights). You can control the hue, and everything else in the room – from the blinds to the digital wall art – using a Samsung tablet.

★ Yotel New York
570 Tenth Avenue, at 42nd Street, New York, NY 10036 (1-646 449 7700, www.yotel.com). Subway A, C, E to 42nd Street-Port Authority. **Rooms** 669. **Map** p398 C24.
The British team behind this futuristic hotel is known for airport-based capsule accommodation that gives travellers just enough space to get horizontal between flights. Yotel New York has ditched the 75sq ft cubbies in favour of 'premium cabins' more than twice the size. Adaptable furnishings (such as motorised beds that fold up futon-style) maximise space, and the bathroom has streamlined luxuries such as a heated towel rail and monsoon shower. If you want to unload excess baggage, the 20ft tall robot (or Yobot, in the hotel's playful lingo) will stash it for you in a lobby locker. In contrast with the compact quarters, the sprawling public spaces include a massive wraparound terrace bar. *Photo p369.*

FIFTH AVENUE & AROUND

Deluxe

Plaza
768 Fifth Avenue, at Central Park South, New York, NY 10019 (1-212 759 3000, 1-888 850 0909, www.theplazany.com). Subway N, Q, R to Fifth Avenue-59th Street. **Rooms** 282. **Map** p399 E22.
The closest thing to a palace in New York, this 1907 French Renaissance-style landmark reopened in spring 2008 after a two-year, $400-million renovation. Although 152 rooms were converted into private condo units, guests can still check into one of 282 elegantly appointed quarters with Louis XV-inspired furnishings and white-glove butler service. The opulent vibe extends to the bathrooms, which feature mosaic baths, 24-carat gold-plated sink fittings and even chandeliers – perhaps to make the foreign royals feel at home. Embracing the 21st century, the hotel has equipped every room with an iPad. The legendary Oak Room and Oak Bar, both designated landmarks, are currently open only for private events, but you can still take afternoon tea in the restored Palm Court. There's also an upscale food hall conceived by celebrity chef Todd English, which includes both old and new cult NYC purveyors, such as William Greenberg Desserts and No. 7 Sub. The on-site Caudalie Vinothérapie Spa is the French grape-based skincare line's first US outpost.

Expensive

Bryant Park Hotel
40 W 40th Street, between Fifth & Sixth Avenues, New York, NY 10018 (1-212 869 0100, 1-877 640 9300, www.bryantpark hotel.com). Subway B, D, F, M to 42nd Street-Bryant Park; 7 to Fifth Avenue. **Rooms** 128. **Map** p398 E24.
When the shows and the shoots are finished, the fashion and film folk flock to this luxe landing pad (it's particularly busy during Fashion Week). In its days as the American Radiator Building, the hotel was immortalised by Georgia O'Keeffe. Although the exterior (which you can appreciate up-close in one of several balconied rooms) is gothic art deco, the inside is all clean-lined and contemporary, with soft lighting, blanched hardwood floors, Tibetan rugs and soothing conveniences such as sleep-aiding sound machines and Bose Wave radios. Further luxuries: travertine marble bathrooms are stocked with Molton Brown products and you can order in from the house restaurant, slick sushi destination Koi.

★ Chambers Hotel
15 W 56 Street, between Fifth & Sixth Avenues, New York, NY 10019 (1-212 974 5656, www.chambershotel.com). Subway E, M to Fifth Avenue-53rd Street. **Rooms** 77. **Map** p399 E22.

ESSENTIAL INFORMATION

IN THE KNOW
BEST FRIENDS WELCOME

New York hotels are increasingly pet-friendly. The Benjamin (see p368), Eventi (see p363), the Surrey (see p371) and Soho Grand Hotel (see p358) are among many that offer special beds, meals and treats – Soho Grand even debuted a dog park, complete with custom-made benches and 'fire hydrants'.

Room design at this small boutique hotel takes its cue from upscale New York loft apartments, combining designer furniture with raw concrete ceilings, exposed pipes, floor-to-ceiling windows and polished walnut floorboards or Tibetan wool carpeting. Guest quarters also feature some of the 500-piece art collection. Everything is designed to make you feel at home, from the soft terrycloth slippers in bright colours to the architect's desks stocked with a roll of paper and coloured pencils should creative inspiration hit. There's no need to leave the hotel for meals, since David Chang's Má Pêche and an outpost of his Milk Bar are on site.

★ Viceroy New York
120 W 57th Street, between Sixth & Seventh Avenues, New York, NY 10019 (1-212 830 8000, 1-855 647 1619, www.viceroyhotelsandresorts. com/newyork). Subway F, N, Q, R to 57th Street. **Rooms** 240. **Map** p399 D22.
Designed by Roman and Williams, Viceroy New York has a cool midcentury vibe. In the snug standard quarters, custom-made iroko-wood cabinets flanking the bed evoke a first-class cabin back when ocean liners were glamorous. You'll find an Illy espresso maker tucked behind one of the tambour doors, while on the nightstand is a Beats by Dr Dre Beatbox Portable sound system that blows away standard iPod docks. The on-site American eaterie, Kingside, is helmed by Landmarc chef Marc Murphy and there's also a sophisticated roof bar with sweeping views of Central Park. *Photo p370.*

MIDTOWN EAST
Expensive

Benjamin
125 E 50th Street, at Lexington Avenue, New York, NY 10022 (1-212 715 2500, www.thebenjamin. com). Subway E, M to Lexington Avenue-53rd Street; 6 to 51st Street. **Rooms** 209. **Map** p398 E23.
All rooms in this pet-friendly hotel have kitchenettes with microwaves and sinks (some suites have full-size fridges), so it's a hit with families as well as business travellers. The decor, in restful shades of beige and cream, is unfussy, with the emphasis on comfort: choose from a menu of ten pillows from Swedish memory foam and anti-snoring to a five-foot-long body cushion for side-slumberers, devised in consultation with sleep expert Rebecca Robbins. Facilities include a hair salon and spa, a good-size gym and a chic, David Rockwell-designed bistro, the National Bar & Dining Rooms, from Iron Chef Geoffrey Zakarian.

Hotel Elysée
60 E 54th Street, between Madison & Park Avenues, New York, NY 10022 (1-212 753 1066, www.elyseehotel.com). Subway E, M to Fifth Avenue-53rd Street; 6 to 51st Street. **Rooms** 100. **Map** p399 E22.
The former home of Tennessee Williams and Tallulah Bankhead, this small 1926 property is like a scaled-down grand hotel: rooms are furnished with antiques, gilt-framed paintings and old prints, and most of the marble-tiled bathrooms have tubs. Many suites are decked out with (non-functioning) fireplaces and crystal chandeliers. Stop by the sedate second-floor lounge for complimentary wine and cheese, served every evening, on your way to dinner at the exclusive Monkey Bar (see p163) – a few tables are set aside for guests every night.

Moderate

Library Hotel
299 Madison Avenue, at 41st Street, New York, NY 10017 (1-212 983 4500, www.libraryhotel.com). Subway S, 4, 5, 6, 7 to 42nd Street-Grand Central; 7 to Fifth Avenue. **Rooms** 60. **Map** p398 E24.
This bookish boutique hotel is organised on the principles of the Dewey decimal system – each of its ten floors is allocated a category, such as Literature, the Arts and General Knowledge, and each elegantly understated guest room contains a collection of books and artwork pertaining to a subject within that category. The popular Love room (filed under Philosophy) has a king-size bed, an ivy-clad balcony overlooking the New York Public Library and reading matter ranging from Ovid's *The Art of Love* to Dr Ruth Westheimer's *The Art of Arousal* (the veteran sexpert is honorary curator of the room's book collection). Nightly receptions dish out wine and cheese, while upstairs in the rooftop bar, creative libations are inspired by Ernest Hemingway and Harper Lee. There's a film library and in-room DVD players if you can't face reading another word.

Budget

Pod 39
145 E 39th Street, between Lexington & Third Avenues, New York, NY 10016 (1-212 865 5700, www.thepodhotel.com). Subway S, 4, 5, 6, 7 to 42nd Street-Grand Central. **Rooms** 366. **Map** p398 F24.
The city's second Pod occupies a 1918 residential hotel for single men – you can hang out by the fire

Yotel New York. *See p367.*

or play ping-pong in the redesigned gents' sitting room. As the name suggests, rooms are snug, but not oppressively so; some have queen-size beds, others stainless-steel bunk beds equipped with individual TVs and bedside shelves inspired by airplane storage. But you should probably know your roommate well since the utilitarian, subway-tiled bathrooms are partitioned off with sliding frosted-glass doors. April Bloomfield's on-site eatery Salvation Taco (*see p164*) supplies the margaritas at the sprawling seasonal rooftop bar.

Other location Pod 51, 230 E 51st Street, between Second & Third Avenues (1-212 355 0300).

UPPER WEST SIDE
Moderate

Hotel Belleclaire
250 W 77th Street, at Broadway, New York, NY 10024 (1-212 362 7700, www.hotelbelleclaire. com). Subway 1 to 79th Street. **Rooms** 240. **Map** p399 C19.
This centenarian landmark debuted a major renovation in 2013. The grand panelled lobby, which retains its original skylight and mosaic-tiled floor, now has a stylish coffee bar. Guest quarters feature wooden floors and details such as padded headboards, Frette linens, iHome iPod docks and bath products courtesy of iconic East Village chemist CO Bigelow. Parents, in particular, will appreciate the refrigerators in every room and the 'media lounge' housing two arcade-game stations and three free-to-use computers.

NYLO New York City
2178 Broadway, at 77th Street, New York, NY 10024 (1-212 362 1100, 1-866 391 6956, www.nylohotels.com/nyc). Subway 1 to 79th Street. **Rooms** 285. **Map** p399 C20.
Launched by former W honcho Michael Mueller, NYLO is short for New York Loft and the airy guest quarters have stacked-plywood furnishings, original art and 'brick' wallpaper that playfully reference the loft-living archetype. The functional style doesn't skimp on comfort, though: beds have a cushy, custommade pillow-top mattress, and in-room amenities include free Wi-Fi and a Keurig coffeemaker to brew your free Wolfgang Puck joe. Deluxe rooms on the top three floors open on to terraces, some with views of the Hudson River or Central Park. In addition to a sprawling ground-floor lounge and a seasonal 16th-floor terrace bar, the uptown arm of RedFarm (*see p120*) is on site.

Budget

Broadway Hotel & Hostel
230 W 101 Street, at Broadway, New York, NY 10024 (1-212 865 7710, www.broadwayhotel nyc.com). Subway 1, 2, 3 to 96th Street. **Rooms** 100. **Map** p400 C16.
For those who have outgrown the no-frills backpacker experience but haven't quite graduated to a full-service hotel, the hybrid Broadway Hotel & Hostel fills the gap. On the ground floor, exposed brick, leather sofas and three large flatscreen TVs give the sprawling communal spaces a slick, urban veneer, but they still follow the traditional youth-hostel blueprint: TV

room, shared kitchen, plus a computer area with four credit card-operated terminals (if you have your own gadget, Wi-Fi is free). You won't find six-bed set-ups here, though: the cheapest option, the small, basic 'dormitory-style' rooms, jazzed up with striking colour schemes and mass-produced art, accommodate a maximum of two in bunk beds. The good-value 'semi-private' rooms offer a queen bed or two doubles/twins, with luxuries like flatscreen TVs, but you'll have to use the shared bathrooms. En suite quarters are also available. There are free linens and towels, a daily housekeeping service and 24-hour reception.

Hostels

Hostelling International New York

891 Amsterdam Avenue, at 103rd Street, New York, NY 10025 (1-212 932 2300, www.hinew york.org). Subway 1 to 103rd Street. **Rooms** 737 beds in dorms; 4 private rooms. **Map** p400 C16.

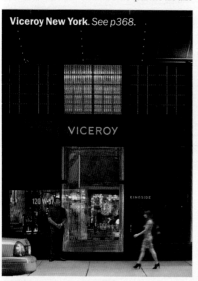

Viceroy New York. See p368.

This budget lodging is actually the city's only 'real' hostel (a non-profit accommodation that belongs to the International Youth Hostel Federation). The handsome gabled, Gothic-inspired brick and stone building – the largest hostel in America – spans the length of an entire city block. Most of the accommodation is in four- to 12-bed dorms, which are spare but clean and air-conditioned with immaculate shared bathrooms. There is also a handful of private rooms that sleep up to four with en-suite facilities and standard hotel amenities including a 32-inch plasma TV, fridge and toiletries (but no in-room phone). You can get to know your fellow travellers in the on-site café, the large shared kitchen, and the backyard and patio. Linens and towels are supplied free, as is the property-wide Wi-Fi.

UPPER EAST SIDE

Deluxe

Pierre

2 E 61st Street, at Fifth Avenue, New York, NY 10065 (1-212 838 8000, www.tajhotels.com/ thepierre). Subway N, Q, R to Fifth Avenue-59th Street. **Rooms** 189. **Map** p399 E22.

The 1930 landmark overlooking Central Park became part of the posh Indian Taj Hotels, Resorts and Palaces in 2005, setting in motion a $100-million overhaul – but it retains delightfully old-fashioned elements such as elevator operators and original fireplaces in some suites. In contrast to the glitzy public spaces, including the mural-clad Rotunda and the Grand Ballroom, the classic rooms are understated, dressed in a neutral colour palette and immaculate upholstery, with modern gadgets including Bose radio/iPod docks. The sumptuous Turkish marble bathrooms are generously stocked with Molton Brown bath products. The Asian influence is reflected in silk bedspreads from Bangalore and contemporary Indian art, but the hotel restaurant is a swanky Italian spot designed by Adam Tihany, Sirio Ristorante.

★ Surrey

20 E 76th Street, between Fifth & Madison Avenues, New York, NY 10021 (1-212 288 3700, 1-800 978 7739, www.thesurreyhotel.com). Subway 6 to 77th Street. **Rooms** 189. **Map** p399 E20.

Occupying an elegant 1920s building that has been given a $60 million overhaul, the Surrey updates the grand hotel model. The coolly elegant limestone and marble lobby showcases museum-quality contemporary art, and guestrooms are dressed in a refined palette of cream, grey and beige, with the addition of luxurious white marble bathrooms. But the centrepiece is undoubtedly the incredibly comfortable DUX bed by Duxiana bed, swathed in sumptuous Sferra linens. The hotel is flanked by top chef Daniel Boulud's Café Boulud and his chic cocktail destination, Bar Pleiades (*see p183*); there's also a luxurious spa.

IN THE KNOW CLOCK THIS

Fancy spending the night in one of the city's most iconic buildings, overlooking Madison Square Park? The Metropolitan Life tower (see p136), is being converted to a 273-room property by Ian Schrager-Marriott brand Edition Hotels (www.editionhotels.com) and should be open by publication of this guide.

Moderate

Hotel Wales

1295 Madison Avenue, at 92nd Street, New York, NY 10128 (1-212 876 6000, www.hotel walesnyc.com). Subway 4, 5, 6 to 86th Street; 6 to 96th Street. **Rooms** 89. **Map** p400 E18.

Purpose-built as a hotel in the early 1900s, the ten-storey Wales is a comfortable, convenient choice for a culture jaunt due to its proximity to Museum Mile. Tucked in the quietly affluent Carnegie Hill neighbourhood just north of Madison Avenue's prime retail stretch, it's also well placed for a posh shopping spree. Standard double rooms are small, but high ceilings, large windows and an unfussy contemporary-classic style prevents them from seeming cramped; about half of the accommodation consists of suites. Guest quarters have been spruced up with designer wallpaper, sleek modern bathrooms and HD TVs. Higher-floor rooms on the east side have Central Park views, but all guests can enjoy them on the large roof terrace.

HARLEM

Moderate

Aloft Harlem

2296 Frederick Douglass Boulevard (Eighth Avenue), between 123rd & 124th Streets, New York, NY 10027 (1-212 749 4000, www.aloft hotels.com). Subway A, B, C, D, 2, 3 to 125th Street. **Rooms** 124. **Map** p401 D13.

Starwood Hotels' fast-expanding Aloft brand pitches to a young, design-conscious traveller whose budget might not stretch to a room at one of the company's W properties. Aloft Harlem was the first hotel to open in the area since the early 1960s. The public spaces combine high-tech amenities (a pair of iMacs, in addition to free hotel-wide Wi-Fi) with colourful, contemporary decor (a scrolling news ticker above the elevators, a pool table in the lobby-lounge). A minimalist approach mitigates tight space in the bedrooms – despite 275sq ft dimensions, standard quarters are outfitted with king-size beds and 42in flatscreen TVs, while bathrooms feature oversize rainfall showerheads and products created by W collaborator Bliss Spa.

Other locations throughout the city.

Budget

★ Harlem Flophouse

242 W 123rd Street, between Adam Clayton Powell Jr Boulevard (Seventh Avenue) & Frederick Douglass Boulevard (Eighth Avenue), New York, NY 10027 (harlemflophouse@gmail.com, www. harlemflophouse.com). Subway A, B, C, D to 125th Street. **Rooms** 5. **Map** p401 D14.

The dark-wood interior, moody lighting and lilting jazz make musician René Calvo's uptown inn feel more like a 1920s speakeasy than a 21st-century lodging. The airy guest quarters, which are named after jazz greats and prominent Harlem figures, have restored tin ceilings and working sinks in antique cabinets, and are furnished with a quirky mix of junk-store finds and period knick-knacks. Four of the rooms are on the top two floors and each pair shares a bathroom. The ground-floor Ellington room has private facilities and a garden.

BROOKLYN

Expensive

McCarren Hotel & Pool

160 North 12th Street, between Bedford Avenue & Berry Street, Williamsburg, Brooklyn, NY 11249 (1-718 218 7500, www.chelseahotels.com). Subway L to Bedford Avenue. **Rooms** 64. **Map** p405 U7.

Small boutique-hotel chain Chelsea Hotels, which operates an ironically retro retreat in Long Island, brings resort style to Brooklyn. In summer, the 40-foot saltwater pool opens on the secluded back patio; there's also a ninth-floor roof bar that takes in the Manhattan skyline. Guest rooms evoke midcentury minimalism with bamboo flooring, taupe leather platform beds and Carrara marble-tiled bathrooms with sustainable toiletries by Italian brand Davines.

Other location Martha Washington, 29 East 29th Street, between Madison & Park Avenues, Flatiron District (1-212 689 1900).

★ Wythe Hotel

80 Wythe Avenue, at North 11th Street, Williamsburg, Brooklyn, NY 11249 (1-718 460 8000, www.wythehotel.com). Subway L to Bedford Avenue. **Rooms** 72. **Map** p405 U7.

A 1901 cooperage near the waterfront topped with a three-storey glass-and-aluminium addition, the Wythe perfectly captures the neighbourhood's elusive hip factor. Since the launch team includes Andrew Tarlow, the man behind local eateries Diner and Marlow & Sons, it's not surprising that the ground-floor restaurant, Reynard, was an instant hit. In many of the rooms, floor-to-ceiling windows offer a Manhattan skyline panorama. Heated concrete floors, exposed brick, reclaimed-timber beds and witty wallpaper create a rustic-industrial vibe, offset by fully plugged-in technology: a cable by the bed turns your iPhone into a surround-sound music system.

> ### IN THE KNOW HOTEL ART
>
> The Wythe Hotel's 50-foot-tall 'hotel' sign was created from salvaged tin signage by local artist Tom Fruin. Some of the rooms look out on to an exterior wall decorated with a Steve Powers graffiti mural that recreates vintage Brooklyn advertising.

Moderate

Nu Hotel

85 Smith Street, between Atlantic Avenue & State Street, Boerum Hill, Brooklyn, NY 11201 (1-718 852 8585, www.nuhotelbrooklyn.com). Subway A, C, F to Jay Street-Borough Hall; F, G to Bergen Street; R to Court Street; 2, 3, 4, 5 to Borough Hall. **Rooms** 93. **Map** p404 T10.

Conveniently placed for shops and restaurants, Nu Hotel has bundled quirky niceties into a classy, eco-friendly package. Rooms are decked out with wood flooring, organic linens and recycled teak furniture, 42in flatscreen TVs and Sonos sound systems for wireless tunes; some are adorned with murals by local artists. Standard rooms are comfortably sized, but the lofty Urban Suites are outfitted with hammocks and a padded-leather sleeping alcove.

Hostels

★ New York Loft Hostel

249 Varet Street, at Bogart Street, Bushwick, Brooklyn, New York, NY 11206 (1-718 366 1351, www.nylofthostel.com). Subway L to Morgan Avenue. **Rooms** 100 beds in dorms; 31 private rooms. **Map** p405 W9.

Set in an arty enclave, this budget lodging fuses the traditional youth hostel set-up (dorm-style rooms with single beds and lockers, communal kitchen and lounging areas) with a fashionable loft aesthetic. In the former clothing warehouse, linen curtains billow in front of huge windows, and there's industrial-chic exposed brick and piping. The patio is the site of free summer barbecues.

QUEENS

Moderate

Z NYC Hotel

11-01 43rd Avenue, at 11th Street, Long Island City, Queens, NY 11101 (1-212 319 7000, www. zhotelny.com). Subway E, M to Court Square-23rd Street; F to 21st Street-Queensbridge; N, Q, 7 to Queensboro Plaza. **Rooms** 100. **Map** p406 V5.

The Z shares a gritty industrial side street with tool suppliers and flooring wholesalers, but the Queensboro Bridge-side setting and largely low-rise neighbours facilitate its most stunning feature:

knock-your-socks-off midtown views through floor-to-ceiling windows. Offbeat details, such as lightbulbs encased in mason jars dangling over the bed, wall stencils of iconic New York images and black flip-flops instead of the standard white slippers, enliven the stock boutique luxury of the accommodation. The sprawling roof bar offers 360-degree panoramas.

THE BRONX
Moderate

Opera House Hotel
436 E 149th Street, between Bergen & Brook Avenues, Bronx, New York, NY 10455 (1-718 407 2800, www.operahousehotel.com). Subway 2, 5 to Third Avenue-149th Street. **Rooms** 60.

The Bronx Opera House showcased the big stars of the early 20th century, including the Marx Brothers and Harry Houdini. Now a hotel, the striking 1913 structure is still a draw for theatre lovers – steps from the subway, it's a mere 20-minute ride from the Great White Way, yet prices are a fraction of what you'd pay for similar digs in midtown. You get a lot more space too: ranging from about 275 to 450sq ft, rooms feature either one king-size or two queen beds. The decor isn't trendy, but comparable to an upscale chain hotel, with a warm, neutral colour scheme and beige leather padded headboards. All quarters are equipped with a refrigerator, microwave, flatscreen TV, iHome iPod dock and free Wi-Fi. Though little remains of the original building apart from the Beaux Arts facade, reproductions of playbills and photos of performers are reminders of its past.

Wythe Hotel.

Getting Around

ARRIVING & LEAVING

By air

John F Kennedy International Airport *1-718 244 4444, www. panynj.gov/airports/jfk.html.*
The **subway** (*see p375*) is the cheapest option. The **AirTrain** (www.airtrainjfk.com, $5) links to the A train at Howard Beach or the E, J and Z trains at Sutphin Boulevard-Archer Avenue ($2.75-$3).
   NYC Airporter buses (1-718 777 5111, www.nycairporter.com; one way $16, round trip $30) connect JFK and Manhattan, with stops near Grand Central Terminal, Penn Station and Port Authority Bus Terminal. Buses run every 30mins from 5am to 11.30pm daily.
   SuperShuttle (1-800 258 3826, www.supershuttle.com) vans offer door-to-door service between NYC and the major airports.
   A **yellow cab** to Manhattan will charge a flat $52.50 fare, plus toll (usually $5) and tip (15 per cent is the norm). The fare to JFK from Manhattan is not a set rate, but is usually roughly the same (*see p375*).

La Guardia Airport *1-718 533 3400, www.panynj.gov/airports/ laguardia.html.*
Seasoned New Yorkers take the **M60** bus ($2.75), to 106th Street at Broadway. The ride takes 40-60mins, depending on traffic, and buses run 24hrs daily. The route crosses Manhattan at 125th Street in Harlem. Get off at Lexington Avenue for the 4, 5 and 6 trains; at Malcolm X Boulevard (Lenox Avenue) for the 2 and 3; or at St Nicholas Avenue for the A, B, C and D trains.
   Less time-consuming options include **NYC Airporter** buses (one way $14, round trip $26). **Taxis** and **car** services charge about $30, plus toll and tip.

Newark Liberty International Airport *1-973 961 6000, www. panynj.gov/airports/newark-liberty.html.*
The best bet is the $12.50, half-hour trip via New Jersey Transit to or from Penn Station. The airport's monorail, **AirTrain Newark** (www.airtrainnewark.com), is linked to the NJ Transit and Amtrak train systems.

Bus services operated by **Coach USA** (1-877 894 9155, www.coachusa.com) run to Manhattan, stopping at Bryant Park in midtown, and inside the Port Authority Bus Terminal (one way $16, round trip $28); buses leave every 15-30mins. A **car** or **taxi** will run at $60-$75, plus toll and tip.

By bus

Most out-of-town buses come and go from the Port Authority Bus Terminal. **Greyhound** (1-800 231 2222, www.greyhound.com) runs long-distance travel to US destinations. The company's **BoltBus** (1-877 265 8287, www. boltbus.com), booked online, serves several East Coast cities. **New Jersey Transit** (1-973 275 5555, www.njtransit. com) runs services to most of New Jersey and parts of New York State. Finally, **Peter Pan** (1-800 343 9999, www.peterpanbus. com) runs extensive services to cities across the North-east; its tickets are also valid on Greyhound buses.

Port Authority Bus Terminal *625 Eighth Avenue, between 40th & 42nd Streets, Garment District (1-212 564 8484, www.panynj.gov/ bus-terminals/port-authority-bus-terminal.html). Subway A, C, E to 42nd Street-Port Authority.* **Map** p398 S13.

By rail

America's national rail service is run by **Amtrak** (1-800 872 7245, www.amtrak.com). Nationwide routes are slow and infrequent (yet full of character), but there are some good fast services linking the eastern seaboard cities. (For commuter rail services, *see p375* **Public transport: Rail**.)

Grand Central Terminal *42nd to 44th Streets, between Vanderbilt & Lexington Avenues, Midtown East. Subway S, 4, 5, 6, 7 to 42nd Street-Grand Central.* **Map** p398 E24.
Grand Central is home to Metro-North, which runs trains to more than 100 stations in New York State and Connecticut.
Penn Station *31st to 33rd Streets, between Seventh & Eighth Avenues, Garment District. Subway A, C, E,*

1, 2, 3 to 34th Street-Penn Station. **Map** p398 D25.
Amtrak, Long Island Rail Road and New Jersey Transit trains depart from this terminal.

PUBLIC TRANSPORT

Changes to schedules can occur at short notice, especially at weekends – check the MTA's website before travelling and pay attention to the posters on subway station walls and announcements on trains and subway platforms.

Metropolitan Transportation Authority (MTA) *511 local, 1-877 690 5116 outside New York State, 1-212 878 7000 international, www.mta.info.*
The MTA runs the subway and bus lines, as well as services to points outside Manhattan. News of service interruptions and MTA maps are on its website. Be warned: backpacks, handbags and large containers may be subject to random searches.

Fares & tickets

Although you can pay with exact change (no dollar bills) on buses, to enter the subway system you'll need either a single-ride ticket ($3, available from station vending machines only) or a **MetroCard**. You can buy MetroCards from booths or vending machines in the stations, from the Official NYC Information Center (*see p383*), from the New York Transit Museum in Brooklyn (*see p208*) or Grand Central Terminal (*see left*), and from many hotels.
   The standard base fare across the subway and bus network on a MetroCard is $2.75. Free transfers between the subway and buses are available only with a MetroCard (for bus-to-bus transfers on cash fares, *see p375*). Up to four people can use a pay-per-ride MetroCard, sold in denominations from $5.50 to $80. (There is an additional $1 for a new MetroCard.) If you put $5.50 or more on the card, you'll receive an 11 per cent bonus, thus reducing the cost of each ride by 27 cents. However, if you're planning to use the subway or buses often, an Unlimited Ride MetroCard is great value. These cards are offered in two denominations, available at station vending machines but not at booths:

a seven-day pass ($31) and a 30-day pass ($116.50). Both are good for unlimited rides within those periods, but you can't share a card with your travelling companions.

Subway

Cleaner and safer than it has been for decades, the city's subway system is one of the world's largest and cheapest. For fares and MetroCards, *see p374*. Trains run around the clock. If you are travelling late at night, board the train from the designated off-peak waiting area, usually near the middle of the platform; this is more secure than the ends of the platform, which are often less populated in the wee hours.

Stations are most often named after the street on which they're located. Entrances are marked with a green and white globe (open 24 hours) or a red and white globe (limited hours). Many stations have separate entrances for the uptown and downtown platforms – look before you pay. Trains are identified by letters or numbers, colour-coded according to the line on which they run. Local trains stop at every station on the line; express trains stop at major stations only.

The most current subway map is reprinted at the back of this guide; you can also ask MTA staff in service booths for a free copy, or refer to enlarged maps displayed in each subway station.

City buses

White and blue MTA buses are usually the best way to travel crosstown and a pleasant way to travel up- or downtown, as long as you're not in a hurry. They have a digital destination sign on the front, along with a route number preceded by a letter (M for Manhattan, B for Brooklyn, Bx for the Bronx, Q for Queens and S for Staten Island). Maps are posted on most buses and at all subway stops; they're also available from the Official NYC Information Center (*see p383*). The Manhattan bus map is printed in the back of this guide. All local buses are equipped with wheelchair lifts.

The fare is payable with a MetroCard (*see p374*) or exact change ($2.75 in coins only; no pennies or dollar bills). MetroCards allow for an automatic transfer from bus to bus, and between bus and subway. If you pay cash, and you're travelling uptown or downtown and want to

go crosstown (or vice versa), ask the driver for a transfer when you get on – you'll be given a ticket for use on the second leg of your journey, valid for two hours. MTA's express buses usually head to the outer boroughs for a $6.50 fare.

Rail

The following commuter trains serve NY's hinterland.

Long Island Rail Road *511 local, 1-718 217 5477 outside New York State, www.mta.info/lirr.* Provides rail services from Penn Station, Brooklyn and Queens to towns throughout Long Island.
Metro-North Railroad *511 local, 1-212 532 4900 outside New York State, www.mta.info/mnr.* Commuter trains serve towns north of Manhattan and leave from Grand Central Terminal.
New Jersey Transit *1-973 275 5555, www.njtransit.com.* Service from Penn Station reaches most of New Jersey, some points in New York State and Philadelphia.
PATH Trains *1-800 234 7284, www.panynj.gov/path.* PATH (Port Authority Trans-Hudson) trains run from six stations in Manhattan to various New Jersey destinations, including Hoboken, Jersey City and Newark. The 24-hour service costs $2.75.

Boat

NY Waterway (1-800 533 3779, www.nywaterway.com) runs a water-transport service that connects Manhattan to Queens, Brooklyn and some New Jersey cities. The East River Ferry runs between Midtown East at 34th Street and downtown Manhattan at Pier 11, via Long Island City in Queens and Greenpoint, Williamsburg and Dumbo in Brooklyn (from $4 one way, $12 day pass). On the West Side of the island, NY Waterway's Hudson River ferries link Pier 79 on 39th Street and the World Financial Center in lower Manhattan to destinations in New Jersey, including Hoboken and Jersey City ($6-$21.50 one-way). Visit the website for ferry routes and schedules.

In addition to its hop-on hop-off service and tours, **New York Water Taxi** (*see p376*) offers a popular shuttle service connecting Pier 11 in Manhattan and IKEA in Red Hook, Brooklyn (2-7.15pm Mon-Fri; 11.30am-8.40pm Sat, Sun). The $5 fare is waived on weekends and for children under 12.

TAXIS

If the centre light atop the taxi is lit, the cab is available and should stop if you flag it down. Get in and then tell the driver where you're going. (New Yorkers generally give cross-streets rather than addresses.) By law, taxis cannot refuse to take you anywhere inside the five boroughs or to New York airports. Green Boro Taxis serving the outer boroughs can now be hailed on the street in the Bronx, Queens (excluding airports), Brooklyn, Staten Island and Manhattan north of West 110th and East 96th Streets. Use only yellow or green medallion (licensed) cabs.

Taxis will carry up to four passengers for the same price: $2.50 plus 50¢ per fifth of a mile or per minute idling, with an extra 50¢ charge (a new state tax), another 50¢ from 8pm to 6am and a $1 surcharge during rush hour (4-8pm Mon-Fri). The average fare for a three-mile ride is $14, but this will vary depending on the time and traffic.

If you have a problem, take down the medallion and driver's numbers, posted on the partition. Always ask for a receipt – there's a meter number on it. To complain or to trace lost property, call the Taxi & Limousine Commission (1-212 227 0700, 8.30am-5pm Mon-Fri) or visit www.nyc.gov/taxi. Tip 15-20 per cent, as in a restaurant. All taxis now accept major credit cards.

Car services

Car services are regulated by the Taxi & Limousine Commission. Unlike cabs, drivers can make only pre-arranged pickups. Don't try to hail one, and be wary of those that offer you a ride. These companies will pick you up anywhere in the city for a set fare.

Carmel *1-212 666 6666.*
Dial 7 *1-212 777 7777.*
GroundLink *1-877 227 7260.*

DRIVING
Car hire

You need a credit card to rent a car in the US, and usually must be at least 25 years old. Car hire is cheaper in the city's outskirts and further afield than in Manhattan. NYC companies add 19.875 per cent in taxes. If you just want a car for a few hours, Zipcar (US: 1-866 494 7227, www.zipcar.com; UK: 0333 240 9000, www.zipcar.co.uk) is cost effective.

ESSENTIAL INFORMATION

Alamo *US: 1-877 222 9075, www.alamo.com. UK: 0871 384 1086, www.alamo.co.uk.*
Avis *US: 1-800 230 4898, www.avis.com. UK: 0844 581 0147, www.avis.co.uk.*
Budget *US: 1-800 527 0700, www.budget.com. UK: 0844 581 2231, www.budget.co.uk.*
Enterprise *US: 1-800 261 7331, www.enterprise.com. UK: 0800 800 227, www.enterprise.co.uk.*
Hertz *US: 1-800 654 3131, www.hertz.com. UK: 0843 309 3099, www.hertz.co.uk.*

Parking

Make sure you read parking signs and never park within 15 feet of a fire hydrant (to avoid a $115 ticket and/or having your car towed). Parking is off-limits on most streets for at least a few hours daily. The Department of Transportation provides information on daily changes to regulations (dial 311). If precautions fail, call 1-212 971 0771 for Manhattan towing and impoundment information; go to www.nyc.gov for phone numbers in other boroughs.

CYCLING

While biking on NYC's streets is only recommended for experienced cyclists, the new **Citi Bike** system (www.citibikenyc.com, 1-855 245 3311) gives you temporary access to bikes at hundreds of stations in Manhattan and Brooklyn. Visitors can purchase a 24-hour ($9.95) or three-day ($25) Access Pass at a station kiosk with a credit or debit card. You'll then receive a 'ride code' that will allow you to undock and ride for 30 minutes at a stretch. A longer trip will incur an extra fee.

The Manhattan Waterfront Greenway, a 32-mile route that circumnavigates the island of Manhattan, is a fantastic asset: you can now ride, uninterrupted, along the Hudson River from Battery Park up to the George Washington Bridge, at 178th Street. The free NYC Cycling Map, covering cycle lanes in all five boroughs, is available from the **Department of City Planning Bookstore** (22 Reade Street, between Broadway & Elk Street, Civic Center, 1-212 720 3667, open noon-4pm Mon, 10am-1pm Wed), or you can download it from www.nyc.gov/planning.

Bike and Roll (1-212 260 0400, www.bikeandroll.com/newyork) is the city's biggest cycle-hire company, with 11 outposts. Rates (including helmet) start at $10 per hour.

WALKING

One of the best ways to take in NYC is on foot. Most of the streets are laid out in a grid pattern and are relatively easy to navigate.

GUIDED TOURS

By bicycle

Bike the Big Apple *1-877 865 0078, www.bikethebigapple.com.* **Tickets** (incl bicycle & helmet rental) $90-$95.
Licensed guides lead cyclists through historic and newly hip hoods: tours include Harlem (the 'Sensational Park and Soul' tour), Chinatown ('From High Finance to Hidden Chinatown') and a twilight ride across the Brooklyn Bridge.

By boat

Circle Line Cruises *Pier 83, 42nd Street, at the Hudson River, Hell's Kitchen (1-212 563 3200, www. cirdeline42.com).* Subway A, C, E to 42nd Street-Port Authority. **Tickets** $29-$41; $20-$36 reductions. **Map** p398 B24.
The Circle Line's famed three-hour guided circumnavigation of Manhattan Island ($41; $27-$36 reductions) is a fantastic way to get your bearings and see many of the city's sights as you pass under its iconic bridges. The company also has a roster of themed tours. The separately run **Circle Line Downtown** (Pier 16, South Street Seaport, 1-212 742 1969, www.circle linedowntown.com) has a more intimate vessel, the *Zephyr*, for tours of lower Manhattan (May-Sept, $15). The two companies' rival speedboats – Circle Line's *Beast* (May-Sept, $29, $23 reductions) and Circle Line Downtown's *Shark* (May-Sept, $28, $19 reductions) – offer fun, adrenalin-inducing and splashy 30-minute rides.
New York Water Taxi *1-212 742 1969, www.nywater taxi. com.* **Tickets** $28-$35; $16-$25 reductions.
Like their earthbound counterparts, New York water taxis are bright yellow. But unlike cabs, they run on a set schedule, and you can hop on and off with a day pass ($31, $19 reductions), enjoying neighbourhood attractions along the way.

By bus

Gray Line *777 Eighth Avenue, at 48th Street, Theater District (1-212 445 0848, www.newyork sightseeing. com).* Subway A, C, E to 42nd Street-Port Authority; C, E to 50th Street; N, Q, R to 49th Street. **Tickets** $44-$159. **Map** p398 D23.
Gray Line offers more than 20 bus tours, from a basic two-hour ride (with 40-plus hop-on, hop-off stops) to the guided 'Classic New York' tour, which includes lunch, admission to Top of the Rock or the Empire State Building, and a boat ride to Ellis Island and the Statue of Liberty.

On foot

Big Onion Walking Tours
1-888 606 9255, www.bigonion. com. **Tickets** $20-$40; $15-$34 reductions.
New York was known as the Big Onion before it became the Big Apple. The tour guides will explain why, and they should know – all guides hold advanced degrees in history (or a related field). Among the offerings is the 'Official Gangs of New York' walk and a weekly 'Multi-Ethnic Eating Tour' that explores the history of the Lower East Side, Chinatown and Little Italy with a little cuisine sampling along the way.
Boroughs of the Dead *1-646 932 0680, www.boroughsofthe dead.com.* **Tickets** $20.
Horror writer Andrea Janes, author of *Boroughs of the Dead: New York City Ghost Stories*, explores the dark side of various neighbourhoods, and offers a spine-tingling tour of Brooklyn's Green-Wood Cemetery.
City Running Tours *1-877 415 0058, www.cityrunningtours.com.* **Tickets** from $35 group tour; $60 individual tour.
A guided four- to 26-mile jog around the city.
Municipal Art Society Tours
1-212 935 3960, www.mas.org/ tours. **Tickets** $20.
Walking tours led by architects, art historians and others reflect the society's focus on contemporary architecture, urban planning and historic preservation.
Urban Oyster *1-347 618 8687, www.urbanoyster.com.* **Tickets** $60-$75 (incl. food and drink).
Urban Oyster offers food-centric expeditions such as 'Brewed in Brooklyn' ($65), which illuminates the borough's suds-making legacy, and a 'Tenement, Tales and Taste' tour ($65) of the Lower East Side.

Resources A-Z

TRAVEL ADVICE

For up-to-date information on travel to a specific country – including the latest on safety and security, health issues, local laws and customs – contact your home country government's department of foreign affairs. Most have websites with useful advice for would-be travellers.

AUSTRALIA
www.smartraveller.gov.au

CANADA
www.voyage.gc.ca

NEW ZEALAND
www.safetravel.govt.nz

REPUBLIC OF IRELAND
foreignaffairs.gov.ie

UK
www.fco.gov.uk/travel

USA
www.state.gov/travel

ADDRESSES

Addresses follow the standard US format. The room, apartment or suite number usually appears after the street address, followed on the next line by the name of the city and the zip code.

AGE RESTRICTIONS

Buying/drinking alcohol 21.

Driving 16.

Sex 17.

Smoking 18.

ATTITUDE & ETIQUETTE

New Yorkers have something of a reputation for being rude, but 'outspoken' is more apt: they are unlikely to hold their tongues in the face of injustice or inconvenience, but they can also be very welcoming and will often go out of their way to offer advice or help.

Some old-fashioned restaurants and swanky clubs operate dress codes (jacket and tie for men, for example, or no baseball caps or ripped jeans – phone to check). However, on the whole, anything goes sartorially.

CUSTOMS

US Customs allows foreigners to bring in $100 worth of gifts (the limit is $800 for returning Americans) without paying duty. One carton of 200 cigarettes (or 100 cigars) and one litre of liquor (spirits) are allowed. Plants, meat and fresh produce of any kind cannot be brought into the country. You will have to fill out a form if you are carrying more than $10,000 in currency. You will be handed a white form on your inbound flight to fill in, confirming that you haven't exceeded any of these allowances.

If you need to bring prescription drugs into the US, make sure the container is clearly marked, and bring your doctor's statement or a prescription. Marijuana, cocaine and most opiate derivatives, along with a number of other drugs and chemicals, are not permitted: the possession is punishable by a stiff fine and/or imprisonment. Check in with the US Customs and Border Protection Service (www.cbp.gov) before you arrive if you're unsure.

HM Revenue & Customs allows returning visitors to the UK to bring £390 worth of 'gifts, souvenirs and other goods' into the country duty-free, along with the usual duty-free goods.

DISABLED

Under New York City law, facilities constructed after 1987 must provide complete access for the disabled – restrooms, entrances and exits included. In 1990, the Americans with Disabilities Act made the same requirement federal law. Many older buildings have added disabled-access features. There has been widespread compliance with the law, but call ahead to check facilities.

For information on accessible cultural institutions, contact the Mayor's Office for People with Disabilities (*see right*). All Broadway theatres are equipped with devices for the hearing-impaired; call Sound Associates (1-888 772 7686, www. soundassociates.com) for more information. For the visually impaired, HAI (1-212 284 4100, www.hainyc.org) offers live audio descriptions of selected theatre performances.

Lighthouse International
111 E 59th Street, between Park & Lexington Avenues, Upper East Side (1-212 821 9200, 1-212 821 9384 store, www.lighthouse. org). Subway N, R to Lexington Avenue-59th Street; 4, 5, 6 to 59th Street. **Open** 9am-5pm Mon-Fri. **Store** 10am-5.30pm Mon-Fri. **Map** p399 E29.
In addition to running a store that sells handy items for the vision-impaired, Lighthouse provides helpful information for blind people (residents and visitors).

Mayor's Office for People with Disabilities
2nd Floor, 100 Gold Street, between Frankfort & Spruce Streets, Financial District (1-212 788 2830, www.nyc. gov/mopd). Subway J, Z to Chambers Street; 4, 5, 6 to Brooklyn Bridge-City Hall. **Open** 9am-5pm Mon-Fri. **Map** p396 F32.
This city office provides a broad range of services for the disabled.

New York Society for the Deaf
315 Hudson Street, between Vandam & Spring Streets, Soho (1-212 366 0066, www.fegs.org). Subway C, E to Spring Street; 1 to Houston Street. **Open** 8.30am-7pm Mon-Thur; 8.30am-5pm Fri. **Map** p397 D30.
Offers information and a wide range of services for the deaf and hearing-impaired.

Society for Accessible Travel & Hospitality
1-212 447 7284, www.sath.org.
This non-profit group educates the public about travel facilities for people with disabilities, and promotes travel for the disabled. Membership, which costs $49/yr ($29 reductions) includes access to an information service and a quarterly newsletter.

ESSENTIAL INFORMATION

DRUGS

Possession of marijuana can result in anything from a $100 fine and a warning (for a first offence, 25g or less) to felony charges and prison time (for greater amounts and/or repeat offenders). Penalties, ranging from class B misdemeanours to class C felonies, are greater for the sale and cultivation of marijuana.

Possession of 'controlled substances' (cocaine, ecstasy, heroin, etc) is not taken lightly, and charges come with stiff penalties – especially if you are convicted of possession with intent to sell. Convictions carry anything from a mandatory one- to three-year prison sentence to a maximum of 25 years.

ELECTRICITY

The US uses 110-120V, 60-cycle alternating current rather than the 220-240V, 50-cycle AC used in Europe. The transformers that power or recharge newer electronic devices such as laptops are designed to handle either current and may need nothing more than an adaptor for the wall outlet. Other appliances may also require a power converter. Adaptors and converters can be purchased at airport shops, pharmacies, department stores and at branches of electronics chain Radio Shack (www.radioshack.com).

EMBASSIES & CONSULATES

Check the phone book for a list of consulates and embassies. *See also p377* **Travel Advice**.

Australia *1-212 351 6500*.

Canada *1-212 596 1628*.

Ireland *1-212 319 2555*.

New Zealand *1-212 832 4038*.

UK *1-212 745 0200*.

EMERGENCIES

In an emergency only, dial **911** for ambulance, police or fire department, or call the operator (dial 0). For hospitals, *see right*; for helplines, *see p379*; for the police, *see p382*.

GAY & LESBIAN

For more gay and lesbian resources, including the Lesbian, Gay, Bisexual & Transgender Community Center, *see pp264-272*.

Gay, Lesbian, Bisexual & Transgender National Hotline
1-888 843 4564, www.glbtnational helpcenter.org. **Open** 4pm-midnight Mon-Fri; noon-5pm Sat.
This phone service offers excellent peer counselling, legal referrals, details of various gay and lesbian organisations, and information on bars, restaurants and hotels. Younger callers can contact the toll-free GLBT National Youth Talk Line (1-800 246 7743, 4pm-midnight Mon-Fri; noon-5pm Sat).

HEALTH

Public health care is virtually nonexistent in the US, and private health care is very expensive. Make sure you have comprehensive medical insurance before you leave. For HIV testing and HIV/AIDS counselling, *see p379* **Helplines**. For a list of hospitals, *see below*.

Accident & emergency

You will be billed for any emergency treatment. Call your travel insurance company before seeking treatment to find out which hospitals accept your insurance. The following hospitals have emergency rooms:

New York Presbyterian/ Lower Manhattan Hospital
170 William Street, between Beekman & Spruce Streets, Financial District (1-212 312 5000). Subway 1 to Chambers Street; 2, 3 to Fulton Street; 4, 5, 6 to Brooklyn Bridge-City Hall. **Map** p396 F32.

Mount Sinai Hospital
Madison Avenue, at 100th Street, Upper East Side (1-212 241 6500). Subway 6 to 103rd Street. **Map** p400 E16.

New York-Presbyterian Hospital/Weill Cornell Medical Center
525 E 68th Street, at York Avenue, Upper East Side (1-212 746 5454). Subway 6 to 68th Street. **Map** p399 G21.

Mount Sinai Roosevelt Hospital
1000 Tenth Avenue, at 59th Street, Upper West Side (1-212 523 4000). Subway A, B, C, D, 1 to 59th Street-Columbus Circle. **Map** p399 C22.

Clinics

Walk-in clinics offer treatment for minor ailments. Most clinics will require immediate payment for treatments and consultations, though some will send their bill directly to your insurance company if you're a US resident. You will have to file a claim to recover the cost of any prescription medication that is required.

Beth Israel Medical Group
55 E 34th Street, between Madison & Park Avenues, Murray Hill (1-212 252 6000, www.wehealny.org/ services/bimg). Subway 6 to 33rd Street. **Open** walk-in 8am-5pm Mon-Fri; 9am-2pm Sat, Sun; also by appt. **Cost** from $125. **Map** p398 E25. Primary-care facilities with by-appointment and walk-in services. **Other locations** 309 W 23rd Street, at Eighth Avenue, Flatiron District (1-212 256 7000); 226 W 14th Street, between Seventh & Eighth Avenues, Flatiron District (1-212 604 1800).

NY Hotel Urgent Medical Services
Suite 1D, 952 Fifth Avenue, between 76th & 77th Streets, Upper East Side (1-212 737 1212, www.travelmd. com). Subway 6 to 77th Street. **Open** 24hrs by appt only. **Cost** from $200. **Map** p399 E19. Specialist medical attention, from a simple prescription to urgent medical care. House calls are available.

Dentists

New York County Dental Society
1-212 573 8500, www.nycdental society.org. **Open** 8.30am-5.30pm Mon-Fri.
Can provide local referrals. An emergency contact line at the number listed above runs outside office hours; alternatively, use the search facility on the society's website.

Opticians

Morgenthal Frederics
399 W Broadway, at Spring Street, Soho (1-212 966 0099, www. morgenthalfrederics.com). Subway C, E to Spring Street. **Open** 11am-8pm Mon-Fri; 11am-7pm Sat; noon-6pm Sun. **Map** p397 E30.
The house-designed, handmade frames on display in Morgenthal Frederics' David Rockwell-designed shops exude quality and subtly nostalgic style. Frames start from around $325 for plastic, but the buffalo horn and gold ranges are more expensive.
Other locations throughout the city.

Pharmacies

The fact that there's a Duane Reade pharmacy on almost every corner of Manhattan is lamented among chain-deriding locals; however, it is convenient if you need an aspirin pronto. Several branches, including the one at 250 W 57th Street, at Broadway (1-212 265 2101, www. duanereade.com), are open 24 hours. Competitor Rite Aid (with one of several 24-hour branches at 301 W 50th Street, at Eighth Avenue, 1-212 247 8384, www.riteaid.com) is also widespread. For New York's oldest apothecary, CO Bigelow, *see p116*.

STDs, HIV & AIDS

For the National STD & AIDS Hotline, *see right* **Helplines**.

Riverside STD Clinic
160 W 100th Street, between Amsterdam & Columbus Avenues, Upper West Side (no phone). Subway B, C, 1, 2, 3 to 96th Street; 1 to 103rd Street. **Open** walk-in 8.30am-3pm Tue-Sat (closes at noon 1st Wed of each mth). **Map** p400 C16.
Call 311 or visit www.nyc.gov for other free clinics.

Gay Men's Health Crisis
446 W 33rd Street, at Tenth Avenue, Hell's Kitchen (1-212 367 1000, 1-800 243 7692 HIV/AIDS helpline, www.gmhc.org). Subway A, C, E, 1, 2, 3 to 34th Street-Penn Station. **Open** *Centre* 10am-6pm Mon-Fri. *Hotline* 2-6pm Mon, Fri; 10am-2pm Wed; recorded information at other times.* **Map** p398 C25.
GMHC was the world's first organisation dedicated to helping people with AIDS, and offers testing, counselling and other services on a walk-in and appointment basis, regardless of sexual orientation. The Testing Center is now located within the new Center for HIV Prevention (224 W 29th Street, between Seventh & Eighth Avenues, Chelsea, 1-212 367 1100). See the website for separate walk-in and appointment-only hours.

Contraception & abortion

Planned Parenthood of New York
City Margaret Sanger Center, 26 Bleecker Street, at Mott Street, Greenwich Village (1-212 965 7000, 1-800 230 7526, www.ppnyc.org). Subway B, D, F, M to Broadway-Lafayette Street; N, R to Prince Street; 6 to Bleecker Street. **Open** 8am-6.30pm Mon-Fri; 8am-4.30pm Sat. **Map** p397 F29.

The best-known network of family-planning clinics in the US. Counselling and treatment are available for a full range of needs, including abortion, contraception, HIV testing and treatment of STDs. **Other location** 44 Court Street, between Joralemon & Remsen Streets, Brooklyn Heights, Brooklyn (1-212 965 7000).

HELPLINES

All numbers below are open 24 hours unless otherwise stated.

Addictions Hotline
1-800 522 5353.

Alcoholics Anonymous
1-212 647 1680. Open 9am-10pm daily.

Cocaine Anonymous
1-212 262 2463.

National STD & AIDS Hotline
1-800 232 4636.

Pills Anonymous
1-212 874 0700 recorded information.

Samaritans
1-212 673 3000.
Counselling for suicide prevention.

Special Victims Liaison Unit of the NYPD Rape Hotline
1-212 267 7273.

ID

Always make sure you carry picture ID: even people well over 18 or 21 may be carded when buying tobacco or alcohol, ordering drinks in bars, or entering clubs.

INSURANCE

Non-nationals and US citizens should have travel and medical insurance before travelling. For a list of New York urgent-care facilities, *see p378*.

INTERNET

FedEx Office *1-800 463 3339, www.fedex.com.*
Outposts of this ubiquitous and very efficient computer and copy centre are peppered throughout the city; many are open 24 hours a day.

New York Public Library *1-212 592 7000, www.nypl.org.*
Branches of the NYPL are great places to get online for free, offering both Wi-Fi and computers for public

use. (Ask for an out-of-state card, for which you need proof of residence, or a guest pass.) The Science, Industry & Business Library (188 Madison Avenue, at 34th Street, Midtown East), part of the Public Library system, has about 70 computers. All libraries have a computer limit of 45 minutes per day.

NYCWireless *www.nycwireless.net.*
This group has established dozens of hotspots in the city for free Wi-Fi access. (For example, most parks below 59th Street are covered.) Visit the website information and a map.

Starbucks *www.starbucks.com.*
Many branches offer free Wi-Fi; the website has a search facility.

LEFT LUGGAGE

There are luggage-storage facilities at arrivals halls in JFK Airport (Terminal 1: 7am-11pm, $4-$16 per bag per day; call 1-718 751 2947); (Terminal 4: 24hrs, $4-$16 per bag per day; call 1-718 751 4020). At Penn Station, Amtrak offers checked baggage services for a small fee for some of its ticketed passengers. Due to heightened security, luggage storage is not available at the Port Authority Bus Terminal, Grand Central station, or LaGuardia or Newark airports.
One Midtown alternative is to leave bags with the private firm, located between Penn Station and Port Authority, listed below. Some hotels may allow you to leave suitcases with the front desk before check-in or after check-out; if so, be sure to tip the concierge.

Schwartz Travel Services
2nd Floor, 355 W 36th Street, between Eighth & Ninth Avenues, Garment District (1-212 290 2626, www.schwartztravel.com). **Open** 8am-11pm daily. **Rates** $8-$10 per bag per day. **No credit cards.** **Map** p398 C25
Other location 4th Floor, 34 W 46th Street, between Fifth & Sixth Avenues, Midtown (same phone).

LEGAL HELP

If you need a lawyer in NYC, contact the New York City Bar Association (1-212 382 6600; www.nycbar.org), which can provide referrals to attorneys practising in almost every area of the law, from personal injury to criminal defence. Outside the city, contact the New York State Bar Association Lawyer Referral & Information Service (1-800 342 3661, www.nysba.org). If you're arrested

ESSENTIAL INFORMATION

and held in custody, call your insurer's emergency number or contact your embassy or consulate (*see p378*).

Legal Aid Society
1-212 577 3300, www.legal-aid.org. **Open** 9am-5pm Mon-Fri. This non-profit organisation provides legal representation for low-income residents.

LIBRARIES

See p158 **New York Public Library**.

LOST PROPERTY

For lost credit cards or travellers' cheques, *see p381*.

Grand Central Terminal
Lower level, near Track 100. 1-212 532 4900. **Open** 7am-6pm Mon-Fri. You can call 24 hrs a day to file a claim if you've left something on a Metro-North train.

JFK Airport *1-718 244 4225,* or contact your airline.

La Guardia Airport *1-718 533 3988,* or contact your airline.

Newark Liberty International Airport *1-973 961 6243,* or contact your airline.

Penn Station: Amtrak *1-212 630 7389.* **Open** 6am-2.30pm daily.

Penn Station: Long Island Rail Road *1-718 217 5477.* **Open** 7.20am-7.20pm daily.

Penn Station: New Jersey Transit *1-973 275 5555.* **Open** 6am-10pm Mon-Fri; 8am-8pm Sat; 9am-8pm Sun.

Subway & Buses *New York City Metropolitan Transit Authority, 34th Street-Penn Station, near the A-train platform, Garment District (call 511).* **Open** 8am-3.30pm Mon, Tue, Fri; 11am-6.30pm Wed, Thur. **Map** p398 D25.
Call if you've left something on a subway train or a bus.

Taxis *311, www.nyc.gov/taxi.* Call for items left in a cab.

MEDIA

Daily newspapers

Founded in 1801 by Alexander Hamilton, the **New York Post** is the nation's oldest continuously published daily newspaper. It has swerved sharply to the right under current owner Rupert Murdoch, it includes more gossip than any other local paper, and its headlines are often sassy and sensational.

The **Daily News** has drifted politically from the Neanderthal right to a more moderate but always tough-minded stance under the ownership of noted real-estate mogul Mort Zuckerman.

Despite recent financial woes, **The New York Times** remains the city's, and the nation's, paper of record. Founded as the *New-York Daily Times* in 1851, it has the broadest and deepest coverage of world and national events and, as the masthead proclaims, it delivers 'All the News That's Fit to Print'. The hefty Sunday edition includes a very well-regarded magazine, as well as arts, book review, travel, real-estate and various other sections.

The **New York Amsterdam News**, one of the nation's longest-running black newspapers, offers a trenchant African-American viewpoint. New York also supports a Spanish-language daily: **El Diario La Prensa**. **Newsday** is a Long Island-based daily with a tabloid format but a sober tone. Free tabloids **AM New York** and **New York Metro** offer locally slanted news, arts and entertainment listings.

Weekly newspapers

Downtown journalism is a battlefield, with the **New York Press** pitted against the **Village Voice**. The *Press* is full of irreverence, as well as cynicism and self-absorption. The *Voice* is at turns passionate and ironic, but just as often strident and predictable. Both are free.

Many neighbourhoods have free publications featuring local news, reviews and gossip, such as **Our Town East Side** and **West Side Spirit**.

Magazines

New York magazine is part news weekly, part lifestyle reporting and part listings. Since the 1920s, the **New Yorker** has been known for its fine wit, elegant prose and sophisticated cartoons. It has also evolved into a respected forum for serious long-form journalism.

Based on the tried and trusted format of its London parent magazine, **Time Out New York** is an intelligent, irreverent, indispensable weekly guide to what's going on in the city: arts, restaurants, bars, shops and more. It's now free.

Since its launch in 1996, the bimonthly **BlackBook Magazine** has covered New York's high fashion and culture with intelligent bravado. **Gotham**, a monthly from the publisher of glossy gab-rags *Hamptons* and *Aspen Peak*, unveiled its larger-than-life celeb-filled pages in 2001. And for more than two decades, **Paper** has offered buzz on bars, clubs, downtown boutiques and more.

Commercial radio

American commercial radio is rigidly formatted, which makes most pop stations extremely tedious and repetitive during the day. Tune in on evenings and weekends for more interesting programming. Always popular, **WQHT-FM 97.1**, 'Hot 97', is a commercial hip hop station with all-day rap and R&B. **WKTU-FM 103.5** is the premier dance music station. **WWPR-FM 105.1**, 'Power 105', plays top hip hop and a few old-school hits. **WBLS-FM 107.5** showcases classic and new funk, soul and R&B. **WBGO-FM 88.3** is strictly jazz, and **WAXQ-FM 104.3** offers classic rock.

WQEW-AM 1560, 'Radio Disney', has kids' programming. **WNYC-FM 93.9** (*see also below*) and **WQXR-FM 105.9** serve up a range of new and classical music. **WXNY-FM 96.3** and **WQBU-FM 92.7** spin Spanish and Latin sounds.

Public & college radio

The city's excellent NPR-affiliated public radio station, **WNYC-AM 820/FM 93.9**, provides news and current-affairs commentary and broadcasts the BBC World Service. **WBAI-FM 99.5** is a left-leaning community radio station.

College radio is innovative and commercial-free, but reception is often compromised by Manhattan's high-rise topography. **WNYU-FM 89.1** and **WKCR-FM 89.9** are, respectively, the stations of New York University and Columbia. **WFUV-FM 90.7**, Fordham University's station, airs a variety of shows, including Beale Street Caravan, the world's most widely distributed blues programme.

Talk radio & sports

WABC-AM 770, **WCBS-AM 880** and **WINS-AM 1010** offer news, plus traffic and weather reports. **WFAN-AM 660** airs Giants, Nets,

Mets and Devils games, while **WCBS-AM 880** covers the Yankees. **WEPN-AM 1050** is devoted to news and sports talk and is the home of the Jets, Knicks and Rangers.

Television

Six major networks broadcast nationwide. All offer ratings-driven variations on a theme. **CBS** (Channel 2 in NYC) has the top-rated investigative show, *60 Minutes*, on Sundays at 7pm; overall, programming is geared to a middle-aged demographic, but CBS also screens shows such as *CSI* and the reality series *Survivor*. **NBC** (4) is the home of *Law & Order* and the long-running sketch-comedy series *Saturday Night Live*. **Fox-WNYW** (5) is popular with younger audiences for shows such as *Family Guy*, *The Simpsons* and *The X Factor*. **ABC** (7) is the king of daytime soaps, family-friendly sitcoms and hits like *Modern Family*, *Grey's Anatomy* and *Dancing With the Stars*.

    Public TV is on channels 13, 21 and 25. Documentaries, arts shows and science series alternate with *Masterpiece* (Anglo costume and contemporary dramas packaged for a US audience) and reruns of British sitcoms.

    For channel numbers for cable TV providers, such as **Time Warner Cable**, **Cablevision** and **RCN**, check a local newspaper or the web. **FSN** (Fox Sports Network), **MSG** (Madison Square Garden), **ESPN** and **ESPN2** are all-sports stations. **Comedy Central** is all comedy, airing *South Park* and *The Daily Show*. **Cinemax**, the **Disney Channel**, the **Movie Channel**, **HBO** and **Showtime** are often available in hotels. They show uninterrupted feature films and exclusive specials; the latter two offer popular series such as *Game of Thrones*, *Girls*, *Homeland* and *Nurse Jackie*.

MONEY

Over the past few years, much of American currency has undergone a subtle facelift, partly to deter increasingly adept counterfeiters; all denominations except the $1 bill have recently been updated by the US Treasury. (However, 'old' money still remains in circulation.) Coins include copper pennies (1¢) and silver-coloured nickels (5¢), dimes (10¢) and quarters (25¢). Half-dollar coins (50¢) and the gold-coloured dollar coins are less common.

All paper money is the same size, so make sure you fork over the right bill. It comes in denominations of $1, $2, $5, $10, $20, $50 and $100 (and higher, but you'll never see those bills). $2 bills are quite rare. Try to keep some low notes on you because getting change may be a problem with anything bigger than a $20 bill.

ATMs

The city is full of ATMs – in bank branches, delis and many small shops. Most of them accept Visa, MasterCard and major bank cards. Some UK banks charge up to £4 per transaction plus a variable payment to cover against exchange rate fluctuations. Most ATM cards now double as debit cards, if they bear the Maestro or Cirrus logo.

Banks & bureaux de change

Banks are generally open from 9am to 6pm Monday to Friday, though some stay open longer and/or on Saturdays. You need photo ID, such as a passport, to cash travellers' cheques. Many banks will not exchange foreign currency; many bureaux de change, limited to tourist-trap areas, close at around 6pm or 7pm. In emergencies, most large hotels offer 24-hour exchange facilities, but the rates won't be great.

Travelex
1578 Broadway, at 47th Street, Theater District (1-212 265 6063, www.travelex.com). Subway N, Q, R to 49th Street. **Open** 9am-10pm daily. **Map** p398 D23.
Travelex offers a complete range of foreign-exchange services. The Times Square outpost stays open late; see website for other locations. **Other locations** throughout the city.

Credit cards & travellers' cheques

Credit cards are essential for renting cars and booking hotels, and handy for buying tickets over the phone and the internet. The five major cards accepted in the US are **American Express**, **Diners Club**, **Discover**, **MasterCard** and **Visa**. MasterCard and Visa are the most popular; American Express is also widely accepted. Thanks to a 2004 deal between MasterCard and Diners Club, all businesses that accept the former can now in theory accept the latter, though in practice many businesses are unaware of this and may not comply.

If your cards or travellers' cheques are lost or stolen, call the following numbers:

American Express *1-800 528 2122, 1-800 221 7282 travellers' cheques.*

Diners Club *1-800 234 6377.*

Discover *1-800 347 2683.*

Mastercard/Maestro *1-800 826 2181, 1-800 223 9920 travellers' cheques.*

Visa/Cirrus *1-800 336 8472, 1-800 336 8472 travellers' cheques.*

Tax

Sales tax is 8.875 per cent in New York City, and is applicable to restaurant bills, services and the purchase of just about anything, except most store-bought foods, clothing and shoes under $110.

    In the US, sales tax is almost never included in the price of the item, but added on to the final bill at the till. There is no tax refund option for foreign visitors.

Wire services

Moneygram *1-800 666 3947, www.moneygram.com.*

Western Union *1-800 325 6000, www.westernunion.com.*

OPENING HOURS

Banks and government offices, including post offices, close on federal holidays. Retail in the city shuts down on Christmas Day and New Year's Day, although movie theatres and some restaurants remain open. Most museums are closed on Mondays, but may open when a public holiday falls on a Monday. New York's subway runs 24 hours a day, 365 days a year, but always check station signs for track or schedule changes, especially during weekends and holidays.

Banks 9am-6pm Mon-Fri; generally also Sat mornings.

Businesses 9am or 10am to 5pm or 6pm Mon-Fri.

Post offices 9am-5pm Mon-Fri (a few open as early as 7.30am and close as late as 8.30pm); some are open Sat until 3pm or 4pm. The James A Farley Post Office (*see* *p382*) is open 24 hours daily for automated services.

Pubs & bars 4pm-2am Mon-Thur, Sun; noon-4am Fri, Sat (but hours vary widely).

Shops 9am, 10am or 11am to 7pm or 8pm Mon-Sat (some open at noon and/or close at 9pm). Many are also open on Sun, usually from 11am or noon to 6pm.

POLICE

In an emergency only, dial **911**. The NYPD stations below are in central, tourist-heavy areas of Manhattan. For the location of your nearest police precinct or information about police services, call 1-646 610 5000 or visit www.nyc.gov.

Sixth Precinct
233 West 10th Street, between Bleecker & Hudson Streets, West Village (1-212 741 4811). Map p3970 D28.

Seventh Precinct
191/2 Pitt Street, at Broome Street, Lower East Side (1-212 477 7311). Map p397 G29.

Midtown South Precinct
357 W 35th Street, between Eighth & Ninth Avenues, Garment District (1-212 239 9811). Map p398 C25.

Midtown North Precinct
306 W 54th Street, between Eighth & Ninth Avenues, Hell's Kitchen (1-212 767 8400). Map p399 C22.

17th Precinct
167 E 51st Street, between Third & Lexington Avenues, Midtown East (1-212 826 3211). Map p398 E23.

Central Park Precinct
86th Street & Transverse Road, Central Park (1-212 570 4820). Map p400 D18.

POSTAL SERVICES

Stamps are available at all US post offices, from drugstore vending machines and at most newsstands. It costs 49¢ to send a 1oz letter within the US. Each additional ounce costs 22¢. Postcards mailed within the US cost 34¢. Airmailed letters or postcards to Canada and Mexico cost 85¢ for the first ounce. The Global Forever Stamp ($1.15) can be used to send a postcard or 1oz letter anywhere in the world.

For faster Express Mail, you must fill out a form, either at a post office or by arranging a pick-up; 24-hour delivery to major US cities is guaranteed. International delivery takes two to three days, with no guarantee. Call 1-800 275 8777 for more information.

James A Farley Post Office
421 Eighth Avenue, between 31st & 33rd Streets, Garment District (1-212 330 3296, 1-800 275 8777 24hr information, www.usps.com). Subway A, C, E to 34th Street-Penn Station. **Open** 24 hrs daily. *Counter service* 7am-10pm Mon-Fri; 9am-9pm Sat; 11am-7pm Sun. Map p398 D25. In addition to operating a counter service, NYC's general post office has automated self-service machines for buying stamps and posting packages.

General Delivery
390 Ninth Avenue, between 31st & 33rd Streets, Garment District (1-212 330 3099). Subway A, C, E to 34th Street-Penn Station. **Open** 10am-1pm Mon-Fri; 10am-noon Sat. Map p398 C25.

US residents without local addresses and foreign visitors can receive their post here; it should be addressed to the recipient, General Delivery, 390 Ninth Avenue, New York, NY 10001. You will need to show a passport or ID card when picking up letters.

RELIGION

Here are just a few of New York's many places of worship. Check online or the telephone book for more listings.

Abyssinian Baptist Church
See p194.

Cathedral Church of St John the Divine
See p177.

Church of St Paul & St Andrew
United Methodist, 263 W 86th Street, between Broadway & West End Avenue, Upper West Side (1-212 362 3179, www.stpaulandstandrew. org). Subway 1 to 86th Street. Map p400 C18.

Islamic Cultural Center of New York
1711 Third Avenue, between 96th & 97th Streets, Upper East Side (1-212 722 5234, www.icc-ny. org). Subway 6 to 96th Street. Map p400 F17.

Madison Avenue Presbyterian Church
921 Madison Avenue, between 73rd & 74th Streets, Upper East Side (1-212 288 8920, www. mapc.com). Subway 6 to 72nd Street. Map p399 E20.

New York Buddhist Church
331-332 Riverside Drive, between 105th & 106th Streets, Upper West Side (1-212 678 0305, www. newyorkbuddhistchurch.org). Subway 1 to 103rd Street. Map p400 B16.

St Patrick's Cathedral
See p159.

UJA Federation of New York
Information & Referral Center 1-877 852 6951, www.ujafedny.org. **Open** 9am-5pm Mon-Fri. This hotline provides referrals to temples, synagogues, other Jewish organisations and groups.

SAFETY & SECURITY

New York's crime rate, particularly for violent crime, has waned during the past two decades. Most crime occurs late at night and in low-income neighbourhoods. Don't arrive in NYC thinking your safety is at risk wherever you go; it is unlikely that you will ever be bothered.

Still, a bit of common sense won't hurt. Don't flaunt your money and valuables, keep phones and other electronic gadgets out of sight, and try not to look obviously lost. Avoid deserted and poorly lit streets; walk facing oncoming traffic so no one can drive up alongside you undetected, and close to or on the street; muggers prefer to hang back in doorways and shadows. If you are threatened, hand over your valuables at once, then dial 911.

Be extra alert to pickpockets and street hustlers – especially in crowded areas like Times Square.

SMOKING

The 1995 NYC Smoke-Free Air Act makes it illegal to smoke in virtually all indoor public places, including the subway and cinemas. As of May 2011, smoking is also prohibited in NYC parks, pedestrian plazas (such as the ones in Times Square and Herald Square) and on beaches. Violators could face a $50 fine.

STUDY

Those who study in NYC have access to an endless extracurricular education, as well as a non-stop playground. Foreign students should get hold of an International Student Identity Card (ISIC) in order to secure discounts. These cards can be purchased from your local student-travel agent (go to www.isic.org or ask at your student union or an STA Travel office).

Manhattan's main universities include: the **City University of New York**'s 24 colleges (1-212 794 5555, www.cuny.edu); **Columbia University** (2960 Broadway, at 116th Street, Morningside Heights, 1-212 854 1754, www.columbia.edu); the **Cooper Union** (30 Cooper Square, between 5th & 6th Streets, East Village, 1-212 353 4100, www.cooper.edu); **Fordham University**, which has campuses in the Bronx and on the Upper West Side (1-718 817 1000, 1-212 636 6000, www.fordham.edu); the **New School** (55 W 13th Street, between Fifth & Sixth Avenues, Greenwich Village, 1-212 229 5600, www.newschool.edu); **New York University** (70 Washington Square South, Greenwich Village, 1-212 998 1212, www.nyu.edu); and performing arts school **Juilliard** (60 Lincoln Center Plaza, at Broadway, Upper West Side, 1-212 799 5000, www.juilliard.edu).

TELEPHONES

Dialling & codes

As a rule, you must dial 1 + the area code before a number, even if the place you are calling is in the same area code. The area codes for Manhattan are **212** and **646**; Brooklyn, Queens, Staten Island and the Bronx are **718** and **347**; **917** is now reserved mostly for mobile phones and pagers. Long Island area codes are 516 and 631; codes for New Jersey are 201, 551, 609, 732, 848, 856, 862, 908 and 973. Numbers preceded by **800**, **877** and **888** are free of charge when dialled from within the US.

In an **emergency**, dial 911. All calls are free (including those from pay and mobile phones).

For the **operator**, dial 0. If you're not used to US phones, then note that the ringing tone is long; the engaged tone, or 'busy signal', consists of much shorter, higher pitched beeps.

Collect calls are also known as reverse-charge calls. To make one, dial 0 followed by the number, or dial AT&T's 1-800 225 5288, Sprint's 1-800 663 3463, or the aptly named 1-800-Collect's 1-800 265 5328.

For **directory assistance**, dial 411 or 1 + area code + 555 1212. Doing so may cost nothing, depending on the pay phone you are using; carrier fees may apply. Long-distance directory assistance may also incur long-distance charges. For a directory of toll-free numbers, dial 1-800 555 1212.

For **international calls**, dial 011 + country code (Australia 61;

New Zealand 64; UK 44), then the number (omitting any initial zero).

Mobile phones

Most US mobile phones will work in NYC, but since the US doesn't have a standard national network, visitors should check with their provider that their phone will work here, and whether they need to unlock a roaming option. Visitors from other countries will need a tri-band handset and a roaming agreement, and may find charges so high that rental or purchase of a US phone (or SIM card) will make better economic sense. Phones can be hired from Jojo Talk (www.jojotalk.com).

If you carry a mobile phone, turn it off in museums and restaurants, and at plays, movies and concerts. New Yorkers are quick to show their annoyance at an ill-timed ring.

Public phones

Functioning public pay phones are becoming increasingly hard to find. Phones take any combination of silver coins: local calls usually cost 50¢ for three minutes. To call long-distance or to make an international call from a pay phone, you need to go through a long-distance company. Most of the pay phones in New York automatically use AT&T, but phones in and around transportation hubs usually contract other long-distance carriers, and charges can be outrageous. MCI and Sprint are respected brand names.

Make the call by either dialling 0 for an operator or dialling direct, which is cheaper. To find out how much it will cost, dial the number, and a computerised voice will tell you how much money to deposit. You can pay for calls with your credit card. The best way to make long-distance calls is with a phone card, available from any post office branch, many newsagents and delis, or from chain stores such as Duane Reade and Rite Aid (*see p379* **Pharmacies**).

TIME & DATES

New York is on Eastern Standard Time, which extends from the Atlantic coast to the eastern shore of Lake Michigan and south to the Gulf of Mexico. This is five hours behind Greenwich Mean Time. Clocks are set forward one hour in early March for Daylight Saving Time (Eastern Daylight Time) and back one hour at the beginning of November. Going from east to west, Eastern Time is one hour ahead of Central Time, two

hours ahead of Mountain Time and three hours ahead of Pacific Time.

In the United States, the date is written as month, day and year; so 8/6/15 is 6 August 2015. Forms that foreigners may need to fill in, though, are often the other way round.

TIPPING

In restaurants, it's customary to tip at least 15 per cent, and since NYC tax is 8.875 per cent, a quick way to calculate the tip is to double the tax. In many restaurants, when you are with a group of six or more, the tip will be included in the bill. For tipping on taxi fares, *see p375*.

TOILETS

The media had a field day when the first pay toilet to open in the city since 1975 received its 'first flush' by officials in a special ceremony in 2008. 'Public Toilet No.1', as the *New York Post* christened it, is in Madison Square Park (Madison Avenue, between 23rd & 24th Streets, Flatiron District) and was due to be followed by around 20 across the city; progress, however, has been stalled. It costs 25¢ to enter the large stainless steel and tempered glass box (beware: the door opens after 15 minutes). Below is a list of other convenient rest stops; for more options, see www.nyrestroom.com.

Downtown

Battery Park Castle Clinton
Subway 1 to South Ferry; 4, 5 to Bowling Green.

Tompkins Square Park *Avenue A, at 9th Street. Subway L to First Avenue; 6 to Astor Place.*

Washington Square Park
Thompson Street, at Washington Square South. Subway A, B, C, D, E, F, M to W 4th Street.

Midtown

Bryant Park *42nd Street, between Fifth & Sixth Avenues. Subway B, D, F, M to 42nd Street-Bryant Park; 7 to Fifth Avenue.*

Grand Central Terminal *42nd Street, at Park Avenue, Lower Concourse. Subway S, 4, 5, 6, 7 to 42nd Street-Grand Central.*

Penn Station *Seventh Avenue, between 31st & 33rd Streets, Subway A, C, E, 1, 2, 3 to 34th Street-Penn Station.*

ESSENTIAL INFORMATION

LOCAL CLIMATE

Average temperatures and monthly rainfall in New York.

	High (˚C/˚F)	Low (˚C/˚F)	Rainfall (mm/in)
Jan	2 / 36	-5 / 23	94 / 3.7
Feb	4 / 40	-4 / 24	75 / 3.0
Mar	9 / 48	0 / 32	104 / 4.1
Apr	14 / 58	6 / 42	103 / 4.1
May	20 / 68	12 / 53	114 / 4.5
June	25 / 77	17 / 63	88 / 3.5
July	28 / 83	20 / 68	106 / 4.2
Aug	27 / 81	19 / 66	103 / 4.1
Sept	23 / 74	14 / 58	103 / 4.1
Oct	17 / 63	8 / 47	89 / 3.5
Nov	11 / 52	3 / 38	102 / 4.0
Dec	6 / 42	-2 / 28	98 / 3.9

ESSENTIAL INFORMATION

Uptown

Avery Fisher Hall *Broadway, at 65th Street. Subway 1 to 66th Street-Lincoln Center.*

Charles A Dana Discovery Center *Central Park, north side of Harlem Meer, 110th Street at Malcolm X Boulevard (Lenox Avenue). Subway 2, 3 to 110th Street-Central Park North.*

Delacorte Theater *Central Park, midpark, at 81st Street. Subway B, C to 81st Street-Museum of Natural History.*

TOURIST INFORMATION

Official NYC Information Center at Macy's Herald Square *151 W 34th Street, between Broadway & Seventh Avenue, Garment District (1-212 484 1222, www.nycgo.com). Subway A, C, E, 1, 2, 3 to 34th Street-Penn Station; B, D, F, M, N, Q, R to 34th Street-Herald Square .* **Open** 9am-7pm Mon-Fri; 10am-7pm Sat; 11am-7pm Sun. **Map** p398 D25. Located on the mezzanine of Macy's, the city's official (private, non-profit) visitors' information centre offers advice, maps, leaflets and coupons, and sells tickets to attractions. For other locations around the city, go to www.nycgo.com/articles/official-nyc-information-centers. **Other locations** throughout the city.

Brooklyn Tourism & Visitors Center *Brooklyn Borough Hall, 209 Joralemon Street, between Court & Adams Streets, Brooklyn (1-718 802 3846, www.visitbrooklyn.org). Subway A, C, F to Jay Street-Borough Hall; R to Court Street; 2, 3, 4, 5, to Borough Hall.* **Open** 10am-6pm Mon-Fri.

A wealth of information on attractions, sites and events in the city's largest borough, plus local-interest books and gifts.

VISAS & IMMIGRATION

Visas

Currently, 37 countries participate in the Visa Waiver Program (VWP; www.cbp.gov/esta) including Australia, Ireland, New Zealand and the UK. Citizens of these countries do not need a visa for stays in the US shorter than 90 days (business or pleasure) as long as they have a machine-readable passport (e-passport) valid for the full 90-day period, a return ticket, and authorisation to travel through he ESTA (Electronic System for Travel Authorization) scheme. Visitors must fill in the ESTA form at least 24 hours before travelling (72 hours is recommended) and pay a $14 fee; the form can be found at https://esta.cbp.dhs.gov/esta).

If you do not qualify for entry under the VWP, you will need a visa; leave plenty of time to check before travelling.

Immigration

Your airline will give all visitors an immigration form to be presented to an official when you land. Fill it in clearly and be prepared to give an address at which you are staying (a hotel is fine).

Upon arrival in the US, you may have to wait an hour or, if you're unlucky, considerably longer, in Immigration, where, owing to tightened security, you can expect slow-moving queues. You may be expected to explain your visit; be polite and prepared. Note that all visitors to the US are now photographed and electronically fingerprinted on arrival on every trip.

WEIGHTS & MEASURES

Despite attempts to bring in metric measurements, you'll find imperial used in almost all contexts in New York and throughout the US. People think in ounces, inches, gallons and miles.

WHEN TO GO

There is no bad time to visit New York, and visitor numbers are fairly steady year-round. However, the weather can be unpleasantly hot and humid in summer (especially August) and, although winter snow (usually heaviest in January and February) is picturesque before it gets dirty and slushy, these months are often brutally cold. Late spring and early autumn bring pleasantly moderate temperatures that are perfect for walking and exploring.

Public holidays

New Year's Day 1 Jan

Martin Luther King, Jr Day 3rd Mon in Jan

Presidents Day 3rd Mon in Feb

Memorial Day last Mon in May

Independence Day 4 July

Labor Day 1st Mon in Sept

Columbus Day 2nd Mon in Oct

Veterans Day 11 Nov

Thanksgiving Day 4th Thur in Nov

Christmas Day 25 Dec

WORK

Non-nationals can't work in the US without the appropriate visa; these are hard to get and generally require you to prove that your job could not be done by a US citizen. Contact your local embassy for further details. Some student visas allow part-time work after the first academic year.

UK students who want to spend a summer vacation working in the US should contact the **British Universities North America Club** (BUNAC) for help in securing a temporary job and also the requisite visa (Priory House, 6 Wrights Lane, London W8 6TA, 033 3999 7516, www.bunac.org).

Further Reference

BOOKS

Architecture

Richard Berenholtz
New York, New York
Miniature panoramic images of
the city through the seasons.
Stanley Greenberg
Invisible New York
A photographic account of hidden
architectural triumphs.
**New York City Landmarks
Preservation Commission**
Guide to New York City Landmarks
Karl Sabbagh *Skyscraper*
How the tall ones are built.
Kevin Walsh *Forgotten New York*
Discover overlooked architectural
gems and anachronistic remnants.
**Norval White & Elliot
Willensky** *The AIA Guide to
New York City*
A comprehensive directory of
important buildings.

Culture & recollections

Irving Lewis Allen
The City in Slang
NYC-bred words and phrases.
Joseph Berger *The World in a City*
The *New York Times* columnist
explores the communities located
within the five boroughs.
Andrew Blauner (ed)
Central Park: An Anthology
Writers reflect on the city's most
celebrated green space.
Anatole Broyard
*Kafka Was the Rage: A Greenwich
Village Memoir*
Vivid account of 1940s Village
bohemia and its characters.
George Chauncey *Gay New York*
Gay culture from 1890 to 1940.
**Martha Cooper & Henry
Chalfant** *Subway Art*
A definitive survey of city graffiti.
Naomi Fertitta & Paul Aresu
*New York: The Big City and its Little
Neighborhoods*
This photojournalism/guidebook
hybrid illuminates New York's
immigrant populations.
Josh Alan Friedman
Tales of Times Square
Sleaze and decay in the old days.
Nelson George *Hip Hop America*
The real history of hip hop, from
Grandmaster Flash to Puff Daddy.
Bill Helmreich *The New York
Nobody Knows: Walking 6,000 Miles
in the City*

Observations and interviews from an
epic trek across the five boroughs.
Jane Jacobs *The Death and
Life of Great American Cities*
A hugely influential critique of
modern urban planning.
Chuck Katz
Manhattan on Film 1 & 2
On-location walking tours.
Gillian McCain & Legs McNeil
Please Kill Me
An oral history of the punk scene.
Joseph Mitchell
Up in the Old Hotel
Quirky recollections of New York
from the 1930s to the 1960s.
Thurston Moore & Byron Coley
No Wave
Musicians reminisce about the
downtown post-punk underground
scene in this nostalgia trip co-edited
by the Sonic Youth frontman.
Adrienne Onofri
Walking Brooklyn
Thirty tours illuminate the culture
and history of the borough.
Sam Stephenson *The Jazz Loft
Project: Photographs and Tapes
of W Eugene Smith from 821
Sixth Avenue, 1957-1965*
Images and conversation transcripts
from the jazz-obsessed photographer's
loft, which became a rehearsal space for
some of the era's greatest musicians.
Judith Stonehill *New York's
Unique & Unexpected Places*
Fifty special yet less-visited spots.
EB White *Here is New York*
A clear-eyed love letter to Gotham.

History

Herbert Asbury *The Gangs
of New York: An Informal History
of the Underworld*
A racy journalistic portrait of the
city at the turn of the 19th century.
Robert A Caro *The Power Broker*
A biography of Robert Moses, New
York's mid 20th-century master
builder, and his chequered legacy.
Federal Writers' Project
The WPA Guide to New York City
A wonderful evocation of the
1930s by writers who were employed
under FDR's New Deal.
Sanna Feirstein *Naming New York*
How Manhattan places got named.
Tom Folsom
*The Mad Ones: Crazy Joe Gallo
and the Revolution at the Edge
of the Underworld*
Engaging ride though the world of
the Mafia during the 1960s.

Eric Homberger *The Historical
Atlas of New York City*
Through maps, photographs,
illustrations and essays, this hefty
volume charts the metropolis's 400-
year heritage.
Clifton Hood *722 Miles: The
Building of the Subways and How
They Transformed New York*
The birth of the world's longest rapid
transit system.
Kenneth T Jackson (ed)
The Encyclopedia of New York City
An ambitious and useful reference
guide for the city.
David Levering Lewis
When Harlem Was in Vogue
A study of the Harlem Renaissance.
Jonathan Mahler *Ladies and
Gentlemen, the Bronx is Burning*
A gritty snapshot of NYC in 1977.
Mitchell Pacelle *Empire*
The story of the fight to build the
Empire State Building.
Clayton Patterson (ed) *Resistance*
This collection of essays reflects on
the Lower East Side's history as a
radical hotbed.
Luc Sante *Low Life*
Opium dens and brothels in New
York from the 1840s to the 1920s.
Russell Shorto *The Island at the
Center of the World*
How the Dutch colony shaped
Manhattan – and America.
**Mike Wallace & Edwin G
Burrows** *Gotham: A History
of New York City to 1898*
The first volume in a planned
mammoth history of NYC.

Fiction & poetry

Kurt Andersen
Turn of the Century
Millennial Manhattan as seen
through the eyes of media players.
Paul Auster
*The New York Trilogy:
City of Glass, Ghosts and
The Locked Room*
A search for the madness behind the
method of Manhattan's grid.
Kevin Baker *Dreamland*
A poetic novel about Coney Island's
glory days.
James A Baldwin
Another Country
Racism under the bohemian veneer
of the 1960s.
Michael Chabon *The Amazing
Adventures of Kavalier and Clay*
Jewish comic-book artists battling
with crises of identity in the 1940s.

Ralph Ellison *Invisible Man*
Epic examination of race and racism in 1950s Harlem.
Jack Finney *Time and Again*
An illustrator travels back to 19th-century New York City.
Larry Kramer *Faggots*
A devastating satire of gay NYC.
Rachel Kushner *The Flamethrowers*
A gritty evocation of the lives of artists and anarchists in the '70s.
Jonathan Lethem *Chronic City*
The author of *The Fortress of Solitude* packs his latest novel with pop-culture references.
Phillip Lopate (ed)
Writing New York
An excellent anthology of short stories, essays and poems.
Colum McCann
Let the Great World Spin
Interconnected stories set in 1970s New York.
Patrick McGrath *Trauma*
A first-person account of psychic decay that floats a critique of post-9/11 social and political amnesia.
Tim McLoughlin (ed)
Brooklyn Noir 1, 2 & 3
Second-borough crime tales.
Frank O'Hara *The Collected Poems of Frank O'Hara*
The great NYC poet found inspiration in his hometown.
Richard Price *Lush Life*
A contemporary murder story set on the Lower East Side.
David Schickler
Kissing in Manhattan
The lives of quirky tenants in a teeming Manhattan block.
Hubert Selby Jr
Last Exit to Brooklyn
Dockland degradation, circa 1950s.
Edith Wharton *Old New York*
Four novellas of 19th-century New York City.
Colson Whitehead *The Colossus of New York: A City in 13 Parts*
A lyrical tribute to city life.
Tom Wolfe
The Bonfire of the Vanities
Rich/poor, black/white – an unmatched slice of 1980s NYC.

FILM

Annie Hall (1977)
Woody Allen and Diane Keaton in this valentine to Manhattan.
Breakfast at Tiffany's (1961)
Audrey Hepburn as the cash-poor, time-rich socialite Holly Golightly.
Dog Day Afternoon (1975)
Al Pacino is a Brooklyn bank robber in Sidney Lumet's classic.
Do the Right Thing (1989)
Racial strife in Brooklyn's Bedford-Stuyvesant in Spike Lee's drama.

The French Connection (1971)
As detective Jimmy 'Popeye' Doyle, Gene Hackman chases down drug traffickers in William Friedkin's much-imitated thriller.
The Godfather (1972), **The Godfather: Part II** (1974)
Francis Ford Coppola's brilliant commentary on capitalism in America is told through the violent saga of Italian gangsters.
Mean Streets (1973)
Robert De Niro and Harvey Keitel shine as small-time Little Italy hoods in Martin Scorsese's breakthrough film.
Midnight Cowboy (1969)
Street creatures 'Ratso' Rizzo and Joe Buck face an unforgiving Times Square in John Schlesinger's darkly amusing classic.
A Most Violent Year (2014)
JC Chandor's absorbing no-bull drama chronicles the trials of an immigrant gas-company owner in scrappy Koch-era New York.
Spider-Man (2002)
The comic book web-slinger from Forest Hills comes to life in Sam Raimi's pitch-perfect crowd-pleaser.
Superfly (1972)
Blaxploitation classic, propelled by legendary Curtis Mayfield soundtrack.
The Taking of Pelham 1 2 3 (2009)
The plot premise may be flawed – in this Denzel Washington/John Travolta remake, as well as in the 1974 original – but it stirs up strap-hangers' darkest fears.
Taxi Driver (1976)
Robert De Niro is a crazed cabbie who sees all of New York as a den of iniquity in Scorsese's drama.

MUSIC

Beastie Boys
'No Sleep Till Brooklyn'
The hip-hop troupe's on-the-road anthem exudes local pride.
Leonard Cohen
'Chelsea Hotel #2'
Of all the songs inspired by the Chelsea, this bleak vision of doomed love is on a level of its own.
Jay-Z with Alicia Keys
"Empire State of Mind"
The Brooklyn rapper's ode to NYC is a 21st-century rival to Sinatra's classic anthem.
Billy Joel
'New York State of Mind'
This heartfelt ballad exemplifies the city's effect on the souls of its visitors and residents.
Charles Mingus *Mingus Ah Um*
Mingus brought the gospel to jazz and created an NYC masterpiece.

Public Enemy *It Takes a Nation of Millions to Hold Us Back*
A ferociously political tour de force from the Long Island hip hop group whose own Chuck D once called rap 'the CNN for black America'.
The Ramones *Ramones*
Four Queens roughnecks, a few buzzsaw chords, and musings on turning tricks and sniffing glue – it transformed rock 'n' roll.
Frank Sinatra 'Theme from New York, New York'
Ol' Blue Eyes' bombastic love letter melts those little-town blues.
Bruce Springsteen
'My City of Ruins'
The Boss praises the city's resilience post-September 11 with this track from *The Rising*.
The Strokes *Is This It*
The effortlessly hip debut of this hometown band garnered praise and worldwide attention.
The Velvet Underground
The Velvet Underground & Nico
Their first album is still the gold standard of downtown cool.
Wu Tang Clan
Few artists embodied '90s hip hop like the Wu, its members coining a cinematic rap aesthetic that influences artists to this day.

WEBSITES

www.timeout.com/newyork
The recently relaunched *Time Out New York* website covers the best of the city, from upcoming museum exhibitions, shows and events to the latest shop openings, plus thousands of restaurant and bar reviews written by our critics.
www.clubplanet.com
Follow the city's nocturnal scene and buy tickets to big events.
www.forgotten-ny.com
Discover old New York here.
www.hopstop.com
Works out door-to-door directions on public transportation.
www.manhattanusers guide.com
An insiders' guide to what's going on around town.
www.mta.info
Subway and bus service news.
www.nyc.gov
City Hall's official New York City website has lots of useful links.
www.nycgo.com
The official New York City tourism organisation provides information on sights, attractions, hotels, restaurants, shops and more.
www.nytimes.com
'All the News That's Fit to Print' from *The New York Times* (limited access for non-subscribers).

Index

INDEX

INDEX

INDEX

INDEX

Maps

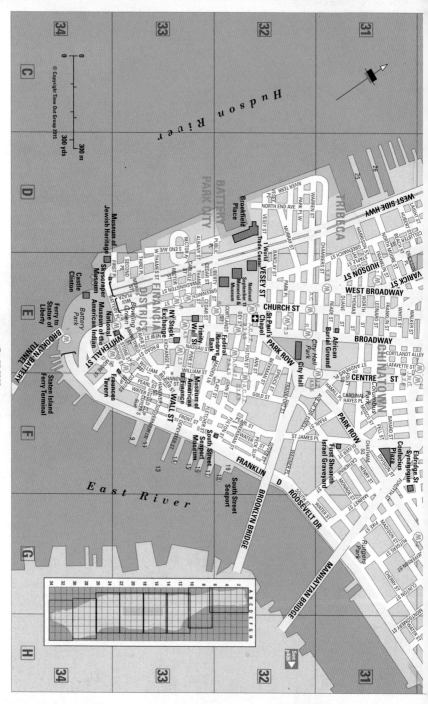

MAPS

Hudson River

East River

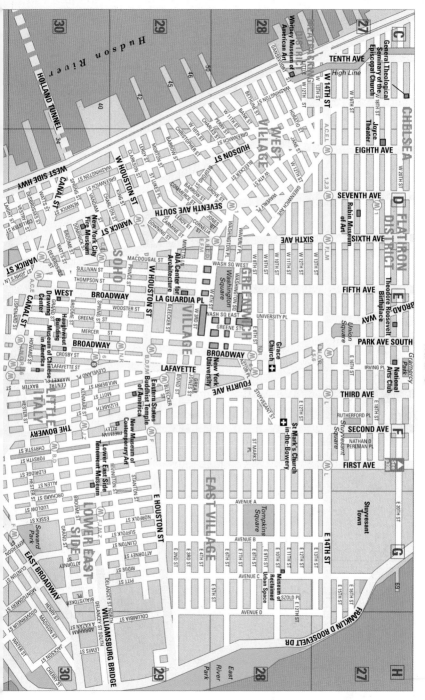

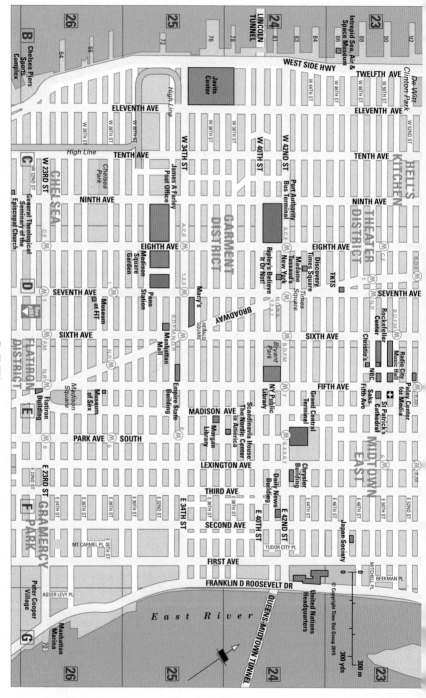

MAPS

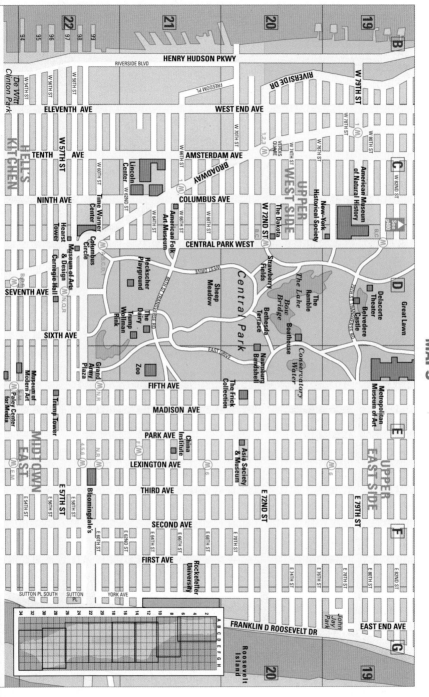

HENRY HUDSON PKWY
RIVERSIDE BLVD
FREEDOM PL
ELEVENTH AVE
WEST END AVE
TENTH AVE
AMSTERDAM AVE
NINTH AVE
BROADWAY
COLUMBUS AVE
CENTRAL PARK WEST
SEVENTH AVE
SIXTH AVE
FIFTH AVE
MADISON AVE
PARK AVE
LEXINGTON AVE
THIRD AVE
SECOND AVE
FIRST AVE
YORK AVE
SUTTON PL SOUTH
SUTTON PL
EAST END AVE
FRANKLIN D ROOSEVELT DR

HELL'S KITCHEN
De Witt Clinton Park
MIDTOWN EAST
UPPER WEST SIDE
UPPER EAST SIDE
Central Park

Lincoln Center
Time Warner Center
Hearst Tower
Carnegie Hall
Museum of Arts & Design
Columbus Circle
American Folk Art Museum
Museum of Modern Art
Paley Center for Media
Trump Tower
Grand Army Plaza
Heckscher Playground
Sheep Meadow
The Dairy
Trump Wollman Rink
Zoo
Strawberry Fields
The Ramble
The Lake
Bow Bridge
Boathouse
Bethesda Terrace
Naumburg Bandshell
Conservatory Water
The Frick Collection
China Institute
Asia Society & Museum
Bloomingdale's
Rockefeller University
New-York Historical Society
American Museum of Natural History
The Dakota
Delacorte Theater
Belvedere Castle
Great Lawn
Metropolitan Museum of Art
John Jay Park
Roosevelt Island

WEST DRIVE
EAST DRIVE
65TH ST TRANSVERSE RD
72ND ST TRANSVERSE RD
79TH ST TRANSVERSE RD

VERDIS DIANE

W 54TH ST
W 55TH ST
W 56TH ST
W 57TH ST
W 58TH ST
W 59TH ST
W 60TH ST
W 62ND ST
W 64TH ST
W 66TH ST
W 68TH ST
W 70TH ST
W 72ND ST
W 74TH ST
W 76TH ST
W 78TH ST
W 79TH ST
W 80TH ST
W 82ND ST

E 57TH ST
E 54TH ST
E 56TH ST
E 58TH ST
E 60TH ST
E 62ND ST
E 64TH ST
E 66TH ST
E 68TH ST
E 70TH ST
E 72ND ST
E 74TH ST
E 76TH ST
E 78TH ST
E 79TH ST
E 80TH ST
E 82ND ST

See p.400

B
C
D
E
F
G

19
20
21
22

94 95 96 97 98 99

2 4 6 8 10 12 14 16 18 20 22 24 26 28 30 32 34

A B C D E F G H

19
20

MAPS

Time Out New York **399**

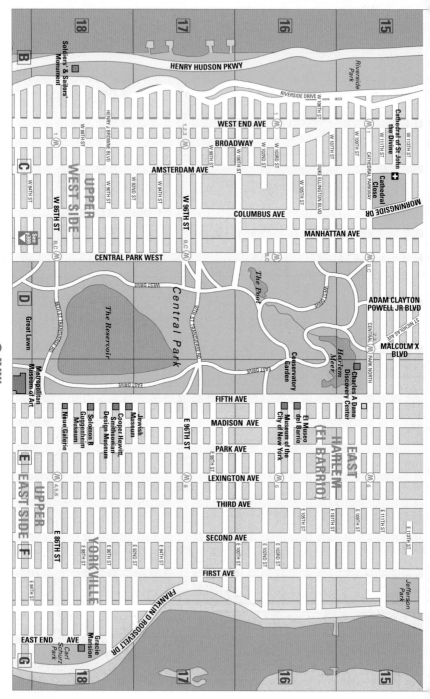

MAPS

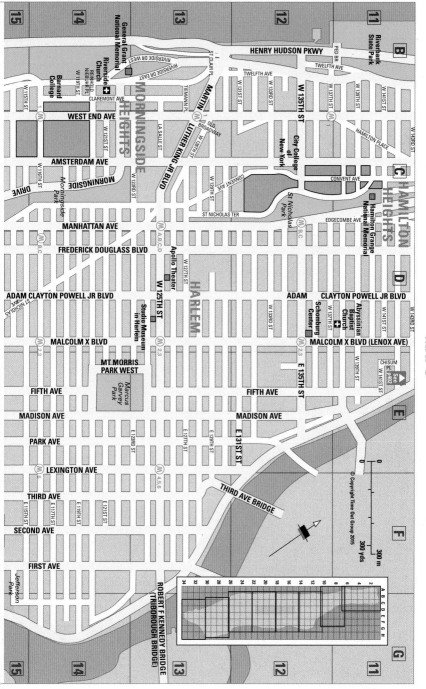

MAPS

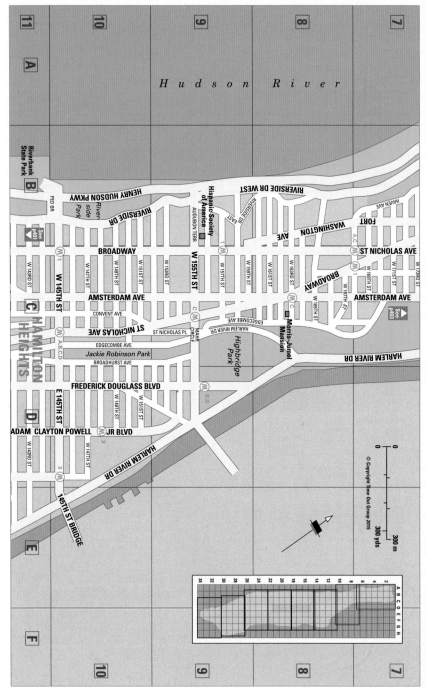

MAPS

H u d s o n   R i v e r

Riverbank
State Park

Riverside Park

HENRY HUDSON PKWY

RIVERSIDE DR

RIVERSIDE DR WEST

RIVERSIDE DR EAST

Hispanic Society
of America

AUDUBON TERR

BROADWAY

W 155TH ST

W 143RD ST
W 145TH ST
W 147TH ST
W 148TH ST
W 151ST ST
W 153RD ST

W 157TH ST
W 159TH ST
W 161ST ST
W 163RD ST
W 165TH ST

WASHINGTON AVE

FORT

HAVEN AVE

ST NICHOLAS AVE

BROADWAY

W 169TH ST
W 177TH ST
W 179TH ST

AMSTERDAM AVE

AMSTERDAM AVE

CONVENT AVE

ST NICHOLAS AVE

ST NICHOLAS PL

MARR
CIRCLE

EDGECOMBE AVE

HARLEM RIVER DR

Morris-Jumel
Mansion

HAMILTON HEIGHTS

Jackie Robinson Park

EDGECOMBE AVE

BROADHURST AVE

Highbridge
Park

HARLEM RIVER DR

FREDERICK DOUGLASS BLVD

E 145TH ST

W 148TH ST
W 151ST ST

ADAM CLAYTON POWELL JR BLVD

W 143RD ST
W 147TH ST

HARLEM RIVER DR

145TH ST BRIDGE

© Copyright Time Out Group 2015

0   300 m
0   300 yds

PED BR

See p401

See p403

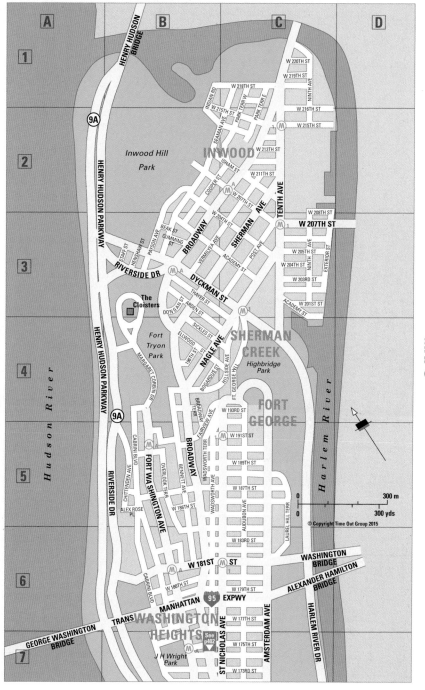

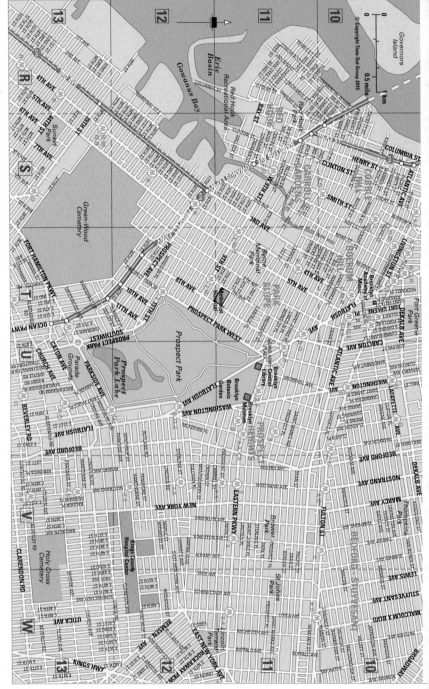

MAPS

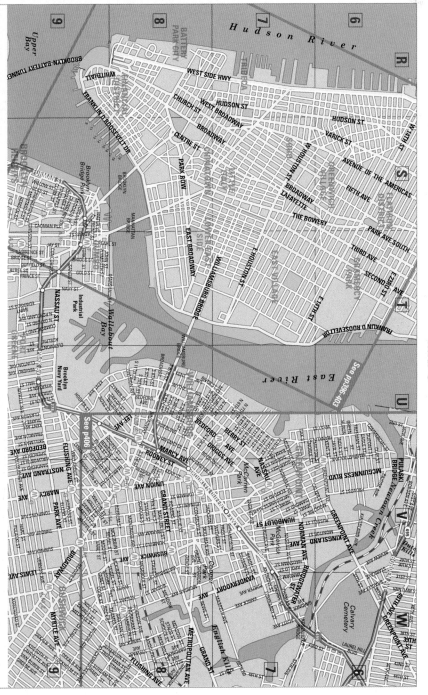

MAPS

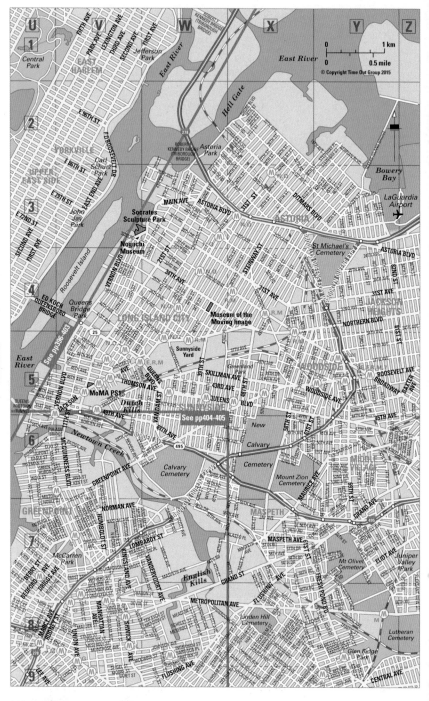

Street Index

STREET INDEX

STREET INDEX

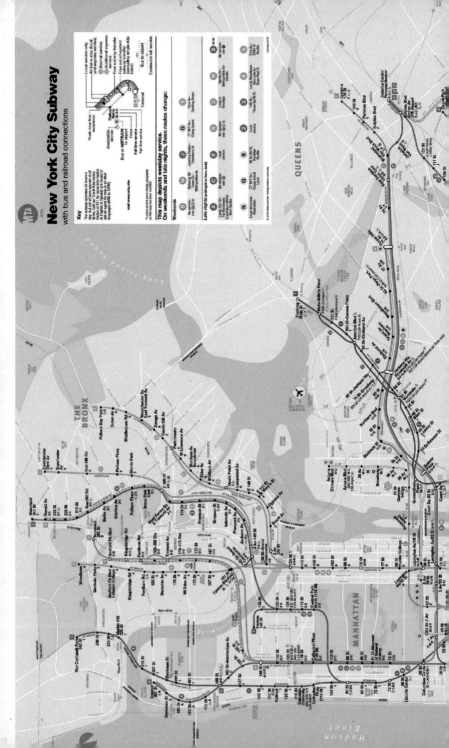

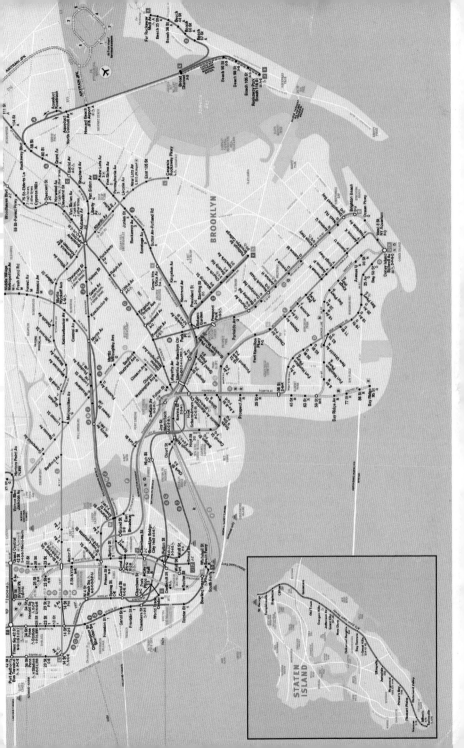

MAPS

Manhattan Subway Map
November 2014

©2014 Metropolitan Transportation Authority. Unauthorized duplication prohibited.

MAPS

Manhattan Bus Map
November 2014

© 2014 Metropolitan Transportation Authority. Unauthorized duplication prohibited.

"*A must-see New York landmark*"
—Variety

THE PHANTOM OF THE OPERA

Broadway's Longest-Running Musical

MAJESTIC THEATRE | 247 West 44th St. | Telecharge.com | 212.239.6200
PhantomBroadway.com